Taking Life Seriously

A Study of the Argument of the
Nicomachean Ethics

Taking Life Seriously

A Study
of the
Argument
of the
Nicomachean Ethics

FRANCIS SPARSHOTT

UNIVERSITY OF TORONTO PRESS
Toronto Buffalo London

© University of Toronto Press Incorporated 1994
Toronto Buffalo London
Printed in Canada

ISBN 0-8020-2953-1

∞

Printed on acid-free paper

Toronto Studies in Philosophy
Editors: James R. Brown and Calvin Normore

Canadian Cataloguing in Publication Data

Sparshott, Francis, 1926–
    Taking life seriously : a study of the argument
of the Nicomachean ethics

    (Toronto studies in philosophy)
    ISBN 0-8020-2953-1

    1. Aristotle. Nicomachean ethics. I. Title.
    II. Series.

B430.S63 1994   171'.3   C93-094629-4

Work on this project was supported by a Canada Council Leave Fellowship in 1970–1.

This book has been published with the help of a grant from the Canadian Federation for the Humanities, using funds provided by the Social
Sciences and Humanities Research Council of Canada.

To my colleagues at Victoria College
whose friendship and tolerance
encouraged my work and endured my presence
from bumptious youth to querulous age
taking life not too seriously
for all these years

Contents

Foreword

The purpose of this book is to display a continuity of thought in the text that has come down to us as Aristotle's *Nicomachean Ethics*.

The project has been with me since my undergraduate days, when neither my tutor, the late W.F.R. Hardie, nor the scholarly world at large seemed interested in the continuity of the text as a developing argument, preferring to expound and criticize parts of the work and show their mutual consistency as bodies of doctrine. This surprised me, since I found the continuity of the argument the most striking and philosophically interesting feature of the work. I eventually concluded that there were five reasons why the overall argument of a work so widely and closely studied for so long had attracted so little attention. First, it has seemed evident on literary grounds that the *Ethics* as it stands could never have been conceived as a unitary composition. Second, Aristotle's way of dealing with topics systematically as he comes to them, without emphasizing the underlying connections, encourages the reader to respond by dealing with them in isolation. Third, many of us are beguiled by the alternative problems of piecing together a single coherent system of 'doctrines' out of the Aristotelian corpus (an approach encouraged by the use of Aristotelian thought in medieval theology, since dogmatic theology lays more emphasis on correctness of opinion than on the coherence of arguments), and of tracing a personal (as opposed to argumentative) line of development from Aristotle's youth to his age.[1] Fourth, it has seemed more sensible to treat all Aristotle's ethical works together, and these works do not share a common plan.[2] And the fifth reason is that (as the reception of my own work has convinced me) few teachers of philosophy are interested in following long trains of argument. Perhaps even philosophers really want opinions, something to believe (or disbelieve) and pass on to their students, not ways of thinking that can be traced and retraced; in any case, they have a natural preference for what can be succinctly stated and tidily discussed.

It is true that much excellent work has been done on the *Ethics* lately, and much of this has dealt with the work as a whole. But the unity these commentators have sought and found is still mostly that of a doctrine, of a unified response to an intellectual challenge. I see that too; but the form taken by this unified response in the *Ethics* seems to me to be the unfolding of a single sequence of implications from a single inescapable starting-point.[3] From this point of view, it is essential that a key thesis may be established and made available in a broad sense at one point, and left open for later refinement. In such a case, though one assumes that the author knows what is coming, it is important that what is claimed and established at the time is only what the argument actually provides, and this is not modified by later developments. That being so, one cannot treat earlier and later passages as separate items in a body of doctrines, nor can one safely infer from a later passage which interpretation of an earlier ambiguity must be correct.[4]

My first attempt to carry out my long-meditated project was completed in April 1967, and shown to some friends. David Gallop made generously detailed comments; Joseph Owens took a benevolent interest. In later years, William Fortenbaugh and Mark Thornton read part or all of the text and made helpful remarks. In forty years of teaching, I have gone through part or all of the *Ethics* with one or more classes almost every year: what I have learned from the suggestions and criticisms of my students is more than I can remember or could enumerate if I did. Like the house of an old fence, my mind is furnished with stuff I have appropriated over the years from sources long forgotten. If you think you recognize some of your own property, you may well be right, and you are welcome to claim it. But I built the house myself.

After a lot of reading and an abortive attempt at rewriting in the late 1970s, I began work on the present version about ten years later. I hope I have profited from all the help I have had and the reading I have done. I have seldom alluded to the immense mass of scholarship that has been devoted to the *Ethics*, especially in the last twenty-five years, unless it directly concerned my project. The *Ethics* is an immensely complex and subtle work, and my contribution here invalidates that other work as little as that work helps mine; all I do is try to show how the pieces of the *Ethics* fit into a scheme which more learned and scrupulous commentaries ignore. On traditionally contested points of scholarship, I have often been content to refer readers to the majestic compendium of R.-A. Gauthier and J.-Y. Jolif (1958). There is a real danger for me in too close an involvement in current debates: the *Ethics* has been so much read and studied that readers tend to think that everyone already knows what Aristotle thought and said.[5] In important respects, it is not clear to me that we do.

For the most part, my work takes the form of a commentary on successive parts of the text. These parts will sometimes be identified by book number and by the traditional chapter divisions as given in most English translations and commentaries. The book numbers do not always correspond to the divisions of the subject-matter – they were imposed by the material requirements of ancient book production – but they are invariable. The chapter numbers lack even that authority, being the work of a medieval translator, but they are familiar and convenient. Following Bywater's Greek text, I refer to them by Roman numerals. There is also a somewhat different set of chapter divisions, the work of a different translator, which I will occasionally cite [in brackets], using Arabic numerals.[6] The internal organization of the text is complex, overlapping, and indeterminate (as shown by cross-references); my own decimal scheme will show what I take the actual articulation of the work to be. Except for fragments from lost works, I follow universal modern practice in given detailed references by the page, column, and line numbers of Bekker's Berlin edition of Aristotle's works. Fragments are cited by their numbering in Rose's Teubner edition of 1886, and where possible by the page numbers in vol. 12 of the Oxford translation (by Ross) and in Barnes's revision of the same.

My project is to show by paraphrase and comment how it might have seemed sensible to write just this text in just this order. I do not write a line-by-line commentary, partly because the text is not linear. Typically, in dealing with a topic, Aristotle describes the phenomena to be discussed, states the difficulties that arise, provides a theoretical solution, and ends by reconciling his theory with the phenomena as described.[7] But he does not always do this, or in quite the same way when he does do it, and different sections of the text call for different treatments. My hope is, however, that everything in the text will be shown, in the end, to be explicable as constituting a single project.

I could not fulfil my task without referring to other parts of Aristotle's work. But such references cannot be more than illustrative, because one cannot be sure that he may not have changed his mind; nor, indeed, am I committed to the thesis that the *Ethics* in its present form is actually his work. The decisive factor is always what can be read in the text of the *Ethics* itself and what it is most likely to mean in its context.

I used to think that my version of the argument was the right one, the only possible way of reading it as a single coherent text. I no longer think that, especially as I keep changing my mind about ('having new insights into') the argument. But the aim is always to give the best explanation of the actual text as a single continuous argument.

I shall assume that the reader has text or translation of the *Ethics* at hand. My aim is not to argue a thesis about the interpretation of the text as a whole, but to enable the reader to see how it actually goes; and for this it is necessary to use my work as a guide to a reading of the text, not as a substitute for it. For ease of reference I have used Bywater's text in the Oxford Classical Text series, and (where convenient) the unrevised version of the Oxford translation by Sir David Ross. The terminology used in the latter is often stigmatized nowadays as misleading, but that hardly matters, because all translations are bound to mislead. The argument, in any case, relies on the Greek original. Crafty and sympathetic readers soon pick up the ways in which terms acquire special senses in their contexts. The Oxford version is the most readily available; besides, use of a new and better English equivalent is apt to mislead translators and commentators into imagining that this is exactly what the Greek word always means, which it never is. The old implausible standbys are less likely to lead us astray. But I have often followed my own preferences, and I have not hesitated to use transliterations of Greek terms unaccompanied by an English equivalent. There is a glossary of these terms at the back. In a similar spirit, I have kept closer to Aristotle's ways of putting things than I might if I were using his thoughts in the context of a contemporary discussion. The result is that my text often has an archaic air, but this is not undesirable; we should not forget that it is a very long time since anyone's thought has been cast in the patterns that Aristotle found natural or congenial.

It is not always possible to separate exegesis from interpretation, interpretation from comment. A few separable passages in which I comment on Aristotle's procedures, rather than expounding and explaining them, are printed in italics; but I have not been meticulous in this.

Taking Life Seriously

A Study of the Argument of the
Nicomachean Ethics

Introduction

1. The Literary Problem and the Present Undertaking

This book is about a treatise on ethics preserved among the works ascribed to Aristotle and called (for no certainly recoverable reason) the *Nicomachean Ethics* (*EN*, or simply 'the *Ethics*').

Nobody has the least idea how the texts of Aristotle's works were produced in the first place. Some, no doubt, were position papers that circulated among his colleagues; some are plainly notes for or records of lectures; but in no case do we know whether he wrote them down, dictated them to a secretary, made notes that a slave or a student edited and transcribed, or what. We do not know whether official or unofficial 'master copies' existed of all or some of them.[1] We know absolutely nothing like that. Discussions of authorship and authenticity tend to treat the works nonchalantly as if there had been autographs prepared for publication. Controversies based on any such supposition are preposterous. We must never lose sight of our ignorance.

In addition to *EN*, a second major treatise on ethics survives under the name of Aristotle, called (nobody quite knows why) the *Eudemian Ethics* (*EE*).[2] The two works have three of their books (V–VII of *EN*, IV–VI of *EE*) in common. Which, if either, is actually by Aristotle? How, in general, are they related? They are preserved mostly in the manuscripts of *EN*, manuscripts of *EE* simply referring the reader to *EN*; but that proves nothing, since *EN* was far more widely studied and anyone who acquired an MS of *EE* would be sure to have one of *EN* already.

Anthony Kenny thinks *EE* is the only authentic version. He argues that *EN* is an alternative version of Aristotle's views on ethics, cobbled together from fragments of his writings centuries later. He gives statistical evidence for identifying the language used in the common books with that of *EE*.[3] The argument of my book requires no decision on the issue. I am taking the actual text of *EN*, as preserved in a manuscript tradition that is nearly unanimous, as an object given for exegesis, *as if* it were the work of an author and *as if* that author were Aristotle. Since the text abounds in references to what has been said already and what remains to be said, I assume that it is intended to be read step by step in the order in which it is written. It is plainly meant to be read as a work by Aristotle, so I refer to its author by that name.[4] Who actually wrote, compiled, arranged, and edited the text is not my concern. The *Ethics* is still taught and read as a single text, and as the standard version of Aristotle's ethics, so it surely makes sense to see how it works *as* an Aristotelian text.

On the question of historical authenticity and the relation between the two treatises I have only two things to say. First, Porphyry, a scholar editing the manuscripts of the philosopher Plotinus in the third century CE, says he is modelling his procedures on those of Andronicus of Rhodes, who three centuries earlier had produced an edition of the works of Theophrastus and Aristotle. Porphyry says that Andronicus, according to his own preface, arranged the surviving texts into 'undertakings' (*pragmateiai*).[5] Since Porphyry elsewhere uses this word of such works as Aristotle's *Metaphysics*, and since there is no earthly reason why Porphyry should be lying or mistaken, it seems to follow that, if the works as we have them are ultimately from Andronicus's edition, their present form is his work.[6] And we have no good reason to believe that any other edition existed, though we do know that many of Aristotle's writings were in circulation before Andronicus's time. We do not know how extensive Andronicus's work was, or on what principles it was carried on; but we are left with no grounds for certainty that the extant form and arrangement of *EN* or any other work are Aristotle's own.[7] I proceed on the assumption that what we have may be treated as an integral work of Aristotle's own; but we have no solid grounds for affirming that it is so.

My second remark will be on the difference between the two works. *EN* retains its pride of place as 'the *Ethics*' and seems likely to do so, if only through sheer inertia and because of its preferential assimilation into philosophical tradition. But Kenny is not the only philosopher who prefers *EE*. My own opinion is that *EE* is a smoother job, more neatly presented, but *EN* is tougher and rawer, more challenging, its tensions and contradictions more exposed. However that may be, there is also a difference of approach, small but vital. Both works start by asking what a good life is, and answer that it is a 'virtuous' life, one in accordance with human excellence. But *EE* is methodologically self-contained. It starts from the term *eudaimonia*, a word primarily applicable only to the well-being ('happiness') of humans, and presents its conclusion in terms of another word (*kalokagathia*) applicable only to humanity, this time in a specific kind of cultural setting. This word resists translation, but means something like 'gentlemanliness.' *EE* thus discusses human behaviour, almost ostentatiously, in its own terms. In *EN*, on the other hand, *eudaimonia* is not a basic concept: it is introduced early on, but it is explained in terms of a more primitive term, *agathon* ('good') – a word that has general application to all animal activity and to any teleological system. *EN* is accordingly grounded on general considerations about the conditions of action and life, and it is these considerations that determine its course. As for the blessed summative word *kalokagathia*, it scarcely appears in *EN*. Once more, we have a working out of the relations between more basic concepts: action, pleasure, perception. This difference between the two treatises looks like one of manner rather than of content; but the reliance on relations between basic concepts gives *EN* a powerful argumentative structure that underlies the phenomenological descriptions in which it abounds.

2. Aristotle's Formalism

Because *EN* proceeds from the perfectly general notion of 'good,' the structure for human behaviour that is developed is schematic and meant to be applicable in principle to all fully developed human lives. Readers often complain that Aristotle resorts at crucial points to merely formal statements, where we would prefer concrete instructions about what to do and how to decide. This is not fudging on his part but, as we shall see, is essential to his undertaking. At the same time, however, his discussion has to be based on the familiar activities and standards of his own place and time, and illustrated by these. What he is concerned with is the formal underpinnings of actual situations recognized and envisaged concretely. The upshot is deeply ambiguous, because we are not always sure whether we should give more weight to his assertions of principle or to his particular evaluations.[8] These ambiguities are, for better *and* for worse, essential to *EN*; we have to make our own decisions about how to read it. If we prefer to read it, as I do, with emphasis on its formal structure – ideas and arguments are what we need philosophers for; only life can teach us about life – the principles we extract may often be at variance with convictions Aristotle expresses without qualification in other works; and, in *EN* itself, we must distinguish between what an argument actually *shows* and the practical applications Aristotle makes of it.

3. The Basic Question

The beginning of the *Ethics* develops a problem out of the familiar basic facts of human life. But it does not explain how that problem arises. We all know that it does arise, and that is enough for the practice-oriented inquiry on which we are embarked. As theorists, however, we can think about the situation, and the interpretation of *EN* is made easier if we do. The relevant work of Aristotle is *On the Soul*, in which he analyses the distinguishing characteristics and basic modes of activity or behaviour of living things in general and of humans in particular. In Book III, chapters 9–10, he discusses the psychological and physiological bases of animal movement. In the *Physics* (II 1) he had already explained that the natural movements of animals, as of all things, are those that can be traced to some source in the animal itself, in the sense that the animal does more than merely transmit mechanical pushes and pulls from the outside. What is specific to the animal movements we call 'actions' is that they depend on perception, the reception of information (together with imagination, the residue of such information). Two things are required. First, the animal must perceive or imagine some object that something could be done about; second, the animal must want to do something about the object (basically, to get it or avoid it). Neither the cognition nor the appetition will lead to action without the other. But, other things being equal, awareness of an object together with an appropriate desire immediately issues in action.[9]

Animals, including humans, thus act because they conceive or imagine a future situation as desirable. But imagination can mislead. The situation obtained may be other than the situation aimed at, or the situation aimed at and obtained may disappoint. This holds for all animals to which action can be attributed (that is, which can properly be said to *do* anything), even for animals incapable of anything like thinking. We say that they learn from experience, and that they act for the sake of some real or apparent good, just as a way of describing the internal mechanisms whereby their adjustment to the environment succeeds or fails. When we are talking about humans, words like *learning* and *good* take on weightier meanings, but the basic structure is the same. As appears from another work, *On the Movement of Animals*, unproblematic human actions follow the same model as animal actions. The model can be presented as a syllogism: a general principle, a perceived fact, and a conclusion. The animal feels hunger; it perceives accessible prey or fodder; without more ado, it eats – *euthus prattei*, 'it acts immediately.' Of course, if it is human, it will consciously identify its feeling as hunger ('I could use a cheeseburger'), may say to itself 'There's a Burger King,' and then *decide* by saying 'I'll go in here' – but, in the absence of rival motivations and perceptions, the action does not need the mediation of any conscious and articulate decision; the action itself is the conclusion of the 'argument.'

What is crucial to the *Ethics* is that, in the account of animal action in the *De Anima*, two complications are immediately introduced. First, in humans, imagination may be replaced by thinking, calculation, knowledge (433a10). Second, in animals with a sense of time, there may be a conflict of motivations: what is attractive here and now must be balanced against what is not immediately attractive but will pay off at some future time (433b8). This is the only sort of conflict Aristotle mentions, and we may wonder why: may there not be a conflict between my desire for a cheeseburger and my equally present desire to stay outside in the sunshine? But a possible answer is obvious: my immediate desires will simply sum as an overriding desire without my having to think about it, human and other animals doing what on balance they most feel like doing. It is only when one has a sense of time that one can balance the overall weight of one's active desires against what one believes will prove more desirable later; and only thus can one engage in strategies.

But what is a 'sense of time'? According to Aristotle in his *Physics*, time is not merely the fact of change and movement, mere continuation and succession; it is the *measurable* aspect of change, the countable aspect whereby events are determinately earlier and later (*Physics* IV 11, 219a32–b1). As the measurable (literally, 'number,' countability) aspect of motion, time is real (219b2–3), but countability is impossible without someone to count, which can only be a living being – and not just any living being, but one with a *mind* (*Physics* IV 14, 223a17–29). A sense of time involves calculation and reasoning, not a mere inarticulate sense of the nearness and remoteness of past and future events. Only humans use language, calculate, reason; so only humans can have a sense of time. The point of the 'sense of time' is not just that comparisons are possible, but that a framework is established within which courses of action can be framed, compared, pursued: the 'deliberative imagination' reduces alternative possibilities to a single standard (*On the Soul* 433b29–434a10). It follows that humans, unlike all other animals, being able to formulate alternatives and to envisage courses of action within the limited span of a lifetime, can think of themselves as living 'a life' and are faced with the question of how to organize that life; and this is an aspect of their general ability to formulate, articulate, and calculate – their possession of articulate speech, *logos*. And time, be it noted, is the same for all minds, so that plans can be not only formulated by individuals but interrelated.

One more thing: though time is defined in terms of counting and calculating, Aristotle does speak of a *'sense* of time': whether he wishes to emphasize this or not, the implication is that our awareness of temporality is direct, functioning as a matter of sensibility, the way the world actually *seems* to us.

It is to the question 'How shall I organize my life?' that the *Ethics* is initially addressed. The passage we are citing from *On the Soul* shows that it is a question that practically confronts every animal with a sense of time, whether the animal thinks about it or not. It is in this specific context that the *Ethics* is best read. The question that confronts Aristotle is how far this inescapable predicament, given a social set-up and political organization and the necessary psychophysical equipment of humanity, suffices to generate an answer to the concrete question of how one should live. I think it does so to a very surprising extent, though, of course, Aristotle's first readers read him, as we do, with a very specific set of sociopolitical circumstances in mind. Be it noted, though, that nothing in *On the Soul* functions as a premise in the argument of the *Ethics* or is alluded to in that work. The *Ethics* rests on its own merits. The account of action in *On the Soul* simply explains why it makes sense for Aristotle to formulate and organize his discussion as he does.

The account of human action we got out of *On the Soul* reveals three ways in which actions can be made more successful. First, imagination can be trained: the agent's envisaging of what is desirable and likely might be made less apt to lead to frustration. Presumably almost all kinds of animals – all those that can learn from experience, including people – can and do improve their performance in this way. In fact, we shall see that Aristotle's accounts of human life are made more subtle and harder to follow by the fact that much practical wisdom is embedded in this subarticulate level of behaviour and experience.

The second way in which success can be improved is by replacing imagination with reasoning. Instead of an envisaged outcome, we have a calculated consequence, which functions as an imagined end. But Aristotle in the *Ethics* is reluctant to use the word *imagination* for it, because imagination is the antithesis of rational thinking.

The third way to improve performance is through the systematic integration of past and present events. Instead of doing what we feel like doing at the moment, we figure out what will give the best outcome overall. It is specifically to the last of these three ways of improving performance that the *Ethics* is devoted. In fact, one way of describing the work is as the systematic exploring of its potentialities and implications. What difference does the sense of time make to an individual who has a limited life span, has the psychological mechanism sketched above, lives among others of the same species in family and society, and belongs to a species that persists unchanged through an unchanging world?

Aristotle is not concerned with 'morality' as philosophers since Kant have understood it. Now we can see why he is not: he is initially concerned with the straightforward problem of how to live a lifetime, as that problem confronts any being that is capable of posing the question. The problem of 'morality' is not a plain problem like that: it is a fancy problem, resting on fancy notions that are hard to explain when they are challenged. One might rather complain that Aristotle does not keep himself sufficiently clear of such mental contortions.

4. The Author

Aristotle was a singular man. Facts about his disturbed and tragic life may be easily discovered from textbooks and encyclopedias, and I will not run through them here. But, since he is the putative author of the *Ethics*, it is worth bearing in mind that he is not just a thinking machine. He writes:

1 / as a full-time philosopher, practitioner of a new profession and exponent of a novel and distinctive way of life;
2 / as a long-time student and faithful follower of Plato, in whose

distinctive thought-patterns his own thinking is saturated, even though he repudiated Plato's most striking theses;

3 / as an alienated man, living in a city (Athens) where he had no political rights and could not own property, and professed admirer of a political order in which he had no part;

4 / as a male in a society in which women were formally excluded from political and economic power, and were discouraged even from appearing in public;

5 / as a rich man, perhaps a very rich man;

6 / as a governing-class man, the lifelong associate of extremely powerful people (notably the ruling house of Macedon, the dominant power in the Greek world);

7 / specifically, as student and tutor, respectively, of the greatest thinker of his day and the most powerful statesman in his day, individuals whose work shaped the world for centuries to come;

8 / apparently, in his old age, as a lonely man, his wife and only son dead, his father-in-law tortured to death, his native city rased to the ground, living in Athens under the protection of an occupying power, himself to die in exile.[10]

In some ways, the *Ethics* is what one would expect from such an author; in other ways, it is not. Its curious blend of optimism and bitterness was not lightly earned.

Two of Aristotle's contemporaries changed the course of history, Alexander of Macedon by his conquests and Plato by his invention of philosophy as we know it. Aristotle was a student and associate of the latter and a tutor of the former. Think about that.

CHAPTER ONE

What Is Best for People
(I i–xii; 1094a1–1102a4)

1.1 The Idea of the Good (1094a1–1097b21)

On the Soul is about what the life of this or that kind of animal *is*. But, if we can ask that question in general terms, we can ask it specifically about humans, and hence about ourselves as individuals and groups. Since our lives are yet to be lived, if we can ask what our lives *are*, we can ask what they *will be* for each of us. That is, any being capable of doing psychology is capable of doing ethics. We can ask how we are to decide about how to live our lives – a question that has no application to other animals. From asking how people can decide we can go on to ask how they do decide; how they should decide; how *I* am to decide. We are engaged in a practical study having to do with the strategies of action. By the same token, what a human life *is* is essentially the life of a being that can ask itself how it is to live its own life. Note, to *ask* itself: a human life is mediated by language.

Is one way of living a human life better than other ways? This is the question to which the *Ethics* as a whole essays an answer. It is a question to which *On the Soul* suggests no answer: all it tells us is that a being with a sense of time must, in effect, make choices among actions and courses of action. By the time the animal dies, we reflect, the concatenated sequence of these choices will have determined what amounts to a lifetime. But we have seen nothing to suggest that any set of such choices is better than any other set. What is a *good* life? The first thing we have to discover is what this question means, what resources we have for answering it, and what limits there are on acceptable answers. That is what the present section essays.

1.11 General Introduction (I i–iii; 1094a1–1095a13)

The *Ethics* begins with a general introduction to practical philosophy, parallel to and reminiscent of the introduction to theoretical philosophy we find at the beginning of Aristotle's *Metaphysics*. Both passages start with a general orientation and proceed to develop the full scope of their subject.

Like most introductions, this one needs to be read (and reads as if it were written) with hindsight, in the light of the complete project it introduces. Some of its key pronouncements strike a candid reader as tendentious, even fallacious. One explanation of this is that Aristotle is careless or cavalier, issuing promissory notes that he will later make good. Another explanation is that such pronouncements are ambiguous, making weak claims that are indeed justified but trivial, while suggesting stronger claims. If so, a large part of the *Ethics* will be devoted to determining *in what sense* these claims will be made good. Especially in the *Ethics*, Aristotle tends to use terms *critically*, not simple as standing for established notions. The concept of pleasure, for instance, is a familiar one and Aristotle uses it in the ways that most of us use it; but, at the same time, Aristotle shows us that such usage is misleading, that the phenomena of pleasure are not really what we tend to think they are. This two-sidedness gives Aristotle's thought much of its power, and is missed by people who want Aristotle to give simple answers to complicated questions.

1.111 The Good as End (1094a1–3)

The *Metaphysics* starts with a ringing declaration: 'All humans are oriented towards knowledge, by nature.'[1] It is about humans, all of them, and their nature. Their orientation towards knowledge is already shown by the way people just like to look at things; when civilization provides leisure, this orientation leads to the development of organized skills, then of sciences, and finally of philosophy, the knowledge of reality as such – the final fruition of the deepest capacity and inclination of humanity as such.

The ringing declaration that introduces the *Ethics*, by contrast, does not start with humans, or with the nature of anything; it speaks not of orientation but of intention, and it does not say how things are, it says how people think they are. (In this it sets the tone for the *Ethics*, in which consensus is vital.)

What I said in the Introduction may suggest that the *Ethics* will start by talking about action, and most people read it as if it did; but it doesn't. It starts with *organized* activities: 'It is generally agreed [*dokei*] that every skill and pursuit ... aims at some good.' Well, of course, that's obvious. What fills the gap in the sentence is 'and in just the same way every action and choice' – and that is less immediately obvious. Of course, choices are motivated, if it is implied that something was chosen instead of something else, to which it was preferred;[2] but is every *action* thus motivated? Aren't there some things we just *do*? The analysis of action in *On the Soul* suggests not – that no animal acts unless an inner impulse responds to an attractive or repulsive object; but that is theory. In fact, this whole first sentence is presented as theory, not as observation, unlike that first sentence of the *Metaphysics*; and that is why the most obvious point had to be made first. But, in any case, as the sequel immediately goes on to show, our whole topic is the organization of activity.

The word *good* is introduced as a defined term and not as a primitive. Does the word add anything? Could we not just have said, 'aims at something'? Does it not indeed follow from the analysis of action in *On the Soul* that the word *good* means no more than 'object of aim' (as Perry defined 'value' as 'any object of any interest')?[3] Not quite. The concept of *the* good enables us to generalize the concept of an object of action, which we could not conveniently do without it. Besides, though the concept of 'good' is introduced by way of that of aiming, good is not made relative to desire. To be desired is not in itself a value. Aims can be misdirected: one can *discover* that one has wanted the wrong thing. Reflection may lead us to use the word *good* only of what proves neither illusory nor disappointing as an objective; we may then distinguish, as Aristotle will later do, between the good and the *apparent* good. It is as if we defined the good not as the objective of action but as the *proper* objective of action.

'Consequently,' Aristotle goes on, 'the good has been well explained as "that at which everything aims." '[4] This looks wrong, in two ways. First, it seems to commit the 'fallacy of composition' – from the fact that each of several things aims at some thing or other, it does not follow that there is some one thing they all aim at – on the contrary, it follows that there need be no such thing, and in the case of actions there cannot be, since our initial thesis was that each action has its own specific objective. Second, it falsely legitimizes the very notion of 'the good' as an overriding or overarching objective. But these misgivings are misplaced. All the sentence says is that, according to these unnamed authorities, whenever a group of entities 'all' have a joint objective, the proper name for that objective in that context is 'the good'; and, conversely, correct use of the expression 'the good' in any context implies a totality of entities of which it is the shared objective. What the totality is will depend on the context. And Aristotle has as yet said nothing to show what his context is. He has not yet announced any subject-matter more specific than that of the relation between actions and goods.

1.112 Means and Ends (1094a3–18)

Every undertaking, it is said, aims at something – some 'good.' But sometimes an activity has no end beyond itself; sometimes an activity is valued not for itself, but for what it will lead to (the end to which it is the means); sometimes its value derives from a wider understanding, of which it forms a part, and it is the outcome (or the ongoing successfulness) of the wider undertaking that is the good that is aimed at. And such undertakings are nested in complex ways: overall plans have sub-plans.

At first, the introduction of an activity that 'has no end beyond itself' looks like a dodge: we began by saying that every activity is aimed at something, and when it turns out that this is untrue, because we do many things just because we want to and not because we expect any good to come of them, Aristotle saves his thesis by calling these activities 'ends in themselves.' But of course it is not a dodge. The very same action that I perform just because I want to I might, on another occasion, perform without wanting to at all, but only because it formed part of a long-term plan or a wide-ranging strategy. In the former case, it has something positive that it lacks in the other cases: a value that I find in it, a kind of 'goodness.' To Aristotle, we shall see that this is crucial, in three ways. First, in talking about responsibility (III v), it is vital to observe that any action is, in a sense, neutral – we can always distinguish between what we are doing and why we are doing it. Second, the discussion of moral weakness in Book VII requires us to distinguish between the action performed and its attractiveness. And third, it turns out that the objectives to which our actions are subordinated as means or as contributing parts always cash out as, themselves, forms of activity – not the Porsche, but driving the Porsche or gloating over the Porsche. Meanwhile, we may reflect that, if one is to decide between immediately enticing activity and long-term strategy, one must be able to distance oneself from the immediate attractiveness of the activity one is considering.

We may note here, although Aristotle does not, that it is already obvious that the way to maximize the value of any action, simple or complex – to get the most out of it – will be to maximize its contributions on all three dimensions: to get the most satisfaction out of it; to achieve the best (and most copiously good) consequences from it; to make it integrate into the most satisfactory and widest wholes. Evidently an individual will do this only by thinking in terms of a whole lifetime and a whole structured community, in which all arts and pursuits are mutually integrated.

1.113 The Synthesis of Ends (1194a18–b11)

1.1131 A Single End (1194a18–22)

Especially in these early paragraphs, Aristotle keeps making what seem to be outrageous statements. I have suggested that when one looks at these closely they prove to have an inoffensive interpretation, and one sees later how they are to be defended. But perhaps one should be outraged. Like Plato, whose *Republic* still scandalizes comfortable liberalism, Aristotle is probably trying to stir things up. Anyway, now he says that if there is an end of what we do, and other things are wanted because of this, this end will be 'the good' (that is, we recall, that at which *all* things aim), the alternative being that we never want anything except as a means to something else, which would deprive desire of any satisfaction. But this is scandalous. This is the first time we have been told that it is *our* lives that are under discussion, that the relevant totality is the life plans of individuals and the overall policies of states. And nothing has suggested what the grammar here insinuates: that there is a single end of all the actions of an individual, or of a state, or indeed of humankind as a whole. Nor is the alternative presented, between unity and emptiness, even compatible with what we have been told; on the contrary, it has been admitted that there are things we just want for themselves. Though these separate objectives may be integrated with others in the ways suggested, there is no reason to think that this holds of most actual lives. On reflection, though, these objections collapse. We have seen that all values cash out into actually experienced values; the sum of these will turn out to have been the end achieved in a lifetime.[5]

The suggestion that 'the good' achieved by a whole lifetime might be simply the sum of the particular goods achieved within that life is less trivializing than it seems, because the 'end' of any animal in Aristotle's teleological biology is not to attain maturity but to *live* the life of its species.[6] So the end of action (in the sense of doing things) should be activity (in the sense of manifesting life, in a sense yet to be explained) – as in Book X it turns out to be. But we need not leave things at that: because of the three dimensions of value we have just distinguished, all the actions of an agent with a sense of time are interwoven, as the original paradigm of hierarchical subordination suggests. Of course, this interconnectedness of an agent's activity may still turn out to be trivial, in the sense that all summations and interconnections are equally good; but this itself would be a valuable conclusion. It is to the developing argument that we must look to see if the implicit unity of a lifetime (and its political analogue) has any significance. Meanwhile, nothing has yet been said to suggest that the actions of a lifetime, whether integrated causally and hierarchically or severally, can have any other kind of value. No sense has been given to the idea that there might be some overall objective for a life beyond the living of that life itself.

1.1132 Ends and Targets (1094a22–4)

We now hear that it will be useful if we can make this 'end (telos) of [all] our actions' a target (skopos) to aim at. But this is absurd and misleading. It is absurd because, if it is the end we are aiming at, it is already our target. It is misleading because what we are aiming at on any occasion is the good relative to a specific desire or intention, and not the sum of all goods, which cannot serve as a single target.

The answer to those objections is obvious enough. The analysis of action in On the Soul shows that any being with a sense of time is already involved in the integration of present and future actions. The sketch of how crafts and skills are organized has shown that they are already integrated into large areas of concern – health care or defence or education. All Aristotle's readers, including ourselves, are already in the midst of massively organized projects: the idea of a human life in which our actions would be separate responses to isolated stimuli is one that bears no relation to reality. But these integrations are performed unselfconsciously, on an ad hoc basis. Aristotle is saying that it would be better to see what considerations are or should be involved – to come clean about the structure of the practical thinking that we already find ourselves doing.[7] After all, as we said in commenting on the first sentence of the Ethics, the statement that all actions and so on aim at some good is a judgment, a theoretical statement. Aristotle is suggesting that we should act on it.

The fact is, as Aristotle will say in the very last chapter of the *Ethics* (X ix), most people do not actually consider the quality of their lives, take responsibility for themselves. They live from hand to mouth, as we say, responding to parental and peer pressure and conforming to educational and legal structures. This is the 'unexamined life' that Socrates in Plato's *Apology* says is not fit for human beings. There is another range of possibilities for humanity that is open to all but secured by few (just as philosophy and the sciences represent a range of intellectual achievement and delight that is open to all but actually enjoyed by few).

Is Aristotle right about this? Is human life better if we think about how to live well, instead of following whatever promptings we happen to have and pursuing whatever projects we happen to undertake? Aristotle does not sufficiently consider this problem. We hear later of the wisdom of Solon whose paradigms of human success were modest and obscure people;[8] what Aristotle does not say and perhaps does not notice is that they were not only unpretentious but apparently unreflective and unselfconscious about how they lived. If it is indeed true that we should make our spontaneous ends into targets consciously aimed at, it is not yet evident in what way or within what limits this is so.

If we reflect that the *telos* of a person's actions is not only the totality implicit in that person's lifelong network of choices but the active realization of the capacities of a human being as such, as explained in *On the Soul* II, it may occur to us that it is probably *not* a good idea to make this *telos* a *skopos*: it would be sensible to think twice before making a conscious objective out of a theoretical explanation of one's behaviour patterns. However, this is rather beside the point, since the context does not encourage us to interpret 'the good' in this way. But there are still two different ways of taking the argument about ends and goals. One is to say that since all one's objectives are going to be integrated in fact, one's conscious aim should be a life in which this is done as efficiently as possible, thus maximizing the achieved good in every possible way. The other way of taking the argument is to say that all ends are subjected in fact to a critique in the light of other ends, so that the supposed overall end of one's actions identified as 'the good' should be subjected to the same critique. One might then conclude that the best thing to do is to thrust this notion out of one's mind, arguing that 'the good' is either a spurious goal or one that is best pursued indirectly.[9]

1.1133 A Sort of Politics (1094a24–b11)

Does it even make sense to think of life as whole, rather than as a mass of loosely integrated events? Is 'the good' as an overriding object of planning in which all values are weighed against each other anything more than a philosopher's fancy? Yes, it is. The study and practice are already in place. Political organizations have to provide for all aspects of human activity and organization, and are prepared to make formal laws about them. This applies even to the scope of scientific research – a point that will become crucial later, because such intellectual activity is going to be assigned a special significance in human life. Aristotle does not spell this out, but it is not the government that actually makes decisions about everything: it is the 'city' (polis) – nowadays, the state as sovereign – that is prepared to decide about everything, including what the government shall intervene in.

The study we have in mind is, then, 'a sort of politics' – it applies to an individual life the same sort of structure of thought that is already involved in political discussions. This is actually a loaded contention, because, as Book I of Aristotle's Politics makes clear, the political organization, despite its comprehensiveness, and despite the fact that it is the setting of all Aristotle's readers, is special and is not found everywhere.[10] It is, precisely, a deliberate organization of social units to achieve a civilized life for the free individuals who are its members. They depend on the structure it provides, but its justification as anything more than a military alliance depends on the quality of the lives it makes possible. Of course, it is better and grander to secure this quality for one's nation and for cities (note the switch from singular to plural, of which more later) – but it is the same sort of thing.[11]

Aristotle seems to be saying that ethics (that is, what we are now doing – neither this term nor any equivalent for it has yet been used) is a branch of politics, and that view is often ascribed to him. But his language, here and elsewhere, is not decisive. One has to distinguish between three things: the political type of thinking, the practice of seeking the welfare of a community to which one belongs, and the practice of the professional kind of politics that statesmen do. At 1094a28 he says only that politics has the character of the kind of thinking we are looking for, being maximally authoritative and architectonic; and at 1094b10–11 he says it is politikē tis, 'a sort of politics.' But that probably means that it is not literally politics: that is what the word *tis* (the closest Greek comes to the indefinite article 'a') most often means in phrases like this – 'politics, as it were.'[12] At 1141b21ff., Aristotle will deny that ethics is the same as what is literally 'politics,' what politicians as such do, and the descriptions of *Politics* III bear this out. In any case, nothing in the *Ethics* looks back to any thesis in Aristotle's political theory or anyone else's: ethics is not a branch of politics in *that* sense.[13] Granted that the lives with which the *Ethics* is concerned are lived in cities, what cities exist to secure is the individual welfare that the *Ethics* investigates.[14]

Though the point is nowhere developed in the *Ethics*, it is worth dwelling on the wording of the comparison between individual and social action. It appears, says Aristotle, to be a bigger and more complete thing to obtain and secure the 'human good' (for this phrase, see § 1.1135) for the city than for one person alone.[15] That seems uncontroversial: bigger, yes of course; more complete, certainly, because more comprehensive. But what is this 'obtain and secure,' or 'seize and retain'? That language has no clear application to the values realized in the course of a life. It is the language of conquest or (more especially) of economics, and will play no real part either in the *Ethics* or in the *Politics*.[16] And what follows is really odd: it is desirable (*agapēton*) to do it for one alone, but 'finer and more god-like' for 'nation and cities' (*ethnei kai polesin*). What is the word 'fine' doing here? It suggests a new whole range of values, one that will be important later but is not explained here. And what about 'more godlike'? We are talking about the *human* good; what have the gods and their attributes to do with it? We know from *Metaphysics* I 2 that intellectual work is godlike, and this in its relation to what is merely human is supremely important for Aristotle, as we will see in Book X; but the divinity in the present sentence seems to be merely that of a war god. It is hard not to relate this to the figure, incongruous in the context of Aristotle's practical philosophy, of Alexander the Great, the God-King (precursor of the deified Roman Emperors, rival of the Persian King), imposing on the Asian empires the Hellenic regime of city life (hence the plural 'cities') and glorifying the Hellenic race (hence the singular of 'nation'), and thus seizing and preserving for his new domains a way of life that he does not necessarily share. If this sort of imperialistic enterprise is what Aristotle has in mind, it is indeed an anomaly in the *Ethics*.[17]

The comparison between self and city, as though politics and ethics did the same thing on a different scale, raises another problem of which Aristotle takes no notice here. If my project as an agent is to

secure and integrate the objectives that I have, this is surely something other people must also do for themselves. It is, after all, only
my own life that I have to live; I can advise and help others, but
cannot live their lives for them. If I am to make my own decisions,
no other person can make my decisions for me. The politician who
makes decisions for the city usurps my prerogative. The alternative,
however, is democracy in the old literal sense, which Aristotle rather
deplores as a sort of communal anarchy (cf. 1161ab–9). In a well-
organized community, people have autonomy, and the firm social
structure provides the situation in which that autonomy is realized.
In my own case, as a university teacher I will never be department
head, let alone dean of my faculty; as a citizen, I obviously will never
be and *can* never be city councillor, let alone member of parliament
or minister – but it never occurs to me to regard this refusal to
appoint or elect me as an infringement on my autonomy and hence
a diminution of my humanity. And perhaps that odd language that
I imagined as contrasting Alexander with his subjects is in point here:
the deans do not run my life and secure my well-being, they impose
and seize and preserve the structure within which I teach my classes
and live my life.

A position like that just stated is available to Aristotle and fits his
thought, but he nowhere articulates it. Its basis is implicit in *Politics*
I, and an aspect of it appears in the justification of legal order in X
ix; but, as we shall see in § 4, it is in the facts of friendship that a
true reconciliation is to be sought.

1.1134 The Human Good

In the middle of the passage we have just reviewed, at 1094b7,
Aristotle for the first time names the object of our inquiry. The end
aimed at by politics, because it would embrace all other ends, would
be 'the human good' (*to anthrōpinon agathon*). What does that mean?

Anthrōpos is a term of very general scope, including all human
beings. The 'good' we are to study is not that for men or for women,
for Athenians or for Macedonians or Stagyrites, but for anyone –
whatever his reasons, Aristotle is very careful to stipulate 'cities' and
not 'the city,' we noted, and *ethnei* means one's tribe or extended
family, kith and kin.[18] But the good is not that of humanity as a whole,
either; it is that of the maximal unit, at whatever level, for which joint
decisions are actually made. (That rules out empires as well as worlds,
at least in an age of limited communications techniques.)

The scope is humanity. It follows that we are not concerned with Greek mores as such; if Aristotle's argument depends on what is specific to a given community, as is held by those who say he is concerned to expound the morality and folkways of upper-class Athenian males, he fails in his professed task. Of course, the question of how I am to live my life is the question of how I am to live the life of the human I am in the place and time where I am. But that question is formally the same for everyone. Our question must be whether anything can be said *in general* about how that question is to be answered. It is because Aristotle knows that that is the question that his work is still agreed to be worth reading, even at this distance of place and time and with our very different attitudes.

Our question, then, is: how am I to live my life? The question, we have seen, does in a way impose itself for any being with a sense of time. What we do not know yet is whether any answer to that practical question is any better than any other. Aristotle is acutely aware of that problem, as we shall see.

Meanwhile, the most important thing of all is this: the implicit stance is that of the person who wants to live the best possible life. We are not concerned, in the first instance, with pontificating and anathematizing, with laying down the law for others. Though Aristotle says much about praise and blame as our responses to the way other people behave, it is the quality of that behaviour itself in the context of an individual's life that is his central concern.

1.11341 Comment: Sexism in Aristotle

Aristotle uses the gender-neutral word anthrōpos *to refer to human beings, and there is nothing anywhere in the* Ethics *that applies to one sex rather than another. But we have seen that he acknowledges that different callings and stations in life call for different behaviour patterns, and he himself is speaking as an adult male to males in a society that excluded women from property ownership as well as from public life. Perhaps what he assumes is generically human actually reflects male attitudes to power, a fact that escapes him because his lectures have no female input.*

Aristotle's treatment of gender is complex; I have dealt with it at length elsewhere.[19] He distinguishes five separate aspects of femininity, which do not necessarily go together. They are as follows:

1 / *the specific sexual differences between male and female animals (including humans) are relevant only to coition and parturition;*

2 / *in many animal species, the sexes are also differentiated in their general physiology and behaviour patterns;*

3 / *among humans, the basic unit is the family, in which the male is the hunter or gatherer and the female is the keeper, and the hunter is the head of the household; this reflects human physiology (men are less sedentary) and the needs of child rearing;*

4 / *in civil society generally, men and women have different ways of life which call for different manifestations of virtue;*

5 / *in cities, women are usually excluded from civic functions and hence from citizenship.*

Since the above are only loosely related to each other, one cannot identify the differences between men and women in a given society with differences between males and females of the human species, and generalizations about 'men' and 'women' would be out of place in a treatise on the human good. The account of phronēsis *and the moral virtues, no less than that of* sophia, *applies equally to all humans (see* Metaphysics XI 9).

Aristotle was a male chauvinist, in the very precise sense that he thought that economic and physiological realities made it normal for males to exercise power, and – this is the crucial point – that to exercise power and leadership in a decision-making position is a sign of general superiority. This is built into his whole project of deciding how to live, *as if one had power over oneself, one's destiny, one's world.*

I take it that the profound implication of feminist thought is that the whole ideology of decision and direction is radically mistaken, needing to be supplemented or replaced by patterns of life based on acceptance and love. From that point of view, Aristotle's ethical philosophy is misconceived. That being so, is there anything in the Ethics *that supports the alternative viewpoint?*

Books VIII and IX of EN *represent a new approach. In fact, they constitute a model for an alternative way of considering the values of human life, one that takes as basic the conditions of cooperation and community. Suppose a treatise on ethics were to start there, and introduce the values of individual striving within that setting as a subsidiary theme. The result would be a radically different perspective on human well-being: if the* Ethics *as it stands identifies male values with generically human values, a consideration of the same material from a perspective defined by friendship and community would yield a corresponding identification of the female with the generically human. It is not easy to see how such a starting-point could have been either practically or theoretically accessible to anyone situated as Aristotle was; but within a few decades Epicurus, some of whose philosophi-*

cal associates were women, worked out a system of ethics which effectively harmonizes both communitarian and individual values. And one of the things this involves is abandoning what emerges as Aristotle's highest ideal, the pursuit of theoretical truth for its own sake.

1.114 Methodological Implications (I iii; 1094b11–1095a13)

The foregoing material has given us a lot of difficulty. Every sentence starts a new train of thought, in effect announces a new topic, the nature of which will become apparent much later if at all. But the translator or expositor of his thought has an extra difficulty. Aristotle's statements are extraordinarily vague and general in scope. Terms are loosely interdefined or undefined. He seems to set out a lot of formal relationships based on the necessary structure of action in animals with a 'sense of time,' and leaves it unclear just what they apply to. Aristotle is aware of this, for the next point he makes is that we can make things only as clear as the subject-matter allows. We are not doing mathematics, where we can stipulate what we mean: we are describing what goes on in human life, where even empirical generalizations are seldom safe. Many commentators discuss Aristotle's work as though he were attempting a precision of statement that would be proof against objections, like a doctoral dissertation. But he is not: the free-flowing handling of the relation between ethics and politics, which we encountered in the previous section, exemplifies the way in which he accommodates the complexities of psychological and social reality.

Aristotle explains his point by borrowing from the fifth-century philosopher Protagoras, as expounded by Plato in his *Protagoras* and *Theaetetus* and developed in the *Gorgias*. In politics, three sorts of values are recognized: what is fine and ideal (*kalon*) as opposed to ugly and degrading, what is just and lawful (*dikaion*) as opposed to what is forbidden by law (written and unwritten), what is good and useful (*agathon*) as opposed to what is harmful and disadvantageous. But different societies have different ideals and different laws, to the point where it is widely held that ideals and laws are a mere matter of consensus and have no objective ('natural') basis. That leaves the good and the useful. This is not a matter of consensus: good fortune is good fortune, it is better to be rich than to be poor, good qualities really are good qualities, courage is better than cowardice.[20] All the same, people can be ruined by their wealth and destroyed by their courage. Working with such variable data, any conclusions we reach will be sketchy. To work in this field, we have to recognize these limitations, and that means we have to know what life is like. In these opening chapters, we can't *explain* just what we are referring to; our understanding has to be controlled by our general understanding of how things go in the world. It follows that young people, who don't have this experience, find such discussions alien.

Aristotle follows this reflection on his subject and the way he had to present it with a closely related but different point, which he presents simply as an explication of it. It is not merely that young people have too little experience of the world to follow serious policy discussions. What they lack is the very concept of a lifetime, a life strategy, a policy; they simply follow their inclinations. It is as though they had no sense of time. As they grow up they will acquire it – but, of course, some people never grow up. And that means, says Aristotle, that discourse about politics is useless to them even to the extent that they can understand it: the purpose of such discourse is to help us formulate better policies, and unless one know what a policy is and is capable of formulating and following policies, listening to such talk is a waste of time. It is useful only to people who are already formulating their projects and performing their actions 'in accordance with *logos*' – with 'reason,' as the translators say. (This is the first time we have come across that word *logos*; it is a key term in the subsequent argument. I discuss it in § 1.212.)

1.12 Happiness as the Human Good (I iv–vi; 1095a13–1097a14)

What we have sketched so far is the idea of an objective that is both comprehensive and final, resulting from the way activities are nested within each other and lead to each other, an idea implicit in the practical thinking that every animal inevitably does if it has a sense of time, and if it is capable of reasoning – as it must be, if it has a sense of time. This objective is the actual objective of politics, and of its analogue in individual life, 'ethics.' Aristotle writes as if no one had actually proposed the notion of ethics before him – or rather, before his mentor Plato and their inspiration Socrates, prophet of the 'examined' life and professed exponent of a 'merely human' wisdom such as might be correlated with our present topic, the 'human good.'[21]

But what are we to say about this vague and elusive notion, the 'human good'? Since it is generically 'human' it cannot be relative to the male sex only, or to Athenian Greeks rather than Spartans or

Persians: specific cultural phenomena must be relegated to the situation in which the person acts. The possibility of giving a general account of the *human* good must depend on the possibility of outlining a general method of dealing with situations, together with a general typology of situations to be dealt with. These generalities can then be exemplified, without prejudice, by one's own local practices.

It is true that 'the human good' has not been made a theme of critical inquiry before, but we have seen that it is what people and states already pursue in an unsystematic way – all we have to do is to convert the unselfconscious *telos* into a conscious *skopos*. So we can get a handle on it by tapping existing notions – as Aristotle is about to say, there is a sense in which people cannot be wrong about what they want, what they suffer from the lack of. We must look at their patterns of thought in this matter, as well as the commonplaces they exchange. To do this, we introduce a new term: *eudaimonia*, etymologically something like 'having a good guardian angel,' but adequately translated as 'happiness.'[22]

1.121 Happiness (1095a14–22)

'Happiness' is just another word for the 'human good' we have been talking about. So why introduce it? Because it is the word everyone uses. We can milk everyday talk about 'happiness' for clues about what people actually think is the best thing people can have in and out of life – the 'pinnacle of goods achievable in action,' as Aristotle puts it at this point. The advantage of the word is that practically everyone does use it, the elite (or 'intellectuals,' *charientes*) and plain people alike, and takes for granted the equation between happiness and 'living well' or 'doing well.' The disadvantage is that the word does not carry its real meaning on its face. No one really believes in guardian angels or fairy godmothers. So most people talk about their lives in terms that are not conducive to critical appraisal. And, in fact, sophisticated people and plain folks give quite different accounts of what happiness is. From our point of view, though Aristotle does not say so, this is all to the good: plain folks hew close to the line of their actual experience, sophisticated people have sophisticated ideas. We can take advantage of both.

1.122 Experience and Speculation (1095a22–b13)

Unreflective views of happiness differ from reflective views in two ways: they consider brief episodes instead of considering a whole lifetime, and they take shallow views of those episodes themselves. Most people, says Aristotle, identify 'happiness' with something 'plain and obvious' like health, wealth, pleasure, and respect, something forced on their attention by the fact that they don't have it and are consequently miserable.[23] Of course, people can wish for anything (as we will see in III iv), even crazy things; but if there is something that regularly turns up on such want lists, we can be pretty sure that it is an essential component in or condition of *eudaimonia*.[24] And, in fact, Aristotle does use these four plain and obvious things as a kind of check-list – whatever our conclusion is, it will have to give them a place. But it is not clear *what* place; the most important thing might be something we did not know we were missing, or did not realize the importance of because we had never been without it.

Many plain people are reflective enough to realize that their thinking follows the above pattern; so, if they are miserable and don't know why, or even if they feel they might be better off than they are and don't know how, they feel there must be some secret of the good life that some clever or saintly person could tell them. So prophets and humbugs and charlatans get a good hearing, and can never be discredited because we can always attribute our failure to profit from them to our own inadequacies – the vague inadequacies that sent us to them in the first place. Aristotle has no time for such spiritual hungers. We are already human beings living the lives of our species, and it is absurd to think that a good life would be something outside the scope of our actual experience. Or is it so absurd? Perhaps this actual feeling of inadequacy, expressed in the traditional contrast between the all-too-human and the bliss of the immortal gods, does answer to a contrast between unrealized and realized values of human life. But thus far we have no content to give to that suggestion, and to countenance it would be to open the door indiscriminately to mystery-mongers of all sorts.

Meanwhile, we have an indeterminate mass of plausible ingredients in the good life, resting on a rough consensus of the experience of plain people, together with the innumerable specific goods embodied in our activities in the ways sketched at the start of our book. What holds this mass together? At this point, we are tempted by the suggestion that there is something else to be invoked – not, this time, a sort of 'pie in the sky,' but something of a different order, an explanatory principle, a theory to show, not how our experience can be found to hold together, but the nature of the simple underlying reality that grounds our diversity. But is such a theory in place? What kind of theory, if any, do we want? Aristotle breaks off to point out that this raises a second methodological problem, though it is one he nowhere really resolves.

1.1221 A Digression on Method (1095a30–b13)

'Aristotle breaks off,' I said; and at the end Aristotle says he has been digressing. But it is only a digression from one point of view. Exactly the same sequence of thought is followed in Aristotle's general treatise on argumentation (*Topics* I 11–12, 104b1ff.), where he follows a discussion of what problems and opinions are worth discussing with a distinction between induction (*epagōgē*) and reasoning (*syllogismos*), just as he does here. So it looks as if he is using a general method of enquiry. In fact, though, the reason for introducing the question at this point in the *Ethics* is stronger than in the general treatise, where it figures as just one in a series of related topics.

Are we on the way to or from first principles, making inductions from facts or reasoning from general truths? '*Even* Plato used to ask that.' The allusion to Plato is very much in point. It was Plato who made Socrates (in the *Phaedo*, 97B–98B) complain that nothing could really be understood until one had a grasp of the universe as a whole, so that one could see why everything had to be as it had to be, and (in the *Republic*, VI–VII) explain why this grasp of absolute goodness was necessary and how it would be used – an explanation in which it appears that such a grasp would, indeed, function as a premise from which deductions should be made. And, as we shall see, it is the Platonic version of the 'self-subsistent good' (1095a27) that Aristotle will specify and attack. So the present point is that Plato was violating his own principles, demanding deductive methods when inductive methods were called for.

Meanwhile, Aristotle does not say in so many words whether we are on our way to or from first principles, although it is implied that the former is the case. We start with the facts, which are familiar from experience. But then it is implied that the facts themselves are principles, or nearly so. So which way are we going? It looked as if Aristotle had a simple point to make, but then he does not make it but says something thoroughly confusing. What is going on?

The fact is, we are not dealing with raw data of experience. When Aristotle speaks of 'phenomena,' he means what is *evidently* so, what everyone can see to be the case, and such general knowledge is embodied in generalizations of small scope: judgments of the worth of health in general, of glory in general. And we will see in Book VI that principles are to be found *in both directions*. The principles of practical reasoning – the unargued premises of moral argument – are of two sorts: a general sense of what is good in life as a whole, and specific insights into the practical character of the situations we are in at a given time. So we cannot answer Plato's question, certainly not in the form it took in the *Topics*. In fact, though Aristotle never puts it this way, most of what we do in the *Ethics* is neither deduction nor induction, but clarification, both of the texture of experience and of the concepts whereby we articulate experience.

It is because clarification is what is required that our actual starting-point is the experiential reality that stands in need of clarification – we need to have been well brought up, or at least to recognize good conduct when we see it.[25] This too is a point from the passage in the *Topics* we have just looked at: 'people who are puzzled to know whether one ought to honour the gods and love (*agapan*) one's parents or not need punishment' (105a5), not argument – the sort of thing we need to argue about in ethics is rather whether one ought 'to obey one's parents or the laws, when they disagree' (105b22).

But does this not beg the whole question? Indeed it does, and we return to the issue in III v. It was just because upbringing without explanation is merely indoctrination that Plato's Socrates hankered after that underlying self-subsistent goodness that Aristotle is complaining about as involving a methodological mistake. A lot hangs, therefore, on Aristotle's ability to debunk the notion, as he tries to do in I vi. But whether the debunking is effective will really depend on Aristotle's ability to differentiate his own methods from a complacent endorsement of the folkways. And neither that problem nor its solution has surfaced at this stage of the discussion.[26]

Aristotle's concern is that one should not suppose that the values of life are something radically other than what we know from experience. Human lives are the lives that humans live; we are real beings living in a real world, not beings inexplicably ill-adapted to the only world we know and designed for a life in a different world with different bodies or no bodies at all. It sounds very reasonable, and I for one am inclined to applaud his contempt for cults that invent fantastic scenarios for their believers. But, methodologically, he is vulnerable, because his whole scientific methodology is weak. It is conceivable that we and our world are such that, to explain us and it, one must make a leap of faith to frame some unlikely-sounding hypothesis with which the explananda conform. True, in ethics, a hypothesis (or dogma) that flew in the face of the facts of our experience and our sense of ourselves would be ruled out of court. But Aristotle's explanation of the prevalence of mystic cults in his own day as in ours – namely, that people are so conscious of their own ignorance that they believe anything charlatans tell them – will hardly do. People are as they are, and one of the things they noticeably are is prone to form religions with otherworldly scenarios. Aristotle, as we will see, has an explanation for the pathology; that it *is* a pathology is something he rather takes for granted. The proper end of humanity's natural orientation towards knowledge is scientific and metaphysical understanding, not some visionary short-cut.

1.123 Ways of Life (I v; 1095b14–1096a10)

'But as for us,' says Aristotle, contrasting himself and his hearers with the useless men Hesiod has described (a little joke there; Ross's translation misses it), let's get back where we left off. Where were we? We said we would take as our data the prevailing views about happiness – popular views, those of the sophisticated, and theoretical constructions. So that is what we now do. But we take them at a higher level of generality than before, when we simply named the unreflective outfall of experience. What we now look at is values considered as ideal *ways of life*, not just qualities or objects of experiences.[27] It turns out that the many and the sophisticated have one each. Ordinary people opt for a life of recreation and enjoyment; superior people go for public life. And then there is the intellectual life, which is something else. And, of course, the life of money making. We waste little time on any of them. None of them has the comprehensive and final quality we are looking for.

Where do these three lives come from? Most obviously, from the tradition expressed in Prodicus's fable of 'Heracles at the Crossroads,' in which the young hero must choose between a life of ease and a life of toil – a life for self and a life for others, to put the same choice in different conceptual terms.[28] Another version of such contrasts is that between Achilles and Thersites in the *Iliad*: it is assumed (or observed) that there are two kinds of people in the world, the classes and the masses, the superior people and the riff-raff, the dominant warrior class and the worthless peasants they hold in subjection. One of Aristotle's problems, though he never acknowledges it, will be to reinstate this class distinction so that it seems to reflect free choices rather than result from destinies of domination and subjection with their associated value systems.

Part of the curse is taken off by the addition of a third way of life, that of 'contemplation,' which cannot be effectively reduced to these class terms. The addition is due to Plato, who is undoubtedly Aristotle's immediate source here. In *Republic* IV, Plato introduces the three ways of life, in the order in which Aristotle gives them here; but he introduces them fundamentally as three motivational or evaluational patterns.[29] The 'life of pleasure' corresponds to the tendency to act on one motive after another in one context after another, without any integration. The political life corresponds to the values of self-preservation, the vindication of the whole self. The intellectual life answers to dispassionate problem solving, the desire to do what the situation as a whole objectively demands – what Plato calls 'justice.' Each of these complexes affords a separate ground for a morality, each has its own satisfactions, each has its distinctive part to play in a good life. This complex analysis, as a whole, pervades the entire *Ethics* in many subtle ways. But, for the present, its components are taken at face value and briskly disposed of. Pleasure and politics are both dismissed as superficial – mere enjoyment does not touch what is human in humanity, public life likewise concerns itself with externals. We are not told what lies beneath the life of enjoyment (it turns out in X vi to be the value of freedom and leisure), but we are told what lies beneath the politician's desire for fame – it is the assurance of one's own worth, so that the underlying true value is that of human excellence and its manifestation in action. And as for the intellectual life, nothing is said about that, though it is included in the general critique as less than final and comprehensive.[30]

The survey of ways of life ends with a rather odd note on money making. This can't be the good life; it is something one does out of necessity (or out of some compulsion?), and money is only a means to an end. Well, one might agree that the accumulation of amounts of money one cannot use is crazy – philosophers and their readers are likely to think that (or pretend to do so). But with this dismissal the whole economic dimension of life is swept under the rug. I will return to this criticism later.

Meanwhile, it is noticeable that while Aristotle denounces money making as the pathology of the economic life, he never mentions the love of power as the pathology of politics, although the phenomenon keeps surfacing in Plato's dialogues. The omission seems odd. It is typical of Aristotle throughout the *Ethics* not to countenance quirks and absurdities; but then one does not see why the economic life is mentioned only in its pathological form. I suppose the reason must be that any value one finds in one's work must come from pride in its products or enjoyment of its activities, and not from the incidental accumulation of the mere means of exchange; but this is not said.[31]

This brief treatment of 'ways of life' is unsatisfactory, to say the least, and Aristotle's irritable dismissal of the topic leaves us wondering why he bothered. But in fact it has furnished ingredients that he will need: pleasure, leisure, glory, and idealism, the primacy of action over condition and of personal over other values. Most important, perhaps, it has introduced the idea of a choice between distinctive ways of life, which will be structurally as well as substantively important in Book X.

1.124 The Good as Universal (I vi; 1096a10–1097a16)

We have now looked at the plain people's viewpoint and that of the sophisticates. Have we said anything about the 'pie in the sky' approach of the gullible who hope some guru will tell them the secret of life? Apparently not, unless Aristotle is being ironic about his own unexplained allusions to the intellectual life. But perhaps there is a 'pie in the sky' aspect to what we discuss next, the postulation of a metaphysical foundation of goodness. Historically, that would make sense: in the *Phaedo* (100C–E), Socrates contrasts his own 'stupid' and down-to-earth theory of 'forms' with the grandiose promise of an all-explaining 'mind' that had once led him to study the writings of Anaxagoras – precisely the authority-seeking mind-set that Aristotle describes.

Be that as it may, what we turn to now is the postulation of a non-empirical somewhat, 'goodness as such,' the understanding of which is supposed to be a prerequisite of knowing what and how anything else can be *really* good, as opposed to merely useful or pleasant in some context. The idea is indeed attractive, as Socrates explains: in our own lives, our usual difficulty in deciding what is really the best thing to do is that we don't know enough – about the consequences, about the context, about our own psychology; so, by analogy, an omniscient Being who knew all contexts and consequences and psychologies and causal relationships would know all about the world, and hence would know what is really good. If that is not true, we are tempted to think, the phrase 'really good' has no definite application and the question of how we should live has no determinate answer. What Aristotle has to show is not merely that such knowledge is beyond our reach, but that the very concept of such knowledge is incoherent, that if there were such knowledge it would not give us the answer to our practical question, and that the practical question has a sufficient answer without it. This is in line with Aristotle's general attack on the theory of 'forms' in the *Metaphysics*: just as a separable form cannot constitute the reality of an individual, so the form of goodness cannot constitute the goodness of a particular life or objective, which must be a *practicable* good.

Aristotle's discussion is highly technical and virtually unintelligible – the conventional wisdom is that it is a condensed version of an earlier critique of his own, the general lines of which would be familiar within the narrow milieu (Plato's Academy) in which it had been composed and was now summarized. Its details do nothing for us today, but we will say something about its general thrust.

As elsewhere, the order of treatment within this enclave in the *Ethics* is not determined by the requirements of the work as a whole, but by its own internal organization. So far as we are concerned (for we have no information as to what sorts of considerations determined the structure of the original critique), the passage consists of a number of independent points directed against the contention that there is something, the general nature of goodness in itself, knowledge of which is certainly necessary and perhaps sufficient for people wishing to make the right decisions about how to live their lives.

Three comments to begin with. First, Aristotle introduces his topic as 'the universal' – that is, goodness as the common property of all good things. But that does not seem to be what Socrates had in mind in the *Phaedo* or what is suggested in the *Republic*, where it looks as if a quite different structure was envisaged, something more like what later philosophers would call a 'concrete universal.' But our second comment is that this may not be relevant because, although the Platonic theory of 'forms' is clearly what Aristotle has in mind, the actual theory being discussed is not attributed to Plato, either here or anywhere else – it is attributed to 'men who are friends of ours' (*philoi andres*).[32] What Aristotle attacks here and in the *Metaphysics* as the theory of forms seems to be an elaborated doctrine of which we have no other evidence, one presumably worked out in the Academy (whose younger members would be more suitably called 'friends of ours' than the hoary Plato) but not really compatible with what is in Plato's dialogues or with what Aristotle attributes to Plato by name. And the third point I would make is that one may wonder whether the demolition job that Aristotle does on the doctrines he dissects here is really directed against the strongest case that could have been made for an objective and universal foundation of all real goodness. The solution to the problem of the objectivity of human good that Aristotle will soon be proposing may look stronger than it is because we have looked at no strong competitors.

1.1241 Goodness as a Property (1095a18–28)

Aristotle's first point is that goodness is not a common property of good things. Good things include good people, good times, good places; and substances and times and places have nothing in common. 'What?' 'Where?' and 'When?' are quite different questions. What the questions have in common is that they may have right or wrong answers, and that some answers are better than others. The kind of practical thinking they call for is quite unlike an attempt to identify and quantify a single quality that all good things might share.

1.1242 Knowing What Is Good (1096a29–33)

Even when we confine ourselves to things (such as people and states of affairs) that might be meaningfully said to have qualities, is there any such thing as general knowledge about what is good? Apparently not. There is an important concept in Greek practical thought, especially in medicine: *kairos*, what we sometimes colloquially refer to as 'the psychological moment,' the exact point at which an intervention has to be made (perform surgery; take the cake out of the oven; call for the question in a political debate; assassinate the archduke; launch a counter-offensive) to get the desired result – not too soon, not too late, and in just the right place and the right time. To know what this opportune moment is, what we need is not general knowledge about the nature of goodness, but detailed knowledge and experience of the relevant skill and discipline – medicine, or cooking, or revolutionary politics, or whatever it may be. Knowing the subject-matter is the same as knowing where all aspects of its goodness lie. So here too: as Aristotle has said before, knowledge of ethics is knowledge of life, not a different sort of specialized knowledge.

To this, one might reply that there is a requisite knowledge of goodness: the knowledge that goodness is indeed this sort of concept, that the things we are now saying are true and important, so that (for instance) discerning the *kairos* calls for information and judgment, not prayer and philosophy. But Aristotle could respond that such a knowledge of goodness would not be properly described as knowledge of the form or idea of goodness itself, which again suggests the wrong model for the mental operations required.

1.1243 Is the Good Good? (1096a33–b8)

The very concept of 'the good itself' is deceptive. To be good, we saw at the start, is to be the proper object of an interest; *the* good is the object of all interests, or of all the relevant interests in the context of discussion. It makes no sense to speak of anything as *supremely* good as if its goodness were somehow quintessential or different in kind from other goods, or somehow explanatory of their goodness, or as if its goodness were of a different order because it was eternal and abstracted from the world of process. Real goods are the objects of actual interests, and that is what makes them good, and there is no other way of being good – just as, Aristotle significantly adds, there is nothing more human than a human being. No postulated entity that would take us out of the domain of actual people living actual lives in which they do actual things for actual reasons is of any concern to us.

1.1244 Intrinsic and Instrumental Goods (1096b8–25)

The notion of 'the good itself' implies that there is only one thing we really want – the unique quality of goodness, which only 'the good' really has, and to which all other goods are merely indifferent means, and in the goodness of which they imperfectly share. This is the clear implication of the language of the 'theory of forms' whenever it is used. But that is misleading. There is indeed a distinction between what we want for itself, and what we want as a means to or a part of other things, as we said at the beginning. And, because plans and strategies can be related to each other, it may be that all our particular objectives are in some sense means to a further objective, *the* good – in fact, this is the case; *the* good for each of us is the good relative to our whole lifetime. But that does not mean that everything we want *in* life is worthless in itself, a mere means to a good life; on the contrary, the goodness of a good life depends on us valuing and obtaining specific objectives within it, which we want for themselves. And the reason we want them for themselves is because each has its own unique value, for which nothing else can be substituted. Once again, the notion of a 'goodness itself' that is the ground of the goodness of all other things imposes just the wrong pattern on practical thinking.

1.1245 The Form as End (1096b25–35)

The foregoing considerations do not dispose of the idea of a metaphysical ground of the goodness of all goods. There may well be arguments for postulating such an entity – a treatise on ethics is no place to determine such a deep theoretical issue. The point here is rather that it does not answer the present question. Our question arose out of the practical problem confronting an agent with a sense of time, who must decide what strategies to use in relating present and future concerns. The only sort of good that concerns us is a good that is within the compass of what we can do and get in actual practice. The supposed ground of all goodness is not that sort of thing at all. For practical purposes, it is no good.

1.1246 The Form as Principle (1096b35–1097a14)

Of course, the proponents of a 'Goodness Itself' that is somehow the ground of all values (never mind how – it is the general form of the argument that is in point, not its detail or proper formulation) did not suppose that it was something people could do or get. The idea is, as we said, that knowledge of the underlying nature of the world as a meaningful system would enable us to distinguish between real and illusory values – a plausible idea. Aristotle's response, in the end, is singularly lame. His reply is that this is not how we proceed. An expert in any field concentrates on the specifics of that field: the better doctors are, the less they talk about disease in general and the more they concentrate on the individual patient under treatment. The trouble with this reply is that it seems to undercut Aristotle's own enterprise in the *Ethics*. It suggests that people should not worry generally about 'the human good' but should concentrate on the job in hand; that it is a mistake to convert one's 'end' into one's 'target.'

How has Aristotle fallen into this trap, if trap it is? Perhaps the best thing to say is that Aristotle's own procedure is dialectical, and the trouble with the universalistic patterns of thought he has been considering is that they are not. His own procedure is dialectical in the sense that the introduction of universal considerations is always in the context of given concerns, and the treatment of given concerns is always to be in the light of holistic considerations. The Plato implicit in the dialogues was a similarly dialectical thinker; the trouble with the 'theory of forms' under attack in the present passage is that it is relentlessly abstract. Whether Aristotle's picture of it is just we have no way of knowing, since we know nothing about it except what he tells us.

Aristotle concludes his treatment with an impatient-sounding remark, which the conventional chapter divisions unfortunately split into two: 'That's enough about that, let's get back to the good we were looking for.'

1.13 The Good: Formal Requirements (1097a15–b21)

Aristotle now offers us a recapitulation, in which, it appears, the data from what people say and think about *eudaimonia* support the formal analysis suggested by the examination of the concept of the good in I i–ii. Happiness cannot be something beyond the bounds of our lives, because all ends cash out into terms of activity. But (I would add) it cannot lie in a *pattern* of activity, because such patterns can always be interrupted and will, in any case, be arbitrarily cut off at death. It follows that happiness must lie in the *texture* of active life. The three attributes that happiness has been shown to have are finality or completeness, adequacy, and being the object of desire – a triad (if the third item is really distinct from the other two) introduced by Plato at *Philebus* 20D.[33]

1.131 Ultimacy (1097a15–30)

From our critique of the three 'lives,' it appears that 'the good' is something ultimate, the final objective of our actions and not something that is really wanted only for the sake of something else, in the way that people want praise as a means to self-assurance. On the other hand, from the critique of the notion of absolute goodness, it appears that the good is something within the domain of practice. But it does not follow from these considerations that there is a single objective of all our actions. On the contrary, there seem to be many such disparate objectives – there were many things that people in different states of deprivation identified as 'happiness,' and our whole discussion began from the existence of a diversity of organized bodies of practice. The fact that '*the* good' is what we want as an end and not as a means to an end leaves it open whether there is one such ultimate end or a multiplicity. But if there is (as there seems to be) a multiplicity, the expression '*the* good' would be applicable to whichever of them was 'most ultimate' (*teleiotaton*). What exactly does 'ultimate' (*teleios*) mean? The question recurs to plague us throughout the *Ethics*. It means 'having the quality of an end' (*telos*), but what it implies is not termination but completeness or perfection. Perfection implies completeness, but that does not entail all-inclusiveness: it might rather be complete correspondence with the relevant ideal. This ambiguity is functional in Aristotle: when we first invoke this value of 'perfection,' we typically do not know which sort of perfection will turn out to be relevant – in the *Ethics*, we have to wait for X vii to be sure. As elsewhere, it is a mistake to force on Aristotle's thesis at this point a determinacy that it necessarily lacks. However we take it, though, this is a cryptic remark, because the expression 'most ultimate' seems as meaningless as 'most unique.' It could mean that what seems ultimate from one perspective might be intermediate from another, in the way that an unexpected summons transforms a completed journey into one leg of a longer journey. Or it could mean that something we once judged perfect fades into indifference in comparison with some more compelling end that a changed perspective makes available to our imagination. In fact, however, the remarks about politics in I ii, together with the project as determined by the theory of action in *On the Soul*, determine a different interpretation, to which we now turn.

1.132 Intrinsicality (1097a31–b6)

Aristotle now makes what seems to me the dubious comment that the expression 'more ultimate' takes a meaning from the fact that something wanted for itself may also be wanted for the sake of something else. Someone who wants to accumulate money for its own sake may also value it for the sake of what it can buy. For such a person, money is less purely an ultimate goal than it would be for a true miser who had no interest in what it could buy. The comment seems dubious to me, though its logic is impeccable in its way, because it seems to put a premium on a narrow sort of single-mindedness.

It turns out, however, that Aristotle has something rather different in mind. He is thinking of the logic of the concept of happiness as he has discussed it. People just use the word *eudaimonia* for whatever it is that they ultimately want – money, health, insight, glory, fun, whatever. But these are indeed the things they *ultimately* want. It follows that if you ask them 'Why do you want to be righteous?' (or whatever it may be) they can truthfully and adequately answer 'I just *do*, that's all.' But they can answer with equal truth 'Because it would make me happy.' If, however, you ask someone 'Why do you want to be happy?' there is no answer: *happiness* is just a word for whatever it is that you want. Happiness is ultimately ultimate, if you like, because to be happy is, by definition, to have everything you want out of life. To say that something would make you *eudaimōn* is not necessarily to specify the end to which that thing would be a means; it is more likely to indicate the completeness of the satisfaction that the thing yields. The currency of the concept of *eudaimonia* is testimony to the general acceptance of the notion that there can be a life that is good in all its parts and aspects. The tendency to equate *eudaimonia* with specific desiderata and ways of life shows in addition that people think that one can say something concrete about what is essential in such a life.

1.133 Completeness (1097b6–21)

It follows from what we have just said that *eudaimonia*, 'the human good,' cannot be something simple. Though we may think some one objective is 'all we need' to make us happy, that cannot be quite true. Suppose we had that one thing. Among all the things that one thing did not embrace, is there *nothing*, however trivial, that we would prefer to any alternative? If there is any such thing, then logically it forms part of perfect happiness. That does not mean that happiness is a mere congeries, of course, which could never serve as a *skopos* and would trivialize the whole argument, but that every kind of choice must be accounted for, every value must be fitted in somewhere.[34] The idea of happiness is of a life that is completely satisfactory and in this sense 'self-sufficient.'

It is perhaps unfortunate that Aristotle perceives that this word *self-sufficient* (*autarkes*) is ambiguous, and clears the ambiguity up by saying that he does not mean that a happy individual lives in isolation. This is unfortunate because readers somehow suppose that Aristotle is saying that the happy life is basically self-sufficient in this rejected sense as well – leaping to the conclusion that this other kind of self-sufficiency must be the real topic, so that when Aristotle says that a happy life is self-sufficient this is what he must mean, his denial being taken as a mere modifying gloss. (The point would then be that the 'self-sufficient' independence would be not that of the individual but that of the householder, able to fend for himself and his family as head of an economic unit.)

The rejected sense, in which happiness is not 'self-sufficient,' would be that in which only what contributed to an individual's welfare would affect that individual's *eudaimonia* and should therefore be taken into account in considering how one should live one's life. That would be absurd, of course. Human beings are social animals; more than that, they are *political* animals, integrated into consciously organized social systems, and are concerned with the welfare of parents, children, spouses, kith and kin, compatriots – a circle to which we need not here set bounds.[35] It is important to notice that nothing has been said, and nothing will be said, to suggest that 'the good' for a human being is to be defined in terms of what affects him or her personally. Careless readers think it has, and consequently they are puzzled when Aristotle immediately goes on to give his concrete definition of happiness in terms of virtue rather than of enjoyment; and then they recover from their puzzlement, and suppose that the later discussion of 'friendship' (*philia*) is a corrective to an account that has previously been self-centred. But that is not what is going on at all. The only way in which the *Ethics* is self-centred is in its concern with individuals asking 'How shall I live?' – or, for groups to which they belong as members, 'How shall *we* live?' But people ask that question not because they are uniquely concerned with their own well-being but because their *own* lives are the lives they have to live, their *own* decisions are the ones they have to make.[36]

Meanwhile, the only sense in which happiness *is* said to be 'self-contained,' and the *only* sense of 'self-contained' that is in point here, is the sense in which *eudaimonia* is, by definition, a good to which no further good can be added because the supposedly added good would *ex hypothesi* be part of happiness already.[37]

Everything we have said so far is formal and abstract, and uninformative, as Aristotle says. His summation of this 'formal requirements' section, itself summative, differs from the one I have presented, which I think shows the way the discussion actually goes. Aristotle himself extracts three theses: the human good is within the domain of practice (*pace* the exponents of absolute goodness), is something ultimate in the fullest possible sense (what is wanted for itself alone, and what everything else is wanted for), and is self-sufficient in the sense indicated.

1.2 Rational Living (1097b21–1102a4 [I 6–12])

1.21 The Definition of Happiness (1097b21–1098a20 [I 6])

Up to the middle of I vii (1097b20) we have only established the equation of the human good with 'happiness,' as comprehensive (representing the best available choice of goods) and self-sufficient (including its own necessary conditions) – the end (*telos*) of all we do. In i–ii, we saw that the task was one of synthesis and clarification; in iv, that it must incorporate good things that are 'obvious' though uncertain; in v, that these seemed to suggest a choice between predominant lifestyles; and in vi, that nothing beyond these is to be looked for. The values involved are comprehensiveness, ultimacy, finality. To secure these, we would have to see how in detail how they enter into our actual lives. The required life must then be, from the beginning, one subjected to critical examination (as Socrates said) – to the use of reason (*logos*), in fact. And the second part of vii shows that indeed it *is*: what is distinctively human is precisely this use of reason. It is the uses of reason, then, that we will have to concentrate on: this is what we have to be serious about. And just that is what human virtue is. But, though we can illustrate all this and fill it out from our experience of life, in itself it remains entirely schematic.

Aristotle begins the present section, accordingly, by saying that what he has said so far is 'a platitude' (*homologoumenon ti*, 'something everyone agrees with'). Do we not need to give the notion some content? Aristotle does not say quite that: what he says people will be asking for is something clearer, more perspicuous. Our schematic account of the formal aspects of the human good, though illustrated by concrete examples of what people say they want, was itself in effect derived by considering the essentials of the human condition – the condition of an agent who has to live a lifetime in one way rather than another in an organized society. What we say next will be of just the same character. The argument to which Aristotle proceeds has a startling and scandalous look, but it adds little to what is implicit in what has already been said or what was implicit from the beginning in the terms of our problem.

1.211 Do Human Beings Have a Function? – The Concept of Ergon (1097b24–33)

Aristotle's next move is outrageous, I used to think. Nowadays I think it is justified, but I think the sense of outrage is valuable, because everything hinges on Aristotle giving what seems the obviously wrong answer to the question: Does a human being, as such, have a 'function'?

I put the word 'function' in quotes because the Greek word used is simply the ordinary word for 'work,' *ergon*, and Aristotle exploits this straightforward meaning; but the associations of the word in our industrialized society make it impractical to use this translation. To grasp what is going on here, rather a lot of explanation is required.

Aristotle seems to be using an argument borrowed from Plato – familiar to us from *Republic* I (352E–353E), wherever Aristotle himself may have got it. Plato uses the concept of work or 'function' just as Aristotle does here, to establish a basis for objective values in human life. The function of any object is what the object does (or can be used for) best – what it alone can do, or what it does better than anything else does. Plato's examples are a domestic animal (horse) and a tool (sickle): the function of the former is the characteristic uses to which horses are put in society, the function of a sickle is the uses for which a sickle is made – though, of course, horses can do many other things, and sickles can be put to many other uses. A good horse and a good sickle are judged by how well they perform these clearly established functions. Plato applies this pattern of argument (he would not, I think, allow that it is a mere analogy) to 'the soul,' that aspect or part of a living thing to which we ascribe its life, its vital manifestations.[38] What, then, is the function of the human soul? To live. What is living, for a human being? Two things. First, the direction of the body; and second, the conscious activities of thought and perception in which the direction of the body is not an issue. A good soul is one that performs these functions well. To do these well is to be virtuous; to 'live well' is to be happy. Virtue is thus the appropriate standard for judging human performance, and virtuous activity is the recipe for happiness.

The last part of the Platonic argument as given above is, and presumably is meant to be, unintelligible as it stands, resting on equivocations and the undefined term *virtue* – the rest of the *Republic* is devoted to defining the concepts used here and establishing the relationships invoked. What Aristotle does is repeat all the main moves from Plato's argument, but change the terms. What he does not do is give the quasi-technical definition of *ergon* on which Plato's argument rested and on which his own argument seems to rely – partly because his first readers will have been familiar with the whole arsenal of Platonic manoeuvres, but partly because he wants to exploit the literal meaning of 'work' in a way that Plato does not.[39]

Aristotle speaks of the function, not of the 'soul,' but of a human being. A function is attributed to humanity, not by way of exemplifying a pattern shared with given examples, but by analogy. And the analogues are very different from Plato's. Plato uses the examples of instruments, animate and inanimate, used by human individuals and communities. Aristotle does not depend on specific examples but cites the facts that parts of human individuals have functions in relation to them (our eyes are for seeing with) and that kinds of humans are named for the work they do (soldiers do the fighting, carpenters do the woodwork, in their communities). So, says Aristotle, would it not be absurd if every part and kind of human had a function that defined it, but human beings as such did not?

Our answer would surely be the opposite of what Aristotle suggests. The parts and kinds seem to be identified by their relation to something else, namely the individuals and societies in question. But surely this is a meaningful relation only because to be a human is *not* itself relative in this way: to be a human is, in Aristotle's own terms, to be a kind of *substance* – the one kind of entity that is what it is without reference to anything else.

In any case, Aristotle seems to be answering the wrong question. Our question was: what is the best way in which *we* can conduct our *own* lives? But the thesis about the function of humanity seems to take a third-person rather than a first-person view, answering the question 'What is demanded of humans by their inborn nature, or by the overall structure in which they are functional units?' And nothing is said to suggest how these two questions might be related.

What is going on here? Well, in the first place, what is a human being? If we look at *On the Soul* II 2, we find that a human being really is what the human being does: the body and soul are identified and described only in terms of how they are realized in activities. It is in terms of the activity of seeing that we identify an organ of vision, the eye, with its visual capacities; if there were no such activity as seeing, the object we call an eye, if differentiated at all from the body as a whole, would be merely a curious complex of tissues.[40] So a human being does indeed have a function, namely, to be a human, to do the things that a human being does and which determine the appropriate description of the human soul and body.[41] And function is not necessarily relative to any surrounding system or organism, such as a body or a society: Aristotle does not actually say that carpenters work *for* the societies they work *in*, and uses the doublet 'work and practice' to emphasize that is the activity itself that he has in mind.

In the second place, Aristotle does not actually assert that humankind has a function. What he says is that, in the case of a technician (significantly, the examples he initially uses are practitioners of what we call the fine arts), who certainly does have a 'work,' i.e., a professional practice, the relevant excellence is to be found in that practice; so *it would seem* that the same would be true of a human being as such, *if* a human being as such has a function.[42] The 'ifs' persist throughout the argument, and are never formally retracted. In fact, of course, after 1098a20 we forget about the hypothetical nature of the context. But it remains uncancelled. The sequel thus depends on neither of two conditions being fulfilled. One is that human beings have no function as such; but this is shown not to be possible. The other condition is that there should be a class of entities whose excellence is not tied to the performance of a function. And this is never ruled out. If there were some deep connection between excellence and unity, as Plato and the Pythagoreans thought in their different ways, we would have to think again about what the best life might be. Meanwhile, however, no clear practical sense has been given to that notion (that was the main point of I vi), and function-based values hold the field.

Aristotle's point is made most clearly, I think, by his statement of the alternative to the hypothesis that a human being has work to do. The alternative is that a human being is 'by nature idle.' There would then be no form of activity, no way of life, more suited to humans than any other. But clearly, though Aristotle does not say so, if that is the case then our question 'How am I as a human being to live?' or 'What is the best way for me as a human being to conduct my life?' has no answer. Or rather, no answer to it can be better than any other. The people who live from impulse to impulse and cannot be bothered with ethical questions are right – or rather, they are not wrong; if we said they were right, we would be praising their life strategy, and thereby underwriting one possible view as to what the function of human beings is. After all, the fact that we can formulate the concept of a good life, and observe the ways in which human activities are in fact purposefully organized, does nothing to show that the concept of a good life has any foundation, or that the purposeful organization of activities makes sense – or, perhaps we should say, has any sense other than whatever sense the organizers and their organizees choose to give it.

Should Aristotle have taken more seriously this alternative, that human life is inherently pointless? One is inclined to think so. It would then be hard, or course, to avoid the conclusion (which used to be drawn by amateur existentialists) that the point of life is its pointlessness; but, with care, that contradiction can be avoided.[43] What saves Aristotle is that the 'function' he comes up with is one that is relatively innocuous, though it has not been found completely perspicuous.

The human function, it seems, is simply to be human – the phrase 'idle *by nature*' comes close to being nonsense. It is by living the life of their species, Aristotle says at *On the Soul* II 4 (415a30), that animals participate in everlastingness. And surely the immortality that the species achieves contributes to the total system of the cosmos. So perhaps we can look at life from two perspectives, that of the liver and that of the totality (just as, we shall see, human excellence can be viewed from the perspective of the individual or from that of the community [§ 2.251], and a carpenter's work is both a personal way of life and a service to the community).

Though the issue is not raised here, the human function has a further duality. We shall see in X vii that humans also participate in everlastingness through their intellectual activity, just as Plato in *Republic* I assigned to the soul a double function, that of controlling the body and that of thinking independently, both of these being parts of the supposedly single function of 'living.'

Nothing in the present passage alludes to any possible duality of human function; in fact, it seems that only a single, unambiguous function would meet the needs of his project. There is no doubt a purpose in nature, and nature can be seen as a teleological order; but what that purpose is cannot be separated, to Aristotle's mind, from what we see actually happening. It simply explains why things happen just as they do: when we can see *what* things do we can see *why* they do it, and vice versa. Moreover, understanding of the cosmic order is not available to the ordinary person with a life to live: what is available for practical philosophy is only what common experience of and reflection on our human life affords. For the time being, all we are given is a possible hint in the two examples of function that Aristotle begins with, that of the specialist and that of the body part: the function of the former lies in his or her own professional life, the function of the latter lies in its being an *organon*, a functioning instrumental part of a living bodily whole.

Meanwhile, too, the single function of humanity must issue in a single activity, itself correlated with a single nature or essence of humanity. To get away from that we will have to assign to humanity a divided nature; and as yet we have no way of making sense of any such notion.[44]

1.212 The Function of Humankind – The Concept of Logos (1097b33–1098a8)

The 'function' of an animal species, we saw, is to live out a characteristic life, coming to maturity generation by generation and realizing piecemeal the physical and psychological potentialities of the animal in its environment. But an elephant (for example) does not ask itself what an elephant's function is; it *shows* what that function is by living out, in collaboration with its fellow elephants, the range of elephantine existence. We, however, are *asking* ourselves what the function of mankind is, so that we can fulfil it. Being human, it seems, is something that has to be worked at. And this itself, I think, is the gist of the answer to the question of what the function of mankind is. In saying what is characteristic of human life, Aristotle goes at this stage for maximum generality. Some commentators give the impression that he has left the way open for some one specific operation, as though it were the sole function of elephants to stamp out flaming ducks; but no such restriction would make sense at this stage in the argument.

Aristotle in effect relies on an analysis that he does not produce for our inspection and criticism. As we would expect, it derives from *On the Soul*. All living things have life, as defined by metabolism and generation; all animals have powers of sensation. (Also, most animals have powers of locomotion, though Aristotle does not bother with that here.) What humans have that no other animal has is *logos*: the function we are looking for must be 'a practical [life] of that in them which has *logos*' (*leipetai dē praktikē tis tou logon echontos*). The noun is *zōē*, 'life' in the sense not of a lifetime but of a manifestation of life – it is simply taken for granted, of course, that the *ergon* is a life – but, as Aristotle goes on to say, not merely being non-dead but actually *living*, as my example of the elephant should have made clear. What is unexplained is the phrase *praktikē tis*. The life is to be a 'practical' one; but what *exactly* does that mean? It is not clear, except that 'practice' fits vaguely with the notion of 'work' (and was coupled with it at 1097b26 and 29). And the force of the article *tis* is equally unclear. Is it meant to give 'practical' a sort of metaphorical sense, as it did with 'political' in I ii? Or is it saying only that it must be *some* practical life, but we don't know which? We cannot say at this point; we can only note that options are being left open.

At this point, we may be inclined to complain that the elimination Aristotle has conducted is unwarranted. Are the things we share with other animals not just as important as the things that set us apart? Is Aristotle not quite arbitrarily expressing the intellectual's typical prejudice in favour of thought as opposed to feeling? Well, no. That is not what *logos* means.[45]

What does *logos* mean? It means 'reason,' our version of the Latin *ratio* which was used in antiquity to translate *logos*. But what does 'reason' mean? It is very hard to say. It is even harder to say what Aristotle meant, before the systematization of Hellenistic philosophy made *logos* seem like a technical term. *Logos* does not mean 'reasoning,' for which the related word is *logismos*, or 'intellect,' which is *nous* or *dianoia*.[46] A look at the article in LSJ shows that *logos* is the noun corresponding to the verb *legein*, to reckon or calculate, to say or speak. *Logos* can mean a computation or calculation, a ratio or proportion, a plea or explanation or formula, 'reason' as a faculty (parallel with appetite or temper, *thumos*), a speech or narration, any phrase or longer utterance, and generally *any* intelligible utterance (LSJ refers us here to Aristotle's own definition of the relevant sense, 'voice that signifies by convention' [*phōnē sēmantikē kata sunthēkēn, On Interpretation* 16b26]). A survey of the article *logos* in Bonitz (1870) shows that Aristotle's usage ranges over the whole of this general terrain. In general, up to Aristotle's time, *logos* means reasoned speech, conceptual and syntactical: language (including mathematics) as the expression of thought, rather than as the utterance of sounds. But it may also cover the aspects of reality to which conceptual or expository speech corresponds: the philosopher Heraclitus called the intelligible aspect of the universe 'the *logos*,' perhaps because he thought of it as the content of his own *logos*, the account he was giving of it. And in *On the Soul* a sense such as sight is said to be a *logos* (424a6), that is, a proportion of two opposite qualities, much as (we will see in *Ethics* II) a moral virtue is. But how is this last sense of the word, 'proportion,' related to the primary sense of 'discourse'? A ratio or proportion is a relationship that can be precisely conceptualized and defined: the *imposing logos* is articulate discourse, the *imposed logos* is the ratio or proportion it defines.

Aristotle, I take it, is using the word in its most general sense, to cover all these phenomena. He is thinking of all those aspects of human life that are mediated by language. The most relevant passage for interpreting the present text is in *Politics* I 2 (1253a9), because the context – a contrast between human and other animals – is so similar. Human beings, Aristotle says there, are the only animals who have *logos*, the power of articulate speech, as opposed to mere voice, *phōnē*. Other animals have cries, whereby they communicate their feelings; humans have speech, so that they can formulate and communicate their ideas about what is right and wrong, what is hurtful and harmful. Only humans have these value concepts, and the common use of these concepts is the foundation of organized human communities, the family and the state.

Any animal, we saw, is defined by its way of life, which is its *telos*. But humankind, it now seems, is defined by the totality of its conceptualizing activity, the total scope of *logos*. But what is that scope? That can be determined only by a serious consideration of human capacities and situations; and the upshot of such consideration should appear in the values endorsed in the most developed human societies, cities.

To see what the implications of Aristotle's emphasis on *logos* are, we should ask ourselves his question: what, in fact, is the characteristic way of life of humans? One answer is that, unlike those of other animals, human life patterns vary from society to society: what is human is precisely this variability, the very fact that the way of life in a society is determined by its culture, its symbol system and the way that system is used. Human life, that is, is conceptually structured through and through: where other animals have nature, humans have culture – not that other animals lack symbol systems (more elaborate than the mere cries that Aristotle allowed them), but they do not have what humans do, the variability that comes from the all-pervasive structuring of life through linguistic and quasi-linguistic codes. The task of discovering what the human way of life in general is can only be the task of discovering the dimensions of and limits to this variability. (One reason why Aristotle never says in the *Ethics* what *logos* is may be that we cannot *say* what it is because it pervades our lives so thoroughly: the discovery of the scope and limits of articulate discourse is a large part of our task.) And this is, in effect, what Aristotle does.

Our talk of culture and symbol systems in the preceding paragraph introduces notions foreign to Aristotle; but the significance he assigns to articulate speech in the *Politics* is really the same as that which contemporary thinkers have assigned to a wider range of symbolic behaviour. For Aristotle, it is the power of articulate speech that is distinctive of humans, that makes possible the very notions in terms of which the question about the good life can be asked and an answer sought, and that is the precondition of political life and thought. It is characteristic of humans that they are symbol-using animals, and that the use of language permeates the whole of their lives.[47] All the questions we can ask of ourselves and others, and all the answers we can give, are formulated in language.

In asking the question how we should live, we are already in the business of asking questions, and any answers we find will be articulated in language. Converting the inarticulate 'end' (*telos*) of our lives into a consciously pursued goal (*skopos*) is largely a matter of *putting things into words* and thus becoming conscious of them. And, as we saw in the Introduction, a being with a sense of time, for whom the organization of a lifetime is somehow a problem, is a being who can locate events precisely within a matrix of change.

If our concern is with our lives as articulated in terms of speech, our task must be a matter of describing and anatomizing the whole scope of what the use of language in articulating our lives is. And that is really what the whole of the rest of the *Ethics* does. As the text from the *Politics* suggests, it thereby provides a sort of anatomy of values. That is really all it does. And it is surprising how much it comes to.

One caveat needs to be added. A critique of the 'life of the *logon echon*' could go in two directions. It could move towards the precise and optimum operation of *logos* in all fields; or it could seek the best operation in the *best* field, if there is one. In effect, Books II–VI pursue the former goal; Book X pursues the latter.

1.213 The Relation of Goodness to Function – The Concept of Spoudē (1098a8–20)

Everyone lives in accordance with *logos*, or 'not without *logos*' – not rationally as opposed to irrationally, or in a way that 'follows or implies a rational principle' as Ross translates it, but in a way that is conceptually articulated, or at least articulated in a way that depends on the way we do conceptualize things. But what is it to live *well*? 'Well' and 'good' are colourless terms, says Aristotle: the work of a so-and-so (e.g., a guitar player) and of a good (*spoudaios*) so-and-so are one and the same, it is just that the good so-and-so does it better. So the human good turns out to be activity of the soul in accordance with excellence ('virtue') – or, if there are several excellences, according to the most complete and excellent of them.

This argument is very cryptic indeed.[48] What are we to make of it?

Aristotle did make two points, which I passed over. He says that the practical life is one of activity, not mere existence – which is important, but was said before at 1095b32, and can surely be taken for granted at this point. (In Books IX and X a lot will be made of the proper interpretation of the word *energeia* ['activity'], but for the moment the point that a good person would still *be* a good person after lapsing into a lifelong coma, and that that is not exactly what we meant by a good life, seems sufficiently obvious.) Then Aristotle slips in the word 'soul,' as if he, like Plato, had been speaking of the function of a soul rather than of a human being; but this too can really go without saying, since strictly speaking it is not the soul but the whole person that acts (*On the Soul* I 4, 408b13–15), and presumably the imprecise locution is introduced simply to show that when we talk about *praxis* and *energeia* we are not necessarily talking about things that involve bodily movement, being busy and bustling about. There is a point to be made there, but the ground has not been laid for it and we can let it go.

What Aristotle says about the colourlessness of the words meaning 'good' and 'virtue' is historically false, as the same point would be in English. Philosophers in Aristotle's day already used these words, as they still do, to mean something so basic as to be undefinable – what is good is what ought to exist for its own sake, what is a proper object of commendation in the most general sense, and so forth. In the English vernacular, however, a 'good' person is (as Nietzsche complained) like a docile child, a 'virtuous' person is one who ostentatiously abstains from messy vices; in traditional Greek usage, a good (*agathos*) man is a brave and public-spirited upholder of civic order, and *aretē* is the kind of rich excellence that is characteristic of agricultural soils, fleeces, horses, and solid citizens. Aristotle is repudiating these associations, as well as any associations that ethical terminology may have picked up from philosophical discussions; the insistence on the colourlessness of excellence is programmatic.[49] Once we know what human life as such is, what the 'function' of a human being is, there is no further information we need to tell us what a *good* life is, and hence what 'the human good' and 'happiness' are. It is the same point that was made in I vi: there is no such thing as the study of goodness itself, as opposed to the study of particular kinds of things that may be good or bad. To know what a good life is, all we have to do, all we can do, is think carefully, clearly, comprehensively, and accurately about life as we ourselves live it and know it in our societies as we know them (they are 'what we best know,' to borrow a phrase from a rather different context [1112a7–8]).

The word Aristotle uses here for the person who does things well is not *agathos*, the colourless word, but a loaded word, *spoudaios*; and he uses the word repeatedly from now on. But what exactly does this word mean? Literally and etymologically it means 'serious' or 'earnest' or 'zealous': being full of *spoudē*, which is 'zeal.'[50] To be good at something, whether it be guitar playing or life as a whole, you have to take it seriously, work at it; and people who take things seriously in any field are themselves taken seriously, they are serious musicians, serious people.[51] And, in an important subsidiary sense that our English word *seriousness* shares, *spoudē* is also contrasted with laughter and playfulness – an implication that will surface in X vi.

The word *spoudaios* is also used, however, of people who are 'serious' in the sense that they are to be taken seriously, worthy citizens; and Aristotle seems to have used it elsewhere unambiguously in this sense.[52] But the argument here requires that it be taken in its former, more literal, sense, and the latter sense is, by implication, derivative. Only people who take a subject seriously, who study it and inform themselves about it and work at it, are worth taking seriously when that subject is pursued or practised or discussed. And I do not know how you could argue with that, if what is under discussion is a matter of expertise, as a specialized function or 'work' would be. Whether the same applies to such a 'function' as we have ascribed to human beings as such is another matter; but of course, as I remarked before, anyone who is reading the *Ethics* must already be supposing that life can be taken seriously in this sort of way.[53]

Aristotle's mention of the guitar player as a paradigm of the kind of relation he has in mind seems to me to show what he means here, if we think of what such playing involves at an advanced level. All guitar players make music, pluck the strings, make sounds somehow in accordance with some of the conventions of music – in the same sort of way that all human beings make plans, make excuses, defend their conduct and attack or deride others, even if only in a haphazard way. But good guitar players work at it – they are serious about it. They develop their own capacities, explore the resources of their instruments, probably take lessons, listen to the performances of more advanced players to find out what they are doing right, invite criticism of their own performances. By being serious about guitar playing they find out what guitar playing really is, and what good guitar playing comes to. There are huge differences in technique and taste, but everyone who seriously studies guitar learns much the same thing, not just by absorbing arbitrary conventions, but by discovering what the resources of guitar playing are. The essential point is that there is really no way of saying what good guitar playing is other than that it is playing as John Williams, or Narciso Yepes, plays, and no way of learning to play guitar well other than by continual practice in the light of what one can see and hear them doing. And you can recognize them. There is no serious doubt that Yepes is a good guitar player.[54] It is only because these things are certainly true that music is possible. And life is like that.

In fulfilling my function of living as a human being 'in accordance with rational discourse' (kata logon), all I can do is to ask in any situation just what that situation is and what it actually calls for from me, in the light of who and what I am, what my resources are for dealing with it and similar situations, and how those resources can be developed. And if I want to know how I can do that, there is no other resource than to observe and listen to the people who are observably making a success out of living their own lives. And there is no real problem about who they are, once we take life seriously enough to try and see what it is all about. It is easy enough to see who is making a mess of things, whose life is a going concern.

But what, when we come right down to it, is Aristotle saying here? He uses the word spoudaios without explanation, and I may be accused of making too much of the guitar-playing example – though why Aristotle should use this particular example if he did not mean his readers to be guided by it I really do not know. The word has four antonyms. It can mean 'solemn' as opposed to 'playful' – but this is plainly irrelevant at this point. It can mean 'serious' as opposed to 'frivolous' or 'negligent.' But it can also (see LSJ) mean 'good at' one's task as opposed to 'bad at' it (phaulos), and (morally) 'respectable' or 'worthy' as opposed to 'rascally' or 'worthless' (poneros). One suspects Aristotle of exploiting this complex ambiguity, and perhaps he is. One could, however, argue that in the long run the last three all come to the same thing: when it comes to living one's life, it is the people who are careless and negligent about what they do who make a mess of their lives, and these same people who are socially worthless and vicious, because it is hard work to be good.[55] Some people take the contrast between 'respectable' people and the rabble as what is basic to Aristotle's thought here and throughout the *Ethics*, and interpret this as mere snobbery. But it is not necessarily so if the project of 'taking life seriously' is possible and legitimate (and has the values of respectability as its outcome), as it surely is if ethics is a subject and if education can be more than technical training. Still, doubts remain.

Are we really justified in taking 'serious' as the primarily operative sense of *spoudaios* here? I think so. Converting one's *telos* into one's *skopos*, the basic description of the project of the *Ethics* in I ii, is precisely being serious about, making the object of conscious attention, the 'political' integration and reconciliation of demands and opportunities that animals with a sense of time cannot help doing anyway. Any other interpretation of *spoudaios*, for instance as the Homeric hero or as the kind of superior being that Callicles sees himself as in Plato's *Gorgias*, introduces new, arbitrary, unexplained ideas unsupported by anything other than the interpreter's presumption about Greek moral/political culture or Aristotle's own supposed class prejudices. The traditional way of reading the passage, however, is to take *spoudaios* here in the sense of 'morally respectable' and to suppose that Aristotle is unselfconsciously endorsing the conventional virtues of an Athenian (or Chian, or Andrian, or Stagiran, or Macedonian) gentleman. But that would make nonsense of everything that has been done so far, and would make wasted labour of Books II–IV.

In deriving the notion of 'virtue' or excellence in performing the *ergon* of mankind from taking that function seriously, the identification of virtue with socially identified and approved patterns is what is expressly repudiated. It will, of course, turn out that the good life in Greece will follow those patterns: the Greek cities do more or less hold together, so they must be doing something right. But the relationship is more or less contingent ('more or less,' because a self-maintaining society really must be doing what is necessary to maintain itself). What 'virtues' there may be and how they are to be established remains to be determined. What has been asserted is that the identification and description of virtues must be derived from the application of thought to the real conditions of life. So, in a sense, we do know what virtue is, because we know what experience has shown to be praiseworthy when practised in cities; but, in another sense, we do not know, because all we have established is the formal notion of 'excellence' in relation to established forms of practice. It remains to derive the familiar 'virtues' from the formal notion, and to show how the former exemplify the latter.

We were asking how Aristotle could justify his apparent switch from a first-person view to a third-person view, from a question about happiness to an answer about virtue – for happiness is basically what I want for myself, whereas virtue is what I want from other people. To show that this transition does not really have that implication is, of course, one of the major tasks of the *Ethics* as a whole. But we can say now that the definition of 'virtue' as excellence dependent on *spoudē* already draws the sting of the accusation. Really to enjoy guitar playing or anything else one has to work at it, to get out of it all that can be got; enthusiasts are happy people. And we will see already in I viii that Aristotle is prepared to give an answer along these lines.

Aristotle is now in a position to recapitulate by a provisional defining formula for the 'human good' (provisional, because it may be modified by a definition of *eudaimonia* at 1101a14): 'activity of the soul according to virtue – but, if the virtues are several, according to the best and completest.' This is disconcerting; nothing has prepared us for a possible plurality of virtues – no conceptual space has been opened up for any such notion.[56] If we think of guitar playing, though, we can see that taking that seriously would call for choices. Some aspects of musicianship are more important than others. Given that all the essentials are sufficiently covered, one tries to go furthest in the most important directions, or the directions most congenial to one's taste and talent. But this too was, in a way, prepared in I ii: finality and comprehensiveness remain an ambivalently dual standard. It is only that this consideration has not formed part of the discussion since the concept of 'function' was introduced.

'And – another thing – in a complete (*teleiōi*) life,' Aristotle adds, as though it were an afterthought (1098a18). It is indeed an addition to the definition; but it is a prime condition from the list of formal requirements we had to meet (§ 1.131), and it was built into the initial formulation of our undertaking in I i–ii. The ambiguity of *teleios* between 'complete' and 'perfect' is particularly troublesome here, because the temporal finitude of human lives is a central factor in all long-term decisions. Is Aristotle milking a laden Greek concept for all that is in it, exploiting an advantage that Greek already has over English, or is he packing resonances and ambiguities into what began as an innocuous word? It is hard to say.

If I engage in an activity and it comes to an end, what is the character of that end? It may be just interrupted, so that I have to stop (or do not even have a chance to stop, as when a coronary terminates a person's eating of his lunch). Or I may just stop and do something else instead. In neither of these cases is the cessation a *telos*, an 'end' in Aristotle's sense. Or I may have completed a construction, which is now perceptibly there as the end I sought to achieve. Or I may have completed a task, which I can look back on as finished. Or I may have completed a performance, in the whole pattern of which (and not just in the contrivance of its terminal state) the value of what I did is to be found. Or I may have completed a feat, such as performing a thousand press-ups, that has no pattern and no outcome, but the continuous doing of which is what I am to be congratulated on. Which of these sorts of completion is that of a 'complete life'? One cannot say. A complete life must comprise all of them. A continuously satisfactory level of activity would be great, especially if we recall the three dimensions of value that in I i bind all our activities together. But a career can have a fine shape to it, too. And surely no life can be continuously or completely satisfactory in this rough world; an average quality, or a few really high spots, may be all it is reasonable to hope for. So 'in a complete life,' as opposed to 'just for a moment,' is all we can say, without specifying what sort of summation or completion is relevant.[57] Built into his whole discussion, though, is a sort of prevailing nostalgia for completeness, perfection, achievement. The emotional tug of this sort of ideal is one I feel. But is it more than an insidious temptation? Should we not be more at home with change, in transitory vicissitudes and indeterminate processes?

1.22 Methodological Caution (1098a20–b8 [I 7])

Aristotle has been moving very fast – my commentary far exceeds his terse and pregnant text. Rather surprisingly, he turns now to a threefold caution about method that seems disproportionately long. The disproportion could be misleading, though; it could be, for instance, that Aristotle, writing in note form, wrote this bit out more fully because he expected what he said to be less obvious and familiar to himself or his readers. What is evident is that it seemed urgent to say these things right now, to avoid dangerous misunderstanding of what has just been said.

The first point is that this is a sketch, merely schematic. What it gives us is something that needs time – but only time – to fill in. I suppose the point is that what he has just said is not substantially informative, it is an agenda; but it is *the* agenda from now on. Activity, soul, virtue, completeness, are the concepts that have to be unpacked, the aspects of life that have to be anatomized.

The second point is one made before, that this is only approximate. Why is it so urgent to say that here? Because it will turn out that what we have specified is not a sufficient condition for happiness. It gives us a formula for the best life, other things being equal. But we must be ready to say 'life's like that' if the formula lets us down. Aristotle shows the same haste in qualifying a slick formula when he gives a definition of virtue in II vi.

The third point is another excursus on 'first principles' (archai). The first thing we said about them was that we had to consider whether we were going from or to first principles. We now remark that there is more than one way of going to them – or rather, of apprehending them: some by induction (well, of course), some by insight or perception, some by a sort of habituation, and so on. And the first principles themselves, equally of course, are matters of fact, not of explanation. It follows, I suppose, that the definition we have just been given, embedded as it is in an argumentative context, is not such a principle. So what are the principles? Actually I said what they are in discussing the previous passage. There is insight into particular situations, and that is a matter of perception. There is insight into the whole system of values we live in, and it turns out that that is a matter of a sort of habituation, because it reflects the habits of choosing we have developed. (At III v, Aristotle mentions the possibility that this too might come from a sort of insight, but that is somewhat problematic.) And what of the 'common opinions' that have been grist to our mill, and to more of which we now turn? I suppose they must be arrived at by induction, though the epistemology of such cultural phenomena is obscure and Aristotle has no light to shed. It is necessary to clarify the matter of 'first principles' here and now because otherwise we might suppose that the defining formula we have introduced was a universal truth reached by induction, which it can hardly be. Anyway, Aristotle concludes, we must be serious about (spoudasteon – work at, be zealous in) getting the first principles right – much of what we want to know will automatically be cleared up if we can do that.[58]

1.23 Harmonization (I viii–xii; 1098b9–1102a4)

Before we get down to unpacking the enigmatic formula we have come up with, there are some urgent matters to clear up. The formula may *be* right, but it doesn't *look* right. The data we used to flesh out the idea of the 'human good' as 'happiness' were couched in terms of the individual's well-being – getting rid of impediments, achieving a rewarding life. They took a 'first person' view of life. But our formula was introduced from a 'third person' viewpoint: we seemed to be looking at humanity from the outside and considered what it would be to excel in the kind of life such a being might live. I said that this discrepancy would vanish in the long run, and that the concept of the *spoudaios* really laid the foundation for its reconciliation; but we really want something to paper over the crack *right now*.[59] This cannot and should not be a substantive answer, because we have laid no ground for any substantive account of what sort of life we are talking about. What is needed is a purely formal account, showing how the formula as such, in its pure formality, is congruent with the popular demands we acknowledged.

We also need, though not quite so urgently, to qualify the insistence on the 'complete life' – not, this time, in opposition to the insistence on the quality of the moment's experience, but in relation to the initial claim that it is better to achieve a good life for kith and kin, for nation and city, than for oneself alone, as the finitude of the individual life might suggest.

There are a few other formalities too, which we will pick up as we come to them.

Ostensibly, what Aristotle will be doing is reconciling his theory with the 'facts' of experience. Actually, he weaves an intricate skein. He is not simply recapitulating I iv–v. There, he was considering what people generally thought desirable, presumably on the basis of their experience. In the present passage he is concerned rather with low-level theoretical requirements, the conventional wisdom of reflective literature.

Aristotle's theory has been operating with a single value, goodness (*to agathon*). But popular literature (reflected in Plato's dialogues, for instance) operates with at least four values: the pleasant, the useful or profitable, and the fine (or noble, or beautiful), as well as the good.[60] How are the other three to be accommodated? Pleasure is the most difficult to fit in, and will occupy us repeatedly. The fine or noble is less problematic, but it is hard to say just how it differs from the good (Aristotle will almost equate it with the good in the guise of the pleasant).[61] But the useful is the most intractable, because what turns out to be useful is largely a matter of luck and has little directly to do with goodness.[62] The values of utility must be shown to be real but peripheral.

Accordingly I ix–x have to do with good fortune – not the activity we defined as happiness, but the circumstances that make such activity possible and cannot be guaranteed; and this discussion naturally settles down to a discussion of the implications of the 'complete life' in which virtuous activity is sustained throughout a vulnerable lifetime.[63] This leads us round to a restatement of our defining formula, with qualifications; and the discussion of fortune and external goods raises the topic of posthumous fate. One would have thought that the initial definition of happiness ruled that out, but if we are going to be considering 'external' circumstances anyway we are getting into the area where what is publicly observable becomes relevant, and what happens to people's relatives and estate after their death is observable by others though not (or not *much*, if you believe in ghosts) by the decedent.

Aristotle's problem throughout this passage is to protect the fulfilment of the human *ergon* as a possible project without losing hold of reality. In the end, the concept of *eudaimonia* calls for a double vision. To call someone happy is to pass a favourable judgment on his or her life as a whole, considered as an observable reality; but what that happiness consists of is in the end a quality of experience. It is only in Book IX that this duality really comes together.

1.231 Valuations (1098b12–1099a7, 1101b31–1102a1)

In one respect, our formula is traditional: it is a cliché that what is part of one's character (or 'self') is more relevant to one's true well-being than what affects one's body, and a fortiori one's external circumstances. And, as regards one's character, it seems undeniable that actually to behave in a certain fashion is more important than merely to have a (possibly inactive) disposition to act in that way. After all, prizes in sports go to those who actually run and win races, not to the fastest runner who happens to be in the grounds. Anyway, you can see this by the fact that one can *praise* people for their disposition, by citing the actual things they do. But you can't praise those activities, you can only celebrate them: there is nothing more to say, except 'The winner!!'

Aristotle really belabours this last point, here and elsewhere. He probably felt that it was the only point in which he had really gone beyond Plato. He carries the demand for centrality in happiness, which takes most thoughtful people from externals to physical fitness and from physical fitness to qualities of personality, that last crucial stage further.

1.232 Values (1098b24–1100a3)

The list of features some or all of which have been conventionally
equated with happiness squares well enough with the previous
account: virtue and so on, prosperity, and this or that kind of mental
endowment in combination with pleasure. The reference to mental
endowments is phrased oddly, though; partly it looks forward to
Aristotle's own analysis in Book VI, but mainly it is a plain allusion
to the problematic of Plato's *Philebus* (assuming, that is, that that
dialogue was written earlier than this passage). Aristotle says his
account must concede the substantial truth of all these claims, though
not, of course, their exclusive truth.

The procedure here is not very convincing. Why should we believe
that Aristotle has included all the plausible candidates? The fact that
his enumeration here matches his enumeration earlier means nothing.
As it is, we note that pleasure is not admitted as an independent
value, but only as an adjunct of other values; and that health is left
off the list of desiderata. Both these omissions will soon be made
good. Actually, Aristotle must have in mind a sort of check-list:
psychic goods may be active or inactive, may be defined in terms of
operation or in terms of enjoyment; goods may be psychic or somatic
or circumstantial, or alternatively non-psychic goods may be somatic
or material or social. The dimensions of value are utility, fineness,
pleasure, excellence (see § 1.2324). These overlapping sets of presumably exhaustive alternatives are what he in fact works through, without announcing that he is doing so.

1.2321 Virtue and Wisdom

Virtue, of course, we have taken care of. Or have we? Not, we might
say, if what the conventional wisdom had in mind was the conventional 'virtues' singled out in conventional morality. But then, it is
not Aristotle's business to save the appearances of conventional
morality, but only to give a place to the legitimate thrust that underlies it. And, in any case, the conventional wisdom should not have
been unconditionally committed to the accepted patterns of behaviour, as Plato pointed out in the *Gorgias* (468Bff.): a person should be
ready, if it is discovered that the supposed best patterns are after all
not the best, to change and go for what is really best – to live by
whatever virtue turns out to be. After all, even Prodicus's simple
fable of Heracles at the crossroads makes the choice not one of be-

haviour patterns so much as of motivations: the pleasure principle as against what looks rather like a Kantian 'sense of duty.'

As for wisdom, the specification of the 'life according to articulate discourse' takes care of that. In a sense, 'virtue' has actually been defined as wisdom, in the way we associate with Socrates, because *logos* is its sole determinant.

1.2322 Pleasure (1099a7–21)

The real challenge to our formula comes from the requirement of pleasantness. Prodicus opposed pleasure to virtue, and our formula made no provision for it. Unless the life we have specified can be shown to be potentially at least as pleasant as any other, our claim that it is the best of all lives is hollow. Aristotle deals with the problem three times (four, if we count the version in Book VII as an independent treatment rather than as a doublet of that in Book X): cursorily and schematically here, succinctly but systematically in Book II, fully in Book X. The same central point is made each time. But, as we shall see, in the later passages we acknowledge a problem that is never resolved, and that is not faced in this first treatment.

The essential point is that the word *pleasure* (*hēdonē* – the point goes through equally well or badly in both languages) is not the name of a particular sort of activity (entertainment, for instance), but is just a word we use for the satisfaction we find in *whatever* in life means most to us. People who are crazy about horses take pleasure in horses. So a person who is crazy about virtuous living will presumably take pleasure in that. The analogy with track events (which immediately precedes the present passage) prepared the way for this: the winner has not only the satisfaction in being the fastest person on earth, but the joy of doing successfully what one is actually doing. And why should there not be such a person, who 'hungers and thirsts after righteousness'? And surely if our formula was correct and pinpoints the quality that what is truly human in human life manifests, actually succeeding and knowing that one is succeeding in this must be the deepest satisfaction of all.[64] And, since (as we said from the start) that quality arises from taking all factors into account and thinking of the structure of one's life as an interconnected whole, the satisfaction should be unsullied by the sense that one may be missing something – as one might be haunted by a feeling that one's devotion to horses is leading one to neglect one's family, for instance.

If we were right about the virtuous life being the best one, and if there really are people who *do* live virtuously (however virtue is specified), then what we are saying simply *must* be true – we would not really call someone a *truly* generous kind of person if they did not really like doing generous things; that would show that they were acting *against* the grain, would rather be doing something else.[65]

The key to this whole argument is that true pleasure is not just what we find titillating or amusing: it is what we delight in, what we rejoice in.

The argument has a specious air. I am inclined to say: life ought to be like that, but it isn't. Actually, Aristotle will return to the issue again and again, not only in the remaining discussions of pleasure but in discussions of responsibility, of weakness, of friendship. He knows it is the point really at issue throughout the *Ethics*. Another way of putting the point is: does humanity *really* have a function, so clearly that we can effectively pose and answer the question whether any one way of living is really the best?

1.2323 Health and Wealth (1099a30–b22)

Aristotle has insinuated that his formula has taken account of all its rivals. But it has done so only if taken with a grain of salt, as Aristotle has said all generalizations in ethics must be taken. Health and wealth and social allies are accommodated by the formula only on two conditions. First, we concede that they must take a secondary place: what is inside us affects us more nearly than what is outside us. Second, we must interpret 'activity of the soul in accordance with a rational principle' in a double way. On the one hand, it means making the most serious use of reason in dealing with personal, social, and political situations. On the other hand, it means being able to deal with such situations effectively and successfully, which means, of course, having the necessary equipment. Once we have conceded that a good person fallen into a coma will not lead a good life, we can go on to say that a handicapped person will not lead as good a life as would have been possible without the handicap – that's what 'handicap' means. A homely, ill-born, isolated, and child-less person is *ou panu eudaimonikos* – 'not the kind of person who is altogether likely to be happy' (1099b3). And then we can say that there are all sorts of things you can't do without vigorous health, lots of money, powerful friends, and lots of luck. (The connection is made, as we shall see in a little while, through the concept of glory.)

But these are just the considerations we said at 1094b19 were so treacherous; they are adjuncts to action, neutral in themselves.

As other philosophers, including Locke and Sartre, would later insist, a person is a person only in a situation, in which alone action is possible. Property and friends cannot be left out of account. One must also, Aristotle thinks, admit that serious misfortunes and deprivations 'disfigure bliss' (not, we note, 'destroy happiness').[66] A person whose life took its quality from the way the person thought and behaved could not be rendered *kakodaimōn* by any but the most serious misfortunes; but it would be absurd to suppose that to contract AIDS or to have one's son convicted of murder might *make no difference* to one. And that's a matter of luck.

1.2324 Honour (1099a22–31, 1099b29–1100a3)

We observed under § 1.232 that one of the grids by which Aristotle is, without announcing it, evaluating his own formula is the spectrum of values: the good, the useful, the fine, the pleasant. All four are tacitly invoked in I v (if we allow money making to stand for the value of utility), but more usually they are reduced to a trio, combining the good either with the useful (if enumerating ultimate values) or with the honourable (if evaluating types of motivation). The latter trio is used in the treatise on friendship (VIII–IX); the former trio is invoked here and at II iii.[67] The life picked out by our formula, we are told, is not only good (by definition) and pleasant (as we have just argued), but also honourable or noble – *kalon* (1099a22). But how does that get in, and why? It is not easy to see.

Roughly, from the way things are said in the present context, it looks as if the *kalon* is the subjective motivational aspect of goodness. If you do something just *because* it is good, and not because it is pleasant or advantageous, it must surely be because to do so represents your ideal: it seems to you to be fine, noble, splendid, etc., to do so. It is, as we said, like the glory of coming first in a race, of manifestly succeeding in what one has set before one as what matters in one's life.

This value of honour, or glory, or the ideal, was not enumerated in the check-list at 1098b23–9. But it was alluded to previously at 1095b27, where it took the vulgar form of 'fame' or 'honour' in the sense of being honoured – *timē*. It was there identified as merely the external mark of the recognition of excellence, which is why it did not persist into the later list. The value it represents is that of the sheer desirability of whatever one thinks highest – the sort of ideal-ism represented by the higher stages of 'love' in Plato's *Symposium*.

Aristotle says repeatedly that virtuous people do the things they do 'for beauty's sake' (*tou kalou heneka*).[68] They see that it is fine, glorious, noble to do that. In the same way, we may say, our serious guitar players play as they do 'for beauty's sake'; they try to play in a way that simply corresponds to their ideal of good playing. This value directly perceived in an action is by no means at odds with the value it derives from its contribution to a wider context – in a sense, it is derived from that – but it is not to be reduced to it either. It cannot be denied, however, that this ideal value tends to be confused or contaminated with 'fame' or 'honour' in its vulgar form. It is in specific reference to the virtues of courage and pride that the *kalon* is invoked as a motive, though Aristotle insists that the same holds for all virtuous actions.[69]

The main difficulty in coming to terms with Aristotle's discourse here is that the Greek word (*kalon*) is much more widely used and more general in scope than any English equivalent. It is in fact the commonest and most versatile of the value words in the language, as perhaps *good* is in English. It is the ordinary word for physical or any other kind of beauty; it is used as we would use 'Fine!' to express agreement. It belongs to whatever is sheerly admirable in any respect or in all respects. It seems to seep into Aristotle's discussion unnoticed. But the part it plays is vital. The fact that a good life is pleasant (to those who find it so) cannot in itself be a reason for preferring such a life to other lives – *anything* is pleasant if you happen to like it. The pleasantness of the virtuous life comes from our being ravished by the very fact of its excellence.

Aside from its incidental uses (as when we say something is 'well said,' 1094a2 and 1098b16), we meet the word *kalon* first at 1099a6 when we are comparing the good person's actions with the athlete's victories; then at 1099a13 and 17 it is used of the good person's actions conceived as what he or she rejoices in. There is no argument. And then, at 1099a32, the word is used to introduce the necessity of wealth and fortune: it is *fine* deeds, *glorious* deeds that one cannot perform *achorēgēton onta*, 'when not adequately fitted out,' – the word for 'fitted out' here is the very specific word used for a very specific Athenian institution, whereby a wealthy man fits out at his own expense a production in the civic theatre.

Finally, the theme is reprised at 1099b26–1100a3: the way in which we made activity central in the good life, with external goods serving merely as adjuncts or equipment, says Aristotle, fits in with what was said in I ii about politics being the all-inclusive practice: politicians try above all to make the citizens be of a certain kind – namely, good – and performers of fine deeds. And that's why animals and children are not called 'happy': they do not have the quality of personality that can issue in such deeds. As was implied in the passage from the *Politics* that we quoted when we were trying to explain the meaning of *logos*, such concepts as 'just' and 'noble' cannot be conceived without the use of an articulate language working on the structure of civilized life that only the city makes possible.

1.233 Comment: The Virtuous Life

One problem for Aristotle is why virtuous people should be so rare. Happiness should be open to all normal people, given a little study and application (1099b18–20); but he seems to take it for granted that most people don't amount to much and never will (X ix). He never explains why this is so, but I think the answer lies in the identification of the good person with the person who is serious about life, spoudaios. *People are serious about the things they take seriously; it never occurs to most people that life itself can be regarded in that way. And why should it? States and social institutions may have as their function to make their citizens good, but in most cases this means no more than keeping their citizens in line while they get on with their own affairs.*

This view of the matter fits Aristotle's view of the development of the state and the invention of the exact sciences (see Appendix). Each is natural: only in the city, the organized political community, can the possibilities of humanity be realized, and science and philosophy are the natural development of the unfolding of the universal human longing for knowledge. And yet cities do not happen, they have to be invented, and the invention is relatively recent and localized; and the exact sciences can be developed only in cities, only in peace and prosperity, which is why they too are recent and local. And it certainly is not true that everyone should, or is likely to, take up philosophy as a career. It is as if Aristotle envisaged in all three areas an elite, defined by privilege (you have to be born at the right place and time to be a scientist, a citizen, and a 'serious' person), but essentially self-selecting.

Aristotle's elitism gives offence nowadays, but should it? He is confronting the same situation that was to evoke Rousseau's dictum that 'man is born free, but everywhere he is in chains.' One cannot see what prevents everyone from being happy, but the fact is that most people are not. If they were, there would be no point in writing the Ethics; *and it would be absurd to hold that writing and publishing such a work will bring about an actual change in the condition of human life. It is not Aristotle's fault that most people do not make the most of the opportunities that life offers, or that life does not offer enough opportunities. One may, however, blame him for not facing the issue squarely and presenting his hearers with a well-articulated position.*

If we look at how Aristotle has now set up his account of the good life, we find a basic value judgment. The good life is one in which the requirements of one's situation (as articulated by logos) *are seriously addressed. But two other areas of activity are mentioned only to be dismissed. These are, respectively, the economic activities designed to secure health and prosperity, and things one does simply because one likes to do them – Aristotle's example was 'horses,' which may stand as an example of an engrossing hobby. Health and prosperity are brushed aside as merely means, merely equipment for the activities in which the meanings of our lives are found; hobbies and recreations will be dismissed (X vi) as 'playful' and hence not serious. Aristotle defends this value judgment, but it may be questioned; I say more about it in § 5.132 and § 6.3.*

1.234 Recapitulation (1099a31–1100a9)

Aristotle's discussion throughout I viii–xi unfolds smoothly and continuously. Despite the promise and intention of my commentary, my own exposition makes its transitions more awkwardly. This is because Aristotle sometimes makes a transition in mid-sentence from one thesis to another or (as in the case of *kalon*) insinuates a topic almost surreptitiously.

The necessity of a modicum of prosperity, which one cannot guarantee, to lead a good life, which essentially is under one's own control, leads Aristotle to introduce at 1099b9 the general topic of how *eudaimonia* is to be had: is it typically something learned by study, or acquired as a behaviour pattern or by some sort of training (*askēsis*), or is it a divine dispensation, or does it come by chance? This, he says, is a notorious puzzle (*aporia*).

Readers may be reminded of the opening words of Plato's *Meno*.[70] But there the same question was posed about 'virtue' itself, not about happiness, and we have seen that virtue is not a sufficient condition of happiness, even if it is the heart of the matter. The fact that it is Meno who there confronts Socrates with the question suggests that it was a topic of discussion in sophistic circles, for Meno is represented as a follower of Gorgias; but the course of the subsequent dialogue shows the careful reader that, in Plato's view, virtue itself requires all the 'methods' of acquisition referred to.

Aristotle brushes the question of divine dispensation aside. One guesses that (like most philosophers since Xenocrates) he does not quite subscribe to popular views about the gods, but he never attacks those views; in practice, he seems to divide the functions of divinity between nature as a single teleological system and pure intelligence as a transcendent principle. For the rest, he here makes the outrageous statement that, since it is better that happiness should come by learning and striving than by chance, it very likely does, since natural things are arranged as well as possible (1099b20). But this is hardly the Pollyannaism it looks like, since 'nature' is to be defined in much the same way as the 'function' of natural objects: an animal, for instance, is to be defined by its way of life, and the appropriate values are simply defined by that way of life, whereas 'chance' is simply our word for things that happen to come about in a way that simulates the effects of natural or purposive action, by coincidence (see *Physics* II 4–6). Chance (and the more inclusive term 'happenstance' [*to automaton*]) is the effect produced when two or more purposive or natural processes or actions, independent of each other, intersect in a way that significantly furthers or hinders the course that one or more of them would pursue anyway. The argument is one of some subtlety, but the upshot certainly is that 'happiness,' the word for the overall objective of human plans, *could not* be the characteristic outcome of chance.

However, though happiness could not be characteristically a matter of chance, chance cannot be ruled out altogether.[71] If there are many independent processes and courses of action in the world, they may further each other and frustrate each other to any extent. We cannot rule out the sort of thing that happened to Priam, the last king of Troy, who at the end of a prosperous and successful career lost everything and everyone. No one uses the word *happy* of someone who ends miserably like that (1100a8–9).[72]

In that last sentence Aristotle has introduced that sudden change in perspective we have remarked on before, from the agent's view to a spectator's view. From his own point of view, Priam, riding high until the final disaster, might well congratulate himself. But Aristotle suddenly introduces the spectator's viewpoint in the word *eudaimonizei*, 'calls or thinks happy,' 'congratulates.' Nothing has prepared us for the view that the right answer to 'What is the best life for me to live?' might be 'The life that impartial spectators would congratulate you on.' A bridge needs to be built here; in Book IX, it will be.

I said 'nothing has prepared us,' but actually something has. Just before we got on to Priam, we were talking about animals and children, who are not called 'happy' because they are incapable of noble deeds – they do not have the relevant value concepts. But, just because they do not have those concepts, it is we who do have them who decide that they are not, strictly speaking, 'happy.' But then Aristotle smoothly continues: in the case of children, we *do* actually call them happy, because after all they will grow up, they are already embarked on lives that will or will not be happy. But that is ambiguous. It may mean that they will lead lives that they will find happy. But it may mean that they will lead lives that an informed and impartial spectator will judge to be happy. And surely people can be mistaken about their own happiness, just because they can mistake what merely seems good for what is really good – and they must be able to make that mistake, because if there is no such mistake to be made there is no real difference between a good life and any other life. And if that is the case, there is nothing in life to be serious about – no answer to the question about how to live well is any better than any other answer. It turns out that the difference between the first-person and the third-person perspectives is trickier than we might have thought.

1.235 The Time Factor (1100a4–1101b9)

The discussion of how happiness is affected by what happens after a person's death has as its context the extension of the concern for happiness to one's associates, not merely oneself as an isolated individual. That we can be concerned for other people is shown by the way we worry about what will become of our children after our death, and make testamentary dispositions, although we will not be around to find out how things turn out. Aristotle's discussion may also, however, be directed against Plato.

If one takes him literally, Plato in the *Republic* and *Phaedo* makes Socrates urge his companions to care for the soul and not for the body, because the soul will survive death and its true destiny is thus incorporeal – in addition to which we may expect to be reborn to a fate which will be governed by our behaviour in previous lives.[73] Aristotle too has specified activity 'of the soul' as being what counts. But insistence on an afterlife and reincarnations would destroy the whole thrust of his argument, draining all activity in this life of value and making it a mere means to a blissful hereafter. All common judgments and valuations of human affairs would then be denied. And the values thus rejected would be those we know from our own experience, whereas what will happen in the afterlife is a matter of conjecture. Ethics becomes a load of old rubbish.

The upshot is that only our lives as we live them and as they are delimited by the death of the soul-body complex call for attention. The way events after our death affect us is metaphorically shown in the vision in the *Odyssey*, according to which the dead have only a shadowy existence, at best a sort of echo of life. We must respect that metaphor in allowing that what happens after our death makes some difference – not to do so, Aristotle says, would indeed be a denial of the value of friendship – but also in acknowledging that when life is over, it's over.

The immediate context in which the question of survival is mooted, however, is that of the parts played by chance and by activity in determining our happiness; and survival becomes relevant because 'chance' is taken not in the specific sense laid down in the *Physics* but as a loose equivalent for what happens to people as opposed to what they do. After our death, we do nothing, but things can, in a sense, go on happening to us. Not long ago, Imre Nagy's body was removed from an unmarked grave and ceremoniously reinterred. In a sense, something was thereby done to him that must affect the way we think of his welfare, even if we don't suppose there is any Imre Nagy to know or care.

Aristotle thus runs together three issues: the difference between what we do and what happens to us, the difference between a first-person and a third-person view of life, and the significance of death. If we accept that to undergo the 'misfortunes of Priam' makes it impossible for one to be considered happy, one is taking what is essentially a third-person view. And if we stand by our judgment that happiness is a quality of a whole life, we seem to postpone judgment until all the data are in, so that the relevant third-person view becomes that of the obituary writer. And that sounds as if we agreed with Plato that it is what happens after death that matters.[74]

Aristotle's solution is to take a strong line, but not to take it strongly. His proposed formula makes happiness both subjectively and objectively a matter of how one lives: to live as well as possible 'in accordance with *logos*,' that is, not merely responding to casual impulses and impressions. But, as we shall argue in Book II, such a life and the character it rests on should be extraordinarily stable and impervious to shock, because the principle of activity will be subject to positive feedback (will be habit-forming) and, though Aristotle does not put it in quite this way, will itself be the principle of doing the best in *whatever* situation confronts one. Such people, in misfortune, will do the best they can, and this doing the best they can is itself the best expression of the life that fulfils them; in extreme good fortune, exactly the same thing. Such people's heads will not be turned by good fortune nor their hearts broken by disaster – not if they are indeed the kind of people we are talking about. (No doubt most people, even most 'decent' people, are *not* like that; but that only shows they are the kind of people who usually fail to succumb to temptation only because the advantages of respectability are too strong.)

We may, then, stick to our formula, says Aristotle, and reiterates it: 'Why then should we not say that he is happy who is active in accordance with complete virtue and is sufficiently equipped with external goods, not for some chance period but throughout a complete life?' (1101a14–16).[75] But what about the exceptions, the people who are unexpectedly broken, or whose misfortunes are so gross that we refuse in the end to call them happy? After all, we never know what may happen, and we did say that happiness was a matter of the *whole* life. Aristotle's response is really a three-layered one. First, we can call people 'happy,' just remembering that happiness is *human* happiness, and we must keep our fingers crossed. That is why we insisted before that generalizations in ethics have to be taken in a special way, corresponding to the variation and approximation of practical affairs. Second, we have a second word to set alongside *eudaimōn* or 'happy': 'blissful' or 'blessed' (*makarios*). So we can reserve this extra word for people who will turn out to be happy to the end (though, as I have remarked already, Aristotle's actual use of this term is loose). But, the third point, it is only of the traditional gods that one has this assurance: the hallmark of divinity is precisely immortality and essential immutability. Only the gods are truly and essentially 'blessed'; so, if we are going to apply the word proleptically to humans who seem supremely to 'have it made,' we must again bear in mind that we are using it in a restricted sense – they are blessed *humans*.

And that, hints Aristotle, is as far as we can go in this matter. All these matters have to be borne in mind, but further fine-tuning would be unprofitable, even if it is possible.

1.236 Praise and Eulogy (I xii; 1101b9–1102a4)

The comments on immortality, though integral to the discussion of
the scope of *eudaimonia*, are actually relegated by Aristotle to a sort
of postscript after the restatement of the formula, because it is really
a side issue. Since personal immortality makes no theoretical sense
and can make no practical difference (a philosopher will not waste
time arguing with people about their religious commitments), we had
better make up our minds first.

A second postscript arises out of the distinction we just had to
make between happiness and blessedness, and has to do with the
rhetoric of the matter. Aristotle taught rhetoric in Plato's school, and
here introduces a professional distinction between 'praise' and something else – 'celebration' or 'congratulation,' perhaps – apparently
made, or one that ought to have been made, by writers of handbooks
on eulogy.[76] The distinction is a good one, but not one anyone nowadays is likely to make much of, since the literary genre in question
is not in fashion. The point is that you can praise a thing or a person
only by saying what is good about it or what it is good for – only,
that is, in relation to something else. But that means its goodness is
being thought of as relative. So there are things that are too good to
praise: God, for instance. 'Praise God, from whom all blessings flow,'
says a famous hymn – but that is, strictly, blasphemy: God is not
good because of what flows from him, like an oil well; God is good
in himself, as in another hymn that begins 'Holy! Holy! Holy! Lord
God almighty!' and continues in that vein without ever specifying
what good he is.

The relevance of this point is that virtue can be praised, because it
is the basis of good deeds; good deeds can be praised, because they
contribute to happiness; but happiness can't be praised, because it
stands in relation to the rest of life as God stands to the world – it is
that to which everything else is referred. The issue was actually dealt
with at 1097a34ff. Aristotle is rather apologetic about mentioning it
here, realizing that his readers are less likely to be interested in the
technicalities of rhetoric than he is.

CHAPTER TWO

Reason in Action
(I xiii–VI; 1102a5–1145a11)

We now have an agenda. We have established the position of 'the best kind of life' as a life of serious or excellent (the ambiguity remains) activity of the living human being as such (hence 'of the soul'), in accordance with reason (or as conceptually articulated) between the life of self-maintenance (important but not valued for itself, hence not included), on the one hand, and the life of entertainment (valued for itself but not important, hence included but not emphasized), on the other – the whole being lived in circumstances adequate to sustain it (its material cause). Our discussion has, from the beginning, had a curious double focus: the entirety of life and the totality of a lifetime, on the one hand, and the quality of action and experience at the present moment, on the other. Nothing will be more important than to maintain a dialectical relation between these two: our life as at is envisaged and implied from moment to moment, and the moment as what it is because our whole lives are implicitly brought to bear on it. Meanwhile, assuming that this structure is in place, what do we have to do now?

The concept of activity seems unproblematic (though we shall see in the end that it is not), and entertainment has been brushed aside, though it too will, in the end, need to be disposed of more definitely. As for external prosperity, we do not need a philosopher to tell us about that. What is obviously on the agenda is the nature and scope of *logos* in the activities of 'the soul.' So obviously what we have to do is consider what exactly the soul is and does, in all the aspects that can be related to *logos*. Then we have to see how *logos* shows up in all these relationships. That should put us in a position to see what it is we have to be serious about. Then, if the result of this inquiry turns out to correspond essentially to what the most respected people (the 'best judges') judge from experience that the best way to live actually is, we can have some confidence in it.

So that is what we do. I xiii through Book VI in their entirety make up the discussion of 'virtue' – that is, what seriousness in the use of *logos* involves. Distinguishing the various uses of *logos* should yield a distinction among things to be taken seriously, hence should discriminate among different virtues; and, since life as a whole is what, in the last resort, we have to be serious about, these should combine in virtue as a whole.[1]

2.1 The Soul (I xiii; 1102a5–1103a10)

The human good is 'activity of the soul in accordance with virtue' – that is, taking seriously the project of living a human life, that is, a life permeated by *logos*. Since only humans live such a life, the word 'human' is hardly necessary, unless it is to remind us that cultural divisions are mutable and to insinuate that gender differences are not basic. And why 'the soul'? We have seen that Aristotle does not always feel it necessary to include this word, but it does serve to remind us that we are talking about ourselves as agents in the world, not about the physiology and chemistry of our bodies as integral parts of the solar system, which will be relevant only as involved in what we do and experience. Sometimes they have to be taken into account, but usually they simply form part of the given situation in and on which we act. Perhaps Aristotle specifies 'the soul' not to satisfy the requirements of his own theory but to avoid some misunderstanding among his original audience – to avoid the inference that 'activity' meant bustling about and taking exercise, or something. Anyway, we did say 'the soul,' and that formally commits us to asking 'What is the soul?'

If we want to know what Aristotle thinks the soul is (or thought it was, when he gave the matter his most careful thought), we go to the opening chapters of Book II of *On the Soul*. There we find two alternative definitions. According to one of these, the soul is the first level of actualization of an organic body – that is, a body organized for unitary action; the second level is action itself. In other words, *soul* is simply a word for what living bodies are (what being alive is) and do. That tells us nothing relevant here, except that (a) when we talk about life, we are not talking about something (such as a 'ghost in a machine') other than what embodied creatures naturally do and (b) what we are is secondary to what we do: 'being alive' is no more than the condition in which we can do the things that living consists in, not something special over and above that.

The second definition of 'soul' is a refusal to define. If you want to know what the 'soul' of a species is, what you must do is find out what the distinct and mutually irreducible manifestations of its life are: digestion, reproduction, sensation, thought, locomotion.[2] All living things have the first two, all animals have the first three, various animals have various versions of them all.

Aristotle does not use either of the foregoing definitions here, except perhaps by implication at 1102a17–23, where a glancing allusion to Plato's *Charmides* 156B suggests that the thesis that underlies the second definition (namely, that to understand an animal one must have a systematic conspectus of the range of its behaviour and how that behaviour is organized) represents the standpoint that politicians need to adopt. All we need to know for present purposes, he says, is something we don't need him to tell us – specifically, that there is a distinction between what has *logos* and what has not. We do not even need to know whether the distinction has any physiological or other ontological basis (1102a26–32). Aristotle simply follows the phenomena.

The explanation of Aristotle's procedure here goes back to the discussion of animal movement in *On the Soul*, which I took as my starting-point in introducing the *Ethics*. Aristotle there claims that motion is impossible without two factors, desire and cognition: we have to want something, and we have to identify something as what we want. There must be input from the environment and some dynamic relation to the environment, because it is in relation to the environment that motion takes place. This analysis of movement cannot be derived from or reconciled with the definition aforesaid. The term 'desire' is used without explanation, and the definition made no place for it; nor is any general term for environmental input easily mapped onto the definition. The two discussions cannot have been designed as part of one continuous discussion, and all attempts to build bridges between them (like this one in *Ethics* I xiii) are full of awkwardnesses. The real explanation of this, I think, is neither the author's intellectual development nor accidents of editorial history, but the fact that animal action, whether of humans or of brute beasts, is an affair of integration with the environment that sustains the animal as part of its world. So an explanation in simply psychological terms makes no sense. With the brutes, we have to consider ecology; with humanity, we have in addition, to think about the social order. There is, there must be, a psychological account to be given – but it is not independently intelligible. Aristotle's functional analysis in the present passage has nothing to do with the 'parts of the soul' that

Aristotle repudiates in *On the Soul* III. We are simply talking about different aspects of human behaviour, all of them attributable to an ensouled body endowed with a functionally separable mind. No ontology of any sort is implied by this or by anything else in the *Ethics*, so far as I can see.[3] When, in *On the Soul* III 10, Aristotle denounces the postulation of 'parts of the soul' to explain action, he is not excluding the admittedly 'exoteric' (1102a25) distinctions between what has and what lacks *logos*, but pointing out that *orexis* operates in *each* of the three 'parts' that Plato postulated. It remains true that *orexis* always requires both input and impulse, and it is the relation between these two that I xiii discusses.[4]

Well, then. We have to say what the soul is, as an entity involving both the use of *logos* and the desirous element that provides the dynamics of action. Since action involves both together, the desirous element must be susceptible to control by reason: we must want what we recognize as desirable, whether that recognition involves simple identification or planning. But obviously this does not always happen. So reason is involved in two ways, in the activity of planning and deciding, and in the affective readiness to do what one decides.

Our actual wishes and desires, as human beings, are for things that are conceptualized in the first place. If the feeling of indignation is a desire for revenge, it is a feeling one cannot have unless one has the complex notions of injury and requital. So, although indignation itself is not in any sense a mode of thought, it is shot through with thinking, and is presumably amenable to further thinking of a more refined and reasonable sort.

In the normal case, one should not be aware of the duality between 'reason' and 'passion' because there should be no tension or discrepancy: one wants to do what one thinks best, and the question whether there are two 'parts' of the soul involved is as practically pointless as it is literally meaningless. But things are not always like that: tensions do occur, and then one 'succeeds' or 'fails' to conform one's feelings and actions to one's best judgment. Aristotle uses paralysis as an illustration. Normally healthy people do not think of their limbs as separate from themselves, but spastics visibly have to cajole and outwit their recalcitrant musculature. It is the visible drama that makes it obvious. It is not clear how far Aristotle wants to push this analogy, but it is clear that he is insisting on the applicability of the dynamics involved. And the insistence is important, because it will be built in (unselfconsciously if not surreptitiously) to the treatment of moral virtues, which deals with different aspects of the character as if they were separate limbs, each of which would be capable of separate training. But there is another side to the analogy, which is more disconcerting. The phenomena of paralysis are exceptional; most of us, as I said, do not have to labour to outwit our recalcitrant physiques. To use such phenomena to explain the relation between the cognitive and the appetitive (or whatever it is) is to suggest that the latter is normally at odds with the former but can be brought under control. Aristotle does not think quite that, as we shall see, but he also recognizes that the development and maintenance of virtue normally do involve some tension. It never becomes really clear why they should.

Aristotle's chief analogy is not with the mind's control of the body, but with the order of authority in a family. As might be expected in a hierarchical and family-centred society like that of Greece, Aristotle envisages a family as normally acting as a unit, with the father taking the decisions.[5] The children would do what father said, not by way of taking orders, but by way of accepting the decisions made for the family. It is not a matter of calculation so much as a matter of identification, as Aristotle says, taking advantage of a handy Greek idiom.[6] But, of course, real children are not always like that. The norm is obvious, but so is its violation.

The twofold analysis of *logos* is the basis of what is to follow: it means that there are two sets of virtues, two domains in which one has to be serious about reason, which we may call 'intellectual' and 'moral,' provided that we allow those words no extra connotations beyond what the argument requires.[7] But the analysis has to be supplemented, and becomes a fourfold scheme, in a curious and tangled way.

The simple dualism of controlled/controlling, or inherently rational and dependently rational, is complicated by adding a third factor, that which is irrational in the sense that its operations are not conceptually mediated at all. The processes of metabolism and growth are vital operations of the organism, hence operations 'of the soul,' but do not enter into our plans because we can do nothing about them – or rather, though that is not said here, they enter only as what has to be provided for because it is the basis (the material cause, in the understanding of *Physics* II 9) on which all our plans depend. This third factor, which operates independently of 'that which has *logos*' (cf. *On the Soul* III, 432b15–16), is introduced as part of the 'non-rational' side of the soul in contrast with the rational, so that the eventual triad is the outcome of the superposition of two dyads, with the common element classed as rational or irrational, according to which way you look at it.

It is worth noting that the triad is developed in this way, because otherwise we seem to have an asymmetry in the treatment – and eventually it turns out that we do. The asymmetry would be a four-fold schema with one element missing: altogether irrational, irrational in relation to reason, reason in relation to the irrational, and (the missing element) purely rational. Or, in relation to the functions of 'that which has *logos*': independently operating, controlling, subject to control, not amenable to control. This duality in the operations of reason is something that Aristotle has not formally introduced, and he still does not do so, though it will be featured in Books VI and X.[8] All we have here is the unexplained statement that there is more than one virtue of the understanding – more than one kind of thinking that one can be serious about and in which we can do well or badly (1103a5–8). At the very end of Book VI, at 1145a7–9, Aristotle will say that the planning aspect of us 'provides for' the purely intellectual aspect, just as I have said that it 'provides for' the metabolism, without directing its operations – with the difference, of course, that metabolism is treated as a merely necessary condition, and intellect is treated as something superior, of which the whole practical life may itself be regarded as a mere necessary condition.

Although the analysis of 'the soul' in I xiii is tangled and intricate, it is presented as simple, because Aristotle wants to draw a simple conclusion: that there are two different *logos*-related aspects of human life to be serious about, with corresponding excellences or 'virtues' – excellences of (controlling) thought and excellences of (controlled) character. The distinction is one generally recognized – the concluding sentence, 1103a3–10, is all in terms of what 'we say.' What follows is, accordingly, a pair of long and elaborate discussions of the dimensions of reason and rational discourse in each of these domains. It is essential to remember that we are not talking about two kinds of activity, let alone two ways of life, but about two aspects involved in every activity, the controlled and the controlling. It is not just that these are inseparable: they are interdependent, can exist only in relation to each other. It is virtually impossible to bear that continuously in mind, but obviously it must be so.

2.11 Comment: Political Analogues

The rational/irrational, controlled/controlling division is clearly political in character, in a sense that is obvious and has lately been brought back into fashion. The shifting twofold, threefold, fourfold scheme that seems to be operating in the present analysis of the soul is, politically, highly evocative.

The basic duality of reason and irrational is obviously the basic political split between rulers and ruled, which seems to be (and may in fact be) unavoidable.

The completed fourfold scheme answers to another pervasive Indo-European hierarchy: priest, king, warrior, peasant, of whom the last-mentioned is of no account, just as the metabolism is left out of practical account.[9] In Plato's Republic, *however, in the shadow of which Aristotle is writing, there is an ambiguous twofold/threefold scheme, just as there is in our present passage, though it is not the same scheme. Rulers and priests ('philosophers' – Aristotle's* Metaphysics *I 1-2 acknowledges the connection, and priests as such are rigorously excluded from the political order by both Plato and Aristotle) are declared to be the same, with the army occupying the ambiguous middle position, and the economic order is excluded from the system of control altogether. But there is a twist: though excluded from power ('not required to serve on committees,' poor chaps), they are full members of the society to which they belong, in which everyone retains a common status. This common status, as Aristotle makes clear in his* Politics, *is the basic idea of the true political organization, the* polis *or autonomous state. The conceptualization of the imaginary society in the* Republic *is inherently (and fascinatingly) unstable, fusing incompatible notions of human community. The complexities to which the instability leads are endless, and form a large part of what lies beneath the detailed treatments of 'virtues' in both Plato and Aristotle.*

2.12 What We Call Virtue (1103a8–10)

I remarked that the last sentence of I xiii is all about what 'we say.' This introduces a new twist into the discussion of 'virtues,' an idea that I have insisted was introduced as a purely formal notion, that of the manner of operation in any field of someone who takes the operationally disclosed requirements of that field seriously. All virtues are thought of as 'conditions' or 'states' (*hexeis*), says Aristotle, including such purely intellectual (not 'character'-related) conditions as 'wisdom.' 'We praise even the wise person on account of his/her *hexis*' (that is, we are saying something nice about what he or she *is*) – 'and, among *hexeis*, the ones that are praised we call "virtues."'

This is a radical shift in focus: what we *call* virtue is what we *do* praise. Fair enough. But there is nothing to show that we praise the right people for the right things, and consequently there is nothing to show that what we call virtues really are virtues. You might say that, in the long run, there could not be a split. In the long run, the standards of guitar playing established by the guitarists who have worked their way to the head of their profession are going to be standards applied by the musical public – what other standards could really sustain themselves? But the link between what is said, what is praised, what is believed, and what is really the case, remains open to question. Received opinions are the data of ethics only because experience is the object of our study, and received opinions reflect experience. But they do not *constitute* that experience. Aristotle has already told us that most people are wrong about happiness.

We will see, then, that what Aristotle does is, in effect, to bring about an intellectual reconstruction of 'the virtues.' His treatment purports to be (and perhaps really is) based on a sort of analysis of what, given the conditions of human existence, the virtues must be; but it takes the form of a *description* in these terms of the conduct that we recognize as desirable because it is what 'our society' endorses. But what is 'our society'? Athens? Aristotle never says so, and he knows that different cities have different standards. Only in a perfect society would conventional judgments be reliable.

2.2 Moral Virtue (II-V; 1103a14–1138b14)

2.21 Two Kinds of Virtue (1103a14–23)

The analysis of the soul shows that *logos* is involved in action in two ways, as directing and as amenability to direction. Obviously, then, if it makes any sense to speak of 'virtues' rather than of 'virtue,' there will be two virtues: directing virtue, and virtue in being directed. The former of these will have to be constructed 'from the ground up,' as it were; but the latter will be constituted by the redirection of something that is, in principle, going on already, because it will have a separate existence as that which has to be controlled by something other than itself. So the first thing Aristotle says is that the 'thinking' (*dianoētikē*) kind of virtue mostly takes its *beginning* as well as its development from conscious process – Aristotle actually says from 'teaching' (*didaskalia*), the sort of thing that schoolteachers do. So it takes time and experience (1103a15–17). But the other kind of virtue, the 'way-of-life' (*ēthikē*) kind, doesn't have to be originated; it simply 'comes about' by the development of habits (1103a17–18).

How can this be, since controlling and being controlled must be two aspects of the same process? We are not told – the question is not even raised here. But we can figure it out. A human child (or an unsocialized and inarticulate adult, for that matter) will develop behaviour patterns on the basis of its experience, as any other animal does. These patterns have nothing to do with virtue. But once the human begins to have things explained to it and acquires the idea of doing things *for a reason*, it will begin to modify its existing behaviour patterns accordingly. As we shall see soon, this means that a transformation has to take place, and the trouble with human life is that the transformation is not always complete. But the viability of the whole notion of 'the human good' depends on the supposition that the natural way for a human being, as a being whose whole life is suffused with symbol use, to develop, is for it to develop habits of acting in accordance with explicit principles – but for these principles themselves to reflect the quality of the entirety of the rational behaviour patterns as they have been developed.[10]

The two-sided account of virtue derived from the analysis of the 'parts' of the soul involved in action proves to be open-ended in at least two directions. First, the account of 'intellectual' virtue bifurcates to introduce the concept of 'wisdom,' excellence in pure or abstract thought. This is unexpected, though we have been given plenty of warning, because, notoriously, Aristotle rejects Plato's doctrinaire equation between sage and statesman, so that scholarly attainments have nothing to do with the direction of policy and hence nothing to do with the analysis proposed in I xiii. It looks as if purely intellectual activity would have to be excluded from the *Ethics* altogether because it has no relation to *praxis*, to the problems of living. But, of course, though it does not help to solve practical problems, it is one of the ways one can choose to spend one's time; and, though it may not be *praxis*, it certainly counts as *energeia*, a human activity, and Book IX will introduce a way of thinking about activity in general that will accommodate intellectual work. And in Book VI we will bring it within our purview by simply pointing out that the dominant value of practical thought, as of any other thought, is truth. Once truth is recognized as a value, we can hardly ignore the fact that it is in the intellectual life that truth reigns supreme. In any case, the most *obvious* operation of 'that which has *logos*' is theory and explanation.

The other way in which the account of virtue proves open-ended is through the discussion of justice. Justice is a virtue, if anything is. But it is not *only* a virtue, and cannot be dealt with in the terms Aristotle chooses for dealing with the virtues: it is a complex social and political phenomenon, covering the whole domain of the formal rules under which agents conduct their mutual interactions within associations. In explaining the virtue of justice, then, we are dealing with the formal rules of social reality. But why should there be any such reality? What is the informal reality that 'justice' formalizes? It is what Aristotle calls *philia*, the whole domain of fellow-feeling and of behaviour controlled by such feeling. It is a vast topic, and one to which our initial stance in the *Ethics*, that of the individual or organized group wondering how best to live its life, gave us no ready point of entry. A whole new perspective is needed, and a fresh start has to be made. But you really cannot discuss justice without discussing friendship, because they are mutually complementary, and you certainly cannot discuss virtue without discussing justice. And it turns out that you cannot really understand the basic values of human life without thinking about friendship.[11]

There is a third way in which the discussion of virtue proves open-ended, which in fact I have touched on above. The occasional recalcitrance of the rational/irrational aspect of the soul (compared by Aristotle to that of a paralysed limb) is a real problem. It is not just the automatic functioning of the metabolism and so on that is beyond the scope of conscious control and unamenable to education. Part of the emotional or desirous system is so as well. Hunger, thirst, the sexual drive, retain a certain basic autonomy, which cannot be eliminated. Does this mean that most people may be 'maimed with regard to virtue' in the way that Book I conceded would (exceptionally) make people incapable of happiness?[12] Aristotle seemed there to deny that this could be so, because it would be an absurd state of affairs. But is it? If virtuous habits must supervene on the vital system of self-preserving responses that keep children alive before they can understand language, maybe the best nature can do by way of producing a rational (*logos*-guided) animal is to produce an animal that can only supplement, and occasionally and partially supersede, its survival patterns with what civilization requires. In Book VII we will find Aristotle conceding that humanity does indeed have a 'double nature,' but this is scarcely compatible with the theoretical attainability of happiness by all who are prepared to take the matter seriously.[13]

2.22 Moral Virtue in General (II–III v; 1103a14–1115a4)

2.221 Moral Virtue and Moral Virtues

Some non-human animals – animals that do not have discursive language – are capable of learning from experience.[14] That is, in

Aristotle's terms, they form habits, routinized ways of behaving. But how is that possible? Only because, in the animal's life, types of situation recur in relation to constant or recurring needs or appetites. Without both constancies, obviously, there could be no such thing as a habitual response. The same is true of humans, except that the recurrent features are named and can be analysed.

It follows that there must be moral virtues. To be or become a certain sort of person, one develops ways of behaving in accordance with a recognizably constant aspect of motivation in relation to a recognizably recurrent type of situation. How the relevant recurrent features are to be picked out and classified is open to question; that there shall be some is a condition of learning from experience.

There are, then, for human beings, moral virtues, though nothing in the above argument shows that these will be the same for all societies and conditions of humanity. But it is also true, as we have seen, that the practical question confronting the language-using species of humanity is always the same, and is not reducible to habit. The question is always: what should I do now? – in my total situation, with my total motivation, only part of which can be reduced to a habituated response. So the only habit directly relevant to a good life can be a habit of asking that question and trying to give the right answer and act on it. Such a habit would be a habit of *choosing*, as Aristotle will explain in III ii. It will not be a 'knee-jerk' response to a familiar stimulus. But learned responses to stimulus are the only possible basis for such a habit, and the less reflective our behaviour is the more it will conform to that pattern.

Aristotle's general account of moral virtue and virtues prescinds, rather bafflingly, from the problem of acting in a complex situation. It assumes that we always act in closed situations in which we can go right or wrong. It confines itself to asking what we can say in purely general terms about what virtue amounts to in such a situation – that is, if we take the situation seriously, what will be the dimensions of our seriousness?

2.222 Becoming Good and Being Good (II; 1103a14–1109b26)

Plato's *Meno* makes much play with Socrates' gambit that we cannot tell how virtue is acquired until we know what it is. By contrast, Aristotle's account of moral virtue in Book II begins with an account of how virtue is acquired and only then offers a definition of a moral virtue, one relatively independent of the preceding discussion. What is at stake here? Well, we know already what a moral virtue will be; from I xiii and from the general consideration of animal life, we know that it will be a state of character that is brought under the control of reason, and that it is not automatically under that control. Aristotle does not argue that point, and does not need to. The first point he needs to make is that virtue formation is a special case of character formation; people form good habits in just the same way they form bad habits. Now we are faced with a problem that pervades Plato's dialogues. Good practices form good habits, bad practices form bad habits. But, if intellectual virtue is mostly a matter of explicit teaching, it looks as if all we can learn in Athens, say, is how to be a good Athenian. If that is so, we have no operational distinction between virtue and conformity.[15] Plato's solution called for a philosophical analysis that would ground such a distinction in cosmology and metaphysics. We have seen that Aristotle rejects that solution. The problem he has posed for himself is this: can the mere formal requirement of seriousness do the trick?

2.2221 Nature and Habituation (II i; 1103a14–b25)

Mental development (*logos* in all its ramifications) supervenes on basic physical development. At first our existence is limited to eating, sleeping, and excreting; then we learn to talk; then we go to school and learn to read and figure. So the intellectual virtues supervene on an already-formed structure of habitual behaviour patterns, the modification of which will be the 'moral' virtues. It will make sense, then, to deal with the moral virtues first. But there are two dangers, which Aristotle does not warn us about. First, we may confuse the pre-rational form of habituation with the form (the habit of *choosing*) that constitutes a virtue; second, we may lose sight of the extremely abstract nature of moral virtue as strictly conceived (as explained in II ii, § 2.22221). I am not sure that Aristotle quite avoids succumbing to both perils.

2.22211 Action, Pattern, Nature (1103a18–26)

Habitual patterns of behaviour arise when repeated actions develop into routines. So they come about in us neither as natural endowments (like instinctual patterns) nor as violations of nature: what is natural is that we should form such patterns. But, of course, though Aristotle does not say it here, there is another sense of 'natural' – that in which the city is a natural development, though it is a product of conscious organization, because it is the environment in which human nature can be realized, in which the full scope of 'that which has *logos*' can be realized. In this other sense, only good habits are natural, as argued in I viii. Bad habits are not within the scope of the human 'function,' it seems, in the way that good habits are. We will have to see if this tendentious claim can be made good (Book IX).

2.22212 Actions and Habits (1103a26–b2)

Action comes first. A kind of action must be performed several times before it begins to be routinized, obviously. Aristotle's examples are instructive: they are brave, temperate, and just actions – corresponding to three of the 'four virtues' into which virtue was analysed in Plato's *Republic*.[16] (The fourth virtue, 'wisdom,' is left out, of course – in Aristotle's terms it is an intellectual virtue, not a moral virtue.) And it is a thesis in the *Republic* (444D) that people become just through performing just actions, as Aristotle says here.

The analogies Aristotle uses are as instructive as his examples: by building we become builders, by playing the guitar we become guitarists. These are not simple responses: they are the uses of complex techniques, in which the mere repetition of learned movements plays a subordinate role. What becomes habitual in builders is the apt performance of builderly assignments in general, even if the precise tasks are novel. They get to know how 'we builders' do things, and spontaneously do things that way. (In a rather similar move, Aristotle says elsewhere that the 'formal cause' of a house is not the architectural drawings or their counterpart in the builder's mind, but the craft of building as objectified in the builder – the builder's own version of knowing how to build; cf. *Metaphysics* XII, 1070b29.)

2.22213 Laws and Habits (1103b2–6)

This is shown by what happens in cities. Legislators succeed or fail according as to whether they succeed in producing good habits of conduct: that is the difference between a good and a bad constitution. So says Aristotle. What is he thinking of?

The thesis is again from the *Republic* (424A–427A), where Socrates says that a well-run city does not have to have laws against everything because people do not want to do the things one would need laws against.[17] But *what* is shown by *what* that happens in cities? I suppose the idea is that actual crimes are penalized so that most people most of the time do not even *want* to do criminal things of that sort – cities are mostly self-policing. Well, so they are.

2.22214 *The Need for Teachers (1103b6–13)*

We become good by doing good things, then, and bad by doing bad things. The same is true of the trades we mentioned. Experience of building badly would make us bad builders – that is why we need teachers.

Aristotle here seems a bit glib. Are there no bad teachers? We know there are. Teachers of music struggle against the effects of incompetent or even perverse teaching. Some children are badly brought up; we are inclined to blame their environment if they turn out badly. Yes; but if you became serious about music you would start by looking for a good teacher. Who is a good teacher? The answer is different at different levels of competence; but at each level there is really no mystery. Is it a mystery in morals? Really?

2.222141 *The Moral Analogue (1103b13–23)*

'It is the same way with virtues': it is in the course of engaging in contractual relations with human beings that some of us become fair and others unfair; it is in the course of acting in terrifying situations and getting used to being afraid and confident that some of us become brave and others cowards. It is the same way with lust and rage: some of us become temperate and gentle, some become dissolute and bad-tempered, depending on how we conduct ourselves. In short, from activities of a certain sort, habits of that sort are developed.

Three things worth noting here: first, the word I rendered as 'engaging' and 'acting' was *prattontes*, engaging in *praxis*, doing things overtly in the world; but the word I rendered as 'activities' was *energeiai*, the technical word for any actual behaviourial manifestation as opposed to a capacity or a disposition. Second, Aristotle gives us three examples. The first is defined by the circumstances of action, bargaining in the market-place; the second is defined by circumstances and appropriate reactions, fear and confidence; the third is defined by the internal condition of the agent, lust and rage presumably finding their own occasions. Both factors, feelings as well as circumstances, are involved in virtues and in the episodes that produce them and conform to them. But the third thing we note is that nothing has been said about teaching. Does the parallel between learning a trade and learning a virtue extend to that as well? We are not told, though we were told beforehand that intellectual virtues mostly come from teaching. Aristotle never quite comes clean on this issue. I suppose he would say: obviously, if a moral virtue is a kind of habit and comes as we have said, it can't come from teaching. It can come from training, in the way we said above (§ 2.22213) that lawgivers try to train the citizens' characters by controlling their behaviour. But that won't quite do, because building and guitaring, which are certainly taught, also certainly come through training. – Or perhaps it *is* all right: building and guitaring contain elements that correspond both to intellectual virtue and to moral virtue, and it is a defect in the Platonic-Aristotelian doctrine of the arts that they overemphasize the intellectual component.[18]

2.222142 Good Beginnings (1103b23–5)

Aristotle's conclusion or afterthought here seems obvious. Since actions lead to virtues, it makes all the difference what habits we form right from the start, 'from childhood on.' But, obvious or not, it is disastrous. We are supposed to be answering the question of how one can secure the good life, which has turned out to mean becoming virtuous. In case we had forgotten, the next thing Aristotle will say will be a reminder of this. But now we are apparently told that what we have to do is retrospectively to have secured a good childhood upbringing – that this is 'everything.' If that is true, though, surely we are neither free to be virtuous nor to be blamed for being bad: our parents and teachers caused us to be so, or 'society' at large made us what we will become.

In III i–v it will become clear that such external influences do not amount to a causal process (such as the modern word *conditioning* suggests) that produces specific habits of good or bad behaviour. The relevant habits are habits of choosing, of sizing up situations and all they involve – the very opposite of the narrow modifications of specific reflexes to which 'conditioning' properly refers. The word used for habit formation, *ethizesthai*, is ambiguous: it could be taken as passive, 'being provided with habits'; it could equally well be taken as middle, 'to provide oneself with habits.' And training, *askēsis* (granted, the word is not used here), is not something that happens to one, it is something one does. If I have interpreted Aristotle right, one starts to become moral when and if one starts taking life serious- ly; this is something one has to do for oneself. It is not clear whether bad upbringing can prevent one from being serious, or good up- bringing impel one to be serious. Aristotle raises the question at III v and does not really answer; at X ix he takes a sort of social determinism for granted.[19]

I think what Aristotle would have to say would be something like the position attributed to Protagoras in Plato's dialogue of that name, which I have mentioned above. Of course, one has to have a decent upbringing, but practically everyone has. Outside a Charles Addams cartoon, almost everyone picks up a way of behaving that will pass muster in society. And this level of socialization is all we need for virtue to be superimposed on, in the way I sketched at the start. As we will see in X ix, most people are not *spoudaioi*, serious about living, and the task of politics is to provide a legal framework (imme- diately educational, ultimately coercive: they wouldn't think of steal- ing, but if they do they may be exiled to Brisbane) in which people live together in an orderly fashion. The exceptions are the people we call sociopaths, who are in Aristotle's phrase 'maimed (*pepērōmenois*) as regards their potentiality for virtue' (1099b19). You don't actually have to be trained in good habits. That becomes obvious when we consider what a good habit is, which is what we will do next.

The trouble is that this remark on early education and the need for a basis of observant behaviour contradicts what was said in I iv about children – that they act at random, responding to the stimulus of the moment, hence do not grasp the notion of a lifetime as a practical unity, hence cannot profitably study ethics and politics. It may be true that they take short views, but the propensity to develop behaviour patterns on the basis of experience is surely something they will share with all other animals that have memory. How could that insistence on childish unreliability be reconciled with the present insistence on early habituation?

A partial solution, not a good one, is to point out that 'from our very youth' (*euthus ek neōn*) does not mean 'from birth';[20] the actual phrase, as Aristotle points out later (at 1104b11), is a reminiscence of Plato's *Laws* 653A–C, where the 'Athenian stranger' says that children begin by being responsive to childish pleasures and pains, and that to get one's pleasures and loves and pains and hates (*hēdonē kai philia kai lupē kai misos*) right 'from the very beginning to the end' of life (*euthus ex archēs mechri telous*) is the prime task of education –

Aristotle substitutes *ek neōn* for *ex archēs*, I suppose because he tends to use *archē* in the *Ethics* as a technical term.[21] To point out where education begins is not quite to invoke social determinism. But I must admit that I wish Aristotle had not indulged in rhetorical over-kill, after saying that early training makes a big difference, by adding 'or rather, *all* the difference' (*mallon de to pan*). I would like to think that it is a marginal scrawl added by some early reader and incorporated into the text by a later scribe – but one must not invoke scribal error to amend a text to suit one's own taste. Still and all, Aristotle cannot have been unmindful of the fact that a good upbringing is not enough, as evidenced by the dismal showing made by the sons of such eminent statesmen as Themistocles (*Meno* 93A–94E).

A better way to effect a reconciliation is to point out that in children it is the habits themselves that are disorganized, not cohesive into a style of life governed by a world-view. The child may then have many organized sets of impulses in its behaviourial repertoire, which can be played off against each other in the way explained in III iii (1113a4–9), just as it will have available many possible role models which it may come to recognize as 'peer pressure' and parental omnipresence recede.[22] A child's habits are trivial and divisive, not a mutually reinforcing system in the way that makes old people 'set in their ways.'

2.2222 Phenomenology of Virtuous Activity (II ii–iv; 1103b26–1128b35)

2.22221 How Reason Enters the Non-rational (II ii; 1103b26–1104b3)

So, virtues come from the formation of set dispositions to act in one way rather than another. But *what* way? After all, bad and good habits are formed by the same process of 'experience' – whatever that is; no mechanism is ever described. So, what is the difference between a good action and other actions?

According to our definition, a good action is one that depends on being serious about the practical use of *logos*, the power articulated in rational speech. So 'it goes without saying' that a good action is defined as one that complies with 'the right *logos*' – and that is all we can say about it now, because the rightness will, of course, be a matter of intellectual rather than moral virtue.

Something more is, however, said. Aristotle reminds us that we began by saying that generalizations in ethics must be imprecise – and this reference to generalization indicates that the 'right *logos*' is, in fact, something that could be put into words as a universal statement. But Aristotle adds that, as well as this 'universal *logos*' (1104a5), there is a *logos* about particulars. And this is even harder to pin down, because particular situations as such are not cases of anything and so cannot fall definitively within the scope of any generalization. Just as in medicine and navigation, when your responsibility is to save the patient or the ship *whatever* may be going on, the task of *logos* is to size up the *kairos*, the moment for action just as it is. And this ability, too, is within the scope of intellectual virtue and not of moral virtue: one must figure out what to do, or grasp it immediately, and then the goodness of the action will lie in doing what complies with both these kinds of thought or insight.

Does that mean that there is nothing useful to be said about moral virtue as such? One might think so; and yet, oddly, Aristotle's discussion of moral virtue turns out to be much longer than his treatment of intellectual virtue. Or is it odd? Not really. The emphasis reflects the truth that what you actually do is what counts, and it is the moral virtue that is directly shown in action. And the greater length of the discussion of practice results from the great variety of situations, the pattern of culture, with which *logos* has to deal, as opposed to the relative constancy and simplicity of the intellectual methods and principles it uses.

For moral virtue strictly as such, however, once you have decided what the right thing to do is, nothing remains except that your feelings (your dynamic impulses) should comply. What are the possibilities here? Everything to do with *how* they comply is decided beforehand by intellectual virtue. The 'non-rational' part of the soul doesn't do any thinking. It only complies or fails to comply.[23] It is entirely a quantitative matter: one can be too eager or too reluctant to comply, or one can comply compliantly; one can actually comply, or one's action can be excessive or inadequate. If you are never frightened of anything, or if you are frightened of everything, you don't have the makings of a good solder; if you always actually run away, or don't actually retreat when you know you should, you are not a good soldier.

I said it is a quantitative matter, but that is misleading. Strictly speaking, quantity is intellectual: to specify 'how much' is a basic and exemplary use of discursive speech (see *Categories* 6). In the absence of a system for enumeration and measurement, there is nothing but an indeterminate 'more' and 'less.' The way reason gets into the irrational is by imposing a 'right amount' on the indeterminately quantifiable – and this, of course, is a *logos* in the distinctively mathematical sense, a ratio or proportion.

The decisions we arrive at on the basis of our thought processes (our intellectual virtues) can be imposed on our feelings and hence guide our actions. By regularly doing this in accordance with a policy, we do not merely train ourselves to be (for instance) less timorous and stingy than we were before: the action that becomes habitual is one that is exactly right – what we are habituated to is to feel in the right way because it is right. In this way, reason is internalized by the reasonless. We develop a feeling for the right.

So, we make ourselves do *x*; we keep making ourselves do it whenever the occasion arises; we become habitual *x*-doers; being an *x*-doer is now second nature to us, and because we are now inveterate *x*-doers we can go on doing *x* without having to force ourselves. It is a self-confirming process, which is why states of character, once established, can be expected to be extremely stable. But it is to be remembered that what is thus developed can never be a blind habituation; what we are habituated to is acting *for a reason*, hence not automatically, and in specific relation to the *kairos* of a unique situation. In fact, on any given occasion, many moral virtues may be involved – as many will be involved as relevant factors are present in a situation.

My account has left out one curious feature. Aristotle's way of making the point that moral virtue as such is entirely a matter of 'how much' is to use the analogy of health.[24] In nutrition and exercise, too much or too little destroys health; the 'right amount' not only keeps us healthy but enables us to do the things healthy people do. Similarly, temperance is maintained by moderation: asceticism and over-indulgence destroy it (1104a11–27). But the analogy seems confused and confusing. Temperance is not something that is 'destroyed by' bad habits; bad habits simply build up vices in the same way that good habits build up virtues. Or is that right? That is what we said at first; but now we have seen that *really* good habits, virtues, are different – they are habits of feeling and acting *in the right way as determined by reason*.[25] That being so, what, if anything, is it that is destroyed by excess and defect? Two answers seem plausible. First, what is destroyed could simply be the mediation of *logos* itself, as opposed to the addictive plunge after the irresistible and immediate attraction. Second, it could be the perception of the situation as it is, the judgment as to what is 'the right amount.' We shall find passages later on to support both views.[26] For the moment, it is probably better to say that Aristotle has been carried away by his analogy, as people so often are.

2.22222 *Pleasure and Pain (II iii; 1104b3–1105a16)*

How can a virtue as a steady disposition to act be self-sustaining (through facilitation, as we have just seen) *as a vital activity in accordance with* logos, not as a dulled repetitive response such as our vernacular usage of the word 'habit' suggests? Well, the actions could not be boring, since they would be responses to the *kairos*, to what was new and unique in each situation as it arose. But what would be self-sustaining? It would not be like a drill; the affect would have to become attached to the principle of rational choice itself. (The relief from this burden, the burden of perpetual earnestness, could only be the 'moral holiday' of recreation and play, as we will learn in X vi.)

To see this, we must return to the treatment of pleasure in I viii. What we call 'pleasure,' it is suggested there, is the quality of satisfaction we get from doing whatever we wholeheartedly want to do. Horse lovers get pleasure from activities centred on horses. So virtue lovers, people who take life seriously as human life, get their pleasure from putting their hearts into the quality of life. It is their second nature to do this, not a duty with which they must perpetually compel themselves to comply. To become a virtuous person is to transfer the locus of all one's pleasures.

What I have just said is not quite right. I said that virtuous people took pleasure in the choice itself. But what is habituated and trained is not the mind that chooses but the feelings that comply. And the feelings, the feelings-in-relation-to-situations that individuate separate moral virtues, are separately trained, insofar as the processes of habituation are an extension of the animals' learning from experience. Our delight in guzzling becomes a delight in regimen because it *is* regimen, a pleasure in eating because one knows (or in the light of the knowledge that) one is eating as one has every reason to believe ('what one best knows,' 1112a7–8) one should.

The transfer of pleasure *through* the transformation of life follows on the transfer of pleasure, by attached pains and pleasures of all sorts, that leads *to* the transformation of life. The manipulation of pleasures and pains, intrinsic and extrinsic, provides the whole dynamic of moral education. This is the entire thrust of II iii, despite the somewhat fragmentary character of its presentation. But there is a serious problem, which the chapter also confronts but does not resolve, because in fact it cannot be resolved. We have seen that eating, drinking, copulating, excreting, and the anger necessary to self-defence, the basic activities whereby an animal species maintains itself in existence, carry a strong initial charge that makes *them* self-sustaining. We do not need to 'put our hearts into them'; if we needed to, the species might be lost through inadvertence, just as we might accidentally die of asphyxia if it were necessary to make a conscious decision every time we breathed. It is these basic and paramount pleasures and pains that lead us astray. Aristotle's wording at 1105a3 is emphatic: it is hard to 'scrub out' this passion (*pathos*) with which life is 'stained.' This *pathos* must be *immediate* pleasure as *undergone*, not an experience associated with reflective appetite; it is the sort of *pathos* that will be contrasted with *hexis* in II v.

It is not true, then, that we are born, as II i suggested, with a neutral capacity of habit formation. We are born with a capacity of habit formation and development and modification, but it is not neutral. On the one side is the tendency of our animal nature to 'do what comes naturally'; on the other side is the drive of our natures as beings with a sense of time and capacity for discursive thought. The basic impulses must be trained and subsumed into a civilized and integrated life, and this is possible and should be normal; but it is inevitable that it should not be invariable.

Moreover, the pleasures and pains that are used as instruments to mould the characters of those who are not interested in moulding their own must, in the first instance, be pleasures and pains that are not already dependent on education. Children are brought up by candies and clouts; adults are kept in line by medals and jails – the means of training are cruder than the qualities the training is meant to achieve, and must be so, for if the subject were already operating on that higher level the training would have been completed.

The transferability of pleasure is a basic tenet of Aristotle's ethics. And it must take this form: that certain crude pleasures are basic and in a sense ineradicable, but a different set of pleasures, those of refined and civilized life, are more fully satisfactory.[27] Humanity has an originating, animal nature, and a completing, rational nature; and there can be no disharmony between the two, except by the sort of malfunction that (in the physical realm) doctors are needed for.

This postulated harmony is a feature of Aristotle's world-view as sketched in our Appendix. In such a system, all values must converge; and the middle of this passage on pleasure is taken up by a brief and superficially cryptic remark on the convergence (1104b30–1105a1) – superficially cryptic, because it exploits a Platonic *topos* which Aristotle has already used. The three values in question are three things that 'make for choice' and 'make for avoidance' – respectively, the fine (beautiful, noble), the useful (advantageous), the pleasant, and their converses.[28]

The form of convergence appealed to here is that the fine and the useful appear in the guise of the pleasant.[29] We *like* things to be useful, we *like* to do what conforms with our ideals. It is because pleasantness is not something intrinsically *opposed to* beauty and goodness that a harmoniously valuable life is possible.

On other views of the world, no such convergence of values need be postulated. On an evolutionary world-view, there is no reason why utility and pleasantness and beauty should converge in any general way – what makes for survival of the genetic material into the third generation is the only thing that counts, and all sorts of stuff may go along with that. For a Christian, there may be a most complete divergence between an agreeable life and a 'virtuous' (or heaven-rewarded) one – an omnipotent spirit may play practical jokes of any sort. It is only in a world that maintains itself as a system that a basic divergence of supportable values is intolerable. But why, after all, is it intolerable? I suppose one assumes that because the world proves to be intelligible, is found to make a certain amount of sense, it must actually be such that complete sense can be made of it: since we can successfully live and do science in the world of nature, we are entitled to say what nature does.

Aristotle had no right to suppose that the world made sense. The fact that (as he thought one could actually prove, *it was not a hunch or a super-stition) the world is everlasting only proves that it has as much order as its everlastingness requires. Incoherence and chaos might prevail all over the place.[30] As a matter of fact, Aristotle, when he gives his mind to the matter, concedes the point – but he does not make much of it, possibly because a pre-mathematical science could not cope with statistical order.*

The doctrine of the transferability of pleasure, as we have seen, requires that we gloss over the admitted difference between the basic pleasures and pains tied to the survival and maintenance of the body in the physical world, on the one hand, and the delights of civilized life, on the other. Fire will go on burning, and it will go on hurting; if it didn't, we would be in grave and continual danger, as people insensible of pain actually are. Aristotle says that someone who was 'confident' and of good cheer when faced with a flogging is not brave but crazy (1115a24), presumably because physical pain and the fear of such pain play an inexpugnable part in normal lives.

The virtue of courage, in fact, gives Aristotle a lot of trouble, and it is in this passage that he meets it (1104b7). He is repeating the thesis from I viii that virtuous people take pleasure in virtuous actions – otherwise, of course, there is something else they would rather be doing, which means that they are not really good but are only pretending or trying to be. So we have to apply that to the brave man in battle, who is 'enduring terrible things.' If he is really brave, what are we to say? That he is enjoying himself? Surely not; he is toughing it out in a dreadful situation. Aristotle suggests that he is 'rejoicing' (*chairōn* – Ross translates 'delights') in it, but then he backs off. At least, he says, such a person is 'not pained' (*mē lupoumenos* – Ross again). I wonder if Aristotle is not bending over backwards here to avoid suggesting that a good person might like fighting. Given the fact that we *are* at war, that as a good citizen of call-up age I *am* in the army, and there is a battle going on, in the thick of which I and my comrades are – and it is the quality of action at the *moment* of action that counts (cf. III i, 1110a12–13) – then, if I am a brave person, a good soldier, is there really anything else I would prefer to be doing? Surely it is not enough to say that I am 'not pained' – there is a sense in which I *am* rejoicing in my ability to hold my place in the phalanx, even if I am not exactly saying Ha! Ha! among the trumpets. But Aristotle wouldn't know about that, any more than I do.[31]

2.22223 What Is Different about Virtuous Action (II iv; 1105a17–b18)

Now, where have we got to? Virtues, it seems, are states of character formed by habituation on the basis of actions, so they depend on the quality of the actions that form them (II i); the quality in question lies entirely in conformity to the various requirements of articulate thought, and is simply a matter of responding to the right degree or in the right amount (II ii). What is the value of such action? Its value is that its being quantified by reason makes a rational person able to think of it as ideal, a triumph of rightness. The good person's pleasures, instead of being random enjoyments of various episodes, are now characteristically traced to this single source: one delights in what one does because of the way it conforms to the rational ideal of the integrated life (III iii). Not only does it have this systematic character (which is actually the 'beauty' that Socrates makes Diotima speak of in Plato's *Symposium*) – if we think of the opening chapter of the *Ethics*, we can see that such actions are useful as well as fine and pleasant, because they are (should be) means to future goods.

That is all very well, but, *ex hypothesi*, the actions of the virtuous person are just the same as the actions by which the virtuous person's character is developed. It is by doing just actions that we become just, as we quoted Plato as saying (*Republic* 444D); but surely, if we do just actions regularly enough to become just, we must already *be* just. Aristotle himself has been rather careful about the way he has actually used the names of virtues in his exposition, but the point remains. What is different about the virtuous action *as an action*? The difference, obviously, must lie, not in the overt action, nor even in the general motivation, which in both cases must be 'to do the right thing' (except that the not-yet-virtuous person may also be influenced by the consideration that 'this is the sort of person I would like to be'); it must lie in the precise relationship to the agent's character and mind.

The virtuous action of the virtuous person is special because it has been brought within the scope of a complete and functioning domain of *logos*, much as the action of the master of a craft is special because it is brought within the scope of operative mastery. It's different when (s)he does it. So what we said in II ii turns out to be misleading, after all. Virtues are built up from actions, to which our attention must accordingly be directed; but the actions that stem from virtues are what they are because they do belong to a life that is conceived as a whole in which all values are mutually reinforcing. Aristotle builds up his case step by step. Part of what distinguishes a virtuous action from the 'same' action done by a different sort of person is the same as what distinguishes expert knowledge from 'beginner's luck': it isn't enough to spell a word right, literacy requires that one *know how* the word is spelled, and know it of one's own knowledge (no prompting, no looking up in dictionaries), and that one know it as a part of a general knowledge of 'how to spell' and of the rules of writing generally.

But the case of virtue goes beyond that, because (as we shall see in Book VI, though Plato and the Stoics would not quite agree) the arts are self-contained enclaves and expertise. The knowledge we spoke of is essential, but not much else. But a virtuous action is such only because it betokens seriousness about life as a whole; one must know (as before) that the act is right, and know it of one's own knowledge, but also one must do it deliberately (we will see what that comes to in III ii), we must do it *just because* it is right, and we must do it as an expression of 'a firm and unchangeable character' (1105a33).

The development of a virtue, it seems, is more than just developing a tendency to perform a certain sort of action: it is making oneself into the sort of person who would, as a matter of policy and self-expression, do just that sort of thing.

But the only way to make yourself into that sort of person is by doing the appropriate sort of action. Learning moral theories, even the sort of moral theory we are doing here, is not enough. It may help, in the same way that going to the doctor may help a sick person. But it helps only if you do what the doctor says.

2.2223 The Definition of Moral Virtue (II v–vi; 1105b19–1107a27)

'And after that one must look at what virtue is' (1105b19). Not 'moral virtue,' we note, but virtue; and we will often find Aristotle indulging in this sloppy and revealing usage. Granted that equation, though, is this not just what we have been doing? In I i–vii we gathered that, since 'the good' is the end of action, virtue is the human quality that issues in genuinely goal-directed behaviour, that is, seriousness in the identification, clarification, and pursuit of goals. And in II i–iv we have discovered what virtue is by explaining how it is acquired. After all that, saying it is time to start examining what virtue is seems very odd. I suppose 'what *x* is' is a technical phrase designating the formal definition of *x*, and what Aristotle means is that he will now define (moral) virtue.

The account of moral virtue follows a pattern rather like that of happiness in Book I (a version of the 'scholastic' pattern mentioned in the foreword). A discursive discussion of general considerations is followed by a formal treatment leading to a definition; which, in turn, is followed by a reconciliation with popular opinion; and that, by some necessary elaborations and explanations that place the definition in its practical setting. But the two treatments are not exactly parallel. What led up to the definition of happiness was a review of received opinions and experiences, with the corresponding constraints on what happiness could be; the definition itself was based on a new factor, the concept of *ergon* and the relation of excellence to that by way of the ambiguous concept of the *spoudaios*, the serious person who is to be taken seriously. In the present discussion of moral virtue, the basis of the opening discussion is familiar facts of experience in the area of education and control – practices generally followed and distinctions generally made, together with the implications of the analysis of the operations of *logos*. What accounts for the difference between the two treatments is largely that at this point in the argument Aristotle has substantive results of his own that he can build on.

When we come to the definition itself, it seems at first that nothing new is introduced. Aristotle seems to be merely restating the basic points made in II i and II ii. This lack of evident progress is inevitable insofar as all he is doing in the *Ethics* is drawing out the implications of the initial problem – examining the extent to which simply being serious about our human condition as time-conscious and discourse-articulating animals generates an answer to the problem of how to conduct our lives. One might say that every real problem thus dictates the terms of its own solution, because what generates the problem is a complex situation, and what is not dictated by a careful and exhaustive analysis of the situation is an occasion for free initiative rather than problem solving. As Aristotle said at the start, the fact that opinions differ and situations vary is a constraint on the scope of informative and normative ethical generalization.

If progress is to be made, then, it is likely to be made incidentally or even surreptitiously. Little caveats and qualifications will be slipped in, or looking at old considerations from new angles will suggest what in effect are new considerations. So it is here. The definition of a virtue simply recapitulates what was implicit from the start – given the facts of personal and social life. But there are such facts.

2.22231 Genus (II v; 1105b19–1106a13)

Aristotle could not give a proper formal definition of happiness because of the global nature of the concept – *eudaimonia* is not a variety of any general sort of thing. But he can give a standard definition of a virtue. A virtue is some sort of aspect of a personality, and a good sort; and a particular virtue is a particular sort of good sort. In short, a definition by genus and difference, the kind of thing you get by a Porphyrian tree, a series of bifurcations of very general kinds (cf. *Metaphysics* VII xii).

Aristotle's statement of the genus of virtue starts with the blunt assumption that there are three things that come about or happen or are generated or 'come to be' (*ginomena*) 'in the soul,' passions and powers and dispositions. Since a virtue cannot (for reasons given) be either of the first two, it must be a disposition (*hexis*). But what is the source of the triad? And what is the force of 'come to be'? It sounds as if Aristotle were relying on some familiar piece of scientific psychology – familiar to his hearers, but not to us. Well, maybe he is.[32] If so, the triad must have been displayed as exhaustively covering the kinds of qualifications of vital agency that are relatively stable but are not inborn – the qualifications that we know virtue has to fulfil.

I do not suppose there ever was any such demonstration, and if there was I do not suppose it would have been convincing. All Aristotle needs to do is to remind us of the obvious reasons why a virtue cannot be a passion or a power. That it *is* a disposition has been explained already; so it cannot be anything else. Not all such differences are worth mentioning. The differences from abilities and emotions are worth specifying because they are obviously important, not because we might have been genuinely puzzled about which of three boxes virtues belonged in.[33] It is important that virtues are not mere passions, because, literally, passions are just things that come over one, things that happen to us; we cannot be blamed for them. What we can be blamed for is for giving in to them, for choosing to act as our feelings prompt us. And it is important that virtues are not mere abilities, because a person can have an ability to act but not act on it. In fact, a person who can do something right is equally able to do it wrong – I can recite the alphabet correctly, but I am equally able to recite it incorrectly.[34] A virtue is a disposition – an *actual* disposition *actually* and *actively* to *do* a certain sort of thing, *whenever* it is called for. If a virtue were a passion, *logos* would be impotent and ethics would be empty; if virtue were an ability, it would be irrelevant to our characters, because we might also have the ability to do the exact opposite – and act on *that*. Aristotle, I think, is not so much performing analysis here as exercising the sort of iterative emphasis that one uses on people who are reluctant to believe their ears: 'Go to jail. Go *directly* to jail. Do not pass GO. Do not collect $200.' In that unforgettable injunction, only the first three words are really necessary.

2.22232 Difference (1106a14–1107a35)

As the 'genus' simply repeats II i, so the 'difference' simply repeats II ii. Moral virtue is a purely a quantitative matter: it is a matter of feeling and acting neither too much nor too little in a certain respect, as *logos* determines. It is the imposition of determinacy on the indeterminate – or rather, we should put it the other way around, because it is the 'irrational' domain of feeling that becomes amenable to the paternal voice. So the virtuous action or response is a mean between extremes – but that could be misleading, as Aristotle explains. Lots of people, though, somehow get the impression that what Aristotle is espousing is just what he is at pains to distinguish it from.

How could so many people be so wrong? It is, in fact, Aristotle's own fault. He does generally have a penchant for intermediate positions: in *Politics* V–VI he extols the middle class, in *Politics* VII–VIII he praises the Greeks for being intermediate between northerners and southerners; in the *History of Animals* I he keeps telling us that 'intermediate' eyes, tongues, and so forth are best. So it is all too easy to equate his 'neither too little nor too much' with the ancient Greek piety of the slogan *Mēden agan*, 'nothing in excess.' If he really wanted to avoid the misunderstanding he warns against, he did not need to use the language that invites it. One suspects him of a certain departure from candour.

One of the things that invites misunderstanding is that Aristotle explains his meaning, as so often, by an analogy from medical practice, and the example he chooses (from dieting) is confusingly close to the moral issue to be illustrated. I would like to pose the relevant contrast in rather different terms.

Let there be a continuum, with a minimum and a maximum value – let them be what you will (a thermometer, with readings from 0 to 100, is a perfect example of what Aristotle has in mind). Let there be some way of measuring and locating points on the continuum – again, let the units be what you will. You can then easily establish the mid-point on the scale (in the example, 50). But this in itself is of no interest, given that both the extremes and the units and method of measurement are arbitrary. You can also establish the 'right' position on the scale for whatever it is you want – but this is not at all likely to be the mid-point, it will be the mid-point only by coincidence. If it is body heat, the 'right' temperature will be 98.4°F. Anything higher than this will be 'a temperature,' as we used to say; anything lower than this will be a low temperature. But, in any case, the reading on the thermometer will be some exact figure, no more and no less determinate than the 'normal' 98.4°.

Contrast this with the determination of the 'right amount' on such a continuum. For this, we need no scale, we only need our judgment. No measurements are carried out. We need have no method of measuring, no units of measurement; there need be no minimum or maximum 'values.' The medical profession establishes, by whatever means, how hot it is normal for a human body to be. Then anyone who is *exactly as hot as that* is at the right temperature, and all patients who are at the right temperature are just as hot as each other. The only formal requirement is that the right temperature shall be somewhere actually on the continuum, not right off the end. (If it were, there would be no 'right amount.') Everyone who is not at the right temperature is either too hot or too cold, and in principle it is always possible to be either one – but in practice, in some cases, the 'right' amount might be at the extreme end of the continuum, if it had determinate ends.

In the kind of case we have just been considering, which is the one Aristotle thinks appropriate to the 'amount of feeling' in virtuous action, only *one* value on the continuum is determined, and it is determined by one's direct standards of 'rightness,' whatever they may be, without any reference to any comparisons or measurements. And a determination of 'wrongness' establishes either excess of deficiency by direct comparison; there is no way in which any determinate quantitative value can be assigned to any deviant position, because no terms have been established in which that could be done. So it is not true that the right amount is intermediate between other equally determinable amounts. *Logos* says right or wrong as it says true or false – there is only one true answer to a simple question, but there are indefinitely many untrue answers. Virtue is not really a mean between extremes. It is the determination of a determinable, which, once made, lies between indeterminate excess and indeterminate defect.[35]

This and only this is what makes Aristotle's project workable, if it is. There is no symmetry between right and wrong answers, virtue is something definite but vice is not. Or so it seems here. But this leads to grave difficulties in explaining the psychology of consistent wrongdoing, and Aristotle never quite faces the problem.

2.22233 The Definition (1106b36–1107a8)

Let us look at our definition. 'Virtue, then' – he says 'then,' so it should all have been said before – 'is a *hexis* of choice (*proairetikē*)' – but *did* we say that before? – 'existing in middleness, the middleness that is relative to us' – what does that mean, exactly? – 'a middleness demarcated by *logos*' – how, exactly? – 'and by the *logos*' – why does he say *logos* twice? – 'whereby the reasonable person (*phronimos*; Ross translates 'man of practical wisdom') – who is he? *have* we heard of him before? – 'would demarcate it' – why bring him in? and *how* would he demarcate it?

We have a lot of questions already, but the definition goes on. 'And it is a middleness between two vices [or defects, *kakiai*], the one by way of excess, the other by way of deficiency' – note the middleness comes first, the betweenness is mentioned and described before Aristotle says *what* it is between; we covered this already – 'and again by one set of badnesses' – note the plural – 'falling short of, and the other set exceeding, what is required' – *to deon*: is that a word we used before? what does it imply? does it imply objectivity, for example? – 'both in sufferings and in doings' – note the careful symmetry of the language; does it have a point? – 'but virtue is both to find' – is there a *procedure of search and discovery*? – 'and to choose' – recognition precedes decision, we notice – 'the middle. And that is why, according to its being and to the *logos* that states what it really is' – the phrase Aristotle uses here is almost a technical term, and is often translated by 'essence' – 'virtue is a middleness, but according to the "best" and the "well"' – why does he use such odd language, or isn't it really as odd as it sounds? – 'it is an extreme' – literally a 'summitness' (*akrotēs*), to mark the parallel with 'middleness.'[36]

That definition is what is called 'Aristotle's doctrine of the "mean"' and is often taken to be his most distinctive contribution to ethics. The wording certainly is extremely tricky. Maybe he did say it all before, but it is hard to be sure. My interpolations indicate where comment or protest seemed to be in order.

2.222331 Choice

Yes, Aristotle did mention choice before – but all he was doing was contrasting a *hexis* with a *pathos* that simply comes over us; so *hexis proairetikē*, 'disposition to choose,' sounds pleonastic. It isn't, because 'choice' is to be taken in a very strong sense; Aristotle will take the matter up as soon as he has this definition properly squared away (III i–iv).

2.222332 'Relative to Us'

As I have suggested, this contrast between an arithmetical (hence objective) mid-point and a point established as right for the occasion is dealt with in a confusing way, though the main point is simple. The phrase 'relative to us' is ambiguous. It could mean only 'in the light of one's temperament,' meaning that to do the right thing will require greater amounts and directions of effort from some people than from others. But it could also mean 'in the light of one's situation in life, life style, life plans, social and economic class, and cultural commitments' and so on.[37] In the latter case, what is right for me to do may not be at all what it would be right for you to do (the very next thing Aristotle does is to explain why this would not justify one in committing downright crimes, 1107a8–17). Since different decisions are, in any case, right only in relation to their unique occasions (*kairoi*), there is no reason why Aristotle should not have meant 'relative to us' in this strong sense. There is no reason at all, in anything he has said, why different people should live in the same sort of way. There is nothing in his argument, for instance, to legitimize the notion of a 'moral law.' Actual societies provide different frameworks within which actions are determinately right or wrong, and the current efficacy or acceptance of such a framework is a factor in the situation. As Socrates says in Plato's *Crito*, one can try to change the way of thinking of the society one lives in, but, if one has not changed it, it continues to provide the situation within which alone one can plan and act.

This is not to say that Aristotle's relativism, even on the second of our interpretations, requires that there be no determinate answer to the question of which social system is best: I am sure he thought the Athenian way was better than the Persian way, and probably better than any other, though it could be improved on.[38] It is only that his theory of virtue and happiness does not *require* that there should be any one way of life or any one form of society that is best. It requires only that, in a given situation, a serious use of reason provides a given person with a determinate answer to the question 'What should I do now?' – to the extent that the action falls within the scope of the virtues.

My discussion here may have been misleading. I have been speaking as if Aristotle were defining virtue in terms of doing the right thing, as one's situation at the moment determines it, and assuming that one's situation is largely defined by one's social relations as the *polis*, the organized community, determines them. But that sounds like equating virtuous action with 'what society demands,' and Aristotle insists that compliance with the legitimate demands of society is not straightforward virtue but 'justice' in a sense that will be defined (1130a13). In V ix, he equates 'being just,' in the fullest sense of that expression, with deliberate compliance with the law, as opposed to deliberate violation of it; but how is such compliance related to acting 'for the sake of the *kalon*'? By making justice one's ideal, I suppose; but then, what does that do to the integrity of the other specific moral virtues? One feels that Aristotle may not quite have got his act together.

2.222333 *The* Logos

The mean is determined by a *logos*. What does that mean here? Ross translates as 'rational principle,' which suggests an overriding universal rule – 'principle' should translate *archē*; I have used the same phrase myself, but it is a hefty overinterpretation. One sees the point: the *logos* must be something that is articulate and universalizable. But actually we know just what *logos* in this context is, or should be. It follows from the account of the human good in I vii that what is required is the most serious use of the mind – all the resources of the *logon echon* insofar as it is applied to the problems of living. Any further stipulation would be wrong in principle, for it could only be some *restriction* on the scope of thought, and that would require one to be *deliberately stupid* about something. So the specification of what the *logos*, the use or uses of reason, is here must be equally general; and it is. We may note a latent ambiguity, however. Both of the main senses of the term are in point: a *logos* in its mathematical sense of a determinate point in the continua of action and feeling is found and applied; but what it is found and applied by is *logos* in another sense, the reasoning power of the agent. Aristotle's use of the singular term may suggest that only one of these is involved or, at any rate, that matters are much simpler than they are.

2.222334 *The* Phronimos

The *logos* in question is the one the *phronimos* would use. But who is he or she? The word has been used only once before in the *Ethics*, at 1095b28, where it was said that the *phronimoi* are the people a glory-hungry person wants to be esteemed by. That is really no help, but it doesn't matter, because we know who they must be: people of intellectual virtue, insofar as that virtue relates to conduct. That follows from I xiii. Only the judgment of such a person could determine the rightness of decisions.

2.2223341 *How the* Phronimos *Would Decide*

What is the *logos* by which the *phronimos* would determine what
virtue required? It follows from what has just been said that we cannot specify. Obviously we cannot, since the decision would be relative to the *kairos*, which is unique. All we can do is what we will do
in Book VI and have partly done already: enumerate the different
ways thinking can go right, and the different things (premises, conclusions, arguments – that sort of thing) it can be right about. That
is why Aristotle uses the optative: the principle by which the *phronimos would* decide.

What Aristotle says about the phronimos *is, in a sense, empty, and
hence disappointing. The same disappointment awaits us in Book VI, when
Aristotle promises to give substance to the schematic notion of 'what the
prudent man (phronimos) would do.' We expect to be told just what it is
that he would do – to be given rules, precepts, guidance. But, of course, that
is just what we cannot be given. What prudent people do is act on their best
judgment in the circumstances they are in, and Aristotle knows nothing of
our circumstances, nor has he any reason to expect that his judgment will
be better than ours. Our hopes for guidance presumed that someone was
better informed than we about what most closely concerned us. It is odd
that so many commentators on the* Ethics *share this disappointment, as if
it would not be absurd for a writer who insists on the way people use their
own rational capacities to usurp the function of those capacities.*[39] *The
reason is, I think, that the commentators are used to the idea of people
sitting in pews and having the law laid down to them by the functionaries
of the God industry. But the presupposition of that practice is what Thomas
Aquinas laid down: there is an objective difference between right and wrong,
but it is far too difficult for human minds to figure out what it is. A paternal God, however, does know what it is, and reveals it, so that the functionaries aforesaid can transmit this saving revelation to the rest of us.*[40]
*Whether that theory makes sense or not is not in question for us here; the
present point is that Aristotle knows nothing of it. Human beings, severally
and jointly, have nothing to go on other than what they can figure out for
themselves; there is no one and nothing else to blame or to thank.*

Why, then, does Aristotle not cut out the middle man? Since we
cannot specify what the *phronimos* does, why mention the person?
Simply to emphasize that there is such a thing as intellectual virtue
and there are right answers in ethics. All *phronimoi* judge the same
way. This is not incompatible with my contention that Aristotle has
left the way open for a certain sort of relativism. What it means is

that any serious and mentally competent person taking into consideration the facts of my situation, my personality and attainments, my social position and the nature of the society in which I have that position, and everything else, would, to the extent of his or her relevant knowledge of the facts, give me the same advice – if I am a virtuous person, every *phronimos* would judge the same as I do. But not every *phronimos* would *do* the same, because *phronimoi* do not resemble each other in character and situation. And, if there is no determinate answer to the question of what I should do, the *phronimos* could tell me what the options are.

I am far from saying that Aristotle thought of his own position as being open in the way I have suggested. He may have thought that all really good people would be like each other – Books VIII and IX sometimes read that way. I am only saying that the ambiguity of 'in relation to ourselves' (*pros hēmas*) leaves it open. What he does leave us with is the impossibility of specifying what the best use of reason is, beyond identifying it with whatever the intellectually virtuous person would decide.

2.2223342 *Comment: Personality – The Problem of Style*

The claim that all phronimoi *would judge the same way has no practical outcome, because situations do not recur: even if the outward circumstances were precisely analogous, which seems impossible, the style of the person deciding would be different. Judgments in the form 'This is what I would do, if I were you' are always speculative, because the antecedent can never be fulfilled.*

Aristotle takes no account of the possibility of alternative moral styles: that different people have different ways of handling problems, and may belong to different subcultures in their community that themselves have different ways of handling situations that cannot be judged better or worse than each other. He concedes that the phronimos *will appear in a different guise in different cities, and will recognize differences in social situation, but never discusses what limits there may be on the unambiguous identification of the* phronimos *or on the morally relevant scope of* phronēsis. *Nothing in what he says in the* Ethics *encourages us to assign normative status to any specific way of life, in the way that used to be suggested by people who thought growing up to be a good person was analogous to an acorn's developing into a mighty oak – the concept of* logos *expressly excludes that; but he leaves no conceptual space for individual personality in his treatment of the good life. Surely it is a matter of the greatest import-*

ance that people are interesting in themselves and interestingly different. It is as if Aristotle confused two positions. One position is that there is nothing to say about such differences, just because they are entirely a matter of preference, however important they may be. The other is that personality differences are simply a matter of personal preference, so that they should not be taken seriously when we are considering how to live, and all good people insofar as they are good are just the same as each other.[41]

Aristotle's 'serious' people are envisaged on the latter model, having virtue but no personality. But in today's open societies, personality seems within limits to be more important than virtue. A great deal of deviation seems compatible with the survival of a society, and may even be beneficial. What Aristotle most seriously ignores is the intersection between style and compliance, between what I owe myself and what my situation requires of me.[42] The concept of seriousness is ambiguous: Aristotle simply assumes that it gives exclusive weight to considerations of the latter sort, because he has never considered the alternative. It may be a quirk of modern civilization that it equates human function with individuality; but it is a defect of Aristotle's treatment that it opens the way to such values but does nothing about them.

Leaving aside the positive values of individual style, which I have been arguing Aristotle's concept of phronēsis *imperfectly accommodates, we are left with the question how the* phronimos *is to be identified. I have agreed with Aristotle that there seems to be no real problem, there is no mystery about who makes a mess of life and who makes a go of it, if you consider the constraints on human life and its opportunities; but then it seems that there is a problem, because those constraints and opportunities do not impinge everywhere in the same way and there seems no compelling reason why everyone should be constrained by them or avail themselves of them – and a serious person might well take that openness seriously into account.*

I think we have to envisage a situation structured somewhat as follows – a kind of structure Aristotle nowhere examines, though things he says sometimes imply something like it. Each individual's personality ('self,' if you will) is formed by interaction with others – with just those people with whom he or she does interact; and each of them has a self that is being formed in the same way. So people grow up in sets of mutually formed people. These sets interact, and the people involved in such interactions will, of course, tell their fellow members about the likenesses and differences they find and the harmonies and disharmonies in which they are involved. By such communication and mutual accommodation a wider community sustains itself. Three things are to be noted. First, nobody has to be 'normal,' even in terms defined by the initial set; one has only to be an interactor, and some interactions can be abrasive. Second, people typically belong to several different sets, and sets themselves are not discrete. And third, the sets an individual belongs to are not random but, in each case, have a complex order (which in any given case can be partly described) which the individual manipulates. Such a society as the polis, *which Aristotle considers as, among other things, a community of communities, is related to its individual members through this sort of dynamic.*

One is not locked into one's original self-formation in such sets as home, school, church, however monolithic these may seem; an adolescent can, and in a modern plural society usually does, exploit the differences among those sets and divide attention among them. But one can also generalize the principles of interaction themselves and form general notions and strategies of success at a higher level of abstraction. This kind of grasp is characteristic of Aristotle's phronimos. Phronēsis *represents a fusion of two ideas: success and failure in interaction, and a grasp of the general principles of interaction themselves – complicated, of course, by a recognition of the imperatives of survival and efficiency for an organism that has an autonomy derived from its sense of time.*

2.222335 Vices

Usually, Aristotle speaks of a virtue as a mean between two (named) vices. Here he says it is between two sets of vices. Probably the reason is to emphasize that a vice, having no determining principle, is not a unity in the same way that a virtue is. But he may be thinking of the special case of courage, and reflecting that other virtues might turn out to be similarly complex.

Aristotle has said what a virtue is; but what is a vice? It is hard to say, though one can say that a vicious person is one who lacks one or more specific virtues. *Metaphysics* IX ix offers some thoughts that may be relevant. A good life, we know from *EN* I vii, is one of activity. Activity is the realization of a potentiality, and is better than that potentiality which is only definable in terms of it and, as it were, exists for its sake. However, just because potentiality is potentiality, it can also be realized in other ways than in the relevant activity (though then, strictly, it is not the potentiality that is realized, but the state of affairs that is the ground of the potentiality turns out to be a potentiality for something else as well). But these 'other ways' are definitionally derivative and posterior to the potency itself – merely coincidental and pointless. So a vice is a mere failure, not a true alternative to virtue, though it may in a particular case constitute a recognizable behaviour pattern. There cannot be a secondary 'quasi-mean' that defines the principle of vicious action. What there is, we will soon be told, is the vicious person's self-congratulatory avoidance of the vice at the opposite extreme of the continuum on which both vices and the corresponding virtue are located. The point is that this avoidance fails to determine a specific condition or action.[43]

2.222336 What Is Required

One is so constantly aware that Aristotle's ethics is not conceived in terms of moral law and duty that one notices imperative language when it occurs. Here, the 'mean' or 'middleness' is called 'what is required.' I do not think this wording has any strong implications; Aristotle used it in I ii, when he said that if we had a target to aim at we would be more likely to hit on *to deon* (1094b24). The human good is *to deon* for our whole enterprise, not because it is our duty, but because it is the norm implicit in our inquiry.

2.222337 Suffering and Acting

When making the point that virtue has to do with feeling as well as the action that is prompted by the feeling, Aristotle designates them by the paired terms *praxis* and *pathos*, doing and suffering. The terms are usually paired in a different way that is not in point here: it is the relation between (for instance) kissing and being kissed. If A kisses B (*praxis*), B is kissed by A (*pathos*). This contrast seems quite irrelevant here; I do not understand why Aristotle puts things this way. I mention the point because it may have an importance I do not yet see.[44]

Aristotle's general point is an obvious one. If the virtue in question is the one involved in temper control, then the required outcome is that I should regularly show myself no more and no less angry than I should; and the basis of this outcome would be that I should train myself to *feel* no more and no less angry than a situation requires, so that in the end I should be able to act just the way I feel, anger-wise, and my anger level will come out right.[45] I cannot see anything wrong with this, given Aristotle's whole method of analysis, but I'm not happy with it.

2.222338 Finding and Choosing

Good people both find and choose the mean. This duality seems to mirror that of 'doing and suffering': the latter pair had to do with affect and action, the non-intellectual side of things, whereas the new pair has to do with the mental side of things, the mental success of discovery and the mental act of choice. This must be a deliberate contrast on Aristotle's part, but it seems out of place. Aren't we talking about *moral* virtue? Yes, we are, but the determinants of rightness cannot be ignored and they are on the *logos* side. We meet this pair again in III ii. 'Choice' we have noted already; 'discovery' will figure as the outcome of the process of deliberation that leads to choice (1112b19).

2.222339 The Best and the Good

The right choice is the best choice. Among wrong decisions, some are worse than others (as all except Stoics agree); so I suppose Aristotle's language is unobjectionable. The point is obviously to counteract the unfortunate associations of 'middle' with 'intermediate' and 'moderate,' as remarked above. I complained because the difference between the one determinate position and the indeterminate stretches above and below that position is more radical than that language suggests. But, of course, other positions on the continuum could be defined, and the fact that one has picked out only one position may give one wrong ideas about the uniqueness of the position one happens to have picked, as we saw in § 2.222335. Aristotle will comment on this in II viii–ix, so there is something to be said for putting things the way he does.

2.22234 Exclusions (1107a8–27)

I have pointed out that Aristotle's position admits a form of relativism that he may or may not have espoused. Rightness and wrongness are a matter of suitability to a unique situation in which the agent's uniqueness is a factor, though the judgment of suitability is presented as objective. Does that mean that there is *no* definable sort of action or response that is *always* wrong? Even so 'consequentialist' a moralist as J.S. Mill, for whom the best action is that which promotes the greatest happiness of the greatest number of people, drew the line at a morality in which nothing was absolutely ruled out.[46] Aristotle's definition of virtue is likewise immediately followed by a specification of kinds of feeling and action that are never right. These are of two kinds.

The first kind of action that is ruled out is the kind that is wrong by definition. It is never right to commit adultery, because the word *adultery* means sexual intercourse of a kind that is defined as forbidden. It is an important fact about Aristotle's society, if not ours, that there is such a thing as adultery. The person who is contemplating sexual liaison and who realizes that it would be adulterous is prevented by that realization from debating the pros and cons of such an indulgence – the question 'how much?' is ruled out as irrelevant. (We shall see in VII iii that it is a symptom of one kind of moral weakness that such realizations are blocked.)

The other kind of action that is ruled out is one that is excluded by the decision process itself. To speak schematically, as Aristotle does, if I have decided what the virtue of generosity requires of me in a certain situation, all other responses are defined as either excessive or defective. We may give them names: they are either stingy or spendthrift. But we have now divided our notional continuum into two contiguous continua; and on these two continua there are no 'right amounts,' because all degrees of stinginess and spendthriftiness are predetermined to be wrong. We could say, if we wished, that spendthriftiness and stinginess are wrong 'by definition,' just as adultery is; but Aristotle treats the two cases as different, because adultery is made wrong by considerations of 'justice' – in effect, contractual considerations, aspects of the social compact – and the term 'adultery' is chosen to indicate that these conditions are violated; spendthriftiness and stinginess are wrong by excess and defect, and the terms are chosen to indicate that the relevant quantitative determination has already been made. There can't be a right amount of an excess or a defect.

That last formulation prompts another thought. If there can't be a right amount of what has already been decided to be an excess or a defect, there cannot be an excess or a defect of a right amount, either (1107a22–7). Well, of course there can't: that's what we were referring to when we said that a virtue was an 'extreme' (*akrotēs*). Is that worth saying, or is it just a rhetorical flourish to complete the symmetry?[47] Perhaps it should not need saying, but perhaps it does. It means that we should never say of someone that he or she is too generous, or not generous enough – and these are things we do say all the time, at least in English.[48] A person is either generous or not generous, and if not generous is either stingy or spendthrift. What we *ought* to say is that a person comes reasonably close to being generous, or is perfectly generous. But these are things we neither say nor think. Perhaps that is because we are not serious about the good life, have not thought through the implications. In II viii–ix, an attempt is made to deal with the issue, and that passage should surely come next. Instead of that, we turn to a list of what Aristotle takes to be the actual moral virtues.

2.2224 The List of Virtues – Preliminary (II vii; 1107a28–1108b10)

Why does Aristotle interrupt the sequence from his definition to the practical qualifications that, as we have just noted, are so urgently required, to insert a list of the actual moral virtues? Did some editor (Andronicus, or whoever) find the list on a sheet of papyrus and stick it in almost at random? Possibly; the list is otiose, it is little more than a prospectus for the examination of the particular virtues at III vi–IV, to which it does not quite correspond. The actual contents of the chapter I will deal with as part of an explanation of the structure of that fuller treatment. My only question now is why a list, explaining how the mean/extreme analysis works in each case, should appear in this place.

The sequence here follows just the same pattern as that which surrounds the other major definition, that of happiness in I vii–viii, where a formal definition is at once followed by reconciliation with 'received opinions,' with the same reason given – that a logical explanation needs to be backed up by an explanation of how it jibes with common experience (1098b10–12; 1107a28–32).[49] There is, indeed, a difference, but it is one I have already explained. The earlier discussion teased the basic notion of the human good out of a mass of received opinions and popular doctrines. But now, since we have stipulated an analysis of the soul, we are able to turn to observable facts (or alleged facts, *phainomena*) in the domain of psychology and sociology. It is this domain that the original discussion of *eudaimonia* determined to be the relevant one. It is still 'politics,' if you like, but the actual field of political action rather than the dialectical world of what politicians say. So instead of the contrast between theory and practice we now have that between the universal and the particular. A formal definition is followed by a 'demonstration' that the pattern in question is exemplified in actual recognizable virtues – not 'the recognized' virtues, by the way, as I will explain later. And the list itself is followed by a corollary and necessary explanations in II viii–ix, much as the definition and harmonization of I vii–viii were followed by the web of explanations about 'lifetime' in I ix–xi.

The list of virtues could not, then, have been conveniently post-poned to III vi, where we might otherwise have looked for it. But the full discussion of particular virtues could not follow directly on the discussion of moral virtue in general, because the treatment of choice simply has to come next; otherwise that concept of choice remains unexplained and the whole concept of virtue may be misunderstood; besides, the reference to the agent's will at II iv remains inadequately supported until the concept of voluntariness is explained in III i.[50] Apart from that, could the discussion in III i–v have been melded with that of the intellectual virtues in Book VI? It looks like it, but no. The discussion of III i–v is concerned with *logos* as directly struc-turing feeling and action, and is integral to the discussion of moral virtue – as we have just seen, the definition of moral virtue includes 'discovery and choice' as an integral part (§ 2.222339). The discussion of intellectual virtue, by contrast, sticks quite rigorously to *thinking* as a domain with its own values – it is an autonomous domain, since its origin is mostly 'pedagogy' (*didaskalia*, 1103a15) rather than habit.

The only real question is whether the list might not have come between the caveats of II viii–ix and the independent discussion that begins with III i. It might (though we would then have wondered why the order of treatment in I vii–xi was being abandoned), but the actual *point d'appui* of the list is the formal definition as such and not the practical caveats that follow. And it is important to the caveats themselves that it should have been established that the triad of one virtue and two opposed vices does correspond to our normal thinking about conduct, since what we will be talking about is how the presence of that pattern in the back of our mind may lead us astray.

2.2225 Implications and Warnings (II viii–ix; 1108b11–1109b26)

The corollaries to the definition of moral virtue look straightforward but a bit tangled. They have to do with the practical implications of the ambiguity in the three-part structure we have been looking at. As in the comparable passage at I ix–xi, there is a central theme, but nothing that looks like a systematic exposition.

The discussion centres on three considerations. First, a virtue and its flanking vices are three named or nameable conditions in which a person may be, and are in this way on a par. Second, a virtue is an extreme, a definite condition, but the vices of excess and deficiency are indeterminate, and in this way are *not* on a par with the virtue.

Third, a virtue as the 'right amount' has no connection with an 'intermediate point' between positions chosen as high and low points on a pre-established scale or continuum.

2.22251 Opposites (1108b11–26)

We tend to arrange our thoughts in terms of binary oppositions – the Greek philosophers more than most; they were always talking about 'opposites.'[51] But in a triad, like that of the virtue and its related vices, each term has two opposites. So people tend to get confused. Cowards think of the people most unlike themselves as foolhardy; so they apply that derogatory term to brave people, who are so unlike themselves. Aristotle does not add here that, in another way, the brave person is more the opposite of the coward than a rash or foolhardy one is, because the brave act on a *logos* and cowards do not, they just give way to fear when the going gets too tough. The coward does not realise that there could be such a thing as courage that acts on a *logos*. Most people do not realize things like that; that is part of what we mean when we say they are not *spoudaioi*, do not take life seriously because it has not occurred to them that any such attitude to life is possible.[52]

2.22252 Which Vice Is Worse? (1108b26–1109a19)

Given that we think of a virtue and its vices as three conditions that are, in a way, on a par, the fact that a virtue may not fall anywhere near the middle of a range of possible responses means that a virtue may be more like one of the vices than the other (it may be the excess, or it may be the deficiency). Aristotle does not say, but I will, that this is likely to happen with those basic kinds of feeling that preserve our animal nature, and remain as standing temptations while we are educating our temperaments. Sexual desire, fear, greed, attract most of us more than their opposite vices, and those opposite vices (such as being undersexed or too fearless or given to undereating) are not the kind of offence that gets denounced from pulpits. They aren't so tempting; but also, they aren't so damaging.[53] Insisting on the symmetry of the two vices can be a mistake.

Recognition of the asymmetry of vices leads to the surprising claim that the person who wants to be good should avoid pleasure (1109a30–b13). We see what is meant; but in the long run, surely, people should relocate their pleasures, not fight them. The ambiguity, or the conceptual confusion, remains to haunt the discussions of Books VII and X: pleasure is a most intractable topic.

2.22253 The Difficulty of Virtue (II ix; 1109a20–b26)

The fact that virtue represents an extreme, and that (as the remarks on adultery showed, 1107a16) the best use of *logos* calls for thinking of *all* the relevant factors ('whom, and when, and how ...'), suggests that virtue and right action are absurdly difficult. Seriousness involves hard work, says Aristotle (1109a24), slyly punning on that word *ergon* ('function,' 'work'). This is an intellectual difficulty; but it leads to a practical difficulty, because, if it is intellectually hard to determine what is right, we do not know what temptations we should resist. The basis of our decision is not perspicuous. It is at this point that Aristotle adduces the facts about some vices being worse than others, and some temptations being stronger than others. Surely we know our own weaknesses! So those are what we should avoid – our 'besetting sins,' they would be called in a different thought-world.[54]

The assumption here is, of course, that we are not yet sure that our feelings are properly adjusted – we may use logos *the best way we know how, but how will we tell when we have it right? Aristotle can only pin his faith to its being a self-correcting process in a world where we can look about us. No one will find him convincing today, because he lacks what Freud and the Prophetic tradition have given us: a psychology of self-deception, of a structure of choice that is not transparent. This loss of faith in any process of reliable self-criticism is one of the things that have led us to mistrust the whole idea of virtue as a real condition of the agent as such. We are reduced to choosing between the idea that life is a perpetual struggle against ourselves, and the idea that virtue is mere compliance with the demands made by social and occupational structures.*

Meanwhile, what are we to do about the difficulty of knowing what to do in complex situations? Some of Aristotle's language here is borrowed from the medical tradition.[55] Doctors have the same problem: the human organism is too complex for complete success to be possible. Doctors do the best they can, and if they don't make too many glaring mistakes that's all we expect.

But how much is enough? Just as our assessment of the right action is up to our sense of the situation, so too is our sense of what is tolerable by way of deviation on any given occasion. 'The decision [*krisis*] rests with perception' (1109b23).[56]

2.223 *The Work of Practical Reasoning (III i–v; 1109b30–1115a3)*

A virtue is a set disposition to feel and to act in the right way in some given respect. Not just to react, but to act, actually to do things, to do them on purpose, deliberately. What this involves is what we have now to see.

I said above that the apparently casual introduction of the word *choose* in the definition of virtue made it urgently necessary to explain what choice is. But actually the discussion to which we now turn is in three parts. The definition of choice is imbedded in a cluster of interrelated definitions, which is preceded by a discussion of the wider concept of the 'voluntary' (*hekousion*) and followed by an extensive mulling-over of the topic of responsibility.

The threefold discussion could have been explained as an account of the nature of choice, together with its necessary presuppositions and its immediate consequences for the general topic of virtue and for the viability of a practical inquiry into how to lead the best possible human life. But in fact the discussion clears up a number of pieces of unfinished business and unresolved puzzles. Already in II i, as we noted at the time, the sweeping proclamation that early upbringing makes 'all the difference' seemed to preclude genuine self-determination and freedom in self making. How is that to be reconciled with the emphasis on choice, on doing things for the right reason, on virtue being open to all? Again, the definition of virtue introduced essential dualities: condition and action, feeling and cognition. How are these integrated in a single lifetime of self-direction? Clearly there will have to be a dialectical exposition of a complex interaction – the matter could not be reduced to a simple statement. Everything here comes out of the discussion in I xiii of what is amenable to *logos* and what is not, the determining and determined aspects of what in some sense 'has' *logos* comprising that part of our lives that is *eph' hēmin*, 'up to us' or 'in our control.'[57]

In general, Aristotle uses a threefold strategy. In the discussion of 'the voluntary' he introduces a *strong* notion of 'what is up to us,' cutting off arguments that disavow parts of the self. In the discussion of choice, he demonstrates that the procedures of deliberation necessarily emancipate those who use them from bondage to any single system of motivation (such as, if one did disavow parts of oneself, one might wish to disclaim – 'that was not the real me speaking, that was my castration complex'). In the discussion of responsibility, he argues that, since in a strong sense our actions are thus 'up to us,' and since our virtues and vices are formed by those actions, our virtues and vices themselves must also be 'up to us' – but, of course, in a weaker sense, because the long process of habituation is not something we can effectively *decide* to carry out at any given time. To put the matter in terms that are more Sartrian than Aristotelian, the decision has to be iterated: just because our decision is free now, it cannot bind our future decisions, which will be free in exactly the same way when we do come to make them; conversely, because our present decisions contribute to the generation of future habits, our present condition is likely to be one of habituation generated by past decisions.

2.2231 Voluntary Action (III i; 1109b30–1111b3)

The word we customarily translate as 'voluntary' (*hekousion*; the person who acts voluntarily is *hekōn*) is not used in a way that is at all close to the way the English word is used.[58] But that hardly matters. Aristotle is not giving an analysis of the 'ordinary language' use of the English word *voluntary*. But he is not analysing the ordinary use of the Greek word either.[59] And I do not see why he should. He is engaging in conceptual clarification (what might be conceptual reform if anyone would listen), to clarify an issue that must arise for individuals who are serious about self-improvement and hence need to think clearly about what is 'up to them.'

Aristotle does not introduce the present discussion as part of the wider setting in which it occurs, but attaches it directly to the immediately preceding discussion of vice. In II ix, much was made to turn on the point at which vicious action ceases to be trivial and becomes blamable (*psektos*, 1109b21). Aristotle picks that word up immediately, and points out that involuntary actions are never blamed; this suggests that a discussion of virtue must consider what makes an action involuntary. And this is also something that lawmakers will need to know about when discussing punishment. The context of the discussion is, in fact, emphatically forensic.

Aristotle is setting himself against a forensic practice that he finds confusing, though its basis is correct. The basis is that we don't blame people for what they can't help. Pleaders in Athenian courts used the contrast between the voluntary and the involuntary to make this distinction: the voluntary is what a person is rightly called to account for, the involuntary is what calls rather for sympathy and gets the suspect off the hook.[60] The practice that Aristotle is objecting to is one that counts as involuntary any action for which one may be excused, or even a reluctant action that in the circumstances may have been justified. What Aristotle wants to do is to substitute for this mess a simple distinction based on his own elementary theory of action, differentiating what falls within our responsible agency from what does not.

It would be a mistake to say, because of the forensic context, that the question Aristotle is dealing with here is entirely or even principally one of legal accountability.[61] We do bestow praise and blame on children and animals; we do not, as a rule, take them to court.[62] He seems actually to be doing several thing at once. He is clarifying the concept of action itself, as we shall see; he is relating the concept of the voluntary to the concepts of choice and virtue; he is exploring the limits of responsibility. Above all, of course, he is charting part of the terrain covered by 'that which has *logos*,' the ways in which our lives are governed by rational discourse in all their surprising variety.

Meanwhile, I was saying that Aristotle reconstructs the concept of the voluntary in accordance with his basic theory of action. According to *Physics* II i, the 'natural' activity of an agent is that of which the origin and cessation can be located within the agent itself. This refers not to the ultimate source of the energy expended, which according to Aristotle is the movement of the earth in relation to the radiation of the sun, but to the cause that explains the single action or activity as such. In any natural entity, such as an organism (a human being, for instance), some of the changes and movements can be traced to specific origins in the organism itself; others can be traced to causes outside the organism, involving the organism only as a material entity with such general properties as mass and a certain chemical composition (rendering it, for instance, inflammable). I do not know whether or not this can be made precise, but it is Aristotle's starting-point. It amounts to a distinction, applicable to any entity of which it is sometimes true that it *does* something, between what that entity actually does and what happens to it. This is the ultimate basis of the distinction between the voluntary and the involuntary.

While the ultimate basis of the account of voluntary action is the *Physics* account of nature and natural movement, its immediate basis is a special case of such movement: animal action is described in the passage of *On the Soul* (III 9–10) which I have been treating as the theoretical background of the *Ethics* as a whole. The source of movement and rest in an animal is twofold: reason and desire, or perception and will. The animal must identify the situation in which it acts, and must be motivated to do something about the situation as thus identified. It follows that action may fail in two respects: the situation may be misidentified (or unidentified), or motivation may be lacking. It is precisely a movement that fails in one of these two respects that Aristotle calls an 'involuntary' (akōn) action. Any well-formed action, that fails in neither respect, is 'voluntary.' So it will be seen that Aristotle draws the net of 'voluntary' action as widely as he can.

Today's philosophers might prefer to say that a movement to which the agent contributes no motivating impulse – for instance, if someone seizes my wrist and hits a policeman with my hand – is not an involuntary action of mine, but no action of mine at all; the assailant is active, but I as the weapon remain inert. And they might insist that an action is such only under a description: to use another of Aristotle's examples, if I give away information that I did not know was a secret, this would not be an 'involuntary' emission of sound like an eructation, but as an imparting of information it is something I did and meant to do, whereas as a breach of confidence it is something I did without meaning to.

We may not want to adopt Aristotle's analysis, but we can appreciate its point. He wants to block the move whereby certain aspects of one's motivation are treated as somehow 'external' to one.[63] What has its origin *in* us must be *up to* us, he says (1110a17–18 – without quite explaining how it follows). One may approve of some of one's actions and characteristics more than of others, but a person as agent comprises all the feelings and thought processes that contribute to action. Aristotle is particularly averse to the practice, common then as now, of identifying oneself with one's virtues and abjuring one's vices. As he pointed out in II i, virtues and vices have the same psychological mechanism. It's a package deal: if I claim credit for my good deeds, I must accept discredit for my failings (cf. § 2.22336 below).

Aristotle's intention is not so much to make censure more stringent than it now is as to clarify the terms on which censure is avoided. Thus, certain actions that would apparently be called 'involuntary' in Athenian courts should rather be thought of as 'mixed.' If a ship's captain jettisons a cargo to save the ship, it may be misleading to say that the action was performed *willingly*, but in the circumstances the captain decided that it was the right thing to do. It was in the circumstances a voluntary action. The question is whether the decision was right – 'what should be endured in return for what gain' (*ti anti tinos*, 1110a30). In the course of a very muddy discussion, the hard-pressed ship's captain is apparently put in the same class as the people of whom we would be most likely to say that they acted under compulsion and coercion, and not freely at all – people who do things under torture or under the threat of torture, or under threats to their nearest and dearest. Even of these cases, Aristotle insists that the person acts 'voluntarily' in his sense. The point is essentially Socratic: assent is actually given. The person finally says yes, finally agrees to betray (or whatever). What we have to consider is whether it would have been reasonable to hold out longer. It may even be ridiculous, Aristotle seems to say, to endure great torment for some trivial gain. At the other extreme, there are cases where sub-mission is (not praiseworthy indeed but) forgivable – where human nature is 'overstrained,' and no one could hold out. Even so, Aristotle says, there may be deeds so terrible that no torment could justify assent – one would simply have to hold out as best one could.[64] Of course, it is not easy to decide the point at which submission is all right, and still less easy to let one's conduct be guided by such a decision. But that is the right way to look at the matter.

Despite Aristotle's refusal to say that assent is literally compelled in such cases, and his insistence that an assent that is given can always be withheld, his treatment of these matters is not rigoristic. In fact, his acceptance that there is almost always a point at which the right thing to do is to give in is possible only because he supposes the power of *logos* to be somehow still operative. But it is obvious that he is leaving something out. He is assuming that the effect of torture and threat is always to extort assent, the power of assent itself being left intact. But what if this is not the case? What if the power of assent and dissent is somehow destroyed or twisted, by drugs or 'brainwashing' or what-ever manipulative techniques ancient ingenuity or modern science may devise? Aristotle does not consider the problem in this context, but in fact an appropriate answer is implicit in Book VII. In such cases we no longer have a case of normal human agency to which moral considerations apply. The situation is pathological; a person whose powers of decision are destroyed is exempt from praise and blame. Where Aristotle differs from us is that we nowadays are less certain of the limits of the pathological, hence less sure of the scope of free-dom and rational persuasion. But one could argue that the principles applicable remain what Aristotle thought they were. Whoever *can* say yes *could have* said no.

The idea of assent is crucially important here. To say yes to a proposition, two things are necessary. There must be a proposition before one; and one must make a commitment. That is why there are two ways in which an action can be involuntary – the analysis in *On the Soul* III is important, but in practice it takes the forms of these two conditions.

The concept of voluntary action as thus conceived circumvents vulgar modern notions of (Skinnerian or Watsonian) 'conditioning.' Saying yes and no cannot be included in a reflex arc. Conditioning must go on at some level more elementary than that which concerns Aristotle. And, indeed, if on Aristotle's account actions are voluntary, and states of character are indirectly voluntary, they must be based on something more simple, lacking the double structure that assent requires. Our impulses themselves cannot be voluntary. There must be something to assent *to*, to decide *between*. And these are what Aristotle relegates to the level of 'passions,' things that just come over us.

If a realistic account of agency and personality prohibits one from disowning segments of one's personal life and endowment as somehow not really one's own, it is even more unrealistic to ascribe causal efficacy to the overpoweringly pleasant or glorious nature of certain of one's objectives (1110b8) – in a word, to 'temptation.' As Aristotle remarks, since all motivation operates as a form of pleasure (II iii), that would again make nonsense of the whole idea of action and agency.[65] The causal efficacy of temptation must be attributed to the agent's susceptibility. External force means external force, really compelling and really external.

Aristotle is, in a sense, taking a tough line. But, in principle, it is above all a clear and definite line. Whatever is part of the agent's psychology is part of the agent, what is 'outside' is what neither is nor depends on that psychology. The agent's assent is assent, whatever the circumstances in which it is given. The effect is that one cannot blame other people for what one does oneself. Nor can one blame the 'society' to which one belongs, as though a mysterious collective personality were the real agent of one's actions (cf. § 2.222142). Aristotle is innocent of this curious modern conceit, but how he might have handled it may be conjectured from Plato's *Crito* (50A–53A). The position Socrates presents in that dialogue is roughly as follows: my city, with its conventions, its language, its laws and folkways, furnishes the way of life which makes me what I am, I am really a dependent part of it. But its laws and folkways and language impinge on me as from without: I can resist them and try to change them as from within. In other and very non-Aristotelian words, as a self-conscious, reflective, and observant being I can be aware of the source of my ideas and customs. But while I share them they are mine.

Aristotle sums up his thoughts on involuntariness through force by allowing an ambiguity to remain. Actions done in emergencies or under constraint are in a sense 'involuntary,' or against one's will, because they are things of a sort one would rather not ever have to do. In the circumstances one did assent, and actions are particulars, so the particular action here and now is voluntary or 'willing'; but the reluctance is real, and must not be forgotten. That is why such actions are said to be 'mixed' (1110a11).

What about actions that are done against or without one's will because of a failure in cognition? It is not general ignorance that makes an action involuntary: ignorance includes ignorance of right and wrong, and such ignorance is no excuse – it is the very defini-tion of bad character. The relevant ignorance is failure to perceive or understand some aspect of the circumstances of the action. Aristotle offers what purports to be a list of such aspects. There is the nature of the agent (oneself), the nature of the action, the nature of the person or object one is acting on. In addition, there is the nature of the consequences, the nature of the equipment involved if any, and the way the action is done ('roughly or gently' – one might miscalcu-late that). He writes as if this were a complete enumeration, but I don't know why. The point seems to be the same as that in the remarks on adultery at 1107a16 and of the mean at 1109a28 – that there are lots of ways of going wrong; but the list implied here does not replicate either of those earlier enumerations. One feature of the list has some interest. Aristotle says that one could not be ignorant of the agent – 'How could one be? it is oneself' (1111a8). One feels like protesting that one may very well forget or not know who one relevantly is, as Pentheus seems to be told in Euripides' *Bacchae* by the god Dionysus that he does not know who he is (line 506). But I take it that this is part of Aristotle's tough line: I am all that I am, and the only relevant distinction is that between me and a different person, one who is somebody other than myself.

Two points remain. First, when identifying the cause of the failure of an action, we go the root cause. If I act in ignorance induced by intoxication or by a blind rage, the ignorance does not render my action 'involuntary' – for one thing, its effect is to make me forget myself altogether, not to mislead me about some one relevant feature of the situation. The cause of my action is my rage or my drunkenness. Such cases need special handling, which they partly get in Book VII. And, second, the Greek terms *hekōn* and *akōn* are contraries, like 'willing' and 'against one's will,' not contradictories. One does not act against one's will unless one is reluctant at the time and penitent afterwards. So, says Aristotle, if one does something through ignorance, though one cannot be said to do it willingly because one did not even know one was doing it, one cannot be said to have acted *against* one's will, *akōn*, unless one is sorry afterwards.[66] One will have to think up some more neutral form of words – '*without* one's will,' or something.

2.22311 Comment: The Tragic Dimension

In discussing actions under duress, I spoke of the point at which it would be 'all right' to give in. But the phrase sticks in the throat, and attempts to find a better form of words fail – Aristotle does not try. These are cases where the agent has to do wrong; we would not feel right about ourselves if we felt right about what we had had to do. It is these 'borderline situations,' the existentialists used to argue, that call all moral systems into question. Aristotle, it is clear, does not think that they do; but they give life a tragic dimension – precisely, as Martha Nussbaum urges, what the Athenian tragedians explored.[67] After the bland discussion of virtue, in which doing right with a good conscience was made to seem difficult but not impossible, we are now confronted with the real world in which even the right answer may not be 'all right.' Just so, after the definition in I vii that made it seem that happiness was in principle within everyone's reach, we were confronted with the 'fortunes of Priam,' the real world of catastrophes and disappointments. And so, too, as soon as we have completed our discussion of human goodness, we will have to be reminded in Book VII of sickness and bestiality and sheer weakness of will. Like Socrates in the Gorgias (473C), Aristotle thinks one's judgment should not be swayed by horrors. But the horrors are there.

2.2232 Choosing (III ii–iv; 1111b4–1113b2)

Like children, animals generally are capable of voluntary action, because the terms in which that is defined are those used in the analysis of all animal action. But non-human animals are not capable of choice, because choice involves conceptual articulation. And virtue is a disposition to choose.[68] The point is crucial. But Aristotle's presentation of it is misleading. To understand what he is saying, we have to read into the present discussion the general discussion of means and ends, and of the special status of 'happiness,' with which the *Ethics* began. Our justification for doing so is that III v demands that wider context.

Aristotle offers us a model with three parts. What it represents is the simplest possible case of deliberate action. Suppose there is something – it could be anything – that we wish to bring about. We call this our 'end,' and for the purposes of our discussion it is our 'good,' the object of our 'wish.' If this something is within the sphere of our possible practice, we start to consider what would have to be done to bring it about; then, what would have to be done to bring *that* about; and so on, through a chain of possible actions, each leading to another, until we come back to something we can do here and now. That process is called 'deliberation.' And the end of the process is a decision, the decision to take here and now the first of the steps that will bring us to our goal; and this is what we call 'choice' (*prohairesis*).[69]

The peculiarity of the model is that, though Aristotle insists on the etymology of *prohairesis* as signifying 'taking one thing rather than another,' the model involves no real choice at all: an agent can only take or fail to take the one immediately practical step through which the proposed end can be achieved, and the model offers no possible reason for not taking that step. The model is as schematic and abstract as the account of the 'practical syllogism' that lays out the schema of an unproblematic action in *The Movement of Animals* (see § 3.112 below) – in fact, the only difference lies in the insertion of an indefinite number of intermediate steps: just as the animal (human or other) that recognizes what it sees as a case of what it wants 'immediately acts,' so here as soon as deliberators realize that there is something they can do to start the process of achieving their end, they immediately decide to do that thing. The function of *logos* here is confined to working out the practicalities, so that reason in this aspect is as much the 'slave of the passions' as David Hume thought it was. Aristotle's discussion includes many things, but it does not include any instructions for modifying the model. Why not?

Part of the explanation must be that Aristotle assumes we are by this time familiar with his general view of the human good, and can rely on us to make the necessary adjustments, which are indeed automatic as soon as we realize that we are being given a set of logical relationships rather than a phenomenology of the decision process. But I think Aristotle stays with this stark model because it already contains what he thinks of as the essential point, and returns to time and again, though his readers generally pay rather little attention. The point is that what one chooses to do is always something of which the value is indirect, derived from the reasoning process. What we act on is never the end itself, always 'what leads to the end.' We do not, in fact, act under the spell of the attractive object. Our desire is mediated. 'Appetite is contrary to choice' (1111b15). And, because choice is the last stage in a process of reasoning, it is the reasoning part of us that chooses.

2.22321 Means to Ends (III ii–iii; 1111b4–1113a14)

Some commentators object to Aristotle's statement that one cannot deliberate about ends. Of course one can: one can call one's aims and objectives into question, and often does. But the objection in this form is misguided. The statement that one cannot deliberate about ends is not a piece of psychology; it is the explanation of what the term 'end' means. To call an end into question is to challenge its status. To do so effectively is to treat it as a means to other possible ends and to ask what those other ends are. This is precisely the point Aristotle made in I vii about *eudaimonia*, the human good: only *eudaimonia* is always and only an end, because of any other end it can always be asked whether it is what one *really* wants, whether it contributes to the life that would really be the best for oneself to live as a human being. But *eudaimonia* cannot be called into question, for the word is used simply to stand for whatever turns out to be the complete and unchallenged end of all relevant actions. And the serious person always acts in the light of this overriding end – that is just what it is to be *spoudaios*, to take one's life as a being capable of articulate discourse seriously. As one reads through these chapters, one realizes that, although Aristotle has formulated a simple model with an arbitrary end-in-view, his whole discussion is framed in terms of the human good as the sole end of practical (that is, non-technical) deliberation.[70]

An objection to Aristotle's linear model of deliberation, according to which what the deliberator does is work out a causal chain from final effect (the end) to precipitating cause (the immediate action), is that it does not take into account the threefold value of actions that was at the foundation of the idea of a good life. According to the crucial introductory statement in I i, an action may have value in itself (it is just what we want to do), or as part of a wider complex of organized activity, or as a means to future goods. The model takes into account only the last of these, as though the choices of a virtuous person were always made with the future only in mind – jam tomorrow, never jam today. But that is absurd: good people do what they do because it is seen to be fine – *tou kalou heneka*. However, an action that is part of a wider program contributes to that program as its overarching objective, and though it may be rather unidiomatic in English to speak of the former as a 'means' to the latter as 'end,' the Greek idiom (*ta pros to telos*) does not jar. I suppose what makes the action fine (*kalon*) is, in the last resort, that it is seen as having to the full that threefold value, so that even the immediately experienced value that is realized in the action is part of the end to which the doing of the deed is the means.

With this in mind, let us consider the simple model of deliberation. That suggested that we begin with a determinate wished-for end and then work back through the steps by which that end might be achieved, as though the actions that constituted those steps were themselves value-neutral. But of course they cannot be;[71] as actions, they have their own value and disvalue, form parts of other complexes, lead to other consequences in addition to the wished-for end – and it is obvious that those consequences might even for us be more important, for good or ill, than the end originally proposed.

It is not, then, as though real-life deliberation began with a simple objective and devised appropriate means. Rather, one begins with an objective, and then works out what one would have to do to achieve that, at each stage sorting out the pluses and the minuses (ends) of the possible moves (the means). As in the case of the ship's captain wondering whether to jettison the cargo, and the person under threat wondering when it would be appropriate to give in, the question is always *ti anti tinos*, 'what is worth what,' a sort of cost-benefit analysis of whatever one sees to be involved. So, once more, whoever says yes can say no: there are always alternatives that can be considered. The fact that we always choose means, not ends, not only insulates us from the raw glamour of tempting and repelling objects, but provides us with the materials for alternative motivations.

The foregoing is true for everyone, serious or not – it is the automatic result of the permeation of human life by conceptualization and articulate discourse.[72] For the serious person, in addition, there is the continual presence as an overriding end of the determination to lead the best human life overall. For such a person, all available values will always be potentially factors in any action, whether they turn up in particular bouts of deliberation or not. As the first sentence of the *Ethics* may be taken to imply, the inclusiveness of *eudaimonia* is part of the concept of 'the' good. But that extra factor is not essential at this point. The dialectic of deliberation as such is all we need, and its effect is summed up in Aristotle's analogy of the Homeric constitutions in which 'the kings announced their choices to the people' (1113a8–9).[73] I take it that what Aristotle has in mind here is what happens in the *Iliad*. Each person present is entitled to offer an opinion. Then the king announces his decision without necessarily giving reasons. It is assumed that all voices have been heard and weighed, but it is the prerogative of the king to do the weighing and to speak authoritatively. A serious monarch will listen closely and judge carefully; but even a biased or frivolous one follows the same procedure and wields the same authority.

Within the individual, of course, the 'decision-making part' (*to hēgoumenon*, 1113a6) is not a separate individual who may have no personal stake in the outcome, as might be true of the king. Choosers commit themselves, and in deliberation the affect and the desire are transferred to the course of action decided on. That is why Aristotle goes to such lengths to differentiate choice from 'opinion' and other unlikely definientia (1111b10–1112a17), and ends up with the definition as a 'deliberate desire of things in our power' (*bouleutikē orexis tōn eph' hēmin*, 1113a11).

An obvious objection to the identification of choice with the outcome of deliberation and the definition of a virtue as a habit of choice is that the concepts of habituation and of deliberation do not sit well together. A habitual action must be a routinized action, and one does not see how the process of comprehensive deliberation could be reduced to a routine, and how if all a good person's deliberations refer to *eudaimonia* as a whole there can be separate virtues, separate dispositions to act. The most one can say is that, once more, habituation is a psychological phenomenon but deliberation is an epistemic structure. One does not have to go through laborious calculations of what is to be foregrounded and what is merely secondary. Just as an experienced driver takes account of the state of the weather and the urgency of the errand and the condition of the brakes while keeping a sharp eye on the traffic and watching for side streets and errant pedestrians, all without having to think about it because the necessary directions of attention and adjustments of response have become automatic without being for that reason anything less than rationally based, so the good person's deliberations may appear as a single responsible decision, articulate but not consciously articulated.[74] And, as for the separate virtues, it may be true that, in a sense, virtue is a seamless whole, but it is none the less true that the dominant considerations guiding one's behaviour are different, depending on whether one is fighting a desperate battle, or endowing a hospital, or making conversation at a party.

One possibly puzzling point remains. In the initial differentiation of choice from various other mental phenomena, much time is spent explaining why a decision cannot be equated with any sort of opinion. Part of the reason for this care may be the prevalent Greek idiom of saying, especially in official contexts, *dokei* ('It seems' or 'It seems good'), as a way of saying 'we have decided' – it is the related word *doxa* that we regularly translate as 'opinion'; part of the reason is the difference between theoretical and practical reason, because the values of opinion are truth and untruth, which are appropriate to intellectual virtue as opposed to moral virtue; and no doubt there are other reasons to do with philosophical debates of the day. In any case, the point seems clear and not worth arguing. But one of the reasons Aristotle gives is that 'we choose what we best know to be good, but we opine what we do not quite know' (*proairoumetha men ha malista ismen agatha onta, doxazomen de ha ou panu ismen*, 1112a7–8); and it is not quite clear just what the point of that is. Of course, it is true that 'opinion' is contrasted with 'knowledge' and there is nothing that is contrasted with 'decision' in that way, and it is true that decision is commitment whereas opinion is not (for 'faith' and 'belief' the Greeks used a different word, *pistis*). But the choice of words seems to identify choice with intuition or certainty, not just with decisiveness (for the contrast, cf. 1146b24–31). I suppose the explanation is that choice as such is the outcome of deliberation, and a complete deliberation is *ex hypothesi* a consideration of all available alternatives. All error and arbitrariness have been excluded: a choice does indeed represent the agent's best available knowledge of what is best. But how good is the best available knowledge? Recent writing about 'lateral thinking' reminds us that the means available for our ends are not a predetermined set, because there may be possibilities no one has thought of; and then there is the problem of how far our ends themselves represent 'knowledge.' The serious person's end is the best possible life: but to know that one would like to live as well as possible in every possible way is not the kind of knowledge on which one could base the claim that what we choose is 'what we best know.'

I do not know just what Aristotle had in mind in that sentence. Perhaps it is not more than this: if I *say doxazō* I am saying 'in my opinion,' and that is a way of saying that I am not certain, that I do not have any firm knowledge or clear intuitions. But the underlying problem of how our wishes are to be evaluated is what occupies Aristotle in the next chapter.

2.22322 Ends (III iv; 1113a15–b2)

'All or most people wish for what is fine (*kalon*), but they actually choose what will be useful.' So says Aristotle in his discussion of friendship (VIII xiii; 1162b35–6). The model of deliberation and choice in III i–v, by establishing a chain between wishing and choosing, seeks to draw the sting out of such cynicism. But it retains a discrepancy between the concept of a wish, which may be for anything at all, and that of deliberation, which is controlled by the norms of practicality and efficiency. The former introduces an arbitrary element which is at odds with the description of the objects of choice as 'what we best know.' Granted that a wished-for end does not become the subject of deliberation unless there are possible ways of achieving it – we cannot even *begin* to deliberate about the past, or (as Aristotle says) the constitutions of distant parts of the world – the model itself seems to exempt ends from criticism.

The exemption, however, is only partial, even aside from the complex interweavings of ends and means that arise from the way deliberation actually works. Wish, certainly, is for the end; but to wish for something is to think of it as good, as a proper object of pursuit (*ephiesthai*, the word used in the first sentence of the *Ethics*). Ends thus immediately become subject to an implicit critique: is what first comes to mind as something I would like, my druthers, really a *proper* object of pursuit, or does it only seem so?

As soon as a wished-for end is brought into the sphere of deliberation, it is made a subject of critical thought even by uncritical people – to start setting about achieving it is at once to raise the question of exactly what it is we want and whether we really want it. Wish-fulfilment fantasies are not the same as plans. And for the serious person the critique is, of course, intensive and wide-ranging. If to wish for something is really to posit it *as good*, the concept of wish is as value-laden as that of deliberation itself. It might be questioned, however, whether the critique is not still internal: a matter of ascertaining what I really want in terms of my plans for my life as a whole. And we cannot, it seems, apply to objects of wish the criterion of the 'mean between extremes,' the 'exactly right for the person as thus situated,' which applies to actions and virtues, because that criterion is strictly relational, and wishes as such are strictly not relational. Not only can I wish for anything at all, I can wish for anything at any time (car owners with bumper-stickers that say 'I'd rather be sailing' do not remove the sticker when a blizzard begins). Such considerations move some commentators to say that what Aristotle really means by the word we translate as 'wish' (*boulēsis*) is something like 'a rational desire for what is good or beneficial.'[75] And the etymology of the word, so close to that for 'deliberation' (*bouleuomai, bouleusis*), encourages this view, making the conceptual discrepancy I spoke of implausible. None the less, a conceptual vagueness and awkwardness pervades the discussion.

How far can an internal critique of ends and wishes go? Aristotle poses the question in a conundrum: is the object of wish the good or the apparent good? In a sense, it is the apparent good, because what I actually wish for can only be what seems good to me, after however much or however little reflection. In another sense, it is the real good, because I have a second-order wish not to wish for the wrong things, however vaguely and superficially I may pose the issue.[76]

Aristotle's solution to his conundrum is that everyone does indeed wish for the apparent good, but in a successful wisher this coincides with the real good. In fact, a good person is one who wishes for the right things. But this solution conceals an ambiguity, with which Aristotle never confronts his reader, whether or not he is aware of it himself. At what level does this coincidence take place? The analogy with sensation and health suggests that the actual wishes of the good person (the word used here is *epieikēs*, not that tendentious word *spoudaios*) are the criterion of value; the contrast with the vulgar suggests that good people wish for the good *as good*, rather than wishing for the good as pleasant, or for the pleasant in the guise of the good. In his discussion of justice, Aristotle suggests the latter view: 'People pray for and go after things that are simply good, but not always good for everyone; but they should not, they should pray that things that are simply good should be good for them too, but choose what is good for *them*' (V i, 1129b4–6). Presumably the *epieikēs* is one who is steadily governed by the principle of wishing for 'what is really good,' like the worshipper who ends all specific petionary prayers with the rider 'Nevertheless, not as I will, but as Thou wilt, O Lord.'

Now the question of the real and the apparent good returns. Does Aristotle hold that someone who is really serious (being steadily governed by the principle of wanting and doing the right thing) is thereby judging by the principle by which the *phronimos* would judge, and is thereby *ipso facto* wishing for the real good, and is hence (with the familiar provisos) thoroughly virtuous? Or is it possible that a person fully serious about the best and most rational life should still wish for the wrong things because the principles of his or her critique are biased through and through, so that, even in applying the self-correcting reflections specified in II viii, the way in which the principles are applied is irremediably subverted? Aristotle will be saying that a person blind to certain facts about life must be 'thoroughly unperceptive' (1114a10). But perhaps we are all biased by our upbringing in ways that prevent us from becoming effectively aware of some sorts of fact; perhaps all views of life are perspectival, and all perspectives are sources of unavoidable error, such as we can detect in others and never in ourselves; and perhaps that is why early upbringing makes 'all the difference' (1103b25). Aristotle seems to hold the former view, that in the normal case a serious approach to life is self-correcting and the *phronimos* effects a genuine identity of real and apparent good. But nowadays the latter view is more widely held, not only because of the self-mistrust engendered by depth psychology but because of earlier religious views of a 'last judgment' in which for the first time we shall be revealed to ourselves as we really are by a truly unbiased because non-perspectival omniscience.

It is to this perplexing problem that Aristotle now turns. He offers no simple answer. He would be a fool if he did.

2.2233 Responsibility (III v; 1113b3–1115a3)

Are virtue and vice 'up to us' (*eph' hēmin*)? Are we responsible for the way we are? The Greek word Aristotle uses, *aitios*, is very close to the English: it implies both causality and accountability. For once, differences in idiom will not threaten to lead us astray.

Aristotle's answer, as I said at the end of the preceding section, is not simple. But it is straightforward. It is given at the start in its definitive form, and never gone back on. That would be unusual for Aristotle if this were an independent treatment of the topic, but it is not; it is in fact the conclusion fully prepared by the preceding discussion of willingness and choice. What prevents the discussion from

being simple is that other considerations are raised and not definitively disposed of. But that is partly because there is no need to do
so; the initial position remains unchallenged, and that is what matters. Since the other issues do not affect the main point, Aristotle sees
no need to discuss whether they are worth taking seriously in their
own right. The difficulty for modern readers is that we may not
agree with Aristotle about what matters, and may be more troubled
by what he leaves undecided than satisfied with what he decides.

As I suggested at the end of § 2.22322, our misgivings seem to
arise from our insistence on taking up impossible positions. We
argue that the truth could be revealed only to a perspectiveless
'God's eye view,' which no human could ever take and which
(because an agent must act as a specific person involved in a specific
situation) is in principle incompatible with practical thinking; or, that
a Laplacean calculator could 'predict' each of our actions, which as
predicted would be predetermined and hence not 'up to us,'[77] or, that
as local modifications of the energy field, we have no real identity
and could not be responsible for anything. Or, most unnervingly, that
since the Fall of Man in the garden of Eden, we have (just as
Aristotle says we have) 'free choice' (*liberum arbitrium*), we could
have said yes whenever we said no, but do not have 'free will' (*libera
voluntas*), because we are in principle cut off (as parts of the Adamic
'mass of damnation') from knowledge of the real good by which
alone we might have directed our lives rightly. Aristotle's confrontation of Plato at I vi disposes of this Augustinian possibility, so far as
he is concerned, because Plato's invocation of the unattainable viewpoint is entirely devoid of content. But Augustine had a detailed
scenario, revealed in inerrant scriptures; and, as the medieval church
found, Aristotle has no arguments against such claims.[78]

2.22331 The Main Thesis (1113b3–21)

It follows from Aristotle's analysis that actions are always chosen as
means to ends; being chosen they are *a fortiori* 'voluntary' and 'up to
us.' And virtues are habits of acting and feeling generated by such
choices; they, too, are therefore voluntary, though not chosen,
because their origin is in us. There is no alternative origin outside.
The word used is *para* ('alongside'), not *meta* ('beyond'); what is
being said is not that there is as it were nothing behind or beyond
our decisions, but that there is no traceable origin *alternative to* the
origin within ourselves, of which the origin is itself within ourselves.

The alternative, says Aristotle, is that humans are not begetters of actions as they are of children – which they obviously are. The point is, I suppose, that our maternity or paternity is not undercut by pointing out that we ourselves have an endless tree of ancestors.

This is Aristotle's essential thesis: our vices and virtues are the outcome of our choices, and whenever we choose to say yes we could choose to say no.

2.22332 Influence (1113b21–1114a3)

Techniques of reward and punishment are not causes of behaviour but ways of influencing choices.[79] We do not apply them to cases where bodily changes and movements are not 'voluntary' – it would be pointless to do so. The principle we go on is again whether the origin of the action is 'up to us' – whether we are 'master' (kurios) of it. Ignorance itself does not render an action 'involuntary' if the ignorance is due to drunkenness, for a person is kurios of whether to get drunk or not; nor if the ignorance (such as ignorance of the law) is due to carelessness, for a person is kurios of whether to take care.[80]

2.22333 Being Careful to Take Care (1114a3–10)

The universal practices to which Aristotle appeals to support his views on responsibility assume that carelessness is itself 'up to us' – we could have been more careful, if we had taken the trouble. But this seems to involve a sort of regress. Suppose a person is temperamentally incapable of taking care? At this point Aristotle makes a point of dubious validity: a person becomes 'temperamentally' careless, he says, by developing a habit of occasional carelessness, just as a person becomes dishonest by getting in the way of repeatedly cheating. The archē is undermined, just as we said at 1104a11–27. But the point is dubious just because in the case of the moral virtues what is to be trained is that feeling aspect of life that is not inherently reasoned but can be subjected to reason. Carelessness, by contrast, seems to be a defect in that which 'has logos' within itself. The mechanism of habituation, so to speak, has been sundered from its material substratum. Aristotle has accordingly to appeal to observation. People must be totally imperceptive not to have noticed that practice makes perfect, that dispositions become ingrained: if they didn't want to become careless, they shouldn't have behaved carelessly in the first place. Just as, if you don't want to get lung cancer, you shouldn't smoke cigarettes. Once the cancer develops it's too late, there's nothing you can do about it now; but that doesn't mean it isn't your fault. You were *kurios*; and you are still *aitios*.

Well, maybe, but Aristotle's favourite use of physiology as an analogue of psychology has surely let him down. The moral virtues can be illustrated from medicine because they themselves involve the body-related phenomena of the feelings; but carefulness is not one of the moral virtues. And we shall see that the moral virtues themselves are not homogeneous in their relation to the body.

Perhaps the thing to say here is what Aristotle will spell out in his discussion of 'weakness of will' in VII iii: such weakness has a physiological explanation in its most typical manifestations, but it has an epistemic structure as well, and that structure is also manifested in types of case where the physiological explanation does not apply. Habits of choice, similarly, are patterns of facilitation in thought and decision, with their own self-confirming motivational structure of pleasures and ideals. We learn in *On the Soul* (III 4) that thought, as such, has no physiological basis: anger would be a desire to avenge a wrong even if it were not also a 'boiling of blood around the heart' (or a squirting of adrenalin around the bloodstream). In this connection, we note that what establishes a firm character is said here to be the relevant *energeiai* (1114a7). And this word is the one that Aristotle uses when he wants to emphasize the non-physical, actively occurrent aspect of behaviour (though he uses it in other ways as well).

One feature of this passage has a bearing on the 'all the difference' that a good upbringing makes. Aristotle clearly assumes here that pernicious habits of choice are not the ingraining of behaviour patterns acquired through conditioning in infancy, but are acquired in years of discretion when one can be called 'thoroughly imperceptive' for not noticing how the world goes. This is in tune with the initial remarks that children act at random, and that politics are wasted on people too immature to have experience of the way things happen. I think we are confused by the closeness of Aristotle's view to a different view that our age finds more congenial. On this other model, a child's behaviour is directly modified by unexplained rewards and penalties; the child then acquires ever more sophisticated insights into the underlying principles on which its 'conditioning' is based, which it then internalizes, and then internalizes the higher-order principles underlying those principles, and finally the principle of moral autonomy itself. (In the analogy from guitar playing, what is first acquired is a discipline of manual movement, followed by a realization and internalization of the rationale at ever deeper levels of the movements that one has already been caused to make.) Aristotle's model appears to do without the initial stage, or to regard it as a form of persuasion and advice, a way of modifying behaviour through adventitious motivation. The child responds to rewards and penalties anyway, and will continue to do so; but what becomes habitual is not the actual behaviour but the tendency to respond to a certain kind of motivation, which is supplemented if not supplanted by a different sort of motivation as soon as the young person becomes able to pose the question of what is the best way to live, acquiring ever deeper insight into situations and ever wider perspectives on life. But one cannot say that Aristotle has posed the issues in a way that is helpful or illuminating when one has raised the questions that are troubling us here.

2.22334 The Impossibility of Reform (1114a11–31)

Just as you can't get a stone back once you have thrown it, but none the less it is your fault that the thrown stone breaks the window, so you can't always throw off a disease you have carelessly incurred or a state of character you wish you didn't have, even if you wish you could (1114a14). The proviso is interesting. The original model of vicious habituation suggested that habitual unfairness would produce a condition that was self-sustaining because it would be self-justifying: one would see things in a way that justified one's conduct. It is now suggested that that need not be so. I may wish I were not an unfair person, but my wish is isolated, no longer connects with my patterns of deliberation and choice. Aristotle does not say that a vicious disposition is always thus irremediable; only that it may be. And it is not clear how much weight he attaches to the possibility that such idle wishes for reform may occur. The whole psychology of reformation and conversion is a blank in his writing: as in the misleading simplistic model of deliberation and choice itself, he seems to envisage complications that he neither takes into account nor rejects as illusory. The fact is, as we remarked above and will see again, virtue is ideally a determinate condition, determined by a *logos*; but vice is just a failure of virtue, with no independent principle of its own.

On balance, it looks as if Aristotle envisages three different conditions in which self-improvement is effectively impossible for the vicious person. In the first, the person's world-view is all of a piece, so that there is no leverage for an alternative pattern of behaviour even to seem attractive. In the second, a person's way of living is so deeply entrenched that an alternative may momentarily seem attractive but gets lost in the established biases of deliberation. In the third, a person becomes addictive, a particular motivation becomes entrenched and pre-emptive. This third case, discussed by Plato in *Republic* IX, is said by Aristotle in Book VII not to be a form of vice at all, but to be located somewhere in a thicket of deviant psychic mechanisms associated with 'weakness of will' (*akrasia*).[81]

2.22335 The Weak Counter-Thesis (1114a31–b3)

People may be responsible for what they become, because they are/were responsible for what made them so. But how is one to meet the objection that those initial choices themselves were beyond our control – that 'everyone acts in the light of the "apparent good," but we are not *kurios* over our imaginations'? What seems to our imaginations to be desirable simply reflects the kind of person we happen to be.

This objection causes Aristotle no trouble – in fact, he does not give it separate consideration. On the model under consideration, the kind of person we are is not the kind of person we 'happen to be,' it is the kind of person we have made ourselves by our chosen activities. The objection is worth taking seriously only if we give it in a stronger form, by arguing against the model itself.

2.22336 The Strong Counter-Thesis (1114b3–25)

Is it really true that we make ourselves what we become? Is it not possible that both the controlling image of what the good life is, and the tendency to feel as we should, are things we have to be born with, so that 'because nature has given us an eye, we see aright' (cf. 1114b6–7)? We note that even here Aristotle does not entertain the possibility that such a power of intuitively correct judgment should be implanted by 'conditioning' – it would have to be a mysterious gift of miraculously correct insight, comparable to the 'divine gift' at 1099b11.

It is noteworthy that Aristotle does not contest this possibility, any more than he rebuts the suggestion of a divine endowment in the earlier passage. Perhaps the explanation for this reticence is that philosophers are wary of accusations of impiety, especially when (like Aristotle) they are politically vulnerable. But perhaps he is prepared to admit that there may be people with naturally sunny dispositions, or maybe even people with gifts of precocious moral understanding comparable to the undeniably real but uncannily mature musical insight of a child like Mozart. But the fact seems to be that he thinks his argument is unaffected. In any case, as he emphasizes, the argument is symmetrical: if it removes blame for our misdeeds, it removes credit for our good deeds in exactly the same way. Of course, this riposte is only polemically effective against someone whose sole concern is to get criminals off the hook; a more philosophical opponent might accept the symmetry and seek to debunk the whole business of praising and blaming, not to mention the enterprise of inquiring into how one should best live (or one might argue that the whole moral enterprise should be rethought in some radically different way). One reason Aristotle can ignore the possibility that good deeds and bad deeds are equally 'not up to us' is that the hypothesis of the *Ethics* is that its readers want to lead good lives, and they could not want that if it did not make sense as an objective – but a person might want to be good and still be glad of an excuse for failure. Aristotle's real argument, however, is that the objection leaves the initial thesis intact. Even if the 'end' is a mysterious product of an imagination over which we have no initial control, it is still true that choices involve saying yes or no, that whoever says yes can say no and vice versa, and that chosen activities become habitual and thus generate states of character, the rightness and wrongness of which are determined by a *logos*. The most we can concede is that if the imagined end is 'natural' we are only 'somehow *partly* responsible' (*sunaitioi pōs*, 1114b22) for our characters, instead of being totally responsible.[82]

To understand why Aristotle is cavalier about this strong counter-suggestion, it helps to think about what it means, especially but not solely in the light of Aristotle's sturdily realistic view of the world. He thinks there is a real world, and things in it – social and psychological reality as well as nature or physical reality – are as they really are; and he thinks that we as epistemically adapted denizens of this world can know its essential features. The good life for a human being is one that consists in using this epistemic equipment in relation to these realities of the human condition, in ways that we are elaborately discussing. The right thing to do on any occasion is determined by these realities. Now, what place is there in this for an 'imagination' that freely and arbitrarily postulates ends? The freedom in the 'way I see things' will surely not displace all the assessments and observations of subjective and objective reality by which I can govern myself. How could it? Even the imagined 'eye' implanted by nature will neither create nor conceal the objects it sees, if it is an eye, though it may afflict me with something corresponding to astigmatism or colour-blindness – or presbyopia. And people with defective eyesight learn to cope with the defects as best they can, because there are real things out there that they need to see.[83]

In the end, the threat of an arbitrarily imagined end (*phantasia tou telous*) makes no real difference. The project of the *spoudaios* is to optimize performance according to the maximal scope of *logos*. Limits on this project will in any case be imposed because *logos* is not ubiquitous and omnipotent. Temperamental and perspectival bias may well be among those limits. The dense structure that Aristotle is exploring is in no way affected.

The concept of an arbitrary *phantasia tou telous* seems also to be misleading in a way that Aristotle might have been expected to mention, and which his first readers might have picked up on. In many contexts, *phantasia* operates only when *logos* is absent, and languishes as information replaces guesswork and measurement replaces estimate. The *telos* of human life as Aristotle has represented it throughout the *Ethics* is not a conjectural ideal. It is an actual human life conceived as reflecting the actual situation of the agent, itself shot through with *logos*. This is in effect guaranteed by the status of *eudaimonia* as a *telos* which coincides with the means that realize it, each of which is subject to critique through deliberation. Or, if one prefers: the *phantasia tou telous* that 'could be anything' and reflects the agent's personality that 'could be anything' cannot be as arbitrary as it is made to sound, because the agent is a real person pursuing real projects in an actual world, and the aspects of wishes that get translated into objects of choice through deliberation are only those that can be integrated into these realities. Above all, in considering what is said in the present passage about the status of ends, we should bear in mind the way in which the idea of the 'human good' is built up in I i–vii, and the conclusion: only *eudaimonia* is always and only an end, and the concept of *eudaimonia* has proved itself susceptible to a critique – the very critique that Aristotle has conducted and will continue to pursue.

2.2234 Conclusion

What is the scope of *logos* as unravelled in these chapters? In voluntary action, there is the identification of the relevant features of the situation, and in difficult decisions the correct estimation of what is to be given up for what – of which, among bad options, is here and now the less bad. And, as part of this, the maintenance of *logos* itself, the preservation of preference rather than abject submission. In wishing, there is the attempt to make one's present conception of the good coincide with what is really good. In deliberation, one must be efficient in working out means to ends and revise one's idea of the end in the light of what one discovers about the means it would necessitate. In choosing, one must preserve the link of motivation whereby one wills to do what deliberation reveals as worth doing. And overall one must maintain a rational critique of the end that our imagination presents to us, the image that may suggest that the sun is only a foot across when it is actually larger than the inhabited globe (*On the Soul* III 3). To be serious about all these will be simply not to be negligent about matters whose practical relevance is obvious when you think about it.

2.23 The System of the Virtues (II vii, III vi–IV; 1107a28–1108b10, 1115a4–1128b35)

The right place to discuss the particular virtues was immediately after the definition of a moral virtue, where they are, in fact, listed. Aristotle postpones his account, for two reasons. It was necessary, for one thing, to interpose an elucidation of the concept of choice and its related concepts if the concept of a moral virtue as a disposition to *choose* was to be intelligible. For another thing, the moral virtues include justice, which is a very special case indeed; the topic of justice includes legal reasoning, which is an elaboration in the public sphere of the topic of moral responsibility in general, which therefore must be discussed first.

I will not comment on the detail of Aristotle's treatment of the virtues, which relies on customs and institutions of his own place and time of which we have inadequate knowledge and which do not concern our lives. I confine myself to his reasons for constructing his system and some of the peculiarities in his handling of it.

2.231 The Differentiation of Moral Virtues

As we have seen, moral virtue is an *epainetē hexis* – in principle, a differentiable disposition that deserves praise; in practice, one that actually is praised by a society that recognizes it. The trouble is that the very notion of deliberation in the light of an overall idea of a good life (the human good) rules out the idea of separate moral virtues: the only relevant disposition is the disposition to make the best choice one can be whatever situation confronts one (§ 2.31121). Aristotle effectively relegates this unity to the sphere of intellectual virtue, but the effect is that moral virtue must also be unified (§ 2.341). And yet there are recognizably different moral virtues.[84] What is the basis of this differentiation?

The obvious answer is that societies, and specifically Aristotle's own, do recognize separate virtues: discourse about virtues is a prime resource of the city as an educational system, which is what Plato (and, to a lesser extent, Aristotle) thinks a city is. People are urged to be brave, to be honest, to exercise a little self-control, as the case requires. But the discussion in I vii absolutely rules this prevalent discourse out as an authoritative source of a list of virtues. A virtue is to be defined in terms of the 'function' of humanity as a *logos*-dominated being, without any reference to social or even personal approval. What other basis could there be?

The basis of a *hexis* is repetition. What is repeated is an occasion for a specific kind of choice. How are occasions of choice effectively classified? It must be not an imposed classification, but one that springs from the conditions of human life themselves. Life must involve recurrent kinds of situation, as determined by recurring circumstances in relation to standing kinds of desire and aversion. Since there plainly *are* different virtues, there must actually be such recurrences.[85] The question is, what establishes our enumeration of relevant recurrences?

It seems clear enough that there must be a number of different moral virtues, because one does not see how one could live in a world in which it was impossible to form behavioural routines in relation to recognizable objects and predicaments. But it is not clear that there must be a determinate list of them. For one thing, different societies might generate different sorts of prominent predicaments, and foster different morphologies of passion. Nothing in Aristotle's philosophy requires that this should not be the case. For another thing, there could be all sorts of overlaps and marginal cases that affect the way habituation and choice operate: the simple model of recurrence and induration that Aristotle uses could be as misleading a simplification as his formal model of deliberation.

In social and linguistic practice, the Greeks, like ourselves, had at their disposal an indefinitely large number of words for 'praised dispositions,' not sharply demarcated from each other, not all equally important, not all unequivocally good. 'Brutus is an honourable man,' says Mark Antony, and leads the crowd to wonder exactly what this honour comes to and how desirable it is. Some of our best entrenched terminology recognizes complex and dubious classifications: calling someone 'a saint' or 'a shit' marks an intricate node in our moral economy. People often develop 'praised dispositions' that we have no word for: 'she has a tendency to ...' we say, or 'he can be relied on to ... ,' followed by specifications that may be of all sorts. One familiar form of words picks a person out as 'the kind of person who would ...' do such-and-such, thus instantly generating a categorization for possible future use.

Although we do really formulate such classifications, it is not clear what their status is. A *hexis* as such is formed by an individual out of the materials of personal experience, and is not likely to coincide with any socially endorsed classification. Maybe so, but Aristotle is doing normative philosophy here, not descriptive psychology; the habits a person forms are set up in a context of social praise and blame, and a serious person will form habits in the light of a conception of the human good.

But why only the human good? What I am serious about, what my virtue concretely will consist in, will be the requirements of my own life, and these will correspond to a specific social situation. In *Politics* I, where social and economic structures are described, we learn that the virtues of men, of women, of slaves, and of children, are different, because the determining contexts of their lives in a household are different. People who give unitary definitions of the virtues are deceiving themselves, says Aristotle there; it is better to follow Gorgias and enumerate the differing states of life and the virtues they require.[86] One may be reminded of Aristotle's observation in *On the Soul* II that it is better to define the 'soul' of an animal species by enumerating its abilities than to define 'soul' in such universalizing terms as Aristotle himself has just used.

If we consider the enumeration of the abilities of an animal species, we can see that they are more general than the related activities: even if every hawk has the same visual acuity, each hawk will see in its lifetime different things from what every other hawk sees, and hawks from specific ecologies will share a common typical range of sights on which the visual faculty common to their species will be exercised. Analogously, we may suppose that every city will provide scope for individual lives and will call for a range of such lives, and that an invariant feature of the human predicament (which is Aristotle's chosen topic) will take on a characteristically different form in each distinguishable type in that range. All humans have bodily appetites that sustain their individual and specific existence, and each serious person confronts the problem of gratifying and controlling those appetites in a social setting; but what this means is not only different for each individual but different for people differently placed in society. The relevant virtue, *sōphrosunē*, is different for men and women (as we have seen), and quite different again for children (as we see in Plato's *Charmides*). The 'human good' requires a seriousness in this area that will be articulated according to whatever necessarily recurrent features of social structures there may be. Aristotle's task in the *Ethics* must be to indicate what the constancies are, what regularly recurrent variations are imposed by constancies in the articulation of human societies, and (what Book II provided) what it is that underlies both constancies and variations.

The recurrence of types of situation in relation to constant motivations does not suffice to establish a phenomenology of the virtues, because of the permeation by *logos* that forms the background to our whole inquiry. *Logos*, we recall, involves the conceptualization of human life, whereby we share our agreements and disagreements about values. That means that what counts as recurrence in situation and motivation will be determined by the accepted applicability of a term (as my remarks about *sōphrosunē* may have suggested). Aristotle, however, does not systematically acknowledge this, because his chosen topic is the *human* good, which is prior to any specific conceptualization. The result is a certain muddiness in his treatment, which comes from his performing a double abstraction, whereby he thinks of moral virtues in abstraction from their intellectual correlates as well as from the social demands and recognitions that actually form their lived substance.[87]

The virtues are individuated and classified, then, by types of situation. These classifications are conceptually based: we have the concept of pride only because we have the concept of honour. And we govern our lives accordingly. But these concepts arise from, and articulate, the cultures in which they are current. Aristotle's picture is one most of which we can still recognize, but not all of it; we can conceive of comparable articulations that would be more familiar or more strange. But I conceive that Aristotle would say that some such articulation there must always be, and in every society the structure of virtue will be the same: taking seriously the structures-for-choice that the life of a functioning community makes available.

Aristotle encounters (without acknowledging it) a problem: his account of what a moral virtue is, in terms of a mean between extremes, cannot be on all fours with his phenomenology of the specific virtues, because the latter is conceptually articulated in a way in which the former is not. The 'demonstration' that the formal account applies to all the concretely acknowledged virtues is bound to be a loose fit. What are our choices here? First, the descriptions might be merely illustrative of the reality that the formal account defines; second, an account in terms of the 'mean' could be arbitrarily applied to behaviour already approved on other grounds; or, third, some inner connection must be postulated between what is observed and what the theory demands. In terms of Aristotle's own personal and cultural commitments, we may suspect that the second possibility is what prevails. In terms of the argument of the *Ethics* as a whole, the first possibility is acceptable. But no doubt Aristotle would want to maintain the third option: that his approvals (as opposed to his mere tastes and preferences) rest on perceptions and judgments of rightness, *recognitions* of means, corrigible by a serious attempt to avoid bias and arbitrariness.

2.232 The List

There seems to be nothing in Aristotle's project or in the way he introduces the notions of 'happiness' and of 'virtue' that precludes him from emphasizing the general way in which 'virtue-thinking' functions in cities, in some of the ways I have been discussing and no doubt others as well, rather than opting for a determinate list of specific virtues. But in fact, notoriously, he insists on there being a definite, systematically established enumeration; he does not even conceive of the enumeration as unfinished business to be tidied up at some future date. In the original enumeration at II vii he says we are to take the particulars 'from the diagram' (*ek tēs diagraphēs*, 1107a32–3), which sounds very specific indeed.[88] At the start of the full treatment, after saying that he will say what virtues there are and what they are related to and in what way (*tines ... kai peri poia kai pōs*) he goes out of his way to add 'and at the same time it will be clear *how many* there are' (1115a4–5) – though in fact he never makes any use in his argument of there being a determinate list, let alone of its precise contents.

How are we understand this demand for a precise list? Such a list corresponds to a clearly articulated society in which there are no fundamental surprises – and this is clearly the desideratum in Plato's and Aristotle's politics, however badly it reflected the political reality they knew.[89] But the concept of *logos* itself, of articulate speech and measurement as opposed to emotional outbursts and guesstimates, seems to require that everything be cut and dried somehow. And, above all, the whole project of the *Ethics* requires that our *telos* become a *skopos*, that we be provided with check-lists and principles of determinacy wherever possible. How can we tell that we are virtuous, unless we have a firm grasp on what virtue involves? As Aristotle has already pointed out (II viii–ix), what Kant would call the 'dialectic of the practical reason' finds endless scope for self-deception wherever the actual principles and content of right decisions cannot be nailed down.

On the other hand, part of the point of enumerating 'the' virtues may be simply to display the richness and complexity of the phenomena underlying our moral vocabulary. In the discussion of prodigality (*asōtia*), for instance, we are reminded of a prevalent type of person who both spends and takes excessively, whose relation to wealth is unprincipled and by no means *tou kalou heneka*, but is not based on a single morbid passion like miserliness or avarice (1121a30–b7).

All this only tells us that a list would be nice to have. It does not explain why Aristotle thinks he has one, or where he got it.

2.2321 The Source of the List

Even a definitive list of *the* virtues would be definitive only for a given society. Most of the most important situations people find themselves in are partly or wholly social situations, so that the recurrences that generate dispositions will be a function of social structures. This does not make Aristotle's account relative in any pernicious way (if relativism is pernicious).[90] Social structures objectively are what they are. Anyone who wishes to write a version of the *Ethics* adapted to the specific conditions of a different time and place is free to do so. Meanwhile, the society in and for which Aristotle writes had proved its viability by its continued existence. So, as before, he could draw on its accumulated experience.[91]

What inputs do we have for a list of virtues? As with the definition of happiness, there are the opinions of the many and the reflections of the wise. Again as before, there are, in effect, three rather than two sources: there is Plato, the author of what Aristotle accepts as wisdom, the state of the philosophic art; there are the uncriticized experiences of ordinary people; and there are the generalizations that reflect the views of the responsible and sophisticated. And, once more, Aristotle can now avail himself of the results of his own reflections. The uncriticized experiences of ordinary people, however, do not get a special hearing in this context: ordinary people are interested in happiness, but they are not interested in virtue, because they are not *spoudaioi*, they are not serious about life.

It is a popular criticism of Aristotle's list of virtues that it is a mere recitation of the prejudices of the Athenian upper classes. But it is not only that, if it is that at all. The very concept of virtue is, of course, an upper-class concept in the first place – that is just what I have been saying, and Aristotle will confirm it startlingly at 1179b7–16; but we must repeat that Aristotle does not invoke any social opinion to underpin his views. At several points, Aristotle remarks that the Greek language has no word for the disposition he is describing; at other points, he remarks that dispositions such as a susceptibility to shame (*aidōs*), a key concept in Greek popular morality, is not a virtue at all (a virtuous person has nothing to be ashamed of). More strikingly, the virtues of 'piety' (*eusebeia*) and 'holiness' (*hosiotēs*) are not on his list, though piety puts in an implicit appearance in the domain of conventional justice (1134b22–4). Actual Greek life was saturated in religion; Aristotle's failure to countenance it shows clearly enough that, whatever he is doing, he is not simply describing the folkways or the prevailing value system.[92]

Another old theory to which I have already alluded is that the Greeks or the Athenians communally recognized a 'canon' of virtues, the one used by Plato in his *Republic*.[93] Aristotle's list would then be an elaboration or correction of this. One cites, for instance, Sophocles' encomium on someone as a 'moderate, just, good and pious man.' But I would suppose that Sophocles was making a point: poets, other than those employed by greetings-card factories, do not *simply* repeat commonplaces. A similar foursome is presented in a fable by 'Protagoras' in Plato's dialogue of that name: piety is an endowment of presocial humanity, justice and moderation are the conditions of social order (courage gets left out, I suppose because everyone knows one needs courage in this world). My hunch would be that this constellation of virtues, in an inchoate form, with 'piety' and 'wisdom' uneasily interrelated, is a product of sophistic thought in the mid fifth-century rather than a traditional notion; in any case, it hardly matters, because the form in which it visibly influences Aristotle is the systematic transformations effected by Plato in his two major works.

Plato uses these four virtue words, whether or not they were already current as a foursome, to schematize his account of virtue in general. In the *Republic* the schematism is that of complex individual and social agents. Such an agent will have plans; it will maintain its own integrity; it will have impulses and motives; and it will have and manifest some sort of organization. It will have four virtues corresponding to these: wisdom for plans, courage for integrity, 'moderation' (*sōphrosunē*) for the impulses and motives and everything else being under control, and justice for the organization actually being the right sort and doing the right things.

The schema of the *Laws* is simpler and does not rely on complexities in the agent. 'Wisdom' becomes the word for knowing the right thing to do; 'moderation' is the word for actually wanting to do the right thing; 'courage' is the word for precisely what we still call moral courage, having the guts to stick by one's moral convictions; and 'justice' is simply the fact of actually doing the right thing.

Aristotle does not mention Plato (or any source or influence for his list, other than the supposed diagram), but in fact he plainly builds his list around the armature of *both* versions of the Platonic schema.

The *Laws* schema is basic. 'Wisdom' remains as 'intellectual virtue,' though it is unified in Plato and split into two by Aristotle. 'Moderation' becomes Aristotle's 'moral virtue' in its entirety. 'Justice' is otiose, in a sense; in Plato it is the resultant of the other three, in Aristotle it appears in V i as that sense of the ambiguous word *justice* in which it can be defined as 'the whole of virtue in relation to other people' (1129a25–b27), not a distinctive virtue at all. And the 'courage' of the *Laws* is not a virtue, any more than shame is, because any virtue implies the will to act in the required way. The 'courage' of the *Laws* becomes the temperamental dispositions of *enkrateia* and *karteria*, 'continence' and 'toughness,' the general abilities to abide by decisions and to endure threats and pain. (In the discussion of choice, at 1111b14–15, we have already learned that the continent person acts 'with choice, but not with appetite'; in the virtuous person, choice and appetite coincide, as Aristotle insisted at 1099a11–21.)

The *Republic* scheme of the four virtues associates them much more closely than the *Laws* scheme does with the specific behaviour patterns that they traditionally imply, and in this guise they form the backbone of Aristotle's actual list. Wisdom, of course, remains as intellectual virtue. Justice as disinterested fair dealing occupies much of Book V. Courage as the virtue of the warrior and moderation as the discipline of the bodily appetites head the list, with extensive discussions. (In the *Politics* these figure as the characteristic virtues of men and women respectively, under different descriptions; but in the context of *eudaimonia*, which is defined as the same for all humans, this approach is precluded.)[94] But then Aristotle adds some other moral virtues, to fill in the gaps. But why should there be gaps? And what are they gaps in?

Plato's schematic treatments expand his four virtues to cover the whole of virtue, treating them rather as powers that can be manifested in any context. Aristotle's approach is the opposite. A particular *hexis* must be defined by a specific sort of recurrent situation and a specific sort of motive. And it is the former that dominates, for Aristotle borrows from the *Republic* (477C–D) the thesis that psychological or epistemic powers are not to be differentiated introspectively but by their fields of operation and their actual effects (this approach to methodological behaviourism is not what most people think of as Platonic, but it is emphatic). In *On the Soul* II 4, Aristotle says that faculties are to be distinguished by their activities, and activities in turn by their objects; so, in the *Ethics*, virtues are determined by actions and actions by fields of operation. The key passage for this is the opening of Book IV, where the virtue of 'liberality' is introduced as the first of the non-Platonic virtues. Liberality is explicitly distinguished as distinct from courage, moderation, and justice; and courage and justice are distinguished as concerned with 'military matters' and 'judicial decisions,' respectively (1119b23–6).

Gaps appear, then, because the coverage of each virtue is shrunk. Courage in the literal sense is simply the special virtue required by and shown on the field of battle. Moderation in the literal sense has to do with the pleasures of 'touching and tasting,' eating and drinking and sex. And I think the gaps appear in what Plato made the sphere of 'moderation.'

As pointed out in the text we began with, *On the Soul* III 9–10, basic motivations for movement can be sorted out into two lots, impulses to seek and impulses to avoid (432b27–9). The basic objects of avoidance are threats, terrors, pains of all sorts. But the only *specific* type of *recurrent* situation in which we have to deal with these is warfare. So courage is a specifically military virtue. What we call moral courage, the practice of facing all threats and terrors cheerfully, has no specific sort of occasion, so it is included within courage as a sort of courage-by-metaphor. But positive inducements and occasions for action among humans are not only much more various than the 'pleasures of touching and tasting' that move other animals, but are related to well-structured and recurrent types of situation in relation to which *hexeis* may be formed. So it is the account of positively motivated action and its virtue, 'moderation,' that generates gaps that are filled with identifiable virtues. Or should we say that they occupy a terrain between 'moderation' and 'justice'? It is hard to say, because although Aristotle insists that justice is a moral virtue (the moral virtue that involves the sorts of things lawcourts deal with), it really does not fit the model, as we shall see.

Is it possible to say what generates the list as we have it, in its departures from the double Platonic base? It should be, if there was indeed a perspicuous diagram, and if the confident boast about seeing 'how many' the virtues are is to be made good.

If virtues are to be primarily differentiated by their objects, a likely source of the list would be a list of different kinds of goods. And we have the rudiments of such a list at 1098b12–14: goods of the soul, goods of the body, external goods. And what are the external goods? Friends, wealth, and political power (*politikē dunamis*) are named at 1099b1; and at 1123b20 the greatest of the external goods is said to be 'honour,' which may be more or less the same as political power in this context. Virtues themselves are goods of the soul, so we may expect there to be moral virtues related to the body, to wealth, to reputation, and to friends. Courage and moderation are related to the body, the preservation of the organism, and there they are in first place. Related to the getting and spending of money are liberality and 'magnificence.' Related to honour are pride and 'magnanimity.' Then we have truthfulness, pleasantness, friendliness, and good temper. Friendliness has to do with friends, obviously; good temper is a sort of converse of that, having to do with enemies. Friendliness, honesty, and pleasantness (sociability) are said to be closely related to each other. The kind of honesty Aristotle speaks of is actually close to pride, and amounts to avoiding pretentions and false modesty in company; sociability relates to behaviour in company, friendliness to real personal relationships. And then we have justice, which, as Aristotle says, is something else again.

It is hard to see how the concluding items in this list could have been neatly diagrammed; I have the impression that Aristotle is basing himself on the fourfold classification of relevant goods, complicated by the need to relate some of the virtues to unpleasantnesses rather than to goods, and by the complication that introduces 'magnificence' and 'magnanimity,' of which more later – but that the whole thing becomes unravelled at the end. I think the reason it becomes unravelled is that friendship gets mixed up with the requirements of the political realm. When one is dealing with people as familiar individuals, the virtue of 'friendship' is called into play. But in a civilized community one deals also with people whom one does not know as individuals. One needs party manners as well as a proper friendliness, and this involves a candour in self-presentation as well as a willingness to be agreeable but not effusive. Actually, justice comes in here, because though justice has been defined incidentally as 'having to do with what the law deals with,' what the law does deal with is people who become involved with each other as strangers within an organized community. And we shall see that 'magnificence' and 'magnanimity' also have to do with life in organized communities as such.

To sum it all up, the systematic justification of the list of moral virtues, in short, might be something like this. The basic motivational equipment of a human consists of motives to seek and motives to avoid. These can be very specific: we have physiologically entrenched urges to avoid pain and the threat of pain, to resist and avenge injury (these contrary impulses are both involved in courage), to copulate, to relieve thirst and hunger. For the rest, the nature of our motivation depends on situations encountered in human societies. We need to be 'adequately fitted out' (1101a15) with property to lead a good life, so we handle stuffs and tools as actual and potential property. We live among people some of whom are strangers, and must be dealt with as such, and some of whom are actual or potential associates, and must be related to as such. In any case, we must preserve the integrity of our social selves as we do of our physical selves, so good temper is added to courage. And our social selves must function in society neither obtrusively nor retiringly, so we need pride. And what about justice? Well, the people among whom we live, like ourselves, have social selves and reputations and property which it is their virtue to safeguard and promote in the right way; and the virtue of justice is that whereby we perform the actions that will promote and preserve the best distribution of these goods. And that about wraps it up.

What is missing from the list? Piety, as we mentioned. Some would argue that a good and prudent person acknowledges some superhuman power in the universe on which all depend and on which all should be rightly related. I do not think Aristotle would deny this, any more than Plato would. Why is it not a virtue? We shall see that it is an intellectual virtue, not a moral one; it leads to no actions. I take it that this is one of the morals of the *Euthyphro*: the alleged will of the gods is actually invoked to defend what is rationally indefensible.

An omission that seems to me glaring is something that corresponds to 'justice' as defined in the *Republic*, roughly 'conscientiousness' – the virtue of carrying out what one has identified as one's specific *ergon* in society, or wherever, neither carelessly nor pedantically but rightly, as a *phronimos* would. The omission is the more odd because, as we saw, Aristotle has grappled with the problem of 'carelessness' at the more fundamental level of self-control and self-improvement. Perhaps this is one case where we can invoke Aristotle's élitist prejudice and class bias. To have a job is plainly servile, to lack leisure. To have something to be conscientious about is to be less than an Athenian *eleutheros*, one of history's self-anointed Free Spirits (like a nineteenth-century Parisian *flâneur* or a Whitmanian Yankee).

Some commentators raise eyebrows at Aristotle's inclusion of the social virtues at the end of the list, as trivial – surely to fail in these is not to be evil and wicked. But here again we see how the association of morality with authoritarian religions imposes an inappropriate perspective: Aristotle is concerned with how to be good, not with whom to denounce, whereas even philosophers who believe themselves enlightened nowadays tend to feel that morality really has to do with lambasting people from a pulpit. These social virtues have to do, as I said, specifically with the conditions and quality of life in a civilized environment. Aristotle's values are centred on the city – the political organization within which alone human life fulfils its potentiality. To grasp the importance of manners as an essential part of morals is Aristotle's distinctive contribution to ethics, not a mere quirk.[95] It is not his fault that his successors lost his vision of civic life, and fell back on the ideal of the good man as a saint in a wicked world.

2.233 The Order of Treatment

Are the virtues discussed in any particular order? Well, the order is substantially the same in the initial list and in the extended treatment, so we may suppose that it is enshrined in that blessed 'diagram.' There is one difference. In II vii, 'friendliness' comes last of the three social virtues, as the most general in scope, next to the equally general virtue of justice, which as we have suggested and will see is closely related to it; in the extended treatment it comes first of the three, immediately after its negative counterpart, good temper. Since Aristotle himself comments on the close affinity among the three, the variation is scarcely significant – sufficient reasons for the different sequences may be found in what I have just said. But is there any system underlying the order as a whole? Obviously, yes. Thomas Aquinas sums it up succinctly: we start with corporeal life, courage being concerned to prevent its interruption and temperance to preserve it, in individuals and for the species; then we consider the external goods, wealth and reputation; then external evils, which are to be met with good temper. And the last three have to do with external activity (I should have said, the social dimension.)[96] More precisely, I think, the order follows the development of civilization.

We start with the individual as a self-sustaining organism, with its self-preserving and self-maintaining behaviour. Then we move on to the economic order, the virtues of property, and then to the level of individual spiritual property, glory and reputation.[97] Then we move up to the level of interpersonal relations in a civilized society, based on mutual recognition of individuals. And finally we come to justice, where the object of concern is no longer the individual's interests or those of particular face-to-face groupings of individuals, but the system of persons itself within which a stable and intelligible order is to be maintained. (This sequence – individual, household, heroic age of alliances between warring tribes, city as community, city as domain of law – is basically that of the opening chapters of *Politics* I.) The whole discussion proceeds in an order of decreasing materiality and increasing abstractness or spirituality, the controlling *logos*, as it were, detaching itself more and more from an independent mass of 'feeling' that has to be brought under control as the original model of a moral virtue (and of the double aspect of *logos* in I xiii) suggested.[98] The detachment goes so far that, as we shall see, justice cannot be made to conform properly to the model at all, but approximates to an intellectual virtue.

Aside from the indeterminacy in the ordering of the three related virtues of social intercourse, two problems remain. First, why does courage come before moderation? Surely the pleasures of touching and tasting are those most fundamentally built in to the organism (hence the difficulty of controlling 'pleasure' as one grows up), and should come first. Similarly, good temper precedes friendliness. A possible but unsatisfactory answer is that in the *Republic* exegesis, on which Aristotle's seems, as I have said, to be an elaboration, courage comes first as corresponding most clearly to a distinctive function related to the well-being of the city (and hence of the individual, by analogy) as a whole. But that won't do as a justification, at least from my point of view, because Aristotle's order of treatment, as I have just explained it, is not compatible with it. The only other explanation that occurs to me is that in the origin of the city in *Politics* I, which is what I was suggesting does underlie the sequence of virtues, it is said that the city comes into existence as a defence organization, to maintain life, and continues in existence to achieve the good life (when people realize how much better things can be in the new circumstances). In fact this, too, is derivable from Plato's *Republic*: a city in which moderation can be exercised, because there is enough food and drink and leisure to be immoderate if one wants to be and to indulge in abstemiousness as a fad rather than from sheer scarcity (what Socrates calls the 'bloated' city), depends for its existence on military security (*Republic* 373D–374A). We make war only in order to be at peace (cf. 1177b9–10); and that is partly why, unlike the exponents of other moral virtues, courageous people do not take pleasure in their courageous acts, except insofar as they find a sort of second-order joy in their ability to endure cheerfully something so terrible (1117b15–16).

The other problem of ordering has to do with the sequence liberality–magnificence–pride–ambition. There is a sort of chiasmus here, not a linear sequence. Why? Most plausibly, so that magnificence and pride shall be juxtaposed, rather than each following (or each preceding) its 'small-scale' analogue. But why should that be? To explain that, I must explain about pride.

2.234 Two Anomalies

Aristotle's actual explanations of his selected virtues are various and intricate. I will not go through them in detail, because to do so would do nothing to unravel the threads of the argument of the *Ethics* as a whole. I merely note that they do not relate in any simple way to Aristotle's formal model, any more than actual decision-making procedures exemplify the simplified model of deliberation. I will, however, say a few words about aspects of pride and courage that readers find bothersome.

2.2341 Courage (III vi–ix; 1115a6–1117b22)

One might expect, since courage is the first virtue to be dealt with, that it would afford a paradigm of the definition we were offered. But this is far from the case. The most notable characteristic of the discussion is its intricacy.[99] This is not because it goes into detail about Greek social institutions and mores, however, on which it offers little information. The intricacy comes rather from the subtlety of the relations between courage on the battlefield (*andreia* is literally 'manliness,' the way one responds to the imperative 'be a man!') and other manifestations of endurance, on the one hand, and other sources of military success (such as desperation), on the other.

One of the things that people find troublesome is the unique emphasis on the battlefield. But this has been explained above, and given that explanation we can simply say that Aristotle treats the word and concept of courage as one of those many terms that are ambiguous, but of which all the related uses are to be explained by one paradigm case, much in the same way that substance is the paradigm of 'being': military courage is the paradigm of courage in general.

What really troubles some people about courage, though, in addition to its obviously anomalous relation to pleasure, is that there seem to be two kinds of feeling involved: aggressiveness, and endurance. But this should not bother us unduly. In the first instance, virtues are defined by the situations that call for them: in the case of courage, those that inspire fear – in a word, dangers. But handling fear really does involve two quite different modes of appropriate response: handling the fear itself, and doing something about what inspires it. And in the military context that involves knowing when to advance and when to retreat – and being able to do either cheerfully.[100]

It is tempting to relate the double nature of courage to the specific military method of upper-class Greeks, the hoplite phalanx.[101] It was a method that called for the utmost discipline – a quality with which the Greek and Greek-trained armies of Alexander overran the neighbouring empires. In the phalanx, the heavily armoured Greek soldier was almost invulnerable: his left side was guarded by his shield, his right side by the shield on the left arm of his neighbour. But this worked only so long as the line was intact. As soon as someone ran away, there was a gap in the line through which inroads could be made. The same was true if someone lost his cool and ran *towards* the enemy. But, although this fact must have made Aristotle's point vividly clear to his upper-class audience (only those who could afford the expensive equipment could join the phalanx), the point seems clear enough without that.

2.2342 Pride (IV iii; 1123a34–1125b35)

For the most part, we can go along with Aristotle's descriptions of the virtues fairly well. It was a long time ago, a different civilization, and the detail of the way of life is, at best, merely quaint; but we expect that, and if we make allowances we can usually see the point of what he says. But at one place many readers stick. This is at the chapter on 'pride' (megalopsuchia). There is a regular virtue of 'ambition,' discussed in the following chapter (IV iv), the self-respect whereby people seek a place in society, with the concomitant recognition, suitable to their actual attainments. But for the very best people there is this very special virtue of pride, according to which one's attitudes and expectations undergo a transformation. One speaks with a grave voice, moves with dignity, greets adversities imperturbably, and so forth. This, it seems, is Aristotle's moral ideal, the counterpart in the practical sphere of the sage – but no, we must not say that: Aristotle does not set up among the practitioners of the intellectual life any such conceited paragon (it was the Stoics who did that). As we read the description of this prince of pomposity, we cannot believe that Aristotle is not being satirical. But there is nothing in the context to hint that he might be. What on earth is going on here?

There is a certain oddity in the account. Nothing anywhere else in the *Ethics* prepares us for it, or is even consistent with it. Everywhere else, we deal with ordinary people going about their ordinary business, and emphasize the importance of seriousness about the life according to reason. Virtue is simply a manifestation of seriousness in integrating the interests and chances of a lifetime. This 'pride,' by contrast, is simply a matter of show, of vindicating a special position for a special accomplishment. This is not merely, as some say, the point at which Aristotle's Greek values become most at odds with today's democratic ideology: the passage is an anomaly in his own work.

Something is going on that is not being said, and we can begin to see what it is if we look at the immediately preceding chapters. There, wealth is subjected to the same double treatment as reputation

is here. There is a virtue of 'liberality' (*eleutheria* – a strange conceptual marriage of liberty and property!), the proper handling of everyday incomes and expenditures, and then there is *megaloprepeia*, 'magnificence,' having to do with very large sums. But as we read the
chapter we see that it is not the magnitude of the expenditures that
is the point. 'Magnificence' is the virtue manifested in *public* expenditures, the endowment of a warship or a theatrical production, or just
mounting a club banquet. These are ceremonious affairs that have to
be done with style. They belong to public life, and that is why a
different set of considerations come into play.

As I said above, I think magnificence and pride are placed back to
back (instead of having pride follow its small-scale counterpart, as
magnificence did) in order to let us see that the cases are analogous.
For, in fact, there is a set of circumstances in which the proud man's
behaviour, though it may not go down well today, would in many
times and places be just what was expected. It is the behaviour of a
great king. For there, in fact, is an 'open letter' of Isocrates to a newly
created king in Cyprus (*To Nicocles*) in which the latter is advised
that just that sort of pompous carrying-on is what is expected and
required. When Shakespeare's Harry became Henry V, he immediately dumped Falstaff; when the Duke of York became George VI, he
never sang 'Underneath the Spreading Chestnut Tree' again. The
ceremonial centre of the state is surrounded with protocol, behaves
with unbroken dignity, and demands special respect.

If Aristotle had said that he was describing the official behaviour
of high dignitaries, I doubt if anyone would have objected. But that
is not what he says. He says he is describing the behaviour that befits
supremacy in virtue *in contrast with* external circumstances. What are
we to make of that?

The answer is to be found in the discussion of monarchy in the
Politics (1284a3–b34). The topic of monarchy is there introduced by
what it then appears would be its sole justification – that there
should be one person in a city who so far excels all the others in all
the virtues as to appear as 'a god among humans.' Such a person
literally cannot cooperate as one among many with the other citizens
– their political capacities and endowments are simply not comparable. The only alternatives are to exile such a person, which would
be grossly unjust, or to make that person sole ruler for life.

The only person fit to be a monarch, then, would be a person on
a quite different level of excellence than ordinary mortals.[102] The
argument on 'pride' in the *Ethics* should accordingly be that the

pretensions that everyone acknowledges to be appropriate to a monarch are actually appropriate to a supremely virtuous person.[103] So a monarch who is actually only a person of average attainments and ordinary virtues but still accepts and expects such homage and behaves in a specially royal way (calling oneself 'We' and wearing hats by Norman Hartnell) has the vice (harmless but foolish) of vanity (*chaunotēs*).

But, if that is what Aristotle means, why does he not say so straight out? A possible explanation would be that he is in a very sensitive position politically, a protégé of the Macedonian royal house in which dignity and virtue were in short supply and a connection of the royal house of Atarneus in which satirists found a target, while identifying himself professionally with the republican mores of Athens. This difficulty, however, did not prevent him from making his position explicit in that passage in the *Politics*.

No doubt I am making unnecessarily heavy weather of this. We do not need to invoke actual monarchy. Other forms of polity have public positions calling for a public manner. So long as we bear the essentially public context in mind, and remember that a public position calls for higher moral and intellectual standards than private life, Aristotle's position is not absurd. The last part of the chapter rings a bell even in our democratic days. People who thrust themselves into public positions for which they are not qualified and in which they do not know how to behave can indeed make proper fools of themselves; and people of great capabilities who adopt an aw-gee-shucks manner and pretend they are quite incapable of filling public positions can be a real pain in the neck.

2.24 Interlude: The Common Books (V–VII; 1129a1–1154b34)

At this point in the Ethics *we come to the three books that also form part of EE (IV–VI), the surviving manuscripts of which simply refer readers to the better-known work. Which work they originally belonged to is an endlessly contestable problem because different factors seem weightier to different scholars. My task is to see what sense can be made of EN as it stands, no matter what its provenance. But it will do no harm to look at some of the possibilities.*

The three books as we have them fit into EN well enough. Book V is an unavoidable sequel to the treatment of the (other) moral virtues, and could not come anywhere else, but it has to be very much a world of its own, largely but not entirely because Plato made it so. Book VI on the intellectual virtues has to come next, to complement the treatment of the moral virtues; but again it is a substantially new topic, and one cannot expect to find textually close connections with what comes after and before. The first part of Book VII complements the study of virtue as a whole with a study of the ways in which virtue is missed – but it is a largely unanticipated topic, though not entirely unprepared, and the author has to 'make a new start' (1145a15). The diverse parts pleasure has played in moral deficiencies seem to call for a full-dress treatment of that topic, and we get it, but it is explicitly introduced only as something political philosophy has to deal with. The endnote to Book VII simply says that friendship is the last remaining topic (which is true in a way, but the headnote to Book VIII assumes that it is following on the discussion of virtue, which would suit a placing after Book IV – but equally after Book V or VI, and not so well where it actually comes, after Book VII. In fact, there is a certain logic to the sequence of topics, but the pieces do not look as if they were written to be read as part of any single literary work, EN or any other. This being so, the attitude with which we approach this part of our project can hardly help being affected by the literary dislocation.[104]

There is much to be said for the view that Books V and VI belong with the Nicomachean compilation (consistently with the opening of Book VIII), but Book VII belongs rather to the Eudemian (for the duplication of essays on pleasure is awkward);[105] *but if once we allow complications like that, we will never stop. The simpler possibilities seem to be the following:*

1 / *the books were originally written for EN (and how they got attached to the other work need not concern us);*
2 / *the books were originally written for EE (as Kenny's statistics of word usage suggest), and then*
   a. *Aristotle was sufficiently satisfied to with them to leave them in the (later) Nicomachean version; or*
   b. *he revised them for the Nicomachean work, and only this revised version survived; or*
   c. *what Aristotle wrote for the Nicomachean version has vanished, and some editor put the Eudemian version (whether earlier or later) in to make up the deficiency – for these topics must, after all, have been covered somehow; or*
   d. *Aristotle did mean to go straight from Book IV to Book VIII, and his intentions were frustrated by a later editor or editors; or*
   e. *Aristotle meant to prepare a revision for EN but never got around to it;*
3 / *the* Nicomachean Ethics *is simply a compilation of originally indepen-*

dent logoi, *minor treatises or working papers, put together by someone (Andronicus or another) who could find no independent work on the themes covered in these books, and was therefore obliged to borrow from the other treatise (which no doubt was a compilation that owed its basic form of Aristotle himself).*

These seven possibilities have very different implications for our undertaking. Option 1 makes any apparent inconsistency something to be explained away, and encourages the commentator to look hard for a consistent reading. So, to a lesser degree, does option 2b. Option 2a will make us resigned to minor discrepancies, but only minor ones. Options 2c and 2e allow that any order that is actually discernible may well answer to Aristotle's original plan, but discourage us from pressing too hard for a strong and far-reaching architectonic. Option 2d means that any pattern we find in the whole is simply our good fortune. And option 3 means that there may well be a pattern, but it may be one devised by an editor rather than by Aristotle himself.

Option 1 is clearly the one that makes my project least heroic. Against it is the computer evidence assembled by Kenny, which, for what it is worth, makes the common books Eudemian, and to my mind has prima facie probability. In favour of option 1 is alleged the fact that the sharp distinction in Book VI between phronēsis *and* sophia *is absent from EE – but then, it is not observed all that closely in EN I, either.*[106]

If option 3 is accepted, the functional interdependencies that I hope to make (and, in some cases, to have already made) persuasive are implausibly extensive. They go something like this: I i–xii prepares and demands X vi–viii, which is based on X i–v, which in turn presupposes VIII–IX; I vii–xii requires I xiii, which prepares for II, which is so written as to demand III i–v; III vi–V is necessary to make II v–vi plausible, and expand II vii; X vi–viii demands VI, without which also III vi–V is misleading; VII xi–xiv is suggested by VII i–x, which is complementary to II–VI (and without which some earlier remarks on akrasia *are not fully intelligible). Thus every part is related to at least one other part, and there is only one substantive discontinuity: there is no way in which Book VII leads into Book VIII. However, Book VIII turns out to mark the introduction of an unexpected new theme, which carries right through into the end of Book X and lifts the whole discussion of the* Ethics *to a new level. The conclusion of Book VII, however, which reinstates pleasure as a possible supreme value and relates pleasure to* energeia, *effectively makes the point which is more concretely and spectacularly established at IX iv and following, which is the final interiorization of happiness.*

*Of the varieties of option 2, 2d is rather attractive. The discussion of the
social virtues would lead smoothly into that of friendship in its more general
sense, and the striking reversal of perspective introduced by the latter would
come nearer the middle of the work and so perhaps give it a better balance.*[107] *Of the omitted books, one could always argue that justice really does
not fit Aristotle's scheme anyway, and that the discussion of moral virtue
really makes any further explanation of* phronēsis *impossible; the material
at the beginning of Book VII is a luxury rather than a necessity (unless you
are haunted by the spectre of Socrates), and the treatment of pleasure in
Book VII is superseded and contradicted by the version at the beginning of
Book X.*

*The idea of a version of EN without the common books has its attractions,
then; but it is not really tenable. Books II–IV have left us with a multiplicity of virtues; the cardinal thesis of the unity of virtue is essential to the
notion of 'the human good,' and only* phronēsis *can establish it. And
without the explicit introduction of* sophia *as a second intellectual virtue
the connection between goodness and contemplation cannot be made. But,
above all, the idea that Aristotle could have composed a substantial work on
this topic without discussing justice is simply preposterous.*

*Between the other versions of option 2 there is little to choose. But per-
haps option 2c has the edge. Neither the discussion of* phronēsis *nor that
of* dikaiosunē *(as we are about to see) is perhaps exactly what is required;
and, above all, there is the presence of two incompatible but similar accounts
of pleasure, of which the second proceeds without any reference to the first.
It can't possibly have been meant that way.*[108] *But Aristotle was a busy
man, and was not preparing the work for publication, so anything is possible.*

2.25 Justice (V; 1129a1–1138b14)

Is justice (*dikaiosunē*) a virtue?[109] If so, is it a moral virtue? It is and
it isn't. In the list of virtues allegedly read off from the 'diagram' in
II vii, justice is not included. Instead, after the list and after the
pseudo-virtues of shame and righteous indignation, we read: 'With
regard to justice, since it has not one simple meaning, we shall, after
describing the other states, distinguish its two kinds, and say how
each of them is a mean; and similarly we shall treat also of the
rational virtues' (1108b7–10, Ross trans.). The ambiguity alone would
not have kept justice out of the list: Aristotle could simply have
brushed the irrelevant meaning aside. The trouble is rather that there
is a problem about how justice is a mean and what it is a mean

between. It does not fit the pattern of the moral virtues, and is never used as an illustration of one. The quoted remark may well be an editorial note added by Andronicus or another – the end of it certainly is, because it refers to the intellectual (*dianoētikai*) virtues as 'rational' (*logikai*) virtues, which is wrong; as we know, all virtues by Aristotle's definition are alike related to *logos*.[110] But the opening of Book V makes the same point: there is a problem about *how* justice is a *mesotēs*.

Justice could not, of course, be excluded from the virtues: it is, in a sense, the supreme and most comprehensive virtue, though Aristotle's references to 'the best and most complete virtue' (1098a17–18 etc.) do not seem to have justice in mind, and Aristotle himself had already written a four-volume work *On Justice* (about which we know surprisingly little).

The basic peculiarity of Aristotle's treatment of justice stems from Plato's enormously elaborate treatment in his *Republic*, the methods and doctrines of which Aristotle took very much to heart.

The *Republic* has a multiple account of what justice is, which can in the end be reduced to two themes.[111] First, there is a formal definition of justice (in psycho-political terms) as the practice of (not rendering to each what is appropriate, as in the traditional view, but) allowing each factor involved to fulfil its own function; and, second, there is an equation (announced in Book I and elaborated in the later books) between justice and the dispassionate use of reason as a ground of action, to be contrasted with appetite or greed (*pleonexia*). This double account corresponds closely to the 'human good' as expounded by Aristotle in his own different terms – making the best use of *logos* as opposed to responding to passion and impulse. And Plato's two formulae support Aristotle's distinction between two linked meanings of the word *justice*, as the whole of virtue in relation to others (or law-abidingness) and as the special virtue involved in the allocation of distributable goods (or fairness). These two formulae and definitions cross over in odd ways. Aristotle does not believe in reified 'parts of the soul,' whose interrelations might constitute the psychic basis of virtue, so his 'whole of virtue' is relegated to the behavioural realm, in accordance with his general tendency to keep things distinct; but the special virtue of fairness that is opposed to 'greed' is simply what Plato had identified with making pure reasoning the basis of action.

If we think of Aristotle's two senses of the word *justice* as a reworking of what Plato had treated as two different levels in the analysis of justice as a constitutive principle of psychic power, we will be in a position to sort out the threads in Aristotle's tangled web.

Aristotle presumably thinks of justice as a moral virtue, or he would not identify his task as that of saying what kind of mean it is, what kind of *praxis* it relates to, and what it is a mean between (1129a3–5). But in fact justice, as Aristotle conceives it (in the narrower of its two senses), is something halfway between a moral virtue and an intellectual virtue. We have seen that the standard-pattern moral virtues are arranged in a sequence that leads away from personal and corporeal concerns to social and interpersonal fields of action; justice takes us one step further. It is like a moral virtue in being concerned with a special field of action, the apportionment of distributables, and accordingly a mean (the fair share) between the extremes of too much and too little. But it is not a mean between extremes of feeling: if it is one's *own* share that is involved, the vice is always that of trying to get too much of good things and too little of bad things; if one is concerned with making fair distributions among other people, there are no relevant feelings of which there could be too much or too little. The only relevant feeling is, as the *Republic* suggests, the intellectual jurist or administrator's passion for getting *the right answer*, the solution to the problem posed – in individual terms, the desire to do the right thing in terms of some publicly accepted standard. It is an orientation to truth, and truth is the distinctive value of the intellectual virtues (1139a28–9; 1139b12). So it is that in the *Republic* the just person is identified with the intellectual – or rather, the intellectual is taken to be the paradigm of a person who is inherently just. What gets in the way of justice is not that the relevant feeling is excessive or defective, but that the dispassionate intellect is disturbed by some passion or other – the judge or administrator, or the individual seeking just treatment, allows personal and passionate concerns to disturb or overturn the relevant calculations. Confusion arises because the private motivation might (though it need not) be a desire for the kind of thing that the 'just' action would have been concerned with the right amount of, and Aristotle is tempted to treat this as the standard case.

The mean of justice, in other words, is not a mean in relation to ourselves (*pros hēmas*), as in the standard moral virtues. The just price is the determinately just price, a fair share is a fair share. Or again: in the standard virtues, the feeling itself is the basis of action, and without such feeling nothing will be done, and this is true whether the feeling is excessive or deficient or just right. But the just action has no other motive than to be just, to do or get the right thing, and Aristotle does not consider that a passion for justice can be excessive, any more than Plato had.[112]

Aristotle's general plan of his discussion of justice is amply motivated. But it does not really fit the expectations that Books II–IV might have aroused. To complete the scheme, one might have expected Aristotle to have talked about the justice of the just individual as sketched in Plato's *Crito* – and, for that matter, implied in the myth of the *Protagoras*, and affirmed by Polemarchus in the *Republic*. On this view, justice in its narrower sense is simply a matter of keeping one's promises and fulfilling one's contractual obligations. Society rests on our abstaining from mutual aggression (theft and violence), but also on our abiding by agreements we have made and living up to obligations we have incurred (*Crito* 49A–E). Book V deals with this only in public contexts, where it is a matter of legal control rather than of personal morality. Such a virtue could not, of course, have been represented as a mean between two vices, but justice cannot be seen in that light anyway.

Why did Aristotle not do things that way? Perhaps because, as Socrates' conversation with Polemarchus suggested, it is hard for such a view of justice to avoid the paradox of rendering evil to the evil, in some form or other, which Aristotle is able to avoid by making 'retributive' justice simply a corrective of bad situations. But still we may feel that a gap has been left. People who fulfil their promises are not covered by the 'broad' sense of justice, because the latter is exhausted by the exercise of specific virtues in relation to others. And none of the virtues Aristotle recognizes seem to cover punctuality in fulfilling obligations one has incurred.

In the discussion we have, Aristotle proceeds on the supposition that justice is a moral virtue, but he doesn't push it. 'The apportionment of distributable goods' sounds specialized, but it isn't really – it applies to everything that one person can have more of than another, provided that the amount one person has is not independent of the amount another person has. This is surely one of the reasons that justice cannot be a standard moral virtue: the sorts of things that may be involved may be the objects of very various feelings and interests. *Pleonexia*, the principle of 'wanting more,' is a standing pattern of conduct rather than a specific passion. One can be pleonectic about anything. Of course, one could deny that, and say that *strictly speaking* greed is always greed for wealth, and to be pleonectic about other things is to reduce them to the status of possessions. But that would be equating justice with liberality, already dealt with as one of the regular virtues. And fairness and generosity are not at all the same. The result is, as we shall see, that Aristotle's laborious distinction between two senses of the word *justice* keeps threatening to break down.

The motive of the just person is to get things right – but to get them right in relation to a supposed normative condition, typically thought of as in some way original, the status quo. Though Aristotle's analyses are always robustly secular, the underlying feeling here is surely religious. Justice as observance of the law is reverence for *themis*, the divine dispensation that functions like a law of nature; justice as fairness is reverence for *moira*, the original allocation of spheres of influence among the gods. In secular terms, these must become, respectively, positive law and the outcome of economic analysis: the 'mean' of justice is somehow out there in the world, as the means of the other moral virtues are explicitly said not to be.[113]

2.251 The Ambiguity of 'Justice' (1129a1–1130b29)

The traditional associations of justice with powerful cosmic and religious sentiment combine with the conceptual imperialism of Plato's *Republic* and Aristotle's own extensive work on 'justice' to make the topic intractable. It certainly cannot be reduced to the compass of any of the moral virtues already considered, and it is hard to see how it can be dealt with within the scope of a work essentially concerned with the problem of how an individual can live the best possible life. The opening of Book V seeks to cut the topic down to size by pointing to an ambiguity in the concept of justice. The word *dikaiosunē* and its cognates are used in a broad sense to refer to virtue in its social or public aspect, but this sense is irrelevant to our present discussion; they are also used to designate a specific virtue within the scope of virtue at large. The concept seems simple and uncontroversial, and one may wonder why Aristotle makes such heavy weather of it – it takes him five pages in the Oxford text.[114] But the frequent allusions to Plato show clearly that it is the dismantling of the Platonic structure that he has in mind. And in fact, as we shall see, his labour is in vain: the distinction he makes will not stay made, and does not provide an effective framework for the actual discussion.

The actual distinction between the two senses is made neatly enough, through the use of antonyms. A just person is the opposite of a lawless person (*paranomos*), and also of an unfair (*anisos*) person; so a just person may be either law-abiding or fair (1129a32–4).[115] At this point in the *Ethics*, our concern is with fairness, not with lawfulness.

So far, so good. But both senses of 'justice' have difficulties, though Aristotle does not show himself to be aware of them. In the broader sense, justice as lawfulness is equated with 'complete virtue, ... in relation to another,' on the ground that cities legislate in favour of all virtue and against all vice, in accordance with the universal scope of politics as originally laid down at 1094a27–b7. But the issue is confused by Aristotle's also saying, as though it were another way of saying the same thing, that justice in this sense is practised in the context of 'the political community' (*tēi politikēi koinōniāi*, 1129b18–19), and virtue practised 'in relation to another' is contrasted with virtue practised in relation to oneself *and one's household* (1130a7, 1129b33) – as though justice as law-abidingness were not a subdivision of virtue in general but its analogue in a separate public realm, so that its proper discussion would belong in a treatise on politics proper rather than in one on ethics. On the other hand, in the narrower sense, 'unfairness' is equated with *pleonexia* (1129a32, 1129b9), the principle of generalized greed, which has no proper antonym of its own. Aristotle says here that the object of greed is those good things you can be lucky an unlucky about, and which may turn out not to be good for you after all (1129b2–7; cf. 1094b16–18); but, as I said in the preceding section, such greed is a general pattern of behaviour rather than the indulgence of a specific passion in a specific context, as a moral vice should be.

When Aristotle writes here of virtue 'in relation to an other' (*pros heteron*), by contrast with members of one's household, it is clear that by the 'other' he must mean something like Sartre's *Autrui*, 'the other as Other,' a person to whom I relate within a community (or else there could be no relation), but as a stranger. The basis of relations to such strangers is that laid down for utilitarians by Jeremy Bentham: each is to count as one, nobody as more than one. But one what? In a sense, the distribution of dividends in a joint stock enterprise is the paradigm: the distribution goes simply by how many shares a person holds, not by who the person is. Equality of contribution is the default value: to the law, each citizen counts as one. All relations with others *as others*, in fact, deal with them not as individuals to whom one is related by personal ties, but as units entitled to equal treatment or in terms (as we shall see) of some supposedly quantifiable magnitude. Like all moral virtues, justice as such is a matter of quantity. Intellectual virtue, as before, determines what the situation is in the relevant terms; the moral virtue of justice is the propensity to act on this determination.

The trouble with the preceding paragraph is that it turns out to be a sketch of what Aristotle makes of justice as a specific moral virtue. But it did not set out to be that. It set out to be an explanation of what was implied by speaking of justice in its *wider* sense as essentially related to the 'other' as such. So there is a very strong internal relation between the two senses of the word, a relation to which Aristotle pays no heed. Are we, in fact, to say that he reverts without noticing it from a discussion of the narrow sense to a treatment of what is really the broader sense? Not exactly that, I think, but it is really very obscure in the end what the distinction is and whether it can be maintained. And yet it seemed so clear, and I was asking why Aristotle made such heavy weather of it!

In the end, the distinction is that between being virtuous in general, insofar as one's virtue affects the public good by its effects on others, and observing in interpersonal transactions that respect for objective status and entitlement that the public good requires. The distinction corresponds to an ambiguity within the Greek notion of law, with which justice is intimately linked: the law commands virtue and forbids vice generally, but courts of law especially enforce respect for entitlements. In Aristotle's day, cities were still codifying their laws, or had done so so recently that it might seem unimportant whether a law had yet got into the books or not. If it had not, it could be called an 'unwritten law,' and that expression is as close as the Greeks got to our modern concept of morality as opposed to law. If a law was on the books, however, the concept of positive law had made enough progress that it would be accepted as a law just because it *was* on the books. Of course, what the law is when the statutes are silent is a matter for dispute even today; but in Aristotle's time the conceptual apparatus itself was more fluid than it is now.

Plato's apparent assimilation of all virtue (and not only 'in relation to others') to justice in Aristotle's narrow sense, the triumph of the calculative intellect with no desires other than that for truth, corresponds to his hypostatization of 'the good' into a self-existent and eternal entity, against which Aristotle argued in I vi. For Aristotle, by contrast, the very fact that justice depends on an objectively and interpersonally ascertainable and calculable norm of right action, which can be expressed in laws and applied in courts, excludes it from the list of standard-pattern moral virtues.

The reason for all these tangles and for the persistence of Aristotle's efforts is that the discussion reflects a profound transformation in Greek values. According to some historians, the Greeks in Homeric times and their aftermath contrasted the competitive virtues for which they reserved the name *aretē* with the cooperative qualities of 'justice.'[116] Plato's ingenious constructions are designed to undermine this contrast by making justice the comprehensive unity of all virtues, so that any heroic qualities that fall outside it turn out not to be virtues at all; and Aristotle seeks to achieve the same effect by less theoretically ambitious measures, making 'virtue' as unfolded in Books II–IV and 'justice' coincide, covering the same actions and qualities, the former when seen in the context of the individual's own life and the latter when viewed from the standpoint of their functioning in a political community.

The complexities we have been working through are not insurmountable, and if the discussion of justice had ended at 1134a15 all would really be plain sailing. At that point the regular treatment of justice in the narrow sense, as a moral virtue, is concluded. In fact, the completion of the topic is twice announced, at 1133b29 and, after a paragraph devoted to the previously announced topic of what *kind* of mean justice is, again at 1134a14–16. The second announcement is the more emphatic but textually the more suspect, for it says we have been discussing the 'nature' (*phusis*) of justice (something of a solecism, because only natural phenomena can have a nature, but not quite impossible for Aristotle to have committed) and also that we have finished our discussion of justice in the broad sense as well. In fact, however, Aristotle goes on in 1134a17–1138b14 to discuss other matters of which the relation to the previous account is left obscure, but which are certainly concerned with 'justice' in some sense or other. And this material in turn ends with a statement that the discussion of justice (this time, together with the other moral virtues) is now ended.[117]

The new material consists of a discussion of the basis of legal systems (V vi–vii) and of certain problems in legal practice (V viii–xi). Is this a treatment of 'justice' in yet a third, unannounced, sense, perhaps tacked on by an incautious editor who failed to see that it had not been adequately provided for? Or did Aristotle himself realize that this material should have been covered, and add it as an unexplained afterthought? Or can it really be accommodated within the definition of justice in its narrower sense, as the propensity to seek one's fair share of shareable goods and evils, so that the second announcement of a conclusion is as premature as the first? In fact I think it can, and that Aristotle develops, without drawing attention to it, an argument to show that it can. But prima facie the case is the opposite, that Aristotle is confronted in 'justice' and its cognates with a set of terms that has not two but at least five meanings. In addition to the two he distinguishes, there are (a) social justice, the state of affairs in which each social class has its rights; (b) legal justice, the practice of the courts; and (c) the system of human relationships formalized by legal and political institutions, as contradistinguished in Book VIII from 'friendship' or the system of informal relationships that constitutes a community (a 'society' rather than a 'state').

The way of reducing this multiplicity appears when we look at the equation of the first sense of justice with 'law-abidingness' at 1129b11–25: the laws exist to promote happiness within a political society, but this (given the definition in I vii) means promoting virtue; therefore, the laws enact morality, and the 'just' person is the wholly virtuous person. But, of course, the state can do this only indirectly, since what produces virtue is the virtuous actions of individuals. All the state can do directly is arrange appropriate incentives and disincentives and – what is relevant here – organize relations between its members, which it can do only by assigning them artificial status that forms a framework within which laws can operate and incentives and disincentives can be systematically applied (cf. V vi).

It is the presence of this artificial framework that makes quantification of human affairs possible, and thus makes justice (in its narrower sense) possible. One can only want the 'right amount' when some scale has been introduced by which amounts can be measured. In fact, the things with which justice in the narrow sense is said to be concerned – privileges, property and security – are just the things that the state controls and through which it exerts its moral pressure.[118] Justice is thus coextensive with the province of law.

We are nowhere told that it will be so, but, in fact, throughout the discussion of justice, the point of view is always that of the supervising government, never that of the supervised or of the humble participants in private transactions. All of our five senses of 'justice' thus turn out to be various aspects of what law (that is, the state power) intends and facilitates.

The whole discussion of justice thus becomes, as one might have expected, not so much a conclusion to the account of the moral virtues as an introduction to a treatise on politics, forming an essential transition from the private to the public, just as the treatise on friendship will effect a transition from the personal to the interpersonal. Both discussions point away from the context of the *Ethics* as such, the individual's concern with the ordering of personal life, to a wider sphere. But justice could hardly be displaced from its traditional status as a virtue, and the order of treatment, postponing the legal to the virtuous aspect, is determined by this position that it retains in the system.

Aristotle ends his study of the ambiguity of 'justice' with a disconcerting proviso. The state's concern with promoting virtue is not only indirect but in a sense compromised: what it is concerned with is education in the *public* interest (*paideian tēn pros to koinon*), with a view to social relations within the community, so that it remains doubtful whether education devoted strictly to the development of the individual is within the state's purview or not, 'for it may not be the same thing to be a good man (*andri*) and a good citizen generally' (1130b26–9). We are told that the discussion is 'postponed,' and perhaps the reference is indeed to the treatment of the topic in *Politics* III; but the thrust of that discussion, convoluted and difficult to evaluate as it is, seems hard to reconcile with the implications of what is said in the *Ethics*.

In the present context, one would expect the problem to be whether state education should intrude into family affairs, and perhaps also whether Aristotle is not allowing for the possibility that the bias of an actual political regime may corrupt its educational system (in accordance with the Thrasymachean view of 'justice' at *Republic* 338E). But the view of the *Politics* is rather that the concern of the state is citizenship as such, as manifested exclusively in the sharing of political power (cf. 1283b42), and that the virtue of a good citizen is manifested only by participation in effective control over the political domain (e.g., 1278b1–5). This is indeed implicit, or partly so, in the *Ethics* (already in I i), and as I have remarked it is the implicit standpoint of Book V; but the relationships are not really worked out.[119]

2.252 Justice as Equality (1130b30–1134a16)

Aristotle's detour through antonyms enabled him to equate justice as a special virtue with fairness, and fairness is the same word as equality (*isotēs*). This is the idea that he introduces and anatomizes now. He does it in a very literal way. 'Equality' is a strictly quantitative notion, and quantity is the domain of mathematics. As Aristotle sees it, two sorts of things can be equal: amounts and proportions. So justice is a matter of equality in amount or of equality in proportion. If I have to make a fair division of a quantity of stuff or a number of things into a number *n* of parts or shares, I can divide it into *n* equal parts, or into *n* parts that are equally proportioned to the magnitude of the *n* entitlements, however that may be determined. And the sharing people (though Aristotle does not say this) may differ in various ways: in what they need, in what suits them, in what is appropriate to them, in what they deserve, in what they have contributed to whatever is going on. In any case, the issue of 'equality' arises only insofar as a precise quantitative assessment can be made.

It is very odd to think of a virtue in just these terms; but even our own looser notion of 'fairness' carries the same implication. A tax, a distribution, a sentence, an academic grade, can be unfair only if it is too high or too low; and that implies that there could be a fair whatever-it-is that would be just right. All Aristotle is doing is spelling that out.

It seems to follow that the basis of injustice must itself be quantitative. I said above that *pleonexia*, the general word for the behavioural principle that lies at the root of injustice, must be equated simply with disregard for justice, and this disregard (as Plato said, and the Stoics would more explicitly argue) can only arise from giving way to some passion or other. But that is going a bit far, because (as Aristotle will be reminding us in the extraordinarily convoluted discussion that begins with V vi) the inward component of unfair behaviour must have more to it than that if 'unfair' and 'unjust' are really going to mean something. If there really is a motive for departing from justice and fairness, as such, it must strictly be the desire to get more of good things and less of bad things, as the plain meaning of *pleonexia* implies. Aristotle accordingly says that the motive of unfairness as such must be the desire for gain as such, and that means that the mere fact of gaining must be the payoff. So unfair actions are committed for the pleasure that comes from gain (*di' hēdonēn tēn apo tou kerdous*, 1130b4).

Aristotle sticks to this formula with such determination that he argues that in assessing a penalty for assault a lawcourt must be assuming that the assailant experiences a 'gain' equivalent to the 'loss' of the victim's injuries. I suppose he would argue, not that this is how courts think, but that this is the only rational justification of the court's procedures, since 'revenge' has nothing to do with justice.[120] But this artificiality is not the worst of it. The real trouble is that in an unjust judgment or distribution the favoured party, who will experience the supposed pleasure from gain, is *ex hypothesi* passive. It is the judge who is unfair, and the judge has nothing to gain from the unjust judgment as such. Such a judge may in fact be receiving a bribe, or popular applause, or gratitude, or merely the gratification of some personal prejudice; but this is not the specific motivation for the unfairness of the judgment as such. Aristotle will grapple with this issue later (1136b15–1137a4).

Although the formula about pleasure and gain is the one required by Aristotle's project as I have construed it, it is part of the sentence that specifies that the field with which fairness is concerned is 'fame and property and security,' 'or that which includes all these, if we had a single name for it' (1130b2–3). What is this genus? Is it those 'external goods' that (unlike friendship) can be included in exchanges and distributions? Or is it that with which the city can formally provide its citizens? Perhaps it does not matter much, but an answer might help to explain just what Aristotle means by 'gain' (*kerdos*). Clearly, Aristotle is using the term in the sort of way people nowadays use the phrase 'the profit motive,' without thinking too hard about what exactly that motive is – it is easy to see roughly what sort of thing it is and what it is contrasted with, and we tend to let it go at that. I suppose the idea is that unfair people, whenever they find themselves in any sort of situation that can be construed as involving a distribution or exchange of anything on which a roughly quantifiable value can be based in terms of that distribution itself, like to get more of whatever it is if it is distributed as a good, and less if it is distributed as an evil.[121] They take care never to give a sucker an even break.

2.2521 The Anatomy (1130b30–1131a9)

Aristotle lays out a simple scheme. Justice calls for equality in relation to situations that involve property and other sharable items. There are two kinds of such situations: one where a set amount or number has to be distributed among a population, the other where individuals exchange property and so forth among themselves. The latter kind comes in two sorts: that where two (or more) individuals agree to an exchange, the other where an exchange is initiated by one party without the other party's consent. Within this last, 'involuntary,' sort, we can distinguish (though it is not at once evident why it is relevant here) between those where the unconsenting party does not know what is going on, the other where the victim knows but is subjected to violence.

So far, so good. But that is not quite what Aristotle says. Actually, he describes the distributive sort of justice as concerned with 'things to be shared by those who are members of the city' or (as Ross has it) 'who have a share in the constitution' (*hosa merista tois koinōnousi tēs politeias*, 1130b32). And he characterizes the rest as 'that which plays a rectifying part in transactions' (*to en tois sunallagmasi diorthōtikon*, 1131a1). But this seems quite wrong. For one thing, a distribution is fair or unfair regardless of whether it has to do with cities and constitutions or not. It is true that justice in class relations in a political organization is very important, and the *Politics* will say a lot about it; but this is the *Ethics*, not the *Politics*, and the restriction is unjustified. If Aristotle had wanted to, he could have made a distinction between the private and the public manifestations, like that which I was arguing underlies the treatment of the supposed moral virtues of magnificence and pride. For another thing, justice in making contracts and establishing prices is not 'corrective' but constitutive: an agreement does not become unfair only when someone tries to alter its terms. (The case is different with the 'involuntary' transactions, which are *un*just from the start and where justice does indeed come in only as a corrective.)[122] What is going on here?

It may well be that the emphasis on state action is simply an unconscious effect of the context. Aristotle has just been saying that the state prescribes virtuous conduct in the private domain, and that its public education is devoted to this end, and has postponed the question whether private education is also a state function (1130b20–9). So we are already thinking about the state power; and we may then simply go on to ask ourselves what the state's mandate is in relation to justice in its specialized form, without realizing that we have somehow changed the question. But at least two other interpretations are possible. First, Aristotle may simply be taking it for granted that justice in *both* forms or senses is the proper domain of state action – it goes without saying. Second, he may be assuming that anyone 'serious' enough about life to be listening to his lectures (or reading his book) will be a member of the ruling class who will naturally look at things from the point of view of those who rule (or who may in their turn be called on to hold office). And certainly anyone who thinks in general terms, as we are doing throughout the *Ethics*, about questions of right and justice, will inevitably be thinking of the procedures of courts and legislative and administrative bodies for whom and for whom alone the principles of justice are an issue.

Aristotle's peculiar procedure, then, has a certain justification, and it enables him to slide into the discussion of legislation and jurisprudence in the later chapters without changing (or admitting he has changed) the subject. But in principle it is objectionable. If justice is anything like a moral virtue, it must be treated from the point of view of the part played by *logos* in shaping the lives of individuals. Later thinkers who think about justice on Aristotelian lines will pay more attention to the value of legality as such in determining rightness even in the form of fairness. Aristotle makes a beginning both in his claim that positive law is a sort of hypostatized *logos* and in his discussion of the natural basis of law at V vii; but his procedures have guaranteed that the issues will be confused at the outset.

2.2522 Distributive Justice (V iii; 1131a10–b24)

The anatomy I have just recapitulated is not tidily laid out in the actual treatment of the topic, though the latter is plainly meant to follow it. The treatment starts with what looks like an attempt to assimilate justice (in the narrow sense) in general to the formula for a moral virtue as a mean between extremes; but, if that is what it is, it involves a paralogism. If injustice is unfairness, i.e., inequality, then justice in the relevant opposite sense will be equality, as everyone agrees it is; and 'equal' is between 'more' and 'less,' a mean. But the 'mean' that defines a moral virtue is between excess and defect of feeling and action, and Aristotle does not explain how that applies in this case. Instead, we have a quite different point about what sort of equality justice involves, which is illustrated by one kind of justice (justice in distributions), and the discussion then slides into an account of this distributive justice, which is finally said to be merely one species of justice, the other being 'rectificatory.' It is not clear to the reader exactly when the discussion stopped being about justice (as fairness) in general and began to be about distributions in particular.

What seems to happen is something like this. Fairness is said, not to be a mean between less and more, but to be a mean in the sense that it involves mediation between two (or more) people; so there must be as many shares in the exchange or distribution as there are people. The minimum allocation allots x to A and y to B – and z to C and so on, if necessary. The requirement that there be two sets of terms, people and goods, with a minimum of two in each, is necessary and applies to fairness in general (1131a15–20). But this really becomes obvious only in general distributions, when equal allocations to unequal entitlements and unequal allocations to equal entitlements both give rise to complaints of 'unfairness' (= 'inequality'). This shows that the equality required is not that of amounts but of proportions: the ratio of A's entitlement to B's should equal the ratio of A's allocation to B's.[123] And Aristotle uses the example (but without saying it is only an example) of the 'just' allocation of powers and privileges in a state, which should go by *axia* – a term that, in addition to its general meaning of 'merit' or 'worth,' specifically denotes position in a hierarchical polity. Aristotle sums up his discussion by reverting to the other sense of 'mean,' according to which a proportional share is unfair if it is disproportionately large or small (1131b16–23). And it is immediately afterwards that Aristotle says that this is only one species of justice, the other being the corrective.

This is all quite chaotic, because several things are happening at once. One way of looking at things is to say that though there are always two sets, each having at least two terms, this can be discounted in situations where all entitlements are equal, as is the case in the lawcourts and the market-place. There is one price for all customers; everyone is equal before the law. So, in these cases, equality is established only among amounts of goods – the denominator is always 1, so we just add and subtract instead of multiplying and dividing.

This seems to be how Aristotle gets from the flat statement that all fairness is proportionality to the distinction between proportional and arithmetical fairness. But, in fact, all three kinds of fairness distinguished in the 'anatomy' involve two sets of terms. Distributions do so in an obvious way, for differentials in entitlements have to be established. But, as we shall see, even in the market-place, where the price is the same for all, there is quality as well as quantity to be taken into account, and the determinant of quality corresponds to the entitlement of persons. (This may seem an odd way of doing it, but what else would you suggest in the absence of any established theory of price?) Only in the lawcourts are all apparently equal – but it turns out that this is only a contingent fact, for an assault on a magistrate is unlikely to be penalized by the same tariff as an assault on a private citizen. Some animals are more equal than others.

2.2523 Rectificatory Justice (1131b25–1133b28 [V 7–8])

Rectificatory justice, as we saw from the anatomy, comes in two sorts, voluntary and involuntary, and Aristotle now repeats that – but in fact he goes on to talk about the 'involuntary' sort alone without mentioning the restriction. And when he goes over to the 'voluntary' sort it is not clear that he is doing so – he seems to be in the middle of a discussion of reciprocity (1132b30; cf. 1132b21, where both the medieval chapter divisions make the split).

2.25231 Righting Wrongs (1131b32–1132b30)

Athenian courts made a procedural break between verdict and sentence, as we see from Plato's *Apology*. In our own legal practice, we make a sharp distinction between the reaching of a verdict, in which the character and previous conduct of the accused are excluded from the deliberations, and the determination of the sentence, where the criminal's character and previous conduct may make a big difference. But Aristotle insists that the judge in 'involuntary' transactions, which it is evident from Aristotle's list include what we call crimes as well as torts, 'looks only to the distinctive character of the injury' (1132a4, trans. Ross), treating the parties as equal – even though he will have to correct this statement, as we have seen, to allow for cases when one of the parties is in an official position.[124] Why this insistence?

In part, Aristotle is simply reflecting Athenian practice, in which offences of one citizen against another, including murder, were treated as interpersonal transactions and not as offences against public order. An offence against the public, as in Socrates' alleged corruption of the youth at large and his rejection of the city's gods, was dealt with by a different procedure (in which, as I said, verdict and sentence were distinct). The only question in interpersonal transactions, then, is how damages are to be assessed.

The way Aristotle puts it is perhaps a bit surprising. He says that what the judge ignores is the moral character of the parties. But moral character is not an issue in distributive justice either: what matters there is relevant entitlement. And one might argue that relative entitlement is taken into account in such cases as those Aristotle mentions, in which encounters between private citizens and officials are not between equals.[125] (After all, it is one thing to knock off a fellow student's hat and quite another thing to knock off a policeman's helmet – and as for knocking off the queen's tiara, I would not advise that at all.) I suppose he might say (he certainly *could* say) that such differences in status are factored into the assessment of injury; but in fact he gives us no explanation at all.

The point Aristotle is making is clearly to emphasize that the law is concerned with the transaction as a transaction, not with the human relations involved. The parties are reduced to elements in an equation. It is this that distinguishes justice from friendship, in which the actual character of the associates is all-important; and the effect is that the city is a double institution, a formal association of citizens and an informal community of comrades, as the later discussion of friendship will make plain.

In explaining the function of a judge, which is to restore the initial equality between the parties, Aristotle says that the artificial concept of 'gain' (*kerdos*) is used for the advantage gained by the offender even in an assault case, so that the judge can be said to restore equality by taking away from the 'gain' and using it to repair the corresponding 'loss.' Aristotle gives us the basis of the calculation, but it seems absurdly overcomplicated;[126] clearly the principle is that the offender gives the victim or the surviving family whatever will count as restoring the status quo, and this can be interpreted as restoring *equality* between the parties only if damages awarded are thought of as corresponding to 'ill-gotten gains.' If fairness is to be literal equality, the fiction must be maintained.

Aristotle goes so far as to say that to resort to justice is to resort to a judge as intermediary, and that for this reason a judge (*dikastēs*) is called a mediator (*mesidios*) in some jurisdictions, the assumption being that the intermediary will be halfway between them, a midpoint between gain and loss; in fact, he derives the word *dikastēs* from *dicha*, 'in half' (1132a19–32).[127]

It is after explaining this notion of equalizing that Aristotle rebuts the common notion that justice involves retribution (*to antipeponthos*), which is the way the Pythagoreans defined justice (1132b21–3). The idea is a natural application of the demand for equality ('an eye for an eye'), but is fundamentally misleading. His initial objection is that such retribution ignores the differences made by status, as remarked above, but his basic objection is more fundamental and is summed up in the remark that it ignores the difference between the voluntary and the involuntary. The point is that 'tit for tat' does not seek to cancel the initial involuntary transaction, but to complete it. Thus its tendency is to initiate (or continue) a feud, not to right a wrong.

People want revenge, he says, because it is the condition of freedom: to suffer an injury without returning it reduces one to the condition of slavery, subjecting one to the other's will. Self-help in 'doing good to one's friends and hurting one's enemies' is a popular Greek idea, testifying to one's freedom and power.[128] But it is plainly a bad idea, just because it denies the difference between involuntary transactions, which ought to be cancelled and neutralized, and voluntary transactions, which should go forward. That is why the injured party submits the case to an intermediary, who stands for abstract justice, the intermediate amount, the personification of *logos* which respects equality 'in proportion' (*kat' analogian*, that is, *ana logon*).

It is in voluntary transactions that reciprocity reigns, that each participant should seek to bring the deal to a completion in which each party gets what is proportionally 'the same.' Basically, it is proportionate equality in exchanges that holds the city together (1132b33–4). It seems to follow from this that, if legal redress is not available, private revenge is a real private and civic good, converting the passive suffering of wrongs into an interactive context for which one assumes responsibility and thus maintains self-respect. But that is not what the legal system is for. Here, as so often, Aristotle refrains from making a strong statement that his arguments seem to have prepared.

Reciprocity, to antipeponthos, is a pre-civilized principle; it is what law supersedes. In it, individuals and injuries both take default values – my eye equals your eye – because this is the only definite value that can be assigned them in the absence of a determinate sociopolitical structure. What law does is, precisely, to raise 'equality' and 'justice' to the conceptual level of logos *and* logismos.

2.25232 Commerce (1132b31–1133b28)

Distributive justice and injustice continue to be practised because distributions have to be made somehow. In Aristotle's favourite example, somebody has to rule, to fulfil the various public functions of the state; a bonanza must be distributed on some principle or other. And the distributions must add up to 100 per cent: all the money must be got rid of, but only the money there is; all offices must be filled, but only the offices there are.

Similarly, rectificatory justice has to proceed somehow. As we have just seen, the meaning of the vital principle of reciprocity is that free people simply will not submit to being passive recipients of injury, as if they were slaves. Consequently, either the principle of revenge will prevail (where there is no law), or the law must follow the artificial principle of assessing 'gains' and 'damages' to act out, as it were, the cancellation of the iniquitous transaction, which from the victim's point of view was 'involuntary.'

The justice involved in market transactions and other freely negotiated exchanges individuals (or between states, for that matter) is quite different. Its principle must be reciprocity, the perception that each party will benefit equally, because that is the only principle on which people will freely enter into relationships. But also, both parties must actually desire to trade: there must be something each wants, something which each is ready to give for it. Otherwise they simply will not enter into the relationship.[129]

It is this double requirement, of equality in exchange and of a common desire to trade, that explains (in Aristotle's view) the use of money. Money (typically a coinage in an imperishable material that has a considerable and fairly constant value and can be cut and moulded into recognizable pieces of a standard size) can be used as a measure to which all exchangeable goods can be reduced (cf. Plato's *Laws* XI, 918B): if I want some lumber from you, I use a monetary term to say how much I want ('a mna's worth'), and what I have to give you for that amount is the corresponding amount of what I have ('a mna's worth of olive oil').[130] Or I can just give you a mna, a mna's worth of currency. And that is the second function of money: it not only provides a measure, it functions as a sort of solid equivalent of wants (needs and desires). How much I want your lumber is shown by how much money I am prepared to give you for it (*beforehand*, says Aristotle), and if I don't have any money (or anything that other people want enough to give me money for) my wanting has, as it were, no social reality. Keeping a stock of money is my assurance that when I do want something that is on the market my want can be effective.

Money can fulfil this second function only if its value is stable – or relatively stable; we will choose for our currency something (like diamonds, and unlike oil) for which the relation between supply and demand varies as little as possible.

What, then, is a just price? According to the present account, it is that which represents reciprocity in terms of wants, or anticipated satisfactions, represented by an agreed price, which expresses the perceived quality and quantity of whatever is to be exchanged. In other words, it is subjective and variable. The amounts can be determined, and perhaps the quality of the goods can be agreed on (in agricultural products, at least, there are established grades); but in addition there are the respective desires of the participants at the moment of exchange, and it is on the anticipated satisfaction of these desires that the voluntary transaction rests. The underlying institution is that of the market, in which individual buyers and sellers come together and bargain with each other. But this bargaining is carried out on the basis of the actual amount and quality of the goods to be exchanged. Aristotle gives us all the materials for this model of a market, but what he does not do is put them together for us. Quality, for instance, as we have seen, is simply identified with the relative merits of the exchanging parties, though it is quite clear that it is quality of merchandise that is at issue. So Aristotle does not actually articulate a theory of value, not even a bad one.

It is clear that a just price need not be based on a free market in the sense considered here. A 'fair price' can be established by regulation; governments have done this from time to time. Justice would be served by specifying how much work and skill it takes to produce a certain commodity, and reciprocity is assured by saying that what that exchanges for is always what takes the same amount of work and degree of skill to produce, according to some formula. Aristotle's apparent insistence that commerce depends on desire is taken care of by saying that if you want the goods you must pay what they are worth – in our industrial societies we seldom bargain, and do not usually feel that this infringes on our freedom.[131] But Aristotle does not mention this possibility. A centralized economy cannot control demand, and price controls work well only in very restricted contexts.

2.2524 Conclusion (1133b29–1134a16)

Aristotle winds up by saying that justice is indeed a virtue, and hence a mean, but not in the same way as the other virtues, 'but because it relates to an intermediate amount,' and injustice relates to the extremes (1133b33–1134a1) – whereas the other virtues were dispositions to make choices in a way intermediate between the corresponding vices, justice is a disposition to make choices fairly, and injustice is a disposition to make choices unfairly by admitting both excess and defect, as the case may be.[132] So, in a case of injustice, there is excess on the one side and deficiency on the other, and just action (dikaiopragia) is intermediate between acting unjustly (and getting too much) and being unjustly treated (and getting too little).

There is something vertiginous in this manipulation of the concept of the mean, in which what looks like the formula for a moral virtue is cut loose from its moorings.[133] But the explanation, as I said before, is simple. In the case of justice, virtuous action is cut loose from its foundation in psychology, so that the perspectives of agent, of victim, and of administrator and lawgiver slide into each other. Instead of the moral motive of action *tou kalou heneka*, for the very splendour of doing the right thing, applying to the way one handles one's other motives, it becomes itself the sole motive.

Some commentators, including Gauthier and Jolif, say that these 'concluding' remarks after the discussion of commutative justice are out of place – perhaps another of those scraps of papyrus supposed to have been stuck in almost at random. But why? We do, after all, need an answer to the question what sort of a mean justice is, and after the anatomy is the right place for it. Showing how different it is forms the necessary basis for the ensuing retractation of the topics discussed in III i–v. The counter-argument would have to be that, despite the proposed anatomy (which actually breaks down), the introduction of the radical distinction between justice and mere reciprocity marks the new topic, which goes straight on from there to deal with 'political justice' as based on artificial systems of value. But that arrangement, though plausible in its own way, would be equally open to objection, because it would leave the anatomy incomplete and the question 'what sort of mean?' inadequately answered.

2.253 Justice, the State, and the Will (V vi to end; 1134a17–1138b14)

The preceding discussion was said to end the treatment of the nature (*phusis*) of justice. 'Nature' can hardly be meant literally; I suppose what it means is the objective reality of justice as a coherent system of behaviour, the ubiquitous social phenomenon that the word *justice* primarily picks out. If so, what follows must have to do with variable aspects of the way societies operate in this domain, or something like that.

The discussion we embark on now is said to be about the distinction between doing something unjust (in the broad sense of 'wrong,' apparently, since adultery is the example) and being an unjust person – a subject already dealt with in II iv. Then we are abruptly told that we must not forget something we were never told, namely, that we are concerned with political justice as well as with justice *sans phrase* (*haplōs*) (1134a24–6); and we start talking about law. What is the underlying continuity here?

The last thing we said about the 'nature' of justice is that it is not a mean in the same way as the other virtues: it is related to a *meson*, rather than being itself a *mesotēs*. But that reopens the question of II iv, where it was being settled in an intermediate disposition that chiefly distinguished the good action of the good person from the good actions of other people. It is still true that the action that issues from injustice is one that is the outcome of choice rather than passion (a formulation not at our disposal in II iv, because we had not distinguished choice from voluntariness, but representing no real change); but the choice distinctive of justice is now seen to be different, as follows.

When we introduced the idea of reciprocity (*to antipeponthos*) we did so as a sort of natural precursor of the kinds of justice that are involved in distribution and in legal rectifications. It is a pre-political sense of fairness that free people rely on in their mutual transactions as the expression of their freedom. The act of a just person might well be the act that issued from a habit of choosing on the basis of that sense of freedom and reciprocity. But that cannot be the whole of our answer, because reciprocity is not the whole of justice. There is also 'political justice'; but political justice rests on the artificial assigning of a sort of quantifiable basis to citizens as members of a constitution and as parties to lawsuits.[134] So presumably what is characteristic of the just person in this sense is some relation to the artificial system of the constitution and laws. It is the relevant ins and outs of these artificialities that will chiefly occupy us from now on.

How does the discussion of the 'nature of justice' as a virtue, now concluded, lead into the convoluted discussions of justice and legality on which we are now embarked? Well, the prime example of distributive justice, one of the two manifestations of the virtue, is the constitutional division of powers in a political organization; and the prime example of corrective justice, the other manifestation, is legal intervention in disputes. But constitution makers need have no involvement in the state for which they legislate, and judges normally have no involvement in the cases they decide; and judges have no interest even in the moral merits of the parties to disputes. The whole connection between wickedness and injustice is thus up for grabs, even apart from the peculiarities of the way in which justice is a mean. Of course, what was said in II iv was true, that a just person is one who deliberately and regularly performs just actions and so on; but what does that come to, in what now appears to be a very different case? We clearly have some unfinished business.

There is the question of voluntariness (of which choice is a subdivision, we saw). The person who receives an unjust share should be the unjust person, for he or she is the only person to whom the desire for 'gain' (*kerdos*) can be relevantly ascribed – but the initiator of the transaction is likely to be someone else, awarding an unjust gain to someone who is passive in the matter.

There is also the relation between legality and rightness. Aristotle remarked, in relation to the 'universal' sense of justice, that the state is concerned with morality only in the public domain, so that the involvement of the state in private morality remains uncertain. But the point was made in entirely general terms: we do not know what it comes to.[135] In *Politics* III, the domain of politics in determining what a good citizen is is subjected to severe restrictions, having to do only with the actual operating of the political organization; but no such restriction has been made here. On the contrary, politics was introduced in I ii as having the human good as its unrestricted domain. Meanwhile, the whole relation between political and moral virtue remains moot. The stipulation on which the positive content of the *Ethics* is based, that there is such a thing as being serious about how to live the best human life, and that this involves guiding oneself by the best use of *logos*, rules out the possibility that the state can legislate morality; and yet the state does enact laws, and respectable people are law-abiding. This really has to be cleared up.

Another aspect of the same problem is the role of the intellectual virtue of *phronēsis* in this domain. In the other moral virtues, the judgment of the 'prudent' (*phronimos*) person is the standard; this cannot be dispensed with, because an action is right only in relation to its immediate occasion (*kairos*), which, of course, cannot be reduced to general terms. But the law deals in generalities, so to act by law is to act *against* the immediate requirement of virtue, and the judge who applies the law must similarly ignore the unique features of the situation. Something must be done about this (and it will be, under the heading 'equity').

Another obvious way in which the account of the 'nature' of justice leaves us with unfinished business is that justice as a particular virtue concerned with loss and gain has now been seen to operate within a peculiarly artificial framework. Judges calculate damages in accordance with a frankly metaphorical notion of 'gain,' and reduce the individuals they deal with to numerical factors in an equation; even commercial transactions proceed by putting a numerical value on one person's goods and skills in relation to those of others, and accept an artificial 'currency' as a medium of exchange; the places of citizens in the constitution are determined not by their individual personalities but by assigning them to one or the other of a set of artificial categories defined by the constitution itself. The nature of this formal system, and its relation to the natural lives of the people who enter into it, is clearly something that urgently needs discussion.

In what follows, the distinction between justice in the narrow sense and justice in the broad sense seems to be abandoned. One could say that it was only intended, in the first place, to apply to the discussion now concluded; but that is not the impression the reader was given. One might better say that the distinction itself proved unstable. It looked like a good idea, separating justice as fairness from justice as universal virtue in the interpersonal domain; but then the interpersonal domain turned out, for practical purposes, to be the *public* domain, and then we found out that in the public domain everything is treated as if it were a matter of gain and loss (and thus a matter for fairness) anyway. Even if we do not go that far, we must admit that, in the domain of rectificatory justice, the offending party may have committed any sort of wrongdoing, injustice in the broad sense, but the justice of the court itself is justice in the narrow sense, as fairness. And the judge can apply this, as we have seen, only by treating the offence as if it were a case of unfairness, translating the offender's wrongdoing as a kind of *kerdos* and the victim's injury as if it were a cash penalty (*zēmia*). So the court effectively transforms the nature of the offence into an artificial equivalent. Once more, the status of this artificial construct is an urgent issue.

All the foregoing issues are discussed as variants of a single question: what is the difference between an action classified as wrong ('unjust') by a given legal system (and its agents) and a really wicked deed? It is within this framework that the basis of law is discussed, and a certain continuity can (we shall see) be made out. But the discussion is certainly not well ordered, and the basis of its articulation is not made explicit. The arrangement in detail seems chaotic, and reduces commentators to despairing conjecture as to what series of textual accidents might have occasioned such disorder. But I think all we have to say is that there are a lot of questions that all have to be answered, and that (as we have seen) the basic distinctions we are trying to operate with keep collapsing. In short, *EN* here presents us with thought in progress, and why not? Nobody thinks it is a work prepared for publication, and it is only in the context of publication that tidiness as such would be an issue. Meanwhile, no other arrangement of this complex material would be a clear improvement, so far as I can see.

2.2531 Illegality and Wrongdoing (V vi–viii; 1134a17–1136a9)

One can do something wrong without being a bad person. What makes the difference? We know already that, from the point of view of the theory of the moral virtues, it is a matter of the state of mind of the agent – the intention and the disposition. But, in the light of what we know about the peculiarities of justice, can we simply transpose that into the context of justice, and say the same thing about the difference between committing an offence (adikēma) and being an evil-doer (adikos)? Not quite, but nearly. To see this we have to make a wide circle through the whole notion of political justice – or rather, to explain how justice itself is a political notion without being a violation of nature.

What seems to be the unspoken basis of the discussion is a favourite sophistic theme from the fifth century: the contrast between law and nature. One version of this contrast has it that law is a matter of convention, so that penalties imposed by law are inherently arbitrary, whereas the penalties imposed by nature (in the form of the actual consequences of one's actions and those of others) are real.[136] So where does justice come in? One answer can be found in the work of Epicurus, in the generation after Aristotle: justice is a set of rules agreed on in a community to secure the common good; the content of the rules varies from community to community; if a set of rules fails to secure the common good, then it does not have the force of justice, but it still bears the stamp of justice.[137] And this is really what Aristotle's solution comes down to. The crucial sentence in this regard is at 1134b18–19: 'Of political justice, part is natural and part is conventional' – followed by a version of the sophistical contrast between those terms. In other words, justice is not contrasted with nature or identified with nature as against convention, but comprises elements of both sorts.[138]

Justice exists only within a political framework. But an offence against justice as established by law is a real offence – there is, in effect, no other justice to be appealed to. To understand the force of this, we really have to look at the beginning of the Politics, according to which the good life is possible only in a political setting, because it is only in such a setting that *logos* as articulate speech and thought about values is possible. There is no properly human nature without some sort of community that is, in at least a vestigial sense, political. So, when it comes down to it, since the law is, in a sense, the basis of justice, the difference between what is illegal and what is a sign of wickedness can only lie in the agent's awareness of and involvement in the violation of the law as such.

Aristotle begins rather obscurely by apparently ruling out the possibility that being *adikos* could simply be explained as committing one of the actions legally defined as crimes, such as theft or adultery (1134a17–21).[139] This won't do, because one could steal something without being a thief, commit adultery without 'adulterer' being an appropriate description of one's character.[140]

I take it that the point of this suggestion is that 'thief' and 'adulterer' are, in fact, legal terms, applicable only to actions that are wrong, as stated at 1107a9–12. An 'ordinary language' philosopher might explain this by making it a matter of linguistic usage – people do not apply the word *theft* to an action unless they condemn it; but Aristotle's point here is rather that a society codifies its condemnations in a system of legal definitions. If you have committed a theft you have certainly committed an offence, whereas you might have done something wrong about which there was no such certainty. That is true, but it is not the point at issue here.

There is indeed a context in which one can inflict a wrongful injury without committing a named offence, and this is in the unstructured, pre-political condition in which reciprocity reigns. A perceived injury then provokes what the victim sees as an equivalent retaliation. The motive here, however, is not fairness, but something to do with personal dignity. In a sense, this is justice (cf. 1132b21, where Aristotle attributes to the Pythagoreans just the phrase he uses here, 'justice *sans phrase*,' *haplōs dikaion*); but 'we must not forget' that what we are talking about is something more specific: political justice, justice in a political system which assigns to offender and victim a formal status of equality (or proportionate rankings).[141] And this is the only proper form of justice. Only individuals freely sharing their lives can be brought into the close quasi-quantitative relations that make real justice possible, and the enforcing of proper compliance with these relations requires explicit law and an impersonal authority to enforce the law. So it is the law, the abstract system, that rules, and not the magistrates, who merely administer it (and have to be paid, in honour and privilege [why not in salary?]). Justice exists only among those who have an equal (or proportionate) share in ruling or being ruled. Political justice, one might say, is the domain in human life in which the *logon echon* has most unrestricted sway.

In *Politics* I and in *EN* VIII x, the city, the community of free and equal individuals sharing their lives, is seen as an outgrowth of the family, itself a community but not based on choice or on equality. In a well-ordered household people are treated fairly. But this is not justice, because neither slaves nor children have independent standing on the basis of which they can be brought into the proportionate relations that are the foundation of proper justice. Only between the free adults is there something like equality of status, but even among them there is not mutual independence. In short, even foreigners can trade fairly, on the basis of reciprocity; family members can behave fairly to each other; but there is no real justice outside the very special context of a city ruled by law.

Aristotle belabours this point, and I belabour it on his behalf, because it is crucial, and determines the answer to our initial question about the difference between an offence against justice and a truly unjust act. The difference can only be in the way offenders relate to the illegality of their acts. Since justice proper has no reality outside the legal order, one cannot appeal against that order to some 'higher' justice.[142]

We cannot, then, set up a contrast between natural justice and positive law: 'and if some things are disgraceful in truth, and other things disgraceful only in repute (*kata doxan*), it makes no difference – neither is to be done' (1128b23). But not all laws are natural. Some things are wrong everywhere, even if there is no law against them (we make laws against them because they *are* wrong), other things are wrong only because there is a law against them (like driving on the 'wrong' side of the road). Ubiquity is not the issue: it could be that everyone was by nature right-handed, and it could still be the case that every legal system in the world required people to use their left hands. In any case, a law is a law.

What a law does, in relation to the problem that concerns us, is to set up a kind of action that is forbidden. Such conduct is said to be 'unlawful,' 'unjust' (*adikon*) – English idiom resists Aristotle's equations here. The assumption is that such conduct inflicts harm (*blabē*), as will appear later (1135b11 ff.), though this is not argued; I suppose the idea is that if no harm is done no one will go to court, since in Athenian law only an injured person (or someone legitimately acting on the injured person's behalf) can bring a suit. In any case, we develop a vocabulary (which Aristotle says must be examined on a later occasion – but, if it ever was, we don't know about it): the law defines a class of actions each of which when performed is an act-of-injustice (*adikēma*).

In the light of the foregoing, we can give a fairly precise answer to our question. The law defines classes of actions that are *adika* and any one of which will be an *adikēma*; unjust people will be those who commit *adikēmata* in a way that shows such actions to be typical of them. A person may commit such an action by accident or unknow-ingly; or without thinking of its illegality; or casually, or deliberately, intending just that aspect of it that made it forbidden – in other words, with malice aforethought. So the law distinguishes, or should distinguish, between misadventures, and mistakes, and acts of wrongdoing; but the acts that are inherently signs of an unjust person are those that are deliberately chosen for the harm they can do – provided, adds Aristotle, that they violate equality; as, of course, they always do, if Aristotle's analysis has been on the right lines.[143]

It is evident to everyone that what Aristotle is doing here is simply revising the discussions of II iv and III i–iv to fit the special context of justice. The difference this makes is that the framework is that of prima facie violations of a code of offences, within a population whose members interact as equals. On further reflection, though, it occurs to us that *EN* has three discussions of the failure of knowl-edge in action: in III i–v, on the nature of action itself; here in V, on the allocation of blame in accordance with degrees of responsibility and conditions of care; and in VII, on the difficulty of maintaining the connections within one's practical reasoning. The question to ask ourselves is not so much whether they agree with each other as whether the omission of material from one of the discussions dam-ages one of the other discussions in its own terms – whether degree of willingness, degree of thoughtfulness, and degree of conscious control, can be segregated to the extent that Aristotle does here.[144]

The really clever bit in the present passage, I think, is Aristotle's casual insertion into this context of the concept of harm (*blabē*): bad people are those who deliberately break the law, not from a spirit of lawlessness or from graspingness (the antithesis of justice as fairness), but from the actual will to do harm, the harm that the law exists to prevent people inflicting on each other.[145] And we note that the proviso of II iv, that bad people act out of a steady disposition to choose in the wrong way, is dropped here. The law is not concerned with character in *that* sense; and, as we have seen, the idea of a state of character that is a general will to do harm, and a habit of doing so, does not fit well into Aristotle's general account of moral virtue.

2.2532 Crime and the Law (V ix–xi; 1136a10–1138b14)

2.25321 The Order of Treatment

A number of points remain to be discussed. The order of treatment is puzzling at first, in the same way that the end of Book VI is: both passages consist of discursive and untidy discussions of the social ramifications of legal and practical thinking, respectively, which cannot be reduced to a system because they arise from multiple mutual adjustments of disparate concerns.

The opening section (1136a10–1137a4 [V 11–12]) raises three questions that arise naturally from the immediately preceding account of the relation between justice and deliberation:

1 / Can a person voluntarily *undergo* an injury, or does the concept of an injury require that it be against (or independent of) the patient's will?
2 / In an unfair distribution, who is unfair, the distributor or the person favoured?
3 / Can one treat oneself unjustly?

It is easy to see that these questions are interrelated. But the discussion of them is broken off, to be resumed without comment in V xi. In between comes an independent discussion of equity (V x) (itself a topic obviously raised by the relation of universal law to particular act), preceded by a discussion of the implications of the relation of justice to deliberation (1137a4–30 [V 13]) that is, equally obviously, a direct sequel to V viii and somewhat more loosely related to the treatment of equity. That is, there is an interweaving of what seem to be two mutually independent sequels to V viii. How is the order of treatment to be explained?

One possibility is that two pages of Aristotle's original manuscript got transposed: 1136a10–1137a4 (V 11–12) is about the same length as 1137a4–1138a2 (V 13–14), about seventy lines, or about as much as would go, written fairly small, on a largeish sheet of papyrus.[146] The original order will then have started with equity (and its introduction) and gone on to the three interrelated problems. The transposition will have escaped notice because the discussion on one of the sheets happened to be a self-contained whole, and the other ended with a complete sentence.

One does not like to rearrange a text instead of interpreting it, unless one has to, and in this case there are two reasons against doing so. One is that whoever edited our present text was obviously a person of acumen and enterprise, and could hardly have failed to diagnose so elementary a mishap if it had really produced a non sequitur. The other is that, although 1137a4–1138a2 (V 13–14) appear in the midst of a continuous discussion, they do so not at an arbitrary point but at the only place where they could reasonably have been inserted as a digression, at the end of the answers to the two questions in which the theme of voluntariness predominates and before that in which it is only one theme among others.

The actual order of treatment is explained if we look at the two other places in the Aristotelian corpus where the subject-matter of V vi–viii is dealt with. In the Rhetoric, it is followed by a discussion of equity, with a slightly different introduction, and the 'three problems' are not dealt with at all.[147] In MM, the subject-matter of V vi–viii is immediately followed by the equivalent of 1136a10–1137a4 (V 11–12) and V xi, and the equivalent of 1137a4–1138a2 (V 13–14) is incorporated into the treatment of intellectual virtue.[148] Both continuations from V vi–viii are equally natural; but the position of the discussion of equity in MM, separate from the discussion of moral virtue, makes no sense. So, if you were the author, what would you do if you wanted to combine both trains of thought and use both continuations? If you start with equity, there is a complete break at the end of it and the discussion of the relation between voluntariness and justice is split into two. But if you put the 'three problems' first, you have no natural way of leading into the topic of equity. Besides, the end of Book V as we have it is a very good ending, bringing the whole discussion of moral virtue round full circle from where it began in I xiii, with a critique of Plato's partition of the soul and an attack on the very heart of his doctrine of virtue, in general, and justice, in particular. Your best solution would be to put equity just where we find it, between the second and third 'problems'; its introduction, treating the relation of justice to deliberation, makes a natural transition from the 'problems' that treat of justice and the voluntary. But the subject-matter of all three 'problems' is, on the face of it, so closely allied that the statement of them could not reasonably be separated – it is in the statement of the solutions that the importance of the difference between the first two and the third becomes evident. In fact, the present arrangement is really the best possible. All that is wrong with it is that the presentation is careless (as it so often is throughout V), leaving a hiatus at the end of V x and failing to integrate the details.

2.25322 Justice and Voluntariness ('Problems 1 & 2') (1136a10–1137a4 [V11–12])

The problems dealt with here seem to contribute little to the advancement of Aristotle's project, but they arise legitimately from the anomalies produced by the insistence on treating justice as a virtue with only one opposing vice. The vice of injustice is motivated by the love of gain, *kerdos*. Justice is motivated by the rational desire for the mean, the right amount. But, as we see from the exchange of armour between Glaucus and Diomede in *Iliad* VI (1136b10–11), people enter willingly into exchanges in which they get the worse of a bargain. What could motivate them? It is the question raised by Thrasymachus in Plato's *Republic* I: not only do they abstain from injustice, they do not even insist on their rights. It is a problem for practical politics. Why do people put up with regimes that treat them unfairly?

Aristotle inserts this problem into the context of the relation between injustice and the will, which in its more general form looks quite different: can a person be said willingly to undergo unjust treatment? Here, the question is not why people willingly submit themselves but whether, if one is literally undergoing something, the question of willingness or unwillingness arises at all. It is a problem around which the Stoics were to build a major theme of their ethics.

Aristotle's treatment of his problem is ravelled and inconclusive, and I do not quite understand it. I provide the best sketch I can and hope it will serve.

2.253221 Can People Willingly Be Treated Unjustly?

Well, they can willingly suffer actions of an 'unjust' sort, consent to have illegal things done to them or accept less than a fair price; but (a) they are not victims of unfairness or wickedness unless unfairness or wickedness (as defined at the end of V viii) has been committed; (b) they are not *wronged*, if they *wish* to have the 'wrong' thing done to them, for it is what they want, and no one *wishes* 'to be unjustly treated,' so it is not *qua* wrong or unjust act that they wish it; (c) since a voluntary action (as defined in III i) is one in the agent's power, one in which the essential source of the action is within the agent, the injuries to which people submit are not voluntary for them – they must wait for someone to come along and injure them. Only the act of submission is voluntary, we might say – but Aristotle does not venture into that territory.

Aristotle supports the thesis that people cannot be wronged against their will by suggesting that one might make it part of the definition of 'harming' that it be against the victim's will (1136b4); but this is an ad hoc suggestion, since elsewhere he finds it enough to define injustice as the willing commission of an illegal injury (1138a8; *Rhetoric* I, 1368b6). The context, however, suggests a more startling interpretation. Aristotle treats the situation as a matter of weakness of will (1136b1). Gauthier and Jolif think he must mean 'softness' (which would fit Thrasymachus's diagnosis in the *Republic*), the victim of injustice merely gives in. But I think the point is rather that the victims in unfair transactions that are freely undertaken are really doing it to themselves, just as weak-willed people really do things that violate their own principles. The victim acts neither on the principle of justice nor on the principle of injustice, but on some motive that is irrelevant to the issue of justice or injustice. 'Anything for a quiet life,' perhaps. We shall see later that something analogous is true of the 'disinterested' perpetrator of an unjust distribution or verdict: some motive extraneous to the merits of the case must be operative. What makes it a case of *akrasia* is not that the victim fails to stand up to the exploiter, but that the victim fails to stand by the relevant moral principles (and appropriate wishes) by which deliberation should be guided. ('Wish,' we recall, in the context of the theory of choice of III ii–iv, is ultimately taken to be the rational formulation of one's overall orientation towards what one best knows to be good.)

2.253222 Unjust Distributors

Is it the unfair distributor who is unjust, or the people whom the distribution favours? Obviously the former. Distributors who favour others at their own expense are not committing an injury against themselves because what they suffer is what they wish; and, whether the unfairness is at the expense of the distributor or of a third party, the fault lies with the distributor who acts and not with the passive recipient of the favour. But also, as we have just suggested, distributors who favour others at their own expense must be getting something out of it – honour, or sheer goodness (*to haplōs kalon*); and if they favour others at a third party's expense, again there must be something in it for them – 'gratitude or revenge,' or some more tangible rake-off.[149] Actually, two points are made here. The first is that the unjust judge or distributor must have some positive reason for departing from the principle of justice, which is, as it were, built into the situation itself – if the 'just proportion' is not respected, there must be some alternative basis for action. The second point is that any alternative basis must belong to the agent's own system of motivation, from which it follows that even an unselfish person must be acting out of self-interest *in some sense* – the very fact that people act unselfishly proves that unselfishness may give satisfaction. The theme is taken up and developed in the discussion of friendship (IX viii).

The thesis Aristotle argues here flirts with the notoriously tricky position known as 'psychological egoism,' in its Kantian form according to which all actions other than those done from a motive of conformity to law must be done from self-interest. Essentially, he can be seen as correcting the Thrasymachean (and perhaps Platonic) equation of injustice with crude *pleonexia*, the logically insatiable desire for 'more.' On the view Aristotle is promoting, to be just *or unjust* is to be rightly or wrongly active in relation to an objective mean, a mean actually embodied in a proportion relating actual people to actual goods. It is true that this proportion is only to be established by means of conventions; but these conventions are not to be relegated to a separate Platonic realm but (as with Aristotle's view of mathematical and quantitative thinking generally) to the world of ordinary experience viewed in a suitable abstractive way. But the Platonic view represents the just as acting out of *love* for the ideal world in which their abstract formulae subsist, and the unjust as acting from greed. Aristotle separates those who act unjustly from those who gain. The latter do in a sense act unjustly, because they carry out or acquiesce in the unjust acts of the distributors, and the distributors do, in a sense, profit, but that is not what makes them unjust. What makes them unjust is their disregard for justice, not their motive for disregarding it. In the strictest and most straightforward senses, the unjust distributor does not, as such, profit, and the favourite does not, as such, act.

2.253223 *Can People Treat Themselves Unjustly?*

It follows from what we have already said that obviously they cannot – what they do to themselves must be what they wish. But further considerations unrelated to the ones we have been discussing bear on this problem, which is taken up independently after the digression on equity.

2.25323 The Unjust and the Unlawful (1137a4–1138a3 [V 13–14])

The discussion of equity, though announced as a fresh topic, is presented within the context of a wider discussion that develops straight out of the distinction between *adikon* and *adikēma*, what is forbidden and what is actually wrong. Concentrating on the former, on universal prescriptions and prohibitions, makes right and wrong seem much simpler affairs than they actually are, both in the context of the law itself (V x) and in the context of virtuous activity in general, which is taken up first.

2.253231 Justice as Virtue (1137a4–30 [V 13])

Concentrating on the *adikon*, on the content of moral or positive law, makes it seem a simple matter to achieve justice, in the broad sense of virtuous behaviour towards other people. The law seems easy to understand ('Thou shalt not commit adultery' – what could be simpler?), so one can see what one has to avoid; what could be easier than to avoid it? It is up to us whether we break the law or not; therefore, it is up to us whether we are good or not. But that is not true. We have already seen that having any virtue is not 'up to us' in the sense that we can attain it by a single decision – to be virtuous is to be the kind of person who acts well 'as the result of a certain state of character.'[150] But, in the particular case of justice, in its broadest sense of abstaining from doing to one's neighbour what the law classifies as an injury, the temptation to oversimplify is especially strong. With the other virtues, the *logos* to be observed is definable only as that by which a sensible person (*phronimos*) would judge; but in the case of justice the law states the *logos*. The *logos* a sensible person would use can be discovered only by becoming a sensible person oneself (which, we shall see, requires becoming morally virtuous), or by asking a sensible person's advice (cf. VI x); the *logos* of the law can be found by reading the law. This apparent simplicity, though, is illusory: the law cannot include rules for its own application – and, if it did, it could not include rules for applying *those* rules, and so ad infinitum. One might as well imagine that one could practise medicine because one had read a textbook.

Justice, in fact, like all the virtues, is something peculiar to the human condition – the condition of a being living a life shot through with *logos* in situations not prefabricated for intellectual analysis, whose life is not constituted by *logos* nor wholly resistant to *logos*, and whose ability to make a proper use of good things (and hence deservingness of them) is neither infinite (as a god's might be) nor zero (as a devil's might be – though Aristotle's cosmos has no place for devils). And the human condition, as we have insisted from the start of the *Ethics*, is such that no universal statements about its values are true without restriction. Every case is a special case – or rather, every case must be treated as a special case because it may turn out to be one.

2.253232 Equity (V x; 1137a31–1138a3)

If the law cannot be applied automatically to individual cases, it must be because there are some actions that plainly come under the wording of the law but are equally plainly not what the law was meant to apply to – or, conversely, are excluded by the wording but should be included. The law is not merely too vague, but too simple.[151] The same will apply to the voluntary exchanges of commerce: unforeseen changes in conditions may render the current terms of a contract inappropriate and its literal fulfilment unfair. In such cases a judge will best apply the law by not applying it, attending instead to 'what the legislator himself would have put into the law, if he had known' (1137b23); and the parties to a contract will best apply it by ignoring its actual terms and recalling its intention. Such departures from the letter of the law are called 'equity,' and we think better of people for thus failing to insist on their rights.

   Our justification of equity gives rise to a problem. The peculiarity of justice in relation to the other moral virtues is its relation to the letter of a law, a precisely and objectively formulated *logos*. How then can equity be praiseworthy (and praiseworthy as an improvement *in justice*) if it abandons this *logos*? Or, if it is praiseworthy, does that not show that justice is no good? But modern commentators on fifth-century Athens observe that the exaltation of justice and the law was the mainstay of the 'bourgeois' morality that had replaced the status-values of archaic feudalism, and which Plato and Aristotle were, in effect, seeking to perfect by incorporating aristocratic ideals into it; so the worth of justice must not be undermined.[152] Aristotle accordingly has to say that there is no contradiction between justice and equity, because the precise formulations of laws and contracts are meant to apply only to the usual case, and are strictly applicable only to the species to which they refer. Equity is simply the recognition of the human condition in the application of laws and contracts to individual cases with all their peculiarities. It does not cancel the law but (as Aristotle suggests when he refers to what the lawgiver would have said *if he had been there*, 1137b23) revivifies it.

In one way, any discussion in English of the relation between 'justice' and 'equity' is misleading. In English, both are words with a strong legal flavour, even if 'equity' nowadays covers a somewhat different range of phenomena from those dealt with here. But the Greek word, *epieikeia*, ranges more widely. At the end of Book II especially, the *epieikēs* figures just as the decent, respectable person, in contrast with the *phaulos*, the low and dirty rascal. Equity, that is, starts out as a word for civilized conduct, the behaviour of people who do not stoop to insist on their rights. Justice is for people who rely on formally quantifiable relationships because they cannot trust each other to do the proper thing. That is very different from the relationship that Aristotle describes, but I am sure it is subliminally present and is very important. In effect, one asks: how can justice be so good, when decent people do not have recourse to it and are not bound by it? And the answer is that what the feelings of decent people impel them to do is not something other than justice, but the proper application of justice itself. It is what justice becomes, we might say (though Aristotle certainly would not), when it becomes a virtue, a habit of behaviour in accordance with what good sense dictates.

The relation between justice and equity represents a pattern that recurs throughout the *Ethics* – not surprisingly, since we have seen that it is the pattern imposed on practical reasoning by the human condition. We find it in politics, in the relation between legislation and administration.[153] In the domain of good sense, we find the same relation between knowing in general terms what is good and bad, and being able to tell on each occasion what it is desirable to do (cf. 1141b14–28). And it is the basis of the original methodological caveat about the limits of moral philosophy (I iii). In all such cases, we are told, it is the ability to make the correct judgment in the particular case that really counts; given that, the ability to formulate the correct generalization is superfluous. In fact, in the general discussion of moral virtue and its ruling *logos* such generalizations play no part at all. And yet Aristotle insists that they exist and are important. The significance of the discussion of equity in the economy of the *Ethics*

as a whole is that it is only here that general rules are not only introduced but given priority. It is the legal and political context that
requires us to convert our unselfconscious procedures into rules and
thus make our *telos* into a *skopos*, stating what the questions are that
our practical policies and decisions are solutions to. Modern ethical
theories are so thoroughly conceived in terms of moral rules and
commandments that we tend not to notice how restricted a part they
play in Aristotle's version of practical thinking.

2.25324 Justice and Self ('Problem 3') (V xi; 1138a3–b14)

Can one do oneself a wrong? That was ruled out by our answers to
the questions whether a person could voluntarily be mistreated, and
whether it was the distributor or the favourite who was to blame in
an unfair distribution. But no easy answer to this question will do.
Suicides are, after all, punished – actually, if they fail; retrospectively
and symbolically, if they succeed. And it seems natural to say of
some people that they 'don't give themselves a chance.' Above all,
the key move in Plato's *Republic* was to remove justice from the
interpersonal realm and transfer it to the internal economy of the
individual, and Aristotle is very much aware of this. According to
Moraux, he had himself retained the Platonic standpoint in his earlier
work *On Justice*, and in the *Ethics* he acquiesces in the transference to
the extent that justice is treated as a virtue of the individual and not
only of the city.[154] In the *Ethics*, though, justice is a virtue *vis-à-vis*
others: particular justice lies in being the kind of person who habitually observes due proportionality in sharing and exchanging with
them, universal justice lies in being the kind of person who abstains
from doing to them what the law defines as an injury – 'both of them
take effect in one's relations with the other' (1130b1). Plato's form of
internalization, in which justice towards others is merely the natural
expression of that due proportionality among aspects of an individual's personality which is the primary manifestation of justice in
human affairs, accordingly calls for some examination.[155]

Why is suicide prohibited?[156] Presumably because it is an injury to
someone, and must this someone not be the suicide? Not necessarily.
The suicide may be disparaged as a coward (1116a13, cf. Plato *Laws*
873C), or blamed for deserting the post assigned by the gods (Plato,
Phaedo 62B–C); but Aristotle thinks that the fact that Athens imposed
a certain loss of civil rights (*atimia*) shows that the offence is one
against the city.[157] Suicide involves justice in its broader sense; in the

narrower sense, people cannot be unjust to themselves because in involuntary transactions it is essential that one party be taken unawares by the other, while in voluntary transactions (sales and contracts) there must be two people between whom a ratio must be established. Anyway, Aristotle concludes breezily, one cannot specify a crime one could commit against oneself. Commit adultery with one's spouse? Burglarize one's own house? Come, now.

In fact, though, we do speak of people as being unjust to themselves. But this is a metaphor. Such people are spoken of as if each were two persons: the 'rational' and 'irrational' aspects are personified, and one part is unfair to the other part. Aristotle does not here say that the personification is itself metaphorical, no doubt because he himself uses it in practical contexts (as in the all-important I xiii), but he does say that the justice involved is like that between master and servant or husband and wife – associations in which there are power relations and spheres of competence and rights and duties, but not the full-blown justice that strictly obtains only within a constitutionally governed state (cf. 1134a24–30). Anyway, if we do accept the language about parts of the soul, we can say that one part does injure another because each part has its own desires, which the other may thwart, and in that way it does make sense that people can be unjust to themselves. The terms of the discussion here seem to be quite specifically those of Plato's *Republic*.[158]

The difference between Plato and Aristotle here is fundamental, despite the latter's willingness to use the former's language. Both Plato and Aristotle reject introspective psychology, as we saw when discussing the differentiation of the moral virtues. No precise statement about parts of the soul can be confirmed. But that is at variance with the requirement that justice refer to a determinate and specifiable quantity. Aristotle bases his account of justice on the assumption that, given the abstraction of an artificial framework, such quantitative determinations are available. But Plato's philosophy rested on the thesis that no precision is attainable *anywhere* in practice: precision pertains to the intelligible world of forms. For Plato, accordingly, it is no objection to the psychologization of practice that proportions cannot be determined within the psyche, since they cannot be determined anywhere. But for Aristotle the objection is decisive. Justice can actually be realized (as Plato denied) in a political organization, and only there. Since this realization is possible, it constitutes the only justice that can be properly so called.[159] For Plato, since no perfect realization is anywhere possible, the use of the term 'justice' in every practical sphere is equally legitimate and equally illegitimate. Priority can therefore be assigned to the structurally most fundamental level. And that level is the individual, for cities are nothing but people living together.

Just before his final resolution of the issue about harming oneself, Aristotle raises parenthetically a question that arises in all cases of injury, but especially here: which is worse, harming or being harmed (1138a28–b5)? Does the suicide suffer more as a murderer or as a murder victim? As a murderer, or course – it is a Platonic question, and Aristotle gives Plato's answer from the *Gorgias*, and in a way that presumes and verifies the caveat given there about not letting tough talk frighten one. There may be occasions where what is generally not so bad turns out to be worse, but that is of no theoretical interest (1138b2).[160]

2.254 Justice: Recapitulation and General Conclusion

The omission of justice from the list of moral virtues should strike us as odder than it sometimes does. The reason for the omission is that, as in Plato's *Republic* and *Laws*, *justice* is simply a word for 'doing the right thing' in general, the behavioural manifestation of virtue-in-relation-to-others – that is, taking personal relations seriously. If justice is to be one virtue among others, we may feel, Aristotle treats it in the wrong way: the vices that correspond to it should be an excessive preference for justice over affection, on the one hand, and an insufficient regard for justice, on the other. What Aristotle lacks is the concept of a specific virtue of law-abidingness as such, corresponding to the missing virtue of conscientiousness we remarked on earlier. But Aristotle could not do things that way, because the calculation of the claims of affection should itself form part of the calculation of what justice requires: in a situation that calls for nepotism, neglect of nepotism is unfair. So Aristotle has to fall back on the idea that an overscrupulous justice is one that leans over backwards to avoid favouring oneself, and so is unfair to oneself, getting the sum wrong in the other's interest.

The law promotes justice, which is the most direct concern of the state. (Economics is the *direct* concern of the household, which remains the basis of economic organization.) But the state cannot directly control virtue, any more than an individual can (see III v). What it can do, over and above setting up an educational system, is set up rewards and punishments to influence the externals of behaviour – the right thing to do, not 'in relation to the agent' but in an interactive context; and *the* right thing, determinately. But determinacy is the domain of quantity. So the state (and its justice, and justice in general) deals with interpersonal relations as quantifiable and treats individuals as units or as quantitatively differentiated. The 'right' becomes the *ison*, the fair or equal, the solved equation.

Insofar as individuals are members of communities based on status and structure (as opposed to comradeship and conviviality), they have or lack the *virtue* of justice, being personally concerned with fair dealing in formal and quasi-formal transactions. But because this is not a mean 'in relation to us,' it must be related to 'extremes' in a quite different way. In fact, there are two ways. There are departures from fairness in situations where fairness is called for but the agent is distracted by some extraneous motivation. But there is also a pair of proper vices in relation to fairness: to seek more than one's share, or less. Only, as Aristotle says, to want *less* is unthinkable; the concept of wanting simply will not accommodate that. Someone who seems to want 'less' must really be wanting *more* of something that is not the ostensible object of the transaction.

The functions of the *logon echon* in relation to justice are distinctive, because they deal with antecedent quantifications. There is the initial establishment of the *logos*, the quantitative system itself, and the relation of this to its unquantified predecessor, reciprocity (*to antipeponthos*); there is the charting of the domain of fairness, and the relation between personal interest and unfairness (since the mean is not 'in relation to us,' the relationship must be more remote than in the corresponding passage in II iv); there is the relation between nature and artifice in establishing norms (the nature of law); there is the relation between the sense of fair play and the observation of ostensively established norms ('equity').

The topic of justice should lead directly into a substantive consideration of politics, dealing with laws, citizenship, and constitutional forms, all of which have been touched on. But we cannot follow that route, because it is essential to deal first with 'good sense' (*phronēsis*, the dominant virtue in individual life) – and besides, politics is too big a topic to handle otherwise than on its own. But also, the consideration of justice as the quantification of relations with the other as Other calls urgently for a treatment of a new and unheralded topic: *philia*, 'friendship,' the affective and operant basis of actual human relations, without which there would be nothing for justice to quantify – in the list of categories, quality and quantity make a pair. *EN* VIII–IX really ought to come right after *EN* V, but this is impossible, because *EN* VI has the more immediate claim. But, in the same way that justice leads into politics, the actual field of organized and quantified relations, so friendship has its proper sequel in the consideration of personal lives. Thinking about the sharing of lives makes us think about life as the field of awareness, but also about individuals as living, graspable personal lives. And the latter enables us to think about happiness as articulated in lifetimes and life choices, a topic we brought up in I v but have not hitherto been in a position to conceptualize. So that is how the argument of the *Ethics* concludes, at X vi–viii.

It remains, however, to reconsider the transition from *EN* V to politics, which was postponed. And we proceed to do that (X ix). But, since we have completed our examination of the lives of serious people, what remains to be thought about is the lives of the non-serious. Aristotle will, in fact, never consider them, such inferior people (*phauloteroi*) are not worth considering – but it is because of their presence in large numbers that law and justice have to be not merely excogitated but *imposed*. And it is on this uncongenial note that Aristotle will conclude his actual transition to a promised treatise on politics, rather unlike the one that has come down to us.

2.3 The Good Mind (VI; 1138b18–1145a11)

Given that the best human life is one that best and most fully develops all the aspects of human life that are shaped by *logos*, the articulate use of conceptual and quantificational systems, and that we have now seen what this comes to in the basically 'irrational' aspects of our selves – in other words, we have said what we had to say about moral virtue and the moral virtues – the obvious next step is to look at the actual use of *logos* that does the shaping. Given that the morally good life is the sensible life, we have to see what being sensible (*phronimos*) amounts to.[161]

Two continuations are possible here. We could simply go on from the totality of what we have been saying, including the treatment of justice; or we could go back to the general definition of moral virtue and make a fresh start by unfolding the implications of the defining formulae we used there. The latter procedure is more in Aristotle's style, and it is what he does.[162] But it does involve a certain awkwardness, and the opening of Book VI is rather disjointed – the first chapter looks like a series of notes, all of them in effect making fresh starts.[163]

In fact, Aristotle goes right back to his initial and most basic formula about avoiding excess and defect, at 1104a12–27, without even mentioning the qualifications that the mean must be 'relative to us' and that the only standard is the judgment of the sensible person – it is not surprising that he comments that that was 'true, but not clear' (1138b25–6). He makes this extreme move mainly to keep his options open, as we shall see. But the subsequent elaborations, and especially the treatments of choice and justice, have covered a lot of what there is to say about good sense (*phronēsis*) already.

According to Aristotle, it is always the matter that individuates and the form that unites. So, in considering the virtues, there is a general formula that is the same for each, and this specifies the contribution of intellectual virtue in determining the mean. The particular moral virtues (which we usually call 'the virtues' without qualification) are individuated by determinable feelings and fields of operation, contextually identified.

Justice, theoretically, is one of the moral virtues. But its domain is unusually broad. In the wider sense of the term, it is indeed 'the whole of virtue in relation to others,' and this in a threefold sense. First, it is the will to avoid injury generally in relation to others, interpersonal relations being considered as a single field of operation; second, because politics and law in a city have as their domain all the concerns of all the people, the will to obey the law as such (to be *nomimos*) is the will *to do right by all* in general; and third, because law ideally seeks the happiness of all, justice is the tendency to seek the welfare of all in the political community (which is so defined as to make it the widest operative association of humans). In its narrower sense, in contrast, justice is the will to deal fairly with all – which in the later chapters of Book V comes close to justice in the broad sense, because the generalities of the law deal with relations insofar as they are formalized, and to formalize them is to quantify them.

Justice, then, is a moral virtue defined in relation to *logoi* that are actually formalized in intellectual terms, in legal practice and theory, and in economic controls and theory. And we saw that the theory of equity requires (as part of this formalization itself) that the operative formulae be observed, not rigidly, but in accordance with a strategic intelligence that keeps the overall objective of welfare in mind.

In describing the *ēthos* of justice, in fact, we have said most of what there is to say about the operations of good sense: legal institutions and market practices show us what *phronēsis* is and how it operates.

What is there for a discussion of intellectual virtue to add? Very little, it seems, beyond pointing out the implications of what has already been said. But three things are possible. First, the actual thought processes of deliberation about means can be separated out, identified, and cultivated, though there will be nothing virtuous about these in abstraction from their relation to a context of virtuous action. Second, the quality of moral insight, the correct identification of occasions for action in relation to a grasp of what the good life is, will be an intellectual virtue, but not one that can be separately cultivated, since it effectively reflects one's basic moral character. And third though it played no direct part in our discussion of moral virtues as such, the persistent reference to political (hence legislative) and legal institutions is enough to show that there is, after all, an architectonic level of generalization in moral thought, even if this has no independent status.

Our account of good qualities of character culminated in a quality that was bound up with legislation and with political practice, and led us to consider those wider fields for the exercise of human wisdom. Also, as we moved on from virtue to virtue, from the control of passion and appetite to the social graces, we progressed to more and more sophisticated qualities, until at last we reached a virtue of practically pure intellectuality: justice and injustice are determined by an *objective* mean, ascertainable by calculation, and to act justly is to be swayed by that calculation alone, so that the desires of oneself and others figure as data rather than as motivating force. So, in our discussion of the part played by *logos* in human life, and in considering how *logos* is, as it were, statically embodied in conditions and situations, we have reached a place where the function of *logos* can be clearly isolated for attention. It remains for us to look at the use of reason itself, an account of which should set the copestone on our account of human excellence. Here we might expect the fulfilment of what went before, the full explication of those unexplained allusions to 'the principle that the sensible person would use' and the like. But, if we expect that, we will be disappointed. There is nothing more to say about the place of reason in practical life than we have said already. And if we had read I xiii we should have known as much. In the distinction there made between the rational and the non-rational, the function of rational control and the operation of the controllable non-rational are identical.[164] There cannot now be any exciting disclosures about the life-directing operations of the good mind. What was said in elucidating the concept of the mean and in analysing the operations of deliberation was not just all that could be said in that context, it was really all that could be helpfully said at all, and the anatomy of justice gave us a full articulation of *logos* in action. The clarifications that follow in Book VI really only make it plain that what has already been said was enough – Aristotle says it was 'true but not clear,' but what is to be made clear is that it was in effect the whole truth. Philosophers cannot tell people what to do; there is no formula that can be substituted for the formed intelligence of sensible people operating with their own insights on their own circumstances.

However, if the account of wisdom fails to give us the formulae and principles we might have liked, it rewards us with something we were not promised: a consideration of those activities of the intellect that have no bearing on practical life. And the introduction of this topic opens up a new range of considerations that do, in effect, emancipate us from what otherwise might seem the disappointingly closed circle of the quotidian.

What, then, is intellectual excellence? As I have just suggested, the answer could almost be teased out of what has already been said about moral virtue. The coincidence of the highest non-rational and lowest rational functions of the soul (I xiii) shows that intellectual and moral vices and virtues must coincide: someone who overeats is *both* greedy *and* foolish. Greed is what makes one think that what is actually too much food is the right amount for one to eat; but it is thinking that too much is right, not greed, that leads one to overeat on any given occasion. (People who eat more than they think they should are not greedy, but lacking in self-control.) That is why actions can be voluntary, although the corresponding virtues and vices are not. But 'thinking too much is right' is not a simple condition. One aspect of it is a misreading or misinterpretation of the situation one is in, a misjudgment about what is fitting. The glutton's folly is simply a general tendency to make misjudgments of this kind. But it may also involve a failure in deliberation, that is, a failure to relate ends to each other, or more simply a failure to take appropriate means to one's ends; for, although the right amount to eat is, in the first instance, a simple matter of metabolism, the right amount to eat *on any particular occasion* will depend on what one is planning to do that evening, whether one is in training, when one can expect one's next meal, the prevailing etiquette of hospitality, and so on. And we remember that three different relations are covered by the means/end dichotomy: steps to a wished-for consequence, parts integrated into wholes, and neutral aspects of actions to be differentiated from their associated values. Insofar as the intellectual processes of deliberation merely have to do with what actions will lead to what consequences, greedy people will presumably deliberate in the same way as anyone else. But insofar as the less hard-and-fast procedures of integration and analysis are involved, greed may more directly affect deliberation by insinuating a false equation between repletion and happiness.

The glutton's folly is objective. Gluttons really are fools, because what they take to be the right amount to eat really is not. The converse of folly, good sense, however much it may depend on having a head unbiased by appetite, and hence ultimately on the condition of non-rational aspects of the psyche, must then be equally objective. It is a propensity to hit on the right amount – that is, to divine *the truth* in this regard. And, since this is so even in that aspect of good sense which is most affected by appetite, one should be safe in saying quite generally that intellectual excellence will be that condition in which one arrives most reliably and efficiently at the truth.

We are now in a position to take our important step forward, one that is familiar to us but was revolutionary when Plato first took it. The description of good sense as that condition in which we best attain truth applies more obviously to theoretical inquiries than to the practical wisdom to which we applied it. But very little has yet been said about any such inquiries in our anatomy of the good life. It follows that excellence in theoretical performances must be quite distinct from good sense; but it is a quite genuine sort of mental excellence. From that, in turn, it follows that there are at least two intellectual virtues, differentiated primarily (just as the moral virtues were) by their field of operation. But the virtue of the theoretical intellect is not a virtue of the controlling aspect of the psyche, because it has nothing to do with the control of the non-rational. We have thus uncovered a stratum of the psyche that was not mentioned in the analysis of I xiii, which we can now complete in a symmetrical form. There are four relevantly distinguishable aspects of the psyche: a non-rational aspect not amenable to conscious control (the functions of nutrition, growth, etc.); a non-rational aspect rationally controllable (the appetites, etc.); a rational aspect devoted to the control of the rational, and thus to the conscious direction of the body; and finally, a purely rational aspect the operations of which are affected only incidentally by what goes on in the body. From this point on, the account of the good life will be complicated by the compresence of these two components, the practical and the theoretical, that have no direct functional interrelation.

The clarification we were promised, then, turns out to be the introduction of the concept of truth itself. And this does two things. It affords the occasion for an elementary anatomy of inquiry; and it opens up to ethical reflection a new dimension of human affairs.

The new dimension, the intellectual life that pursues truth for its own sake, stands in no predetermined relation to practical life and the truth involved in that. The values of moral virtue were not initially subordinated to the demands of social utility, nor is the urgency of practical affairs cited there – in fact, as we shall see, the urgency of practical affairs is seen as detracting from their value in VI viii. And we may add (though it is a point of which Aristotle does not avail himself) that the impetus of the natural orientation to knowledge alleged to be basic to humanity in *Metaphysics* I i carries us forward on the road to science and philosophy. Besides which, every one of Aristotle's hearers and readers is strenuously engaged in intellectual work, and it would be dishonest in them to disavow its value.

2.31 The Duality of Wisdom (VI i–vii; 1138b18–1141b23)

2.311 Wisdom and Its Objects (VI i–ii; 1138b18–1139b13)

A lot of material is laid under obligation in Book VI, and my account of its basis has been correspondingly discursive. But Aristotle's own introduction of the intellectual virtues and their duality is brisk. Essentially, he just says that the account of moral virtue needs to be completed by a complementary account of intellectual virtue, and that the objects with which intellectual virtue is concerned are of two kinds that differ so radically that (in accordance with the Platonic procedure laid down in *On the Soul* II 4) they differ correspondingly in their operations and must be assigned to two different faculties. But he says this disjointedly, presumably because the insufficiency of the account of moral virtue does not in itself require that there be identifiable intellectual virtues – that follows rather from the previous analysis of the psyche.

2.3111 The Criterion (VI i; 1138b18–1139a17)

'We happen to have said previously,' Aristotle begins, that the mean between excess and defect is determined by the 'correct *logos*,' and this is what he will now expound. And he adds something that is 'true but not clear' – that in all such cases what is required is to 'look away' towards the target (*skopos*) and strain or relax accordingly, as though one were bending a bow to hit a distant mark with an arrow. Actually, this version of the 'mean' is not one he has used before; in Book II, the analogy was rather that of steering a boat between hazards, in which the dynamics are very different, although the word *skopos* was used (at 1106b32). The language is taken from Plato's *Gorgias* (503D–E and 507D), where ideal virtue is the 'target' to which one is to 'look away' and towards which one is to 'strain' (though Plato, of course, has nothing about relaxing, since he is not concerned with means between extremes). It is Plato's alleged vagueness, then, that is glanced at; and the target is to fill the place of Plato's permanently absent world of ideas.

Aristotle says that we must say what the *orthos logos* is, and what its *horos* is – apparently a twofold inquiry, then. A *horos* is a boundary marker, or a definition. And in this context it looks as if it should be the same as the 'target.' Aristotle does not explain the duality; can we guess? Well, from I ii, where the utility of ethics is said to be that it converts the overall end, the *telos*, that we already unselfconsciously pursue in the necessary integration of all our objectives within a single lifetime, into a *skopos* defined by a life plan, the *horos* of wise people should simply be the true vision of the best possible life, their *eudaimonia*.[165] And the correct *logos* should be the accurate and swift performance of the intellectual operations that secure this. These two, and the relation between them, furnish the required analysis of *phronēsis*. But Aristotle does not say that here. He introduces the intellectual virtues as a fresh topic.

2.3112 Intellectual Virtue and the Concept of Truth (1138b35–1139b13 [VI 2])

2.31121 The Intellectual Virtues (1138b35–1139a17)

The opening of Book VI, with its casual air, introduced by the adversative particle *de*, looks more like an appendix or a footnote than the start of a new topic. What we come to now looks much more like such a beginning (the introductory particle is the non-committal *dē*). We are reminded of the previous analysis of the psyche, and the corresponding distinction of two sorts of virtue, those of the character (now dealt with) and those of the mind (*dianoia*).[166] We are now invited to make a second division within the part of the psyche that 'has *logos*.' It is laid down as a postulate that phenomena of which the principles cannot be other than as they are, and phenomena of which the principles can be other, must be 'contemplated' by separate parts of the psyche, on the ground that cognition requires affinity between the knower and the known. Once more, the language and procedures look very Platonic. To these two 'parts' we are invited to give the names 'scientific' (*epistēmonikon*) and 'calculative' (*logistikon*), respectively, on the grounds that calculation and deliberation are the same and no one deliberates about things that cannot be altered (cf. 1121a21–6). These two parts will have different functions, and hence different virtues, for virtues are 'best conditions' in relation to function wherever a function can be identified.

This is easy enough to follow, but it does seem a bit glib. Is there not a kind of 'calculation' that has to do with pure numbers, which are *ex hypothesi* unchanging? And does not science take changing particulars into account, wondering why they occur or even whether they do occur? Perhaps the insistence that it is the *principles* that are unchanging takes care of that; but, in that case, are not the 'principles' of changing particulars themselves unchanging, so that Aristotle can write about practical problems in general terms (including the general problem of the limits of generalization)? Perhaps it is this sort of difficulty that makes Aristotle introduce his distinction as a *postulate* (*hupokeisthō*, 1139a6); it is the following section that will make the hypothesis good.

It is important not to loss sight of the principle laid down here: that there are two and only two intellectual virtues, one of which does not enter into the practical life.[167] It is only through the unity of good sense that the good life is unified, and only because it is unified that the project of ethics is viable. When we are discussing courage (or any of the moral virtues) we speak as if brave deeds were performed in a context into which no considerations enter other than dangers and how they are to be met. But, in real life, what determines the right thing to do is all the considerations that are relevant to the particular concrete situation. There may, indeed, be many occasions on which only a person's courage (or generosity, or whatever) is tested; but there are others that tax other virtues as well, and one of the things a person must decide is the relative weight of these others. Without the exercise of good sense we cannot tell what these are; in fact, it is the mark of good sense that one never loses sight of any of the factors that are relevant to one's situation. Our good sense is tested whenever we act, and through the unity of our good sense our moral qualities are indirectly unified too – which is why the Platonic Socrates tends to argue that wisdom is the only virtue, because any other virtue (such as courage) exercised without regard to wisdom is no virtue at all but may be a menace to its owner and to others. The passions that affect one's good sense are the *whole* of one's character at the time of action.

The necessary unity of good sense leaves us with a problem. Since there is no place in good sense for purely intellectual excellence, which is, none the less, a virtue in its own right, the ideal of *eudaimonia* seems to fall apart.[168] A makeshift effort to patch things up will be made at the end of Book VI, but the necessary conceptual unity will not really be achieved until Book X, when considerations based on the discussion of the concept of friendship make a new approach possible – and such an approach is needed, for a life spent doing philosophy is after all a life, even if Plato did let Socrates in the *Phaedo* call it the 'practice of death.' But, for the time being, in these opening discussions, the purely intellectual virtue of *sophia* is treated as not directly relevant to our discussion, which remains within the parameters of practical life where it began. *Sophia* is introduced only as a foil to *phronēsis*, which remains the focus of interest.[169]

2.31122 Truth (VI ii; 1139a17–b13)[170]

What is the function of the two 'parts' of the psyche that have reason? To attain truth – this is the function of all thinking (1139a39). But it is only in a parenthesis and after much beating about the bush that Aristotle gives this simple answer to the initial question. In fact, the exposition seems singularly confused, though there seems to be nothing in the subject-matter that makes the confusion necessary.

In theoretical activity, truth is simply a matter of asserting and denying the correct things. In practical matters, it is not so simple. What corresponds to assertion and denial here is pursuit and avoidance, and these involve recognition and motivation working together. Aristotle introduces the discussion by what looks like a reminiscence of the basic analysis of action from *On the Soul* III 9–10. But I'm not sure it is. There are, he says, three things in the psyche that are responsible for action and truth: perception, desire, and insight (*nous*). But perception is not the basis of action – beasts (*thēria*) have perception, but have no part in action. This cannot just mean that sense perception is inert in the absence of desire: it must mean that *nous* (itself inert in the absence of desire) goes beyond perception – as indeed it does: what one has in mind must be perceived or envisaged as good, as an end (1139b2). But Aristotle wants to go beyond this – the earlier analysis of moral virtue pointed to a peculiar fusion of desire and insight. A moral virtue is a disposition to *choose*, and choice is a desire (*orexis*) not merely occasioned by but suffused with deliberation. What the mind recognizes as its objective must be identical with the object of desire. So (the point tends to be lost in translation) the notion of the correct use of reason, *orthos logos*, splits into two: the *logos* must be true, the desire must be *orthos*. And in our 'political' context, we recall, the end envisaged is not any old end, one of the limited objectives of technical thought, but 'good practice,' *eupraxia*, excellence in practical life itself. In one sense, the origin of virtuous action is the end as thus envisaged; but, in another sense, it is the originating fusion of thought and desire in choice, which can be thought of either as 'desirous insight' or as 'reasoning desire.'[171] And this sort of an origin is what a human being is (1139b5).

How are we to take this last sentence? Is it a mere rhetorical flourish to finish off the conceptual pyrotechnics? Not necessarily. We can take it quite literally. It is only in human beings, neither in beasts nor in gods (or angels), that we find this fusion of thought and appetite. And we can take this for a necessary truth: whatever characteristically operates in this fashion is essentially human. If a computer does so, a computer is human; if a six-nosed bug-eyed Martian does so, the six-nosed bug-eyed Martian is human.[172] This is going to be important in the denouement: it entails that philosophy is not a characteristic human activity. It is more like what gods do (or would do).

The modes of behaviour by which the two 'insightful parts' (*noētikōn moriōn*) most achieve truth, then, will be the virtues of the pair of them.

2.312 Elimination (VI iii–vi; 1139b14–1141a8)

We are now told that we are to make a fresh start and go over the same material again.[173] What we now hear is that there are (not two virtues or three 'things in the soul that control action and truth' [1139a17] but) *five* things whereby the soul 'gets things true' (*alētheuei*) in assertion and denial: art, good sense, intuition, knowledge, and wisdom. We proceed to examine their credentials. In fact, since

there are only two intellectual virtues, Aristotle conducts an elimination, though he does not announce it as such. Why does he do
things this way? Since 'supposition' and 'opinion' are excluded from
the list of five, as not being infallible, we may suppose that he is
working from some accepted list of seven items – he expects the
provenance to be familiar to his audience. Gauthier and Jolif (pp.
435–6) argue that here, as well as in VI ix–xi, Aristotle is simplifying
and organizing the list of intellectual virtues current in the Academy,
together with the other words for intellectual excellences accepted by
Plato and here treated as aspects of good sense; and that may well
be the case. But there should be a systematic point as well; and, by
analogy with the 'elimination' that shows that moral virtues are
neither abilities nor passions but dispositions, the intention should be
to point out some crucial aspects of what the two intellectual virtues
are. And this is certainly done, though not in a way that will make
today's philosopher happy.

The distinction between art (*technē*) and good sense was made
already in Book II, and is fundamental: art is subordinated to practice
(1139b1–4), for it is a matter of perfection in achieving ends that are
themselves indifferent except insofar as they are themselves means
to the practical end of a good life. And the virtue of *sophia*, the excellence of the theoretical intellect, incorporates two mutually independent accomplishments, the ability to grasp the premises on which
theories are based and the ability to grasp the articulation of the
theories themselves. So that gets rid of three of the five candidates,
one by subordination and two by subsumption.

The elimination has a certain untidiness. On the one hand, art is
excluded from good sense, whereas intuition and knowledge are
included in wisdom; on the other hand, an analogue of the distinction
between intuition and knowledge is to be found within good sense
also, since one must have a grasp or vision of the good life as a
whole as well as having the ability to deliberate effectively in the
light of that vision. One can, however, make a case for doing things
this way, on the supposition that what Aristotle still has principally
in mind is the place of good sense in the practical life, with 'wisdom'
serving merely as an external paradigm of intellectual order – it
being conceded that if this is what Aristotle is doing he fails to
inform us that this is so. I return to this shortly.

A difficulty today's philosophical reader has with this discussion
centres on the word *alētheuein*, to 'get things true.' It sounds as if
there were methods of certainly achieving truth. But we may be more

inclined to think that there are ways of eliminating various sorts of error and that there may be ways of increasing one's chances of achieving truth (heuristics), but that, if the connection between truth and the terms Aristotle uses here is invariable, it is not because there are infallible methods for getting things right but because there is a *conceptual* connection. Someone who claims to have an 'intuition' is claiming to have attained truth without argumentation; but the claim may prove false, and then the claimant will have to admit that it was not an intuition after all. Similarly, if I say someone *knows* something, I am saying two things: first, that the person has appropriate grounds for thinking it true; and, second, that it really is true. Aristotle's discussion insinuates that somehow there are techniques such that, if they are correctly applied, the result will be infallible and indubitable. Maybe he doesn't think that, and maybe it is true – what is disconcerting is that he seems oblivious to the problem, which has been at the centre of epistemological concerns since a few years after his death. The result is that we may feel that his account of the intellectual virtues is completely wrong: either he is wrong about the difference between good thinking and bad, or he is wrong in believing that 'good thinking' is within the scope of human capabilities.

2.3121 Knowledge (Epistēmē) (1139b18–36)

'Knowledge' is the first candidate to be considered, because in Aristotle's usage it represents the ideal of a science, in which universal conclusions are drawn by valid arguments from premises of which the truth is certain. Four points are made here. First, the premises themselves must be arrived at otherwise than by argumentation – in fact, by 'induction' (*epagōgē*), a term somewhat mystifying then as now, but in any case standing for some process of getting in a position to see something. Second, knowledge can be taught (*didaktē*), a term that, in Plato as in Aristotle, stands specifically for what teachers do (*didaskalia*) in classroom-like situations, and which therefore consists of what can be stated in universal terms without 'hands-on' demonstrations. Third, since knowledge is *ex hypothesi* certain, its objects must be such as could not be otherwise, and must hence be eternal (i.e. timeless). And fourth, teaching depends on previous knowledge. It follows immediately (though Aristotle need not say this again) that *epistēmē* cannot be the virtue of the practical intellect. But it follows also that it cannot be the virtue of the theoretical intellect, for it cannot provide itself with the premises it requires. And it further follows that a science is of limited scope, not concerned with its own limitations or its own relationship to other sciences or the overall scope of the knowable. This last point is not made here (though it is one of the lessons of the *Posterior Analytics*), but it is relevant, because it is precisely analogous to one of the limitations of art (*technē*), the next candidate to be considered.

2.3122 Art (Technē) (VI iv; 1140a1–23)

Technē and *epistēmē* bear a certain likeness to each other. *Epistēmē* is understanding. To grasp the structure of a theoretical area is to understand a field, to be in possession of it, to 'stand over' it as the etymology of the Greek word suggests, regardless of its relation to knowledge as a whole or to my own concerns. Similarly, to grasp an art (*technē*) in its ideal totality is to be master of a practical field, regardless of what contribution that field makes to the good life.

'Art' was a fundamental term in the epistemology of both Plato and Aristotle, and appears in various guises. In the opening chapter of *Metaphysics* I, it represents the crucial phase in the development of characteristically human thought patterns. It represents the stage at which a reliance on experience is supplemented by research into causes and effects and the relation of practice to universal principles – which, as we just saw, can be taught. Teaching makes the cumulative development of knowledge possible by the development of systematic chains of reasoning. But 'art,' in this sense, is merely a transitional phase in the development of thought, being overtaken by an abstract theorizing that is emancipated from all practical needs and circumstances and simply satisfies the impulse to explore the bounds of the knowable. One might, however, on that basis, suppose it to be the virtue of the practical intellect, since it lifts practice to its highest level in terms of intellectual organization. But that would be misleading, since, as Aristotle repeatedly says, it is less practically important to know the relevant general principles of an art than to be able actually to do the right thing for the given occasion.

The present discussion of *technē* takes a quite different tack. Art is not an intermediate stage to science, because it is concerned with changeable things. One then might expect Aristotle to say what I suggested, that art is not the virtue of the practical intellect because the values it exists to promote are merely postulated as desirable, their real value being determined by a correct view of what the best human life is and requires.[174] But what he actually says is very differ-

ent – partly, no doubt, because the later discussion of *euboulia* will
show that *phronēsis* also is related to an end that it does not establish.
Art and good sense are both concerned with changeable things, but
their fields of operation are not the same. Art is concerned with
making (*poiēsis*), good sense is concerned with doing (*praxis*). Art is
a disposition to *make* things with a true *logos*.[175]

What is the difference between making and doing? The former is
said to be a matter of bringing into being and contriving and providing for things whose origin (*archē*) is in the maker and not in the
thing made (1140a11–14); but we are not told what 'doing' is. I suppose making is the production of some result beyond the operation
of making, whereas doing is an activity conceived as without result.
The separation is often obvious – the sculptor's activity of making is
the very activity it is, but is designed to produce a statue that is
distinct from the process of its making. But one wants to say that
every making involves doing, and vice versa. The activity of making
the statue is something the sculptor does, and that activity has to be
considered as an activity within the whole context of the sculptor's
life and the life of the community, whereas the same activity is a
making the value of which is relative to the worth of what is made
in relation to the relevant standards. And there is a sense in which
every action is a 'making,' it makes at least *a difference*, produces an
effect in the world that is other than itself, even if that effect does not
fall within the scope of any recognized or formalized art.

Aristotle's insistence that making and doing are different, so that
neither is included in the other, seems acceptable if one takes it as
making the conceptual distinction I have just made. But it involves
an awkwardness. In I i, Aristotle says that the means-end distinction
is threefold, with the relation between an action and what it brings
about as one of its three aspects. He illustrates this with examples of
arts. But in the same context he seems to subject politics to the same
analysis, and by the present account politics cannot be both an art
and the highest form of *praxis*, as the argument requires it to be. The
same difficulty recurs in III iii, where the paradigm of 'deliberation'
is the calculation of how to bring about a desired result, which on
the present separation of doing and making would seem to fall
within the scope of art and not of good sense at all. What I would
like to say here, and what I wish Aristotle said, is that any form of
strictly consequentialist ethics, treating actions as the means to bring
about desirable ends distinct from themselves, reduces doing to
making and thus removes the former from the scope of good sense

altogether, so that it cannot as such be considered a part of the good life. But Aristotle does not say that, though he does not show how the conclusion is to be avoided.[176]

Metaphysics I allows for 'arts for living' (technai pros diagōgēn), which must include all recreational activities that involve organization of skill. Since these belong to 'art,' their operations must be excluded from the scope of good sense, and hence from the virtuous concern of the serious person. That is basically why Aristotle excludes cultural pursuits from the purview of his Ethics, as I keep complaining. The late C.J. Ducasse introduced the concept of 'endotelicity,' the property of having a purpose that is both serious and self-contained, to circumvent Aristotle's reservations on this score.[177]

The trouble is that Aristotle's account is simplistic, ignoring the subtlety and complexity of the ways in which logos enters life. His account of the moral life is intricate but the life itself is empty, consisting (as he points out) only of responses to crises and taking no account of leisurely times – but the conclusion he seems to draw from this is that a serious person's leisure will take the form of a similarly serious use of the mind to consider the nature of intelligible reality. This, together with the current state of scientific research, leads him to ignore the creativity of science, making no allowance for the need to frame imaginative hypotheses (like those of Democritus) which might be subjected to verification (strictly speaking, to falsification). As modern historians of science often complain, he sticks too close to what he takes for common-sense observation, unconscious of the element of bold conjecture in his own work. It is really his separation of art from good sense and from wisdom, and his neglect of the possibility that imagination may have a positive part to play in the life of the mind, that enabled Aristotle to figure as the enemy of intellectual progress in the great ages of scientific discovery.

2.3123 Good Sense (Phronēsis) (VI v; 1140a24–b30)

The treatment of *technē* relied on a neat distinction between doing and making, in terms that made the former relevant to virtue in a way that the latter is not. So the obvious thing to do next is to give an account of excellence in doing that parallels the account of excellence in making. The name for this is 'good sense' (*phronēsis*), and it is not surprising that this turns out to be the virtue of the practical intellect. In fact, Aristotle's treatment is reminiscent of the way 'ordinary language' philosophers of the 1950s discussed value words.[178] It is as if *phronēsis* were, in the first instance, definable as whatever was required for excellence in practical thinking, but, in the second instance, a recognizable style of thought, so that an account of the descriptive content of the condition would at the same time serve as a norm by which practical thinking could be judged. And this is more or less the way Aristotle handles the topic, beginning with a description and proceeding to a conceptual elimination that leaves good sense in the uncontested position of intellectual excellence.

The parallel with 'art' leads us to expect that the definition of good sense will use the same formula, but with the word *doing* substituted for the word *making*. And it nearly does, but not quite. In defining art, the *hexis* was said to be 'with a true *logos*'; but, in defining good sense, the epithet 'true' is taken away from the *logos* and applied to the *hexis* itself (1140b5–6): 'a disposition that is true, together with *logos*, a matter of action in relation to the good and bad things for a human' – the nuances of the Greek diction won't go into idiomatic English. (A little later the same words are used in a different order, as if to emphasize the separateness of the items included: 'a disposition, together with *logos*, truthful, in relation to the human goods, practical' [1140b20–1]). Why is this more contorted formulation adopted? The obvious answer is that since this is to be the virtue, and intellectual virtues by definition attain truth, the truthfulness must be attributed to the disposition itself, and not merely to the *logos* that goes with it; and we may add the more practical consideration that, whereas in the case of art the reasoning has to be unmisleading but the end is arbitrary, in the case of virtue the end itself must be really good and thus truly conceived.

Aristotle's order of treatment is not that suggested by the contrast with art, but follows the indications of the treatment of moral virtue, where it was said that the correct *logos* was that by which the person of good sense would judge.[179] So we start by asking: what can we say in general terms about people of good sense? That they deliberate well – moral virtue was a disposition to choose well, and choice is the outcome of deliberation. The end of their deliberation is a worthy one (*spoudaios* – the ambiguity between seriousness and respectability is particularly apposite here), and not relative to a technical context. And their deliberation is general in scope. As the opening passage of the *Ethics* insisted, they refer their choices to their articulate vision of the good life as a whole, just as politicians are expected to refer their decisions to every aspect of the welfare of all the citizens.

The material adduced here is familiar to the point of tedium – the distinctions between making and doing and between the mutable and the immutable are gone through again. A new twist appears, though, when Aristotle says that, because of the difference between doing and making, doing has no end beyond itself – it is 'good action' (*eupraxia*) itself that is the end. And that, he says, is why we attribute good sense to Pericles and people like that – because they can *think about (theōrein)* what is good for themselves *and for humans in general*, and we think that politicians and people who run households are like that. What is the argument here? It seems a non sequitur. The argument would have to be that because good action (as opposed to making) has no determinable external objective it must have as its guiding value goodness in action in general – a concept which, once formulated, can be applied not only to the generality and sum of one's own affairs, but to the affairs of all the groups of which one is an active member, and hence to the affairs of other people and groups in general. In thinking of one's own life, one thinks of an exemplification of human life, and hence of human life as such.[180] After all, species exist only as embodied in individuals, so that to think adequately of an individual is to think adequately of the species to which the individual belongs. However, though this seems to be what the argument must be, Aristotle does not make explicit what the ground of his inference actually is.

After the apparent equation of good sense with excellence in deliberation, Aristotle rather abruptly says that this (the considerations expatiated on in our preceding paragraph) explains why the Greek word for 'moderation' (*sōphrosunē*) seems from its etymology to mean 'what preserves good sense' – failure in moderation, which means succumbing to pleasure and pain, destroys 'this kind of judgment,' that is, judgment about what is best for humans in general. What is destroyed by character defects (for we learned in II iii that all character defects can be explained as defective conditions in relation to pleasure and pain) is the first principle (*archē*) of action, one's grasp of the end for the sake of which everything is to be done.

This may seem bewildering at first, since this 'grasp of an end' that depends on character seems at odds with the reasoning processes of deliberation. But everything is in order. It was to make room for this manoeuvre that the word 'true' in our definition was transferred from the *logos* of the *hexis* to the *hexis* itself, as I pointed out; and in the preparatory treatment of choice Aristotle insisted that choice (the outcome of deliberation) was a fusion of thought and desire, and that this fusion was the *archē* that defined a human being (1139b3–5) – and that excellence in action (*eupraxia*) required both character and thought (1139a34). In other words, the bewildering-looking transition in the passage before us has been thoroughly prepared, with all the relevant terminology in place.

In the definition of moral virtue in Book II, the emphasis was always on the judgment of the moment, with no reference at all to 'moral laws' or general imperatives such as preoccupy recent ethical theory. But at the outset of the whole discussion of virtue Aristotle said that moral virtues come by habituation and intellectual virtues by teaching – which, he says, is why the latter come with maturity. What can be taught is abstract and universal; action is individual. How are we to reconcile this apparent contradiction? Well, as I said already, the reference to 'the *logos* by which the sensible person *would* decide' already universalizes the principle of judgment by prying it loose from the actual *krisis* in the *kairos*, the context-bound decision. And then in the treatment of justice the whole domain of virtuous behaviour towards other people is dealt with in terms of law and the quantifications that make law possible; and we will see in X ix that the whole legal system replaces individual judgment for people who do not explicitly make the good life an objective. We will see further that sensible people can apply their *logos* to the lives of others, giving advice; and this is possible because people have their humanity in common. Again, what makes it possible to define virtues is that types of situation recur and the human equipment of feelings and motives is constant. Besides, in the preliminary discussions of Book I we introduced the general models of the three ways of life, and the terms in which they could be criticized; and also we took it for granted that one could enumerate 'the good things in life' and generalize about how they enter into individual lifetimes and situations. There is, in fact, a great deal of material about generalizations of one sort or another, quite enough to justify the claim that intellectual virtue as such is teachable. What is not teachable is moral virtue and the insight into ends and situations that reflects such virtue. It is truly remarkable, though, how peripheral this 'lawlike' aspect of ethics appears to be in Aristotle's discussion. When he brings it up, it is practically always in connection with law and politics, never in the form of moral imperatives used to structure individual values.

In this elimination of putative virtues, the treatment of good sense ends with a sort of coda (1141b21–30), recapitulating the main conclusion and adding some reinforcing remarks. Neither the necessity nor the bearing of these additional ways of being sure that good sense is neither art nor scientific knowledge is clear to me. I don't know what it means to say that there is a virtue of art but not of good sense. Does it mean that one can be more or less good at carpentry or medicine, but not more or less good at good sense? If so, one might rejoin that that is true only because 'good' sense is perfect by definition; all the aspects and parts of good sense are things in which one may do better or worse. One's deliberations may be more or less clear or swift, one's grasp of a situation or of the structure of a good life may be more or less acute or comprehensive: are these really matters in which it makes sense to speak of 'perfection'? But Aristotle might rejoin that the intellectual virtues are defined as the dispositions whereby the two forms of reason achieve truth, and truth is an absolute: what is not false is true. I suppose that's right; and I also suppose that that is a good reason for rejecting this model of intellectual virtue.

Then Aristotle makes the old point that a voluntary failing is less of a defect in artistry than an involuntary defect, whereas the opposite is true of good sense as of all virtues, which suggests that good sense is itself a virtue. That is true but hardly necessary at this stage in the discussion, one might think: it is as though Aristotle felt he needed to show in how many ways the concept of *phronēsis* was like that of other virtues, so that the systematic claim that it is one of the two intellectual virtues would seem more like a recognition of reality than like a piece of philosophical jugglery.

The next point Aristotle makes is startling, because what he does is take the claim that good sense is the virtue of one of the two parts of the soul that have *logos* and rephrase it in Platonic terms, derived specifically from the *Meno* and the *Republic*: the part of which it is the virtue is the opinion-forming (*doxastikon*) part, for it is opinion that is related to what is contingent. Part of the oddness of this very odd sentence lies in the isolation of contingency as the relevant feature, rather than the context of practice – this is a reversion to the language and thought of *Republic* V in which the 'two worlds' theory of knowledge and reality is expounded in its most trenchant (and least Aristotelian) form. The use of Platonic formulations makes sense, even if we do not accept (as I, obviously, do not) the Gauthier–Jolif position that Aristotle's chief purpose hereabouts is to set the Academic conceptual scheme in order: it was, after all, Plato who followed Socrates in highlighting the concept of intellectual virtue itself through the paradoxical thesis that all the virtues can be reduced to wisdom.[181] But what strikes me most is the reminiscence of the thesis put forward at the end of the *Meno*, that virtue is not teachable because it as a matter of correct opinion as opposed to knowledge – which is why, specifically, people like Pericles (named in the present discussion as the paradigm of *phronēsis*, as we saw) cannot teach their children to be good. The *Meno* is an enigmatic dialogue, but one way of reading it is to the effect that, on the one hand, virtue cannot be 'taught' because it does require training (a possibility mooted by Meno in the opening sentence, but never taken up) as well as knowledge; while, on the other hand, people like Pericles cannot teach the knowledge side of it because they don't have knowledge (only a 'philosopher monarch' would have that) but have merely internalized the folkways and acquired the requisite experience – the point about experience being that, as Aristotle observes in *Metaphysics* I 1, it functions below the level at which universal formulations, and hence teachability, begin. On that reading, Aristotle would here be giving Plato the lie direct, as we might expect: what Pericles has is indeed intellectual virtue, the appropriate excellence of the practical intellect, which operates in the realm of opinion where truth depends on feeling no less than on reasoning, and with which the abstract formulations of mathematics have nothing to do.

Plato rejects the thesis, which in his *Protagoras* is expounded by Protagoras, that the whole city 'teaches' virtue in the same way that a community of native speakers 'teaches' children a language, by saturation and unanimous precept, because this process maintains not virtue but the vicious circle whereby the current folkways perpetuate themselves – folkways the excellence of which Protagoras takes for granted. Aristotle embraces this circle in part because the procedures whereby human societies maintain themselves define what humanity is: the elements of all good must be found there in however stunted and distorted a form. But Aristotle, no less than Plato, needs something to break the circle. Plato invoked the vision of 'the form of the good,' in effect the eventual knowledge of the universe as a unique functioning system. What breaks the circle for Aristotle, though, is that, at any given time, agents find themselves in determinate, concrete situations that call for specific responses from them; and he will show in *Politics* III–IV that the forms of political organizations can and should reflect the specific circumstances in which they are planted and the ways of life that they must accommodate. One might object that in many circumstances there is nothing to determine a specific response; but to that objection the sufficient answer is that in such circumstances the question 'What is the right thing to do?' has no application. The question presupposes a specific situation calling for something to be done *about it*; and people who say we are all always in situations of that sort may be suspected of having bees in their bonnets and axes to grind.

Finally, the discussion of good sense ends with a cryptic remark to the effect that good sense is not *merely* a *'hexis* with *logos'* because one might forget such a disposition but one cannot forget good sense. That seems to be true – one can forget how to fix a flat, but one can't forget the difference between right and wrong – but I don't quite see the point of it here, unless it is just to remind us that 'good sense' is a reflection of a person's personality as a whole and in all its articulations, involved constantly in all deliberations. Which is true, and could be a good way to wind up the discussion; but the point is not made explicitly, and I have the impression that Aristotle is once more responding to what he thinks is an erroneous formulation espoused by someone in his circle.

2.3124 Intuition (Nous) (VI vi; 1140b31–1141a8)

Of the five candidates we began with, two remain, *sophia* ('wisdom') and *nous* ('intuition,' or 'insight'); and we have one place to fill, that of the virtue of the theoretical intellect. Obviously that is going to be wisdom. Wisdom includes scientific knowledge, the grasp of deductive systems. But such systems are derived from principles that they do not establish. So 'intuition' remains to be the word for that whereby we grasp such principles. Aristotle is brisk about this, but even so makes heavy weather of it; the elimination he presents is succinct but complex – pointlessly so, I feel.

Why is *nous* introduced at this specific point? Granted that it is complementary to *epistēmē* as an element in *sophia* and has to be dealt with before the latter, wouldn't it have been natural to deal with these three concepts in succession and then proceed to *phronēsis*, or to deal with the 'art and good sense' couple first and then deal with this triad? In a way, yes. But the present order has its attractions. *Epistēmē* really had to come first, as the chief claimant, and *sophia* last as the winner. Art follows knowledge because they form an epistemic pair, as we saw, and good sense follows art for the same reason. So there is nowhere else for intuition to go.

The treatment has its problems, though. Good sense has its principles, its *archai*, just as wisdom has – its first principle seems to be its grasp of an overall end. Why was not 'intuition' then introduced (since after all we have just been talking about good sense) as that which grasps first principles in both areas? In the anatomy of good sense that follows this elimination and conceptual clarification, the word *intuition* will indeed be used in relation with the first principles of practical reason – eventually, the individual recognitions that are the 'principles' of practical reasoning at the other end. So why is that not said here? I think the answer is twofold. First, as a matter of method, Aristotle is anxious to preserve the complete separation of practical and theoretical questions, which Plato had confused, and to use the same word for what occupies the same position in relation to each would make *nous* a relative term rather than one of the real somethings with which a thinker actually achieves truth. And second, it really would be an equivocation: the place of an axiom or definition as foundation of a deductive system is not the same as that of a grasp of the nature of the human good, because the actions of which a human life consists are not deduced from anything but are individual deeds in unique situations.

Aristotle's treatment of intuition here is puzzling because it is so laconic. The word *nous* plays an important role elsewhere in his writings, and one that seems at odds with its restricted scope here. From his lost (early?) work *On Prayer* we have an isolated quotation that 'God is either *nous* or something even beyond *nous*,' and in *Metaphysics* XII the unmoved mover is said to be *nous* intuiting itself and spoken of in terms that take it for granted that it is a supreme deity.[182] Again, in the systematic exposition of the faculties of the psyche in *On the Soul*, the term *nous* is used to stand for the entire faculty of thinking. How are we to explain this discrepancy between the narrow scope of *nous* in the present passage and its exuberant expansion elsewhere?[183] Is Aristotle using the word here in a special sense for a very restricted purpose, without regard to what he says elsewhere? Or must we say that this passage comes from some otherwise unexemplified period in his literary life?

A sort of solution to this puzzle is perhaps possible. In the passage in *On the Soul* it looks as if *nous* really stands for the grasp of concepts: we can just take it for granted that a being that has attained the level of conceptual abstraction is capable of operating discursively on that level, just as a being endowed with sense perception is able to construct for itself the external world and is ipso facto endowed with desires and aversions. And it will be suggested in *Ethics* X that the need for discursive thought is a product of human weakness. This would be a sketchy statement of what was to be a standard thesis of more firmly monotheistic systems: only a corporeal being capable of deliberation is capable of *epistēmē*, the laborious demonstration of conclusions from hard-won premises, for a purely intellectual being would grasp all the necessary connections immediately, as a single intuitively conceived whole. *Sophia*, in which systems are demonstrated from first principles, is after all one of the human virtues, a perfection of specifically human nature.

2.3125 Wisdom (Sophia) (1141a9–b8 [VI 7])

It follows by elimination that 'wisdom' (*sophia*) will be the word for the excellence of the theoretical intellect. But the elimination was unnecessary. Of course it is. The word *philosophy* means the pursuit of wisdom, and was coined (in Pythagorean circles, it seems) to mean the systematic pursuit of the most basic understanding of the most fundamental realities of the world – it being assumed that such understanding was not readily attainable. *Sophia* is the word for what philosophers would do if they could, and what that is depends on the shifting ambitions of philosophers as science and speculation get wider and deeper.

Aristotle's way of introducing the topic, however, is by way of everyday language. *Sophos* is a word applied to experts, the most accomplished practitioners of any field of skill. But it is also applied to people who show comparable gifts in less restricted contexts. It is a word for the most 'precise' or 'accurate' (*akribestatē*) kind of knowledge; and this must be the best inferences from the best premises – *nous* plus *epistēmē* equals *sophia*. But what are the 'best' premises? The most clearly ascertained? Aristotle's word is *timiōtata*, 'most honourable' – the idea is clearly that the topic of wisdom in the unrestricted sense should be that which we regard most highly. (Ross uses the word 'highest,' but that is not explicit enough.)

On the face of it, this should equate wisdom with theology, if there is such a thing. Aristotle makes the equation only incidentally, however. What he says is that wisdom is thus differentiated from good sense, even in its most comprehensive form as statecraft, unless one supposes that human beings are the most venerable entities in the universe. But they aren't. Even if living things are the most venerable of physical things, and humans the most venerable animals, other things outrank them, are more godlike – most obviously, the constituents of the cosmos.

Aristotle is being very cagy here, and rightly so: it cannot be part of the definition of philosophy that its subject-matter should ultimately prove to be of this or that kind. All we are committed to here is the presumption that no inhabitant of the cosmos can ontologically out-rank the cosmos as a whole. Even so, Aristotle may be going too far, or in the wrong direction. The essential difference between wisdom and good sense is surely that good sense is fundamentally practical rather than theoretical. But I suppose the point is that, as Aristotle says here, good sense (and its diminished forms in animals other than humans) is limited by its practical aim to the lives of the practitioners and their associates; wisdom would be limited to that subject-matter if it should happen that the practitioners did indeed exemplify the most venerable kind of reality in the cosmos, which would be odd (*atopon*). (Aristotle, we note, does not actually say it would be impossible, only that the possibility is too absurd to take seriously.)

The emphasis on the exalted status of wisdom and its objects will be important in Book X, but as it stands it is almost perverse. It almost misrepresents the tradition to which it belongs. Plato in the *Republic* (475B–485B) emphasized rather the scope and universality at which science and philosophy aim, even though the unchanging nature of fundamental truths inspires awe and lifts their student to a higher level of being. Similarly, in Aristotle's main programmatic statement in *Metaphysics* I 1–2, the line of ascent that takes us through the arts and sciences involves universality as well as abstractness. At the end of *Metaphysics* XII, the objective of philosophical contemplation seems to be the universe as a unified system, in which the fact of its unity and its unifying ground are obviously complementary. And in a famous passage in *Parts of Animals* (I 5), the mundane richness of specialist inquiries is balanced off against the exalted poverty of theology. In fact, I suppose, in the universe as Aristotle conceives it the philosopher arrives at the knowledge of the most rarefied and exalted realities only through more and more comprehensive syntheses of phenomena using more and more recondite principles, following the original impetus that takes us from experience to art in the first place.

Note where the elimination of presumptive virtues has left us. Book VI began with the call for an account of the *logos* that is complementary to moral virtue and directs it. But, by the time our elimination is complete, we see that moral virtue and good sense together are contrasted with *sophia*, the other intellectual virtue. Since from the very beginning we have been concerned with the moral life as the field of practical reason, this seems to make wisdom extraneous to our concerns. And yet, wisdom is *ex hypothesi* a 'higher' excellence of human beings, being concerned with more exalted objects; and, from the practical point of view, 'wisdom' is conceptually a perfection that is recognized as such in every particular domain of skill and in life generally. But, by the same token, wisdom takes us away from the commonplace to a more rarefied sphere of activity. And it was important to our initial discussion of happiness in I vii–xi that happiness should be within the compass of ordinary human activity, available to all who are not disabled.

We seem to have landed ourselves in a predicament. But, in fact, we were already in such a predicament, though we took no note of it. Good sense and moral virtue had already taken us out of the domain of the commonplace, because, although they are in theory accessible to ordinary people, most people take no account of them. Most people live unselfconsciously from day to day within the confines of law and the folkways ('unwritten law' in Aristotle's usage).[184] The very idea of living the 'best possible' life is an elitist idea; its consummation in politics involves the idea of leadership, which entails superiority in the leader over the led. Aristotle in his *Politics* resists this implication by enunciating the political ideal that each citizen in turn should rule and be ruled, lead and be led; but the idea has a utopian flavour.[185] And, perhaps more important, the next main division of the *Ethics* will introduce the notion of moral weakness (*akrasia*): not everyone lives up to their ideal of the good life all the time. In fact, it may occur to us that hardly anyone does. As with the 'authenticity' that existentialists talked about in recent decades, the normal condition of humanity turns out to be a highly unusual one. Most people have no effective ideals, though they know what ideals are; those who do have clearly envisaged ideals fail to live up to them. The fact that, if they did, there would be a further ideal of intellectual excellence that cannot even be envisaged until peace and plenty provide leisure for a privileged class hardly takes us further into the stratosphere than we already are.

It is true, however, that the relation of wisdom to good sense leaves us with a problem, to which we return after considering the internal workings of good sense.

There need not be and cannot be a determinate anatomy of *sophia* to fill out the schematic outline Aristotle has given us. Such an anatomy would consist of the whole content of Aristotelian philosophy – in the same way, I would argue, that the same material would furnish the substantive content of *nous* to flesh out the laconic remarks in *On the Soul* III 4–8. There can, however, be an anatomy of *phronēsis*. If practical wisdom can be exercised by individuals on their own behalf in relation to the 'human good,' it can be exercised on behalf of any group of which one is a member, such as family, tribe, and city. And if one an exercise it for them, one can exercise it for any other individual or group to whom one is mentor or adviser, ex officio or out of good will. And then, one can exercise it for anyone at all, simply by empathizing with their aims and views. And if these are all possible, one can consider the skills of deliberation in abstraction from any practical concern – this will form part of our anatomy of *phronēsis*, because there is plainly no other context in which Aristotle could suitably discuss it. And once this abstraction has been made, one must say something about its complement, the true grasp of the *archē* on which deliberation must be anchored if it is to be a part or aspect of virtue. And how about the enlightened imagination that discerns the *kairos*, the situation as moment of action? There is a lot to be said here, and Aristotle is about to say it.

2.32 The Anatomy of Good Sense (1141b8–1144b1)

After eliminating false claimants to the position of 'intellectual virtue,' Aristotle slides into an anatomy of one of the two successful claimants, *phronēsis*. It seems to work like this. In clarifying the position of *sophia* Aristotle explains why it cannot be the same as *phronēsis*, not even the ruling kind of *phronēsis*, which is statecraft – or is it? And before we know it we are launched on a rambling discussion whose aim is uncertain until we learn at 1144b1 that our discussion of *sophia* and *phronēsis* is now ended; so that is what we must have been doing. We start with a simple contrast between the concerns of *phronēsis* and those of *sophia*. But this is essentially a commonplace; and why should we be reverting to *phronēsis* at all? What has happened is that *sophia*, now recognized as the most refined and conceptually sophisticated use of mind, turns out to have a dual structure, involving conceptualization (insight) as well as argument. And this suggests a comparable structure for *phronēsis*, which in the light of the development of Books I–V must still be the main topic.

Just as the actual substance of theoretical wisdom is scientific understanding (*epistēmē*), so the substance of practical wisdom is 'good counsel' (*euboulia*) – a new term, the anatomy of which is what Aristotle now provides. He is thus able to give the idea of *phronēsis* some content at last, as he could not do before the elimination and the *sophia* analysis. The discussion is remarkably tangled, however; Aristotle seems to be fighting on several fronts at once, repeating many points he has already made in *EN* and elsewhere.

Not surprisingly, the structure that emerges reflects the anatomy of deliberation in III ii–iv. Deliberation begins with a wish for something assumed without argument to be desirable – if rightly, on the basis of some form of insight; if wrongly, as the product of imagination. At the end comes choice, a decision to act, which again should reflect insight because it involves the direct recognition that this particular action and no other has the desired characteristics that call for it to be done.

We can see how and why Aristotle gets into a discussion of *euboulia*. But why is the discussion itself so convoluted, and why does he introduce such apparently peripheral topics as advice and judgment? This does not really become clear until we reach the evaluation of intellectual virtue at VI xii. It then turns out that Aristotle, without quite saying so, has been answering the question: what is the controlling (*kurios*) kind of *phronēsis*? My difficulty with this is that the question seems unnecessary, owing less to the necessities of the case than to Aristotle's personal conviction that authority is the only alternative to disorder.[186]

Whether Aristotle's question is well posed or not, his answer is that what is *kurios* is insight into the fact; he keeps coming back to this, but then he keeps sliding away from it because, from another point of view, all inquiries must be controlled by a grasp of the universal end. Insight, apparently, operates at both ends, but not in the same way.

What gets Aristotle into a discussion of 'understanding' is the consideration that we deliberate always on the *supposition* (*hupolēpsis*) of the goodness of an end. We do not always exercise our practical reasoning powers in the light of the end presented by our own moral characters: we can advise other people about their problems from their own points of view. What we do then is not strictly deliberation as Book III originally defined it, but it is certainly practical inquiry or quest (*zētēsis*) of a sort. And, as Aristotle goes on to say, all these states and activities, which are a sort of fall-out from *phronēsis*, converge on a single point: they all centre on the grasp of an individual case. The function of all this discussion is to get us away from the wish-dominated (and statecraft-dominated) model of *phronēsis* and deliberation to a model that preserves the dominion of particular insights into practical affairs.[187]

2.321 Good Counsel (1141b8–1142b33 [VI 8–10])

Sophia, which divides into insight and understanding, has to do with the highest and most honourable things – in the last resort, with the divine (1141b2–3). If *phronēsis* is to be strictly comparable, it must likewise be concerned with the most exalted things in its own range. But Aristotle's definition was more general: 'a truthful tendency, with *logos*, to take action with regard to things good and bad for humans' (1140b6–7, slightly varied at 1140b20–1). The definition, trickily worded as it is, has to have this greater generality because the virtue of good sense is needed in *all* the contingencies of life, as they come along: practical people do not have the option, as theorists do, of picking and choosing among their topics. The place for an analogue of *sophia* remains open, however, and at 1141b12–14 Aristotle fills it with another trickily worded formula, each word of which could use a commentary: 'one who is given to hitting on what is the best for a human being among practicables, in accordance with reasoning.'[188] What this defines, however, is not good sense but good counsel (*euboulia*) in its most general sense (*haplōs*), where good counsel is verbally equated with excellence in deliberation. We note the insistence on the *processes* of reasoning, because it is after all deliberation we are concerned with; but since it is *the best* that is to be attained a true grasp of principles must be involved as well, so that the analogy with *sophia* extends to its duality as well.

The relation between these two complex concepts, good sense and good counsel, is not simple; and the ensuing discussion switches back and forth between the two in a way that seems pointlessly confusing. Aristotle does not clear up the confusion but makes it worse confounded, confronting the reader with a string of assertions merely linked by the phrase 'and another thing' or 'on the other hand' (*eti de*).

The basic trouble with this discussion is that the evident structure of *phronēsis*, the deployment of *logos* in active contexts, is stated in an oddly hedging or veiled way. The *work* of good sense is deliberation, Aristotle says (1141b9–10), but such thinking must be done in the light of true insight into nature of the good and (above all) into the particular situations that confront the agent. Neither of these kinds of insight, however, is something a person can *work* at. At the particular end, situation-recognition is clearly epistemic in character, the fruit of experience, and experience is funded memory that comes with time (so long as one is not 'totally unperceptive,' 1141a10). But

Aristotle says little about it, beyond what can be gathered from the first part of Book VII. He does not say whether such recognitions are explicit or inexplicit, whether the appropriate values are correctness or relevance or comprehensiveness or what. At the universal end, on the other hand, the premise in the form of 'the end, i.e., the good, is of such and such a kind' (1144a32–3) is simply a reflection of moral character, with no specific epistemic identity. Presumably it is inarticulate (how could one put a view of life into a verbal formula?), but Aristotle does not even say that much. In fact, I suppose because it is indeed not epistemically grounded, he tends to exclude it from his discussion, writing as if it were not a *part* of dianoetic excellence at all. He writes almost as if it were as extraneous to intellectual virtue as the external goods are to moral virtue: an indispensable adjunct rather than an integral constituent.

2.3211 Good Counsel in General (1141b8–1142a30 [VI 8–9])

It sounds from the definition as though good counsel means a tendency to reason truthfully about practical things in general, since its topic is 'what is best for humans.' But Aristotle repeats (1141b15–20) his old line about good sense being concerned with the *facts* of life, so that, though the universal and the particular are both desirable, it is knowledge about the particular case that is more important – if one has to choose. And not just knowledge of the facts, either, of the sort that a clever child might memorize: in mathematics, it is knowing what to say that matters, which is why children can be mathematical prodigies, but in practice one has to see what one has to *do*, which takes experience (1142a11–20) and the sort of conviction that arises from that. Perception is what is involved – not like sense perception, but the kind of perception that sees that 'the last is a triangle' (1142a29).

The immediate aim of that last bit is to contrast *phronēsis* with *sophia* again – the concern with particulars precludes it from being either *nous* or *epistēme* – but as soon as he has said it Aristotle backtracks: this sort of insight into particulars is not perception as a part of good sense, but *in contrast with* good sense. One sees the point – only *euboulia* is the *work* of good sense – but surely Aristotle has here become tied up in his garters.

How are the two allusions to mathematical thinking related? It might be easier to tell if we could be sure what 'the last is a triangle' refers to.[189] But perhaps the argument goes like this. Youths can do mathematics, just as children can learn their lessons, because all they have to do is get the words right in a verbally structured setting. The problems they have to solve are already precisely formulated. Practical problems are not like that: it takes experience to discern what there is in one's present situation that is problematic, and what the problem is about which something has to be done. But this painfully acquired shrewdness is not something that can be learned in a classroom, as an 'intellectual virtue' worthy of the name should be. So it cannot be part of good sense, but must be separated from it as a kind of perception. However, it is not at all like sense perception; it is more like recognizing an obvious truth than like hearing a noise. And then it seems suddenly to occur to Aristotle that geometry also involves a kind of perception, the recognition of obvious truths (like the slave in the *Meno* realizing that a square can be divided into triangles as well as into squares). But recognizing truths about geometrical figures is something that takes place essentially in the context of mathematical inquiry; and Aristotle goes on immediately to say that good counsel is itself a form of inquiry (*zētēsis*), though not just *any* sort. Insights into situations are not just isolated intuitions that could occur in the same form outside a context of inquiry.

2.32111 Politics and Individual Life (1141b22–1142a11)

Despite the supreme importance of the particular case, Aristotle says, there should be an architectonic or organizing or (in Ross's version) a 'controlling kind' of *phronēsis*, and it looks as if that should be politics.[190] The initial definition of good sense seemed to identify it with the ability to think about (*theōrein*) what is good for oneself and for humanity in general, as exemplified by the statesman Pericles – an ability ascribed to economists and politicians (1140b8–11). But did it really? A closer look shows that that was only what people generally think. It now turns out that we were wrong. The distinction between architectonic thinking and hands-on thinking does not distinguish politics from private affairs, but turns up within politics itself as the difference between constitutional lawmaking and day-to-day decision making.[191] And the nitty-gritty of political life itself is traditionally contrasted with good sense, which minds its own personal business, as a quotation from Euripides reminds us. The fact is, politics as we know it involves the same sort of thinking as good sense, but its defining properties are different: it operates in a special way in a special sphere (politics is a trade, political science is an academic discipline, though Aristotle does not have quite those thoughts). The insight sensible people have into their own affairs is a genuine exercise of intelligence (*gnōsis*), but quite different from that.[192] And yet, how could it not be more generous, more noble, more glorious, and sign of a higher power to concern oneself with the good of the community as a whole rather than confining oneself to one's own private affairs? (In setting this opposition up, Aristotle does not let us forget that there is a transitional area, that of the family; it contributes nothing to the discussion, but it is fatal to forget it.) This apparent paradox, however, is easily resolved: since one's individual life is lived within family and city, one cannot separate the individual good from the common good (1142a9–10). This is a surprisingly muted statement of the theme emphasized in *Politics* I, that a good human life cannot be lived outside a civic structure.

2.3212 Good Counsel as Inquiry (VI ix; 1142a31–b33)

I suppose what we have just learned is that the distinction between the architectonic kind of good sense and other kinds cannot be made in terms of power relations, but has to be a matter of the logical structure of the thought processes involved, as indeed the analogy of *sophia* suggested. What remains is to examine that structure; and, as usual, what we have is a contribution to formal analysis rather than description and recommendation of a way of life.

The work of good sense then, as we said before, is good counsel, excellence in the process of deliberation that links our assumptions about the good to our perceptions of our situation. The process is a quest (*zētēsis*), but not just *any* quest, for inquiry in general has as such no practical point.

The word 'quest' or 'inquiry' may take us by surprise: where did it come from? Looking back, we find it just after the quotation from Euripides about good sense in private life: people who have that are understood to *search out* what is best for themselves and believe that that is what they ought to do – they are rational egoists, in fact (1142a7). What they are right about, and why we pay them the compliment of calling them sensible, is not their self-centredness but the fact that they inquire systematically into a good by which they think it is right that their action should be guided.

What can we say about excellence in deliberation? We have seen that it is the analogue of *epistēmē*, but of course it is not *epistēmē*, it belongs to the practical realm. It is correctness in the actual processes of practical thinking – not just serendipity or shrewdness or quick-wittedness, and not just having the right opinions (even the right opinions about what should be done), but performing the operations of practical reasoning in the right way. That means, of course, that one's reasoning should neither be valid though unsound (1142b19–26), nor reaching a true conclusion by invalid means (1142b26–7), but logically correct; and, since we need to reach a decision, efficient as well. The processes are the same whether the end in view is right or wrong, and there is a sense in which good counsel is good counsel whichever the end may be; but the person to whom we attribute good counsel without qualification (*haplōs*) is the one who has the true end in view. But it is the *phronimos* as such who has that true view; the *euboulos* as such simply takes that end for granted, acts on the supposition of its truth. How far it is practically possible to deliberate in the light of an end that does not truly represent the sum of one's experience and convictions is a question Aristotle does not go into; it is a problem that civil servants after a change of regime do not always succeed in solving, even if they try.

Tricky as it is, the theoretical separation of the processes of logically correct and efficient deliberation from the 'supposition of the end' is what makes the separate consideration of advice and sympathy possible. And in the context of politics, it also acknowledges the *Meno*'s point that, in practical affairs, correct opinion is as good as knowledge – though in Aristotle's version the difference between the two has nothing to do with 'reasoning about the explanation' (*Meno* 97B–98A).[193]

2.322 Understanding, Advice, and Judgment (1142b34–1143a24 [VI 11])

'Understanding' has, in effect, the same scope as good sense, but is not literally practical; the conclusion is not a decision but a criticism. And 'sympathetic judgment' (*sungnōmē*) is the basis of equity. Equity was previously said to be a reinterpretation of laws by reading the lawmaker's mind rather than following the letter of the law; but here the meaning may rather be that the judge attends to whether offenders meant well rather than to whether they knowingly violated the law. (The Greek text is apparently corrupt, but it seems not to matter vitally.)

These very brief remarks open up an important topic that Aristotle does not expand on. We do not, it turns out, have a sharp distinction between thinking that is immediately practical, and preoccupied with contingency, and thinking that is impersonal, theoretical, and universal. People think about each other's affairs, as well as their own, and pass judgment on them even when there is no occasion to. And the judgment they pass may involve simple comprehension, or it may involve an element of sympathy as well. The sharp distinction between thinking based on justice and thinking based on friendship does not represent a real-life dichotomy between the reflective and the practical, the personal and the impersonal.

2.323 Intuition (1143a28–b5)

Anyway, as Aristotle says, all these dispositions point in the same direction or converge on the same point. Understanding, judgment, good sense, and insight are ascribed to the same people. They all have to do with particular cases. And, since, as we have seen, there is no necessary connection between such insight and a personal insight into 'the human good,' the intuition or insight into particulars must be the actual basis of all practical thinking. We knew this from the start, of course: from the first paragraphs of the *Ethics* it was evident that the overall good 'at which all things aim' could not undermine the actual values people find in particular situations, and that a good action is done for its *own* sake, because it *is* fine. The knowledge of the good never achieves an independent and distinct identity such that it could be involved in a genuine dialectic of deliberation.

But is that really what Aristotle says? 'Intuition is of the ultimates in *both* directions,' he says (1143b35–6); and does this not mean that we need *nous* both to see the universal in the particular and to grasp the overall truth, which in this case would be the conviction that 'the good is of such-and-such a kind'? I for one used to think that was what he meant, because it seemed so obviously right; but the text here clearly rules it out. In theoretical science, *nous* grasps the most basic indemonstrable axioms; in practical thought, what is basic is insight into contingent particulars, for these are the first principles, the *archai*, of purposiveness. Universal judgments are derived from particulars, and particulars call for perception, i.e. *nous*.[194] It could not be more explicit.

2.3231 Nature and Good Sense (1143b6–14)

The first time we emphasized the importance of particulars in *phronēsis*, we suggested that this might be why young people may be good at mathematics but not at politics – the former needs only skill in manipulating uninterpreted symbols, the latter calls for experience in interpreting situations. (In fact, says Aristotle, even philosophy and natural science require more understanding of the real world than mathematics does.) That shows, incidentally, why the distinction between the overall end of action and particular goods cannot be maintained: young people experience one thing at a time, just as older people do, but they don't understand their experiences, don't relate them to other events and to the whole fabric of life. To grasp life as a whole is to grasp each event as related to other events.

Now, when we say that all the dispositions we have distinguished converge on one point, it turns out that that point is the particular situation; and particular situations are a matter for insight, something that comes only with time. So we tend to think that these dispositions are a matter of natural maturing, we just grow into them. It follows that we ought to attend to the sayings and opinions of experienced and older people (or people of good sense), no less than to arguments: because experience has given them an eye, they see correctly.[195]

This is surely rather strange. What is the point of deliberation, originally said to be the chief work of practical wisdom, if experience is just as good? Or are we to say that experience somehow subconsciously builds up the skill in establishing connections that the expert in deliberation consciously cultivates? Well, yes, I suppose we are. Just as moral virtue grows in people who are well brought up and conscientious, so good sense grows in people as the ways the world works are brought forcibly and persistently to their attention.[196]

One must not go overboard here. Aristotle does not actually say we should take the word of wrinklies for anything, only that we should listen to them respectfully. The mere fact that experience has given them an eye does not mean that they are always looking in the right direction, or even that they are keeping their good eye open. And, when it comes right down to it, is this acknowledgment of the advantages of experience anything more than another version of the thesis that right opinion is as good as knowledge, so long as it *is* right? Still, we are rather left wondering what the status of good sense is. And that is the question to which Aristotle now turns.

2.33 The Value of Intellectual Virtue (1143b18–1144b16)

Having emphatically closed off the discussion of the two intellectual virtues, Aristotle starts what looks like a major new discussion, that of the utility of these virtues, by listing obvious difficulties (*aporiai*) that have to be faced. But in fact there is little that needs to be said. Indeed, it seems strange that at this point Aristotle should raise the question at all. The same question could have been asked of the moral virtues, but was not. The moral virtues are desirable by definition – the virtue of anything is simply its most desirable condition, and what we said of the moral virtues was mostly an account of the formal properties that followed from that definition. So why does the question arise for the intellectual virtues? Aristotle immediately points out that to call them virtues is already to affirm their desirability. On the other hand, if we take 'useful' literally as referring to instrumental value, no attempt was made to show that moral virtues are useful in that sense. Such an attempt would belong not to ethics but to political and social theory. But it turns out that Aristotle has three points that he is using this question to introduce, one about good sense, one about wisdom, and one about the relation between the two.

The point made about the worth of wisdom is that it makes people happy simply by being actualized, since activity in accordance with excellence in the manifestation of *logos* is happiness. This brings us suddenly back from the long detour through the varieties of excellence to the main theme of the *Ethics*, the activity that is happiness. The whole account of the virtues, though by no means a digression (as some have called it) was in a sense a blind alley. Everything we said about them showed how rational they were, but did not show how they contributed to well-being. An idealist would act thus, a well-brought-up person would be ashamed not to act thus; but how is a person's life richer for acting thus? The argument of I viii insisted that acting thus should bring inward peace; but was that convincing? Why should we call it peace, rather than stagnation?[197] To make further progress, we must consider the nature of consciousness and the relation between consciousness and pleasure, a theme we will be able to approach only by way of the unlikely route of a discussion of the true nature of friendship and love. That discussion will explain why it is wisdom whose exercise is said here to form a part of happiness, and not good sense, though good sense is a virtue too.

Is it really true, though, that intellectual virtues must be desirable just because they are virtues? Yes, if the argument is to be trusted; but Aristotle has warned us not to trust arguments that affront our sense of reality. Good sense must indeed be desirable, if the argument of the *Ethics* is to be trusted at all, because the presupposition of the whole investigation is that for any living being with a sense of time the question 'How shall my life be organized?' and 'What should I do now?' inevitably arise. A propensity to answer these questions in the right way, if there is a right way, is then obviously desirable. But the virtue of theoretical reason, *sophia*, has no such conceptual connection to human well-being and the inevitable dynamics of life. The intellectual virtues are defined as propensities to achieve truth, and though, if one is going to ask theoretical questions, true answers are doubtless the best sort to have, we have been presented with no argument to suggest that one is better off asking such questions in the first place, or that, if one does, there is any value in the asking other than the fun of working out an answer to meet arbitrary criteria. So far as we can tell, wisdom and its pursuit might be a moral irrelevance, at best a form of recreation. Only if the 'function' of human beings requires them collectively to serve as the self-knowledge of the universe, which I think is implied by Aristotle's world-view, even if he did not himself think of it that way, do scientific and philosophical thought take on any significance.[198]

Nowadays one might say something like the following. The ability to develop technologies and cultures, which is the basis of human life, is inevitably also the ability to speculate and reflect on the nature of the world. But such speculation and reflection are a mere by-product or side-effect of the valuable, practical parts of human thought, with no value of their own. They have no survival value, but are causally inseparable from what does have survival value. This position, or something like it, is commonplace today. It was not available, of course, to Aristotle. But the values it implies were asserted shortly after his death by Epicurus, according to whom the only value of scientific theories was reassurance, so that preoccupation with their truth was to be avoided.[199]

Aristotle, in short, has performed a sleight of hand. Good sense has been shown to be desirable. Good sense has been defined in terms of truth. The acquisition of truth is thus shown to be the criterion of desirability in intellectual matters. And the highest truth must be the most desirable kind. It is a non sequitur, because what made truth desirable in good sense was its relevance to practical life, not its status as truth.

2.331 Excellences Not Virtues (11444a20–b17)

The demonstration of the value of the intellectual virtues rests on their definition as the states whereby we reliably grasp truth by the best methods; and this demonstration is best carried out by reminding us of what happens in the domain of practical life when we have the truth without the methods or the methods without the truth. What we are then left with is either an unprincipled cleverness or a fortunate temperament. Aristotle incorporates sketches of both conditions in his treatment.

2.3311 Cleverness (1144a24–36)

The way is opened for a consideration of cleverness (*deinotēs*) by the description of the derivative forms of good sense, judgment and sympathy. Those endowments, though sundered from consideration of one's own good, are by no means divorced from consideration of the *human* good: we can advise other people, exercise good judgment in their affairs, enter sympathetically into their plans and predicaments, only because we, like them, are human, and take as our reference point their best knowledge of the human good as it applies to them. Mere efficiency and logical cogency, sundered from connection with such knowledge, is mere cleverness, and this is not in itself an admirable characteristic. One can be too clever by half.[200]

The existence of cleverness in abstraction from any context of moral seriousness may remind us that there is one question that Aristotle fails to raise which is rather damaging to the optimistic version of his position, according to which virtue is within everyone's reach (1099b19): how is skill in deliberation acquired? Character is formed by experience, which, at the same time and by the same process, forms the insightful judgment that is the first principle of action. But what of deliberation? It requires the faculty of cleverness, and is nothing but cleverness in the service of good ends. But how does one get to be clever? The intellectual virtues are supposed to be developed by teaching (1103a15); but how does one teach people to be clever? It is hard to teach people who are not clever already. And in calling cleverness a faculty (1144a23) and referring to it (apparently) as an 'eye' (1142a29–30), Aristotle seems to assimilate cleverness to such faculties as sight, which one has to have before one can exercise them. Again, one has the impression that Aristotle has not fully worked out his epistemic model for good sense.

2.3312 Natural Virtue (1144b1–16)

The point Aristotle wants to make about good sense in this discussion of the value of intellectual virtue is that the account we originally gave of the moral virtues was, in one respect, an account of them *together with* good sense: the presence of the *orthos logos* and of the good sense that determines that *logos* was included in the definition, just as the analysis of deliberation was included within the discussion of virtue though it formed no proper part of it. But it would have been possible to consider what the strictly moral aspect of moral virtue would be in isolation, and we recognize it as something familiar: natural good nature, an inborn or spontaneously developed propensity to mean well. Some people seem to be born with their hearts in the right place. So we have to recognize the existence of this natural virtue alongside virtue in the strict sense, in which what is done not only coincides with what reason would dictate but actually is dictated by reason.

A few years ago it was fashionable to assign to this 'natural virtue' an important role in Aristotle's ethical theory. But that was surely a mistake. It is only one paragraph to set against the elaborate and protracted discussion of the moral virtue that goes with good sense, and Aristotle's treatment is not encouraging. Unless people have the good judgment to tell them what the right thing to do is, their well-meant endeavours may be harmful to themselves and other people.

Natural virtue is not be confused with the 'eye' that Aristotle has told us untutored people acquire from experience. Cephalus, in Plato's *Republic* I, is surely meant to be the paradigm of such a person; although he cannot say what justice is, he expresses himself as convinced that the desire to do right should be the dominant motive in his life. Natural virtue, by contrast, is just a temperament one happens to have, not based on any idea or dominant motivation at all. It is not a habituation to the best choice as such, but to some pattern of behaviour that merely happens to coincide in a certain area with what virtue would prescribe. It is, says Aristotle at 1144b13–17, a separate *hexis* alongside of virtue proper in the domain of practice, just as cleverness is a separate something alongside of good sense in the domain of thought.[201]

The recognition of an apparently innate disposition to mean well in one sort of context or another sorts ill with what seemed to be Aristotle's initial position in Book II, that the human character is formed by habituation from a neutral predisposition to form habits. But Aristotle did not actually say that the initial condition was neutral; on the contrary, he said later in Book II that people are more tempted (in general, and as individuals) to one sort of departure from the mean than to others, and that some departures are worse than others, from which it follows that there could be people whose natural predisposition draws them in one or another kind of situation towards what is, in fact, the mean. Aristotle's theory of habituation really requires no more than that character be malleable, that innate temperament where it exists have no determining force.

Aristotle remarks at 1144b8–9 that beasts and children have such natural dispositions; we find the same thesis in his *Histories of Animals* VIII 1; he says there that in children such tendencies are the seeds of what will later be virtues. But then again, in *Rhetoric* II 12–14, he has a brilliant series of stereotypes of the temperaments characteristic of the young, the old, and the middle-aged. Presumably the terse formulation of the *Ethics* is meant to be compatible with the folk psychology of these more extensive and picturesque passages; but it may not be quite clear how the reconciliation should be carried out. I suppose Aristotle would simply say that the facts of natural endowment and development provide the material out of which the serious person must construct a character and a life.

2.34 The Unity of Virtue (1144b17–1145a11)

Book VI is complementary to the main argument of Books II–V, completing the account of virtue in general, and it ends by returning us to this wider context. The return is effected by way of the account of cleverness as an aspect of thought, which leads into an analogous account of 'natural virtue' as an aspect of habitual behaviour – and we find ourselves back discussing 'virtue' in general and adopting the loose form of words according to which only moral virtue is actually given that name. But the return to the wider context does not remove us from the topic of intellectual virtue, which remains the subject actually under discussion. The unity of moral virtue itself depends on the integrity of good sense, which itself depends on the apparently unstatable premise 'since the good is of such and such a kind' – unstatable, because it stands for the underlying awareness of all our values which is realized only in the way we see particular situations and problems and reflects the moral virtue of which it is itself the unifying factor. As if that were not confusing enough, we have still to take account of our discovery of a second intellectual virtue, theoretical 'wisdom' (*sophia*), which clearly represents the most sophisticated manifestation of *logos* but for that very reason can have no integral relation to practical life. Good sense cannot, therefore, control or embrace it; but some firm relation between the two must be established, or good sense faces an impossible (even a nonsensical) task.

2.341 The Unity of the Moral Virtues (1144b17–1145a6)

The account of 'natural virtue' said that people of fortunate temperament, if well instructed and appropriately prompted, will always
cheerfully do the right thing; but we must beware of them, because
we never know what they will cheerfully do next. We may add that
they will not be really good people, because the reason they use is
not their own and they can be led astray by bad advice. They do not
do the right thing, as really good people do, for the reason that they
see that it really is the right thing. And it is at this point that
Aristotle, apparently casually, introduces the essential and striking
feature of his account of virtue to which I have already drawn attention. Since good sense is single, its necessity to moral virtue means
that the latter is also single (1144b32–1145a2). The different 'virtues'
cannot exist separately, though the 'natural virtues' that are the
temperamental predispositions to them may so exist.

2.342 Wisdom and Good Sense (1145a6–11)

When we were discussing the value of the intellectual virtues we
insisted that wisdom was desirable as a constituent of happiness. The
omission to mention that good sense is also such a constituent might
be attributed simply to a desire not to be tedious. The contribution
of good sense to happiness was, after all, obvious from the beginning. It is only wisdom that needs to have its claim vindicated. But
a stronger interpretation of this reticence is suggested by the third
point Aristotle makes about his two virtues, which concerns the
relation between them. It was said already, at 1094a28–b7, that politics controls all other activities, including the sciences, by controlling
the conditions in which and the extent to which they are cultivated.
But politics is the same *hexis* as good sense, so that this subordination
suggests that wisdom is subordinate to good sense. This, Aristotle
now assures us, does not follow, for to make arrangements for wisdom to be realized is not to claim superiority over it, any more than
to provide for public worship is to claim superiority over God.

This doctrine, as stated, is innocuous. It leaves it open for us to
assert later that intellectual pursuits are the most delightful and
valuable of all, but does not require us to do so. But the exclusive
emphasis on the contribution of wisdom to happiness does suggest
the stronger interpretation, that the *sole* function of good sense, both
in private and in public life, is to make the intellectual life possible.
In Book X we will see Aristotle resisting without complete success

what is evidently a strong temptation to say precisely that. The passage before us will not of itself bear the stronger interpretation,[202] but other passages in the Aristotelian corpus permit themselves more emphatic language.[203]

The stronger interpretation is, of course, ruled out by the actual terms in which practical life was introduced and described – hundreds of pages of exposition cannot be assigned to oblivion by a single paragraph. But, even without that, the introduction of the intellectual life as the field of one of the two intellectual virtues, and hence as an important ingredient in human well-being, introduces into Aristotle's account a weakness of which we encountered a less serious form already. What comes of the notion of a good life, valuable in all its dimensions and such that anyone not 'crippled for virtue' can attain it, if its most valuable aspect is not only beyond the reach of all but a few savants but such that it can be open only to a minority supported in leisure by the labours of others? No doubt the good life, as Aristotle has described it, is *in practice* one open only to a leisured class, supported by slaves, but that dependence forms no part of the description. The dependence of *sophia* on *phronēsis*, by contrast, is explicitly necessary. How is this to be reconciled with 1139b4–5, which equates humanity with that kind of source of action that is equally describable as desirous insight or as thoughtful desire – an equation that would exclude the unimpassioned intellect from humanity altogether? The answer to be given in Book X is obvious, and taken up already by implication in Book VII: what we call the human (*anthrōpinon*) is the all-too-human (*anthrōpikon*), and humans are capable of something further than humanity. Being an obvious answer, however, does not make it a good one, though that does not mean that Aristotle could not have given it. As it stands, it is a palpable fudge. Meanwhile, the detachment of intellect from any physiological basis (*On the Soul* III 4) means that there can be no functional correlation of practice and contemplation: all we have is the demand for a quite indeterminate provision of leisure. There is no question of a way of life that shall include both the practical and the theoretical in any particular way. That question has not even been mooted, let alone settled.

We have now completed the treatment of virtue that began with I xiii. Have we also completed our positive treatment of *eudaimonia*? Book VII and Books VIII–IX could be said to be business left over from that discussion, but not to be parts of it. The account of virtue itself, however, is a survey of what there is to for a *spoudaios* to be serious about, in an integrated way corresponding to the integration of the human soul. But the original definition of happiness at I x also said, first, that it involved the *highest* virtue, if there is more than one, and, second, that it must be manifested in a complete life. But that raises two issues: first, the comparative evaluation of actions; and, second, the organization of a life, the overall allocation of interests and activities in a lifetime. Nothing has been said about either of those. In Book X, something will be. The discussion will not hark back directly to I x; it deals with those problems in the light of all that has been said in between. And the evaluation of activities makes no sense otherwise than in connection with a discussion of ways of life, because it is the latter that show what choices there are and in what contexts they have to be made.

CHAPTER THREE

The Pathology of Practical Reason (VII; 1145a15–1154b34)

From one point of view, the conclusion of the treatment of virtue would have been the place for Aristotle to stop. There is a clean break: all we are given by way of introduction to what follows is 'The next thing to say, making a fresh start, is ...' Always in ethics there is the danger of saying too much. Aristotle's insistence on the correct use of reason being that which the person of good sense would make leaves much scope for flexibility. Granted that determinate situations call for definite solutions, there could be large areas of life in which good sense dictates that one may do as one pleases – in fact, this must be so if the intellectual life is truly contingent on the availability of leisure. From that point of view, anything else we say can only foreclose on possibilities for living that would better have been left open.

There is, however, as we have seen, a lot of unfinished business, some of which is urgently required by what has gone before. Most urgently, the ideal of virtue as a coincidence of true judgment and correct desire in a mutually reinforcing circle leaves us with a question. What are the alternatives to virtue? By definition, vice and vicious activity are excessive or defective by the appropriate standard. But how is that possible? Is it that the vicious person is mistaken about where the mean lies? If so what could be the content of such a mistake? The original reliance on 'seriousness' suggested that attention to one's situation and the will to do right sufficed to indicate what was to be done: how could there be alternative solutions to the problem of how to live one's life, of which only one was correct? What could the criterion possibly be?[1] The alternative seems to be that vicious people do not seriously try to formulate ideals of a good life as a whole. I think this is what Aristotle does think: bad people may believe they are doing the right thing, but this belief has not been subject to criticism.[2] This view seems to leave no room for any such concept as 'evil' or 'wickedness,' but perhaps we are better off without such concepts. In any case, though, the question has not really been addressed yet.

Another piece of unfinished business is indicated by the fact that, both in virtue and in vice, desire and reason are in harmony. Good and bad people delight in doing what they do and in what they tend to do. But surely not everyone is like that. In fact, Aristotle's model of moral improvement and his whole project in the *Ethics* depend on people being dissatisfied with themselves, having the idea of a life better than the life they are already living. I have already noted how ill at ease we are with Aristotle's ideal of virtuous people delighting in their excellence. But we shall see that he leaves it open to us to believe that most people are neither virtuous nor vicious, but spend their lives struggling more or less successfully with inclinations that are at odds with their highest ideals.

The possibility of discrepancy between plans and longings suggests that we had better look at pleasure again, because pleasure is what tempts people. That suggests that a virtuous life is an austere life. But pleasure is natural (we spontaneously take it as a sign that things are going well for us, just as we take pain as a natural warning to stop whatever is causing it), so that a virtuous life, being by definition the life in which what is most truly human in us is most fully expressed, should be the most pleasant of all. We affirmed as much in I viii, and we glanced in II iii at the psychological machinery involved; but conceptual clarification is called for.

That is more or less the unfinished business that Book VII deals with. Other problems, as we have seen, are dealt with in Books VIII–IX, and call for yet another fresh start; they will be introduced in due course.

3.1 The Anatomy of Wrongdoing (VII i–x; 1145a15–1152a36)

The new topic is announced as the distinction between three behavioural conditions to be avoided: wickedness, weakness of will, and beastliness. But an examination of the second of these reveals the existence of a fourth condition, 'softness,' which needs to be distinguished from weakness; and the bulk of the treatment is explicitly devoted to a discussion of weakness and softness with their opposites, strength and hardness (announced at 1145a34, signed off at 1152a36). This anatomy of wrongdoing really is a new topic, and makes a fresh start in the sense that it draws little on what has been said before; but, as I have been saying, it does arise as a natural and necessary complement to the whole topic of virtue, in which the coincidence of reason and desire is thought of as unproblematic.

Aristotle's architectonic for the relations between controlling reason and that which reason controls, following the schema of I xiii, is a direct application of the underlying analysis of action from *On the Mind* III 10; it is quite systematic, but is not reflected in the dynamics of the text. He brushes aside the problems of vice (considered already, he claims) and beastliness (postponed), and plunges into a consideration of notorious problems arising from Socrates' thesis that 'no one goes wrong on purpose.' But I will begin by expounding the architectonic.

First, then, in the controlling/controlled relationship, we may contrast the condition of a being that has no independent desires to control with the condition of a being with desires but nothing to control them. The former condition is that of the gods (and, we may add, of angels and any other supposed incorporeal beings);[3] the latter is that of dumb animals. But we have to concede that there may be beasts in human shape – human beings in whom, congenitally or as the result of disease, the effective power of rational speech is absent.[4]

The second contrast to be made is that between humans whose perceptions and desires lie within the normal range of human goods, and those who lie outside this range – those whose lives and habits strike us not as wicked but as perverse or sick or simply inhuman. I do not know how, if at all, the lines are supposed to be drawn here, but what Aristotle has in mind is the existence of people whose tastes and habits are so bizarre that we cannot relate to them at all, we do not condemn them because we cannot understand how any human being could share them. It is as if the machinery of the mind were out of order. There are physical monsters; why not moral monsters?[5]

The beings contrasted in those pairs lack the normal controlling/controlled couple. Among people who possess both, we may first contrast those who regularly act on principle with those who have no principles to act on. This is the contrast between the virtuous and the vicious. But alongside this contrast is that between those who manage to force themselves to act on their convictions and those who fail to do so, who regularly violate the principles they acknowledge. These are the 'self-controlled' and the 'weak of will,' respectively; the former are not virtuous, because their desires remain at odds with their good sense, and the latter are not vicious, because their principles remain intact despite their failure to live up to them. Both of them are too susceptible to immediate impulses – in fact, to pleasures.

There is another pair of people who are differentiated by their resistance to pain: weak or 'soft' people, who do not persist in virtuous courses in the face of threats and discomforts, and enduring or 'tough' people who find it temperamentally easy so to resist and persist.

The preceding two pairs are all cases where good sense is intact but defects in the emotional apparatus lead to results other than a good life. But strength and weakness of will are shadowed by two defects of the reasoning process. Some people are stubborn, in the sense that once having made their minds up they are reluctant to change their minds, whatever new evidence or arguments may be adduced. Other people are labile, easily persuaded by whoever talks to them last. It makes no difference to the dynamics of these conditions whether the results are good or bad. Aristotle uses the example of Sophocles' *Philoctetes*, where Neoptolemus is talked out of the noble plan he had been talked into – or talked out of a cruel deception, whichever way you like to think of it. A case like this is hard to fit into Aristotle's general view of good sense, according to which one's view of the good reflects one's character; but I take it that Neoptolemus is persuaded to substitute a false *hupolēpsis* of the good for his own, or misdirected into a plausible misidentification of the relevant moral aspects of his situation. In *EN* X ix, we learn that well-meaning youths can be persuaded to change their lives for the better, so why should they not also be susceptible to persuasion to do worse?[6] But *of course* people can be talked into things; the oddity, if there is one, is that Aristotle pays so little attention to this possibility in the *Ethics*.[7]

3.11 Weakness of Will (1145a35–1152a36)

The main point of the anatomy I have outlined is to place the phenomenon of 'weakness of will' (*akrasia*) in a rich conceptual setting, and to anatomize that phenomenon itself. Weak-willed people act against their own moral convictions; but if a conviction is convincing, what can prevail against it? Surely the principles I actually act on must be identical with what I really think best for myself and for humanity as I exemplify it. As Aristotle deals with this problem, it becomes evident that what is at issue is the place of pleasure and temptation, and the complexities of the ways they lead people astray.

In fact, it is an elaboration on the same topic that was treated in II iii, but now from the perspective of adult life rather than that of character formation. One result of this emphasis is that Aristotle writes as if 'overindulgence' (*akolasia*) were a synonym of 'vice' (*kakia*) in general – an equation which greatly weakens the presentation of the *Ethics* as a whole, and is still common.[8]

Having announced this problem as the focus of his discussion, Aristotle offers us a full-scale formal treatment of it (1145b2–7), more or less in accordance with the 'scholastic' pattern sketched in the foreword. In the present case, however, Aristotle is not answering a single question but is unravelling a hitherto unexamined set of relationships within which the Socratic problem is placed. Consequently, the answer to that problem, despite its practical significance, does not serve effectively as a centre around which the discussion can be organized. We have a resolution of difficulties and a reconciliation of the phenomena, without being promised or provided with any core doctrine or definition.

3.111 The Conceptual Question

Akrasia is a tendency to be led astray by an excessive desire for things that in their place are naturally good – or by a desire for an excess of them. And by 'led astray' we mean that weak people, unlike bad people, are convinced that what they are doing is wrong, but do it anyway – pleasure and desire lead them to act in a way that violates their convictions. But Aristotle observes that whether one is called weak depends on what kind of desire it is. His discussion is two-sided. From one point of view, it is simply a description of how the Greek word *akratēs* was used. But at the same time it is an account of the facts that the usage reflects. And these facts are facts about the place of reason in human life – the circumstances in which people are reasonably thought to lose rational control over what they do.

To a considerable extent, the explanation depends on the necessary physiology of self-preservation. *Akrasia* in the literal sense is a loss of self-control in relation to the pleasures with which *sōphrosunē* (in the literal sense, as expounded in III x–xii) is concerned: the pleasures of touching and tasting. In discussing pleasure and virtue in II iii, we noted that no animal can survive unless its body keeps it informed (so to speak) of its need for food and drink. And no species can survive unless their bodies keep a fair proportion of its members reminded of the need to procreate. That is, there must be a set of desires that precede analysis and decision making. It is not surprising that there are a lot of people in whom these mechanisms of desire are not adequately under control.

There is another set of passions in relation to which people regularly lose self-control: people lose their tempers, see red. We use the same word *akratēs* of them, but add the qualification that it is their anger they can't control. Anger, according to some of the doctors of Aristotle's day, was a bodily phenomenon, a 'boiling of blood around the heart' (*On the Soul* I, 403a31), but Aristotle insists that the phenomenon is not so purely irrational as gluttony and lust. An ungovernable rage is said to be half rational, like slaves who listen to only half an order and rush off to execute it before they hear the rest. The point of this analogy must be that lust and gluttony are triggered simply by the sight or imagination of the desired object, whereas anger requires reflection on a situation in relation to our own involvement, a kind of mental activity only a reasoning animal is capable of. But people with uncontrollable tempers then go blind, as it were, and react to that partial analysis without regard to what they perfectly well know the situation really calls for.

In this connection, Aristotle throws in what looks like a countervailing consideration from popular morals. We tend to think rather better of the hot-tempered weakling (let's use that word to render *akratēs*, regardless of idiom) than of the lustful one because an ungovernable rage so obviously does make a person lose control, whereas someone overcome by lust may (in a sort of moral trance, I suppose) lay devious plans for seduction.[9] Is that really true? I don't know: I don't see why it should not be the case that some people in the grip of an 'insane' rage concoct murderous plots, while other people, overcome by the lust to touch or taste, rape or guzzle without regard for the consequences. Perhaps what Aristotle is recording is no more than a literary stereotype, or an accident of folkways that are more tolerant of some forms of uninhibited behaviour than of others.[10] However that may be, the significance of this passage is that the effective absence of the weaklings' good sense does not leave them as simple reactors to simple stimuli; they are left with a whole system of thought, but one that operates in a sort of moral limbo. Something of the same is suggested by Aristotle's comparison of the weakling with a drunkard reciting the verses of Empedocles: the drunk is not doing philosophy, but is doing something that involves quite complex mental operations.

Just as any animal must have inbuilt mechanisms to prompt it to eat, drink, and copulate, so any animal must have inbuilt mechanisms to defend itself in extremity: there must be reactions (the boiling of blood round the heart, the release of adrenalin) to obliterate caution and sensitivity in emergencies. So the parallel between *akrasia* in the most literal sense and *akrasia* with regard to anger is reasonable, and may well be reflected in usage. In the context of civilized life, however, which is the context in which we live and in which our languages took their mature forms, these necessary pieces of any animal's survival kit are simply one range of feeling among others, one field of activity among others, related to one set of virtues and vices among others in the context of an overall life that is the unique field of good sense. So the concept of *akrasia* should be extensible to analogues in the cases of any other pleasure – that is, any other kind of action and value that enters into the good life. And so it is. We also speak of inabilities to resist other prima facie goods, most notably the external goods such as property and reputation. Some people show moral weakness in the face of salespeople who exploit a consumerism and acquisitiveness that does not represent their true values – so much so that some governments allow people to cancel any sale contract within twenty-four hours, to allow the glamour of the occasion to wear off. But we never use expressions like 'no self-control' of such people without specifying 'when it comes to' whatever the allure may be, whereas we may say of violent-tempered people no less than of gluttons that they 'have no self-control' without further qualification. But what about people who just can't resist doing good, can't resist loving their parents or their children? Is Mother Teresa a weakling when confronted by poor children? It looks very much like it. But we would never dream of using the word *akratēs* in such cases, Aristotle says. Why wouldn't we, though? I'm not sure; but it may be that money and fame and possessions are things one wants for oneself, that relate to one's own well-being; people who can't help caring for other people or for some impersonal ideal, even if we think they are making fools of themselves, are not in that category.

Aristotle's treatment here is suggestive, but not quite satisfactory, perhaps because a psychological account is run in harness with a linguistic observation. One can see that the persistence of biologically necessary appetites in a cultured animal could give rise to the phenomenon of *akrasia* in a physiological way that Aristotle will sketch. But if we accept that special aetiology, we are left with no explanation for an analogous weakness for money or publicity. Morally the pattern is the same, and differs from the pattern of excessive mother-love; but why is the pattern exemplified? Here, as so often, we feel the need of a more complex account of motivation, one less committed to rationality.[11] We hanker for Freud, or for someone else who can show how the mind operates with primary processes that are essentially symbolic. The love of money can become an irresistible urge cut off from its possessor's life ideal because money stands for something of which the attraction stems from an unconscious and primitive level that ought to become integrated into the plans of the ego but does not always become so.[12]

3.112 The Moral Psychology of Weakness

The problem of *akrasia* as Socrates saw it was: How is moral weakness possible? The function of reason in human life is to be the decision maker; knowledge is naturally in control (for Aristotle the rational grasp of the human good would have this function), so isn't it absurd that it should be 'dragged about' by desires and fears?[13]

One possible answer to Socrates Aristotle rejects out of hand. It's no use saying that 'knowledge' is not involved on the ground that there is no such thing as moral knowledge, even though the definition of *epistēmē* in Book VI warrants this answer, and even though it is (as we shall see) right in a way. Socrates' point is that what is alleged to happen is that people act against their own most complete moral convictions, so that one wants to say that weak people do what is to the best of their beliefs what they should not do. But our account of virtue and good sense in the *Ethics* seems to have ruled this out. A theoretical account of moral convictions in terms of moral laws, categorical imperatives, commandments, and so forth makes it easy to see that someone could intellectually endorse the law but act on a quite different set of motives. But the whole gravamen of Aristotle's account was to identify the envisaged good with the whole commitment and habituation of the person. Socrates is right: a serious explanation is called for, redefinition won't do it.

Actually, it is Socrates' choice of the high-powered notion of 'knowledge' (*epistēmē*) that points to the solution of his paradox. At any given time I have a lot of knowledge that I have acquired and not forgotten but do not have in mind. Such knowledge is not 'dragged about' but simply bypassed. It is conceivable that there could be situations in which my deepest and firmest convictions do not come into play, either because they do not come to mind or because the connection between them and my present situation is not effectively made. This could in principle happen with the standard case of *akrasia*, because, as we saw, it involves immediate responses to stimuli perceived as pleasant at a pre-reflective level. And, as we just suggested, it takes two forms. In one form, the process of 'deliberation,' the connection of means with the ends of life, does not even get started. In the other form, deliberation takes place, but does not reach its terminus in 'choice' in the strict sense of that term, the fusion of reason and desire. The desire relating to the end is displaced by a different desire.

In this presentation, Aristotle allows no place for moral struggles, 'wrestling with the evil one' and so forth. His whole strategy depends on the moral principle and the akratic desire bypassing each other. Weaklings may well repent when they come to themselves – in fact, they will inevitably do so – but their lapses will not themselves involve any agonistics. Plato, in the *Republic* (439E), describes someone who is angry with his eyes for succumbing to an obscene lust, in a way that opens the way to moral wrestlings if it does not actually include them; but Plato was more inclined to split the personality into antagonistic parts than Aristotle was. Could Aristotle have included a reference to moral struggles if he had found it necessary? Or has his introduction of softness and hardness (a matter of resistance to pain and intimidation experienced as external) suggested the only area in which such fighting is admitted? On the logical level, no direct conflict can be introduced; but on the physiological level, a direct confrontation would be possible. It would be analogous with the efforts of a person fighting off sleepiness or drunkenness.

What actually happens in moral weakness? What are the situations in which a person's moral convictions can be bypassed? The answer has two sides. One is in terms of what we might call 'human nature' but Aristotle does not, the psychological and physiological events. The other side is in terms of what Aristotle calls nature (1147a24), the nature of human beings as rational agents. This corresponds to what we might call the epistemics of the situation.

What happens is that a 'practical syllogism' takes over. This is a much simpler phenomenon than deliberation. It is derived from the model of animal (as opposed to specifically human) action formulated in *On the Soul* III 10, and makes no reference to any *logos* or to the complications introduced by a 'sense of time.' The practical syllogism is expounded in *The Movement of Animals* 701a6ff., and is part of a model whereby animals may be subject to mechanical necessity as much as though they were worked with levers and strings.[14] The animal is in a state of desire for something having a certain character (food, for instance); it perceives or imagines something as having that character; it immediately pursues that thing. The situation represented by the practical syllogism is presumed to be quite unproblematic; the action is immediate, not in the sense that no time elapses, but in the sense that, given the desire and the recognition, there is nothing to stop the animal acting – the conclusion *is* the action. The model does not apply to deliberation, or to any complex system: it applies to human beings only in the unproblematic and closed contexts of *technē*, where a definite solution to a given problem is sought, or where a context of action is similarly closed off from its context and from the general problematic of life. There is a universal premise and a particular premise, such that a case is brought under a rule and a conclusion at once follows. For application to human situations, Aristotle gives the major premise in a truly universal form: beings in a certain condition should pursue (or avoid, as the case may be) situations having a certain character. And the minor premise is doubly subsumptive: 'But I am in that condition, and this has that character.' Pursuit (or avoidance) follows at once.

Aristotle's own example of the sort of rule that operates in a practical syllogism is given in alternative versions: 'Everything sweet is to be tasted,' or 'Everything sweet is pleasant.'[15] It should be obvious, even without the equivalent formulations, that this 'rule' is not something people *say* to themselves or put into any words, it is a built-in or acquired preference, such that anything perceived as sweet is perceived as attractively consumable. The point is that, as Aristotle says, nobody has a moral rule that *contradicts* any version of that 'rule.' Being sweet or sour is not a morally significant characteristic; if our principles forbid us to eat, it will be because the object perceived or imagined as sweet will also be perceivable as fattening, or distracting, or in some other way unsuitable for immediate consumption. It is not the principle that contradicts our principles, but the action that violates them; and it violates them because the desired object has characteristics other than those that make it desirable. There is nothing in the closed circle of the practical syllogism that violates our convictions. What goes against our convictions is that there should be any such enclaves at all.[16] That there are such enclaves is, however, not surprising: the pattern of action to which the weakling succumbs is simply that of the person who pursues 'each successive object as passion directs' in I iii (1095a2– 11).[17]

'No one goes wrong on purpose,' *oudeis hekōn hamartanei*, was the Socratic slogan. If taken literally, that is a truism, one cannot really make a mistake deliberately. So how can the appearance be saved? One can lean a little on the word *hekōn*, the word we translate as 'voluntary' and analysed in III i – though Aristotle himself does not invoke that analysis here. The origin of the action is, in cases of moral weakness, in the agent – the limits of what counts as 'in the agent' have been set as widely as possible. So, if the action of the morally weak person is to be in some legitimate sense involuntary, it can be so only because of ignorance of the circumstances of the action. And this is the solution that Aristotle in effect provides: the weakling does not have practically available the relevant facts of the matter. But how can this be, when the desired object is in plain view or vividly imagined, and must be so in order to exert its fatal attraction? We have been looking at the machinery Aristotle provides. But it opens up a can of worms. Whatever is done is done under a certain description: a killing that would be murder from one point of view is an 'execution' from another point of view. Aristotle's account of the difference between good sense and moral weakness relies on the former being correct and the latter a deviation, in much the same spirit as he contrasts reason and perception (which see and conceive things as they really are) with imagination, which seems to see things in ways determined by the imaginer's subjective condition. But how can this distinction be maintained, in the practical situations that concern us here? We could easily suppose that what morally weak people lose sight of is just their settled conditions and policies, good or bad, and sometimes Aristotle seems to want no more than that. But most of the time he seems to want the dictates of good sense to be not only authoritative but true, as the analysis in Book VI requires. And yet weaklings see truly, in a way; what they are tempted by is something that is really there. They merely fail to see relevantly. To make his case, Aristotle has to suppose that there really is one thing that it would be right for a given person to do on a given occasion, determined by the facts of the matter; and the facts of the matter have presumably to be determined by the relevant system of laws and virtues, which is actually established within a community, and is itself subject to a critique in terms of the economic, military, and political conditions of existence of the state. Well, we have been over all this before, and will no doubt be over it again. It is equally hard to see how it could be right and how it could be wrong. But really, it doesn't much matter. Phenomenologically, the difference between acting realistically as the situation one is in requires, and acting in a selfish or deluded or self-indulgent fashion is perfectly plain.

It is possible to think of the moral deliberations of good sense as themselves constituting a complex of practical syllogisms, rivalling the one in the enclave. Whether one thinks of them in that way or not, it is evident that in *akrasia* that system is inoperative; something prevents us from effectively noticing the aspects of the situation that should bring it within the scope of our moral convictions. So Socrates was, in a way, right after all. Knowledge is not dragged about, it is simply bypassed. But how is this possible? The explanation is a change in our bodily condition, as when people go to sleep or get drunk or even go mad (1147a15ff.). And people recover from bouts of *akrasia* in the same sort of way that they recover from drunkenness or wake up – it is not a specifically moral question, Aristotle insists, but a physiological question (1147b6–10).

Obviously, the foregoing account leaves weaklings in a morally equivocal position. We blame them, but we are sorry for them too, as with sentries who fall asleep on duty: they are supposed to stay awake, whether they can or not. But Aristotle's account is unsatisfactory. The 'natural' version in terms of epistemic connections ranges more widely than the physiological version that is supposed to provide its operative mechanism. The latter requires that there be specific toxins or other physical influences that flood the system. We can well believe that, in the case of rage, or sexual desire, or hunger or thirst, the needs of the organism as a self-maintaining system trigger a condition that temporarily controls our perceptions, and hence our actions, until the emergency is past and we get back to normal – and then we realize what we have done, like Sophocles' Ajax recognizing the slaughtered sheep. But can we really postulate such a mechanism for all the other sorts of obsession that Aristotle brings into his discussion? No doubt these are only *akrasia* in some metaphorical sense; but what difference does that make? They not only really happen, they are common. Perhaps we all have our little weaknesses, with regard to which we are not fully rational. How are they to be explained? If we need a physiological theory to account for *akrasia* in the strict sense, don't we need a physiological theory here too? But it would be implausible to postulate one.[18] If, on the other hand, we concede that all or most people, or even just *quite a lot* of people, are akratic in respect of money, or baseball cards, or whatever, and that this is just the shape their lives happen to take with no need of further explanation, why do we need a special physiology to explain an inability to resist the pleasures of touching and tasting? But perhaps Aristotle would say that we don't *need* such an explanation – we just happen to have it.

3.113 *The Scope of Weakness*

How widespread and how pervasive is weakness of will? Aristotle does not say; but the answer surely affects how we think of his enterprise. The impression left by the account of *eudaimonia* in Book I was that a good life was effectively within the scope of whoever wanted it: all one had to do was to try systematically to deal intelligently with every aspect of life, and the resulting life would be happy and rewarding, because the values built in to such an endeavour are the most rewarding of all and the least dependent on the accidents of fortune. A modicum of worldly goods and freedom from crippling diseases and blemishes were all that is required. Later we learn that without a good upbringing the goal will be unattainable, but it looks as if that only meant that the pursuit of the goal will not seem initially desirable. Provided that the 'modicum of worldly goods' doesn't rule out most of the world's population, as in fact it may well do, prospects don't look too bad; nor should they, because Aristotle must be right in insisting that it is ludicrous to suppose that the human species is such that most of its members are excluded from the characteristic way of life in which the potentialities of the species are realized (1099b18–21; cf. § 1.233). But the whole enterprise rests on the supposition that one's life can be effectively governed by the will to do good, the idea of a life in which every action is as valuable as it could be from the point of view of a being with *logos*. That supposition makes sense if the alternative to virtue is vice. One can avoid vice, if Aristotle is right. But can one avoid the lapses that arise from the closed loops of recurrent obsessions and intoxications? And, if one can avoid them, can one do so only by expending much effort in resisting them? In either case, one will not be happy and cannot be virtuous, even if one's good sense remains unimpaired. (It is possible that it should be unimpaired, since the deliberations and the choices that they entail are unaffected by unchosen and undeliberated lapses.) It was partly worries of this sort that led the Stoics, a few decades later, to conclude that virtue and happiness are almost impossible, since the incursions of passion are ubiquitous.

Aristotle gives not even a hint of how he would answer such a question. On one view, the prevalence of weakness and other deviant conditions might be such that the ethics of virtue would be a remote ideal, leaving most of us to deal with a real world of temptations and backslidings in which happiness is beyond our grasp. Leaving aside the Stoics, Aristotle would not be the only philosopher to admit of such a pessimistic reading. Kant's stipulations about categorical imperatives might leave a scrupulous person in despair. Sartre's anatomy of 'bad faith,' while leaving open the way to a life of authenticity and a clear-eyed morals of freedom, seems more realistically to assign almost everyone to a dialectic of self-deception. And so on. Should not Aristotle have provided us with an ethic of weakness?

Well – perhaps not. The ethic of virtue provided us with a clear articulation of values, together with clues for its adaptation to different lifestyles and circumstances. The prevalence of weakness does not provide us with any alternative articulation.

3.114 Which Is Worst?

Bestiality and sickness, moral weakness, softness, wickedness – which is worst? You might think it was bestiality, because we invoke that only when we are so horrified by an action that we cannot associate it with humanity at all. The same applies to madness and sickness, except that we invoke them when we conceive that the agent might recover or might realistically be thought of as recovering sanity. Softness is just a matter of temperament, not in itself a matter for moral judgment – it's more a matter of what philosophers lately have taken to calling 'moral luck.' Moral weakness might be thought worse than wickedness, because wicked people might reform, but weak people already know they are doing wrong and do it anyway – so they are incurable.

Some of the judgments in the preceding paragraph could be reversed, and Aristotle thinks they should be. The things 'bestial' people do are unspeakable, but we don't exactly *blame* them – it wouldn't do any good, they are impervious to reason, they are not responsible. As for the incurability of akratic people, that is only provisional – if their unfortunate appetites would let them alone, they would do just fine. But wicked people think they *are* doing just fine, they don't see any point in virtue, they think their own condition is virtue – not because they have an alternative *logos*, but because they don't see that a *logos* is involved.

Aristotle thinks this second set of evaluations is the right set (as well as being the one that we actually endorse, if we use this conceptual apparatus at all). But I am inclined to think that it was important to mention and explain both sets. Life is not all that simple. There are valid points of view from which different evaluations can be made, there are bases for different reactions. We need to bear that complexity in mind. Every case must be disposed of, every situation must be met, somehow or other. But that does not mean that the rejected alternatives have nothing to be said for them, or that we will be acting more intelligently if we suppose that that is the case. Sometimes the upshot of an argument should be, not 'This, so not *that*,' but 'This; not forgetting *that*.'

3.2 The Snare of Pleasure (VII xi–xiv; 1152b1–1154b34)

The anatomy of wrongdoing led to a disconcerting conclusion. The weakling's 'true supposition of the good' becomes inoperative because an 'apparent good' intrudes, not by subverting good counsel but in the form of a practical syllogism more characteristic of the unreflective beasts. That is, moral motivation is short-circuited by an independent subsystem that can only be the sort of immediate response to pleasure or pain that was operative in infancy. This fact leads Aristotle to give immediate consideration to pleasure *as evil* – not in contrast with pain considered as good, but together with correspondingly immediate pain. We already know from I viii and II iii what to say about this: it is not pleasure that is evil, but the wrong kind of pleasure. But we have not really thought about pleasure, and it is time we did.

The editorial hand that prepared our text was uncertain whether this was really a new subject or not: the last words of Book VII describe the topic concluded as 'continence and incontinence, pleasure and pain' with their respective natures and values, although the opening words of VII xi invoke the Olympian standpoint of the political thinker, 'architect of the end,' for whom pleasure is one of the topics that must be taken up in its own right.[19] And we are reminded of the established connections between pleasure and virtue and between pleasure and happiness, the latter reinforced by another of Aristotle's implausible etymologies (1152b1–8).

This announcement of pleasure as a general topic is not followed by the sort of inquiry we might expect. Aristotle plunges directly into a defence of pleasure against its detractors, which turns into a discussion of the peculiarities of bodily pleasures and concludes with what looks like a lament, more Platonic than Aristotelian, about the unfortunate duality of human nature.

The passage as a whole is a deviant form of Aristotle's 'scholastic' expositions. Normally a sketch of the phenomena, the accepted state of the field, is followed by a statement of the difficulties (*aporiai*) to be resolved; then we have Aristotle's version of the truth of the matter, followed by a demonstration of how his theory resolves the difficulties and accounts for the phenomena. In this instance, however, the 'phenomena' consist of an elaborately articulated three-part statement of the case against pleasure, and this is followed by a complex rebuttal within which the theoretical position is embedded;[20] then, instead of a harmonizing passage, we have a sort of addendum explaining how the whole controversy has arisen.

3.21 The Literary Problem

It is in connection with the discussion and defence of pleasure at the end of *EN* VII that the problem posed by the 'common' books V–VII is most acute. There is another full-dress treatment of pleasure at the start of Book X. If Books V–VII were originally part of *EE*, the material we have examined so far might simply have been held over pending revision; but can we say that of the two treatments of pleasure? Well, we may reply, someone must have thought so; an interpolating editor could easily have terminated the interpolation after the discussion of *akrasia*.[21]

It is indeed easy to argue that the double treatment is inevitable. The first treatment is a defence responding to the implications of the preceding chapters, the second treatment lays the groundwork for what comes after it and is prepared for by Book IX; and each treatment is adapted to its function in its place.[22]

It is hard to believe, though, that the two treatments of pleasure in their present form were designed to stand together in a single discourse. Not only do they overlap too much for that; there is also a discrepancy in style. The account in Book VII, like the preceding treatment of delinquency, treats the problems it raises dialectically (or 'organically') rather than in logical sequence. The account in Book X is much more systematic, and has a quite different tone. There are also fundamental points at which the accounts contradict each other. In the present passage, pleasures are said to be activities; in the later treatment, they are inseparable concomitants of activities. Correspondingly, in the present passage pleasure as such is (or may be) always good; in the later passage, whether pleasure is good or not depends on the quality of the activity it goes with. The difference is of radical importance, though subtle and hard to evaluate. It is easy to see why someone might, in a 'defence of pleasure,' wish to isolate the pleasantness of pleasures as an always-desirable object of experience, and in a more finely tuned treatment deny that the isolation is really possible (or desirable); it is impossible to believe that anyone would make such a correction without drawing attention to it and explaining its necessity.

Finally, the emotional tone of the two passages is different. Book VII concludes on a pessimistic note, speaking of a necessary conflict of pleasures that corresponds to an apparent discrepancy within the human psyche. The passage in Book X is more positive, putting the conflicts discussed throughout Book VII behind it. Book VII seems to be haunted by the spectre of a Platonic metaphysics, a ghost which in the daylight of Book X has been thoroughly laid.

One thing is clear: the two treatments of pleasure were not revised in the light of each other to take their respective places in a series of discourses conceived as a single whole. But two treatments of pleasure were necessary, placed as they are now and containing the essentials of what they do now. Aristotle could easily have reconciled them. But he was a busy man, and did not know that he had twenty fewer years to live than Plato.

3.22 The Defence of Pleasure

3.221 The Concept of Pleasure

The concepts of pleasure and enjoyment give philosophers a lot of trouble, and their Greek counterparts (hēdonē, apolauein) were equally intractable. Philosophers have persistently tried to isolate a single problem and a unitary concept, which may roughly be posed as follows: can we reduce all reasons for action (or one large class of such reasons) to terms of the amount of pleasure yielded? And, if so, what do we mean by 'pleasure'? This may be a wild-goose chase, but one can see more or less why thinkers (including Epicurus and Aristotle) get involved in it. In the first place, one contrasts all reasons for action that can be specified without referring to the agent's personal likings with those that cannot be so specified, and lumps the latter together under the heading of 'pleasure.' In the second place, one reflects that, in a different sense (or in just the same sense, if one is a strong reductionist), whatever one does shows what one wants to do, otherwise one would have done something else; and what one wants to do is, in a sense, one's personal liking, so that too is pleasure. The concept of pleasure thus has to accommodate three things: the sorts of activities that are customarily singled out as pleasure; the whole class of activities that are done for what are plainly personal reasons; and the whole class of activities of all kinds, conceived as motivated, and hence (because, as a matter of sheer logic, one cannot be directly moved by other people's motives) as personally motivated. The moral philosopher may now be faced with a dilemma, which haunts Aristotle here. On the one hand, if people always do what pleases them most, one is at a loss to find a compelling reason to choose one way of life over another; on the other hand, if some values are independent of pleasure, one is at a loss to recommend them to people preoccupied with living their own lives.[23]

One may embark on the wild-goose chase for a unified theory of 'pleasure' by treating as mutually equivalent a wide range of such expressions as the following: 'I will do x and not y,' 'I prefer x to y,' 'I like x more than I like y,' 'x pleases me more than y,' 'I enjoy x more than I enjoy y,' and 'x gives me more pleasure than y.' The next move may be to take the last of these expressions as if it meant something like: 'There is something called "pleasure," which I like (and which is the only thing I like or anyone could like), and of which x gives me a greater quantity than y does.'[24] None of these equations are very persuasive, and the interpretation proposed for the last is gratuitous. But the temptation to embark on the chase lies in the undoubted fact that in deliberation we do weigh different considerations against each other, and that there must accordingly be something like a common measure of weight to make that weighing possible. And what could that be if not the amount of pleasantness, the intensity and duration and widespreadness and purity of pleasure? The force of this temptation is revealed in Plato's *Protagoras* before Aristotle, and its rationale is explored by Epicurus after him.

If one does think of pleasure as homogeneous, one is faced with the problem that now confronts Aristotle. Pleasure is undoubtedly the undoing of the weakling, and pleasure-loving people are perhaps the commonest type of wrongdoers. But does that not suggest that all pleasure is evil? Even if it is not, it must sometimes be evil, or it could not be a temptation.

Aristotle in effect escapes from this argument by speaking of 'pleasures' rather than of 'pleasure.' Pleasures are things one enjoys doing; the word *pleasure* merely singles out the fact of their enjoyability.

Different people enjoy doing different things. In fact, there is no activity of which it is inconceivable that someone might enjoy doing it. Therefore, since one must do something, and the distinction between good and bad ultimately reduces to a distinction among activities, it is not possible that all pleasures should be bad – unless, as no one would maintain, what made an activity bad was the very fact that one enjoyed it. If there are good activities, there are good pleasures.

What is it we like about things we like doing? Here, surely, the search for the unit is the delusion – what we like about them is in each case what is specific to them; that is why it is *them* we want to do and not something else. But a minimal (though not quite vacuous) answer to the question would be that it is the doing of them that we like. We value them as activities. From this point of view, all pleasures are good. If we call a pleasure bad, or less than perfectly good, it is presumably not because of its immediate value as activity but because of its effect on other people, or because of its effect on our later condition, or because it prevents us from engaging in some other activity with a (higher) value of its own. Pleasures, then, are activities as such. But what makes an activity enjoyable, as such? Aristotle suggests that it is the lack of internal or external impediment: what we enjoy is the free exercise of our unimpaired faculties.[25] If that is correct, the connection between virtue and happiness is well on the way to being established – the activities that best fulfil human function should be the most purely pleasant; but at present it is no more than a suggestion. Meanwhile we can say that if the best thing in life is an activity or a complex of activities, and if people can enjoy any sort of activity, there is no reason in principle why the highest good should not be a pleasure, or a system of pleasures, even though pleasure as such would not be the highest good.

So much for pleasures. Is pleasure then good? If by pleasure we mean what makes activities pleasurable, the fact of their enjoyability, the answer must be that it is. Whatever one may say of an activity in other respects, and however one describes pleasure, the fact that an activity is enjoyable is always a good reason for doing it and never a reason against doing it.[26] If we mistrust pleasure, our reason for doing so is our recognition that the excellence of the reason that pleasantness affords is likely to blind us to other considerations.

3.222 The Defence

In the first part of *EN* VII, defects in the synthesis of reason and desire were attributed not to stupidity but to pleasure and pain, enjoyments and dislikings, and especially to the pleasures of the body – the ambiguity of Greek *hēdonē* in this regard is the same as that of English 'pleasure.' Pain was dealt with incidentally in III i–v, but needed no special treatment: pain hurts and deters, that's what it's for, its action is obvious and direct. It is not pain but pleasure that is the focus of our concern now, not only as the motive to vice but as the source of the behavioural disturbances we call *akrasia*. This suggests that pleasure as a separable factor in life is always bad; and yet we saw in I viii and II iii that the good life must be a pleasant life and that moral education is a matter of learning to take pleasure in the right things. So the apparent evil of pleasure must be systematically disposed of. The case against pleasure is stated in VII xi; xii–xiii refutes that case; xiv identifies the source of the problem as the prominence of the pleasures of the body, in isolation from the good life to which they should be contributing – essentially Plato's argument from *Republic* IX. Then, from 1154b20 to the end of the book, this isolated prominence is associated with a tragic duality in human nature, providing an unhappy ending for the whole discussion of *EN* so far. The remainder of *EN* gives us an alternative ending, a happy ending in which the duality of human nature is defanged and the restlessness of the human condition is put down not to the warring of two psychic elements but to simple fatigue (cf. § 6.42).

What seemed to be wrong with pleasure in the context of *akrasia*? Four things: (a) it fogs the mind; (b) it grounds a motivation opposed to that of virtue (cf. 1109b3–12); (c) it distracts one from one's overall plans and ideals; (d) it supports the uncultivated, animal levels of the personality.

The case mounted against pleasure in VII xi incorporates those four points and goes beyond them. To begin with, three positions need to be distinguished: that no pleasure is good, that few pleasures are good, and that, even if all pleasures are good, the best thing in the world cannot be pleasure. Of these, only the first needs rebuttal, the second can be conceded, and the third requires a more nuanced response. We note that the terminology switches back and forth between 'pleasure' and 'pleasures,' and I will say more about this presently; meanwhile, what relates most directly to the discussion in

VII i–x is the first position, which incorporates six theses rather than the four distinguished in the previous passage. First, pleasure is a process, and processes as such are never good. This point was not made in the *akrasia* discussion, because it is a theoretical point, not one of the accepted phenomena. Second, temperate people avoid pleasure – a version of (b), but, as we saw already in II iii, mistaken. Third, good sense avoids pain rather than making pleasure a positive motive – a version of (c). Fourth, pleasures are hindrances to thought – (c) again, with overtones of (a). Fifth, there is no *art* (skill or technique) associated with pleasure, as there would be if pleasure were a good – a version of (d), but not in itself persuasive, since it depends (as the first objection did) on theoretical considerations that require to be established. And sixth, pleasure is proper to the lives of children and brute beasts – a quite straightforward version of (d).

The key is the first objection, that pleasure is a process. The point is a simple one, though it becomes complicated by Aristotle's metaphysics and by the mixed condition of everyday life. A process as such is a movement or change (*kinēsis*) in state, position, or whatever, from one condition to another. A change is defined by its end state, reached by some process from a relevant initial state (otherwise, what we have is not a change but simply a number of different events). While a process is going on, it is incomplete. So, if pleasure were (for instance) a restoration of bodily equilibrium, it would be the achieved equilibrium that was the relevant value. Contrasted with movement is activity, an active state of being that is fully realized at each moment, the vital manifestation of human potentiality. The case against pleasure would then be that all pleasure is process, and thus can have no value in itself.

Though the distinction between movement (*kinēsis*) and activity (*energeia*) is clear and simple in itself, it becomes confused because Aristotle does not distinguish clearly between two propositions: (i) all the things people do are either movements or activities, and nothing is both; (ii) some of people's activities involve movements (or, under some description, *are* also movements), but not all, the others being 'activities of motionlessness' (*energeiai akinēseōs* or *ēremias*, cf. 1154b27), such as listening or thinking. The objection to pleasure as movement relies on (i), which is quite implausible, and is to be met by holding to (ii) and saying that pleasure *as pleasure* is activity, not movement, even though what a person is taking pleasure in may well be a movement itself. But there is also an implication that pleasures that do not involve *kinēsis* are better than pleasures that do.

The contrast between movement and activity may remind us of the problem we encountered in the discussion of 'art' in distinguishing making from doing. Everything one does involves making something in *some* sense; and in making anything one is constantly *doing* things. And one of the things one may be doing is engaging in the ongoing activity of making whatever it is one is making, conceived as a project of which one never loses sight. Correspondingly, pleasures, the things people enjoy, may well be processes; the bodily pleasures clearly are so, being obviously inseparable from the physiological changes which are themselves thought of as supplying deficiencies; but the delight in them, the enjoyment, is a state of being, an activity, and from that point of view the pleasures are activities (1153a7–10). But we have known ever since I i that the good must in the last resort be activity; the way is open for the best pleasures to be the best things there are within the compass of human life.

3.223 Pleasures

Pleasure as activity, as the active enjoyment of what one is engaged in, is good; pleasures, conceived as processes we go through in the course of our lives, may not be. But we tend to use the term 'pleasures' in a collapsed sort of way to refer to the episodes of enjoyment that enter into our lives. Now, given that 'pleasures' are simply enjoyed or enjoyable activities, and that any activity may be enjoyed, we would not be able to generalize about 'pleasures' (as we do) if people did not tend to enjoy the same sorts of things – if there were not some particular kinds of activities that people recognize as 'things one enjoys doing.' And we do find that the name 'pleasures' is commonly appropriated to the pleasures of the body (1153b33–6), which are the very pleasures that figured so largely in our moral pathology. People who object to the notion that pleasure is good are usually thinking of pleasures of this kind. 'Good people avoid pleasure' – what they really do is abstain from sensuous excess, not abstain from the delights of doing good. 'Pleasure interferes with one's activities' – the pleasure of doing x interferes with doing y, but not with doing x, and what is usually meant is that (for instance) long lunches cut into the working day. 'Only beasts and children, not adult humans, are interested in pleasure' – it is the sensual pleasures alone that appeal to these inferior beings.

When we generalize about pleasures, we are, of course, thinking about the recognizable events and happenings in which people are engaged; and this may be part of what makes people say that 'pleasures are mere processes.' Now, even if that equation held, it would not follow that pleasures could not be good, since we know from I vi that processes could be as good as anything else (especially if we included the initial and terminal conditions as parts of the process). But though pleasures as events and episodes may be processes, pleasures as pleasant stretches of experience are not. Processes have histories; they proceed fast or slowly, have beginnings and endings and intermediate stages. But none of that is true of the pleasure we take in them. One does not enjoy oneself fast or slowly. At any time, one is enjoying oneself just as much as one is: the enjoyment is logically complete at any moment.[27] If we say that pleasure increases, what we mean is that at a later time we are enjoying ourselves more than we did at an earlier time. Pleasure, in short, is a *state* of mind that is what it is when it is.[28] If we combine that idea with the assertion that enjoying oneself is something one does, we are on our way to a theory of human activity according to which what one does is basically always to have a certain state of mind. The development of that notion will be the last and perhaps the most important part of the central theme of *EN*, how *logos* enters into human life.

3.224 Two Natures (1154a22–b34 [VII 15])

The arguments against pleasure that we have considered really assumed, as we saw, that the bodily pleasures are all the pleasures there are.[29] The assumption is untenable, but reflects the fact that these are what come to mind when we think of 'pleasures.'[30] That fact is a stumbling-block for us, since virtuous activities as done by people who are enjoying doing them (because they have the deep satisfaction of getting things right, of 'having their act together') are the most natural pleasures and really deserve the name far more. How is it that their place has been usurped? Because the bodily pleasures are so obtrusive. It is this obtrusiveness that makes people think of them as bad, which in themselves they are not: most people are so strongly tempted to overindulge in them that it is wise to resist them.[31]

People uninterested in virtue will never discover its natural pleasantness. But everyone is familiar with the pleasures of the body, for two reasons. First, the hungers that such pleasures satisfy are both inevitable and painful.[32] Second, they are the first pleasures we know, as infants whose experience is confined to the bodily functions.

Besides, they are violent pleasures. We have seen that, in general, the pleasure we take in one activity gets in the way of rival activities: music lovers cannot concentrate on their studies when music is playing, moviegoers stop eating popcorn when the action gets exciting. This being so, one can have recourse to food or drink or sex to find distraction from trouble or grief.

It begins to look as if the development of morally virtuous habits requires one to be trained against the bias of the initial basis of one's nature. The reason why humanity is called the 'political animal' is that without educational and social pressures one cannot achieve the only sort of life that will fully satisfy the developed self.[33] The human being is a biological animal on which a social animal is superimposed.

Aristotle's way of describing these phenomena is to say generally that things are *incidentally* pleasant if they relieve defective or pathological conditions, but *naturally* pleasant if there is a 'nature' whose action (*praxis*) they evoke. But then he says something very disconcerting. Human nature, he says, is not simple. There is 'something else' in it, insofar as we are perishable. If our nature were simple, the same action would always be the most pleasant, as god always enjoys a single pleasure, a pleasure of rest and changelessness. But human nature, being shabby (*ponēros*), requires change. If one element or aspect does something, this is 'against nature' to the other nature (or 'to the rest of our nature,' *tēi heterāi physei*).[34]

The introduction of a twofold 'human nature' in irresoluble conflict seems incompatible with the original project of the *Ethics*. It is also hard to see what exactly is meant. On the basis of what has gone before (at least as I have expounded it), the conflict should be between the animal nature and the social nature, the former belonging to 'nature' as the domain of natural science as Aristotle understands it and the latter being human 'nature' as the teleological fulfilment of the mature individual in the most favourable (i.e., political) environment. And the animal nature would be normally 'included' in the other in the sense that the appetites are socialized. But the reference to 'perishability' suddenly introduces a different duality: that of the godlike intellect and the all-too-human nature that is both animal and social. It is this latter duality that is suggested by the duality of intellectual virtue in Book VI and the description of good lives in Book X. The idea that the all-too-human is somehow 'against nature' (*para physin*) is familiar from Aristotle's popular (and, in most people's view, early) writings.[35] But what is it doing here?[36]

The texture of the writing is too close for us to invoke editorial botching – it looks as if Aristotle has suddenly forgotten what he was talking about.

Two alternatives seem attractive. First, the contrast with mutability may imply a duality of pleasures between those that are concerned with the bodily processes themselves and those that are not – and the pleasures of all virtuous activities would be of the latter kind, since they refer to a wider context and a more comprehensive end. In that case, the paradigm of divine pleasure is in place as indicating the nature of the contrast being made, a contrast that will take on a different tinge when we consider the intellectual life itself (just as the concept of leisure will take on a new and deeper meaning). The other alternative (perhaps simply a different way of putting the same thing) is that the duality is simply that from I xiii, between the part of the soul that has *logos* directly and that which does not.

In itself, the contrast between the unity of god and the 'perishable' nature of humanity does not require any duality in the latter. The point of our perishability could have been simply that we are engaged with changing situations, and our pleasures could not be those possible if we were not so engaged. From this point of view, the statement that human nature is double, and hence vicious, is gratuitous (as well as being incompatible with the initial project). If humanity has a 'function,' human nature must have a unity – in fact, we have seen what it is. The ideas of virtue and happiness make no sense if human nature is itself base and villainous. The trouble is that no direct rebuttal of the blackly pessimistic point of view presented here is to be found anywhere in the *Ethics*. We break off to discuss friendship, and never revert to the topic of the divided self. The phenomena are taken up again in Book X, but without any suggestion of conflict. If there is a solution, it has to be read between the lines. It is as if another, depressive Aristotle had interrupted his manic alter ego and then held his peace.

Whatever the 'two natures' are, it is obvious that they ought to represent a distinction between animal values and civilized values at some level: some version of the polarity and tension between nature and culture. It is odd that EN VII *should end with the tension unresolved. If what Aristotle says is true, to be a human being is just to be a being whose nature has this duality. Why should this be a depraved or inferior version of something else, rather than the singular nature of a being with a unique two-sided 'work' in the world? Aristotle speaks as if the universe would be a better place if there were no people in it. But from what perspective would this be an*

*improvement? Darwinian views of evolution and Christian myths of the
Fall can provide such perspectives; Socrates in Plato's* Phaedo *can insinuate a mythology in which souls are condemned to imprisonment in bodies
by unidentified deities operating unexplained penal systems; but Aristotle
has nothing to appeal to.*

If human nature has this two-sidedness, one of the main tasks of
phronēsis will be to effect a wise reconciliation. But nothing was said
about that in Book VI. And in the present passage, if you think about
it, the presupposition is that there is no such thing as *phronēsis*: there
is simply an unbrokered and unmediated conflict between two separ-
ations. One may sympathize with Aristotle's mood, but in the context
of the *Ethics* the passage makes no sense at all.

There is a sense in which the end of *EN* VII brings the whole work
to a tragic conclusion. The unheralded introduction of a new topic,
friendship, starts a train of thought that makes it possible for *phronēsis* to perform its mediating role, but the pessimism of the present
passage is unequivocal. The parallel with *Republic* IX is striking, in its
contrast between divergent ways of life and disparate 'parts of the
soul.' But the Platonic passage is a real conclusion to a continuous
argument (*Republic* X is a coda that adds little and changes nothing),
whereas the Aristotelian passage is almost an irruption, a cata-
strophic denouement that contradicts the tendency of the whole.
Perhaps we should simply say that here too Aristotle shows his
acceptance of tragedy, that, in this world where virtue and happiness
and a decent prosperity should be open to all, there is much to fill
us with pity and fear: disasters and losses, weaknesses and perver-
sions, hard choices and unavoidable evils, and, in the end, no gain
without some loss that can never be made good.

CHAPTER FOUR

Love, Consciousness, and Society (VIII–IX; 1155a1–1172a15)

The massive discussion of 'friendship' (*philia*) appears as an anomaly in the scheme of the *Ethics*.[1] Nothing in what has gone before suggests any such continuation. The agenda announced in Book I was completed at the end of Book VI, and Book VII reached a conclusion. Friendship introduces a new, unheralded value – a value, by the way, usually and disastrously omitted from contemporary academic treatises on ethics. It is not prepared for by the analysis of animal action in *On the Soul* III 10, where the problems of ethics are shown to arise for any animal with an awareness of time. However, the topic of friendship occupies the same position in *EE* as it does here, so it would be rash to assume that these two books are an independent treatise, wrongly inserted by Andronicus or some other editor.

The *Ethics* is most plausibly seen as (and is said in X ix to be) integrally related to a sequence on politics, so that something has to be said somewhere about the basis of society in individual life; and that is one way of seeing the topic of these two books. If it had to be done by way of a digression, it would have to be in the only place where a digression can reasonably appear in a Greek treatise, where there are no appendices: immediately before the final topic that leads the work to its triumphant conclusion.[2]

Without an account of friendship, the appearance of justice in the world is a mystery, and the growth of the city from the extended family would be unintelligible. Humans are social animals; if they were not, families would dissolve as soon as sex and the nurturing of children were over. The account of individual happiness in *EN* I–VI took for granted established and permanent relationships. How are we to account for them?[3] There must be, as we know there is, a world of feeling in which we live, as necessary to happiness as virtuous activity. And to show how this can be we must somehow reduce feeling and action to common terms. And we do. And when we have done it we find we have redefined the concept of practice itself in such a way that we can bring intellectual activity within its compass; so the digression on friendship turns out not to have been a digression after all. The concepts of happiness and friendship are mutually accommodated to make a new conception of the good life possible.

There is in reality another piece of unfinished business, though we have been given no hint of it. The opening of the *Ethics* introduces the idea of a single 'good' at which 'all things' aim, and which turns out to be a maximization of virtuous activity in a single life; and in III v the idea of a single view of 'the good' mirroring an overall excellence of activity and functioning as the unique object of 'wishing' played a crucial part as a basis of deliberation. But, when we came to Book VI, it seemed almost to have vanished: a basic 'perception' that might also be called 'intuition' in relation to particular situations replaced it as the epistemic basis of good sense. We are left to reflect on the Platonic question so quizzically mooted in I iii: are we on the way to first principles, or on the way from them? There, too, the particular facts of experience seemed to be the basis; and yet, in I ii, the study of ethics seemed to promise to make the good life, the *telos* implicit in all our life strategies, into a *skopos*, a goal we could aim at. At the end of Book VI, we still have heard nothing about how this could be, although Aristotle has not seemed aware that there might be a difficulty (and perhaps, after all, there is none). It is actually in the discussion of friendship that we find something that may help. The analysis of friendship zeroes in on the thesis that a friend is, in a specified sense, a 'second self' – the phrase has become such a cliché that it takes an effort to realize how outrageous it is. But if a friend is a second self, our attitudes to our selves can be based on our attitudes to our friends: a self is a primary friend. That is, the habit of thinking objectively about our friends as entire individuals gives us a model for thinking about ourselves and our well-being as integrated wholes, not in what would otherwise be the obvious way, perspectivally, as actively engaged in this relation and that.

Aristotle seems unaware of any problem. He simply presents friendship as what it is, something obviously essential to the good life. Only in retrospect do we see that the actuality of friendship gives a new perspective on life: it enables us to see that human activity is essentially a matter of awareness, and this perception enables us to compare ways of life from a single point of view, that of what we may term 'the quality of consciousness.' This is not a mere quirk in the *Ethics* – the same position is implicit in *On Sleep* (454a1–7) – but it is a position not easy to reach from the common store of commonplaces and controversies about happiness.[4]

A certain looseness of fit between Books VIII–IX and the rest of the *Ethics* should not bother us, since we have seen that Aristotle has a regular 'scholastic' procedure for articulating major topics, regardless of their immediate context. But we may ask what precisely there has been in the antecedent material that calls for any treatment of friendship at all. There are at least three things. First, there is the appearance of 'friendship' as an item in the list of virtues, where what is said is far from an adequate account of the concept as Plato and others had discussed it. Second, there is the discussion of justice in a broad sense as comprising the whole of virtue in relation to other people, thus implicitly raising the question of what makes these other people such that one should relate to them at all. And, third, there is the repeated claim that the *phronimos* is best exemplified by one whose foresight and concern extend to the nearest and dearest rather than to oneself alone, and ultimately to one's fellow members in a political community. This implicitly raises the question of how individuals come to be related to others as they are to themselves, as objects of concern, and which individuals are involved in the relation. What is the ground of the nearness and dearness of one's nearest and dearest?

Since the status of friendship as virtue is mentioned by Aristotle in his own introduction in VIII i, I will postpone that to the next section and say something now about justice and *phronēsis*.

Justice is a matter of seeking to obtain the right amount of something in a relationship. But this assumes that relationships with others already exist to be regulated. A system of justice is thus sustained by a web of camaraderie. The 'others' involved must be really other – one cannot, Aristotle insisted, be just to oneself – but clearly they must be positively related to one in some practical context. Aristotle insists that the formal relationships of justice and the informal relationships of friendship go together. In one important aspect, in fact, the architectonics of the two treatments are the same, The discourse on justice distinguished a loose general sense of justice (as right-doing) from a specific sense (as fairness), and both of these from a crude reciprocal relationship (*to antipeponthos*) that is not yet justice. Somewhat similarly, the discussion of friendship distinguishes friendship proper, the relation between individuals who choose to spend their lives together, from a more general relationship of amicable cooperation incidental to activities jointly engaged in, and both of these from the family relationships in which continual mutual proximity is enforced by the conditions of life itself. Then, in Book V, the 'disputed questions' on justice lead to the conclusion that all questions of justice, in the broad sense no less than in the narrow, are really matters of quantification; and the 'disputed questions' on friendship lead similarly to the conclusion that friendship in all its forms is a matter of shared experience, and thus resists the stipulations and quantifications that proved essential to justice.

In the matter of *phronēsis*, the 'political' wisdom that provides for happiness by the use of reason in the integration of goods, we have been told that it is better to do this for one's associates or (in the literally political context) one's fellow citizens. But this is viewed simply as an extension of what one would otherwise do for oneself alone. That is, one looks after the affairs of others not as others but as if they were one's own. One acts for an association, a *koinōnia*, for which and to which one is responsible. But what is the basis of such an association? Families (and the nations into which extended families grow) and states make formal relations necessary, because of the cooperation called for by tasks that have to be shared and predicaments that have to be jointly endured. But the relationships set up go beyond these and establish a will to live together, without reference to any specific benefits that may accrue. It is this general, unforced willingness to share lives that establishes the groupings within which good sense is exercised for a common good. This lack of reference to any specific pay-off is what makes individual friendships based on 'virtue' more genuine and lasting than those based on pleasure or profit. The unforced sharing in a shared good is the basis of society and is what Books VIII and IX explore.

The concept of friendship as implicit in social life is problematic. The best life, we know, is that which most fully develops the highest excellence of the *legon echon*. But that means that the best life for me is that which most fully exercises my own rationality, especially if I do so for those with whom I share my life. But then, what about those others? We were wondering in § 1.1133 whether my thoughtfulness on their behalf does not diminish their own lives, which, no less than mine, should give effect to their own thinking. The *Politics* suggests that it does diminish them if a political leader acts as a dictator, but not in a proper city: a true political community preserves the autonomy and self-respect of its members. In the economy of a household, a slave's autonomy is denied, a child's is postponed, a wife's is held in abeyance.[5] But the general solution prepared in the present passage is that autonomy is not abridged where no contrast between self and other is felt (just as one is not oppressed by compliance with law as such, because one's own reason prescribes compliance). The softening and elimination of the contrast between self and other is what friendship is.

The fact that consideration of friendship pushes the *Ethics* beyond the bounds set by the analysis of action in *On the Soul* III 10 leaves many readers feeling that a previously egocentric ethic is being supplemented or modified by a more altruistic viewpoint. But we saw in § 1.133 that *eudaimonia* was not based on self-interest to begin with (see also § 4.632). The illusion that the *Ethics* has hitherto taken an egocentric line is further weakened when we reflect that happiness is the exercise of virtue, and the entirety of virtue in relation to others is 'justice,' which is the same for all and implies a community of interrelating individuals among whom relations of fairness obtain. Nor should we forget that the excellence of the good life is enhanced if it is pursued for 'the nation and cities' (1094b10). Besides, we were warned against misinterpreting the requirement that happiness be self-sufficient; and we must, in any case, remember that household and city are also functioning natural units, each having its own independent system, each no less independent and self-sufficient than its individual members.

Philia has to be a topic in the *Ethics* because without it the relation between individual and group is ungrounded. Given that family and city begin from necessity and continue for the sake of a good life, we need to see what makes this possible. Books VIII and IX establish that fellow-feeling and self-feeling are grounded on the continuity of reason in individual and group. The idea of the self is a product of reflection (IX iv). Without this reflection, the 'sense of time' is unexplained because the relation of future to past is itself ungrounded. The outcome of VIII–IX is twofold: first, the equation of life with sensation and thought; second, the derivation of the sense of self from the recognition of other people. It is very relevant here that thinking is conceived as internalized language, rather than language as externalized thought. But these themes remain to be developed.

In sum, the continuity of ethics with politics, and the fact that individual lives can reach fruition only in cities, mean that a strong bridge must be provided from individual concerns to social concerns.

The concept of virtue provides a bridge, but not a strong one. If virtue is defined in terms of social needs, its place in an individual's values becomes either obscure or a matter of doctrinaire postulation; if virtue is defined in terms of self-development and self-realization, its social value is correspondingly gratuitous. Just *why* should the zeal of the *spoudaios* be devoted to the common or public good? What is needed is a demonstration that social values and personal values necessarily coincide. We have had a demonstration that a good life *can* be pleasant because anything can, which applies even to virtue socially defined, and we have had a sort of demonstration that the activities of virtue as self-realization *must* be pleasant; but these together do not suffice to show that the activities of virtue conceived as social must be pleasant. Justice cannot provide the connection, because as conceived in terms of the public good it is concerned with externals, a system of correct choices rather than of controlled passions. Justice provides the mechanism of social life, but not its power.

4.1 The Order of Treatment

Aristotle emphasizes the closeness of the relation between justice and friendship, and in both subjects a broad sense is distinguished from a narrow sense. The broad form of *philia* is a warm feeling that arises from any recognized sharing of activities or experiences; the narrow form is a reciprocated affection for someone with whom one wishes to spend one's days. Since it is the good person who forms true friendships of this latter sort, we could say that serious people, who develop and cultivate the resources of their *logon echon*, cultivate and take seriously the value revealed in community and in acts of cooperation, making a virtue of this necessity.

The immediate parallel with justice is hardly evident. In justice, the broad sense, the other-directed aspect of virtuous activity in general, is contrasted with a specialized virtue that cultivates the specific value of fairness, which seems at first to have no connection with it. But as the discussion proceeds we learn that the special virtue of justice-as-fairness is rooted in the recognition that all humans are equally human: it amounts to making a virtue of, cultivating the value of, the recognized equality of all participants in a *polis* – outside of which, says Aristotle, there is literally no justice to be found.

The city, the community within which our lives take shape, supports both friendship and justice, the sharing of life and the exchange of recompenses and rights; and the formulation of the mean for a particular virtue is always relative to a situation constituted in part by the presence of recognizable others. The special virtue of justice-as-fairness and the special relationship of personal friendship-in-virtue confirm and thematize the two implicit bases of social and political life.

The discussion of justice began with the general and proceeded to the particular. In friendship, the order is reversed: we start with the special and particular, and move on to the general. More precisely, we start with the definition of true friendship, and proceed through the quasi-friendship of 'community' to its origin in the conditions of unavoidable cohabitation. The reason for this reversal is that the *Ethics* is centrally concerned with the quality of individual life, with which individual friendships are most directly concerned; in the case of justice, the formal relationships of exchange are of less intimate concern than the social aspect of individual virtue.

In the discussion of justice, the treatment of both general and special senses of the term is followed by a brief remark on the ur-form of justice, 'reciprocity,' after which we embark on a chaotic-seeming series of considerations relating to how justice fits into the course of private and public life. In the discussion of friendship, the treatment of both individual and communal manifestations is followed by a sketch of the conditions of cooperation out of which friendship may arise, which is accompanied by a pathology corresponding to failures in cooperation (a passage to which the treatment of justice affords no real parallel), after which we embark on a ram-shackle-looking series of notes and problems bearing on the relationship between friendship and happiness. This whole passage forms a sort of sandwich, in which more miscellaneous material encapsulates a sequence of chapters (IX iv, viii–ix, xii, arising out of the definition of true friendship as mutually recognized reciprocity in affection), which suggest the view that human life consists most centrally of reflective activity – the basis of Book X, and what makes the comparison of lifestyles in X vi–viii possible.

The close connection between justice and friendship does not, of course, mean that the two discussions should be similarly organized, as the specific problems that arise and perspectives that open up are very different and have their own dynamics. In particular, the whole treatment of friendship may be seen as a response to a difficulty that is never clearly stated: how can the concept of friendship as a sharing of life be reconciled with the status of friends as chief among the *external* goods? (This is actually just the same problem that is posed for justice in *Republic* I – how can justice be both the central human virtue and 'another's good'? – but Aristotle ignores it, presumably because Plato had disposed of it already.)

To get a hold on the organization of *EN* VIII–IX, we must stop thinking about justice and ask directly what form Aristotle here gives to his general 'scholastic' schema for full-scale inquiries: phenomena, problems, theoretical statement, reconciliation. Here, in place of the phenomena, we have a statement of conventional encomia; the problem announced is whether friendship is for the akin or for the alien (an essentially physical and metaphysical version of the 'suppressed' difficulty I mentioned in the last paragraph); the theoretical statement takes the form of an elaborately hierarchical anatomy of human associations. This perhaps corresponds to the elaborate anatomy of the uses of *logos* in I xiii–VI, and is accordingly followed by a pathology corresponding to Book VII. Such an anatomy dissolves problems rather than confronting them, so there is no concluding passage of harmonization and reconciliation; rather, as remarked above, there is a morass of elucidations and elaborations in which no systematic relationship to what has gone before leaps to the eye.

4.2 Introduction (VIII i; 1155a3–b16)

The real reason why the topic of friendship makes a wholly new start is not that an egocentric standpoint is abandoned for an altruistic or universalistic one, but that friendship on the face of it is not an action-based concept at all, and does not enter into the context opened up at *On the Soul* III 10. In any case, Aristotle scarcely attempts to justify it in terms of what has gone before, saying only that friendship 'is a virtue, or goes with virtue,' and going on to show how it is 'most necessary to life' (whatever that means) in quite general terms. If we choose after all to regard these books as an independent treatise that has become incorporated in the *Ethics*, we have a choice. We can think of the reference to virtue as an afterthought added on the reasonable ground that in Book VII we are still pursuing the implications of that topic, in which case the account of the 'necessity' of friendship will have been part of a general explanation of why the topic is an important one; or we can suppose that the original introduction has been replaced by a few cursory remarks judged more suitable to a work on ethics, so that the material from the original treatise starts with the 'disputed question' at 1155a32.

4.21 Friendship as Virtue (1155a3–4, 28–31)

One should not, perhaps, make heavy weather of a single clause, but is it true, in the terms of the *Ethics*, that friendship is a virtue or 'with' virtue?[6] The reference can hardly be to the specific virtue asociated with *philia* in IV vi, which was the mean between churlishness and effusiveness, the 'right amount' of sociability within a context in which social relations are established. The right amount is what mattered, the feeling itself being, of course, no more virtuous than any other feeling. In the present passage, it is the propensity for social feeling itself that is extolled, and to have many friends and favour them is said to be glorious without any hint that there could be any excess in that direction. What Books VIII–IX do is, rather, to explore the whole range of feeling of which the virtue of *philia* is a mean, a feeling which is simply a function of interaction and not a 'disposition to choose, lying in a mean.' It is hard to see how the author of Book II could have written these opening words.

4.22 Friendship as Necessity (1155a4–28)

The word translated as 'necessary' (*anagkaion*) is faintly ambiguous. It can indeed mean that, and seems at first to mean that here; but it can also mean something more like 'intimately bound up with,' and that meaning seems to tinge what is said a little later.

To say that friendship is necessary to life or even to a good life is not to justify its treatment here, as the author claims. It may be true that 'without friends no one would choose to live,' but, the same could be said of the other 'external goods,' health or money, without which no life is 'sufficiently equipped' but which are not judged worthy of extended discussion in *EN*. And the claim is misleading. Friends do come in handy in the ways mentioned, and friendship among the citizenry is something that does make a government's task easier; but to say that is to miss what will be the whole point of friendship in the good life. In short, this passage shows why friendship in general is important, and thus introduces a general treatise on the topic; it does not show why friendship should be discussed at this point of the *Ethics*, or indeed at any other point.

4.23 The Concept of Friendship (1155a32–b16 [VIII 2])

Aristotle mentions three controversies about friendship: whether it is based on affinity or on complementarity; whether wicked people can be friends; whether there are radically different kinds of friendship. Such mootings of 'disputed questions,' as in Book I of *On the Soul*, are often used for conceptual clarification, to give the reader an idea of where the target concept fits into philosophical questions (for not every usage of a word is relevant to such problems), and may be independent of the substantive discussion that follows. But that is not quite what happens here. The following passage uses the methodology of *On the Soul* II 4: abilities and states are identified by the actions they issue in, and the actions are identified, where possible, by their intentional objects. So here, the nature of love is explained by the diverse kinds of loving behaviour, and these are differentiated by the objects to which they are directed, the varieties of 'lovables' (*philēta*). This differentiation is explicitly introduced as an approach to the third controversy, but effectively offers a way in to the other two as well and is basic to the whole of the positive treatment. And it is only the first of the three questions that offers any conceptual light.

Aristotle's concept of *philia* does not coincide with any in the English repertoire. It includes all mutual loving and liking, including that between members of a family, for whom English would find a different word (probably 'love'). Mutuality is built more strongly into the English word than into the Greek: the Greek prefix *philo-* is used wherever we would use the suffix '-lover,' *philein* is 'to like,' and a *philos* may be someone you like or someone who likes you, not necessarily both.[7] The connotation of the word is perhaps best fixed by the thesis of Greek popular morality that one should 'help one's friends and harm one's enemies.' In fact, the Homeric usage of the word has nothing to do with interpersonal relations, but stands for what is one's own: Odysseus addresses his *philon ētor*, 'his *own* heart.' My friends are my *own* people. This will be important in Aristotle's treatment too; but what friendship as discussed by Aristotle really is is fixed less by 'ordinary language' than by the course of the discussion itself.

The conundrum of whether *philia* is based on likeness (affinity) or difference (complementarity) answers itself in the concept of appropriation: before one has what is *philon* it is most other, because it is defined by one's lack of it; after one has it it is assimilated, so that if it is still distinguishable at all it is the *least* other.[8] And that is really why it is appropriate to call a friend a *heteros autos*: not a 'second self' so much as a self/other, the most other when absent and the least other when present.

4.3 True Friendship (VIII ii–viii; 1155b17–1159b24)

4.31 Anatomy of Friendship (VIII ii, iv–v; 1155b17–1156a5, 1156b33–1158a1)

Friendship is a relative (*pros hen*) concept: that is, it is used with reference to a paradigm case in which the idea of friendship is truly realized. This paradigm case is that of 'best friends,' pairs of individuals who are devoted to each other and spend as much of their time together as they can. How can we characterize their relationship? First, each likes (and loves) the other; each must find something about the other lovable (and likeable). What this is we shall see shortly. Second, the liking must be recognized: we are not friends if I like you but you don't know it. And, third, the liking must be reciprocated: unrequited love does not constitute friendship. Thus far, all seems obvious, but from it Aristotle draws a controversial conclusion: that the basis of true friendship is likeness (1157a33ff.), and that associations based on complementarity are likely to be unstable and evanescent (IX i). In any friendship not based on likeness, the motives of the parties will be different, and this is almost bound to lead to misunderstandings. Likeness, then, is a fourth feature of friendship.

This contention is typical of Aristotle, and can be made to look plausible. After all, if friends want to be together, they must want to do the same things; if they are different kinds of people, what they do together must go against the grain of one of them. But one might object that in matters of friendship life is at its quirkiest, and that schematic arguments are out of place here. The contention runs counter, as Aristotle recognizes in his 'disputed questions,' to a traditional view (persuasively presented in Plato's *Symposium*) that one loves what one lacks, as the parched soil yearns for rain (1155b2–3). But the *Symposium* was concerned, not with *philia*, but with love, *erōs*, sexual desire and desires that are akin to that.[9] Such attachments are reciprocated only contingently; even when mutual, they do not constitute a genuine friendship, for the parties are attached not to each other's personhood but to the satisfaction of their own respective needs. One of the things that such attachments lack is a fifth note of friendship, permanence. True friends stick by each other through thick and thin. And this permanence is partly due to the fact that forming a friendship represents a policy, a series of decisions, not merely the growth of a mutual sentiment. Really to love people is to wish them well for their own sake, and such wishing involves a commitment of the whole personality, a practical judgment that must reflect a state of character rather than a mere passing emotion (1157b29–37). So, even if friendship is neither virtue nor 'with' virtue, it has something important in common with virtue.

Although friendship requires reciprocity, the basic fact in friendship is one person's active love for another. This is obvious to Aristotle, since a person's life is essentially made up of what the person does. Life is activity, what else? What happens to people affects them only by being taken up in a certain manner into their vital activities. So loving matters more than being loved.[10] One might think otherwise: people need to be needed, like to be liked, and in one popular view one needs friends simply to rally round one and offer support in these and other ways. But Aristotle rejects this idea, asking us to consider a mother's love for her child, which is independent of the child's ability and willingness to respond and reciprocate (1159a28–33), and the supposed fact that people feel kindly towards their beneficiaries and resent their benefactors.[11] Indeed, if the active side of friendship were not paramount, one could not sustain friendships at a distance, where assurance of returned affection depends on an occasional letter.

The characteristics of reciprocity, permanence, and activity, put together, show that the normal friendship is the sharing of life. Best friends are people who spend all their time together, and the truest friends are those of whom it is said that they are 'inseparable' –

We wore one hat, smoked one cigar,
One standing at each end.[12]

All of these characteristics – love, acknowledgement, reciprocity, likeness, permanence, activity, and sharing – are of the greatest importance for the concluding part of the discussion of friendship, in which the compatibility of friendship with self-love and the necessity of friendship to the happy life are vindicated.

4.32 The Basis of Friendship (VIII ii–v; 1155b17–1158a1)

The heart of *philia*, then, is its active part; and activities, we know, are discriminated by their objects. What are the objects of love? In answering this question, Aristotle indulges in some fancy footwork. What we are looking for the object of is not friendship itself, since that is a mutual bond; it is *philēsis*, which can only mean, 'liking' here, though it is not a word in common use.[13] The object of this 'liking' is not the *philon* – a word that, as we saw, connotes own-ness as much as fellowship – but the *philēton*, a verbal noun with no colour of its own. Aristotle writes as if he had in mind the abstract object of liking in general, of 'pro' attitudes as such, not the concrete object of a personal attitude, much less a personal partner in a relationship. On this understanding, it seems reasonable to say that the objects of liking are three: the pleasant, the useful, the good. Some things one likes simply because one likes them, one finds them agreeable or 'pleasant.' Some things one takes a 'pro' attitude to because they help one get what one wants. But some things one 'likes' simply because they compel one's admiration, one thinks them good. One might have expected the word 'fine' (*kalon*) rather than 'good' in this context (cf. § 1.2324), but Aristotle prefers the latter for three reasons. In the first place, he needs a word that will naturally cover the special case of good moral character, which is what he is actually interested in. In the second place, the word *fine* introduces a suggestion of subjectivity, which he is anxious to exclude. And in the third place *kalon* as applied to people connotes personal beauty (it is the word Attic potters applied to the pretty boys to whom they dedicated their designs) rather than admirability of character.

All this seems reasonable enough. The thesis that the three 'objects of choice' are the pleasant, the useful (*sumpheron*), and the fine (*kalon*) was laid down at 1104b30, and there seems no reason why they should not also serve to classify the objects of 'pro' attitudes. But the shift from *philia* to *philēsis* seems to change the subject from a relation between persons to an attitude towards external objects. What one is friends with is an individual person, not any aspect or attribute that the person may have.[14]

Well, does it really matter? Attractions among human beings are no exception to the general rule: some people one cultivates for the use one can make of them, others because they are fun to be with, others because one thinks highly of the kind of person they are. And it is obvious that the requirements of true friendship are not met by the first two. Friendships such as business partnerships, based on utility, are not based on liking at all, have little of activity about them, do not involve living together, and are likely to be no more permanent than the prospect of the advantage foreseen. Friendships based on pleasure (Aristotle plainly has sexual partnerships mainly in mind) come closer to genuine friendship: it is something about the other person one likes, and as someone one likes to be with. But one likes the person, not as a personality, but as a source of gratifications: as the body ages or the wit sours, the attraction will evaporate. Only the friendship based on the other person as a person, the friendship based on character, really has the characteristics that define true friendship. Your character is not something other than what you are, and your excellence is not something other than what you are. Character is durable, too, and the friendship that is based on it should last.

The disturbing thing about Aristotle's argument here is that he equates friendship based on character with that based on virtue – an apparent consequence of his reduction of the beloved person to abstractly favoured attributes. This leaves no place for sheer congeniality. Plato, in his *Lysis* (221–2), had introduced congeniality as a basis of friendship, only to abandon it as indistinguishable from similarity; Aristotle never considers it. One might think it came under the heading of 'pleasure,' but we saw that Aristotle confines that to such more superficial attributes as sexual attractiveness or a gift for repartee. He recognizes (1172a1–8) that, since friends like to do things together, chess players tend to be friends of chess players; but his formal treatment allows no place for anything between the friendship based on true moral worth and that based on mere sensual gratification or mutual amusement. Just so, we may think, he recognized earlier (I viii) that some people just loved riding horseback and that was what life meant for them – but the *Ethics* as a whole is written as if human beings were not like that at all.

That Aristotle should treat character-based friendships in terms of virtue is understandable, given the orientation of the *Ethics* as a whole and its leading themes. Virtue is the most stable of character traits, since it alone is based on a consistent and self-sustaining principle and involves no inner tensions, and it is, of course, the most objectively valuable of characteristics and hence the least likely to pall. A person who has developed a taste for true excellence is hardly likely to change it for a different taste. And it is the least superficial of characteristics: people's characters are in an obvious way more centrally *them* than even their love of music or baseball.[15] But such friendships, says Aristotle, will be slow to ripen: it takes time to get to know what someone is really like through and through.[16]

The emphasis on true virtue as the basis of the truest friendship still strikes us as strange. Virtue is so *insipid*. Is there any way of mitigating this? One might try the following. Actual friendship, like actual wishing in Book III, is based on the apparent rather than the real good (1155b21–6), though ideally it aims at the real good and in a good person actually does so. People, we may then say, make friends of those they think agreeable (though they may be disillusioned about this),[17] of those they believe to be useful (though this is often an illusion), and of those they believe to be good because they answer to their own aspirations and standards – that is, they find them congenial. But good people's notions of what good people are like are true, and what they find congenial is virtue.

This way out seems not to work. I may very well find someone congenial though I do not think them wholly admirable, and I may admire people without finding them personally agreeable. We might do better to consider that only two people can be each other's best friend, and not every good person is a friend of every good person. How do such people become friends? I suggested before that a good person will still have a distinctive lifestyle (involving love of particular kinds of recreation and so on). Good people who love chess, to use our earlier illustration, will find friends among those good people whose tastes run to chess and, among chess players, will prefer to spend time with those whose characters they find admirable. The virtue component is invariable; the lifestyle component may be what we please. But we could go even further and suggest that (equating virtue with seriousness) one may find a person's style of seriousness itself congenial, loving the individual way he or she goes about solving life's problems and meeting its challenges.

Though we may find Aristotle's emphasis strange, it is not without precedent.[18] And it is at least arguable that the liking for any character other than a virtuous one, or for any other reason than that one believes it to be virtuous, is irrational and really subject to all the instabilities of a friendship built on pleasure. Besides, if the idea of human virtue can really be educed from the bare idea of seriousness in the use of *logos*, one can urge (as Aristotle seems to have thought) that there cannot be any such thing as a positively bad character – characters fail only through indeterminacy, inconsistency, and frivolity. And our protestations on behalf of congeniality are idle. What exactly *is* congeniality? We have not said anything definite enough to vindicate a place for it in an Aristotelian scheme. Our remarks on 'style' are a gratuitous and self-indulgent intrusion into his thought-world. A distinctive notion of congeniality must rest on a notion of individuality and the supreme value of being, not a good specimen of humanity, but just the very person one is. Such a notion is distinctively modern, we may think; but then we call to mind Odysseus on Calypso's island, longing to see the smoke rising from his own home.

Meanwhile, the emphasis on virtue is central to the scheme of the *Ethics*. Our problem must be to show how friendship finds a place in an ethic grounded on the individual's *eudaimonia*. But *eudaimonia* was equated with (the best kind of) virtuous activity. To bring friendship into happiness we must therefore stress the active side of it, but must also make it characteristic of virtue. And insofar as friendship is based on likeness and sharing of activities, only another virtuous person's activities will be sufficiently like those of a virtuous person to be shared. Only a friendship based on virtue thus falls within the definition of a good life. Nor should we ignore the function of *logos*. The sequence pleasure–utility–goodness represents a scale of more sophisticated and far-reaching reflection. Pleasure involves immediate reaction to directly experienced characteristics. Utility requires a calculation of partially shared goals over a limited range. Goodness evokes choice and long-range commitment. Analogous is the sequence of communities, from the family that arises from immediate need, through the trading partnership that is relatively stable though provisional and limited in scope, to the full sharing of life in a *polis* united by a common understanding of the human good.

But all this is merely a formal solution to our problem. We are no closer to an account of how friendship actually can and does contribute to happiness. That question remains for § 4.5.

4.4 Community (VIII ix–xii; 1159b25–1163a23)

Aristotle distinguishes three forms of friendship: 'comradely' (*hetairikē*), the mutually chosen companionship of individuals, which is what we have been considering; 'familial' (*sungenikē*), based on the natural predicaments of kinship; and 'communal' (*koinōnikē*), generated by the circumstances of cooperation (1161b11–16). In a broad sense, it is cooperation that generates all friendship, the subjective counterpart of the bare fact that human beings do not live in isolation from each other but live knowingly and willingly as social beings; but it is not simply a matter of the amount and circumstances of shared life, because blood ties are qualitatively different from any sharing of activities, and community always involves some sort of formal agreement (*homologia*, 1161b15) as opposed to the spontaneous togetherness found in the other two.

Of all friendships, the individual relation founded on virtue is the rarest, since the requirements are so stringent, but it is also the strongest and purest form. It is by its standard that all other friendships are recognized and judged. So we started with that. But a complementary approach would start with the most widely diffused and therefore presumably least intense form, the communal or associational relationship. Insofar as genuine friendships always involve shared activity, this weakest form would be the fellow-feeling that is engendered among those jointly participating in any enterprise involving any cooperation in the pursuit of any objective whatever. The bond is still shared life, but instead of the direct *reciprocity* of two individuals we have the diffused and general mutual goodwill that prevails in a community at large and is the by-product of the pursuit of a *common* objective. The essence of this goodwill is enshrined in the classical political concept of 'likemindedness' (*homonoia*, Latin *concordia*), the mutual acceptance that is the condition of all successful social action and which it is traditionally among the chief tasks of any government to promote (1155a22–6). The relationship between friendship and 'living together' that we previously examined turns out to be reversible: mutual love is expressed in shared activity, and shared activity engenders a modicum of mutual affection.

4.41 Justice and Comradeship (VIII ix; 1159b25–1160a30)

The wider the area over which one person cooperates with another, the stronger the bond of feeling. But this suggests an interesting relationship between justice and friendship. Justice as it turned out to be in the latter part of Book V, a set of rules and presuppositions facilitating the handling of relations between strangers on an artificial basis, must be proportionate in its scope to the amount of activity to be shared.[19] If few activities are shared, there will be little to regulate: a book club can get by with a handful of regulations covering a few transactions within a tiny area of life. But then, since justice and friendship alike are proportionate in their extent and intensity (respectively) to the amount of cooperation involved, they must be proportionate to each other.[20] Social and legal relations go hand in hand. This seems to contradict the encomium in VIII i, where friendship is said to make justice unnecessary (1155a26–7), but each statement is right in its way. Justice is really unnecessary only in true friendships between pairs of individuals; and even among individuals, 'friendships' based on utility on both sides, or on utility on one side and pleasure on the other (as in commercial sex) are unlikely to be workable unless based on fairly specific agreements as to the rights and obligations of the parties (cf. VIII xiii–IX i). One might express this by saying that there is a rather high threshold below which friendship alone does not obviate the need for justice, a threshold that can never be reached in a community of such proportions that its members are not all personally acquainted with each other.[21]

The thesis of the last paragraph is too simple, because both 'justice' and 'friendship' are ambiguous. Close friends and family get by without careful reckoning of who owes whom what, their friendship makes justice unnecessary; but they have, in fact, innumerable ties felt as binding, just because they are so close. Again, a close working agreement is often entered into without a contract, because all parties know what is going on, their friendship makes 'justice' unnecessary; but, after a while, people forget and develop other interests and the world changes. A formal contract then becomes necessary, not to introduce new obligations where there were none before, but because it has become necessary to make existing obligations explicit.[22]

The essential difference between justice and friendship, as Aristotle conceives them, is that friendship is almost entirely a qualitative affair, but justice, in its overriding concern with the 'equal,' is wholly quantitative. That is why there can be justice where there is no friendship: so long as two quantities, however disparate, are measured by a common unit, they can be brought into a common proportion, and this 'proportionate equality' is what justice requires.[23] But friendship requires *actual* equality (VIII vi–vii, especially 1158b30–3): if there is too great a disparity between people, they simply cannot be friends. Justice is based on the reciprocal exchange of its cruder antecedent, *to antipeponthos*, a relation between agents who recognize each other but whose mutual concern does not go beyond the transaction in question; friendship, by contrast, depends not on exchanging but on sharing. There is, indeed, exchanging in friendship, since attention and love from one partner are met by attention and love from the other, but these exchanges are not transactions in which one gives up what the other gets. Even so, if one does try to interpret the friendship between extremely unequal people in terms of exchange, and hence as it were to make their friendship *intelligible* by treating it as something like justice, one can see that, if the laws of commutative justice are applied to such a case, there will be a wide disparity between the attention and love that the greater owes the lesser and that which the lesser owes the greater. And this is what Aristotle says, that relations between unequals are preserved by being handled in terms of such quasi-justice and reciprocity, but too great a disparity makes sharing impossible and at this point such relationships break down (VIII vii).[24]

Although in face-to-face transactions justice simply lays the foundations of a 'proportional equality' that is really no equality at all, but merely commensurability, in the context of a whole community 'justice,' in the rather different sense of the systems of rules and obligations and rights that bind them all into one articulated whole, is indeed an equalizer. It lays the ground of joint action, and to that extent should be accompanied by a modicum of feeling (the 'we' feeling) that Aristotle in this laxer context recognizes as a form of *philia*. It unites people as equals and thus generates camaraderie. Each is equally an element in this complex, and this gives all the same reason to say 'we' in the same sense, and thus to think and feel 'we.'[25] But face-to-face justice, mediating between individuals, need have no such implications. The fact that I am entering into an exchange relationship may have no effect on my feeling for you – though our sharing in the experience of bargaining may. In fact, in any transaction involving me with you, we are likely to figure partly as opponents and partly as comrades. To this deep ambivalence Aristotle shows himself as insensitive on the one side as Sartre does on the other.[26]

All human associations are designed to achieve some common end, which determines not only the extent but also the nature of the 'justice' (the rules and regulations, overt or tacit) and hence also of the friendship that obtains among their members. But there is one association which is unrestricted in its aims: as stated in I ii, the political organization exists to secure welfare overall, its laws are general in scope, and the friendship that prevails among its members is correspondingly unspecialized. It may then be taken as the paradigm of friendship in the communal form, just as the friendship of two good people is the paradigm of individual friendships because it rests on the love of what is, in general, lovable rather than on the coincidence of contingent predilections. This being so, we might expect to find that the basic forms of political organization are the basic forms of human association and reflect its necessary conditions. We might further reflect that these conditions would issue in the fundamental forms of friendship. But this point we are left to make for ourselves. Aristotle pursues a different line of inquiry, to which we turn shortly.

The political organization, unlike more specialized associations, is designed to secure welfare *in general*. In the crucial passage (1160a9–14), Aristotle gives it as the accepted view that this welfare is defined in terms of common utility (*to koinēi sumpheron*); the following lines add that the state also has as its accepted function the provision of common amusements.[27] But this does not rule out the possibility that the true function of the state must be to secure what Aristotle himself would identify with true welfare, *eudaimonia* as it really is, and this we know to be virtuous activity. If that is so, as Aristotle says elsewhere, the end of the state must be to secure the virtue of its citizens as well as facilitating the corresponding activities – the state is, above all else, an educational institution. And if *that* is so, the perfected form of friendship among fellow citizens, and thus the perfected form of associational friendship in general, will be like the perfected form of individual friendship, a partnership in virtuous activity founded on virtue. In its subjective aspect it will be a sentiment that crowns partnership in action in the same way that, we will be told, pleasure crowns the virtuous activity of the individual (1174b29–33). Friendship here, like pleasure there, is a sign of the facilitation of action.

4.42 Necessity and Cooperation (VIII x–xii; 1160a31–1162a33)

One can now see what the value of friendship is to a community and to the individual members of that community, though the answer has not yet been spelled out. We have also seen that friendship comes into the world as a by-product of cooperation. But we still do not know why and how friendship comes into the world, because we do not know what makes people cooperate. In the *Politics*, where the conditions of cooperation are the main topic, we read (1252b29–30) that political communities are generated for the sake of life and exist for the sake of the good life: necessity drives people to set up a form of organization in which they thereupon or subsequently discover an inherent value.[28] So the question of how friendship comes into the world is related to the question of what drives people to establish cities. And, since cities are still being founded, we can answer that. Considerations of defence lead tribes to settle in walled concentrations. But that does not answer the question of the origin of friendship, because a rudimentary organization, the tribe, was there already. So our question is rather, how do tribes start? And the answer to that is known. A tribe is (or has as its nucleus) an extended family. And at the centre of the extended family, of course, is the basic family.[29]

What we want to know, then, is what the cement is that binds the family together, and what the impulse that generates it. The question does not seem too hard to answer, but we may make it a bit more complex and precise. What demands explanation is specified by an analysis of the political organizations into which tribes are transformed. And these are traditionally of three kinds: monarchical, based on the absolute superiority of one; aristocratic, based on the principle of specialization or the recognition of a diversity of complementary superiorities; and democratic, based on the equal status of a group's members simply as members.[30] And the prototypes of these relationships are all to be found within the unit family of husband, wife, and progeny.[31] The relation between parent and child is one of domination; that between husband and wife is one of specialization, for the husband does not interfere in the store-room and the wife keeps out of the shop; that between siblings is one of tempered equality, for no brother has authority over another but the older brother has a certain responsibility and status.[32] In state and family alike, if these relationships are governed by justice they engender love, if not they engender hate. A tyrant and a tyrannical father; the rule of arbitrary or irrelevant privilege, and a henpecking wife and a meddling husband; siblings who yield to rivalry, and democracies that pay no regard to merit – these are all notorious occasions for spite and strife.

The question how friendship comes into the world now reduces to that of the nature of the necessity underlying each of the three types of family relationship.[33] Of these, the relation between parent and child is, in a sense, basic (1161b16). We might point here to the dependence of children on parents, the protracted helplessness of the human young that goes with the complexity and ubiquity of culture; and, in the case of siblings, to the common situation of dependence and environment into which they are thrown together. But Aristotle says nothing of that. He attributes necessity only to the relationship between man and woman, the sexual urge that leads to an association that is later continued partly because of the mutual convenience of the division of labour in the household and partly because the children, if any, may form a common bond.[34] Besides, if they are lucky, they may get to like each other. What Aristotle does say of the other two bonds is something very different: that their strength depends on *identification*. Siblings recognize a common origin; parents see in children a continuation of their own lives, children see in their parents the authors of their being. The family lineage is an extension of the self.[35]

It is only in a sense, I said, that the parent-child relation is basic. What it is basic to is the family as blood relationship, the blood that is thicker than water. Mother and father are blood relations only because each is a blood relation of the children. What gets the whole thing going, though, is the natural pairing impulse of humans as of other sexually reproducing animals – an impulse so natural that people think that friendship between man and wife is natural too (1162a16–17). But the inference, as we learn from *The Generation of Animals*, is too hasty: animals are essentially sexual only in the business of reproduction itself.[36]

However that may be, the family relationship is an extension of the self. And this gives us the clue that leads us on to the final account of the nature of friendship, according to which a friend is a 'second self.'[37]

4.5 Friendship in the Real World (VIII xiii–IX iii; 1162a34–1165b36)

The crucial difference between justice and friendship as modes of human relationship is that justice obtains between any two people operating within a common political framework: whatever their differences, they can be united by being brought into a common quantitative relationship. The heart of the relationship is 'proportionate equality,' which is not really equality at all: it is commensurability, the existence of something like a common measure that applies to both. We call it 'equality' because *ison* means 'equal' as well as 'fair,' and because the parties are 'equal before the law,' standing in the same relation to the legal system that assigns each the same place, the place we call 'standing' before the law. Friendship, by contrast, depends on actual equality as recognized by the participants, the feeling that makes them think of themselves and each other as 'us' regardless of any formal relationships between them. Consequently, differences among the participants do not, as with justice, merely specify the terms of the relationship; they actually endanger it. And the kind of difference it is governs the kind of danger, and hence what must be done to avert or minimize it.

The dangers to friendship are of two kinds. In the friendships between individuals, they arise from the different requirements each may have in the relationship, and the consequent fragility caused by changes in the situation; in friendships arising from a shared condition, they arise from the limits on the extent to which the condition is actually shared. Aristotle deals with these matters in a protracted discussion of the casuistry of friendship, the limits within which friendship can be sustained.[38] He clearly thinks the matter important (or simply interesting; it has a sort of gossipy fascination). Perhaps its chief importance lies in that, as he says, friendships between people who acknowledge their social inequality are sustained by recognizing the inequality and accommodating it (IX i).[39] This is one of the ways that friendship sustains justice, and hence social reality underpins the political order.

Intercalated with this discussion of the pathology of friendship and its remedies is a consideration of the ways in which friendships with their personal commitments may conflict with each other (IX ii). This is carried out in terms of justice, rendering to each what is due. Aristotle does not say so, but this is because as soon as different relationships present rival claims we must distance the claimants so that we can adjudicate between them. A *philos* is not only a *philos* but is related to us in other ways as well, because even the closest friends and lovers are living together in a real world of complex relationships.

The whole section concludes with the saddest topic of all: what happens when friends change? Aristotle's trust in the durability of virtue (and hence of friendships based on character) falls foul of his awareness that people may change even to the point where, with the best will in the world, estrangement cannot be avoided. If we can't live together, we can't, and that's that (1165b30), though we will retain a certain lingering affection – unless the breach is caused by excessive wickedness.

These chapters relate to the discussion of the varieties of friendship as VIII iv–vi did to the treatment of friendship proper, reminding us of how mixed and complex personal relationships are in social reality. In thinking about these matters, we as readers have to exercise our 'understanding' and 'judgment,' even if our 'good sense' is not engaged: Aristotle presents us with imaginary cases and types of complex relationships, confident that we will be able to judge what he says about them – what the relevant factors are likely to be, what our decision would probably be – even while conceding that, of course, we would need to know the actual situation before making up our minds.

This section as a whole is one of those passages, rarer perhaps than in Plato but common enough, where Aristotle shows himself aware of the ambiguities and intricacies of social life. We cannot refrain from making the relevant distinctions, laborious as that may be, as best we can (1165a33–5).

4.6 Love and Consciousness (IX iv–xii; 1166a1–1172a15)

The last main division of the treatise on friendship is perhaps the most startling passage in the *Ethics*, and one that affords a key to the general tendency of the whole work. It is here that Aristotle develops the theory of activity, proposing a way of viewing human life that reveals the most fundamental way in which *logos* enters into human life. This is through self-awareness, the perception and thought that have perception and thought as their object.[40] In this reflexivity we see how finality and value are present in human activities, thus substantiating the distinctions among modes of goodness and means/end relations that were made but not supported in I i.

Friendship, we saw, depends on love, on likeness, on recognition, on reciprocity, on activity, on quality of characters, and ultimately (and from a different viewpoint) on sharing of life. These requirements (*ta philika*, 'the friendly things') are now recognized as being fulfilled most obviously in people's relationships to themselves, insofar as they consider themselves as objects – that is, to the extent that they can be self-aware.[41] A friend is thus virtually a 'second self,' serving as a projection of the ego.[42] One can know this second self as one cannot know one's real self, so that a friend can be a means to self-knowledge, and an indispensable aid to the happiness that only a fully conscious existence can afford. An unshared activity, it seems, cannot be a complete activity at all; or, at least, beings who share none of their activities cannot be fully conscious, and hence not fully aware, in any.

For all its audacity, this passage is not unprepared. Its themes are activity, self-cultivation, idealism (action *tou kalou heneka*), harmony, the joy in living, and the conceptual normativeness of the virtuous person; and these have been leading themes of the *Ethics* throughout. But only now are we made aware of the single end to which they were tending.

In the first movement of the treatise on friendship (dealt with in § 4.3), we saw that the conditions of friendship issue in the activities of shared life. The second movement (§ 4.4) reversed the implication, showing how the sharing of activities issues in friendly feeling. Now in this final movement the implication is reversed again, and we are shown how a purely internal (self-regarding) attitude within a good individual issues in the external relationship that we know as friend-ship.

This last movement is based on a doctrine of self-love that is derived from the two earlier movements. The first movement taught us that one can really like people only for what they are – that is, for their virtues, which are accessible to us only in their actualization in virtuous activities. We love them, as it were, for being what they do. We may infer that a true self-love can only be a love of what we are, of our virtues or what we take to be our virtues, which again are accessible to us only as activities. But our activities are accessible to us, we may think, only as states of consciousness; for whereas our bodies as bodies *move*, changing their position in space, it is we as people who are active, and what in this activity is distinguishable from bodily movement can only be what Aristotle calls 'perception and thought,' our state of awareness at a given moment. Aristotle, as we have seen, thinks of human life as permeated by the *logon echon*: everything is mediated, experienced as verbalizable and calcu-lable, a subject of reflection – except, no doubt, the experience of life itself, which is immediately enjoyed. But *what* is thus enjoyed is the experience of life as mediated and mediating, because that is what human life is. (The denser the mediation, the stronger the immedi-acy.) Hence the original emphasis in Book I on 'activity *of the soul*,' an expression that seemed at the time otiose. The soul itself, accord-ing to *On the Soul*, is the actualization of the body; the body as *a body*, and not merely as assemblage of limbs and vessels, is soul. So bodily feelings are not immediate, unless perhaps when they are pathological (as in *akrasia*): they are funded, they are experienced as within the life of which they are part. 'Sensation and thought,' then, are not something abstracted from and essentially external to the life of the organism, as if on the screen of a TV monitor; they are the medium within which activities are carried on, except for those unconscious processes of digestion and growth that are outside the reach of the *logon echon*.

From the second movement of the treatise we gather that friend-ship is proportionate to justice, which in turn is proportionate to amount of shared activity. But since, in a sense, we share all our own activities, we may say that in that sense people are their own best friends.[43] A friend is a second self only because oneself is one's pri-mary friend. But Aristotle wants to say that this applies only to a character that is not at odds with itself: self-love requires a self to be loved, and this must depend on integrity of character.[44] But integrity of character is the mark of the virtuous person. That seems to follow from the way in which the definition of virtue was reached: virtue requires and results from being serious about one's life *as a whole* – even a harlequin life could be virtuous, but only by being consistent in the method of its harlequinity, so as to form a single object of serious attention. Thus from each of the two earlier movements we draw the same inference, that a true self-love is the prerogative of a good person. But self-love can be nothing else than love of one's life, and how else could we define happiness than as loving one's life or having a life one loves?[45]

4.61 Self and Other (IX iv; 1166a1–b29)

The *Ethics* differs from many modern discussions of morality by resolutely taking the first-person view: the question posed is how one should live one's own life, not how other people should behave, and the assumed stance is that of the person wondering what the best life to live is and how to live it. But now, if my relation to my own life is somehow the same as that of my relation to my friend's life, the gap between first-person and third-person views is bridged. In at least one case, I can wonder how another person should live, and can consider how I should live as if I were another person. This transition of viewpoints is, or ought to be, thematic. One of the things it does is cut the ground from under Kant's 'antinomy of the summum bonum,' the divergence of virtue and welfare supposedly resolved only by the hope of an 'after life.' (Not that Aristotle allows any room for such an antinomy in the first place.) That antinomy posits an unmediated life of feeling and a feelingless life of rational calculation. As a person, I find within myself the source of rationality in the moral law; as an object of observation, I see myself as I see others, a hedonistic component in the all-embracing system of causes and effects. Aristotle rather uses the basic experience of friendship to bridge the gap between aspiration and observation. From Aristotle's point of view, Kant can appear rather childish; from Kant's point of view, Aristotle is uncritically naïve.

That what we believe of friendship is true of good people's relationships to themselves, and of everyone's relationships to themselves insofar as they approve of themselves, is argued on the basis of five obvious characteristics of friendship.[46] First, people do, and wish for, whatever is really best for their friends. But people always wish for and seek what they think is best for themselves; and good people seek what is *really* so. One wishes friends well for their own sakes, and good people wish themselves well for the sake of their true selves – for Aristotle, despite his rejection of attempts to exclude passions from a person's real self, accepts the Platonic evaluation of the planning and thinking aspects of people as the truly human, that with which we *cannot but* identify ourselves (1166a16–23). What this means we can see if we recall the account of the 'human good' in I i–vii; good people consider their best interests in the longest run, make the quality of their lives as a whole a conscious object, deliberate in the interest of all their values, whereas bad people fail to integrate their lives and indulge the impulses of the moment or follow short-term advantage – they 'don't see any harm in it,' as we say.[47]

Second, we think that people want their friends to go on living, for their own sakes, and would wish them to do so even if they lost all contact with them. So, too, good people find their own existence good and wish it to remain unchanged;[48] and, again, they wish this for the 'true' self, the thinking, planning, and controlling aspect. But bad people, though they may enjoy themselves at least some of the time, cannot approve of (take delight in) their existence as a whole; or, if they do, they approve of it not for the sake of their own true selves, but only for the sake of the incidental pleasures with which their lives are garnished.[49] In this connection we recall the insistence (1157b29–37) that friendship is more than just mutual liking, but involves policy: to wish people well for their own sakes is to make a choice and involves the whole character. So good people's relationship to themselves is one of dispassionate benevolence, involving a commitment of character to their own well-being. Good people have assumed responsibility for the quality of their own lives; this, I would add, is part of what we mean by calling them 'serious' (*spoudaioi*).

Third, we say that friends enjoy each other's company. And good people are happy when alone, enjoying pleasant memories and needing no distraction, while bad people are cheerful only in a crowd of cronies who help them forget themselves.

Fourth, we think that friends share each other's tastes; and good people 'share' their own tastes, in the sense that their tastes are consistent, unlike those of bad people who must reject with one part of themselves what another part enjoys.

Fifth and last, we think that friends grieve and rejoice together. And good people are as consistent in their moods as in their tastes, never having to regret what 'seemed like a good idea at the time,' whereas bad people are full of remorse. Evil simply is not lovable, since 'good' was defined as the object of desire in general (for every sort of desire or tropism or 'pro' attitude there is a corresponding sense of 'good,' and the more unequivocal the desire the less qualified the sense of 'good'). From this it follows that bad people cannot love themselves.[50] Only good people, then, can have tolerable lives.

The derivation of the relation of friendship from that of good people to themselves seems outrageous and even paradoxical. What is literally true of the allegedly derivative relationship is only true by metaphor of the supposedly primary one. Perhaps the primacy is only psychological (as David Gallop has suggested to me), as when the supremely unjust are said in *Republic* IX to be friendless because they are at enmity with themselves. Who would want to be around self-hating people? This certainly seems to be the position of 1166b26–9, where it is said that vice makes one unlovable both to oneself and to others, and it is easy to infer that the former causes the latter. However, Aristotle's argument makes better sense if the relationship is conceptual or ontological: the fact that such relations obtain within individuals establishes a prototype that can then be recognized in interpersonal relations. But if it is conceptual or ontological priority that is intended, ought not Aristotle to have said so, conceding that it is from the familiar and factual relation of friendship that we actually derive the more recondite and metaphorical notion of self-love? Perhaps, but on reflection we can see how Aristotle comes to take up the position that he does. After all, the individual *is* primary, in the sense that friendships, being relations between individuals, necessarily assume individuals as relata.[51] That said, the paradoxicality of Aristotle's position is its main point. It is because these relationships are only imperfectly realized within individuals that friendship is necessary. If friendship is formed on the model of self-love, self-love can be brought to fruition only on the model of a friendship between independent individuals who can take an objective view of each other. Humanity is social by nature, after all, which means that the potentialities of individuality can be realized only in social relations. Humans can think about themselves clearly only by using as a model the other people whom they begin by treating as 'second selves.'[52] So one can see what Aristotle is getting at. But to me the whole passage seems glib, too clever by half.

4.611 Aristotle on Vice

By the time he gets around to saying that bad people cannot love themselves, Aristotle has forgotten his starting-point, which was that people may think themselves good mistakenly – *kakia lanthanei* (1150b36), their badness escapes their notice. In fact, it seems impossible that people should ever truly think of themselves as bad people, since a bad person can simply be defined as the kind of person one wouldn't want to be (from whatever the appropriate viewpoint may be). One has to conclude that Aristotle has no consistent theory of vice, and in fact nowhere really confronts the problem. At the crucial point, in Book VII, he sidesteps the issue, relying on a distinction between vice and moral weakness (with side glances at pathological and subhuman conditions and at temperamental weaknesses), without ever looking at vice itself – he says he has looked at it already, but has he? And in the present passage he seems to be in his high-minded phase, in which he thinks that because a bad life must, by definition, be an unnatural life, it must actually impose strains on those who live it, so that bad people must be at least intermittently and obscurely aware of their own deficiencies. How can they help noticing that something is amiss, any more than they can help noticing that they are liable to the censure of their fellows?[53]

What Aristotle says here about vice seems to be what one would expect him to say about weakness of will – compare 1150a22 and 1150b29–30, where it is explicitly said that the *akratēs* repents but the *akolastos* does not, whereas at 1166b24–5 it is the *phauloi*, the bad, who 'groan with repentance.' True, *phaulos* is a word less specific in meaning than *akolastos* and does not connote downright rascality as *mochthēros* does, and it might perhaps include moral weakness; but in that case Aristotle's whole argument falls to the ground, because it leaves us with the possibility of people who are cheerfully and wholeheartedly bad, which is exactly what he is concerned to exclude.[54]

The simple opposition of good and bad people in the present passage looks back to the basic moral psychology of I xiii (another passage that uses overtly Platonic concepts), where the irrational element in the soul is presented as having a dynamic of its own, capable of acting in opposition to reason, rather than as a morally neutral quantifiable as in Book II. Either this element in the soul is under control or it is not, so that a person is either good or not (1102b14–23). And if the irrational is out of control, presumably the affected person must be somehow aware of conflict (even if you cannot actually see the conflict, as you can see a paralytic limb failing to respond), because the *logon echon* that should be controlling it is certainly present. But I xiii leaves open the possibility that the *logon echon* might have the *alogon* under control, but control it in the interests of a mistaken idea of the good, a possibility mentioned in III v.[55] It is useless to say that *logos* is inherently a principle of rightness – if one can calculate, one can miscalculate; if truth is possible, error and deception must be possible too. In fact, four sorts of error are, in principle, possible. A passion might be occasionally and arbitrarily unruly; a passion might be autonomously organized independently of the *logon echon*; reason might control a passion mistakenly; or a person might be morally weak, loss of control being a temporary departure from an established norm. Aristotle has simply failed to pay systematic attention to these possibilities or any others he may recognize.

The way out of this labyrinth begins to appear when we look at the formal definition of virtue in Book II. It there appears that the common notion that there is a simple and symmetrical opposition between vice and virtue is an illusion. Virtue established the mean from which vice is a departure. Vice has no principle of its own. The vicious person simply fails to be *spoudaios*, does not think things through, either fails to see that there is a mean or fails to use all available data to establish what the mean is. But since the data are, in fact, available (they are simply a description of the actual social and psychological context of action), bad people can only maintain their conviction of their own rectitude by averting their attention from what is there to be seen. Their *kakia lanthanei*, they don't notice it, but in the longer run and at a deeper level thay can't *help* noticing it.

What makes the position oulined in the preceding paragraph tenable is that in Aristotle's world there is no possible place for radical evil. What, indeed, could radical evil be? It would have to be something like an alternative possible world order, opposed to the order that prevails but somehow relevant to it, like the backward-spinning world of Plato's *Statesman* 269A–270A or the alternating cosmogonies of Empedocles. I do not think that would make sense to Aristotle.[56] For him, either the world is such as to determine a single way of life (or ordered set of alternatives) as good, or it is not. If it is not, one cannot say what *eudaimonia* is and the project of the *Ethics* has a negative outcome. But, if it is, all views of human life other than that determined as good by the sort of argument that Aristotle uses are demonstrably incoherent and simply incapable of determining a way of life that can be judged satisfactory.

The point is that the proper motive of the moral agent as such is 'getting things right': such actions must be done *tou kalou heneka*, because of their fineness, and what is fine about them is that they are done because deliberation shows them to be right and not from any unmediated appetite for their immediate object. It follows that there is no counterpart motive for vice: there is no intelligible motive such as 'getting things wrong.' Vicious people either don't care, being locked into the maximization of personal advantages as they come along, or don't care *enough*, allowing their hunches, the 'conscience' or 'common sense' that enshrines the biases they happen to have, to tell them what is right or wrong. In fact, it is just because there is no independent principle of evil that Aristotle's whole project is feasible.[57] There is no danger that in the course of one's deliberations one might stumble on the wrong principle by mistake.

There is in fact, as we saw in § 2.222335, a metaphysical explanation of the indeterminacy of vice: it is always some sort of failed actualization of the potentiality for virtue. I think Aristotle has this in mind, and has omitted to reconcile it with the principle laid down in III i, that humans in general are equally capable of forming virtuous and vicious habits (though individuals may be temperamentally predisposed in one direction or another). Because of this omission, he has not distinguished between people who mistakenly believe themselves to be good because they have not thought the matter through with enough care or energy or honesty, and people (like those envisaged in X ix) for whom the issue of vice and virtue has never even arisen (cf. § 2.22251, n. 52).

4.62 Goodwill and Unanimity (IX v–vi; 1166b30–1167b16)

Aristotle next delineates two concepts related to friendship, goodwill and unanimity.[58] Both are 'imperfect' in the sense that they do not require or issue in that active sharing of life that is true friendship. The former is no more than an attitude on which no action is based; the latter is indeed a coincidence of thought and consent issuing in common action, but in which (as in the Sartrean 'series' mentioned in § 4.4, n. 19) those associated are side by side rather than face to face. These relationships are like friendship in being based on character, not mere fancy, and are likely to obtain only among good people. What they lack, in their different ways, is direct mutual involvement, the decision to spend time with one another. They are based on conditions rather than on actions.

The relation of goodwill and unanimity to friendship is systematically but not functionally the same as the relation of understanding and judgment to good sense in Book VI. The latter pair are imperfect in that they do not affect behaviour by being related to the agent's idea of the good. Their inclusion furthers the analysis of good sense, which it follows, by highlighting the unique place of insight into situations as the epistemic foundation of action; and it is followed by the themes of the unity of virtue and the direct contribution of the intellectual virtues to the good life. Does the account of goodwill and unanimity play a similar part in the discussion of friendship? Hardly. If it does, it is because it leads directly into the chapter on beneficiaries and benefactors, which introduces the idea of self-love as the hinge on which friendship turns; and this in turn leads to an inquiry into the real values of friendship as an element in happiness.

The foregoing analogy between the strategies of Books VI and IX is somewhat loose, and I am not sure I have got it right. But, in any case, what these two conditions lack can be most clearly seen from considering the relationship between a benefactor and a beneficiary; and that brings us to what is really a new topic.

4.63 Friendship and Activity (IX vii–ix; 1167b17–1169b19)

The following chapters embody two alternative but overlapping sequences of thought. According to one, as we have just seen, the topic of quasi-friendly relationships leads (by way of benefaction) to that of self-love (IX viii), and that in turn to a string of inquiries into the contribution of friendship to happiness (IX ix–xi), the essential point being that friendship enhances reflective self-enjoyment (IX ix). But the key theme is the priority of activity in friendship (broached in VIII viii, resumed in IX vii); what IX viii does is to show how the primacy of activity enables us to conceive of a self-love that is not only harmless but admirable, and IX ix further develops the notion of activity and expression thereby opened up. So we may also consider IX vii–ix as a treatment of the topic of 'friendship and activity,' with IX x–xi as merely incidental comments on ways in which friendship enters into the good life. My treatment follows this alternative emphasis.

4.631 Giving and Receiving (IX vii; 1167b17–1168a27)

One might think that beneficiaries would be well disposed to their benefactors (would love them, if not necessarily like them) more than the other way round, out of gratitude. But it is generally agreed

(*dokei*) that this is not the case. Why not? Because the recipient of
one's benefaction is a constant reminder of one's efficacy as well as
of one's goodness. Just as poets love their poems and parents their
children, because they are their own handiwork, extensions of themselves, testimonies to their own existence, manifestations of their own
activity, and therefore they love their work because they love their
lives – in the same way, people love their beneficiaries because they
love existence.[59] Activity is better than passivity, and beneficiaries are
reminded of their weakness and dependence. Besides, to tell the
truth, the benefactor comes off better in the exchange. The beneficiary
has most likely received property or pleasure, but the benefactor has
the glory, *to kalon*; and while in anticipation we look forward to
pleasure more than we do to doing good, in retrospect it is what we
have done that gives the deepest satisfaction.

This observation confirms and explains what was already said of
friendships in general. It is in loving, and in the continuing commitment of oneself, that the value of friendship resides, and the love of
our friends is just another form of the love of ourselves. But our
friends, unlike our beneficiaries, represent not what we have done
but what we are.

4.632 Friendship as Self-Love (IX viii; 1168a28–1169b2)

Since we now see that altruistic behaviour is in one's own best interest, we are in a position finally to dispose of one half of the paradox
of friendship, how to reconcile with the preciousness of friendship
and the values of social life the postulates of an ethic derived from
a theory of action based on individual desire. Reconciliation is possible because such desire is not necessarily a desire for external goods
or for anything in which the agent's gain is another's loss. It is true
that 'selfish' and 'self-centred' people are condemned, but that name
is applied exclusively to people who define their interests in terms
of utility and amusement, and thus try to appropriate too great a
share of goods and services that may be in short supply, and with
respect to which their gain is likely to be at another's expense – an
expense that does not figure in their deliberations. No one objects to
people appropriating 'more than their fair share' of glory and virtuous activity, because these are not really shareable goods. The agent's
gain here is everyone else's gain too.[60] And that is the form 'selfishness' would take in the life of someone whose interests were defined

in terms of a happiness recognized as consisting of virtuous activity. Such people *ought* to be 'selfish,' if that means seeking to do what they judge best for themselves – though, since they act *tou kalou heneka*, in that the actions they propose appeal to their idealism, it will not be their own well-being that they have as the actual target of those actions. The 'self' such people love best will be the true self constituted by their thinking and planning activity. True self-love (*philautia*), we may say, involves the frame of mind introduced in IX iv, in which one's life becomes an *object* of concern, its qualities considered in abstraction from immediate involvements.[61] The condemnation of selfishness belongs to the context of 'justice,' in which all transactions between people are construed as trade-offs of quantifiable possessions. Friendship does not see things that way. Not all human relationships are transactions between strangers; and, even in those that are, more than commercial considerations are involved.[62] In friendship, the contrast between selfishness and altruism does not obtain.

4.633 Friendship and Autonomy (1169b3–1170a13)

The same line of argument readily disposes of the other half of the paradox of friendship, that happiness was defined as self-sufficient but a friendless life would be unlivable. Mostly the apparent paradox is dissolved by what was said about the relevant sense of 'self-sufficient' in Book I.[63] For the rest, we need say only that good people are not typically dependent on other people to bail them out or keep them going, but they do need people to be good to and, above all, to be good *with*. They must be active; but few activities, even among those characteristic of good people, can be carried on in isolation.[64]

What, after all, does a supremely happy person want out of life? Or rather, since to speak of 'wanting' like that may suggest that one can be supremely happy and still in want of something, how do happy people choose to spend their days? In the contemplation of good actions of their own! The answer is unprepared, and rather scandalous. Happiness was defined as performance; how did contemplation get in there? Part of the answer is that the word used is not *eudaimōn* but *makarios*, 'blessed' as the gods are blessed, and it is less scandalous to speak of such blissful beings as essentially contemplative – after all, as Aristotle will say at 1178b8–22, one can't really think of gods as *bustling about*, and it has become a commonplace (especially since Aristotle's introduction of the Unmoved Mover in

Metaphysics XII) to think of the divine activity both as the paradigm of blessedness and as contemplative. If we permit ourselves to apply this paradigm of blessedness to human life, we can see why happy people need friends. Since friends are like second selves, in contemplating their actions one is virtually contemplating one's own good actions; but it is obvious that one cannot really make oneself and one's actions an object of attention and observation as one can those of one's friends. So friends are not only occasions for self-love but means to self-knowledge.

That argument really won't do, though. We are godlike only insofar as we are contemplative, but our human actions (despite the conceptual revision that will be attempted in § 6.423) are not like that. Our awareness of ourselves as doing them will either be a nonthetic awareness (like our awareness, in seeing, of our activity in seeing as well as of what it is we see [*On the Soul* III 2]) or a thought process that will be separate from what it is we are aware of ourselves as doing – in which case we will have to do two things at once, and what we know will be less than the whole of what we are doing. On the other hand, we can be conscious of a friend's action without being self-conscious about it. Well, one sees the point of the argument; but it does seem a little slippery.

4.634 Activity and Consciousness (1170a13–b19)

The implications of the foregoing sequence of arguments about the relationship of friendship to self-love are summed up in a long, serpentine argument that seems to be meant for a formal demonstration of the value of friendship to a good person.[65] Aristotle calls it a 'physical' equivalent of the preceding argument – that is, one that brings out in the most directly relevant form the underlying structure of which the superficial manifestations have been phenomenologically described. (It shows and orders the middle terms by which the relationships are carried.)[66]

The basic premise of this argument is one that, in effect, justifies the reference to 'contemplation' which puzzled us just now: that human life is essentially a matter of perception and thought. The premise, being a premise, is not argued for, but the underlying view is not obscure. What is characteristic of animal life is self-motion, but the motion is merely a change in the position of the body, and not as such a part of the strictly vital process, to which it belongs only because the movement is occasioned by an integrative perception. Animal life can thus be defined by the power of perception; and to this, in the case of humanity, is conjoined the power of thought.[67] Thus a human life can be thought of as a continuous flow of consciousness: a live human is not one whose body may move, but one who is capable of thought and feeling, and this is true even although such consciousness may be possible only in conjunction with certain bodily movements. Feeling and perceiving are things we do, ways in which we are active, and the activeness of all our activities lies herein. Whatever we do forms a part of *our lives* only in the guise of a perception or a thinking.[68]

Aristotle uses a second pair of premises for which we have not been prepared, and which also lacks justification: that life is determinate for good people, and that what is determinate is good. (Conversely, life for bad people is indeterminate, and so is pain, so that painful and evil lives are undesirable because the indeterminate is bad.)[69] The general justification of the equation of the determinate with the good is treated as a Pythagorean commonplace (1106b29–30), and no doubt was too familiar from Plato (e.g., *Philebus* 24–6 and 64–5) to need discussion; but the determinacy of the good life was established by the uniqueness of the mean that defines it. Only the good life can have any shape and order to it.[70] But this is also, by the same token, the only life that really is a life, that achieves what a life is capable of. We can therefore say simply 'Life is good' without committing ourselves to saying that their lives are good to evildoers. It is to the good that what is really good is good.

From these premises we may derive the conclusion that perception and thought are good to good people, so that the reflexive perception and thought of these in themselves will be doubly good (remember that the *form* of a thought or a perception is the same as that in what is thought of or perceived, it is only the matter that is different); and, since a friend is a second self, so will one's awareness of them in one's friend be.[71] But the good life must contain all that is good (or it would not be *the* good life); therefore, a good person's life must include friendship. Q.E.D.

The oddness of these contentions will be taken up later. Meanwhile, I note that the argument seems more valuable for its new premises than for its old conclusions. This is not really surprising, because in any string of Aristotelian syllogisms the conclusion is what one starts with, and science proceeds by the discovery of 'middle terms,' and hence of new premises rather than new conclusions (cf. *Post. An.* II 2 etc.). All the same, the conclusion (something of which we were never in doubt) does seem inadequate to the portentous-looking premises. It looks as if the argument is introduced partly to introduce these premises and partly to give Aristotle an opportunity to rehearse his encomium on friendship. But actually the argument carries a bonus. Since it is in awareness of awareness and thought that the value of this extended self-consciousness lies, one must suppose that *perfect* friends will spend their time together primarily in activities in which this awareness is most thorough and direct – in the sharing of words and thoughts (1170b11–12). So the intellectual life, praised at the end of VI as stemming from the highest intellectual virtue, is also characteristic of the highest friendship.

4.6341 Notes on Sharing (IX x–xi; 1170b20–1171b28)

The next two chapters add little or nothing to the main line of argument, but consider problems that seem to arise from the central thesis that friendship enhances life through sharing of awareness. I say 'seem' to arise because they have really been disposed of in the initial accounts of what friendship is; but they are interesting enough in themselves.

If sharing awareness is good, one would suppose it would be good to have as many friends as possible, whereas in fact true friendships are confined to small groups.[72] But there is no contradiction here after all, because the size restriction merely arises from the practical impossibility of large groups having the requisite degree of affinity and being able to spend the appropriate amount of time together – crowds are temporary assemblages, and the scope of their common concern is limited to the game to be won or the windows to be smashed (IX x).

Again, one would think that friends would shun one another in grief, because the grief would be intensified by sharing; whereas everyone knows that fair-weather friends are no friends at all, and friends are a comfort in affliction. But the solution is simple. Rather than both sharing the grief of the afflicted, the unafflicted should comfort the suffering by their presence, and the afflicted for their part should not thrust their misery on their friends but wait for their friends to rally round (IX xi). Aristotle recognizes that friends comfort each other by their mere presence but does not consider whether this may not be so even when both are grieving.

4.635 The Shared Consciousness (IX xii; 1171b29–1172a15)

In X vi–viii, the praise of the intellectual life is followed by a recognition that unintellectual lives may be satisfactory. So here, after saying that partnership in intellectual pursuits constitutes the most penetrating sharing of consciousness, Aristotle recognizes that with unintellectual people what is shared is whatever is enjoyed. People go jogging or hunting or philosophizing together because that is what life means to them, and that is what they value life for (1172a2). Sharing life is sharing pleasures. Such sharing is not to be confused, evidently, with the friendship 'for the sake of pleasure' that was contrasted with friendship 'for the sake of virtue,' and said to be based typically on sex and wit ('fun to be with'); it belongs to that area that Aristotle fails to accommodate systematically, that of congeniality.

It would seem then (cf. 1170b10) that in friendship one somehow incorporates a friend's consciousness with one's own by sharing thoughts and actions, which insofar as they are actions of a person are modes of consciousness. Thus friendship is an enlargement of consciousness and hence an enhancement of life. But it seems to follow that friendship between bad people is an evil, however pleasant it may be, for as a partnership in evil it must reinforce them in their evil ways and involve mutual corruption, just as a friendship between good people is a mutual incentive to improvement.[73]

In all of this we see a striking analogy with the account of pleasure to be worked out in the next section of the *Ethics*. We have the same insistence on activity as consciousness, and the corollary that, as activities vary, so the friendships and pleasures bound up with them vary too: the worth of a pleasure or of a friendship depends on the value of the activity that is enjoyed or shared. In both cases the activities of the intellectual life are singled out for commendation; they are the most purely active because they involve the body and its movements least, and afford the fullest scope for sharing consciousness, and hence the most profound companionships. The oddity is that the treatment of friendship comes first. The conception of activity as consciousness is abstracted from the treatment of friendship as shared consciousness, instead of the identification of enjoyment with unhindered awareness leading to the idea that such enjoyment can be enhanced by sharing. But we have seen how this is to be explained: self-awareness is intelligible only on the analogy of the awareness of others, just as thinking is explained as internalized

speech. Self-awareness may come first ontologically or psychological-
ly, as I have been arguing, but in the order of explanation it comes
later.

Is Aristotle confusing (or am I confusing in his name) two quite
opposed notions? To share someone's activities is quite opposed to
being aware *of* that someone as a person, and to enjoy oneself is not
only different from but may be scarcely compatible with being self-
conscious and reflecting *on* one's activities. The answer to this suggestion is to be found in IX ix, and is based on the relation between
pleasure and intelligence worked out in the *Philebus*. It is argued in
that dialogue that to enjoy pleasure without intelligence would be to
lead the life of a whelk, and would be something that no human
would choose, the reason being that one would not know *that* one
was enjoying oneself. Human pleasures, it seems, are propositional:
humans rejoice in *the fact that* something has happened, or is happening, or will happen, and much of the *Philebus* is given over to the
consideration of these intellectualized enjoyments. An unconscious
pleasure is a subhuman pleasure. That is the point of the remark in
IX ix that animal life is defined by the capacity for perception, human
life by the capacity for perception *and thought*. To be human is to
think about what one is doing, to make one's activities objects of
conscious reflection at the same time as one is conscious *in* doing
them.

That is how human life can be unified, how we can build the idea
of 'the good for humans' into the idea of 'the best life for humans,'
happiness. We can speak of 'the good for fishes' (1141a23), because
fishes can be healthy and free from parasites and well fed, but we
cannot speak meaningfully of 'the good *life*' for fishes. Fishes can
only perceive and have pleasant perceptions that they cannot even
find pleasant. A fish's *telos* can never be its *skopos*, it can never be
happy (or unhappy either).

If we could not be conscious *of* our actions we could not attribute
any inherent value to them, much less relate them in an articulate
manner to the sum of values we find in all the actions of our lives.
To be aware of our thought, to think about what we are doing, are
not separate from the thinking and doing of which we are aware and
about which we think; they are simply the characteristic human ways
of doing and thinking (bearing in mind that nature holds no non-
human ways of thinking). The human way of enjoying an activity is
to say to oneself: I am enjoying this.

In saying that 'human pleasures are propositional' I may have gone

too far, though Aristotle does not help much. There is a clear difference between (for instance) consciously and intelligently enjoying an
activity one is engaged in, so that one relishes all the nuances of
one's activity and of the situation itself, and explaining and describing to oneself in a formulated internal discourse what one is doing
and what is so great about it.[74] Both Plato in the *Philebus* and
Aristotle here seem to think that the self-knowledge characteristic of
intelligent human action involves at least the possession of judgments
that could be put into words, otherwise one would not know what
one was at; but they do not suggest that one has actually to say to
oneself what it is one knows. Aristotle speaks of 'perceiving and
intuiting' (*aisthanesthai kai noein*) that one perceives and intuits
(1170a31–2); and *noein*, as we have seen, typically stands for the non-
discursive grasp of principles and situations which (we may now
add) must be propositional in the sense that it can function as a
premise in discourse.[75]

*What confronts us here is not a failure by Aristotle to say precisely what
he means (or even my failure to divine his meaning), but a grey area in
everyone's epistemology. How do we mark the gradations between an awareness of something, a conscious awareness of it, a self-conscious awareness
of one's consciousness of it, a dwelling on the quality of one's consciousness
of it, an articulate formulation of what one is conscious of in it, and so on?
And is it a matter of gradations, or of different kinds of awareness? I do not
know of any accepted or acceptable criteria by which accounts of such
matters are to be assessed: consequently, I do not know how Aristotle is to
be criticized or how his whole discussion of friendship is finally to be
assessed.*

One serious question remains about the general doctrine of friendship now developed. We have just remarked that it is not clear what
'perception and thought' are in this context. We must add that we do
not know what is meant by 'sharing.' Are we entitled to say more
than that friends recognize in each other something like themselves,
and respond empathetically to this likeness? The argument that
seemed designed to get beyond this was somewhat as follows: good
people's lives are pleasant to themselves; therefore the contemplation
of such a life is the contemplation of something pleasant, hence itself
pleasant; but good people are related to their friends as to themselves, therefore take pleasure in contemplating a friend's life. But
there are two false moves there. First, the respects in which good
people's relations to their friends are like their relations to themselves
are irrelevant to the point at issue; second, the awareness of one's

own activity is 'from the inside,' hence fundamentally different from the awareness of another's activity, however like that activity may be to one's own. Identity is not the limiting case of resemblance, as Aristotle seems to recognize when he bases family affection not on community of situation but on consanguinity. How then is the transition from likeness to identification to be effected? The direct answer is that sharing of experience rests upon likeness but is not it. After all, I am not *sharing* experience in the required sense, which involves living together, if what I am experiencing now is qualitatively identical with what someone else experienced at some different place and/or time (or even if it is identical with what someone else is experiencing here and now without me knowing about it). There are two ways of sharing experience, I suppose. One is the face-to-face exchange of talk and thought, the other is the side-by-side sharing of action and experience. In the former, we join in doing a single thing in which we take different but interdependent roles; in the latter, we do separate but parallel things in a single situation. In both of these our experience is that of taking part in a larger whole that involves us both. But our sharing is not such that my share diminishes your share, and it is not experienced as an infringement on our autonomy. Our sharing represents not a diminution but an expansion.[76] So your experience must be a sort of supplement to my own. And it can be such a supplement only because I can be aware of my own experience as itself a possible object of awareness (at the same time as it is that which I am aware of).

Does that resolve the problem? Perhaps not. People cannot literally share each other's experiences, if that means feeling each other's tickles and toothaches in just the same way that they feel their own. No doubt I can be aware of another person's feelings, but surely I can be aware of other people's feelings whether they are my friends or not. As Aristotle says in the opening chapter of his *Poetics*, the arts of representation depend on the controllable possibility of recognizing what other people are feeling and hence simulating such feelings in various media. And that has nothing to do with the special relation of friendship. What sort of sharing does he have in mind? Well, there are special relations of sympathy, such as those that are said to unite identical twins;[77] but nothing is said to suggest that they are what Aristotle is thinking of. Then there are the mutual understandings that develop in long-standing marriages and other close alliances, where much goes without saying. This is notoriously a source of great comfort, but again nothing Aristotle says alludes to this sort of thing.

Perhaps, though, there is something between the sharing of a feeling like an itch and the sharing of a thought or a feeling simply by recognizing what it is. When you say 'It's cold,' I share your thought even if I don't feel cold myself, because I understand what you say by, as it were, inwardly repeating and decoding the words 'It's cold,' so that I have the same thought even if I don't have it in the same way. But if I am just like you, when I hear what you say I not only have the same thought by way of entertaining and decoding it, I will think it in the same way you do (even if you thought of it first, or said it first). When we laugh at the same joke, the closer my life is to yours, the more I will find it funny in just the same way you do.[78]

4.7 Conclusion

Aristotle's account of friendship covers a great range of phenomena. He says many good things, much that is original, much that is profound. But still one may object to the whole approach. One questionable move is that whereby an individual's choice of an intimate friend is assimilated to the fellow-feeling that unites compatriots meeting by chance in a foreign land.[79] Richard Wollheim, for instance, thinks it wrong to equate a friend with a 'second self.' What friendship depends on is the capacity to perceive and the willingness to respect the differences between people: 'Friendship lies in a response to the singularity of persons.'[80] And surely that or something like that is true. If all friendships were based on likeness in virtue, not only would all pairs of friends be like one another, but every pair would be significantly like every other pair. Can Aristotle really have thought that that was the case?

No less directly opposed to Aristotle is W.H. Auden:

A vice in common can be the ground of a friendship but not a virtue in common. X and Y may be friends because they are both drunkards or womanizers but, if they are both sober and chaste, they are friends for some other reason.

The experiences which friends can share range from the grossest to the most subtle and refined, but nearly all of them belong to the category of the Amusing ...[81]

Dear old pals! Jolly old pals! Give me the friendship of dear old pals! But it is pointless to say that Auden does not mean by virtue what Aristotle means, and in fact has no clear conception of virtue at all, and that he simply assumes that friendship 'for the sake of pleasure' is the only kind there is. For a discussion of friendship, the emphasis on virtue that is appropriate to a treatise designed for people anxious to live the best possible life is out of place. Most people, as Aristotle himself insists, are not concerned with improving the quality of their lives, but live from moment to moment or from decision to decision within the framework of law and customary morality. Such people are concerned with justice, only because justice is concerned with them. But they are directly concerned with friendship, no less than idealists and saints are. Their concerns may come closer to Auden's notions that to Aristotle's. Aristotle would despise them, and no doubt he would have little respect for Auden. But, whatever may be the case in his general discussion of the human good, his contempt in the context of friendship has neither ground nor authority.

CHAPTER FIVE

The Worth of Pleasure
(X i–v; 1172a19–1176a29)

It is obvious that an account of pleasure is needed as complement to
the account of virtue. The equation of the good life with one of
virtuous activity is empty unless that life is also the most 'pleasant,'
in the sense that no other can be more deeply rewarding. And so it
should be. Virtue or excellence is defined, in relation to any undertaking or activity x, as doing x well. And to do x well is to do it as
people who are serious about x do it (or try to do it, or aspire to do
it). But that means that the standards for x are internal to x, whether
x be an art like crocheting or human life itself. But that means that
being virtuous in relation to x is the same as getting the most out of
x as x. And how can getting the most out of x not yield the most
satisfaction that can be got from x? Those who are virtuous in relation to x will surely enjoy it, relish it, appreciate it, to the full. How
could it be otherwise?

Human life is life governed by *logos*, the use of articulate thought
in the widest possible sense. What that sense is is revealed only in
the anatomies of which most of the *Ethics* is composed, supplemented
by the reflection that the more advanced functions of the soul effectively incorporate the less advanced functions. Human life is saturated by culture, by chosen and articulated ways of life, and culture
is articulated by language. Even non-discursive modes of awareness,
the 'perception and thought' that are the stuff of our conscious existence, take forms that already incorporate all the complexities of
culture – we see 'the son of Diares' and see him directly *as* the son
of Diares, although nothing in what meets our eyes shows his identity or paternity, or suggests that such things as kinship systems exist
(*On the Soul* 418a20ff.).

If all this is so, the characteristic pleasures of a human life will be
pleasures taken in the components and structures discerned in such

a life when taken seriously, reflective pleasures of sensation and thought. The pleasures of a virtuous life, as thus conceived, will be those of perception and thought at their best and in their deepest concern with the most rewarding objects. And what are those? Those that give the most scope to the deployment of the abilities in question, whatever that may turn out to be – neither here nor anywhere else is it the task of ethical analysis to give useful tips that will substitute for the wisdom of experience. But we can say that what gives the most scope will be what gives the most *human* scope, that which is most deeply and fully integrated into the life that seriously explores and exploits the possibilities of the *logon echon*. So, when Aristotle speaks of the 'best' objects, the word he chooses is the one that means 'most serious' (*spoudaiotata*, 1174b22).

The best life will be that which gives the deepest satisfaction to those who take life seriously. But *all* activities, when engaged in seriously and wholeheartedly, are pleasant, whatever form the 'taking seriously' may take and whatever the appropriate kind of pleasure may be. There may be many modes of zeal, many ways of taking things seriously, and a corresponding variety of kinds of pleasure, satisfaction, gratification, enjoyment – Aristotle's account does not take note of this aspect of the matter, but it requires it, and it should not be ignored.

Pleasure has been discussed three times already (I viii, II iii, VII xi–xiv), but it is the present discussion that complements in the required way what was said about virtue, and the account of activity in Book IX is the appropriate lead-in. If human life is defined as activity, and human activity turns out to be primarily perception and thought, and perception and thought in a virtuous life involve reflexivity, the quality of life as experienced will lie in the quality of reflexivity. As self-awareness is a cognitive charge on naïve experience and cannot have a value separate from that, so delight and enjoyment are an affective charge on the self-aware experience. Pleasure is neither to be separated from nor identified with the activity in which pleasure is taken. And, as we saw, the analysis of experience on which this account depends could be given only in the new context of friendship.

The new and definitive treatment of pleasure is a retraction of the one in Book VII, to which it never refers. That was a defence of pleasure against the attack implicit in the account of *akrasia* (most explicitly at 1150a9–13); the new treatment grounds itself (X i) on the whole of the *Ethics*, especially the foundational passage in II iii, and adds that philosophical discussion of the matter has been skewed by moralizing – a comment that could well have been directed against the Book VII version.

The introductions of the two accounts are subtly different. In Book VII, the professed stance was procedural: pleasure is within the purview of the political philosopher as 'architect of the end,' it is the very stuff of moral virtue, it enters into the idea of happiness. In Book X, we come down to earth: pleasure is part of our biological endowment to begin with, then it is an instrument of education, in maturity it is again the stuff of moral virtue. Then Book VII explains that controversy surrounds the issue whether all, some, or no pleasures is good; Book X avoids what will turn out to be a misleading reification of pleasure and simply says that the value of pleasure is controversial. The new stance is cooler, more distanced; it is not surprising that the melodramatic conclusion of Book VII is nowhere approached.

The layout of the new discussion purports to be as follows: in X i, we are told that the value of pleasure is in dispute, and that the dispute is vitiated by the tendency of participants to say what they think they should instead of trying to establish the phenomena. Then X ii–iii, according to a remark at the end, reviews what people say on the issue. But that is not quite what it does. Rather, Aristotle states certain claims, which he then immediately refutes: that pleasure is the sole good (intellectual maturity is good too), or that it it cannot be good because it is indeterminate or a mere process (neither is true in the required sense), or that some pleasures are bad (bad 'pleasures' are not real pleasures but only seem such to bad people). In X iv we are told the truth of the matter: the precise (and very tricky) ontological status of pleasure is established, and that resolves all the evaluational disputes and (X v) enables us to set up a valuational hierarchy of pleasures. It is this hierarchy that grounds the final discussion of happiness in X vi–viii.

What has happened is this. Because the account in Book VII began as a defence, it had to end positively, with the possibility that pleasure can be good or even the best of all things (counterpoised against the subversion of our 'second nature'). But the upshot will not do. If pleasures are simply unimpeded activities or realizations of the natural state, the concept of pleasure can contribute nothing to the explanation of their value: an account of pleasure will only be an account of activity from the subjective standpoint. Pleasure as such, then, if it can be dealt with at all, must be approached more tangentially. And this is, in effect, what the new account of pleasure does.

Book VII argued that pleasure was not movement but activity (an analysis elaborated in X iii–iv). But IX ix urged that all animal and human life *as lived*, as activation of the activation of an organism as such, is activity as experienced; if pleasure were good, all activity would be good. Pleasure can only be a sort of epiphenomenal resultant of activity, in which the value or disvalue must lie. It is hard to make concrete sense of this, but that does not matter; however elusive the nature of these familiar facts, the argument is ineluctable. Axiologically, though not ontologically, pleasure vanishes into thin air.

In X ii–iii, an antimony is elaborated and resolved. On the one hand, pleasure must be good – good as an end and not merely as a means. For one thing, if one gives pleasure or enjoyment as a reason for doing something, no further explanation is needed; one does not have to say why one wants to enjoy oneself. For another thing, absolutely everyone, wise or foolish, regards pleasure as a good, and it is merely silly to pretend that any argument can be stronger than this consensus.[1] On the other hand, the popular stereotype of moral decision (as in that fable of Hercules at the crossroads) is a choice between what one *should* do and what one feels like doing – between virtue and pleasure.

There is no contradiction here, only an ambiguity. That pleasure is good as an end in itself does not entail that there are no other such ends. In fact, there are. Again, the fact that one often chooses between duty and pleasure does nothing to show that pleasure is not good. The enjoyment of *any* activity, good or bad, enhances one's tendency to persist in that activity as opposed to others (that, one might say, though Aristotle does not, is what pleasure is for): when pleasure is bad, it may be because the enjoyed activities are depraved and should not be persisted in, but it may only be because persisting in the enjoyed activity is incompatible with doing something else that one's ideals or plans require.

The above resolution of the antinomy depends on a subtle ontology of pleasure expounded in X iv, developed out of the simpler contrast between process and activity sketched in Book VII. We saw that a specific action in which pleasure is taken, such as a game of tennis, may be a process with an articulate shape, a sequence and conclusion, but our pleasure in the game is just what it is from moment to moment, the degrees of pleasantness have no causal connections between them. Nor is pleasure ever the conclusion of a process: if the game ends in a victory or a healthy glow, the satisfaction we take in that is not itself an outcome caused by previous feelings of satisfaction or dissatisfaction, it is simply a relishing of the concluding situation as we now perceive it in the light of the way the game went. Pleasure does not even literally come into being, for 'coming into being' is itself a process. So pleasure, we said, is more like an activity, such as seeing (as opposed to scanning or perusing) or walking (as opposed to making a journey on foot). Though performing a visual examination of something involves a sequence and procedure, throughout the time I am performing it my visual apparatus is active, and at any moment it is completely active in just the way it is. If I take a walk to the post office, my journey has a history, but all the time I am walking it is just completely true that I am walking, that is the form my activity takes. And that is true of pleasure: my pleasure at any moment is simply the form my affective condition takes at that moment. So far, so good: it seemed to follow that pleasure is an *energeia*, a manifestation of the vitality of a vital entity. But that, it now turns out, was a mistake. Any activity whatever can be found pleasant; its pleasantness simply lies in its enjoyability, which follows on its freedom from a certain kind of inhibition and in turn enhances and reinforces it. To be an *energeia* on its own, pleasure would have to be something distinctive, the realization of a capacity in relation to a distinctive kind of object; and this it cannot be. In other words, pleasure isn't anything in itself, has no independent existence, cannot be either good or bad 'in itself' because the expression 'in itself' has no application to it. It is, as it were, the apparent good in the apparent good. As an encourager and enhancer, it is good if what is encouraged and enhanced is good, bad if bad. And what enables us to realize this, as I said above, is the Book IX equation of active life with sensation and thought, which enables us to distinguish the experience of playing tennis from the body movements that (as it were) subtend the experience.

If activity is reduced to terms of sensation and thought, and pleasure belongs to unimpeded activity, we have to ask what an impediment to activity could be. And it is obvious that it must be something wrong with the perceiver (the sense organ, or something analogous to that), or something wrong with its object, or a failure in the relation between the two. There is nothing else it could be. But where here is there room for pleasure? It cannot be any of these and it cannot be anything separate from these. It must stand to them in some altogether peculiar relation; and this is what Aristotle will say.

On this account, pleasure, whatever it is, is coextensive with life insofar as anything in life is going well. Aristotle can even climax his discussion by saying that the question of whether we live for pleasure or have pleasure for the sake of life is one we may set aside 'for the present' (1175a18–19). But, if this is so, there will be three kinds of pleasure, corresponding to three kinds of activity. The pleasures of virtuous activities will be good, those of vicious activities will be bad. But there are all sorts of activities, as Aristotle says, that people enjoy and equate with life itself, things they just enjoy doing that are in themselves neither virtuous nor vicious, like making music – or playing tennis. Pleasure in such activities is not vicious. In fact, it is just the kind of pleasure that everyone agrees to be good, a consensus that Aristotle allows to be authoritative. So what could be wrong with it? Only, as we saw, that in enhancing its proper activities it must inhibit all alternatives, and these might be activities that virtue required, that one's overall view of the good life embraced.[2] Such pleasure is then desirable, but only in one's spare time, as recreation. And to make recreation one's whole aim in life would be precisely to make the choice that Hercules rejected at the crossroads. So the very next topic we will have to take up, after the topic of pleasure, is the concept of recreation. And that is precisely what Aristotle does.

The whole discussion of pleasure, which I have now traced, seems to me curiously elusive. All the movements strike me as in a way compelling, but at the end I cannot see what, if anything, has been said. In the following sections I will look more closely at some of the more important aspects of the argument, and comment on its implications.

5.1 Pleasure as Supervenient (1174b31–3)

The statement in Book VII that pleasure was an unimpeded activity of the natural (that is, non-defective) state of the organism was already ambiguous. Did it mean that one's enjoyment of eating strawberries is the very same 'activity' as the conscious eating of them? Or is the enjoyment a separate activity, so that one is doing two things at once, enjoying and eating? Neither answer is satisfactory. Enjoying oneself is obviously not something to do, in the way that eating or swimming is; but if the activity that is the enjoyment of doing something is the same as the doing of that something one does not see what is added by giving the something an extra name. In any case, as we have seen, Book X withdraws the equation of pleasures with enjoyed activities. Being enjoyed can hardly be *the same as* being unimpeded, even if they go hand in hand: if I am doing just what I did before, only I enjoyed it then and am not enjoying it now, I may wonder what has gone wrong, and the 'going wrong' would doubtless be an impediment; but I can know that pleasure has failed and not know what the impediment is. Aristotle thinks the untenability of the equation is clearly shown by the new, more sharply focused notion of what an activity is. Activity in humans is equated with perception and thought, the condition of awareness at any instant. But 'it would be absurd to *identify* pleasure with thought or perception, but because it is not found separately some people think they are the same' (1175b33–5).[3] Pleasure must be either something one is aware of, or a special mode of awareness, not the awareness itself.

That pleasure cannot be equated with activity in any simple way is evident from the argument of Book I. The good life, the life of perfected activity, is such that no addition could improve it. But Plato showed in the *Philebus* (20–1) that pleasure could not constitute such a life, because pleasure would be improved by the addition of *noēsis*. It is no use saying that *noēsis* at its best is invariably pleasant, because it would still be valued even if it wasn't – no one would choose to be an ignorant child again, no matter how pleasant a childish life might be (1174a1ff.).

Our enjoyment of an activity is neither our awareness in it nor something different from that awareness that might conceivably exist without it (it is not conceivable that I might enjoy eating strawberries without actually eating strawberries and being aware that I am doing so). The only possibility left is that when conditions are right, pleasure 'completes' the activity, not by any causal contribution such as the relevant physical condition makes, but 'as a sort of supervenient end, like beauty to those in their prime.' But Aristotle does not elaborate, and the famous simile is hardly illuminating. It is not even clear what phenomenon Aristotle has in mind, let alone how he would interpret it.[4] The most likely point is that pleasure is no more and no less separable from its associated activity than beauty is from the physical features of the beautiful person. You can give the vital statistics, and you can be sure that anyone *exactly* like that would be equally beautiful;[5] but you could not tell just from the measurements that the measured person was beautiful, or why beauty was present when it was found to be so.[6] Similarly, if an activity is repeated with the same object and the agent in the same condition, pleasure will follow, but we cannot say why an activity answering any such description should be pleasant. However, if this is what is meant, the analogy is scarcely helpful. The relation between beautiful features and the resultant beauty might well defy any but an empirical account (just as relations between light-rays and perceived colours do), but the analogy with activities and the pleasure we take in them would hold only if we could specify the activity in physicalistic terms, and that is just what the distinction between *energeia* and *kinēsis* prohibits us from doing. If, then, we take pleasure as being the experience of an experience, how can we avoid treating it as a separate experience, hence a separate activity? But that is just what the analogy seemed to be devised to help us avoid doing.

Perhaps I am making an unnecessary fuss. All the analogy does is emphasize that pleasure is not a link in a causal chain, not even a terminal link, but an epiphenomenal resultant in the total experience. It is true that the analogy does not help us to explain what pleasure *is*. But, in a way, that is something we all know; in another way, we have seen that it isn't anything; in yet another way, Aristotle has told us a great deal about it. Perhaps our dissatisfaction stems from Aristotle's failure to give us any relevant categorization of *ta en tēi psuchēi ginomena*, 'things that go on in the mind' (1105b20), in which pleasure could be assigned a niche. But I am not inclined to blame him for that, because I have not the least idea of how to set about constructing one.

In the end, I think the objections to Aristotle's ontological account of pleasure reduce to two. First, in his own terms, he does not make it sufficiently plain on what the issue depends whether pleasure is or is not an *energeia*, and as opposed to what else – I said that the concept of *energeia* is basically simple, but basics are not always enough.[7] Second, in our terms as well as his, there is an over-easy assumption that 'pleasure' is a workable psychological category. Aristotle supposes that values and motives can be sorted without significant remainder into a few bundles, such as the 'pleasant,' the 'useful,' and 'beautiful' (see § 1.2324 and § 2.22222 note 28). But on what principle does this classification depend, and in what circumstances is it sufficient? Without the sort of anatomy that Aristotle provides for the equally sprawling category of *philia*, we really do not know. However, the same objection could be levelled against virtually all philosophers, from Plato to Mill at least, who have written on pleasure; and perhaps that means that it is not really an objection.[8]

Throughout X iv, a double connection is supposed. Activity, equated with 'perception and thought,' has, when perfected, pleasure as its invariable concomitant; but the perfection is itself supposed to be the concomitant of a relation between the appropriate agency and its appropriate object.[9] If pleasure fades, it is assumed that the activity must have become 'blunted,' and this either because the object has changed or because the agent has succumbed to fatigue.[10] The apparent suggestion that perfection in agent and object alike can be independently specified, and that any failure in pleasure can be determinately traced to one or the other, is surely mistaken and has aroused protests.[11] But the analysis, as we saw, can be read as purely formal: since pleasure cannot have any dynamic of its own, any failure in pleasure must be caused by some change in object or agent or in both. Nor could anything more concrete be demanded from a theoretical treatment. We cannot predict what the relevant perfections will amount to; as in virtue and the good life generally, only experience can be expected to show what is actually enjoyable. Some people get enormous pleasure from doing crossword puzzles. But what exactly makes a puzzle a really good puzzle, and what is it exactly in solving that solvers enjoy? It would be a long story, but there is nothing *mysterious* in it; solvers can tell you just what is right or wrong with particular setters and clues, and why.

5.2 The Evaluation of Pleasure (1175b24–76a29)

Evaluation of activities results in a twofold evaluation of pleasures. In the first place, since pleasure enhances enjoyed activities and inhibits others, we have to abandon the Book VII position that the pleasantness of an activity is always a point in its favour and substitute evaluation of pleasures according to the worth of the actions enjoyed (1175a28–36).[12] In the second place, the identification of activity with the perception and thought it embodies enables us to grade pleasures by the inherent worth (dignity, purity) of the mode of awareness involved. Among the senses whereby we are aware of form, sight is purer and therefore better than touch; among those whereby we are aware of quality, hearing and scent are better than taste. And thought is purer and better than any (1175b36–1176a3).[13] The underlying idea may be that the 'distance' senses are less bound up with the body and hence extract form from matter more neatly than the 'contact' senses; but that seems a bit silly, especially when we reflect that what is felt and savoured in stuffs and flavours is not 'matter' but form in relation to some further matter. It would make better sense to say that sight and hearing are our means of access to the kind of information most related to our plans and reflections, the kind of *logos*-related 'perception and thought' most characteristic of our human life – for it is the differences between the pleasures of different animal species that Aristotle considers next (1176a3–9).

Although I have tried to justify the schematic nature of Aristotle's treatment here, it leaves me uneasy for a reason to which I keep returning. The evaluation seems unrelated to the substance of what it evaluates, paying no attention to the actual ways in which enjoyments vary. Aristotle keeps remarking how people vary in their pastimes, and we may think he is going to talk about that here, because he does mention that the ways of life of different species are heterogeneous – but when he goes on to say that in the human species individual ways of life are heterogeneous too, he turns out to mean no more than that nasty people like nasty things just as sick people have distorted perceptions (1176a9–15).

Even Plato in *Republic* IX, to which the hierarchy of awarenesses may be traced, paid more actual attention to the diversity of enjoyments than Aristotle does here. But he might retort that he could not consistently have done otherwise. Pleasures have no existence of their own; a comparison of pleasures as pleasures could only be a comparison of activities, and to do that would be to do the whole of the *Ethics* over again. One can ask whether a particular person prefers music to fishing, but that is a question of individual preferences among pursuits and lifestyles. Only the two hierarchies he uses introduce comparisons that are both established independently of any supposed Bentham-like calculus of amounts of pleasure and also clearly relevant to the evaluation of pleasurable activities as such.

5.3 Pleasure and Happiness

Pleasure is not unimpeded activity but has no existence in separation from it. The evaluation of pleasure must therefore reflect the evaluation of activity, and we have seen how the direct evaluation of particular activities proceeds. But the *Ethics* as a whole shows how the human good is a life of activity, a happy life in which each activity plays its part. How does the immediately experienced good in activity, which is pleasure, relate to the overall good that is happiness?

5.31 Pleasures and Lifetimes

The relation of immediately experienced pleasure to the whole quality of a life as lived by a being with a sense of time is glanced at in the observation that 'one cannot be pleased with the pleasure of the musician without being a musician, nor with that of the just without being just' (1173b29). But it is not clear what Aristotle means by this. He could be making the merely grammatical point that one cannot enjoy skating without skating, or the psychological point that pleasures supervene on activities in such a way that the distinctive pleasure of skating is inseparable from the actual activity of skating.[14] But (especially if one takes *mousikos* here to mean, as it often does, 'educated person' rather than 'musician') he is more likely to mean that one can have the pleasures of a particular kind of person only by being that kind of person. This would be consistent with his general position that a just action of a just person is what it is only when done in certain specified conditions, which make it a different kind of activity even if the outward and visible action is the same. Being a just person is more than behaving justly on a given occasion; being educated is a condition manifested over a lifetime. Even so, the point is not quite clear. Is it that the musician's pleasure involves bringing the active recollection of past musical experience to bear on the present occasion, or is it simply that only a musically educated person is capable of having the kind of experience that is now being enjoyed? But in either case the point is that pleasures cannot be regarded as isolated incidents. The experience of a moment is what it is as an integral part of a lifetime. Since activities are conceived in psychic terms as awareness, and not in social terms as pieces of significant behaviour, the activity one enjoys is the expression of the person one is. Thus pleasure and happiness, though fundamentally different concepts, come to be virtually equated when the quality of a good life is considered. In the characteristic activities that represent the kind of person one fundamentally is, one finds the meaning of life, 'what life is' for one, and it is in these that one takes pleasure.

5.32 Pleasure and Virtue

The convergence of the very diverse concepts of pleasure and happiness, which we have just noted, is illustrated by a passage in the *Politics* that seems to refer to the present discussion: 'if we were right in saying in the *Ethics* that the happy life was that lived in accordance with unimpeded virtue ...' (1295a35) – or, indeed, 'an unimpeded life lived in accordance with virtue'; the syntax is loose, but the point is not affected.[15] Since the word *unimpeded* occurs nowhere else in his writings, it looks as if Aristotle has misremembered what he said about pleasure and activity as a saying about happiness and virtue.[16] If so, the concepts must be very close in his own mind, which would make him more of a hedonist than he usually seems to be. But it is not so. Any unimpeded activity is indeed crowned by pleasure and may be called 'a pleasure'; but unimpeded *virtuous* activity is happiness. (The substitution of 'virtuous activity' for 'virtue' is nugatory, if you think about it.) For happiness is a lifelong affair, and virtue is a lifelong condition. We saw already in I viii that the 'impediments' to virtue that poverty, disease, and disaster afford preclude happiness. We now see that a continuously virtuous life free from such obstructions (and, no doubt, from the obstructions of *akrasia*) will be consistently delightful.

Any activity that is 'unimpeded' in the appropriate sense will be pleasant in the sense that the agent will certainly enjoy it.[17] That says no more than that there must always be some reason why one fails to enjoy what one is doing. But it does not follow that every *sort* of activity that anyone ever enjoys is properly termed 'pleasant' or 'a pleasure.' If that were so, the term *pleasure* would have no distinctive application, since *any* sort of activity may be enjoyed by someone. When applied generally, the adjective *pleasant* is applied to the kinds of things that 'normally' give pleasure. But what is the implied norm? In Books II and VII, we said that the norms most often used are familiarity and salience: 'pleasures' are activities of the sorts that most people realize they find pleasant or seek out as pleasant, specifically those accompanying fulfilments of bodily needs. In our own usage, I think, 'pleasures' are the sorts of things one does *for no other reason* than that one enjoys them, and more especially that are commercially and politically recognized as being such – what Aristotle calls 'amusements' (*paidia*, 1176b9): circuses, to go with one's daily bread. In both cases, the norm appealed to is obviousness to ordinary people, prominence in ordinary lives.

Aristotle rejects this norm. For people serious about life, serious people set the standard. What they think right is really right, what they think good is really good. It is not that their dictum establishes what is good: rather, they see clearly (because they have taken pains to see) what really is the case, both in the world and inwardly in the humanity that they fully and accurately exemplify. The activities they prefer are those characteristic of humans as human, not of humans as animals, or even of humans as chess players. Only the activities they enjoy deserve the name of 'pleasures,' because they are not the incidental but the normal sources of gratification.

The argument that only good people's pleasures deserve the name does not in itself imply that they enjoy what they do more than bad people enjoy their own pleasures. But that further implication is carried by the contention that only the just can enjoy the pleasures of justice, because that means that the moment's experience is reinforced by the experience of a lifetime. At 1153b9–19, Aristotle spelt it out: every *hexis* has its activities, some of those activities are unimpeded, no activity is perfect or complete when it is impeded, and happiness implies perfection (which is why happiness requires freedom from the 'impediments' of poverty and misfortune). Again, it was argued in IX iv that bad people must be distressed when they survey the quality of their lifetimes. The pleasures of such people must accordingly be such that past and future are blotted out in them (as in the sexual act); and these must, despite their intensity, be impoverished experiences because of that lack of temporal resonance, so that 'perception and thought' have but a narrow scope in them. Without this further consideration, though, the contention that only good people's pleasures are worthy of the name seems empty. If it does not mean that good people enjoy the pleasures of virtue more than anyone else enjoys anything else, it is no more than a futile terminological recommendation about how the word *pleasure* is to be used, or a moralistic recommendation that people ought to enjoy doing what good people do.

If we accept that bad people can never be really at ease with themselves, so that they can enjoy themselves only so long as they do not look beyond the present moment, we can see that their pleasures can never be wholehearted or go very deep, they can never really be enjoying themselves to the full. But what about those salient pleasures of hobbies and recreations? Like the arts, they involve neither vice nor virtue but are independent action systems of their own. So, though they are activities performed and enjoyed for their own sakes, and all value in the *Ethics* is ultimately grounded in the worth found in activity, they too will surely lack temporal resonance and suffer from a certain thinness, and Aristotle is inclined to discount them.

The way Aristotle talks about the pleasures of virtue, tracing them back to a handful of perfected hexeis, *suggests that because virtue can be specified in general terms a good life can be adequately described in terms of those generalities, as if it consisted entirely of 'being brave' and 'being just.' But, though the bias in his argument keeps pushing him in this direction, he never quite gives way. He knows that real virtuous actions are not performed in the abstract but in concrete situations, and that each action is a specific engagement with an actual state of affairs, and he does allow a place for pastimes. Saying that the pleasures of the virtuous are those of humans as humans, not humans as animals or even humans as chess players, is true but misleading. They enjoy the pleasures of human animals as human, of chess players as human: sensuality and play are not excluded but subsumed.*

What is more important is that Aristotle never considers the satisfactions and rewards of the economic activities in which then as now almost everyone spends most of their lives. 'In the sweat of thy brow shalt thou eat bread' was spoken as a curse. But though most livelihoods are irksome and full of stress, and many are hellish, it is not the fact of their economic necessity that makes them so. Many useful jobs are full of satisfactions and it is not clear what, if anything, prevents all from being so (as utopian socialists have long urged). And it is certainly distinctive of human intelligence that it is exercised in work, in culturally developed and organized patterns of the production of goods and services. This side of life is excluded from Aristotle's account, mostly no doubt in careless snobbery, but basically because we are to assume the stance of people deciding how to live their lives. To be in a position to make such a decision, one would have to be at one's ease, delivered from the necessity of making a living. The whole economic sector is accordingly relegated to the necessary precondition of the good life. But that is a viewpoint no longer accessible to us. Integral to the modern view of the human condition is our recognition of ordinary lives and of the ordinary activities of which such lives consist. The transvaluation is part of the Judaeo-Christian world-view, and most familiar to us is the rhetoric devised by Protestant egalitarianism: 'Who sweeps a room as for Thy laws makes that and th' action fine.' But if the action is dignified it can be relished and deeply enjoyed.[18]

The pre-eminence assigned to the pleasures of the virtuous life can be defended on the ground that they have all three dimensions of the means/end relation differentiated in I i: they are prized for themselves, they contribute to further ends, they are integral parts of a good life for individuals and societies. And our awareness of these extra dimensions no doubt forms part of the activities themselves and thus affects the pleasure we take in them. Mere pastimes, we were saying, are like the arts in lacking temporal resonance: one or more of these dimensions is lacking, except to the limited extent that they are indeed integral to a life of virtue. But this defence of the pre-eminence of the pleasures of virtue is not conclusive. A devoted chess-player contributes to the ongoing life of the chess-playing world, and each game facilitates future victories. More importantly, Aristotle's own examples of multidimensionality were taken from the world of work: saddlers could take deep delight in the quality of their work, in its relation to the craft and mystery of saddlery, in the wider world of horse breeding and the contribution of a well-saddled cavalry to the defence of the city and so on. The fact that harness making is not a leisure-time activity no more deprives it of life values than the fact that generalship flourishes only in response to the horrors of warfare deprives courage of the status of virtue.

What is missing from Aristotle's account is any recognition of the public workplace, the economic city. His account of virtue and happiness focuses on the essence of humanity, the life of rational intercourse of which the only proper locus is the city as such. Vocational life is conceived as centred not on the city but on the private household, the oikos, an economic unit unconcerned with the human good as such, its values not subsumed in those of the city.

As economic life centres on the household, the life of entertainment centres on the individual, whose personal quirks and tastes again have nothing to do with essential humanity or with the city. Humans may have hobbies and jobs, but these do not affect their basic humanity and an analysis of the human good can discount them. One sees the point; but I think it is a bad mistake, an aspect of what I have called Aristotle's neglect of style (§ 2.2223342).

One can, of course, insist that a human being is human first and a chess fiend second, and chess is no more an essential part of the good life than a chess club is necessary to a good society; and even saddlers, though society needs their saddles, are fulfilling a role that is not necessary to a virtuous life. But why should not one maintain that since chess and music and many other pastimes are blameless and (to their devotees) delightful, the good life must include such activities as alternatives? Humanity is imperfectly realized unless the spectrum of such refinements is filled out. In a society each of whose members did nothing but what it was necessary for everyone to do, life would be thin. Aristotle's claim that a virtuous life needs no ornament but is delightful in itself would be specious, if that were what he meant. Similarly, as Plato realizes when he describes the 'bloated city' of his Republic, a rich and full life requires the availability of a wide choice of alternative trades and vocations. Socrates affects to regard such variety as sickness and the taste for it as childish, but on his own showing it is only in such a city that philosophy is to be found.

The clue to Aristotle's treatment of such vocational satisfactions is his apparent conviction (itself no doubt a product of the class bias in his society and the actual relations of production it reflected) that people cannot enjoy themselves while doing something useful. Accordingly (for the connection see Rhetoric 1370a12–14), working for a living is necessarily distasteful as *well as crippling to the character (see* Politics *1337a33–b21, and Plato's* Republic *590C). The assumption seems to be that because saddlers have to make saddles even when they feel like doing something else, they can never feel like making saddles.* Homo faber *is a concept that Aristotle lacks. But he might have reflected on the implications of his own recognition (1097b25–30) that carpenters have a characteristic practice and function, and that this furnishes the analogy for the characteristic function and practice of humanity at large. He might then have asked himself whether this might not bring people's vocational lives within the general scope of virtue, happiness, and pleasure as he develops them.*[19]

Suppose one concedes that a good society does need both a chess club and a musical organization (or their analogues in other cultures) to make these variants of the good life available to the citizens. Should one then take the further step, and say that if the variability of culture is too great to be accommodated in a single society, the happiness of the world depends on its containing a comprehensive variety of social and cultural orders, all mutually accessible, so that people of the greatest variety can find their own (equally virtuous) niches? I am sure Aristotle would have refused that step, even if it had occurred to him, for the reasons given in Plato's Crito: *people are what their societies make them, we cannot pick and choose among ways of life. But the reason most commonly given for the refusal, that human nature determines a single way of life as the only one appropriate to a given environment, is unjustified unless we define virtue as what is thus invariant. And this, we have seen, Aristotle does not do. The invariant 'function' of humanity is the deployment of the uses of reason, and nothing is said to suggest that an optimum deployment may not admit (or even demand) options.*

We have been encountering difficulties that arise because some of Aristotle's formulae suggest a narrowness of view that runs counter to the implicit breadth of his original project and commitments. Some of these difficulties may be put down to my own frivolity in supposing that a good life should remain at some deep level uncommitted, leaving open 'options' in which one has no real interest. Some may reflect a rather careless tendency on Aristotle's part to follow his own bias or Academic dogmas rather than the implications of his professed position. Some may be due to really contradictory tendencies in his thought. But some may arise from our unrealistic expectation that Aristotle should spell everything out, so that succinct statements are mistaken for his last word. Surely we should follow the general principles laid down and interpret specific remarks in the light of those principles. Of course, this may lead us astray, both in interpreting what Aristotle thought and in interpreting what his texts mean: one cannot tell what is a principle and what is a mere boutade. But at least we should try to give each of his statements a meaning that supports and is supported by what has gone before.

5.321 Pleasures and Lives

Moral virtue in conjunction with good sense is not the only virtue there is. Wisdom is a virtue too, and in the double evaluation of pleasant activities the premium placed on purity of apprehension prepares a unique place for the intellectual life, just as the emphasis on moral virtue prepares a privileged place for the pleasures connected with that. The 'unplaced' pleasures of activities that we simply enjoy as ways of passing the time remain anomalous, though they retain their place as objects of our zest for life; they are what we turn to next, and to accommodate them we will have to introduce a new value, leisure, which will change the whole perspective of our inquiry. These three kinds of praiseworthy and blameless pleasure, it is time we reminded ourselves, correspond to the three popular 'lives' briefly canvassed in I v, and which in effect provide the subject-matter for the rest of the *Ethics*.

CHAPTER SIX

The Good Life and the Best Life: Outline of a Discourse (X vi–viii; 1176a30–1179a32)

We are now prepared for the conclusion of the whole enquiry. The human good, the 'end of human affairs' (1176a31–2), was initially determined to be a lifetime in which the characteristic resources of humanity were most fully deployed, and this meant living the life in which activity followed all the aspects of *logos* as fully as possible, opting always for the 'highest' and 'most complete' alternative. In the last three books we have satisfied the demand that a good life be a pleasant one by contrasting human activities with mere body movements and identifying them with their conscious aspects, arguing that pleasure is simply a matter of satisfactory quality in reflective perception and thought. The consequence of that is that the sort of life commonly called 'virtuous' and equated with doing good deeds is reduced to a common measure with the other ways of life (that of amusement, and that of intellectual life) that had been singled out in I v as its plausible rivals: all three ways of life are active and (in that sense) involve *praxis*, all three are articulated in terms of perception and thought, all three as activities are completed by pleasure when 'unimpeded.' The three ways of life are fully comparable; it remains to ask which is the most satisfactory. But we should bear in mind that the initial selection of three lives rests at present only on an alleged consensus, and that the concept of a 'life' itself reintroduces a scale of thinking that we have not been using since I xii.

The present passage is introduced as a sketch of *eudaimonia*, as if this were a separate topic – the only remaining one. But we note that Aristotle does not treat it as such by following a version of his 'scholastic' pattern, nor does he introduce any new material. What we have is, in effect, what we should expect, a synthesis.

Aristotle's actual introduction is brusque – 'The things about the virtues and friendships and pleasures having been said, it remains to expatiate in outline about happiness ...'[1] The three topics mentioned do indeed cover everything from I xiii to IX, but is Aristotle merely saying that only one topic remains? The connection is closer than that. The last words of X v reintroduced the theme of I vii–x, the paradigmatic status of the good person's life: the true pleasures come from the best activities of the highest virtue; other pleasures are such only in a secondary sense and to a fractional extent. So now we turn from the parts to the hierarchical whole.

The last words of X v erected a hierarchy of pleasures on the basis of a hierarchy of activities with a double basis, the worth of the activity itself and the refinement of the thought or perception of which it essentially consists. Put together the criteria of sheer pleasantness, of refinement, and of worthiness, and what you have is the prima facie claims to pre-eminence of the lives of enjoyment, of intellectual activity, and of 'the rest of virtue,' respectively.[2] And, from a slightly different angle, we find that the life of 'the rest of virtue' is actually introduced in X viii as depending on friendship (as that was identified in VIII ix with the lives lived by humans together in their humanity; see also 1125a21–2), whereas it is the intellectual life that represents the acme of virtue – so that from this point of view the three lives correspond to the three topics that are here said to be what the *Ethics* has covered so far.

I remarked that the notion of a way of life or lifetime, which is tacitly reintroduced here on the basis of I v, has never really been examined. We took it for granted that a being with a sense of time and a limited life span has to make choices in terms of that one life to be lived, that people are judged happy or otherwise on the basis of their whole lives, and that actions are what they are because of the ways they fit into larger patterns that are ultimately those of the city and the individual's life span. But what sort of evaluation does this support? Speaking of a 'lifetime' suggests a biographical narrative, a CV or a *Who's Who* entry; or it may suggest that people's lives are something distinct from the people who live them, like works of art they construct. But that can't be right; Book VI contrasted the values of art with those of good sense, and activity as such is a matter of the state of mind as realized at each moment. What is characteristic of a lifetime cannot be its shape, then, it can only be the overall tendency of a person's concerns and preoccupations. This is suggested by Aristotle's language in the crucial passage 1178a6–10, where 'the life according to *nous*' is contrasted with 'the life according to the rest of virtue.' Still, we may wish he had devoted more attention to the matter.

6.1 Introduction (1176a30–b8)

In his recapitulation of what has already been established, Aristotle goes right back to what was said about *eudaimonia* before the subject of the *ergon* of human beings was brought up: that it must be a life of activity, and that it must be sought for its own sake and not as a means to some further end.[3] 'Virtuous activities' are now introduced as plainly fulfilling both requirements. As we have seen, these are the only activities in which agents have a clear grasp of what they are doing, and hence the only activities in which the 'perception and thought' of what they are doing can be wholly delightful. But Aristotle at this moment ignores the fact that this claim has been established, and proceeds as if it were still an open question whether some other life might not have an equally good claim to be one of happiness.

The reason for going right back to 1097b21 must be that the ensuing arguments about function and seriousness are suspect in some way. I take it that the trouble is that the connection between seriousness and what is conventionally recognized as 'noble and good deeds' (1176b8–9) is contingent, not to say factitious. To identify happiness with a life 'in accordance with virtue, and if there are more than one virtue, in accordance with the best and most complete' (1098a16–18) does not decide the issue in favour of the behaviour described in II–V. In fact, those books do not determine a specific way of life, but say how situations and challenges of all kinds are to be met. So the issue of *eudaimonia* has not really been faced; it is thought to have been so only by those who assume that the argument about seriousness and human function is a defence of conventional Greek norms. But why should it be? As the Sceptics would argue some centuries later, we do not need a philosophical *argument* to teach us what we learned at mother's knee.[4] So all Aristotle says here is that virtuous actions 'are thought to be' (*dokei*) of this kind; whether they are really so is a question we must now tackle head on, bearing in mind *everything* that has been said up to this point. All the concrete results of the *Ethics* have, in fact, been established phenomenologically rather than by argument, which has simply set up the relevant formal structure. Consequently, after recognizing the claims of *aretē*, we are free to offer 'pleasant play' as an alternative ideal which also 'is thought' (*dokei*) to be an end in itself. Part of the point here is that, at I v, the claim of 'pleasure' was not supported (as it now is) by apparent compliance with the criteria for happiness, which had yet to be formulated. So the question remains, in a way, open. To settle it, it looks as if we need only repeat what has been said already; but that, as we will see, is not quite the case.

6.2 Pastimes (1176b9–1177a11)

We have repeatedly noted Aristotle's emphasis on activities people engage in whenever they can, just because they want to, and of which we can even say that this is what life means to them. Such activities certainly seem to meet the basic requirements of the good life we have just laid down. They are activities chosen for their own sake – they are certainly not useful, for if anything one damages one's worldly prospects by indulging in them. It is noteworthy that Aristotle thus places them in the context of utility and not that of worthwhile activity; the virtuous *praxis* with which they are contrasted is in itself no more conducive to health and prosperity. In fact, his language is ambivalent throughout. Right at the start, at 1176b8–9, there is a verbal contrast between the 'serious' and the 'playful' – but 'serious' here is being used with the connotation of 'virtuous,' thus automatically suggesting that amusing oneself detracts from one's virtue. Again, at 1176b12–14, Aristotle repeats the slur from I v that it is 'the many' who envy such people, and 'tyrants' who like to have them around – though in expressing this apparent disparagement he uses precisely the three words by which the *virtue* of 'ready wit' was defined at 1108a23–4.

6.21 The Tastes of Tyrants (1176b12–24)

The pastimes in which people love to spend their days were originally exemplified by 'horses' and 'sightseeing' (*theama*, 1099a9–10), to which I have added chess and tennis. But Aristotle never really meets the challenge of such innocent enthusiasms, which their lovers take so seriously; instead, he cites (surely irrelevantly) the 'bodily pleasures' (1176b20) and, for the rest, uses the disparaging word *play* and alludes generally to the tastes of children. The idea is that the evidence in favour of 'the life given over to enjoyment' must be derived from the practices of people who are rich and powerful enough to do as they please without regard to public opinion or economic pressures, and what those people enjoy is mostly naughty or frivolous. The pastimes that we should be considering are accordingly not looked at but are found guilty by association, brushed aside with a gross combination of irrelevance and *petitio* by the remark that 'virtue and *nous*, from which serious activities originate, do not lie in the exercise of power' (1176b18–19): pastimes represent the life-choice of inferior people, *phauloi*, not of the good and serious-minded. If that were all there is to it, there would be no reason to bring the matter up: it is because virtuous activities are not the only prima facie candidate for a happy life that the issue of the status of pastimes was raised at all, so the mere fact that the latter are not virtuous activities is not conclusive evidence against them. It turns out, however, that what is characteristic of inferior people is not that they engage in pastimes but that they give up their lives to them; such activities have their place in the lives of the virtuous, which means that they have a value of their own, and this value turns out to be a new and important one.

6.22 Recreation (1176b24–1177a6)

A strong argument in favour of pleasure (or at least some pleasure) being good was that every animal and human acts as if it were. It is not really possible that what everyone thinks good should not be so, since good is definable only as the object of desire. But that confronts the downgrading of amusements with a serious objection: since everyone desires them, and they are not useful, everyone must desire them for their own sakes, and this is just the sort of thing everyone cannot be wrong about. It is really trifling to argue that the idle rich are evidence only for their own depraved tastes. Ordinary people watch TV because they like watching TV; watching TV has a value we have not yet come to terms with. And the value that Aristotle finds for these activities is apparently that of recreation, rest, time off (*anapausis*). We engage in these pleasant pastimes to recruit our energies for more serious pursuits, like a Scottish professor playing golf, because we get tired, no one can be continuously active in the same way for very long.[5] A life in which serious pursuits are undertaken for the sake of relaxation seems absurd; a life in which we 'unwind' occasionally so that we can return refreshed to our serious pursuits makes sense. Aristotle might add that recreations are commonly thought to be 'ends in themselves' because they have no *specific* function that depends on what is actually done: whether we play poker or go fishing makes no difference whatever, nor is there any specific kind of serious activity that any of these trivial pursuits facilitates – any recreational activity fits one for any serious undertaking.

I said that Aristotle *seems* to equate amusement with recreation considered as rest from one's labours; but it is not clear that he actually does so. Ross makes him say at 1176b34–5 that 'amusement is a sort of relaxation,' but what Aristotle says is that playing (*paidia*) is like resting (*anapausis*), and what one rests from is specifically labour (*ponein*): that is, he is using the relation of a rest-period to physical labour as an analogy of the relation between amusement and serious undertakings. What he says is, in fact, confused by this analogy, which he has in mind before he states it. He wants to say that only the virtuous are 'serious' (so that the alternative meaning of *spoudaioi*, 'respectable people,' is no real ambiguity), because people who are not serious about living are indeed *phauloi*, worthless and negligible. But he seems to forget temporarily that the 'serious' life is the happy life and has its own profound pleasures, because the reason he gives for thinking the identification of amusement with happiness absurd is that it would require one to 'take trouble and suffer hardship all one's life in order to amuse oneself '(1176b29–30). One supposes that he has not really forgotten it: what he means is that if there were no happiness in virtuous activity all of one's life except one's scanty leisure hours would be mere pointless effort and misery, and that would be absurd.

The effect of Aristotle's treatment of amusements is to assign them no value other than that of recuperation. This is to treat them as means, not as ends, not as parts of happiness. But they are not carried out *as* means to any further end. A busy person may justify taking time off from whatever that business may be on the ground that a change is as good as a rest, but when that time is taken the activities the time is spent on are simply enjoyed, cultivated with enthusiasm.[6]

Aristotle's treatment implies that in a good life as little time as possible will be spent on recreation: one can hardly wait to get back to 'serious' activities. One sees what is meant, and one can acknowledge the worth of the life pattern suggested – that of the scientist who cannot wait to get back to the laboratory, for instance. But what is there in Aristotle's account of the virtuous life to justify this? If the function of humanity is the life that exploits the full resources of the *logon echon*, and if the value of an activity is ultimately that of the quality of sensation and thought it involves, why should it not be part of that function to develop sophisticated cultural pursuits for their own sake? Why should science and politics take all our time? Aristotle seems simply to have fallen into the trap of identifying serious pursuits with those that are taken seriously by administrators – an alternative version of the error he warns us against, of equating power with wisdom and virtue.

If we allow enough weight to the stipulation that an account of the good life for humans must cover lives that everyone could live, lives that could be ordinary, the very triviality of recreations and amusements may recommend them to us. The requirement that the best actions be undertaken because they are fine or noble, *tou kalou heneka*, may nudge us too far in the direction of honour and glory, activities that are valued because they are exceptional. But exceptionalness is not an ideal that it makes sense for everyone to pursue, as we may see when we reflect on the absurdity of the young chieftains in the *Iliad*, each urged by his father to 'always be the best and be superior to the others,' *aien aristeuein kai hupeirochon emmenai allōn*.[7] Aristotle, as we have seen, seeks to neutralize the associations of the *kalon* by identifying what is truly glorious with what is just (a requirement with which all can comply), and reducing it to a motive, the subjectively perceived counterpart of the good. But these are tricky moves; and in the present passage Aristotle gets into a muddle. He has simply taken it for granted that virtuous activities add up to a demanding program that would take all everyone's time, a lifetime of strenuous toil, even if all economic needs were taken care of. But why should that be so? In fact, it is not so, if the virtuous activities in question are those within the domain of *phronēsis*, because, as we have already been told and are about to be told again with greater emphasis, that domain includes the provision of leisure for scientific and philosophic contemplation. Besides, as we shall see (§ 6.4231), the scope of *phronēsis* does not determine any particular program. And does Aristotle seriously think that *everyone* who has any leisure time should fill it with intellectual work, or that anything more than a minimum of leisure time should be assigned only to people with the capacity and taste for scholarly pursuits?

6.23 Slaves and Serious People (1177a6–11)

In the initial critique of the life of pleasure at I v, the bodily pleasures were stigmatized as suitable only to beasts. But what is said now is that even a slave can enjoy them – and everyone agrees that slaves cannot be happy. True, everyone does agree on that; but surely one's reason for doing so is not that slaves are an inferior kind of person but that they have to do as they are told and submit to whatever their bosses impose on them. Aristotle says elsewhere that, whereas the free members of a household live constructively organized lives, the slaves, when they are not carrying out orders, act 'at random' (*Metaphysics* XII, 1075a18–22) – they are not in control of their own lives, and therefore cannot engage in long-term projects, but must find the value of their lives in acts of which the value lies in themselves without any relation to larger unities.[8]

Bodily pleasures are not integrated in any positive way into the larger patterns of life. If this objection is to be extended to our ostensible topic, recreational pastimes, the latter must be supposed equally incapable of such integration. Now, in a sense, that is not true, as I argued in § 5.32. To the chess player who lives by and for chess, each game has its own value, its value as part of a 'life in chess,' and the contribution it makes to a career as chess player with its own triumphs and setbacks. The argument must be that such a career has no significance beyond itself. If one granted the significance of chess, one could grant the significance of every game of chess in all three dimensions. But how can one grant that? It remains a game; and games and pastimes are just what cannot be taken seriously. This is, in fact, Aristotle's objection: a life of amusements is not serious, and to 'take it seriously' would show that one was childish, did not know what life was about. Everyone agrees that serious matters are worth more than frivolous matters, and nothing can be worth more than happiness.

The difficulty with the position just outlined is that the criterion of seriousness is not examined. The serious life was identified with the exploration of the scope of *logos* and the attempt to apply it systematically to every aspect of life, and the moral virtues were arrived at by analysing the contexts and contents of practical life. But, granted that one should be serious in meeting all one's obligations, why should one not be equally serious about the things one freely chooses to do, especially since we now know that what matters in life is actually the quality of experience? Aristotle too easily assumes that serious matters are those with which bosses and bureaucrats are concerned, matters relating to the general well-being of people and societies. Activities that do not contribute to that really exist in self-contained enclaves, cannot be taken seriously because they do not specifically relate to the general good. The bureaucrat's error is to equate the goodness of life with the structurally good, to dismiss as 'frills' the activities that make up the lives for which bureaucracy makes provision.

6.24 Leisure

The 'new and important value' I mentioned at the end of § 6.21 is
that of leisure (scholē). The concept is introduced only retrospectively,
at 1177b5 where the life of moral virtue is contrasted with that of the
intellect as *lacking* it. 'We are busy that we may have leisure' (*aschol-
oumetha hina scholazōmen*), Aristotle says there – a judgment that
seems sharply at variance with Anacharsis's advice to 'play in order
to be serious' (*paizein hopōs spoudazēi*) at 1176b33.[9] The point is that
the actions characteristic of moral virtue are reactive, responding to
situations as they arise rather than expressing the agent's free choice,
whereas one engages in leisurely activities spontaneously. (We may
be reminded of the ship's captain in III i, who jettisons the cargo
because it seems the right thing to do in the emergency – but it is not
the sort of thing one would choose to do if things were going well.)
The concept of leisure is akin to that of freedom, but is not identical
with it: free people, unlike slaves, 'exist for themselves and not for
someone else' (*Metaphysics* I 2, 982b26); but slaves, whose lives are
not their own, may well have time of their own, and that is leisure
time. The fundamental value of leisure was implicit in the *Ethics* from
the start, because it is only people who are free from present commitments who can ask 'What shall I do now?' or even 'How shall
I live my life?'; but it is only now that this is brought to the reader's
attention.

The introduction of the concept of leisure makes retrospectively
plain what is not clear at the time of reading, the overall argument
in X vi. Every life has (needs) periods of free time, when we can do
what we like, engage in the practices and pastimes we love. The
trouble is that such 'playful' activity is contrasted both conceptually
and practically with the serious activities of 'work' (including the
human 'function'). So leisure and seriousness, *spoudē* and *scholē*,
exclude each other. But then it occurs to us that the 'highest' virtue,
that of the most rarefied and exalted states of awareness, is 'wisdom,'
the exercise of which is philosophy and science. But philosophy is,
above all, an activity of leisure, for two reasons. In the first place, as
Metaphysics I 1–2 shows, philosophy begins only when the division
of labour provides for a leisure class (originally a priesthood) with
time to engage in it; and in the second place, as *On the Mind* III 4–5
shows, the workings of the intellect have no functional relation with
the physical necessities of the body. The upshot is that we have three
possible lives: the life of pleasure is leisurely but not serious, the life

of moral virtue is serious but not leisurely, the life of the intellect has both values (and from this point of view represents perhaps the most complete [*teleios*] virtue as well as the most exalted).

The life of pleasant amusements, as we saw, is allowed only the value of relief and recuperation, in comparison with the virtuous activities that achieve pleasure through serious commitment. But when we come to look at the virtuous life we find that it has the defect that it *needs* recreation; and this brings to our attention the hitherto neglected value of leisure. But then we may reflect that this value is one that intellectual activity (*theōria*) *almost* has, for the reasons given. Not altogether, though, because even *theōria* is something we tire of, need a change and a rest from – recreational pastimes count as 'leisure' in relation to this 'serious' use of leisure. In fact, 'leisure' turns out to be an elusive notion, a relational term connoting always some unspecified freedom from some pressure or other. But this is never worked out; the concept of leisure is never subjected to the kind of critique that is directed against the concept of pleasure. It may be partly because of this that the place of recreational activities in a happy life is dealt with so inconsistently.

Aristotle cannot resist pointing out that leisure, common to contemplation and recreation, seems absent from the life of active virtue; but this has implications that perhaps he misses. We have seen that he allows no place at all to the satisfaction of a job well done, or for the simple enjoyment of the exercise of skills and strengths in necessary employment. And his best excuse for that neglect is that workers are not at leisure, their pleasures have no significance because their lives do not reflect the system of their choices. If they can get a kick out of marinating octopus for the taberna's customers, well, jolly good luck to them, but Aristotle's leisurely readers have larger issues in mind. If, however, the lack of leisure does not exclude the morally virtuous from *eudaimonia*, Aristotle has no sufficient reason for ignoring lives that derive their satisfaction from the serious exercise of the *logon echon* in a craft or trade. It would, of course, be absurd to expect anyone of Aristotle's background miraculously to adopt a position so characteristic of our own day. But the result is that the *Ethics* can have little direct practical interest for us. We may admire, we may be stimulated or inspired, but we are not inclined to follow.

6.3 Excursus: Leisure and Three Lives

We have seen (§ 5.32) that Aristotle's specification of 'three lives' of enjoy-

ment, theorizing, and practice is superimposed on a different threesome that he does not mention. He provides us with the material for a view of the good life in which vocational, avocational, and moral/political pursuits are integrated as three different subsystems, each with its own complex of values integrated in all three dimensions, and forming one system under the architectonic of good sense or political wisdom. But he does not provide the articulation of that system itself. He mentions economic necessities and leisuretime recreations only parenthetically in the intervals of his own conventionally virtue-oriented preoccupations. I have insisted that this procedure is inadequately defended: it is as if Aristotle had fallen victim once more to his prejudice in favour of whatever can be classified as 'intermediate' (§ 2.22232), serious autonomy being favourably placed between unwelcome necessities and licentious frivolities.

Some new light is shed on Aristotle's procedure here by the peculiar nature of his newly introduced ideal of scholē. It seems so obvious: civilization, culture, happiness, dignity – all rest on the possibility of so organizing our lives that we can have a breathing space, can stop and think about what we should be doing. That is, everything depends on the provision of leisure. But leisure can be provided in three ways. One way is to set up a leisured class of priests or parasites, whose necessities are provided by the surplus generated through the toil of others.[10] Another way is to organize toil in such a way that all or most people have spare time. A third way is to make economic activity itself leisurely enough that it is not oppressive, the rhythms of work themselves being spontaneously generated and modified.

Humans must eat in any case. Aristotle's reaction to this necessity is to relegate it to the worthless side of life that goes without saying, just as the processes of digestion and breathing escape conscious control. But another response is to integrate the necessity, the actual provision of edibles at the point of consumption, into the actual processes of social life. Like all other activities, the processes of care have three dimensions of value. They bring about desired results, they form part of the ongoing life of the society of intelligent animals, they have their own quality as activities of mind and body. In a well-integrated life there would be no clear distinction between what is work and what is not work: even at the most toilsome moments, the labour is not imposed but is part of the life that is one's own and the expression of oneself. Aristotle misses all this completely; it was the achievement of Stoic ethics to rediscover it and encapsulate it in the concept of the oikeion, that which belongs to one's own being as a rational animal. And this shift of perspective is reflected in a revision of the concept of a trade or technē, which the Stoics understood to be not a self-contained system of which the value is merely hypothetical but an organization of activity in the light of some end that is recognized as making a contribution to human life.[11]

According to On the Soul II 4 *and* Coming to Be and Passing Away, *the whole point of human existence is to perpetuate the specific form, to keep humanity going. The individual's individuality seems irrelevant to this, so the account of the human good should be perfectly general, its content indifferent to specific political constitutions and choices of occupation and lifestyle. But Aristotle agrees that people* are *individuals,* do *have jobs and hobbies and personalities – what life means to us is the particular activities that we take seriously. One cannot be human without being a specific kind of person. Surely, then, our generic account of the good must not only make general provision for the dimensions of diversity (cf. § 2.2223342), but must recognize the maximizing of diversity in individual development as an important aspect of the human function. This is what Aristotle fails to do. In this as in so many things he follows Plato's example in the* Republic, *where the ordinary lives of ordinary people are mentioned but not discussed because they are not called into question – the crafts are basically right as they are, and people will live well if they have a good society to live in. So Aristotle no doubt supposes that people are already adequately serious about their vocations and avocations; what they are not serious about is the overall picture, so that is what needs discussing (cf. § 1.233). If that is how Aristotle came to distort his picture of human life, it is a bad mistake, because in the* Ethics *all people are alike, responsible for their own lives; the task of integration is one that each must perform.*

Aristotle would not, I think, be greatly disturbed by the foregoing strictures, even if he were to accept them. He would simply say that the virtue of the phronimos *extends to these questions too, that changing situations open up new fields for the* logon echon. *Whether that would be an adequate response is another matter.*

6.4 Virtue (X vii–viii; 1177a12–1178b32)

Now that the life of pleasure has been disposed of, the way is clear for virtuous activities as the stuff of happiness. In principle, these are any activities for which we deserve to be praised as good people (as we do not for our recreations), but in fact we have imposed a three-fold limitation: that they be realizations of our function as human beings, that these realizations take the forms described in I xiii–VI, and that in cases of conflict a criterion of 'completeness' be applied. So the only question really open is whether theoretical truth or practical rightness is more important.

6.41 The Highest Virtue (X vii; 1177a12–1178a8)

We have seen that the unstated assumptions of the context provide
a way of answering the question of which Aristotle does not avail
himself. Serious pursuits are preferred to playful, leisure is preferred
to business. This leaves a conceptual space for the serious use of
leisure. Only science and philosophy (*theōria*) are acknowledged as
filling this space.[12] Why? Jacques Maritain pointed out that creative
and imaginative uses of the mind (specifically, the fine arts) have
been recognized and revered since the Renaissance as an important
and characteristic element in human life – certainly part of our
human function as Aristotle conceived it.[13] And what about the
celebrations of love and friendship? The importance and independent
value assigned to *philia* cry out for such recognition. But Aristotle
will have none of it. Why not?

Obviously, the main reason is historical: Aristotle speaks out of an
established tradition, and no social reality made such thoughts available to him. In particular, the closed universe he thought he lived in
did not encourage him to place any intellectual value above that of
discovering the truth about reality. But the key factor is surely that
the operations of the intellect are self-starting in a way that nothing
else is. All animal movement involves response to a real or imagined
stimulus that is envisaged as good; without such a stimulus there
will be no action. Perception depends on the presence of a percep-
tible object; imagination is, in some way, a residue from perception.
Only intellectual activity, though dependent on imagination for its
materials, is operationally self-starting. It is essential to thinking that
one should be able to think about anything at all, without the presence of any object. Thought must be autonomous, and in *On the Soul*
III 5 is ascribed to an aspect of *nous* that somehow makes all its own
objects and is itself somehow timeless and impersonal. The practical
attribute of leisureliness and the metaphysical attribute of timeless-
ness go together.

6.411 Power and Perfection: The Primacy of Mind (1177a12–18)

Aristotle does not make the connections we have just made. His way
of introducing the topic is direct. He simply cuts out the alternatives
by picking up a formula from I vii and interpreting in a way already
used by Plato as a defence of intellectual pursuits – a defence which
is one of the most striking and durable features of the view of life
which Aristotle shared with him. The happy life was initially iden-

tified as a life of *praxis* in accordance with 'virtue' (the values generated by serious attention to what one is doing) – and, if there are several virtues, the best and most complete (*teleiotatē*) (1098a16–18). The effectual identification of *praxis* with *energeia* and the interpretation of the latter as really a matter of states of awareness means that a life of thinking is, in its own way, a practical life. The requirement of 'completeness' was ambiguous: did it mean perfection (in itself, at that stage of the argument, an unintelligible notion), or did it mean comprehensiveness, as of one who saw life steadily and saw it whole?[14] The latter reading makes more sense, but in this reprise at 1177a12 Aristotle tacitly rejects it. He does not even use the word *teleia*. He simply says that it is reasonable that the virtue involved in happiness should be the 'best' (or 'strongest,' *kratistē*), and that this would be the virtue of the 'best' (*aristou*). The best what? The best part of the soul, apparently; it is probably *nous*, but in any case it is the ruling and leading element and that which, being most related to divine (timeless) reality, is itself as close as we can get to being divine. It is the activity of this according to its native (*oikeia*) excellence that will be the best life. And now the adjective 'complete' is reintroduced – but the noun it governs is 'happiness,' not 'virtue.'

The language used here is flatly incompatible with anything we have seen before in the *Ethics*. It is egregiously Platonic, suggesting the model of *Phaedo* and *Republic* I where a single soul has two functions of which one is not really *oikeion* – the use of that word in this connection is from *Republic* 610E–612A. And what precisely are the implications of the words *kratistos* and *aristos* here? Both can be translated as 'best,' but the former suggests supremacy and dominance whereas the latter connotes, rather, exaltation and venerability. Aristotle seems to be making no sense at all; it is not surprising that commentators treat this passage as a hangover from his youth, but it is the rhetorical vagueness and looseness rather than the immaturity that strike one most.[15]

From the point of view of the overall argument of the *Ethics*, this curious passage is not merely retrograde. Transferring the epithet *teleia* from virtue to happiness is an important move. Hitherto, happiness was an absolute; but now we learn that one happiness can be more complete than another, so that in the end it becomes a relative notion and the best life is the 'happiest' among happy lives.

Meanwhile, *teleia* is ambiguous as between completeness and qualitative perfection. If we prefer the latter meaning, we find that the life of the mind comes out on top of all three of the hierarchies of X v: it is most delightful in itself, concerned with the most important objects (divine and eternal truths), and exercising the most refined mode of cognition. But what is the most 'complete' happiness if that means 'inclusive'? We saw in I x that this can involve fullness of years – but that is not something we can control. But what of comprehensiveness of content? As we have pointed out before, this is not something a philosopher can decide for us; it is for our own good sense to choose, just as political power determines how time and resources are to be spent in the city – and this includes the provision and use of leisure for the life of the mind (1094b1). The relevant strategies must be worked out, on the basis of such evaluations as Aristotle is providing, in the actual situation (including temperament and talent) the individual is in. As we shall see, the injunction to maximize the life of the mind is indeterminate (§ 6.423).

The relevant *ergon* of humanity lies in the saturation of life with 'reason,' which as we saw entails the intensification, focusing, and integration of one's self-aware activities. This requirement is adequate to specify a happy life: it is enough that we find a way to be serious about this, and the outcome of such seriousness might be any of an enormous variety of possible ways of living, depending on one's circumstances and perhaps also on free choices. But this certainly does not specify the *best possible* life, either in relation to one's own circumstances or absolutely. Aristotle's argument has specified in the most general terms the normal and necessary deployment of the human faculties. Wondering what we must *do* leads to a conclusion determined by the necessities of action and interaction; once we start wondering what we should *believe* about the world we are launched on the journey that leads no less inevitably through mathematics and the physical sciences to metaphysics. There is more to life than that; but everything else is contingent, occasional, and in a way optional. Good sense will surely recognize that the relevant moral virtues will be exercized when there is occasion to do so; when there is no occasion to do so, one will be at leisure for contemplation; when contemplation becomes wearisome, we are ready for recreation. But what counts as leisure is for good sense to decide. It is their good sense, not their wisdom, that dictates whether on a specific occasion the studies of the wise must be postponed or interrupted for emergencies or even for meals.

6.4111 The Advantages of the Intellectual Life (1177a18–b26)

In coming to terms with Aristotle's pre-emptive move in favour of the intellectual life, it is helpful to recall *Metaphysics* I 1–2, the fundamental statement of his attitude to philosophy: the fundamental human orientation towards knowledge expands in scope as leisure grows, and it is the organization of civic and economic life rather than technical advances that provides this leisure. Philosophy, though not common in the world's rough history, is the natural fruition of a basic human interest. One may even wonder whether the requirement that happiness be 'widespread' (*polukoinon*, 1099b18) has to mean that many people actually achieve it, or only that it depends on something universally shared, so that anyone *might* have it. All the same, it is distasteful to read Aristotle's presentation of his own preferred pattern of life (and that of his audience, presumably) as if this were an ideal for everyone.[16]

The encomium on the intellectual life is meant to show that it has all five qualities shown to be necessary to happiness in Book I: activity of the best virtue (1098b17), stability (1100b11–17), pleasantness (1099a7–31), independence (1097b6–20), and being sought for its own sake alone (1097a16–b6).[17] Essentially it repeats Plato's evaluation of pleasures in Book IX of the *Republic*. Aside from the introduction of the concept of leisure, it holds little of new interest; but we may note how Aristotle shows himself conscious of having gone overboard in explaining how the philosopher needs no colleagues. Immediately he retracts – of course, it is better to have colleagues, he says, but one doesn't actually need them (1177a32–b1). We are free to reflect, if we will, on his lonely years on Lesbos, and on his supposed remark that 'the lonelier and more isolated I am, the fonder I become of stories' (fragment 668 Rose) – a person of solitary temperament, then, but not unaware that for Plato and his circle philosophy was a communal enterprise.

6.41111 Contemplation and Leisure (1177b5–15)

It is only at this point that Aristotle, as we have seen, introduces leisure as an important value, in pointed contrast with seriousness. That is, he introduces it after the affirmation of the values of the intellectual life has entrenched the hierarchy by refinement of cognition as opposed to the one that seems to look to utility. But this downgrading of what will be called 'the rest of virtue' does not eliminate it from consideration; it only points to the existence and general acceptance of an alternative valuation, one that corresponds to the primacy of the *nous* with which in our reflective moments we primarily identify ourselves. Nor can this alternative valuation be dismissed, as we are tempted to do, as a throwback to Aristotle's early days before he had thought of the material in Books II–V: it is expressly formulated as a correction of that.

6.412 The Substance of the Intellectual Life: The Discovery of Science

Many of today's commentators are puzzled or offended by Aristotle's praise of *theōria*, which I have rendered as 'the intellectual life' but is most often translated 'contemplation.' Perhaps they take Aristotle to be thinking of some discipline of religious meditation, a monastic *vita contemplativa*. But it is obvious that he is talking about scientific and philosophical inquiry of the sort to which he and Plato and their colleagues devoted themselves, and which formed the substance of his theoretical works – an activity which he regularly describes in the terms he uses here. Since the whole of our scientific civilization looks back to the movement they inaugurated, one can hardly fault him for judging it to be both profoundly important and immensely satisfying.

Aristotle's readers today are not conscious of themselves as participating in a revolution, a turning-point in the history of the world. Science is not vital truth, it is that boring stuff that is droned out in classrooms. But in Plato's day the successful application of mathematical models to astronomy made it seem possible, for the very first time, to know and establish the actual truth about the timeless structure of reality. We have no hope of understanding Aristotle unless we can recapture something of the overwhelming excitement that both he and Plato felt and rightly felt.[18]

Readers who take Aristotle to be making propaganda for the enjoyability of academic life as they know it are surprised by his statement at 1177a27 that those who know may be expected to have a better time of it than those who inquire. This seems unrealistic: the fun surely lies in the chase; when the discovery is made it loses interest. But to Aristotle the deep excitement comes with the realization that the hitherto unsuspected truth about the world can be known and that one actually knows it. Reports on such experiences sometimes come to us today, as when the discoverers of quantum mechanics suddenly find that a large number of previously disparate theorems in physics form part of a single intellectual structure. The point is not so much that contemplation is more fun than investigation: the word Aristotle uses, *eidosi*, does not denote the activity of contemplation but the condition of knowing – even in the work of inquiry, the significant value lies in the certainty that what is being unveiled and is progressively more and more in one's possession is the truth. It is not at all like the fun of doing a crossword puzzle, where there is no value in what is known.

It is bewildering and disheartening to find today's scholars writing that 'in Book 10 of the *Nicomachean Ethics* he seems to believe in a rather immoderate indulgence in contemplation of the immutable,' or that 'the way he links "the good man" with "the good for man" as far as the *theoretic* life is concerned ... does not have much contemporary relevance once we have denied the reality or feasibility of a life devoted wholly to unproductive contemplation.'[19] So much for those useless wastrels, Newton and Einstein! These scholars may be right to denounce the existence of scholarly pursuits and the universities that sustain them; but then, how do they justify their own existence? And how can they expect us to be ignorant of or indifferent to the importance that is actually ascribed to science and 'higher education' throughout the world today? The only explanation I can think of is that they have indeed allowed the word *contemplation* to suggest a sort of religious exercise, perhaps influenced by the use made of Aristotle by Catholic monasticism for which the paradigm of *theōria* would be the Beatific Vision of the Creator. But what has that to do with Aristotle, for whom the excitement and sense of understanding, as his logical writings show, comes from a sense of one's grasp of the connectedness of things, through the discovery of middle terms in demonstrations?[20]

6.4121 Intellectual Life as Human Function

I noted that the concept of 'function,' which Aristotle uses to give substance to the idea of happiness in I vii, does not figure in X vii–ix. All the same, there is an obvious sense in which *theōria* is the supreme activity of the *logon echon*, and as such is pre-eminently the human *ergon*: it is a central constituent in what humanity is for, answering to one of the two intellectual virtues. And at 1178a7 the life 'according to *nous*' is said to be what is most proper (*oikeion*) to our humanity; as such, it answers most closely to the criterion for human function.

When Aristotle thinks in terms of function, he does so primarily in terms of the internal functioning of a system, how it works. But functions can also be understood in terms of a system's relation to a wider system, to which it contributes: at 1097b25–33, function is exemplified not only by the practice of an expert artisan but also by the relation of an organ to its organism – just as, in his works on nature, the 'final cause' of an animal is defined by the fulfilment of its capacities as a member of its species, but on occasion is extended to a consideration of how it contributes to the ecology.

Jonathan Lear remarks that 'purely physical considerations of the interaction of mind and the world would suggest that contemplation is a higher form of activity than the non-contemplative *active* living of a human life. And so it should be; for man is by nature a systematic understander of the world. In the non-contemplative life, the innate desire to understand never gets fully satisfied.'[21] If we think of the world as Aristotle conceives it (see Appendix), we see that, though Aristotle never says so, the human mind in relation to the cosmos of which it forms a part has a second function, as knower of the world. Without the human mind to conceptualize and theorize, the world order is unknown; and that means that, as a world order, it does not exist. Fortunately, since the cosmos is everlasting, there always have been and always will be humans. Science and philosophy thus have a supreme importance.[22]

At the beginning of our discussion of X vii, I wrote as if Aristotle had noticed a possible niche to be filled by activities that were both serious and leisurely, and wondered what such activities might be. I then considered that in another time and place he might have allowed to creative imagination the place that he reserved for *theōria*. But that was quite misleading. He starts with a reasoned conviction of the overwhelming importance of scientific and philosophical activity in the world, and confronts the task of showing what the value of this tremendous innovation is in relation to the values already established for *eudaimonia*.

6.413 The Apotheosis of the Sage (1177b26–1178a8)

The intellectual life is called the life 'according to *nous*,' that in which insight is the dominant value.[23] This leaves open the question whether intellectual activity can be a full-time occupation – and we now learn that it cannot.[24] We humans can undertake it only insofar as there is something in us that is superhuman or 'divine' (*theion*).

Modern readers find that the association of the life of the mind with divinity sticks in their throats, either because God is so exalted that such association is blasphemous or because any reference to gods is redolent of primitive superstition. But there it is. The terms of the association are derived from *Theaetetus*, where philosophy is described as involving 'likeness to god,' and is a standard Platonic (and presumably Pythagorean) theme to which Aristotle often recurs: its most articulate statement is in *Metaphysics* I ii, where an approximation to divinity is the concluding stage in the process of refinement and strengthening of intellectual processes, reinforced by the famous postulation in *Metaphysics* XII vii of an intellect that is nothing but the awareness of its own activity. The argument is perhaps innocuous, suggesting not that gods exist and happen to be intellectuals, but that any sophisticated notion of divinity envisages a kind of existence that on reflection turns out to be nothing other than that which philosophers take as their norm. Since gods are conceived simply as embodiments of the ideals we ourselves take to be the highest, philosophy in fact answers to an ideal universally acknowledged to be supreme. But what exactly did Aristotle mean by 'divine,' and what did he expect his hearers and readers would think he meant? Not Blake's 'Old Nobodaddy,' obviously, and presumably not the Olympian deities as Plato's Euthyphro conceived them.

It is a commonplace that the Greek word *theion* can be applied to anything that lasts for ever, as the immortal gods do, and may carry no implication beyond that; but Aristotle, whether literally or metaphorically, speaks definitely of gods as living beings. What are we to make of this? *Generation of Animals* 732a2–10 offers a clue, where in a biological context the operation of form (not as such subject to change) is said to be more 'divine' than that of matter. The plain fact is that, so far as Aristotle can see, the operations of the intellect do not involve bodily movement; they take place within the operations of nature, but are not part of nature because nature is a system of movement. Purely intellectual operations are literally supernatural, though they are, of course, a perfectly ordinary constituent of the cosmos.

Aristotle's language is equivocal. *Nous* is that in us which is most divine and hence non-human – but is at the same time most *ourselves*. The paradox is conscious; but what does it mean? Does it mean, for instance, that we identify as 'ourselves' that with which we would wish to identify ourselves, hence our ideals, but consider as 'human' that which we empirically find in ourselves? Perhaps; but what are we, if not human? And what are humans, if we are not? One answer could be that a being with a sense of time is a being that envisages itself as becoming other than what it now is, and that necessarily distinguishes between what it discovers itself to have been and what it aspires to become. But the straightforward answer is that Aristotle means just what he says. We identify ourselves with the controlling aspect of us that thinks and plans (1166a16–23), but we are also the confused, passionate, and fleshly creature that experience also confronts us with. Whether gods exist or not, we think of them as like that reasoning and controlling aspect that is the part of us we identify with ourselves.

When we look at Aristotle's language we find that he does not usually say that philosophers at work are actually gods or godlike. We have to bear in mind that a life of *pure* intellection is something of which we have no knowledge. We cannot think otherwise than discursively, on a basis provided by imagination. Aristotle says at 1166a18–23, quite consistently with what he says here, that we would not want to be gods, because we would then no longer be ourselves.[25]

In the *Theaetetus* (176A–B), philosophers are enjoined to escape their mortal nature by 'assimilation to god, as far as possible' (*homoiōsis theōi kata to dunaton*). The corresponding phrase in Aristotle makes no mention of any deity to whom likeness might be achieved, but says we should '*eph' hoson endechetai athanatizein* – 'to the extent that is open to us, live an immortal life.'[26] The question is what exactly that last phrase means. *Athanatizein* with its *-izein* termination should mean 'to play the part of an immortal,' to do the sort of things immortals do or would do. Words in *-izein* can be freely coined, and generally refer to the continued practice of the activities of whatever noun the termination is attached to: *kitharizein* means 'to play the *kithara*,' be a guitarist; Thucydides (III 62) uses the word *attikizein* to mean 'to belong to the pro-Athenian party.'[27] On that analogy, *athanatizein* would mean no more than to declare oneself to be on the side of immortality; the more likely interpretation would be 'to do the sort of thing immortals do' or would do. In any case, the phrase has no ontological implications. What is contrasted with it at 1178b7 is *anthrōpeuesthai*, a word presumably invented by Aristotle to mean 'to act as human beings act.' It is worth noting, too, that the limiting phrase *eph' hoson endechetai* imposes a quantitative rather than a qualitative limitation; the implication is that one spends as much time as one can (without fatigue) on the 'timeless' pursuits of the intellect; all we really have here is an alternative description of a life in which one spends as much time as possible doing science and philosophy.

6.414 Aristotle's Elitism

Today's readers, even if they can adjust to the apparently theological language, still find Aristotle's elitism troublesome. What jars in the elevation of the intellect is partly, as I remarked in § 6.4111, that what the resources of philosophy are called in to exalt is the way of life chosen by Aristotle's own circle; one might have been more sympathetic if the favoured life had been a different one, from which Aristotle had for some reason felt himself debarred. It is useless to say that the argument of the last books of *EN* had led ineluctably to this conclusion; the objection is precisely that this denouement depends on a shifting of terms. Given the presentation, it is made to seem inevitable that the intellectual life should occupy the place it does. But, despite all the hints and warnings that Aristotle has planted along the way, it runs against the universalistic and inclusive tendency implicit in the original project.

Three things need to be remembered. First, it was indeed left open from the beginning what sort of unity the human good would have. Second, science in Aristotle's time was a recent discovery, overwhelming everything else with its revelation of a new possibility for humanity. Turning-points in our lives do push all other considerations into the background in just this way (cf. § 1.133 n. 37). And third, as we will soon see, the theorist cannot live by theory alone, and as a person with a body and a society is subject to the same constraints as everyone else.

All the same, we are left uneasy. The human good, as Aristotle insists, should be within the reach of practically everyone who cares to take the trouble; that is part of the reason why exceptional prosperity was deemed unnecessary. But, granted that most people do not and will not, in fact, take the necessary trouble, is it even thinkable that everyone should take up science or philosophy? Even if the economic problems were solved, is such a life within the capacity of most people? Does it not require special gifts and a special temperament? If so, are we saying that happiness is only for a minority? What is puzzling is that Aristotle says not a word about this – unlike Plato in the *Republic*, who says the appropriate qualifications are specialized and rare. Did Aristotle really think that philosophy was something anyone could do if they had a mind to do it? Or did he rather think that people on the whole do not resent differences in gifts, so that if (say) the best life on earth were that of an opera singer people without good voices would cheerfully accept that such a life was not for them? What disconcerts us is that Aristotle seems quite unaware that anything needs to be said on the matter, just as he seemed untroubled by the rarity of seriousness and its occasions (§ 1.233).

Aristotle is indeed to be faulted for not saying where he stands on this issue. But to blame him for elitism is absurd. He does not disparage people without intellectual interests, as he does people lacking the moral virtues. He simply gives reasons for saying that they will not be as happy as they might be. That is a factual claim. Either what he says is true or it is not: as he says, experience decides. He is not telling us how he would like things to be, only how he thinks they are.[28] We are not living in a world that must strike us immediately as the best of all possible worlds, but in the only actual world.

Aristotle's account of the intellectual life and its place in human life generally has given rise to a great deal of controversy. I do not propose to deal with that here. My exposition of the argument of *EN* as I see it will suffice to make my position clear on many issues, and the others cannot be relevant to my project. And in my view, many of the most hotly debated questions simply evaporate if one takes into account the whole argument as Aristotle develops it.[29]

6.42 The Rest of Virtue (X viii; 1178a9–1179a32)

After the apotheosis of the sage we return to practical life. The life 'according to mind' and the life 'according to the rest of virtue' sound as if they should belong to two different kinds of people; but careful reading shows that the two ways of spending time are thought of as belonging to the same person, who has to accommodate both.[30] They correspond to the 'two natures' warring within the same individual at the end of Book VII, but instead of a tragic ending the conclusion here is a reconciliation. There is no tragedy because, instead of being victims of an irreconcilable conflict, we simply exemplify in one way and another the fact that corporeal beings cannot be continuously active (1175a4, 1176b35, 1177a22). One might as well take relief from practical life with intellectual activity, relief from thinking with practical work, relief from seriousness generally with recreation, relief from waking with sleep. So our primary stance is still that of the individual asking 'What shall I do with the one life I have to live?' What is new is that our answer has to accommodate the discovery of the intellectual life as culmination of the human orientation to knowledge.

The line of argument in X vii–viii goes back and forth in a kind of dialectic. It runs like this. Happiness is, after all, activity 'according to virtue,' and it is reasonable that this should be the 'most powerful' virtue, that of the best in us. But the best in us must be what has most power and is most related to the highest reality – that is, the divine. But this must be what in us is itself divine or has most affinity with the divine. Complete happiness must be activity in accordance with the virtue that is most truly *ours* (*oikeian*), the true self we have just described. But this activity, being godlike, is too 'powerful' to be human (1177b26). However, because it is the best and controlling element in us, it would seem to *be* each of us after all. So the life of the mind is indeed the exercise of 'our' virtue, and is the happiest of all; but the life according to the rest of virtue is happy too, because it is the exercise of the corporeal and social beings that we also are. As scientists and philosophers, we will not be much dependent on external circumstances, but as humans living among humans we will choose to do virtuous things, and for this we will need external goods (as explained in Book I). The point finally is that we are not gods, but some of the things we can do are god*like*, and it is in these that our chief happiness lies; but insofar as we are human and not godlike there are other things that concern us, and these contribute to our human happiness as well.

The point is, I take it, that when we are at leisure we can do as we will, and it is when there is leisure that the intellectual life is discovered and pursued; but to be at leisure is not something we can choose at will. 'Only a god would have this privilege.'[31]

6.421 The Human Composite (1178a9–b3)

The account of intellectual life ends by calling it 'happiest'; this implies that other lives may be happy, but less so. I wrote as if this were a revision of the concept of *eudaimonia* as *the* human good, and hence unique; but is it? Different happy individuals live different lives, consisting of different activities, and it would be merely silly to contend that these must all be good and pleasant in the same way and to the same extent. But, if that is so, it can hardly be denied that some describable kinds of happy life will be better and pleasanter than others.

The next sentence contrasts this 'happiest' intellectual life not with a determinate alternative way of life but with happiness in general, life 'according to the rest of virtue' (or 'the alternative virtue' *tēn allēn aretēn*). There is a double contrast: the 'divine' is contrasted with the 'human' (*anthrōpika*), the soul/body 'compound' with the 'separated' (*kechōrismenē*) mind.[32] It is obvious that this does not distinguish the philosopher and scientist from other people, because philosophers and scientists have bodies and are human like everyone else. The 'lives' can only be patterns of activity.

Paying too much attention to the conventional chapter division here may mislead us into supposing that Aristotle is making a sharper distinction between two kinds of people than he really is. The sentences contrasting the two lives are a bridge passage in the middle of a unified account of happiness. The emphasis in X viii is never on a life devoid of intellectual pursuits; Aristotle keeps returning to the relation between the practical life and the life of mind. This is, of course, because the practical life has been discussed at great length already; all we need to say about it here is that it is 'secondarily' happy. The only point that needs to be made is the superiority of intellectual activity.

At 1178a5 the life 'according to the mind' was called the most connatural (*oikeion*) to humanity, with the mind being 'most of all the human being' and its life correspondingly 'happiest'; the life 'according to the rest of virtue' is happy 'secondarily,' its activities being merely 'human' in that they arise from the necessities of interpersonal intercourse and (apparently as an afterthought) the management of the body.[33]

The effect of associating ordinary life specifically with the soul/ body 'compound' is that the moral virtues are described (as they are in *Politics* VII) as essentially related to other people. This is understandable – Book V began by remarking that the term 'justice,' as a blanket term for moral behaviour, is equivalent to the whole of virtue in its relation to others. But it is not the way the moral virtues were introduced, defined, and discussed. How are we to explain the change in viewpoint? One could say that the substance of the present passage comes from an early, Platonic, phase in Aristotle's development, to which the *Politics* contrast obviously belongs, and which is signalled by the appearance of the *Republic*-sounding phrase *to prepon hekastōi* ('what is fitting to each') at 1178a13. But, in any case, the present context needs to emphasize the social and situational context of moral virtue because the main point is the way the practical life lacks 'leisure,' autonomy; in the main discussion of moral virtue this approach was out of place because what was then relevant was to show that virtuous activities are the basis of values discovered within individual experience. It was not necessary to make the obvious point (now emphasized) that valour is called for only in war; it was necessary to show that, in situations where valour and its opposites are called for, it is valour alone that makes satisfactory sense as a life policy.

6.4211 The Humanity of the Sage (1178b3–7)

Aristotle's language here is carefully nuanced. The *theōrōn*, the person actually engaged in *theōria*, will not need external goods *for this activity*, but as a human being living among others will choose to perform virtuous deeds, and will need such things *for human life* – the phrases are parallel.[34] The crucial point, we note, is not the need for human companionship (philosophy is actually a communal activity), but the need for material possessions – the emphasis is on materiality, as at 1178a1 when we are adjured not to discount the mind because it is small in bulk (*onkōi*).[35] In contrast with the emphasis throughout these last books on the status of activity as a matter of sensation and thought, the emphasis here is all on actually getting things done: people need money and power to do the things that will make the reality of their virtues evident to themselves and others. The counterpart of Aristotle's insistence on the abstractness and otherwordliness of scientific activity as such is his emphasis here on the concrete actuality of practice in real situations. If you put it that way, it becomes absurd to think of these two kinds of activity as belonging to different beings.

6.422 What the Gods Do (1178b7–28)

After dealing with the double nature of human life, it seems redundant to start talking about the gods again. Surely we said enough about them in the encomium on the intellectual life! But no; a second look shows that nothing was said there about 'the gods' as actual entities with a way of life, only about the 'divine' entity in human thinkers. Even in the present passage, there is nothing to suggest that gods exist; what is said is all about what 'we' think. We suppose the gods to be happy (1178b9), we ascribe certain actions to them (1178b10), and conclude what the activity of god 'would be' (1178b22). This is not about our knowledge of supernatural beings; it is about what we suppose to be appropriate to a being that we suppose to be 'blessed' (*makarios*) and supremely happy. The point is a conceptual one: we find it absurd to ascribe any sort of activity to such a being other than thinking.

The argument is hardly a cogent one. We start by saying that gods must be alive, hence 'active' in Aristotle's special sense; their activity cannot consist of practice or manufacture (which involve interpersonal transactions in a material world), and what is left if not thinking? To this argument, one objects that it supposes that the stated options are exhaustive, either of possible activities in general or of possible divine activities, whereas they actually state alternatives familiar from specifically human life. Then we say that the gods are supposed to be supremely happy. To that contention, the objection is that happiness was defined specifically as the *human* good, so that, strictly speaking, gods are not happy at all. Then we say that the human activity that comes closest to this will be the height of human happiness, to which the objection is that the unattainable happiness of a different kind of entity is an inappropriate ideal for humans whose nature is human. And the clincher is that animals are not thought to be happy, and the reason for this has to be that they have no share at all in *theōria*. But that is objectionable too, because what we said in Book I was that animals are not said to be happy because they do not formulate choices and plans, do not engage in practical reasoning.

And who, finally, are the 'we' who make these suppositions about the gods and their happiness, and who find it degrading to ascribe to the gods such human virtues as courage, justice, generosity, and temperance?[36] Not Homer and his readers, and surely not the population of any actual city. 'We' must be Plato and Aristotle and their circle, and the philosophical tradition that looks back to Parmenides and Xenophanes.[37] Aristotle is preaching to the converted.

6.423 *The Extent of* Theōria *(1178b25–32)*

What Aristotle was really doing in the passage we have looked at is redefining *theōria* in such a way that animals have none at all, the gods have nothing but, humans occupy various positions in between, and the more one has of it the happier one is: happiness is always a sort of *theōria*.

Assigning priority to the life of the mind meant that the whole argument of the *Ethics* must be reassessed. It was one thing to remark, almost parenthetically, that the intellectual life has its own value, for which political and private policies should allow a place of its own; it is quite another thing to make that life the paradigm of human happiness. To do that, Aristotle must provide an alternative interpretation of human existence in which the relative valuation of lives will make theoretical sense. And so he does. The interpretation of human action in which an 'activity' (as opposed to the body movements it is embedded in) is equated with the state of awareness – the perception and thought – that makes it part of a life consciously lived, and the incorporation of this interpretation into the theory of pleasure, does just that. Aristotle is now suggesting that this consciousness itself is really *theōria*, 'contemplation,' although this way of looking at it is not usually taken until we come to the organized ways of activity to which the terms 'contemplation' and 'intellectual life' are customarily applied. Mere seeing and hearing are not *theōria* in this extended sense; what is required is consciously seeing, seeing and knowing that one sees. Happiness extends as far as this kind of awareness extends and no further: animals have the full use of their senses, but they are not 'happy' because they are not reflectively conscious of the quality of their immediate experience.[38] Only a god could engage in a contemplation quite divorced from empirical experience and involvement, which would be perfect bliss; other lives partake of happiness insofar as they are 'likenesses' of this activity. So we have a single scale to which all happy lives can be referred. The best life one can choose and live for oneself will be the one that incorporates the best and most *theōria* that is within one's purview.

So happiness 'would be a kind of contemplation [*theōria tis*].' But what exactly does that mean? We are reminded of the reference to 'a kind of politics' in I ii: a sort of politics, a kind of politics, something like politics, metaphorically politics. So perhaps all that is being said here is that we can speak of 'happiness' only where we can identify some phenomenon that has *some* of the character distinctive of *theōria* in its full and literal sense, and the possible scope of the happiness available will be commensurate with the scope of the *theōria* in question.

6.4231 *The Political Life*

The virtuous activities described in I–V, with their three dimensions of value, amount to a happy and satisfactory life affording full scope to a serious person's diligence and enthusiasm. But they do not amount to a distinctive and determinate way of spending one's days. They enter just as fully into the life of a philosopher or a person of leisure (a chess player, for instance) as to a 'practical' person. To see that this is so, one has only to look at what Aristotle says and think about what he is actually talking about. What, then, is meant by a 'life according to the rest of virtue'? If it is more than a life that responds appropriately to the demands of situations as they arise, it must be a life that seeks out such occasions. This is not mentioned in X viii, where a person who emphasizes practical virtue does no more than make sure that its exercise is effective and conspicuous (*dēlos*). But we were repeatedly told before that it is more satisfactory to achieve happiness 'for the people and cities' – to go into politics as a leader in peace and war. That is why the 'virtuous life' was identified from the start as that of honour and glory: not so much because of the scale of achievement involved as because this represents a career, a shape chosen for one's life, independent of personal predicaments that may or may not arise. But what do such people do with their lives? They furnish the conditions of happiness, arrange the affairs of the community as such, contrive defence, facilitate economic affairs, provide for education, maintain a judicial system. So this is, in a special sense, a *life* according to 'the rest of virtue.' But Aristotle nowhere says so; on the contrary, he indicates in VI viii that career politicians are suspect, that their actions are felt to be somehow extraneous to happiness and good sense.

The success of the city makes room for leisure. In the world as we know it, politicians are kept busy as we stagger from crisis to crisis. But suppose they managed to achieve a secure, self-maintaining, well-regulated community? How would the politicians, the bureaucrats, the military, put in their time? In intellectual, recreational, and artistic pursuits, I suppose. What else? Hannah Arendt's idealization of a supposedly Greek ideal in which people spent all day standing around and doing politics for the sake of politics is at the same time realistic for things as they are and preposterous for things as they should be.[39] But then, things never will be as they should be.

6.4232 *The Hierarchy of Lives*

> For forms of government let fools contest;
> Whate'er is best administer'd is best.

Aristotle would not agree. In his *Politics* III one is struck by his gratuitous assumption that some one form of government must be the best. So here he assumes that some one kind of person must be best and happiest. But is this so? It may be possible to recognize a paragon in a particular respect, but can we imagine someone who would be a paragon in every respect? Aristotle recognizes that people follow different life patterns, but does he recognize even the possibility of different ideals? One suspects that the idea that value is relative to function would rule this out; but one feels that Aristotle simply has an unargued propensity for hierarchies.

Aristotle's whole discussion, even if we accept his discounting of vocations and avocations, provides material for a hierarchy of good lives that is more complex than the simple dichotomy between mind and the rest of virtue. There are not two good lives, but traces of at least seven to which he has given countenance. First, of course, is the intellectual life. Then, among the practical lives, comes that of the 'proud' individual, the natural ruler, supreme in all talents, virtues, and worldly circumstances.[40] Then perhaps there are people like Pericles, supremely able to theorize effectively about human life and put relevant policies into effect for nation and cities (1140b7–10). Then there is the life of intense and integrated experience, moral and other, but without the rare extreme of heredity and fortune that marks the *megalopsuchos*. Then there is the life of the person of prosaic but precise virtue, doing just the right thing for the right reason. Then come the people who fill the bill of the virtuous life because their errors lie within a tolerable range.[41] Below these come the people who, in default of sound judgment but full of goodwill, take the moral sense of their mentors for guide rather than their own. They too are virtuous in their limited ways: they live not only *kata logon*, 'in accordance with reason,' but *meta logou*, 'with reason,' though the reason they go by is borrowed (cf. 1095b3–13). Perhaps, though I am not convinced of this, we should include in our list any people there may be who have 'natural virtue,' whose disposition leads them always to do the right thing without thinking about it – I am unconvinced because it seems obviously absurd to suppose that there could be such people. And superimposed on these degrees is another differentiation: at each of the lower levels, it is more splendid to act in the public realm than in the private sphere (1094b7).[42] A life can be permeated with reason, and charged with value, to various degrees and in various fashions: a life so permeated will be, in its way and its degree, a happy one, and none the less happy because someone else enjoys a more intense or less clouded happiness. We were told at the beginning: humanity is not meant for bliss, and to do well enough is all we are entitled to expect and all anyone is entitled to expect from us.

6.5 Peroration (1178b33–1179a16 [X 9])

Just as in Book I, the identification of happiness with virtuous activity is followed by a double insistence on the dependence of such a life on external prosperity and on the limited scope of the prosperity required. Nothing is new here, but the language is different: the virtue in question is now intellectual virtue, and the point made is that the intellectual's nature is not 'self-sufficient for thinking' but, being human, requires maintenance and care for the body.

Famous names are now invoked to support the downplaying of wealth, and by implication the whole argument of the *Ethics*. Significantly, the names are those of Solon and of Pericles' friend Anaxagoras, both of them associated with the days of Athenian greatness; Aristotle wants to leave his audience smiling. And the appeal to authoritative opinion leads naturally to the signing-off admission that, after all, experience is the only true authority here.

People who want to save Aristotle's secular self from contamination with old-time religion would gladly end the *Ethics* with the words 'otherwise, it must be taken for mere talk.' But in fact the text has a pious conclusion: a person who acts 'according to *nous*' and cares for it (*therapeuōn*, the same word that was just used for the care of the body) will be not only in the optimum position but 'dear to the gods.'[43] Here at last the gods seem to appear in person: only a real deity, surely, can love and reward its devotees. But even here Aristotle is cagy. A conditional sentence intrudes: *if*, as is generally agreed (*dokei*), there is any care for human affairs on the part of gods (not *the* gods, we note), it would be reasonable for them to return the favour and care for the people who care for the mind – and plainly that applies mainly to the wise. So the wise are the most god-beloved, hence the happiest. Here as before we can, if we will, interpret 'god-beloved' as one more descriptive (and metaphorical) epithet applicable to the happy savant, with the stuff about divine affection and gratitude little more than a flourish. Plato's *Republic* too, we may recall, has as its final words a pious little piece about loving and being loved by the gods. I am sure the parallel is no accident.[44]

CHAPTER SEVEN

Postscript: The Transition to Politics (X ix; 1179a33–1181b23)

The last words of X viii, in which the wise person wins the favour of the gods, are plainly written as a peroration. The present chapter treats the issue as settled and effects a transition to a discourse on politics which (the last words tell us) is about to begin. The *Ethics* ends, as it were, with a colon: 'Let us begin by saying: ...' Whatever one thinks of the transitional sentences in the *Ethics* generally, this at least cannot be the contribution of an editor, but represents an author's insistence that urgent business awaits, the second half of our 'philosophy of human affairs' (1181b15).

What is announced is certainly a treatise on politics, but that is not how it is introduced. Once again the *Republic* provides the model: it is all very well to explain what happiness is, but our concern is practical, and we have yet to see how happiness is possible. The *Republic* passage is 471C–473E, where Socrates announces that 'philosophers must be kings.' Aristotle's solution is that philosophers should study the principles of legislation.

Here for the first time in the *Ethics* Aristotle shifts from the position of idealistic individual to that of responsible adviser. The move is not from individual ethics to public politics, but from the problems of leading a life to those of laying down principles for people generally.

With well-brought-up youths, there is no problem, they are anxious to be good and need only to be instructed and encouraged. But most people are not like that. They respond only to force, and have been brought up by people like themselves. What they need is coercion, but coercion in the interests of reason and without personal bias – in a word, law. Law does for adults what education does for children. It is best if each family is legislated for by its own head; but people with the requisite interest and concern should extend their efforts to the community at large (because, as we have just seen, family heads among the 'many' are not doing the job).

But who knows how to legislate? Not practical politicians, not public educators; in fact, nobody does. Aristotle must start from scratch, by compiling data on how cities are in fact organized and subjecting this material to a critique that will extract the relevant principles.

What makes it easy for people to acquire appropriate behaviour patterns is the fact that there are laws penalizing deviation. Aristotle writes as this were simply an expansion of the point that most people are not interested in the good life and have to be kept in order by legal control, but actually the point is significantly different. The ability to become good if one wants to, and perhaps even the project itself of leading a good life, largely depend on the sustaining framework of the laws. The laws apply to and benefit everyone, not only the selfish and thoughtless masses.

In laying out this transition passage, Aristotle makes heavy use of the problematic of Plato's *Meno*. Meno's opening conundrum about the three ways in which virtue might be acquired appears at 1179b20; and the argument that neither the purported professionals, the sophists, nor the practical experts, the practising politicians, provide the required education is a straightforward (and hence anachronistic) paraphrase of the end of the dialogue. But there is a significant departure from the *Meno* in one crucial regard. In the dialogue, it was argued that virtue could not be 'taught' by general classroom-like methods (*didachē* at 1179b19) because no one had the relevant knowledge of the underlying truths: politics as we know it is a matter of mere opinion, successful hunches and experience, which cannot be taught in this way. The implication was that someone like Plato with a knowledge of timeless truths and eternal realities might establish what virtue really is and thus be able to teach it; and the *Republic* passage has the same implication. Aristotle's parallel claim, insisting on the extraction of principles from historical data, replaces Plato's abstract theoretical 'recollection' with a kind of reasoning that remains practical, abstracted from our actual knowledge of affairs but not (as in Plato's formulations) pertaining to a separate domain.

Aristotle presents us with the world we know, in which most people are ignorant, stupid, malicious, selfish, greedy, irresponsible, and short-sighted, and will always remain so. They are not serious about making their telos into their skopos. The task of practical politics and social engineering is not to remedy this situation but to cope with it. The world order is fundamen-

tally unchanging. Few philosophers really reconcile themselves to the world, but Aristotle does, even though he uses judgmental language of the villains, slobs, jerks, and scoundrels who make up the majority.[1]

The idea that most people are not deeply and continuously reflective about the conditions of social existence and are kept in line by custom and by social pressures seems reasonable enough, and it does seem to follow that social guidance and reform will be the work of a reflective minority. Less acceptable is Aristotle's suggestion that most people would be selfishly hedonistic if left to themselves, and are prevented from being unacceptably so only by the intervention of legislators who impose laws with penalties. The self-sustaining pressures of customary morality and individual goodwill are left out of account. Classical Greek writers often write and think like this: everything rational and functional in human affairs is asserted or assumed to be deliberately introduced by some individual. Typical of this is the Athenian tendency to call the prevailing morality 'unwritten laws' and to ascribe the laws, written or unwritten, to 'Solon' or some such cult figure. One supposes this comes from the fact that the laws had only quite recently begun to be codified: one saw morality, as it were, condensing around one in the form of the work of identifiable legislators; it was an easy transition to think of the substance of what was condensed as also being the work of namable individuals. But the effect is disconcerting: the mass of humanity is identified with irrational desire, whereas rationality is localized in a few dominant lawgivers. As with Plato in the Republic, *it is not clear whether Aristotle has really thought out the implications of this way of talking.*

The elitism of Aristotle's concluding chapter is troublesome, as so often. But it leaves a mixed impression. From one point of view, an upper class, leisured and idealistic, is contrasted with industrious, 'banausic' people dominated by the love of luxury and the fear of pain.[2] *This contrast appears most strongly when it is said that the latter are* naturally *motivated by fear* as opposed to *shame (1179b11). From another point of view, though, it is not a class matter of all: anyone can make the effort to lead a good life, though few people actually do. Again, from one point of view the majority of people are denounced as pleasure-loving and base (1179b12); from another point of view, the point is rather that most people do not take long views but simply respond to the immediate situation with its opportunities and demands. Aristotle's arrogant and insensitive remark that most people are selfish and require coercion could be softened by saying that most people most of the time have to respond to immediately pressing situations; the function of the laws is to ensure that immediately pressing situations have compatibility with the general good among their most pressing elements.*

The thesis that everyone could lead a good life if they really wanted to may be rejected on the ground that it falsely supposes that it makes sense to try to improve the quality of one's life – that some ways of living are better than others. The Greek intellectuals mostly thought it did make sense, that they were building a civilization more enlightened than what surrounded them – the 'funeral speech' that Thucydides ascribes to Pericles is a good expression of this viewpoint. Some people nowadays find this offensive: how can one culture assert its superiority to another culture? But the alternative is that there is no such thing as reform, that nothing counts as an advance (as opposed to a change of fashion) in science or philosophy, that the concept of a 'good life' has no content beyond compliance with arbitrary norms. All ideals are empty ideals. Can one really accept that? Probably one can; possibly one should (in whatever sense of 'should' remains available). But, if one does, that means one of two things. Either humanity has no 'function' – but we have seen that Aristotle admits that possibility, with its corollary that it renders his project nugatory – or the human ergon is such that all human lives fulfil it equally well. If the function of humanity is to live in accordance with 'reason,' it may be that all human lives are linguistically mediated, and hence saturated with 'reason' in the only sense of that term that begs no questions. In principle, that seems quite possible. Does anyone really want to accept it?

Afterword

If Plato nicknamed Aristotle *Nous*, 'Mind,' it is less likely to have been a compliment to his intelligence than a playful reference to the key concept in his epistemology (see § 2.3124, n. 183). Aristotle thought Plato's theory of ideas was empty, introducing mere twitterings as the supposed objects of thought (*Posterior Analytics* I 22, 83a33). It is a plain fact about humans that they have the capacity (*nous*, 'insight') to discern the realities that make up the real world and its constituents, in their interrelatedness, on the basis of the evidence of the five senses that perceive everything that is there to be perceived (*On the Soul* III 1). The content of *nous*, the *noēton* ('intuitable') as such, is the realization of reality.

Reality, for Aristotle, is the realization of potentialities. What is fully real is fully realized, has all its potentialities fully developed. At the asymptote of realization, so to speak, would be a reality that is completely realized with nothing separable in it that could have been an unrealized potentiality. The relevant concept of realization is worked out in *Metaphysics* VIII; and in *Metaphysics* XII we learn that a realization without potentialities, a pure actuality, would be a mind (*nous*) thinking itself – and that the existence of such a mind is necessary to explain the cosmos, though it plays no actual part in the specific operations of that cosmos.

The word I have translated above as 'realization' and 'actuality' is *energeia*, a key term in the *Ethics* where it is most naturally rendered as 'activity.' We learn there that human life is a matter of activity, not merely potentiality (or 'virtue'), and that the inner reality of that activity is sensation and thought. It is easy to see that the reality of such a life is most fully expressed in pure thinking (*theōria*); and this is called the life of *nous*. The view of life endorsed in the *Ethics* is thus locked in to the epistemology that Aristotle spent much of his life elaborating.

It is because the best life, the most living life, is one of fully developed activity, and this must be the life most successfully saturated with perception and thought, that the key value term in the original exposition was zeal, seriousness, *spoudē* in its most general sense. The person who takes life seriously, with diligent energy and attention, who is not slack or idle and does not take life 'as it comes,' is the person who gets the most out of life and thus does what is required to fulfil the human *ergon*, to realize the potentialities of humanity.

The metaphysical and epistemological aspect of this complex of thought is not spelled out in the *Ethics*, but it is basic to what is going on. The intimate connection between *spoudē* and *energeia* is what gives the *Ethics* its point.

I have now done my best to show how far the *Nicomachean Ethics* can be read as a unified enquiry from beginning to end, in which every component is in the place that the development of the argument requires and has to be read in the light of that argument.

I have not tried to show that the text was written at one time, or was ever intended to be presented to any public in its present form. The former of these is unthinkable; the text is patently a scissors-and-paste job. But a person preparing a complex and novel text on a big topic is bound to proceed piecemeal, and different bits will inevitably present different emphases and different nuances of doctrine until the final polish is put on. Serious philosophers are changing their minds all the time; that is what philosophizing is.

I have not sought to show that the *Ethics* is consistent. Much depends, as we have seen, on the flexibility of the key terms, and it is not always clear when flexibility becomes equivocation. There are also deep ambivalences. A work on ethics that was free from such strains or that pretended to resolve them would be quite worthless. To pretend that our difficulties in life are not really difficulties at all would disqualify a writer from serious attention.

I have not sought to show that the *Ethics* offers sound guidance on how to live our lives today. It does not. Aristotle's basic conceptions have no purchase on an evolutionary world, a world without fixed species. Aristotle thinks of humanity as a stable reality that maintains its place in a fundamentally unchanging world. Homo sapiens as we know it is a passing phase, manifestly unable to sustain itself in its environment; the human propensity for discovery and invention and change seems unequipped with any feedback device, so that we are dubious dwellers in our world. We might be tempted to say that humanity as we know it is a disaster, except that we cannot justify any standpoint from which a disaster could be identified as such. Humanity as a self-changing phenomenon cannot meaningfully be assigned any 'function.'

Setting aside the ecological problems, Aristotle's economic suppositions, identifying the (basically agrarian) 'household' with its in-built hierarchy as the ubiquitous unit of supply and preservation, lack any privileged status in the flux of today's economic conditions, and the vision of society that goes with them is useless in a world of massive technology and electronic interchange. In short, the *Ethics* is an eminently interesting work, but interesting primarily as a daring theoretical construction and secondarily as a collection of seductive half-truths. Its power as a vision of rational living is unexcelled, and does not diminish. But it is only a vision.

The *Ethics* is based on a fallacy. Because we have to make decisions in our lives, and do so in the light of all our circumstances and prospects, we frame the ideal of an autonomous life in which such decisions are decisive; because we are beset by accidents and irksome constraints and demands, we frame the ideal of leisure, a life free from demands and interruptions. But the content of this double ideal is not a human life at all; it eliminates all the conditions of life of an intelligent animal in a world of scarcity. So in the end Aristotle leaves us with three false ideals: the ideal of a life of sheer fun (the falsity of which Aristotle recognizes), that of a purely political life of 'virtue' (equivocally endorsed), and that of a purely spiritual and intellectual life (extolled except for its being 'too high for a human being'). What is missing is any sense of how all these levels of freedom and culture are dynamically related to the life of the animals that we are. Aristotle recognizes the problem but he never confronts it. I think he succumbs to a simple fallacy. Because the problem of how to use our freedom arises only insofar as a solution of our economic problems sets us free, Aristotle slips into supposing that the economic problem can be solved and put behind us as individuals and as societies. But of course it cannot: whatever arrangements we make must be remade and revised continually, because we have to eat every day, all our lives.

Aristotle knows this and shows that he does; but he allows himself at crucial places to write as if he did not. Perhaps we should say: human beings cannot always choose, but, when and insofar as they can, what Aristotle says is what has to be borne in mind. I suspect that all moralities have to be seen that way, not as directions for life but as guides to the uses of freedom.

All this, though, is beside the point. Who am I to say why and how you should read the *Ethics*, or how in general moralists should be read? My task has been to show how, on my view, the text as we have it functions best. I have completed that task. On important issues of practical wisdom I have no reason to suppose my judgment is any better than anyone else's.

Appendix: Aristotle's World

Aristotle's picture of the world is different from those of his medieval and modern interpreters. Predominantly, later commentators have believed in a created world, the deliberate and planned product of an all-powerful being. To do right has been to do this being's will, to know the world is to know its plan. It is thus appropriate to speak of 'moral laws' and 'laws of nature,' and this affects the way we think even when we consciously repudiate the model. In this created world there is a beginning and an end of history, a scenario (typically including fall, salvation, and judgment) of which we may have some inkling.

In the post-Christian era, everything in this broad picture changes. Earth has a history of which the future is obscure but has no preemptive moral significance; human and other animals are changing products of natural selection. The past is no guide to the present because conditions keep changing. Changes in technology and in the gene pool mean that we have to keep finding new answers to the question of how we should live our lives, though any 'decisions' we reached would represent the outcome of the real pressures, themselves incalculable and uncontrollable, generated by the situation as it is and as we see it. In such a world, to identify a persistent value is to discredit it, because its persistence shows that it reflects an obsolete phase of physical and social reality.

Aristotle's world is neither the product of a divine plan nor the field of unpredictable and open-ended change. It differs from both in ways that may deeply affect our view of his project in the *Ethics*. The following is a list of some important features of his world-view – some of them the common property of his place and time, some of them conclusions he came to on his own.[1]

1 / The physical universe is of limited size; the central earth and the surrounding heavens are unique. But it is everlasting. Consequently, the world is not open-ended, but constitutes a self-maintaining system in which, in the short or long run, situations return cyclically. Humans can recognize these recurrences, identifying animal species, seasonal changes, planetary orbits, and so on. Science is thus possible; it consists of the identification and explanation of these constancies and regularities.

2 / The heavens maintain themselves in a steady state, the heavenly bodies revolving in constant orbits. The species of living things cannot maintain themselves in such a state: individuals age and die. But species themselves are everlasting parts of the world, because species on the whole breed true. Immortality is the traditional perquisite of the gods, and through continued reproduction living things participate in divinity, towards which they are oriented (*On the Soul* II 4, 415a26–b3). The eternal maintenance of the actual species, as of the overall system, is divine, and has no other basis or purpose than its own actuality.[2] The world has no secrets.

3 / What an animal actually *is* is its life, the full manifestation of the way of life characteristic of its species – the full manifestation being that of the unmaimed and healthy adult. The value and reality of living things lie in activity, the active manifestation of vital capacities.

4 / Change as such has reality only as achieving and maintaining realities, the actual manifestation of states of perfection ('a change' can be isolated and identified only by a definite initial condition and a definite terminal state).

5 / The individual as such has no value, and has only incidental reality. Different specimens of a plant, for instance, will all vary, but these variations are of no consequence to the scientist. But the reality of the species is maintained solely as the general nature that is manifested not otherwise than *in* these individuals. The features of the individual that make it a more or less perfect specimen of its species are what matters, what is real.[3]

6 / This being so, it is not necessary that all seeds should germinate, that all offspring should reach maturity, that all adults should be good specimens. All that is necessary is that the species should be maintained.

7 / The future has not happened yet, the past has. What's over is

over, so all life must be future-oriented: what chiefly governs events is the 'final cause,' the drive towards the future manifestation of mature perfection and activity. But this future manifestation is operative only because it manifests what has already been achieved, and all the formative forces for its reproduction are already effectively in place. Future novelty has no operative place in Aristotle's 'teleology'.

8 / An animal's life is its *way* of life, and this depends on its perceptions, its appetitive awareness of its environment (and of its internal states, though Aristotle is vague about this). Life in humans is a matter not only of perception but of thought as well; thought involves not just recognizing, but conceptualizing, theorizing, inquiring, and the like.

9 / The only animals in which thought occurs are human animals. If scientific thought is to be knowledge of the world as it is, human thought must be able to think truly about anything whatever, so that its epistemic character cannot reflect the distinctive properties of any physical substance. Thought occurs only as a neutral power to abstract from individuals the properties they manifest, and to remember them. Abstraction and memory require a perceptual apparatus, but are not themselves the work of that apparatus.

10 / The world contains as one of its permanent parts a kind of animal – humankind – that knows the world. Without humanity, the world system (what science discovers) would not be known at all. In fact, the world would not exist as a system at all; there would be no way in which its essential and constituent features would be separated from accidental phenomena.

11 / A pattern of duality pervades Aristotle's major systematic works. Typically, we are presented with a self-contained system based on physical reality, but hints are dropped that the system is not all there is, and it eventually appears that 'mind' has to be introduced as a sort of reality extraneous to the workings of the system but necessary to it. The *Physics* presents a self-contained system of the natural world, but in Book VIII we learn that the system itself is inexplicable without postulating a non-physical 'unmoved mover,' and a similar move is made in *Metaphysics* XII, where we learn that the self-sustaining movement of the heavens (and hence of everything else) is inexplicable unless it depends on orientation towards a self-thinking

mind. In *Generation of Animals*, the physiology of reproduction needs, in the case of humans, to be supplemented by the appearance of mind in the human child 'from outdoors,' in a way inexplicably associated with male insemination but not biologically connected with it. In *On the Soul* the soul is shown to be the 'actualization of the organized body' – except for mind, which cannot be functionally related to any body part. In the *Ethics*, science, the activity of an animal-borne mind in knowing the world, is celebrated as the highest happiness. The invocation of mind as a necessary factor in any field of reality is a striking and constant feature of Aristotle's thought.[4]

12 / Since mind is not the operation of a physical system that can be investigated, there is not much that can be said about it – one is reminded of the way in which 'the good' is said to be 'beyond reality' in Plato's *Republic*: obviously, what is beyond reality is not real and cannot be directly discussed. A mind without animal embodiment is identified or associated with 'God' (*Metaphysics* XII 7, 1072b25ff.); an embodied mind is the most 'godlike' of things. In all spheres, pure mind has to be postulated to account for physical and epistemic systems, but adds nothing to the actual working of those systems; it has no structural implications.

13 / Only mind realizes eternal reality; only embodied mind working on the data of perception can abstract concepts and do science (by discovering 'middle terms') and hence *explain* the world.

14 / Just as not all tadpoles grow up to be mummy and daddy frogs, but some do, and that is enough, not all humans become scientists, or even become good manifestations of forethoughtful and responsible life – but some do, and that is all the world requires.[5]

15 / Without human scientists to know it, the system of the world would be unknown and would have no distinct existence. But science is possible only in the leisure provided by a stable and well-ordered society. Such a society depends on a political type of order, and not all human tribal groupings achieve such an order. Egyptian mathematics and Greek philosophy are a kind of achievement that is not at all common. Civilization is, to Aristotle, a recent phenomenon: he speaks of 'the first governments' (*Politics* III 15 x and IV 13 x). He is very conscious of history and his own place in it not many generations after the

origins of philosophy (as recounted in *Metaphysics* I), the maturity of which he identifies with his own synthesis of Plato, Democritus, and Empedocles. Only in the Greek world had philosophy been discovered and developed, and only by a handful of people. Only in Plato's school had any sort of systematic and critical science been done. In *Ethics* X vii–viii, Aristotle is acknowledging and defending the unique nature of this activity. *Of course* philosophy and science are supremely important, of course they occupy only a few people, of course they pertain to a special way of life found only in philosophical schools.[6]

16 / We seem to be involved in a blatant contradiction here. How is this historical emphasis to be reconciled with the 'steady state' view of the universe, according to which humanity has existed from all eternity and all its potentialities been completely realized throughout? The answer is that civilizations rise and fall, succeed each other as individuals do. Cities are founded, but the city has always existed. There are two phenomena to be explained: the existence of cities, as the necessary environment for the development of the most truly human capacities; and the origination of cities, through accidents of necessity and invention, at a place and time when those capacities were not realized. So the need for security leads to the foundation of cities, cities make leisure possible, leisure makes science possible: the universal human 'desire to know' (*Metaphysics* I 1) comes to fruition in metaphysics as soon as it finds its opportunity.[7] The arts have had to be rediscovered infinitely many times, because civilizations are repeatedly wiped out by catastrophes – notably by wholesale climatic changes and changes in water level in different parts of the world, leading to floods and desertification (*Meteorology* I 14).

17 / The place of catastrophes in cultural history links up with the discussion of individual catastrophes in *Ethics* I ix–xi. It is the fact of the weakness of individual animals that leads to their death, depriving them of their part in everlastingness and divinity. Cultural activities function only intermittently; the function of human contemplation is not carried out at all for much of the time, and while it is in abeyance the system of the universe is as if it did not exist. But that does not matter, any more than it matters that many human lives never achieve happiness or end in disaster. The important point is that (because the real world will always be there to be perceived)

the system of the universe is there to be understood and will be known again as soon as circumstances are right; *eudaimonia* remains an objective within the ordinary compass of human endeavour, and will be achieved whenever things go well. It is not Aristotle's fault if we live in a world in which things do not always go well for people.

In a curious way, I think the prevalence of catastrophe is necessary for the achievement of *eudaimonia* at the practical level, because the latter depends on political deliberation, the energetic securing of well-being for oneself and for 'race and cities.' In a continuously benign environment, civic life would settle down to the 'cycles of Cathay' in which all political problems would be resolved. Aristotle objects to the political life that it lacks leisure, but he claims that it is a form of happy life, no doubt the commonest form; and it is a form of happiness that, in a sense, leisure precludes.

The objection that Aristotle's view of human happiness is 'elitist' almost answers itself in the light of his theory of social development and catastrophe. *Eudaimonia* is the full and unimpeded use of *logos*, a life with and according to thought applied to one's circumstances. Only moderate external means are necessary. But a city does offer opportunities that a village or an isolated farmstead does not, a metropolis offers opportunities that a small town does not; the development of a leisure class and the development of scientific culture make possibilities available that are not available in a commercial entrepôt. There is a sense in which the relation of the rest of life to scientific knowledge is that it 'provides for it to come about,' but that does not at all mean that life is pointless otherwise: humankind is the unique *logos*-using animal no less in other contexts. Aristotle's definition of *anthrōpos* is as an animal *dektikon epistēmēs*, 'apt to receive scientific knowledge' (*Topics* V 4, 132b1), not as an animal whose self-realization requires that this aptitude be exercized.

Aristotle envisages a finite, stable, and knowable world which simply is what it is, in all its specificity. Such a world, as a system and in its parts, affords grounding for no other value than that of being intensely and purely what one has it in one to be and can be known to be. It supports the value of *energeia*, the full realization of specific potentialities, and the value of *spoudē*, the curiosity and energy needed for, and directed towards, the discovery and realization of these potentialities by a being endowed with *logos*, a being with a sense of time.

Notes

Foreword

1 For an astonishingly detailed and successful study of this development, see Rist 1989.

2 This procedure is followed by Broadie (1991) in her profound and
penetrating critique of Aristotle's views.

3 Richard Kraut (1989) purports to deal with the *Ethics* as a whole, but
his main concern is to establish (as he magnificently does) the internal
consistency of Book X and its compatibility with the position outlined
in Book I; the actual line of development from beginning to end is
neither sought nor followed. In an earlier day, Grant's edition (1874)
starts off by explaining how the work unfolds, but does not follow
this insight through in the actual commentary.

4 In the *Posterior Analytics*, Aristotle urges that you don't know a fact
unless you have the argument that establishes it, which suggests that
what the fact actually *is* is not independent of the reasons for accepting it.

5 At its worst, this tendency shows itself in the reliance on 'proof texts'
to show what 'Aristotle's doctrine' on a topic was. This can descent to
sheer buffoonery, as may be seen from Modrak's account (1987, 4–9)
of recent controversies on Aristotle's theory of mind, which shows
how divergent views can be developed by exclusive attention to the
wording of isolated texts.

6 Douglas Hutchinson tells me that these chapter numbers are first
used in print in the third collected edition of Aristotle's works, published in Basle in 1550. For their medieval origins, see Gauthier and
Jolif 1958 (I 82*, n. 245): 'on voit apparaître dans le texte au cours du
XIVe siècle les deux divisions qui ont subsisté jusqu'à nos jours, l'une
transmise par Argyropoulos et Lefèvre d'Étaples à Zell, à Didot, et

aux éditions anglaises, l'autre par Th. Zwingger et Duval à Bekker et aux allemands.' It is worth dwelling on this because almost all editors and translators include their preferred chapter numbers without comment, irresponsibly leaving their readers to infer that the corresponding articulation reflects Aristotle's own decision.

7 The widespread notion that this fourfold pattern is Aristotle's normal procedure may be influenced by the explicitly fourfold layout of an article in such works as Aquinas's *Summa Theologiae*; I will refer to it in the text as Aristotle's 'scholastic' layout.

Introduction

1 The usual way to 'publish' a book in antiquity was to hold a public reading. The manuscript from which the reading was given constituted the author's 'book,' from which copies might or might not be made. Plato's dialogues were presumably introduced to the world in this way. Aristotle's scientific writings evidently were not, so the criteria for their existence and identity are nebulous.

2 There is also a shorter but substantial treatise covering much of the same ground, the *Magna Moralia* (*MM*). Scholarly opinions differ as to whether this is Aristotle's work (see, for instance, Cooper 1973 and Rowe 1975), but in practice everyone treats it as a reasonably faithful and well-informed but not necessarily wholly reliable source for Aristotle's views.

3 Kenny 1978. A review by T.H. Irwin (1980c) overturns much of Kenny's argument, but my impression is that the statistical reasons for associating the 'common' books with *EE* hold the field. See further Gottschalk 1990, 68 n. 69.

4 Conversely, I occasionally refer to 'the editor' when it is preparation of the final text rather than composition of its content that is in question, without meaning to imply that the editor must be someone other than the author.

5 Porphyry, *Life of Plotinus* xxiv 9.

6 Ibid xiv 4–6; the *Metaphysics* is also called a *pragmateia* by Plutarch, *Life of Alexander* 6. But reference to LSJ shows that the word was used in other senses as well, and Rist argues (1989, xiv–xv) that all Andronicus did was group such treatises as *EN* together with other treatises on similar subjects, respecting their textual integrity. On Andronicus generally, see Gottschalk 1990, 55–64.

7 Various discussions in *EN* are linked together by editorial notes. These often seem to show little insight, and have commonly been

assigned to some uncomprehending editorial hand. But I think such a compiler would provide better explanations. To me, these notes look like more or less casual explanations of transitions in a manuscript, as if the author had simply gone on to the next main topic, leaving a proper account of the relationships for oral improvisation, and had later jotted down the first explanation that came to mind.

8 A similar situation arises with Kant's ethics, in which I for one am not always sure how to divide my understanding between the formal statements about the categorical imperative and the maxims of actions, which are purely formal, and Kant's unwavering conviction that he often knows what the maxims of certain kinds of actions actually are.

9 For detailed discussion of this basic theory of action, see Nussbaum 1978.

10 Compared his supposed statement (preserved by a grammarian), 'The lonelier and more solitary I am, the fonder I become of stories' (fragment 668 Rose); and consider his repeated references to the surliness and unfriendliness of the elderly. These are not the utterances of a cheerful temperament.

1 What Is Best for People

1 Martha Nussbaum (1986, 273–5) says that the term I have here rendered 'oriented' (*oregesthai*) basically means the 'reaching out' of a desirous animal to an object of desire in its physical or social environment, this idea being associated with Aristotle's physicalism. But in this passage of the *Metaphysics*, the desire is not for the knowable in the world as known, but for knowledge itself, the word for knowledge (*tou eidenai*) being one related to vision. Analogously, the corresponding word in the opening sentence of the *Ethics* is one connoting not desire but active pursuit, not a response to attractive stimuli, as in the cases that Nussbaum has in mind, but an active embarking on projects and undertakings.

2 The word translated 'choice' here can also mean 'project,' and in this sense Aristotle applies it to his *Ethics* (1179a35), which he also calls a 'pursuit' (*methodos*). In fact, all four words can apply to his own work, which is 'in pursuit of' the good – we seem to be confronted with an elaborate pun (cf. Burnet 1900, 6n).

3 See Perry 1923, especially p. 115.

4 The Oxford translation has 'rightly,' not 'well,' and that is certainly what the word *kalōs* means in an analogous passage in the *Politics*

(1295a35). But it is not the primary meaning of the word, and it is odd to ascribe correctness to such an ambiguous saying.

5 The point that Aristotle has left it open at this point whether the 'end' of a life is simple or multiplex is made by Engberg-Pedersen (1983, 30–2).

6 See *On the Soul* II 4; also § 1.211 and the Appendix.

7 In the *Gorgias* (507D) Plato uses the same word, *skopos*, to say that everyone should aim at the same thing; but here the target to be aimed at is not a quality of life but *the principle itself* that everything should be subordinated to the ideal of a virtuous life. The corresponding *telos* here is, as the argument of the dialogue as a whole shows, the universal desire that one should attain whatever is *really* good in life. The relation between Plato's and Aristotle's uses of this metaphor is worth reflecting on.

8 1179a9; the reference is to Herodotus's anecdote of Solon and Croesus, *Histories* I 30.

9 Following a similar argument, one might question whether the expansion of one's range of concerns from oneself to one's fellow members of human groups deserves the unique status that Aristotle seems to assign to it. One might consider transferring one's concern to the whole ecological setting of which one forms a part. The rhetoric associated with such a transfer is nowadays familiar, though the logic of the relevant argument remains obscure.

10 See Appendix.

11 Aristotle is presumably addressing himself primarily to denizens of Athens, where participation in public political activity was traditionally part of the good life – see Thucydides, *History* II 40. It is worth recalling that Aristotle as an alien was debarred from such activity; his failure to allude anywhere in the *Ethics* to such restrictions on citizenship and public life suggests that his remarks on the value of giving one's activities a wider context are to be taken as perfectly general, and do not refer to the specific activities we know as 'politics.'

12 For instance, *On Dreams* 459b4, *alloiōsis tis*; *Politics* 1295b1, *politeia bios tis poleōs*; *Rhetoric* 1355a4, *pistis apodeixis tis*. See Wedin 1988, 202, n63.

13 The three opening sentences of the *Politics* curiously parallel the opening sentences of the *Ethics*: all communities exist to achieve some good, we hear, and the most authoritative and comprehensive community, the city (*polis*), exists to achieve the most comprehensive good, the general welfare of its members. (The missing term here, 'community' (*koinōnia*), is used in the *Ethics* in just this sense and this context, but not until Book VIII.)

14 Aristotle's language vacillates throughout: for instance, at 1152b1–8 he writes as if we were discussing politics, but at 1177b6–10 he contrasts 'political' activities with those that form part of a satisfactory life.

15 The word translated as 'complete' here is *teleios*, literally 'having the character of a *telos*,' which, as we have seen, means 'end.' But there are two ways of being *teleios*: completeness is one, the other is perfection, coincidence with the relevant ideal. *Teleios* virtue might be the highest virtue, or it might be inclusive of all particular virtues; a *teleios* life might be glorious though short, or it might require a full tale of seventy satisfactory years. The ambiguity is pervasive.

16 The economic context is primary: the economic unit of human life is the self-sustaining household, which has two functions: acquisition and preservation (*Politics* I 8). Does it follow that warfare is an economic phenomenon rather than a political one? Plato, *Republic* II 373Dff., suggests that it is.

17 Aristotle never alludes overtly to Alexander's conquests, with which he was so closely connected (cf. Chroust 1973, vol. 1), but writes as though cities like Athens were still independent, the last word in political development. Why is this? Partly because of the irrelevance of empire to the quality of everyday life (see previous note), partly, no doubt, because the topic was both painful to his readers and dangerous to himself. But see § 2.2342 below (on IV iii).

18 *Ethnos* in Aristotle tends to mean the ethnic community, but can mean a nation or state or any other general association larger than the *polis*, the self-contained city-state in which an assembly of all citizens can participate in the direction of affairs (Mulgan 1977, 141 n22).

19 Sparshott 1985. For an up-to-date survey of the place of women in Athenian society, see Just 1989. It should be borne in mind that, although Aristotle lived in Athens and was addressing Athenians, his family connections were with societies in which the legal and social position of women may have been significantly different.

20 At *Republic* 505D, Plato's Socrates makes the related point that people may be satisfied with mere appearance in relation to the first two of these values, but insist on reality when it comes to the third. I will say more about these three values in § 1.232 and elsewhere.

21 Plato, *Apology* 20C–23B. For Aristotle's estimate of Plato's originally, see his poetic encomium on Plato (Fragment 673 Rose, p. 2463 Barnes).

22 There has been a fashion of preferring other translations, such as 'human flourishing,' largely on the ground that the Utilitarian philosophers equated happiness with 'pleasure and freedom from pain' and

less sophisticated people equate it with a passing sense of euphoria ('happiness is a warm puppy'). But the English term has traditionally been used in serious discussions with the same generality as the Greek term and has the same core sense, and the everyday use of the Greek term suffers vagaries like those of the English word, so 'happiness' remains by far the best rendering. One caveat is necessary: the Greek word always represents a judgment on the quality of a person's life as a whole, and never (as the English word often does) merely expresses the way a person happens to be feeling at the moment. One *is* or *is not eudaimōn*; it makes little sense to say that one *feels eudaimōn*. But it makes perfect sense to say 'I feel so happy!'

23 Since these everyday notions about happiness reflect what people find missing from their lives – that is, impediments to well-being – they imply an ideal of a pleasant life as one that is free from all such impediments. That goes far to explain Aristotle's equation of pleasure with 'unimpeded activity' at 1153a15.

24 Aristotle's list is not made up out of whole cloth nor is it derived from observation; it is conventional, closely resembling the list Plato uses at *Euthydemus* 279Aff., for instance.

25 Myles Burnyeat (1980, 72–3) insists that even here the point is that by *doing* good we learn what goodness *is* – 'practice has cognitive powers, in that it is the way we learn what is noble and good' – in the way explored in II i–ii.

26 Note that the present remarks on the prerequisites for profitable study of ethics and politics are quite different from those in the previous methodological comment in I iii. The previous point was that one needs a grasp of life as a whole, as opposed to a tendency to react to immediate stimuli; the present point is that one needs to have internalized basic morality.

27 Broadie (1991, 24), in line with Ross's translation, says that the contrast is between what people say and how they actually live; but Engberg-Pedersen (1983, 7n.) suggests a quite different translation: 'For people seem reasonably enough to understand the good and *eudaimonia* on the basis of the (well-known) lives' – that is, presumably, they make their choice among preformulated ideals. The Greek certainly could mean that, but I do not think Aristotle did.

28 The fable is known to us as narrated by Xenophon in his *Memoirs of Socrates* II i, 21–34. The figure personifying the life of ease says her friends call her *eudaimonia* but her foes call her vice (§ 26); the personification of the life of toil says that following her will lead to the 'most blissful' (*makaristotatēn*) happiness.

29 These are what Plato presents as three 'parts of the soul,' but motivational patterns is what they are, and the *Republic* makes much more sense when that is recognized. In *On the Soul* III 10, Aristotle notes that each of these three 'parts' has its own motivational complex of recognition and appetition.

30 This reticence follows a general pattern in Aristotle's thought, which will be mentioned in our Appendix. Also, since Aristotle begins with what is 'familiar to us' rather than what is knowable in itself (cf. *Physics* I, 184a16–20; *Metaphysics* VII, 1029b3–12), it is fitting that philosophy should not enter the discussion until the argument calls for it, at the end of Book X.

31 If one adds the money makers and the intellectuals to the politicians and the plain people, one has four classes or castes: the warriors and feudal nobles; the wise men and priests; the traders and manufacturers; the peasants and workers. But Aristotle shows no sign of awareness that he has introduced this social stratification, which strikes us as so venerable (see § 2.11 below, citing Cornford 1912).

32 Ross's translation refers to 'Platonists' at 1096b10, but no such word occurs in the text. This is of a piece with his substitution of 'Plato' for 'Socrates' in the translation of *Politics* II: in general, in Ross's translations of Aristotle, the occurrence of the words *Plato* and *Platonists* are as likely to represent Ross's private opinion as they are to render what Aristotle wrote.

33 The word translated 'desire' here is the word used in the first sentence of the *Ethics* – *ephiesthai*. The doubt about the status of the third member of the triad extends to the present passage in the *Ethics*: it is arguable that Aristotle makes only two formal requirements of the 'human good,' finality and self-sufficiency – in which case my § 1.131 and § 1.132 are not true parallels.

34 See Stephen R.L. Clark (1975, 154), who cites *Metaphysics* V, 1024a23: 'Wholes are not mutilated by the privation of just any part.' Scrupulous accounts of the way all parts and conditions of *eudaimonia* fit together into a complex hierarchy are given by Kraut (1989) and Broadie (1991).

35 Aristotle says 'wives,' not 'spouse.' He is speaking in a male-dominated society; he assumes that his hearers and readers are males. However, if linguistic adjustments are made, there is little in the structure of his argument that makes provision for any difference between men and women. On his principles, there should be none, though one may be living in a society in which such differentiation is a social fact.

36 Nowadays, when the global economy is unified, the 'us' for whom
we are obliged to make decisions extends in a way to the whole of
humanity; but Aristotle knew of no context in which such involvement would be realistic, so that he can say unselfconsciously that
Spartans do not deliberate about constitutional reform in Scythia
(1112a28).

37 Note that the requirement that happiness embrace all the goods one
aims at does not entail that one should aim at everything one considers good. Someone devoted to a well-rounded life might discover
something – some ideal, some noble cause – in comparison with
which everything else seems unimportant. One's whole perspective
may change. It is even thinkable that an account of 'the good for man'
might stipulate that such a burning interest might dominate a
person's life. Equally, such an account might exclude such pre-
emptive priorities as incompatible with the requirements of the
human condition. (On pre-emptive values in general, see the discussion of Socrates' view of the relation between virtue and happiness in
Vlastos 1991, ch. 8, especially 209–14.)

38 Plato's use of his definition is criticized as tendentious by W. Charlton
(1970, 102–3), but his strictures are unreasonable. The definition is not
introduced as self-explanatory: the examples are given in response to
the complaint 'I don't understand': they are not mere ornament, then,
but are designed to show just how the definition itself is to be understood. And the notion of function was prepared beforehand by the
innocent-sounding introduction of the phrase *haper pephuken ergazes-
thai*, 'its natural operations,' at 352A5–6. With Plato as with Aristotle,
close attention to the actual course of a discussion is called for.

39 Nussbaum (1978, 81) warns against equating Plato's account of function with Aristotle's; the former leaves the point of a functional
account unexplained, while Aristotle's account is 'always given with
reference to a containing system.' My text and the preceding note will
show that I am not convinced that this is the right way of putting
what is indeed an important difference.

40 The same thing is said at *Meteorology* IV 12 (390a10): all things are
defined by their *ergon*, without which their names do not literally
apply to them. See also *Politics* I 2 (1253a21–5), where function is
identified with relationship to a whole.

41 There are verbal connections here, which translations necessarily
obscure. The word for 'activity' (*energeia*) is closely related to that for
'function' (*ergon*), as though we were to say 'functioning' – Aristotle
emphasizes this connection at *Metaphysics* IX, 1050a22. But *ergon* is

also intimately related to the word for a bodily organ or an instrument or tool, *organon*; and this connection too is emphasized by
Aristotle (*Generation of Animals* I 2, 716a23–7). I do not know how
close these connections would have seemed to the ordinary user of
Greek in Aristotle's day.

42 The connection between excellence and function is asserted in *On
Heaven* II 3, 286a8: 'everything that has a function exists for the sake
of the function.'

43 Suppose that, if humans have a function, it is such as Aristotle pro-
poses. To say that 'humanity has no function' then represents a decision to abstain from the rational organization of one's life, or at least
to abstain from supposing that such organization is incumbent on
one, not a judgment that such abstention is itself incumbent.

44 In the (presumably earlier) *Protrepticus* (fragment 6 Walzer; pp. 34–6
Ross; p. 2411 Barnes; not in Rose), Aristotle seems to argue that if
humanity has a *single* nature that must be the intellect, so that the
unique function of humanity is to attain truth. The argument of the
Ethics, as we see, is entirely different.

45 In Book X, the human 'function' is effectively redefined as 'the life [*bios*
this time, not *zōē*] in accordance with insight' (1178a7), and we are told
that 'happiness extends as far as contemplation does' (1178b28), but
these are new moves, not explications of what *logos* means.

46 According to Aristotle (*On the Soul* III, 427b14), *logos* is a *necessary condition* of *dianoia*; it is by no means the same as *dianoia*.

47 For this pervasiveness, compare the well-known dictum of Karl Marx:
'The *forming* of the five senses is a labour of the entire history of the
world down to the present. The sense caught up in crude practical
need is only a *restricted* sense. For the starving man, it is not the
human form of food that exists, but only its abstract being as food; it
could just as well be there in its crudest form, and it would be impossible to say wherein this feeding-activity differs from that of animals'
(Marx 1959, 101).

48 Someone has tried to clarify it by a recapitulation, placed in square
brackets as an interpolation by Bywater's text and Ross's translation,
and quite right too, because it includes disastrously irrelevant notions,
notably that the life we have in mind is that of an adult male.

49 LSJ's entry under *aretē* makes the word seem colourless, but perusal
of the examples in Stephanus suggests rather the coloration suggested
in the text.

50 LSJ say the original sense of the word is 'haste,' but they offer neither
evidence nor argument in support of this.

51 For the meaning of *spoudaios* see Aubenque 1963, 45–8. On the connection between being serious and being taken seriously he writes: 'Le *spoudaios* est l'homme qui inspire confiance par ses travaux, celui auprès duquel on se sent en securité, celui qu'on prend au sérieux' (p. 45), and he justly castigates all those scholars who have identified the *spoudaois* with whatever kind of hero took their fancy.

52 In *On Good Birth*, fragment 94 Rose (pp. 61–2 Ross, pp. 2423–4 Barnes), Aristotle uses the word throughout in a sense that seems to unite moral probity with noble birth.

53 Aristotle cannot have suspected that people would be reading him *as a school text* – that is, without regard to the truth of his ideas, and without thinking seriously about the aspects of life he is referring to.

54 And so, mutatis mutandis, was Jimi Hendrix, I suppose. The point is that people really concerned with his kind of music and musicianship would be in doubt about his merits only in a deeply discussable way.

55 'Being serious is something you have to work at' (*ergon esti spoudaion einai*), 1109a24; in II iii we learn that excellence goes with what is harder (*chalepōteron*), and II ix warns us against taking the line of least resistance.

56 It is also disconcerting to find that the reference to *logos* has vanished; but this is no doubt because 'virtue' has been implicitly defined in terms of the operation of the *logon echon*.

57 Gauthier and Jolif (1958, II 59) insist that *en biōi teleiōi* here means 'in a perfected, matured life' and not just 'throughout a lifetime.' But this is untenable: the phrase is explicitly contrasted with 'a single day and a short time' (compare 1177b25, where we meet the phrase 'the length of a *bios teleios*').

58 Note the verb derived from *spoudē*. Here, at least, I trust no one will want to say that what is in question is respectability rather than energy.

59 Consider our exemplar, the serious guitar players. What are they serious about? Pleasing the audience? Or what? Why do people bother to learn the guitar anyway?

60 This is not the same triad as the one attributed to Protagoras in § 1.114 above. For more about these triads, see § 1.2324 below.

61 Compare Plato's treatment of 'the good' in the *Republic* with his treatment of 'the beautiful' in the *Symposium*. Are they the same, or aren't they?

62 The tragic implications of this theme are the subject of Nussbaum's *The Fragility of Goodness* (1986).

63 This holds for all living things, as Aristotle conceives them: three of

the four 'causes,' the final, formal, and efficient, are within the dynamics of the species as a 'natural,' self-sustaining entity, but the 'material' cause, the sufficiency of food and other environmental conditions adequate to sustain that dynamic and the absence of destructive interventions, is not within that internal dynamic itself. See *Physics* II 7ff.

64 See 1117b15–16: 'It is not in *all* the virtues that the activity is pleasant, except insofar as it achieves its end.' Aristotle never warns against the dangers of complacency and self-congratulation, if he is aware of them.

65 Some commentators object here in the name of stern morality, saying that really good people are those who act well though sorely tempted to act otherwise, because that proves that their *will* is good though their *appetites* may not be. Aristotle rejects the argument, because it supposes that there is really no such thing as a good person, hence no such thing as virtue – that humanity is a botched job.

66 *Thlibei kai lumainetai to makarion.* The verbs imply abrasion and disfigurement as opposed to structural damage. The noun phrase *to makarion* is one never defined by Aristotle; sometimes it seems to be just an elegant variation for *eudaimonia*, sometimes to be contrasted with it as the kind of blessedness the gods enjoy. Often, as here, it is equivocal.

67 Neither of these triads is quite the same as the 'political' triad borrowed from Protagoras (see § 1.1114), in which pleasure does not appear but legality does – I suppose laws are civic and arbitrary in the same way that pleasures are personal and arbitrary. For a more elaborate treatment of these value spectra, see note 28 to § 2.22222.

68 Cf. 1115b12–13 and 22–4, 1119b16–18, 1120a23–9, 1122b6–7.

69 Virtue and happiness are in everyone's reach, says Aristotle; but his voice is the voice of Plato's colleague and Alexander's tutor (see Introduction), and that must make it hard for him to communicate with the likes of us.

70 The *Meno* is a highly sophisticated dialogue, and one Aristotle often cites, though it is sometimes misrepresented by being placed relatively 'early' in Plato's career and hence by implication immature.

71 See Nussbaum 1986, especially ch. 11.

72 In Aristophanes' *Frogs* (1182–7) Euripides quotes the Prologue to his *Antigone*: 'Oedipus was at first a happy (*eudaimōn*) man ... but then he became the most miserable of mortals.' But Aeschylus protests that he can never have been happy, since even before his birth Apollo had predicted that he would kill his own father.

73 One must not forget that the immortality which the *Phaedo* arguments purport to prove is impersonal: its content is knowledge of universals that are the same for all, and has nothing to do with particulars or with personal recollections.

74 It helps to remember here that Aristotle takes a strongly realist view of knowledge: a true judgment is one that is supported by the facts as they are (*On Interpretation* 9, 19a33), so that the truth-value of predictions is equivocal at best.

75 This definition differs from the formulation at 1098a16–18 in that (i) the word 'happiness' is substituted for the phrase 'human good,' (ii) the reference to 'soul' is omitted, (iii) the reference to 'complete' virtue is incorporated without fuss, (iv) the reference to a 'complete' life is included rather than being added as an afterthought, and (v) the stipulation of prosperity is included.

76 Cf. Anaximenes Rhetor 35, p. 80.18 Spengel/Hammer (Radermacher C71): 'As for the strong, the beautiful, the well born, and the rich, it is not fitting to praise them but to felicitate them (*makarizein*).'

2 Reason in Action

1 Some writers (e.g., Monan 1968, 109) take this whole discussion of the virtues to be a digression, but plainly it is not: it is, as Aristotle says, the substance of what the definition of happiness specifies. Perhaps these commentators are partly motivated by the need to combat the once-popular view that the *Ethics* is essentially a morality of virtue. John Rist claims (1989, 187) that the overall discussion of virtue is announced as starting with the beginning of Book II, but he is wrong. The beginning of I xiii makes that announcement; what is announced at the beginning of II is the separate discussions of moral and intellectual virtue prepared in I xiii.

2 These abilities or 'faculties' are not separate parts or entities, even though Aristotle himself sometimes uses language that suggests that. They are simply an animal's abilities to do what it can do, and what it can do depends on what it does do, and these actions are differentiated by their actual objects and operations. Speaking of actually extant faculties makes no more sense than speaking of 'parts' of the soul: the soul is simply the livingness of an actual living body.

3 Modrak (1987, 9–15) argues that attempts to trace a development in Aristotle's thought about the soul through separate phases cannot be sustained from his technical writings: he 'treats psychological hylomorphism and psychophysical instrumentalism as complementary

hypotheses.' The history of the controversy on this issue bears her out, I think.

4 If this is right, Rist (1989, 183) misses the point completely.

5 The model is laid out and explained in *Politics* I.

6 One 'takes account' of father and friends – as opposed to doing one's accounts (1102b31–3)!

7 'Virtues of character' and 'virtues of thinking' are less far from the implications of the Greek terms.

8 It was, we recall, a key feature in the passage in *Republic* I in which Plato introduced the concept of 'function' of the soul.

9 The fourfold analogy was pointed out in Cornford 1912; see note 31 on the previous section for its further manifestation in the 'ways of life.' Cornford does not explain, however, in what form this caste system was known to the Greek world or why it is nowhere overtly referred to.

10 This should yield a Pareto-optimal solution, a way of life in which no possible change could yield an improvement, though there may be other solutions that would be equally optimal. Aristotle does not deny that that is the case, and says things that suggest that, in a way, he would accept it, though he does not consider the question. (The word 'principle' in my text here is used very loosely, by the way, to include any maxim or explicit formulation of a behaviour-guiding verbal formula.)

11 The complementarity of justice and friendship is like that of justice and 'temperance' (*sōphrosunē*) in Plato's *Republic* IV, where justice is the cold fact of social cooperation, and temperance is the willingness of all to cooperate.

12 The theory of 'original sin' in fact holds that all unredeemed persons are maimed in this way (in Augustine's version, they are incapable of envisaging goodness in a way that would set their wills free), so that the concept of virtue has very little application to natural humanity.

13 For some relevant considerations about the theoretical underpinnings of Aristotle's position, see the Appendix.

14 *Metaphysics* I, 980b26.

15 In Plato's *Protagoras*, Protagoras says that people learn virtue as they learn their mother tongue, by picking up the prevailing mores – but then, he assumes that what the prevailing mores embody is really virtue. In the *Meno*, Socrates says that correct opinion is as useful as knowledge (a point to which Aristotle keeps returning), but points out that one never knows whether a mere opinion is correct or not.

16 Authors persist in postulating an ancient 'canon' that Plato is merely

repeating, but the evidence does not support them. See Sparshott 1970.

17 Rather a dumb thing to say, actually – see *Ethics* V vii. But Plato's point is that the conventions and conformities necessary to make communal life possible will be spontaneously developed and followed, not imposed and enforced.

18 The Platonic use of the 'craft theory' of virtue is examined by Irwin (1977). For the theory of the arts in general, see Sparshott 1982b.

19 He returns to the question, briefly and enigmatically, in X ix (1179b23–35).

20 Contrast the more explicit language at 1105a1–2, where it is said that pleasure 'has grown up with us all from our infancy' (*ek nēpiōn suntethraptai*), where the word specifically implies incompetence; *ek neōn* just means 'from youth,' 'since we were new.'

21 A more striking parallel with Aristotle's diction is at *Gorgias* 510D, where Socrates uses the phrase *euthus ek neou ethizein* – someone wishing to curry favour with a tyrant should 'accustom himself, from his youth up, to feel the same pleasures and pains as his master.' Note that the 'youth' in question is a period that the schemer can still incorporate in his life strategies; note too the significance of sharing pleasures and pains, a recurring theme in the *Ethics*.

22 Compare Nussbaum 1986, 285: in educating children, 'we begin the educational process not with a creature who is simply there to be causally affected and manipulated, but with a creature that responds selectively to its world via cognitional *orexis*, and whose movements are explained by its own view of things, its own reachings-out for things as it views them.'

23 This cannot be quite right, since a moral virtue is a habit of choosing and its compliance must accordingly have an element of rationality built in. See Fortenbaugh 1969 and 1975.

24 It is tempting to attribute Aristotle's frequent use of the analogy of health to his membership in a medical clan, and there is no doubt that this approach is naturally congenial to him. But Plato also has frequent recourse to the parallel between physical health and moral 'health' or virtue. One excuse must be that the parallel is striking, and that physiological facts are observable in a way that the corresponding psychological facts are not. But we should add that medicine is a systematic study of human life, the only repository of human wisdom that is not vitiated by human passions. Socrates, in the *Apology*, does not extend his sceptical cross-questioning to doctors, any more than he does to mathematicians.

25 Note that nothing corresponding to this is true of bad habits, which are thus in a sense inexplicable. We shall see that Aristotle never finds a satisfactory solution to the consequent problem of explaining vice.

26 See, however, VI xii (1144a34–5), according to which 'wickedness ... causes us to be deceived about the starting-points of action,' the starting-point in question being 'since the end, i.e., the best, is of such-and-such a nature' and further described as 'the eye of the soul.' But this still leaves it unclear just how this 'eye' is formed and corrupted.

27 The same contrast between basic pleasures and truly satisfying pleasures was to be made fundamental and elaborated by Epicurus.

28 The good, the pleasant, the useful, the fine, and the just tend to occur in Aristotle in triads: good, just, pleasant; good, useful, pleasant; good, fine, pleasant (cf. §§ 1.1114 and 1.2324). I am not aware that these relationships have ever been systematically explored. Gauthier and Jolif (1958, II 125) suggest that a conflation of the present passage with 1155b18–21, 1152b26–7, etc. yields a fourfold schema: the *kalon* is what is really valuable in itself, the *hēdu* is what is apparently valuable in itself, the *agathon* or *chrēsimon* is what is really valuable in relation to an agent, and the merely utilitarian (*ōphelimon*, or *chrēsimon* in another sense) is what is apparently valuable in relation to an agent. I think that is rather clever. For a less schematic view of the relationship, see Myles Burnyeat 1980, 86–7: 'Pursuit of pleasure is an inborn part of our animal nature; concern for the noble depends on a good upbringing; while the good, here specified as the advantageous, is the object of mature reflection ... A good upbringing makes the noble a part, perhaps a chief part, of the pleasant for us. Aristotle's lectures are designed to take the next step, and make the noble a part, perhaps the chief part, of one's concept of the good (cf. *EE* 1249a11).' Well said, except that Burnyeat overlooks the fact that *kalon* in Greek is a much less specialized word than 'noble' in English.

29 In another context, one might argue that only what is useful to mankind should be regarded as truly beautiful and glorious (as Socrates argues in Xenophon's *Memorabilia*, III viii and IV vi 9), or that pleasure is something good in itself (cf. *EN* VII xii–xiii), or that pleasure and beauty are indicators of what is, in one way or another, naturally good.

30 See especially *Physics* II 4–6, which explains how fortuitous occurrences are assigned unwarranted significance because they fit into familiar teleological patterns.

31 I have always suspected that he was shipped off to Plato's Academy at the age of seventeen to avoid military service in the Macedonian army.

32 D.S. Hutchinson (1986, 14–15) points to *Categories* 8b25–10a26.

33 Note that powers and dispositions are both defined in terms of passions, and passions are identified as 'what pleasure and pain attend' (1105b23); a psychic dynamic is thus being articulated, though, so far as I can see, no actual use is made of it.

34 I can do it backwards, and once amazed a tableful of drunken soldiers by doing so – but I could equally well recite it backwards *wrong*.

35 Contrast the case of the senses, as Aristotle conceives them in *Sense and Sensibilia* 3 and elsewhere. A sense is a *logos* between extremes, colour is black or white or some mixture of the two – but any such blend is just as much a definite colour as any other blend.

36 The virtue is a condition of 'middleness' (*mesotēs*, an abstract noun) and what it relates to is the middle or 'mean' (*meson*). The same language, establishing the same relation between the terms, is used at 1133b30–3. Like everyone else, though, I will call the virtue itself a 'mean.'

37 Meno, when asked to define virtue, replies by saying that different stations in life call for different forms of behaviour. Socrates in effect asks for the common factor that makes all the called-for forms virtues, but does not deny the truth and relevance of the observation. In *Politics* I, Aristotle argues that the different positions of father, mother, child, and slave in the power structure of the family call for different virtues. But one must be cautious here. John Rist, commenting on *Politics* 1325b4 and 1277b20ff., observes (1989, 304 n. 28) that 'there are different *kinds* of virtue like justice, moderation, courage, different in men and women. (A man would be a coward if he was as brave as a woman, a woman a chatterer if she was only as decorous as a good man.)' One sees what is meant, but what is said is incoherent in terms of Aristotle's definition. Virtue is never a matter of degree. Both men and women must be brave and decorous – exactly as brave and decorous as their situation requires. Their way of life, which is presumably not unrelated to their psychology and physiology, requires different behaviour patterns from them.

38 In V vii, Aristotle makes some sketchy remarks on the variability of laws. What he says leaves all the practical questions open. A city could make a law that everyone should be left-handed, but ...

39 A few years ago, commentators on Aristotle's praise of the contemplative life used to wonder why he did not tell us whether a wise man will 'stop thinking and pull a drowning man out of the water.' But that, of course, would be for the *phronimos* to decide in the light

of the situation. If it is perfectly obvious that he should, that will be just as obvious to him as it would be to Aristotle.

40 Thomas Aquinas, *Summa Theologiae* I IIae, q. 91 a. 4.

41 Somebody said: 'If people obeyed all the laws, they would never have time to do anything else.'

42 His caveat against rigorism in II ix (1109b18–23) does not fill the bill, because it only allows for a degree of permissiveness without considering the possible relevance of another range of values.

43 It is precisely this state of affairs that is revealed in Book I of Plato's *Republic* where Socrates' 'justice,' a determinate policy based on insight, is contrasted with Thrasymachus's *pleonexia*, the indeterminate desire for 'more' – more than what, or how much more, one cannot say, so that this is a recipe for folly and incapacity. I explore this theme in Sparshott 1966.

44 Doing (*poiein*) and suffering (*paschein*) figure as separate items on Aristotle's list of ten 'categories,' *Categories* 4, 2a3–4.

45 I would then be in a position to comply with Augustine's slogan *Dilige et quod vis fac*, 'Love and do what you will.'

46 The 'greatest good' depends on security, and this requires that some things will *never* be permitted; and the natural desire for pleasure and freedom from pain is supplemented by an equally natural sense of indignation (Mill 1861, ch. 4).

47 Aristotle's language is extremely terse and epigrammatical, in ways that (partly because English is less highly inflected) cannot be approximated in translation. A reference to the original will often show why Aristotle says what he does by revealing brusque antitheses and terse asides, the power and pregnancy of which may depend on their abruptness. Is rhetoric here pretending to do the work of argument? Possibly. But the movement of thought and the movement of language are not easily separated.

48 See note 37 above.

49 That this list forms part of the explanation of what virtue is appears from the fact that the phrase linking the list to the definition is the same as that which links the 'genus' (II v) to the 'difference' (II vi): *dei de mē monon ... alla kai*, 'we must, however not only ... but also.'

50 Much light may be shed here by the comparison of the *EN* and *EE* discussions of virtue in Rowe 1971, ch. 3. In the *EE*, he explains, we have a succession of definitions of virtue successively incorporating the concepts analysed in *EN* III i–v. Looking at Rowe's material, it occurs to me that the effect is that *EE* never clarifies the idea of a moral virtue strictly as such or articulates the kind of thinking it

involves. This would support the view I put forward in the Introduction, that *EE* is a smoother job but does not bring out the basic
issues.

51 This at least is the impression Aristotle gives of his predecessors – see
Bonitz 1870 s.v. *antikeisthai*.

52 This seems to be the position implied by X ix, but it may be closer to
the truth to say that people mostly do realize that there could be such
a thing as acting on a *logos*, but not steadfastly; it is only an occasional inkling. But the theory of vice implied by the present passage
is incoherent; cowards who think the brave are foolhardy must think
that they themselves are *right* to be as they are, but Aristotle does not
explain either how their position can be determined by a (faulty) *logos*
or how the concept of rightness can attach itself to a position that is
not so determined. The people envisaged in X ix are in a sense *beneath*
both vice and virtue. The whole issue will be taken up in § 4.611.

53 Anorexia nervosa, which can be fatal, is not a vice but a disease, in
the way that Aristotle will point out in VII v. The point about the
asymmetry of vices is charmingly made by J.O. Urmson: 'It is an
insult to Aristotle's good sense to make him say that taking insufficient pleasure in the pleasure of food, drink, and sex is a moral vice,
though he regards it as an *ēthikē kakia*' (1973, 160). Urmson does not
offer an alternative translation, or explain why Aristotle could not
have held that our contemporaries were as capable of moral misjudgment as his own.

54 The metaphor of straightening a curved piece of wood by bending it
in the opposite direction recalls the analogy of the paralytic limb in I
xiii. But the dynamic here suggests that a virtue results from a correct
blending (*krasis*) of opposed forces – see Clark 1975, ch. 3 §2, and in
general Tracy 1969. Note then that, in cases where the natural tendency is stronger in one direction, virtue will be practically identified
with pulling in the opposite direction. This explains the erroneous
notion that a woman's moderation is a greater moderation than a
man's, and a man's courage a greater courage than a woman's. The
result is that in a way the idea of excess and deficiency are reversible:
'excessive' moderation is restraint, but the excess that moderation
avoids is overindulgence.

55 Aristotle's phrase 'aims at the intermediate' (*stochastikē tou mesou*,
1109a 22–3) echoes the phrase *metrou tinos stochasasthai* in the Hippocratic treatise *Old-Fashioned Medicine*, 9, where (as in *EN* II vi) the
measure in question is a mean between too much and too little food.
In the same context, Hippocrates, like Aristotle, says that it is *ergon* to

make a precise determination in complex issues; and, also like Aristotle (1109a22–3), he uses the analogy of steering a ship in danger. Of less immediate relevance is Hippocrates' remark in this same chapter that 'bad physicians ... constitute the great majority,' just as Aristotle holds in X ix that bad people do. It is hard to believe that Aristotle did not write the present passage with the Hippocratic passage in mind – unless, of course, the latter is a later forgery whose author had the Aristotelian passage in mind.

56 The association of judgment with perception as mean comes from *On the Soul* II, 423b30–424a7 – see Olmsted 1948. *Krisis* is the ordinary term for judgment or discrimination; I do not know how relevant it is that it is also a technical term in medicine, meaning the 'turning-point' in a disease at which the patient's condition changes decisively for better or worse, but the word does appear in the same Hippocratic work that Aristotle is alluding to in this passage (*Old-Fashioned Medicine* 19).

57 The use of the first person – 'up to *us*,' not 'up to *one*' or 'up to *the agent*' – is significant as determining the practical context. If one thinks impersonally, one can theorize that every agent does what the present situation causes to be done. But, in practice, at every moment, we have actually to do one thing rather than another, by taking into account what we can and what we cannot do something about. Aristotle's repeated insistence on the *practical* nature of the present inquiry makes determinism a non-issue. Penal legislation causally affects the behaviour patterns of the citizenry by altering the factual consequences that people will take into account in their decisions (cf. 1113b21–30).

58 'Intended' comes closer, as J.O. Urmson points out in what I think to be the most sensible exposition of Aristotle's thought here – Urmson 1988, 42ff.

59 The treatment of the topic in *EE* comes closer to doing this, concentrating on something like 'ordinary language' analysis where *EN* focuses on forensic issues.

60 For the forensic relevance of involuntariness, one may compare Plato, *Apology* 26A and *Lesser Hippias* 372A, but the standard reference is the elaborate exposition in a real-life legal situation, Demosthenes' speech *On the Crown* 274–5. Demosthenes adds that a sound policy that fails through no fault of its promoters should not attract 'sympathy' as an involuntary action would, but participation in their chagrin – a point akin to Aristotle's.

61 T.H. Irwin (1980b) implies that it is; but he is not confining himself to *EN*, let alone to this passage in it. The passage on voluntariness in

V viii is, of course, explicitly concerned with the legal issue – it is part of the discussion of justice, not simply an elaboration of the present passage.

62 H.D.P. Lee (1937) reminds us that (according to Aristotle's *Athenian Constitution* 57) homicide was dealt with in Athens by three separate courts, depending on whether it was premeditated, or involuntary, or justified. The classification is hardly exhaustive. One wonders where premeditation would fit into the discussion of *EN* III i–v; Lee suggests that Aristotle's discussion of 'choice' in II iv may be tailored to fit it (p. 139).

63 1110b9–15 makes the different point, that one should not regard the pleasant and good objectives of one's action as exercising compulsion on one just because they are 'external' to one.

64 Aristotle must surely have had in mind his father-in-law Hermeias who died after torture but got the word back to his comrades that he had done 'nothing unworthy of philosophy' (cf. Düring 1957, 272–83) – assuming, that is, that the story is true.

65 See note 16 above. On the personalization of passions and involuntariness, see Just 1989, 177–181 (citing E.R. Dodds [1951] and K.J. Dover [1974].)

66 Plutarch (*Seven Sages' Symposium*, 147A) has an anecdote of a youth who threw a stone at a dog. He missed the dog, but the stone accidentally hit his stepmother. 'That's not bad either,' he said.

67 Nussbaum 1986, 42. She cites the case of Agamemnon who was compelled to sacrifice his own daughter – his fault is not that he did so, but that he did so without a qualm. See, in general, Nussbaum 1986, ch. 9.

68 It seems to follow that, since voluntariness suffices for praise and blame, not every praised disposition is a moral virtue. No more it is: we are praised for experiencing shame, but it is not a virtue (IV ix).

69 The word is ambiguous. We saw that in I i it could mean something like 'project'; and in *Politics* III, 1280a32ff., where it is said that slaves have no *prohairesis*, it should mean something like 'life-plan.' Aubenque (1963, 119–20) argues that in Book II it cannot mean what it means here, but only 'l'engagement intérieur de nôtre être'; but to take it so is to reduce *EN* to a pile of rubble.

70 We will see in VI iv that it is definitive of an 'art' (*technē*) that its end is good *ex hypothesi*, it is both rational and arbitrary, not to be called into question in the practice of the art but only in the context of politics, which has the task of deciding whether and how far any art shall be studied and practised in the society (cf. 1094a27–b7).

71 At 1142b25–6, one of the ways a deliberation can be defective is that it reaches the right objective through the wrong means.

72 This holds true even for non-serious people – as Plato suggests in the *Phaedo* (68C–69D), even self-centred people can usually see that certain lines of action would be counterproductive, and civic morality gets by on that basis (with or without legislated penalties to weight the scales).

73 The political analogy is prepared by the preceding phrase 'that which has been decided upon as a result of deliberation' (1113a4, Ross translation). Although the English version is not exactly mistaken, the Greek *to ek tēs boulēs krithen* could equally well (or better) mean 'what was decided in the senate' – the senate, or *boulē*, being the deliberative body that prepares motions for the popular assembly. The underlying thought is that, whereas in a democracy the sovereign will of the people has the final say in what the deliberations of the wise have recommended, in a monarchy the royal will has the final say on policies that subordinates (who may or may not be wise) have recommended. It is, I think, this inversion that prompts the choice of the word *dēmos* for those to whom policy is announced. In Homer, the *dēmos* does not get a look in at all. (The crucial importance of this passage was pointed out to me by W.F.R. Hardie.)

74 At 1117a18–22, discussing courage, Aristotle says it is accepted that it is more a characteristic of the brave to keep their heads in a panic than in a foreseen danger: the former reaction must come from the virtue itself, the *hexis*, whereas the latter could be 'from preparation.' What is one to say of this? Does the truly virtuous person deliberate at lightning speed? Or is it the case, as J.S. Mill thought, that experienced people do not have to work through all the possibilities every time? Or is Aristotle only reporting an accepted view (*dokei*) from which he himself dissents? In any case, he seems to be less than explicit about the relation between habit and deliberation. If a virtue is a habit of choice, is it also a habit of deliberation? Perhaps in my example of the experienced driver we should distinguish three possibilities: (1) the novice has to try to think of everything at once every time, and is in a constant fluster; (2) the bad driver responds directly to the most salient feature of the situation, ignoring everything else; (3) the good and experienced driver takes everything instantly into account (as the Stoics were to say, the right action is the one you can give a full explanation of *afterwards*). Perhaps in the end we should say that the impulsive action and the deliberate action are both revelatory of character, but in different ways: the former shows what

is most deeply ingrained, the latter shows the scope of the values to which a person is committed. I suppose we are always suspicious of sudden generous impulses: Phalaris may have let someone off the brazen bull, but if he did it on a whim we are not inclined to give him credit.

75 Kahn 1988, 239.

76 The topic is familiar in folklore through the misfortunes of those who are magically granted 'three wishes.' The third is usually needed to undo the effects of the first two.

77 I put the word 'predict' in scare quotes because an actual prediction would take time and energy; if you want to predict what I do your brain will have to work faster than my brain – you will have to catch up with me first. If you *really* want to know what I am going to do, you can ask me and I will look in my diary.

78 Aristotle would not be left without a response. He could say that committing oneself to the scenario compiled by the officials of this or that firm in the god industry is just what he means by not being serious about the use of *logos*. Just so, it's no use consulting your stockbroker and then wagering your fortune on a lottery.

79 David Furley must have overlooked this passage when, relying perhaps too heavily on 1103b23–5 (§ 2.222142), he wrote: 'It is odd that Aristotle never (to my knowledge) asks himself why the discipline of parents and teachers is not to be taken as an external cause of man's dispositions' (1967, 194). The reason he never asks himself is that the answer follows from what he clearly says. Such discipline surely neither mechanically compels victims to act nor prevents them from acting, but gives them strong reasons for choosing to act, the prospect of reward and punishment being something they take into account in assessing the situation. If discipline were believed to be causally efficacious, citing a bad upbringing would automatically ensure acquittal or a suspended sentence for a wrongdoer. Since that is not true of any actual or possible jurisdiction, Aristotle was not obliged to waste words on the possibility.

80 Aristotle stipulates that the law should be one everyone ought to know, and easy to find out (1113b34) – presumably the underlying principle here is the one invoked in the discussion of the voluntary, that one must exercise judgment as to *how much* care should be taken to avoid *what* errors. The question is resumed in the discussion of legal responsibility in Book V.

81 At 1111b13, Aristotle says that the *akratēs* acts 'with desire, but not with choice.' But it seems possible that the overwhelming desire

should coincide with the kind of choices the agent used to make when still capable of choice.

82 For partial responsibility and contributory causes, W.F.R. Hardie refers us to *On the Soul* II 4 (416a9–18), where Aristotle says that the natural process of combustion may be a contributory cause of nutrition, but the real cause is the soul, the vital process of the body that converts nutriments into usable forms and distributes them functionally throughout the body (Hardie 1968a, 276). The analogy suggests that our partial responsibility for our actions would be confined to providing crude motive force, while the actual form of our activity was contributed by whatever formed the 'natural end.' That is not a very plausible scenario.

83 When Aristotle says that our choices reflect 'what we best know,' the word for knowledge is the one he uses in *Metaphysics* I 1 for the knowledge towards which all humans are oriented by nature.

84 For the technical possibility of there being separately distinguishable moral virtues, see Hutchinson 1986, 11–13.

85 Ramsauer observes (1878, 113) that Aristotle uses whichever of *three* ways of defining virtues lies readiest to hand: by the passion involved, by the action performed, and by the object related to.

86 *Politics* 1260a9–33. Socrates is explicitly attacked on this issue, probably with *Meno* 71C–72A in mind.

87 The abstractness of the treatment appears from 1177a30–2, where we hear that all moral virtues have to do with relations with other people – something that, in the exposition of the moral virtues themselves, is confined to justice (1129b31–1130a8).

88 What diagram? Either the 'we' must be his original audience, or Aristotle's original text had an illustration which did not find its way into the manuscript tradition.

89 See MacIntyre 1982.

90 Something that is 'relative' because it stands in a specific relation to something real is as objective and definite as anything else. One should not be misled by the slimy form of words according to which something that is merely believed to be the case is said to *be* the case 'relative to' the 'belief system' in question.

91 'If Aristotle wishes to show the form of virtue he cannot reasonably take artificial virtues as his subject: he must begin from what his public are likely to accept' (Clark 1975, 89). If that is so, Aristotle's list need not be complete, but it must seem to be such that any missing virtues can be readily supplied – it must be comprehensive in principle.

92 One can get a better idea of what a description of the actually prevalent conceptualization of the virtues was from the catalogue of weaknesses and eccentricities in Theophrastus's *Characters*; but even that is
probably closer to being a typology of the characters in the Greek
'New Comedy' than to being a caricature of everyday life. For
Aristotle's departure from accepted notions, see Dirlmeier's commentary, and especially his comment on *praotēs* (1962, 383).

93 See Sparshott 1970 for a detailed treatment of all this.

94 In *Politics* I, the household of husband, wife, children, and slaves is
treated as the basic economic unit. There are two functions: getting
and keeping. The male, being more vigorous, does the getting, and
courage is the virtue most called for. The female does the keeping,
and needs *sōphrosunē*.

95 *Rhetoric* 1366b1–3 has the same list of virtues except that it omits
truthfulness, politeness, and friendliness. It is obvious that this list
(like that of the ten categories) is approximate and provisional, diagram or no diagram. Fortenbaugh (1968) remarks that making friendliness and politeness virtues is odd, because they are not really dispositions to choose, they are ways of behaving in social contexts where
no choice is at issue.

Shame (*aidōs*) is a toughie. It cannot be a virtue, because it is an
attitude towards one's failings, which presumably will not survive
one's attainment of a fully virtuous condition. And as Stewart
remarks (1892, I 370), 'If one takes credit for being ashamed, one
palliates the action one is ashamed of, and is more likely to repeat it.'
Gauthier and Jolif (1958, II 321) observe that what Aristotle calls *aidōs*
here is more often called *aischunē* – *aidōs* in Plato's *Charmides*, for
instance, is something more like the shame-facedness of a well-
brought-up child before its elders and betters. All the same, a discussion and conceptual placing of shame is called for, because, since
it is hard to be right all the time, there must be a proper attitude to
oneself and others on occasions when one has gone wrong.

Introducing the concept of *nemesis*, however, seems ill advised. It
may have got in as follows. Since it is the fact of offence that gives
rise to 'shame,' there ought to be some appropriate reaction to
offences on the part of others on occasions when the personal involvement of 'indignation' would be out of place. But *nemesis* can
hardly be located on a mean, because other people may either succeed or fail, and may do so either in accordance with desert or not. A
good person's failure, a bad person's success, are disturbing; a good
person's success, a bad person's failure, are satisfying. There are just

too many variables here; the 'virtue' pattern is being stretched beyond its limits.

96 Aquinas 1949, 94.

97 'Liberality' (*eleutheriotēs*, presumably the characteristic virtue of the free individual) is said to concern everything that is measured by money (1119b27), so it can hardly be based on a psychological disposition. People with this virtue take care of their estates *to maintain their liberality*; the virtue is a matter of policy in a way that the preceding virtues, courage and moderation, are not.

98 This progression from materiality to spirituality is emphasized by Joachim (1951).

99 Much of the detail, as Dirlmeier points out (1962, 339) is taken from Plato's *Laches*.

100 David Pears (1980) completely misses the point that courage as a military virtue calls for doing the right thing (*to deon*) and feeling the right thing in a particular situation, as determined by the *kairos*. Hence he talks only about two 'feelings' in the abstract, of which the means must be on the same or different scales; he never even mentions the fact that a brave man must be enduring as well as daring, both of them in the right way, in attack and in retreat.

101 But see Nestor's exhortation in the *Iliad* IV, 303–5: 'Let no charioteer, trusting in his horsemanship and courage, think to advance and fight the Trojans on his own; and do not fall back either. You will be weaker that way.'

102 The argument had already been prepared in Plato's *Statesman*, where a distinction is made (with an eye on the *Republic*) between governments in which it is assumed that governors and governed are different kinds of being, like shepherds and sheep, and those in which it is not. The implication of calling King Agamemnon 'shepherd of the people' (*poimena laōn*), as Homer does, is that he is not a human being like his subjects.

103 This (1124a4) and 1179b10 (where it is said to be out of reach of the populace at large) are the only places where *kalogathia*, the special word for the quality of a fine Athenian gentleman, appears in the *Ethics*.

104 Our view of the literary problem may well be affected by today's common practice of cobbling together journal articles and calling the result a treatise, often with much less regard for consistency and repetition than Aristotle or his editors show.

105 Moraux 1951, 80–1, citing Léonard 1948.

106 In favour of (1) also is the fact that what is probably the oldest list of

Aristotle's works, attributed to Ariston at the end of the 3rd century BCE, includes an *Ethics* in five books, which can only be the *EE* without the common books – from which Gauthier and Jolif (1958, I 56*, n142) infer that *EN* must already have existed *with* the common books, though there are no mentions of it.

107 The supposed transition from virtue to friendship would actually be affected by the remarks on shame. Shame, in relation to virtue, sets up a new positive/negative couple to match courage/temperance and good temper/friendliness: shame is the negative effect of a good person on someone trying to be good, friendship is the positive effect of one good person on another. But if this sequence had been in the author's mind one would have expected friendliness to take its place at the end, next to friendship proper, as it does in II vii.

108 Dirlmeier (1962, 495) contends that one cannot infer from the double treatment of pleasure that *EN* was not conceived as a whole: he cites the incorporation of the 'Thrasymachia' and the double treatment of poetry in the *Republic*, a work unquestionably intended for publication.

109 *Dikaiosunē*, 'justice,' is a noun derived from the adjective *dikaios*, 'just,' which means someone with a penchant for *dikē*. *Dikē* means recompense for an offence against hierarchical and topographical order – in short, for the violation of boundaries. It also stands for the system that is thus violated. 'Justice' as thus conceived becomes a word for the stable virtue of established societies, as opposed to the heroic virtue of individuals and chieftains. The translation 'justice' is usually the best: the Greek concept, like the English one, is ambiguous between law-abidingness (what courts of justice administer) and fairness. The Greek word, however, also does most of the work that English reserves for the word *right* (and its derivate *righteous*). Correspondingly, Greek has no word with quite the flavour of 'right' and 'rights,' words we associate with Teutonic traditions rather than the Latinate 'justice.' The conceptual equipment of both languages is rich, confusing, and complicated. Two things to be noted are: (i) Greek legal institutions were elaborate but imperfectly codified; (ii) correspondingly, the Greek concept of law and the lawful (*nomos, nomimos*) covers basic social norms as well as formal systems and has less of the connotation of *correction* than *dikē* has. What Aristotle is doing in Book V is not simple and could not be simplified, because he is dealing with the institutionalization of norms in societies that are conceived of as stable, whereas in fact they are fluid, not to say chaotic.

110 *Logikon* in this sort of sense tends to be Hellenistic, and specifically Stoic.

111 Actually, the *Republic* conducts an analysis and vindication of 'justice' (as opposed to selfishness) in *five* stages. First, Cephalus equates justice with paying one's debts to humans and gods, without analysing the basis of such debts. Second, Book I equates justice (as fair dealing) with intelligence and strength, because it accommodates all claims and recognizes all factors – but the defence is specious, because the equation is applied in an arbitrary way. Third, Book IV equates justice with political and mental health – but the analogy with health is undefended, so that the related values are left hanging in the air. Fourth, in Book VI the intellectual passion for getting right answers to problems is said simply to override the personal motivations that lead to injustice – but this indifference stands in no organic or functional relationship to the specific institutions it underwrites. Fifth, in the metaphysical and epistemological construction of Books V–VII, justice is to be grounded in a grasp of the world as a total system in which everything is as it must be, a grasp that would afford the only secure basis for values. Aristotle's *Ethics* is clearly written in the light of this wide-ranging dialectic, which today's readers often miss because they forget that the whole dialogue is about justice and ludicrously treat the 'search and discovery' in Book IV as an independent inquiry.

112 It seems that there cannot be a *pleonexia* or uncontrolled appetite for justice, because justice is essentially concerned with control, so an excessive concern with justice (at one level) would be corrected as unjust (at a higher level). But students discern in the *Republic* an unbridled concern for justice as opposed to other values, whatever Plato may say – and they are right, insofar as the city that is constructed with exclusive regard to the value of 'justice' (on the basis of an association of functioning adults, rather than loving families and comrades or autonomous individuals) is presented as though it were designed to embody all humanly important values. Aristotle's concern for this problem appears in his discussion of equity, which is precisely the second-order justice that corrects the formalism and intellectualism of first-order justice; but in the end it is the architectonic function of *phronēsis* that defines what moral virtue comes to on any occasion, and this must apply in principle to justice. But I do not think Aristotle has thought this through: his method makes him play down the ways in which justice is not really one of the moral virtues at all.

113 On this aspect of justice, see in general Lloyd-Jones 1971.

114 Gauthier and Jolif (1958, II 335–6) suggest that Aristotle is newly dis-

cerning an ambiguity where previously there had been a confusion;
but their evidence shows only that *pleonexia* was generally thought to
be lawless (*para nomon*), which is not very startling.

115 One of the reasons why Aristotle proceeds by way of antonyms may
well have been to introduce at the start the essential equation of justice with 'fairness': the Greek word for 'fair' is the same as the word
for 'equal' (*ison*).

116 See Lloyd-Jones 1971, 1–2, and references there given.

117 Ross translates *tōn allōn tōn ēthikōn aretōn* as 'the other, i.e., the other
moral, virtues'; but it could equally well mean 'the other virtues, i.e.,
the moral virtues,' acknowledging, as it were, that justice is not on the
list.

118 I take it that 'security' (*sōtēria*) includes such personal immunities as
the citizen's immunity from flogging, a constant threat to slaves and
the unprivileged generally (cf. Acts 22: 24–9).

119 This is perhaps not surprising, for a philosopher who was to spend
his maturity teaching in Athens under the auspices of a Macedonian
governor. It was left for the Hellenistic schools to work out what
ethics must become in a real world of power politics.

120 Vinogradoff, however, argues (1908, 6) that 'in Greek law, and not
only in Aristotle's jurisprudential statement, the matter is usually
treated as one of redress complicated by penalties.' He may be right,
for all I know.

121 The point is that you may not want the prize in the competition, and
it may be something no sensible person would want, but if you are an
unfair person you will try to get it and cut corners in order to do so.

122 My text here perhaps betrays a liberal bias. A Marxist could argue
that 'justice' is simply a piece of bourgeois ideology, as follows: on
the one hand, the concept of a 'just' price or a 'fair' contract represents the intervention of the ruling class and its ideology to distort
whatever basis of cooperation would otherwise be in place; on the
other hand, the assumption that an 'involuntary' transaction represents an injustice that must be reversed assumes the view of the
courts, the tools of the ruling class, that define 'justice' (as Thrasymachus maintained) as whatever that class has sanctioned. But Aristotle,
though not a liberal, is not a proto-Marxist, and assumes throughout
the legitimacy of the state power and (as my text here suggests) the
possibility that the power and other relations it regularizes can themselves be just.

123 At 1131a31, proportionality (*analogia*) is defined as equality or fairness
of ratios (*isotēs logōn*) – heavily charged language indeed!

124 The translated phrase is *pros tou blabous tēn diaphoran monon blepei ho nomos* – literally, 'the only difference the law looks at is that of the injury,' in a sentence which has just referred to the differences made by the moral quality and respectability of the victim. Ross's version misses the verbal connection.

125 One might have expected Aristotle to say here that offences by and against officials involve the city and not merely individuals as such (the position clearly stated in the Aristotelian *Problems* XXIX 14, 952b28–34, as well as Demosthenes' *Against Midas* 41), but he does not; he writes as if they were indeed individuals, but on different levels.

126 W.F.R. Hardie (in a tutorial) said of this passage that Aristotle sounded like someone with no talent for mathematics showing off how much mathematics he knew.

127 This hermeneutic use of quite implausible etymologies seems to have been a fad (see Plato's *Cratylus*). It is one of the few things classical philosophy has in common with what is nowadays called 'literary theory.'

128 For the popularity of this idea, familiar from Polemarchus's use of it in the *Republic* (332A–336A), see Dover 1974.

129 We will see that this applies in a way even to friendships between individuals; but in the case of true friendship, in which all the friends want is each other's company, the element of exchange effectively vanishes.

130 Compare this report from Devonshire in the late nineteenth century: 'Within the last twenty years I have seen an account set out between a blacksmith and a farmer without any reference at all to money. On one side there were horseshoes, ploughshares, etc., and on the other side, pork, butter, geese, etc. And both parties reckoned the items up, and saw that the totals balanced. They seemed to have some weights and measures in their mind that are not found in books, say, four horseshoes make one duck' (Torr 1979, 11).

131 I say 'apparent' because I cannot see that Aristotle actually says that the reciprocity of demand that makes a transaction possible must be established by agreeing on a mutually satisfactory price according to the three variables of quality, quantity, and desire, rather than by a common willingness to pay and accept here and now the pre-established price for the goods. But the fact that reciprocity is introduced as the basis, and is conceived as fundamentally pre-legal, strongly suggests the view I take here.

132 Note that being related to a specific *amount* is an intellectual matter, in the sense that it rests on calculation.

133 Abraham Edel (1982) is the commentator who best appreciates and displays the flexibility of the ways in which Aristotle plays with his 'technical' terminology. In the present case, however, it is hard to see why calling justice a mean between doing and suffering injustice is more than a *jeu d'esprit*.

134 See *Politics* I, 1253a37–8: 'Justice (*dikē*) is ordering (*taxis*) of a political community, and justice (*dikaiosunē*) is determination (*krisis*) of the just (*dikaion*)'. *Taxis* is marshalling, the sort of order manifested by a military unit on parade.

135 Probably the best thing to say is this: insofar as we distinguish a public from a private domain, the state is concerned only with the former.

136 Antiphon 87 B 44, Diels-Kranz.

137 Epicurus, *Principal Doctrines* 31–6. (Some sources say 'occupies the terrain' rather than 'bears the stamp'; cf. Arrighetti 1973, 135n.)

138 Aristotle, like Plato, never really confronts the possibility that the content of a set of laws may actually be deleterious: as Stewart observes (1892, I 493), he speaks as if only morally indifferent things could be conventionally just, not things evil in themselves.

139 Ross's version of 1134a19 seems entirely wrong to me; it is certainly an interpretation rather than a translation. The Greek seems to say what the sense requires, viz. 'This is not what makes the difference' – the *this* in question being the fact of belonging to a nameable category of offence.

140 One thinks nowadays of Sartre's *Saint-Genet*, according to which the young Jean Genet, believed to have stolen something, is called 'a thief' and takes this to be a description of his nature, which he then decides to live up to – or something like that. But Sartre's point is not the same as Aristotle's. Aristotle thinks that people who steal and keep on stealing really do become the kind of people who are properly described as thieves, their choices become habitual in a self-confirming policy that may become so ingrained as to be irreversible. Sartre denies that this happens: consciousness has no inertia, a lifetime of stealing does not make one subjectively a thief, though that is certainly the way others will see one. But Sartre admits that, in practical terms, it makes little difference, because the habitual thief functioning in a thievish environment has no practical alternatives – he can change, but at what cost!

141 'We must not forget,' Ross's translation of *dei de mē lanthanein* at 1134a24, suggests falsely that the point has been made before; but it has not. 'It must not escape our notice' is just as good a translation of the Greek, depending on context. The point that justice proper exists

only in a city or something city-like is a new one. But of course we are doing 'politics' all the time, so we should have known it all along, and 'forgetting' is not an impossible way of describing our neglect.

142 When in Sophocles' *Antigone* the heroine protests against Creon's edict that it was not Zeus who proclaimed it, and the god of justice did not lay down such laws for humanity, she was out of line. If Creon's edict violated justice, it was because it violated the fundamental law of the society. (For a somewhat different perspective, see Nussbaum 1986.)

143 It is possible, however, that Aristotle here means no more than that a deliberately harmful act may not be unjust if its aim is to redress an imbalance, either in accordance with reciprocity or within the framework of a penal system.

144 Sorabji (1980, ch. 17) has an extensive argument to the effect that this argument in *EN* V viii is closely related to *EE* as opposed to *EN* III i–v. But since he completely ignores the relevance of these discussions to their contexts, his argument is less than conclusive.

145 Students of Plato will note that Aristotle reverses the Platonic/ Socratic equation of 'harming' with 'making worse' (e.g., *Republic* I, 335B–E): Aristotle equates harming with violating (legitimate) interests, the integrity of which is, as we saw, a requirement of freedom and is safeguarded by reciprocity in the absence of legal redress. In this argument, Aristotle's commitment to the existential priority of the household, the economic unit of survival, moves him towards the position that would eventually be developed by John Locke in his *Second Treatise on Government.*

146 According to Kenyon (1951, 48–52), the unit of manufacture for papyrus was the single sheet (*kollēma*), the standard size being about 10 × 7.5 inches, and it was marketed in rolls for literary works but in single sheets for short documents. Marketed rolls would be stuck together or cut up as necessary.

147 *Rhetoric* I. 13 corresponds to *Ethics* V vi–xi, but there are major differences because the treatises are about different things: the *Ethics* persists in thinking of justice as a sort of virtue, the *Rhetoric* takes an unabashedly legal/forensic point of view. The *Ethics* discusses law only so much as is necessary to make the single point on which the discussion here turns – in fact, it leaves out some obvious points about the law that would have made the course of discussion easier to follow. The *Rhetoric* leaves out the matter of *EN* 1136a10–1137a4 and V xi, which has no bearing on law as such, and introduces its treatment of equity with a discussion of 'written' and 'unwritten' laws

– that is, the legal version of the distinction between law and morality, which *EN* 1137a4–1138a2 discusses from the moral point of view.

148 *MM* mentions equity in II 1 (1198b24–34), associates equity with good judgment (*eugnōmosunē*) at 1198b34–1199a3, and proceeds to relate good judgment (*euboulia*) to *phronēsis* at 1199a4–13. Various questions about justice are raised in II 3 (1199a14–b35), including some roughly corresponding to *EN* 1137a4–1138a2. The 'three questions' are raised in I 33, 1195b5–1196b3. A good reason for treating equity in the context of intellectual virtue is that the distinction between justice and equity follows from that between the 'controlling' or rule-framing and 'particular' or judgment-passing spheres of good sense. (Whether authentically Aristotelian or not, *MM* serves our present purpose, which is to demonstrate an alternative way of ordering the materials under consideration.)

149 Aristotle thinks it worth noting that if a judge gives a wrong verdict through an honest mistake, or a lawgiver passes an unjust law through inadequate information, the action is not 'unjust' from a legal point of view, *kata to nomikon dikaion* (1136b32–4), the *judgment* is not unjust. What he needs here is the more explicit distinction between procedural justice and substantive justice – a fair procedure may lead to an unfair state of affairs. As it is, he merely contrasts *nomikon* with *prōton*, 'primary,' which is hardly explicit.

150 The converse case, Aristotle remarks parenthetically, disposes of the paradoxical contention of Socrates against Polemarchus (*Republic* I, especially 334A) that the just are best able to be unjust, since to do wrong one must know what is right to be sure of avoiding it. The fact is that a single decision is not enough to make someone a good *or* a bad person.

151 Aristotle's best statement on equity is that in the *Rhetoric* (I 13, 1374a27ff.), where he says, for instance, that the written law may require correction by equity either because of careless draftsmanship or because of unavoidable vagueness – life would be too short to specify just what is and what is not a weapon for the purposes of 'armed robbery.'

152 See Adkins 1960, especially chs 4 and 9.

153 Aristotle equates the relation between law and equity with that between law (*nomos*) and edict (*psēphisma*) (1137b27ff.), though in real life an edict, a vote of the assembly, is not an application of standing law so much as an ad hoc decision to deal with a situation, even if such a decision will not be valid unless it is within the scope of the existing laws.

154 See Moraux 1957, 8.

155 It may be relevant here that Plato lacks the theory of proportionality that makes Aristotle demand four terms to constitute a proportion. According to Heath (1931), the general theory of proportion as found in Euclid V was the work of Eudoxus (pp. 190–1), though the theory of proportions among whole numbers had been developed by the Pythagoreans by the end of the fifth century (pp. 51–7).

156 Aristotle's statement that 'the law does not command a man to kill himself, and what it does not command it forbids' (1138a6–7, Barnes's correction of Ross's disingenuous rendering) is odd. Stewart (1892, I 533–4) says that it is true of customary as opposed to statute law that one is effectively forbidden to kill anyone one is not ordered to kill. Joachim (1951, 161) has a marvellous suggestion that he ascribes to Cook-Wilson: originally the text read 'does not allow,' not 'does not command,' but OYK EAI was misread as OYKEΛI, which means nothing, so someone corrected it to OY KEΛEYEI – and then someone inserted the 'explanatory' phrase about commanding and forbidding, to make sense of the result.

157 What is this alleged offence against the city? Michael of Ephesus (p. 69, 22–3) says that the state is deprived of the suicide's services – but that is to interpret the justice involved as 'particular,' whereas Aristotle's context requires it to be 'universal,' and implies a relation between state and citizen that is more Byzantine than Hellenic. The 'dishonouring' (*atimia*) involved required that the suicide's hand be buried separately from the body (see Aeschines *In Ctesiphontem* 244), which suggests that it was conceived as a ritual offence; and Vinogradoff (1922, II, 182–5) argues that Athenian law differentiated the laws about ritual cleansing of pollution from laws about the punishment of such offences as murder, to which considerations of *mens rea* were relevant. Probably Aristotle has simply got it wrong. He resolutely refuses to consider that Athenian law incorporates archaic and superstitious elements, hoping, I suppose, that if he ignored them they would go away.

158 At 1138b8, Aristotle says that the rational and irrational parts of the soul are contrasted *en toutois tois logois*. The phrase is ambiguous. Some translators (Ross, Gauthier–Jolif) take it to mean 'in these ratios'; others (Rackham, Dirlmeier) say 'in these writings,' sc. those that make the distinction. If the latter is correct, the reference is presumably to the *Republic* and perhaps to Aristotle's own *On Justice*. If the former is correct, the reference is to despotic and domestic relations. The use of the word *diistēmi* rather favours the latter version; against it is the absence of any suitable antecedent for *toutois*.

159 The difference between Plato and Aristotle here reflects their gen-

erally different view on classification. For Aristotle, since forms exist as embodied, organized classes tend to be focused on paradigm cases, words of multiple application being used with one exemplary case in mind. For Plato, since forms exist perfectly in themselves, exemplifications are judged by their assumed approximation to completeness.

160 The language is odd: *ouden melei tēi technēi*, 'it makes no difference to the science.' What science is this? If it is 'politics and ethics,' this is the only place I know where Aristotle actually uses this word of his own investigations, despite what commentators say. Since at this point Aristotle is using a medical illustration, the reference may be to medical science (already introduced at 1137a16).

161 *Phronēsis* and *phronimos* are traditionally translated 'prudence' and 'prudent' respectively, but English idiom has taken a turn that makes these renderings unsuitable. Ross uses 'practical wisdom,' which is accurate but conceals the relevant fact that the Greek term is a word in everyday use; I prefer 'sensible' and 'good sense.' The *phronimos*, in Greek usage, is brainy, intelligent, sagacious; Aristotle's use of the term is his own, and his explanations are sufficient.

162 Gauthier and Jolif remark (1958, II 440) that the treatment of intellectual virtue follows the same pattern as that of moral virtue: a general discussion leading to a definition is followed by treatments of the particular virtues.

163 Gauthier and Jolif (1958, II 440) observe that 1138b35–1139a3 look like the original introduction, with 1138b18–34 stuck on as an extra introduction without regard to the continuation; I would add that 1138b18–20 look like an alternative to 1138b20–5.

164 This identity follows a common Aristotelian pattern, for which see *Physics* II 3. Aristotle does not think that reality consists of a discrete series of instantaneous states of affairs of which the earlier cause the later; whatever exists is temporally extended and is temporally divisible ad infinitum, so that the more closely we look the more cause and effect appear as simultaneous.

165 The word *horos* is used in a similar context in a passage from Iamblichus rather implausibly conjectured to be quoted from Aristotle's *Protrepticus*: 'what is a more precise measure or boundary (*horos*) of good things than the *phronimos*?' (fragment 52 Rose, p. 33 Ross, p. 2408 Barnes). The passage sounds like a half-baked assemblage of Aristotelian verbiage to me, though.

166 We must not forget that the adjective for the 'intellectual' virtues is *dianoētikai*, 'thinking,' a word that definitely connotes the processes of reasoning rather than the fact of insight (*nous*); and these virtues, we were told, owe most to pedagogy.

167 The point is obscured in what in some ways is the best short commentary on the *Ethics*, Sir David Ross's table of contents to his translation, where he describes the five candidates for the two places as
'the chief intellectual virtues,' and such subsidiary capacities as
'judgment' as 'minor intellectual virtues.' There is no shred of justification for this in Aristotle's text. There are several moral virtues
because appetites and passions, as such, are centrifugal and terminate
on their diverse objects; but the function of intelligence is to integrate,
and Aristotle needs some ingenuity to show that there can be two
rather than one.

    Stewart in his commentary (1892, II 33) says there are five intellectual virtues because Aristotle says, at 1103a9–10, that every laudable
disposition (*epainetē hexis*) is a virtue by definition; but surely this
could not weigh against the explicit statement in the text here.
Stewart also says they must all be virtues because Aristotle nowhere
says they aren't, which hardly seems a cogent argument. One might
equally argue that they can't be because he nowhere says they are.

168 I say 'seems to' because even at this stage it is not clear that it does.
Since virtue is relative to function, and the human function is to live
in accordance with *logos* as a whole or at its best, being serious about
performing this function *initially* requires seriousness not about this or
that aspect of *logos* but about the whole, including all relevant values
and interrelations. The relation between speculative and practical
reason is a proper part of what serious people will think about, in the
course of determining the optimum life strategy. Discussions of the
issue are reduced to absurdity by people who write as if wise and
good people would let this part of their thinking be done for them by
Aristotle, who should provide them with a 'recipe' (the word is that
of Engberg-Pedersen [1983, 95]), as though he were a physician prescribing a laxative.

169 It may look as if theoretic wisdom is as extraneous to ethics as the
existence of an 'unmoved mover' is to the science of nature, which in
itself is concerned only with things in motion even though those
things could not exist without there being other things that are not in
motion. The natural scientist excludes the latter from consideration
even though reflection shows that they must exist.

170 Gauthier and Jolif observe (1958, II 442–3) that the structure of this
passage parallels that of II v–vi: the genus is *hexis*, the species is
determined by function, which in the case of the intellectual virtues is
the attainment of truth.

171 Note the switch from 'insight' (*nous*) to 'reasoning' (*dianoētikē*). Choice
is a momentary 'insight' suffused with desire, or a desire suffused,

not with insight, but with reasoning – the *process* is involved. The reason for the doublet here is to accommodate this double aspect of the thinking involved in choice: it is both insight and reasoning-generated, but of course it cannot be a reasoning-generated insight. What sustains the insight is the desire, which is both occasioned and occurrent.

172 The point is made by Irwin (1980a, 49–50).

173 I wrote at this point, 'A comment that sounds more like that of a desperate editor than that of a confident and organized author' – but then I recalled how often I have said and done things like that in my own lectures. Monan (1968, 64) observes that *EN* VI abounds in false starts: after dividing the parts of the intellect on two separate principles (scientific versus calculative on the basis of contingency, contemplative versus practical on the basis of aims), he introduces the 'five states' on yet another basis.

174 The distinction is made along these lines in Plato's *Charmides* 173–4.

175 Ross renders *logos* here as 'a true course of reasoning,' but that is too restrictive: it may be what Aristotle has in mind, but it is not what he says.

176 Aristotle's distinction between *poiein* and *prattein* hardly reflects Greek usage, in which 'What are you doing?' was *Ti poieis?* The distinctions between *facere* and *agere*, *faire* and *agir*, 'make' and 'do' in European languages are generally untidy and reflect a more subtle discrimination than Aristotle allows for.

177 For endotelicity, see Sparshott 1982b, 64, and references.

178 Compare Hare 1952, and see especially Nowell-Smith 1954 on 'Janus words.'

179 *Would* judge, not *does* judge. It is a counterfactual condition: the supposed judgment of the *phronimos* operates like a law, even though in the concrete case we cannot formulate an appropriate generalization to represent what this idealized person would say, other than 'In every case exactly like this in all relevant respects, do exactly this.'

180 Relying on earlier uses of the term, Pierre Aubenque observes: 'La *phronesis*, c'est le savoir, mais limité et conscient de ses limites; c'est la pensée, mais humaine, et qui se sait et se veut humaine' (1963, 160).

181 Everyone says this. But it is a sobering experience to go through the Platonic texts and see exactly what Socrates does say about this equation. The upshot comes closer to saying that wisdom is a necessary condition of virtue, but not a sufficient condition, though it is the only condition Socrates usually wants to talk about.

182 The fragment is from Simplicius's commentary on Aristotle's *On*

Heaven – fragment 49 Rose, p. 58 Ross, p. 2403 Barnes. John Rist (1985) has an ingenious argument to show that this work never existed, the supposed quotation being a garbled reference to a Plotinian version of *EE* VIII 2. Well, possibly, but he forgets to explain how the non-existent *On Prayer* came to be mentioned by Diogenes Laertius, and a direct reference to Plato's calling the good *epekeina tēs ousias* seems as likely for Aristotle as Rist's elaborate chapter of accidents seems for Simplicius.

183 It is alleged that *Nous* was Plato's nickname for Aristotle (see Düring 1957, 109). Some take this for a compliment, others think Plato meant he was a smart-ass. I think it just as likely that Plato would have been alluding ironically to the young man's penchant for harping on the concept of *nous* as his basic term in epistemology.

184 Moral virtue and political activity 'provide for the existence' of philosophy, we will be told, by providing the necessary order and leisure. Perhaps we should say that the spontaneous life strategies of unreflective folk 'provide for the existence' of practical philosophy in much the same way. The very fact of compliance with the prevailing culture implies the use of cultural compliance as a critique of life, and this is inseparable from the critique of culture itself: to know what to do one must know what one is *supposed* to do. Aristotle's discussion does not, however, actually base itself on this critique; the standards inherent in the everyday life of unreflective people are acknowledged only at the beginning (I iv–vi) and the end (X ix) of *EN*.

185 Athens had a democratic constitution under which officials were chosen by lot. But they did not rely on a lottery in selecting their military leaders, with the result that the generals acquired political leadership.

186 This conviction comes out clearly at the end of *Metaphysics* XII, where he uses a political metaphor from Homer to insist that the orderliness of the world must depend on the single ordering activity of an unmoved mover; in his arbitrary insistence in *Politics* I that every family must have a head; and in his assumption that in every city somebody must be ruling, even if people take turns to do so. Never mind that the mover he has described cannot exert any ordering activity; that man and woman, having different spheres of activity in the household, have no occasion for mutual subordination; and that a division of powers in a state works well enough with no overall centre of authority! But his authoritarianism does not change the fact that the *Ethics* is basically concerned with how people are to achieve happiness in living their own lives; Sarah Broadie's searching and

profound investigation of Aristotle's ethics (1991) is vitiated throughout by her assumption that he is preoccupied by how people are to
exercise power over other people.

187 It is this insistence on the priority of insight into the situation that
will make the Socratic 'paradox' of weakness of will so easy to dissolve in Book VII.

188 The word 'given to hitting on' (*stochastikos*) is the word used at
1109a30 for hitting on the mean in moral virtue.

189 Very likely the point about the 'ultimate' triangle is that you can split
plain rectangular figures into triangles but you can't split a triangle
into anything else that has fewer sides – you can *see* that you can't.

190 The 'must' and 'controlling' of Ross's version are significantly misleading: Aristotle does not say there must be, he says there would or
should be – one would expect it, I suppose, on the analogy of wisdom. And the word rendered as 'controlling' is not a general word
for domination but *architektonikē*, 'architectural.' Political thinking in I
ii was integrative thinking about interests and strategies; but what an
architect does is rather control and organize the activities of individual workers. That is, the metaphor recognizes more explicitly than the
former passage the autonomy of the particular act.

191 At 1152b1–2, Aristotle will say that the political philosopher is the
'architect of the end' with reference to which we call things good or
bad without qualification. I suppose the assembly passes decrees
which constitute a critique of individual actions, the senate or constituent assembly passes laws that constitute a critique of administrative
decrees, and the philosophers like Aristotle perform analyses that
generate a critique of the general ideas with which such bodies operate. But Aristotle keeps telling us that philosophers do not purport to
lead other people's lives for them.

192 *Gnōsis* is what the Delphic oracle told people to exercise in their own
affairs when it said 'Know thyself.' It is not a term with a fixed use in
the epistemology of the *Ethics*: Aristotle is performing the old philosophical trick of getting himself out of a tight argumentative corner
by introducing an undefined term.

193 What ties down the statues of Daedalus, in Aristotle's view, is the
stable character of the virtuous person.

194 Compare the statement on concept-formation in *Posterior Analytics* II
19, 100a16: 'It is the particular that is perceived, but the perception is
of the universal.' As the rest of that book shows, the difference is that
in theoretical studies the perception of the universal is not yet the
acquisition of the related definition or axiom, which requires a great

deal of work. In practical thinking, the universal remains in a sense latent in the particular – as soon as we think of the universal in abstraction from the relevant particular we lose connection with practice.

195 The words 'or people of good sense' (ē phronimōn) at 1143b12 quite spoil the run of the argument. How nice it would be ascribe them to scribal meddling. Burnet (1900), who did not suffer fools (other than himself) gladly, did so; Gauthier and Jolif's argument for their retention is singularly lame.

196 This does not sit well with the claim at 1103a15–17 that the intellectual virtues mostly come from teaching, and that *that* is why they develop with age.

197 The same problem confronts Plato at the end of *Republic* IV. Socrates seeks to establish a connection between the inner harmony he identifies as 'justice' and 'just' behaviour towards others. But he makes no serious attempt to explain why that inner harmony should be in itself a source of joy. Why should a happy life not rather require inner turbulence, disquiet?

198 This aspect of the duality of human function (cf. § 1.211) is taken up in § 6.4121 below; see also Appendix.

199 Epicurus, *Letter to Herodotus* 78–80 and *Principal Doctrines* 11–12.

200 The word *deinos*, which in contexts like this unambiguously means 'clever,' can in other contexts mean 'strange' or 'terrible' (the dinosaurs are terrible lizards, not clever lizards). It seems to have acquired its meaning of 'clever' by way of its application to preternatural skills, including skill at speaking.

201 Literally, a separate 'species' or 'form' (*eidos*). Aristotle has just called cleverness an ability or faculty, but good sense is not a faculty; it is not clear to me what the genus would be of which cleverness and good sense are both species.

202 Gauthier and Jolif in their commentary on 1144a3–6 say that the parallel passage of *EE* 1249b 9–16 shows that wisdom produces happiness as healthiness produces health, whereas good sense produces happiness as a doctor produces health. But, as well as flatly contradicting the whole treatment of the concept of *eudaimonia* in Book I, that is precisely what Aristotle does *not* say in the present passage.

203 *EE* 1249b 6–23, *MM* 1208a 5–20. But the Eudemian passage refers only to external goods, and the authenticity of *MM* doctrines is always open to question. Burnet (1900, 287) quotes a scholiast who represents Theophrastus as saying that the relation of *phronēsis* to *sophia* is like that of slaves to their master: 'They do everything that has to be done

in the house, so that their masters may be at leisure ...' But this may well be a paraphrase of the *MM* passage, which the scholiast may have attributed to Theophrastus. Anyone who would hang a dog on such evidence must really have it in for dogs.

3 The Pathology of Practical Reason

1 Richard Robinson observes (1945, 279–80) that Aristotle fails to recognize that two serious people can disagree about morals, assuming that one of them must be wrong: 'He says that vicious people do not know they are vicious (hē men gar kakia lanthanei). But suppose one day he came across the supposedly vicious person saying to a friend "Aristotle does not know he is vicious"?' Robinson does not, however, say just how vice could elude serious efforts to detect it, or tell us just what the content of the serious disagreement he has in mind might be.

2 J.A. Stewart argues (1892, II 173) that the vicious man cannot deliberately pursue present pleasure (as 1150a20 suggests) because deliberate choice would pursue pleasure not as an immediate object of desire but 'in relation to a system of life.' He concludes that vicious people are really 'chronic weaklings.' His point is logically telling, but mistaken; why cannot people be hedonists on principle, deliberately abstaining from criticizing their own appetites?

3 The *Protrepticus* seems to have spelled it out: in the Isles of the Blest, there would be no need for any of the virtues except *sophia* (fragment 58 Rose, p. 46 Ross, not in Barnes; the actual source is Augustine's citation of Cicero's *Hortensius*).

4 The reference to brutes that 'lack discourse of reason' is so well entrenched that we tend not to question it. But is it in place? Non-human animals have ways of life and naturally tend to conduct themselves in orderly fashion. I suppose we have to say that 'beastly' people have non-human ways of life; human life is culture, and a human life without *logos* and culture is disorderly or pathologically ordered. Matters are complicated by Aristotle's invoking of the idea of a 'natural slave' in *Politics* I 4–6: the only kind of human naturally suited to slavery would be one devoid of controlling *logos* but with an emotive equipment amenable to direction by the *logos* of others. Aristotle observes that Greeks believe that some non-Greek nations are all like that, which is why they enslave them; but what he has in mind seems not to be the 'beastliness' spoken of here.

5 Since theoretical reason has no physiological basis, Aristotle has no

way of accommodating the idea of theoretical insanity. But he and his contemporaries were too thoroughly ignorant of relevant physiology even to be aware of what their difficulties might be.

6 Compare Plato's remarks in *Republic* VI (494B–495B) on how easily idealistic young people are misled.

7 He did, of course, teach rhetoric, and wrote a book about it, not to mention his work on logical fallacies.

8 It is built into the phrase 'the permissive society,' recently much used by preachers: the evil 'permitted' is always bodily indulgence, never malice or envy or unfairness.

9 Compare what Achilles says to his mother about ungovernable rage (*Iliad* 18, 109): it seeps in like honey, fills one like smoke, the world would be better without it.

10 A British person working in Greece has commented to me on how normal and acceptable it was in Greece to express rage in a screaming match, and how safe a young woman was from sexual molestation in the streets. Someone raised in a Greek city and someone raised in a British city would be exposed to quite different norms of inhibition.

11 My own feeling is that 'moral weakness' needs also to be considered in the context of free imagination. People are all party crazy, their rationalizations operate in terms of arbitrary obsessions. Aristotle is talking about some species quite different from the one of which I have the misfortune to be a typical specimen.

12 Lack of Freud also appears in the treatment of the non-rational conditions of sickness and bestiality. Aristotle can only treat these as sheer mechanical failures, of which no explanation can be given. Someone terrified of mice is just bonkers; as Aristotle sees it, the fearing mechanism has gone haywire. But this will not do for us: a fear of mice is a highly organized phenomenon. Surely it *means* something.

13 The reference is to the specific language of Plato's *Protagoras* 352 B–C, but Aristotle ascribes it to Socrates without hesitation.

14 John Rist holds (1989, 182) the *Movement of Animals* is a later work than this part of *EN*, so that its account of the practical syllogism is clearer. He may be right about the dates, but the difference is accounted for by the different subject-matters of the two works; *akrasia*, whatever we make of it, is a matter of confusions and complexities.

15 On the face of it, these can hardly be alternative versions of the same premises, since one has a prescriptive element that the other lacks, as David Gallop reminds me. But the point is, as Stewart and other commentators insist, that appetite goes immediately for pleasure

without deliberation; in the absence of other considerations, pleasure is prescriptive.

16 The place of the 'practical syllogism' in Aristotle's practical philosophy is controversial. The view presented here, that 'practical syllogisms' lie outside the domain of moral reasoning rather than representing the components into which such reasoning should be analysed, is not the only one. The best discussion is in Nussbaum 1978, 'Essay 4: Practical Syllogisms and Practical Science,' pp. 165–220.

17 Burnyeat 1980, 83–4 has an illuminating exposition of this point.

18 The phenomena Aristotle is concerned with may be considered in the light of Tourette's Syndrome, or the effect of L-dopa on patients with post-encephalitic Parkinsonism (see Sacks 1973, especially p. 92 n1). The personality remains intact, the tics are independent; but some patients ignore them, and some 'manage' them, in which case they appear as 'mannerisms, affectations or impostures,' leading to a fission of the entire personality. Aristotle's distinction between normal and disturbed functioning masks a more intricate state of affairs, of which even Freud's analysis is a misleading simplification. The operative dynamics of human behaviour involve interactions among a variety of chemical and functional subsystems in the context of the organism as a whole. This part of *EN* is best seen as sketching a general strategy for coping with the stresses and strains involved, rather than as a descriptive psychology.

19 This language seems dubiously Aristotelian to me: in the light of § 2.32111, should we say that someone who 'philosophizes politics' is the 'architect of the end'? The provenance of these signposts around the text is always questionable.

20 The presentation of objections and rebuttals is rather a tangle. Ross's translation incorporates a helpful guide (of which Barnes's revision unfortunately omits all but the analysis of the objections themselves); Gauthier and Jolif (1958, II 771–9) give an admirable account of how the particular puzzles and objections relate to controversies of the day.

21 This argument is not conclusive. On the one hand, no sane person would undertake the immense labour of copying out unnecessary chapters by hand; on the other hand, it is less trouble to write 'insert *EE* IV–VI here' than to write 'insert *EE* IV–VI, but leave out the bit that starts *Peri de hēdonēs kai lupēs.*'

22 The consensus of recent authors favours this view; cf. Rorty 1980, 5; Broadie 1991, 314; Dirlmeier 1962, 586–7.

23 The difficulty lies not in persuading such people (they may not listen,

but so what?) but in justifying one's position in demonstrably relevant terms.

24 In these reductions, everything seems to hinge on the interpretation of some one expression – in the present formulation, 'I like ...' But there has to be some undefined term here: in Aristotle's terms, desire has to be one of the basic faculties of the psyche. Somewhere around here the wild goose is nesting.

25 What about rock climbing and crossword-puzzle solving, where the overcoming of difficulties is what we enjoy? In those cases, what is an impediment to the *process* of climbing the cliff or finishing the puzzle constitutes the very *activity* we enjoy. See Suits 1978.

26 Not all twentieth-century philosophers buy this argument, but some do. See, for example, Baier 1958, especially ch. 4.

27 There is an ambiguity here. When I am enjoying a game of tennis I am playing, what I am enjoying at any given moment is not just the stroke I am performing but the game I am playing, the present project within which my particular strokes, hopes, fears, fatigues, plans, and so on are aspects or phases. I experience the process of the game as a single activity. It is perhaps in reference to this totalizing aspect of experience that one speaks of such protracted enjoyments as 'enjoying oneself.' But Aristotle says nothing about that, so his discussion of the whole issue is unsatisfying.

28 The English phrase 'state of mind' may suggest passivity and imply quietism. Aristotle's own language has no such implication, and is better represented by the phrase 'state of being' that I used before. A conscious state of an organism is for him an *energeia*, the activity of the living being as alive and aware. He thinks of the 'soul' as the form, the realization (*entelecheia*) of the body as organized for life, and he thinks of living activity as the realization of the soul; hence what I call a 'conscious state' is not something divorced from the organism's movements and actions, it is the inward aspect of the embodied life as the organism lives it. But in *EN* VII Aristotle is not focusing his mind on this analysis from *On the Soul* II, even if he has already for-mulated it. That analysis does not definitively replace an earlier dualism; it is a nuanced reinterpretation of the same phenomena.

29 There are at least two other arguments that do not rest on this assumption: that all pleasure (and all pain) is a disturbance of the impassive equilibrium that wise people maintain; and that pleasure taken in wrong actions strengthens the tendency to perform them. Aristotle thinks the former of these is simply wrong, but the latter is valid, and it is largely for this reason that Book X withdraws the

contention that the pleasantness of an action is always a point in its favour.

30 The same fact is presupposed throughout Plato's *Philebus*, in which the priority of these pleasures is attributed to their violence. But that violence is associated with their impurity, their admixture with pain. Most of the dialectic of pleasure developed by Plato in the *Republic* and perfected in the *Philebus* is retained by Aristotle – assuming, that is, that the late *Philebus* is not itself a response to Aristotle's early work – and survives in Epicurus.

31 At 1172a29–b7, Aristotle will give this as one reason why moralists denounce pleasure.

32 The myth that a good appetite is painful persists, not only among philosophers but even among scientists. Thus W.H. Thorpe writes: 'Even the hunger drive amounts to something more than the immediate effect of the hunger pangs or hunger contraction' (1963, p. 18). Can't one enjoy one's food without having been so hungry that it hurts?

33 One should probably go further: without the specific civic pressures of a free city, in which all citizens participate in the direction of affairs, one cannot develop the autonomous life in which *logos* is fully exercised.

34 Aristotle adds that if both are in equilibrium, what is done is neither pleasant nor painful (1154b23–4). That seems to me to be nonsense.

35 See *Eudemus* fragment 41 Rose (p. 18 Ross, p. 2401 Barnes): 'Life without a body is natural for souls, and is comparable to health; life in a body, being against nature, to disease. There, they live in accordance with nature; here, against nature.' See also *Protrepticus* 15 Walzer (p. 52 Ross; not in Rose).

36 A particular difficulty is that the 'corruptible' element is apparently said to be *inside* the other nature (1154b22), rather than the mind coming into the psychophysical complex from 'outdoors' as in *Generation of Animals* II (736b28). If the present passage belongs with *EN* VIII–IX, the 'other' element might be something other than the perception and thought mentioned in IX ix – perhaps the autonomous passions implied in I xiii, the 'low passions' of 1169a14–15. Maybe this is a fuss about nothing: the intrusive element could be 'in' the soul as a whole. There is, however, a persistent ambiguity of dualisms in this discussion, between that of mind versus psychophysical organism and that of *logos*-permeated organisms versus anarchic passion – neither of which is quite the same as the contrast in Plato's *Phaedo* between the desire-driven body mechanism and the operations of the immortal life principle.

4 Love, Consciousness, and Society

1 There is no good translation for *philia*. The context shows the meaning well enough. For some discussion, see §4.23 below.

2 The *Republic* has a digression similarly placed: the treatment of drama in Book X has no organic connection with what immediately precedes or follows it, but comes at the last possible place before the theme of immortality introduces the concluding apotheosis of the just.

3 This is notoriously the question that harpooned Hobbes's *Leviathan* – the initial contract on which society is said to rest presupposes a practice of intercourse and language already in place.

4 This passage of *On Sleep* identifies sleeping and waking as alternative states of the organism; someone who is awake always perceives something, either externally or internally. 'Perception' in this extended sense must be what we would call 'consciousness' or 'awareness,' a concept for which Aristotle's language affords no special term.

5 This is not quite the same as what is said of interpersonal relations in the family as such, in *EN* VIII x.

6 The sentence linking Book VIII to its antecedents looks like one of those in which the editor (whether Aristotle or another) is trying to make sense of the *unexplained fact* of continuity present in the text (see Introduction, note 6).

7 Greek, like English, has a wealth of expressions for love and kindred emotions and relations. Among them: *philia*, affection; *erōs*, desire; *storgē*, maternal brooding care; *pothos*, yearning; *agapē*, esteem or appreciation (but see Spicq 1953); *himeros*, longing. What *philia* actually means is determined in part by the availability of this repertory for contrast. One's *philoi* include one's near and dear, including kin; in this context, it is the closeness that counts (see Cooper 1980, 334 n. 2), which is no doubt why Aristotle in these cases emphasizes the blood relationship rather than the sharing of experience. On the other side, 'friendship' in English carries a definite connotation of absence of affinity, so that we have to speak of 'married love' or 'parental love' for a relationship that would be called 'friendship' were the participants not kin. Conversely, 'love' tends to carry a connotation either of sexual involvement or of consanguinity. These conceptual tangles make it hard for philosophers (and others) to write about interpersonal relations without muddle or oversimplification.

8 This is what Aristotle says about food in *On the Soul* II 4, 416a19–b9.

9 The metaphor of soil and rain is, in any case, only a metaphor, and Aristotle's remark in context that he is not concerned with such

physical phenomena but only the relations between people may pro-
voke the thought that sexual attractions are, as we like to say, a matter of 'chemistry.'

10 If friendship is really reciprocal, could one not say that my active
awareness of your love for me is as important in my side of it as my
love for you? Perhaps, and Aristotle might have thought of that; but
my feeling for you is clearly direct and primary.

11 Since unrequited love has been contradistinguished from friendship,
the argument seems weak. Even in Aristotle's own terms, we have no
reason to suppose that a mother's tender care (storgē) is identical with
the active ingredient in friendship. And nowadays we would probably postulate an instinctive 'bonding' component in maternal care for
the neonate that would put it outside the terms of Aristotle's discussion. But such questioning of the example of maternal devotion leaves
the main contention untouched.

12 G.K. Chesterton, 'A Dedication: To E.C.B.' (1987, 13).

13 In addition to the two passages in EN, LSJ cite only one in Alexander
of Aphrodisias, and one in Plotinus. The word itself is simply the verbal noun from the verb philein (to love, kiss, like, approve of, be affectionate towards ...), as philēton is the adjective. At EN IX v
(1166b32–5), it is confined to personal affection stemming from personal acquaintance, which makes it seem like the active side of philia;
but the context here seems to rule that interpretation out.

14 Remember the suppressed aporia I mentioned: is a friend an external
good or a companion?

15 The assertion that virtue is more central to a person than a love of
music seems doctrinaire. It seems to rest on the metaphysical conviction that my essence, what makes me what I cannot cease to be
without ceasing to be myself, is to be a human being (as correctly
defined). I could cease to love music and still be me, but when I lose
the attributes of humanity I no longer exist as the being I was. But
this does not carry the argument, because I could turn into a rascally
or worthless human being and still be me; and a true music buff
might be recognizable by the shape and intensity of musical tastes
rather than by anything more conventionally constitutive. It is hard
not to beg questions in matters of this sort.

16 Aristotle makes no allowance, as we might do, for the belated emerg-
ence of quite unsuspected sides to a person's character, provided that
that person is virtuous: phronēsis is an undivided unity, and so
therefore must moral virtue be, and there is no place for change to
find a toe-hold. But this doctrine can afford only a hollow assurance:

if a person starts to act in an unexpected way, it shows that the apparent virtue formerly manifested was, after all, only a 'natural' virtue, or that the person is now acratic in the respect in question. That is, it is true *by definition* that a virtuous character is consistent: if a character shows itself inconsistent, that proves it was not virtuous. The definition does, however, have a practical point: people who are virtuous act deliberately and idealistically, and their actions are predictable in the sense that we can be sure they will not proceed from whimsy or unconsidered appetite. It makes no sense to make the practice of deliberation merely one sort of impulse among others. David Gallop reminds me of the way lawyers keep warning their clients of how people do change, how even the best people cannot be trusted to behave virtuously twenty years from now – no one's actions are predictable in the long term.

17 Plato in the *Philebus* makes much of the notion of 'false pleasures.' Today's philosophers rejoin that a pleasure cannot be false: one enjoys what one enjoys. That may be true, but there are all sorts of ways in which pleasures lead us astray, even in their experienced qualities; and that is what Plato is saying.

18 See, for instance, Theognis I 17: 'What is *kalon* is *philon*, and what is not *kalon* is not *philon*' (cf. also I 113). The relation between friendship and virtue is insinuated in Plato's *Lysis*.

19 It is instructive to consider here the contrast between 'group' and 'series' elaborated by Jean-Paul Sartre (1960). His views on the unreality of consciousness as such require him to hold that cooperation in pursuit of a common objective cannot engender any true fellow-feeling: in fact, since each is related separately to the objective, the possibility of conflict and mutual exclusion is always present. True comradeship arises only fitfully, when the common objective is so urgent and engrossing that the shared relationship is all that matters, so that the participants no longer have any relevant differences but form a 'group in fusion.' In less extreme situations, true groups are formed only by the members thinking of themselves as 'a group' from the objectifying standpoint of some potentially hostile Other. Aristotle, by contrast, thinks of people as conscious animals rather than as embodied consciousnesses, and regards the divergence of interest that might break down the solidarity of the 'series' not as an ontological fate but as something to be avoided by social and political engineering; and the feelings that sustain a group as a group are not an overwhelming epiphany or a conceptual construct but a natural function of the extent and intensity of cooperation.

416   Notes to pages 280–2

20 John Rawls remarks (1971, 491–2) that this proportionality presupposes that the conditions of cooperation are just, otherwise interaction
will only increase resentment. No doubt Aristotle is thinking of the
free cooperation of individuals, which will not take place if the conditions are unacceptable.

21 The *Republic* (425A–E) suggests that good education makes elaborate
legislation unnecessary: rights and duties need to be spelled out only
when people lack sufficient goodwill to ensure that they spontaneously do what is best. But, in the absence of a specific agreement, members of large associations may have no way of determining what *is*
best. And the position eventually put forward in the dialogue is not
that popular goodwill makes administration unnecesary but that administrative goodwill makes regulation of administrators unnecessary.

22 See Hannah Arendt's remarks (1963, 259ff.) on factory soviets after
the Russian revolution: they worked well in the short term, but were
destroyed by the impetus of their own procedures.

23 Is not this incompatible with the contention that justice and friendship
co-vary? No; the framework of justice can exist before any active
relationship is established.

24 What is Aristotle thinking about here? Presumably the inequality is in
power and status. A structural relationship makes a personal relationship impossible. But should it and does it? Can't a king have personal
friends with whom the question of status is simply ignored? As
Aristotle says, can't a free person be a friend of a slave, not as a slave
but as a person (1161b2–8)? Aristotle had slaves and spent much of
his life at royal courts, and the negative tone of his discussion perhaps reflects the experience that a king remains a king and a slave
remains a slave, and these facts can be ignored only by a carefully
sustained limitation of intercourse that itself militates against real
friendship. If the power relationships are kept in mind, the friendship
can be sustained. Beau Brummel maintained a friendly relation with
the Prince Regent until he asked the Prince to ring for the servant.
The Prince did so, and told the servant to call a cab for Mr Brummel;
and that was the end of that.

25 That whoever says 'we' feels 'we' is admittedly a Sartrian rather than
an Aristotelian thought; but it seems a legitimate interpretation of
Aristotle's argument here.

26 Cf. note 19 above.

27 An obvious dislocation in the received text (1160a19–23 seem to be an
alternative version of 1160a18 and 23–30) does not affect the general
sense of the passage.

28 One needs to be a bit careful here. We can say why a particular city comes into existence and why it continues, but 'the city' in general did not come into existence; there have always been cities. What are to be explained are two recurrent phenomena, two standing features of the world: the generation of cities, and the existence of cities. So too, we should not ask how friendship comes into the world, it was always there.

29 This account of the origin of the city is in *Politics* I and in Plato's *Laws* 680.

30 The classification of constitutions is found in Herodotus III 80–3 (where it is put in a Persian context), and becomes standard: it is found in Plato's *Republic* VIII and *Statesman*, as well as *Laws* III. Note that the description of 'aristocacy' defines its defensible principle, not the actual practice of deferring to upper-class twits.

31 Aristotle is here merely simplifying *Laws* III. At 1160b9–28, he introduces what looks like a covert critique of the theory of political degeneration developed by Plato in *Republic* VIII: instead of the sequence monarchy–aristocracy–oligarchy–democracy–tyranny developed there, he insists that the likeliest degenerations are the simplest, in which each lawful form of government passes over into its lawless counterpart, so that monarchy tends to pass straight into tyranny. It is because Aristotle's scenario is so much more plausible than Plato's that the *Republic* utopia is so strenuously rejected by superficial readers, who refuse to take seriously the features by which Socrates distinguishes it from its opposite.

32 We observe that Aristotle considers relationships between brothers, and says nothing about sisters. His theory cannot accommodate the extreme sexual discrimination institutionalized in Athenian and other Greek laws. See the next note.

33 We might have expected a fourth, the boss–slave relation, since Aristotle includes this among the basic family relationships in *Politics* I. One reason for its exclusion here is given at 1161a32–b8 in a slightly different connection: there can be no friendship between boss and slave as such, for that relationship excludes and denies their common humanity. They can be friends only as human beings, that is, by ignoring the power relation. But there is a second, deeper, difference between *Politics* I and the present discussion. *Politics* I is about *oikonomikē*, the structure of the minimal self-contained economic unit, the family farm with its patriarch and its division between gathering and preserving functions. The topic of the present passage is *sungenikē*, relationships depending on blood ties. This changes every-

thing: slaves are now excluded, the function of patriarchy is minimized, the children are integral to the system and not mere replacement parts.

34 'Necessity' for Aristotle, especially when he is thinking carefully, tends to be equated with the material cause, that without which some end will not be achieved. But he also equates it with mechanical processes. In the case of sex, without procreation there will be no family; but it is also true that the sexual urge is a compelling force.

35 In this, Aristotle is reversing what is often taken to be a standard emphasis of Greco-Roman antiquity, in which it is said that the family, the Greek *genos* and more especially the Roman *gens*, is conceptually and emotionally primary and the individual is thought of as merely a participant in and continuer of the family. The standard reference is Glotz 1904.

36 This biological drive is perhaps included among the 'physical' relationships which we have seen Aristotle excludes as irrelevant to his concern. The supposition that sexual relations are essentially friendly may be what accounts for the mistaken notion that the basis of friendship is complementarity, as we saw above.

37 Aristotle does not say so in so many words, but the general tendency of *Politics* IV suggests that each of the three analogues of family relationships has its own justification in its own context: kingship in power relations, especially in war; specialization in economic affairs of all kinds; democracy in committees and discussions of general policy. They can and should all exist together, and should not be thought of exclusively as founding rival types of constitution, as the Greek tradition habitually does. One might also say, though Aristotle does not, that the affectionate feelings generated by these relationships differ in kind: democracy gives rise to camaraderie, specialism to a mutual respect, and monarchy to reverence on the one side and what one can only call providence (*pronoia*) on the other.

38 VIII xiii to IX iii are plainly a single discussion; the division between the books here is merely a matter of the length of papyrus rolls. The treatment of the hazards of friendship is in some ways parallel to the treatment of the hazards of virtue in VII i–vi – but not, I think, in any interesting way.

39 Is it worth remarking that the topic of friendship among unequals does not move Aristotle to consider relations between humans and domestic animals? Were it not for Odysseus and his dog Argos in *Odyssey* XVII, one might say that to pay attention to such matters is a peculiarity of modern sentimentality.

40 This language is reminiscent of the 'unmoved mover' of *Metaphysics* XII, whose sole activity is self-awareness. I suppose the idea is that human happiness is the conscious living of a good life, and hence depends both on there being a good life and on there being a consciousness of it – and the consciousness is not separate from what it is conscious of, just as one's awareness that one is seeing something is not separate from one's seeing it, and hence from the 'it' that one sees (*On the Soul* III 2). A perfectly blissful consciousness would have to be one in which this division was not even thinkable, hence an awareness (*nous*) that was nothing but being aware of being aware (*noēsis noēseōs*). This may make no sense to us, but we would not expect it to. Nor does it need to; it is an inference formally required by things that do make sense.

41 What Aristotle actually begins by saying is that the attributes of friendship (*ta philika*) towards others seem to have 'come from' those attributes toward oneself. What sort of relationship this 'coming from' is we are not told. This seems to presuppose that *ta philika* are recognizable in abstraction from their interpersonal context, a rather breathtaking assumption unless one supposes a 'form of friendship' on the Platonic model that could be manifested in any sort of embodiment. Gauthier and Jolif (see note 46 below) take the whole of IX iv–vi to be a mere polemic against Platonic notions, in which profound-seeming remarks occur as it were by accident; but the passage does not read to me like a polemic.

42 It is hard to convey the scandalous nature of this passage because the idiom whereby 'the self' is a substantive is so thoroughly at home in today's English: when I talk to myself, we calmly swallow the implication that there is a 'self' that I talk to. But this reifying use of emphatic and reflexive pronouns had not taken hold in Aristotle's Greek. On the other hand, I confess that my phrase 'projection of the ego' is one that has no clear sense, and any unclear sense it had would be one that could not be ascribed to Aristotle. We have no clear ways of talking about these matters because we have no clear ways of thinking about them.

43 The argument is scandalous in that it destroys the contrast between oneself and other people: interpersonal relations take their character from holding between different people, and oneself is the only person with whom one cannot share anything. In Book V, we rejected the notion of justice between me and myself on just these grounds: we allowed only for the metaphor by which 'interpersonal' relationships may hold between different 'parts' of a person's character, an excep-

tion that seems inapplicable here. However, Aristotle does not explicitly endorse the formulation that oneself is one's own best friend (cited as the implication of certain proverbial expressions at 1168b10), substituting relatively innocuous forms of words. Since in friendship we have to do with attitudes, it is certainly possible for people to take up an attitude towards various aspects of themselves, or to themselves as objects of thought.

44 To make this go through, in the light of the fact that we can certainly make friends with inconsistent people, we have to consider that other people are present to us unified by the recognizable bodies they present to the world, but this guarantee of unification is not available to us in our own case, we have nothing but our conscious unity of personality to go on. But this may lead to the reflective consideration that we are to others a corporeally available entity as they are to us, and that the true unity we are aware of in them is that of their personality. This topic is a matter of endless discussion under the head of 'personal identity,' eminently suitable for beginning students in philosophy.

45 'Loving one's life' sounds like contentment with one's lot, one's passively assigned 'station in life.' But that is not what we mean, and has been ruled out from the beginning by the way *eudaimonia* was defined in I vii.

46 Gauthier and Jolif (1958, II 726) argue that these are five *definitions* of friendship proposed in the Academy, all of them based on disinterestedness rather than on the sharing of lives. But their authority seems to be Von Arnim, relying on *Magna Moralia* 1211b40, so people whose faith in *MM* is imperfect will want a bit more evidence.

47 This interprets *kakia lanthanei*, 'the badness goes unnoticed' (1150b36).

48 The argument here has surprising affinities with the sophistical thesis scouted in the *Euthydemus* (283), according to which wishing people to change is to wish for their death, since it is wishing them to cease to be (what they now are).

49 Compare I viii, where a good person's life is contrasted with others as needing no *addition* of pleasure.

50 The following words, 'if to be thus is the height of wretchedness, we should strain every nerve to avoid wickedness [*mochthēria*] and should endeavour to be good [*epieikē*],' 1166b27–8, are said by Dirlmeier (1962, 269) to be the only hortatory remark in *EN*.

51 If I had never seen other people but had imperfectly reflecting surfaces in my surroundings, I might be able to figure out what my face looked like. But only when I actually saw a face would I really know

what a human face looks like. But without already knowing more or less what I looked like, I would not know that the face I now saw clearly was what my own face looked like.

52 Stewart (1892, II 353) says that good people's relations to themselves cannot precede in time their relations to friends, because good people can exist only in cities which are themselves based on friendship. But cities depend on the diffuse and low-grade *philia* of a community, and the high-grade *philia* of good individuals depends on the city.

53 One might think that public censure, to which Aristotle often appeals, is irrelevant to the question of vice and virtue because the latter are carefully defined without any reference to what people may approve or disapprove. Might there not be societies so ill run that bad people are there thought to be good people? But even there one might expect them to find their lives less than perfectly satisfactory, because one would not know how to fault a social order in which the approved behaviour yielded complete satisfaction to all those who followed it. By such viability the way of life would prove itself to be natural.

54 David Gallop, who draws this contradiction to my attention, thinks it may show that *EN* VIII–IX must have been written before *EN* VII, at a time when the distinction between vice and weakness had not been formulated. It does seem unlikely that anyone who had thought of the distinction in Book VII would have written the present passage. (Gauthier and Jolif [1958, II 734] sort it out as follows, in terms of the typology of Book VII: the *phauloi* of 1166b3 are the wicked, the *komidēi phauloi* of 1166b5 are the 'beastly,' and the people referred to in 1166b6ff are meant to be wicked but are actually morally weak: the *hoion* at 1166b8 means 'viz.,' so that the 'morally weak' referred to there are taken as typically *phauloi*.) Of course, if *EN* VII originated in *EE*, which is earlier than *EN* as a whole, the present passage would come from a very early phase in Aristotle's career, which would be consistent with it representing an internal debate within the Academy. It is perfectly possible that such a passage could be included in a later compilation without being thoroughly revised.

55 Richard Sorabji cites (1980, 267 n34) the following passages in which people acting viciously are convinced they are doing the right thing: 1127b14, 1134a17–23, 1135b25, 1137a4–26, 1138a20, 1144a27 and 35, 1146b22–3, 1148a17, 1150a20 and 24, 1150b36, 1151a7 and 13–26, 1152a6 and 24 – much more often than they are said to be inadvertent.

56 I doubt that such an idea can be clearly formulated otherwise than in a thought-world in which it seems possible that the world order is at

.   once established by an entirely arbitrary will (endlessly affirming I
    AM) and at the same time indisputably good.

57 Iago's 'Evil, be thou my good' makes no sense. All Iago is likely to
    have meant was that he would give free rein to the jealous resent-
    ment that he happened to feel, without caring whether it was right to
    do so or not. But, as Plato observes in *Republic* X, playwrights do not
    have to imagine precise meanings or realistic psychologies for their
    characters – only visual and auditory presences.

58 The Greek terms, *eunoia* and *homonoia*, are etymologically related to
    each other (and to *pronoia*, 'providence'). The common component,
    -noia, connotes something like 'mindfulness' (it is also part of our
    word *paranoia!*). I cannot think of any way of suggesting this connec-
    tion in English; nothing hangs on it, but the terms do make a more
    obvious couple in Greek.

59 Cf. Plato's *Symposium* 206–9 and *Republic* 330 C, as well as *EN*
    1120b13–15. Note the transformation this topic undergoes. The *Sympo-
    sium*, concerned with *erōs*, the love of what one lacks, makes poets
    love their poems and parents their children as earnest of their future
    immortality, the preservation of their memory and life; the present
    passage, concerned with *philia* and shared life in the present, makes
    them earnest of one's present existence and vitality and potency – one
    lives oneself out in them. The two emphases seem equally well or ill
    based on familiar stereotypes of authorship and parenthood.

60 Aristotle glosses over the fact that there may be competitions in vir-
    tue, since occasions for heroism may be in short supply (as Aristotle
    will sardonically suggest at 1177b6–12). He points out that, in such
    cases, the better part may be to give up to one's friend the opportun-
    ity for distinction ('Here you go, Tosh, your turn to throw yourself on
    the grenade – I've got a VC already'). But he fails to consider whether
    it may not be even more meritorious to forgo on a friend's behalf this
    very sacrifice of opportunity ('No, that's all right, Chev, I don't need
    a VC, you go ahead') ... and so ad infinitum. These refinements of
    lifemanship are doubtless better avoided, but the implicit difficulty
    about 'selfishness' remains. Aristotle can sustain his case because
    there are very few people who actually value virtue above cash or
    safety. I suppose two *really* virtuous friends would avoid emulation
    altogether, and just toss for the honour or something; to *compete* for it
    would be reduce it to the level of an external good.

61 The true self whose interests are to be promoted is identified at
    1168b31f. as the 'most authoritative' part or aspect of oneself, *hautou
    to kuriōtaton* – as in any organized entity (*sustēma*). Is this the reason-

ing, thinking part of oneself? Yes, I suppose so (cf. 1166a16–23, 1177a12–15); but the formulation fits the context, it is *whatever* in oneself makes one a single organized person. As (in *On the Soul* II i) the soul makes the body an organism and hence truly a body, so the habit of considering one's life as a whole constitutes it an integrated lifetime, and hence truly a life.

62 Mark Thornton reminds me that even in commercial transactions 'self-love' would not be reduced to the quest for a good bargain; virtuous people retain their virtue in the market-place.

63 The 'independence' of good people, a nebulous notion indeed, must not be confused with the logical 'self-sufficiency' of *eudaimonia*. The latter requires only that happiness be so defined as to include all aspects of well-being, on the ground that it cannot be the only thing that is desired for itself alone and never for the sake of anything else unless it actually leaves nothing else to be desired.

64 This whole issue is admirably discussed in Cooper 1980.

65 Burnet (1900) gives a formal analysis of this argument, revised and included by Ross as a footnote in the Oxford translation. I follow Hardie (1968, 332 n1) in simply pointing the reader in this direction.

66 'Physical' explanations are contrasted with 'dialectical,' and also with explanations drawn from extraneous disciplines. Thus physical explanations in ethics have to do with the structure of practical reasoning and its basic premises (cf. 1147a24, § 3.112); these are contrasted both with explanations drawn from physiology and with 'dialectical' explanations that rely on popular stereotypes and other presuppositions about what is the case – the sorts of explanations laypeople give each other and orators rely on.

67 Cf. *Protrepticus* 7 Walzer, pp. 36–7 Ross, pp. 2412–13 (B 73–4) Barnes (not in Rose); other parallels are cited in Gauthier and Jolif 1958, II 756.

68 This is implicit in the equation of human 'function' in I vii with a life of the *logon echon*, which is dependent on perception. Everything is mediated by language and language-like symbolisms.

69 Aristotle says he will explain these alleged indeterminacies later, but I cannot see that he does. The explanation of the indeterminacy of pain is the same as that given for the indeterminacy of vice: if pleasure is unimpeded activity, this is possible in respect of any situation only in one way, that in which all relevant perfections coincide. Any impediment may destroy pleasure and introduce pain, which is thus possible in an indefinite number of ways. The argument has something absurd about it: the toad beneath the harrow knows that every pain is

determinately just the pain it is, and every vice is just the vice it is, but it will pass muster so long as we pose the contrast in general terms. The argument may be directed against the contention in the *Philebus* that pleasure and pain are equally indeterminate, both being unquantifiable forms of psychic disturbance. Aristotle, by making pleasure an *activity* of 'the soul' (that is, of the organism in its unity or its intellect), in which vitality is realized, rather than a psychic epiphenomenon of a corporeal condition, destroys the basis of this argument by removing the symmetry between 'pleasure' and 'pain.'

70 This assumes that the 'major premise' of a bad person's life is neither a different premise from that of the good person nor its contrary, but its contradictory (cf. § 4.611). Good people think it incumbent on them to act thus and so, bad people see no reason why they should. Aristotle says things that suggest otherwise, speaking at 1146b22 of people who 'judge that one should always pursue the present pleasure'; that certainly sounds positive and definite enough, but this is something of an illusion unless 'present pleasure' means something more definite than Aristotle formally allows that it does. If pleasure is simply whatever immediately attracts, the supposed positive principle comes to no more than having a policy of allowing no principles to stand in the way of doing what one feels like – being the sort of person whom Aristotle refers to as 'the scoundrel who follows worthless feelings' (*ho mochthēros ... phaulois pathesin hepomenos*, 1169a14).

71 Wedin (1988, 141), referring to *Metaphysics* 990b24, has some penetrating remarks on the sense in which two people can have the same thought, and the sense in which they cannot; and later, in connection with the self-thinking mind of *Metaphysics* XII 9, on the impossibility of thought without a determinate object and the consequent impossibility for humans of direct self-thought (p. 265).

72 The joys and dynamics of crowds and throngs perhaps arise from the feeling that one has more close friends than one could possibly have really, *alle Menschen werden Brüder*.

73 One may well ask how the friendship of bad people can be pleasant, since evil is inherently unlovable. If it were not, bad people could be at ease with themselves, which Aristotle denies. Are we then to say that friendships between bad people must be either for pleasure or utility, or else rest on such innocuous shared pursuits as pool? But of such superficial friendships the objections Aristotle levels would scarcely hold.

A fine distinction is made at this point, which Aristotle does not elaborate here (or, I believe, elsewhere). Because bad people are unstable (*abebaioi*) they share in worthless things (*phaulōn*); and their mutual imitation makes them wicked (*mochthēroi*), I take it that the first point is that the pleasures they share are trivial, idle, unconstructive, and soon abandoned, but their mutual influence ('daring' each other and so on) leads them into positively vicious action. Perhaps vice (having no *mesotēs* of its own) cannot sustain itself within a personality, but can do so in gangs with a traditional practice. Aristotle's view of vice then becomes easier to follow if one thinks of bad people as young delinquents rather than as Napoleons of crime – a concept Aristotle could scarcely have formulated (and not just because Napoleon had not been born or Moriarty invented).

74 It has long been common to say that people construct and construe their lives in terms of narratives that they tell themselves. Neither Aristotle nor any of his contemporaries had thought of that. This makes it hard for us to figure out what they are saying and what they are not saying about the role of language in self-knowledge.

75 This would not be true of a god or any incorporeal thinker, presumably.

76 This is why TV comedies have laugh tracks, to simulate the sharing that is the joy of laughter in a theatre or cinema. Only the devil laughs alone.

77 Compare also Oliver Sacks's quotation of a post-encephalitic Parkinsonian patient: 'When you walk with me, I feel in myself your own power of walking. I *partake* of the power and freedom you have. I *share* your walking powers, your perceptions, your feelings, your existence. Without even knowing it, you make me a great gift' (1987, 248). The central difficulty with Aristotle's treatment of friendship (as with his whole *Ethics*, and anyone else's ethical theory, for that matter) is that his undertaking obliges him to impose a schematism on a mass of material of extraordinary diversity. Useful as such schemata may be, at certain points one has to rebel and say 'Life is not like that.'

78 The difference made by sharing partly explains the split made in Book X (but not in Book VII) between an activity and the pleasure that crowns it. I can take pleasure in perception simply as the actualization of form; the pleasure is mine in a way that the perception is not, because if my condition is normal the form of the perception comes entirely from the object perceived, only the matter being contributed by me as percipient. But, in general, only good people are normal. Bad people will not see or think of things in the same way as each other, except by coincidence of history or circumstance.

79 Am I alone in finding this contention overstated? If one is lost in a country where one dislikes the natives and does not speak their language, a face and voice from home may certainly be welcome. But if I am enjoying the unfamiliar life and managing to communicate, the last thing I want is to be latched on to by a hoser from Toronto who will insist on talking about the Blue Jays.
80 Wollheim 1984, 277.
81 Auden 1962, 402–3.

5 *The Worth of Pleasure*

1 This argument is also used by J.S. Mill (1861), and is met with the same objection, that it confuses what is preferred with what is preferable. What Mill actually says is that you can't *prove* that pleasure is desirable, but everyone desires it, and that is the best *evidence* you could have. You would need a really bizarre view of the world and of the place of humanity in it to suppose that a motivation so universal is a baseless sort of error. But Aristotle is entitled to the argument in a way that Mill was not, for Aristotle thinks we are living in a real world, and in Mill's day it was thought acceptable among educated people to substitute for reason and experience the fanciful and self-serving lucubrations of priests and prophets. Not that Aristotle was ignorant of such things (cf. 1095a25–6); it just did not occur to him that educated people might be expected to take them seriously.
Aristotle's actual sentence here (1172b36) is ambiguous, and could be taken to mean generally that what everyone believes to be true must be true. But there is no reason to suppose that that is what is meant here, since no such thesis is maintained by Aristotle elsewhere, whereas he does constantly hold that practical problems arise within acceptances based on actual predicaments (which can only be based on perceived values).
2 Aristotle uses as example the inability of aficionados of the flute to concentrate on their studies when they overhear a flute being played. Aldous Huxley provides an ironic illustration in *Point Counter Point* (1928, ch. 3).
3 At 1175b33, we are told that pleasure and activity are so indissolubly linked that it is debatable whether they are identical. But the criteria of identity in such cases are nowhere specified. (In general, one might wonder how one could form the judgment that A always went with B if A and B were literally the same; if A and B co-vary, they probably form part of a single system, but presumably not the *same* part.)

Book VII holds that pleasures *are* activities but what is good as pleasure may be bad as activity, whereas Book X, claiming that pleasures are not activities but their completions, holds that if the activity has a certain value its completion must have the same value. The explanation of this apparent inconsistency is that a mere completion is too insubstantial to have a separate value of its own, but an activity has enough robust reality to be considered under two aspects. The underlying rationale is that pleasure and activity are, in any case, so closely linked that they must be either one thing under two aspects or two things under one aspect, so that if their distinctness is denied on the axiological plane it must be reintroduced on the ontological plane.

4 'Beauty' in the quoted phrase renders *hōra*, and 'in their prime' renders *akmaiois*. But it is not clear exactly what those words mean. To be *akmaios* is to be in one's prime but, depending on context, this may be fulness of vigour or the high point of sexual attractiveness. *Hōra* literally means 'season,' but in Plutarch's *Life of Agesilaus*, 34, this is explained as the time when people look most pleasing (the transition from boyhood to manhood), and in Aristophanes' *Birds* 1723 it forms a doublet with 'beauty' (*kallos*). One sees more or less what Aristotle has in mind, but it is not clear just how different the meanings of the two terms are, and this is crucial. Is the point meant to be that *at a certain age* charm supervenes, or that charm supervenes on the physically attractive features of (some) people who attain that age – or simply that what we call 'the prime' is a more general condition that comes to people at a certain time of life? Perhaps Aristotle would be content to leave the relation between pleasure and activity in a similar ambiguity; but, if so, the reader has a legitimate grievance.

5 Does beauty depend entirely on physical features, or does it depend partly on such things as vivacity or expression? If the latter is accepted, Aristotle's unhappily multivalent simile becomes less helpful than ever.

6 The argument in the text here is no doubt influenced by Frank Sibley's famous article 'Aesthetic Concepts' (1959) and the massive controversy that persisted through the next decade about the relation between such aesthetic properties as beauty and the measurable physical properties on which they must somehow be based. Aristotle had not read Sibley.

7 John Rist (1989, 110–12) shows how Aristotle's concept of *energeia* changes – partly as a result of his thinking about pleasure. But he does not take *EN* IX ix into account.

8 The general notion of enjoyment seems unproblematic, in that we

know what it is to enjoy doing something – obviously the relation will not be describable in terms of any other relation to which it might be reduced, but will be a basic and pervasive aspect of human life, so it should not bother us that it often leaves us at a loss for words. But it is not clear that the notion of enjoyment covers everything we mean by 'pleasure' when we are thinking of sexual activity, for example. Both Plato and Aristotle meet this difficulty by distinguishing between pleasures that involve bodily disturbances and antecedent or accompanying discomforts and those that do not involve them. This makes the distinction extrinsic, a matter of contexts and contrasts. But I do not find this very convincing. Again, I am not sure how Aristotle's theory of pleasure accommodates the phenomena of cheerfulness (*chairein*) and euphoria.

9 Ross's translation at 1174b14–19 twice uses the word 'organ,' so that pleasure is made to depend on the best condition of organs and objects. But Aristotle uses no such word, though he does say that one may speak indifferently of a (sense) activity or of that in which the activity is. The difference is important, because if we say that visual pleasure depends on the state of the 'organ' it sounds as if we are talking about 20–20 vision (so that the preferred visual object should be something sharply defined and finely detailed). The text can be read more generally as saying that not the eye but the seer must be in the best condition, so that Aristotle is well able to accommodate Coleridge's 'Depression' ('I see, not feel, how beautiful they are'), even if he does not actually take moods into account.

10 See *Metaphysics* IX 1050b22–8 for the claim that the maintenance of activity involves fatigue for all beings that have the capacity for inactivity, and Thorpe 1963, p. 349, for the contention that continued activity both facilitates and inhibits continuation of activity of the same sort.

11 Kenny (1963, 149) notes that if the goodness of the object is so defined as to include enjoyability nothing is explained, whereas if it is not so defined Aristotle's claim seems false. He thinks that making the criteria of enjoyability independent of specific occasions (appealing to the normal tastes of normal people with normal eyesight) may dispose of the objection; but I see no need to be even as specific as that.

12 The same point was made about friendship, when the consideration that bad people ought not to make friends was eventually allowed to obliterate the initial contention that friendship as such was always good (1172a8–10).

13 Though this is consistent with the repeated claim that the pleasure of

a god would be the pleasure of pure intellection, I am not convinced that this remark is not an interpolation: it goes against the thrust of the passage, and the context is better without it.

14 Aristotle would not accept the view that since activity is essentially perception and thought there is no real difference between skating and dreaming or hallucinating that one is skating: *aisthēsis* and *noēsis* are modes of objective cognition, not subjective conditions.

15 The phrase *en tois ēthikois* might be rendered 'in our discussion of individual behaviour' rather than 'in the *Ethics*' – we cannot be sure that it alludes to an already named work.

16 Ramsauer (1878, 488) remarks that the substantive reference is not so much to 1153a12ff. as to the formula for happiness at 1101a18ff., 'activity in accordance with complete virtue' etc. – compare 1153b16, 'no activity is complete [*teleios*] when it is impeded.'

17 Enjoy it, or take some deep satisfaction in it; even the bravest man, Aristotle says at 1117b15–16, does not enjoy himself on the battlefield, though there is nowhere he would rather be.

18 This modern view of the human condition is explored in Taylor 1989. The quotation is from George Herbert's poem 'The Elixir.'

19 One recalls Plato's reference to the injured carpenter who demands speedy treatment from his doctor because he has no leisure for invalidism (*ou scholē kamnein*), he has a job to do with without which *life is not worth living (ouk elusitelei zēn)* (*Republic* 406D–E). The language is interesting from our point of view: note the ambivalent attitude to leisure, and the apparent equation of worthwhileness with profitability. This sorts well with Socrates' assumption in *Republic* I that arts have two aspects, function and recompense; but note that, in the context, the carpenter's attitude is contrasted with frivolity and idleness.

Unlike Aristotle, Plato writes like someone living in a world full of people with real lives to live; but, again unlike Aristotle, like someone who does not live in a family. This may have something to do with the fact that Aristotle was an alien in Athens, a man with no homeland, no neighbours, familiar only with his family and his philosophical associates.

6 The Good Life and the Best Life: Outline of a Discourse

1 1176a30–1; the words 'forms' and 'varieties,' in Ross's translation, have no counterpart in the original and may be misleading.

2 'The rest of virtue' covers moral virtue together with *phronēsis*; one tends to think of it simply as moral virtue, but that is a bad mistake.

3 The equation of an activity with the perception and thought involved in it makes this distinction between actions and their consequences ambiguous. The consequences of doing something are, in way, the result of the actual movements involved in the material world; the perception and thought, as *energeiai*, are what they are and can have no consequences, though they may be remembered and regretted or rejoiced in. But Aristotle says nothing to show that he made this distinction, and in fact it has no obvious practical point.

4 This is the implication of Sextus Empiricus, *Outlines of Pyrrhonism* I xi 23–4.

5 The strongest evidence for this is the phenomenon of sleep, and Aristotle's most confident and emphatic affirmation of the principle is at *On Sleep and Waking* 454a29–32, where it is applied to the *ergon* of perception. Presumably the function of humanity, virtuous activity, is similarly incapable of continuous exercise, and this will be as true of the moral virtues as it is of the intellect.

6 The relation between happiness and contributory means or components actually has to be much more complex than this; see the meticulous and exhaustive treatments by Kraut (1989) and Broadie (1991).

7 *Iliad* VI 208 etc. Homer gets round this by assigning to each young man a battle of which he is the hero, as in Andy Warhol's world where everyone is a celebrity for fifteen minutes.

8 What Aristotle says is that 'no one allows a slave a share in happiness, if not even in life [*ei mē kai biou*].' What does this mean? Slaves are certainly alive; what they do not have is precisely a *bios*, a life to live. Rist (1989, 249) would like to emend *biou* to *nou*: 'The slave cannot be happy because he has no intelligence (or mind).' But Rist is thinking of the 'natural slaves' who are incapable of organizing their own lives (*Politics* I, 1252a34). Real slaves are not like that; they are ordinary people who have been purchased or captured. To make the point perfectly clear, the word used in the present passage is *andrapodon*, the very etymology of which points to status slavery; the word in the *Politics* is *doulos*, which has no such connotation.

9 The conceptual tension is resolved in the discussion of pleasure at *Rhetoric* I 11, where Aristotle says that 'serious' acts 'involve compulsion and force, unless we are accustomed to them, in which case it is custom that makes them pleasant' (1370a12–14) – the word for 'custom' being the one we translate as 'habit' in the discussion of moral virtues; and of 'serious games' that 'some of these become pleasant when one becomes accustomed to them, while others are pleasant from the start' (1371a3–5). But it is never safe or easy to reconcile the

Ethics with the *Rhetoric*, since they allow fundamentally different relative weights to precision and plausibility.

10 Aristotle's initial stipulation of the happy person's need for external prosperity said that such a person must be 'adequately fitted out' (*hikanōs kechorēgēmenon*, 1101a15, repeated at 1177a30). It is time to cash the metaphor out. The reference is to the way Athenian theatrical producers were provided with funds to mount their productions. So, whose treasury defrays the expenses of individual happiness?

11 For a somewhat free-wheeling account of the Stoic concept of art, see Sparshott 1978.

12 At 1177a17–18 Aristotle says this has been stated already. It is not clear that it has; certainly it was not asserted where we would expect it, at the end of Book VI. But in the light of 1170b11–12 in Book IX, not to mention I v and many other hints along the way, anyone who is surprised by the announcement here must be (to use an Aristotelian phrase from III v) 'completely imperceptive.'

The word *theōria* resists translation. It is the regular word for sight-seeing, spectatorship at a theatrical or sporting event, 'seeing the world' as a tourist; in affairs of the mind, it can mean theory as opposed to practice, cognizing a reality that is there to be cognized as opposed both to fanciful speculation and to discursive explanation. Aristotle's use of the term has to be related to his ideal of a perfected science as stated in *EN* VI iii and vi–vii and elaborated in *Posterior Analytics*, a deductive system corresponding to the timeless structure of the real world; I have accordingly sometimes rendered the word as 'science and philosophy.' The customary translation, 'contemplation,' is accurate but wholly misleading.

13 Maritain 1930. His argument is concerned directly with Thomism, but it is directly relevant to Aristotle.

14 At 1101a14, recapitulating this formula, Aristotle omits the require-ment that the virtue be the 'best' and simply stipulates that it be *teleia*, with the sense of this word being fixed as 'complete' rather than 'perfect' by his adding in the same sentence that it be exercised 'in a complete life' (and by using the adjective in its positive rather than its superlative form as before).

15 For the thesis that this passage is a Platonic survival see, for instance, Monan 1968.

16 As recruits in the British Army in July 1944, my intake were expecting to serve in the infantry in the Burmese jungle. One other recruit and I had identification numbers belonging to a different series from the rest; when asked why, we explained that we had been selected to

study Japanese. The general reaction of our fellow recruits was expressed by one who said 'Give me —ing Burma!' Aristotle's praise of the intellectual life puts me in mind of that young man.

17 See Gauthier and Jolif 1958, II 878–9.

18 See Vlastos 1975. The most sympathetic and illuminating treatment of Aristotle's attitude to his own work is Lear 1988 (for the point at issue in this section, see especially p. 311).

19 Urmson 1973, 161; Wilkes 1980, 354.

20 Again, the best guide to how Aristotle's mind works here is Lear – but in a different work (1980).

21 Lear 1988, 133. He goes on to say that 'the highest level of human soul will be found in the mind of the person who is actively contemplating the essence of human life.' This may be true, and makes the important point that in such reflection we have an analogue of the 'thought thinking about thinking' in *Metaphysics* XII; but it needs to be balanced against Aristotle's insistence that humanity is not the greatest thing in existence.

22 Contemporary readers tend to miss this, because even if they are not theists they are brought up in a theistic ambiance: the world order is fully realized in the mind of the God who created it. Recognition and rejection of this set of ideas usually involves a hard-headed refusal to think at all about such matters as the implications of the possibility of science.

23 To see what life 'according to *nous*' is, see Book VI (cf. note 12 above). *Nous* enables us to formulate true axioms and definitions, and the life 'according to' it is one governed by concern with such principles and whatever may be deduced from them, that is, the practice of philosophy and science as intellectual disciplines. It is worth noting that Aristotle does not use the expression 'theoretical life' (*theōrētikos bios*), but only 'theoretical activity' and 'life according to *nous*.'

24 The language used is significant: throughout this chapter the virtue of speculative reason has been called the *kratistē*, 'best' in the sense of most high-powered and related to the aspect of oneself that has the same sort of supremacy. But what we are now told is that this life and virtue are too high-powered (same word, *kreittōn*) for humanity.

25 After a valuable review of Aristotle's language here, Michael Wedin concludes (1988, 211) that 'so far, then, from showing that we ever do anything that the gods do, the most *EN* X shows is that we sometimes do something like what the gods always do.'

26 The language of the *Symposium* (207D), which applies to human aspiration generally and not specifically to philosophy, is closer to

Aristotle's: what is sought by the 'mortal nature' (*thnētē phusis*, just as in the *Theaetetus*) is 'to exist for ever and be immortal, as far as possible'; and this is said to be possible only through procreation (just as it is for animals according to Aristotle's *On the Soul*), or through the metaphorical procreation of creative work. But what Aristotle is saying is something else again.

27 For the significance of this verbal termination, see Schwyzer 1959, vol. 1, 722–36. I have not found anything comparable on verbs in *-euein*; but see note 34 below.

28 Even more absurd is the complaint (found in the correspondence column of the *Guardian Weekly* in the fall of 1992) that Aristotle shows his élitism by denying slaves a part in happiness (1177a8). Does the correspondent really think that slaves are fortunate to be enslaved? Does he think it is Aristotle's fault if they are not?

29 The problems are fully discussed, and for the most part excellently resolved, by Richard Kraut (1989).

30 The linguistic point that one person can be said to have two 'lives' is made convincingly by Rist (1989, 186), citing *Politics* 1256a40ff. and Plato's *Laws* V 733D–734E.

31 The 'privilege' (*geras*) the gods have, according to this tag from Simonides, is that of being *esthlos*, of having excellence as a secure possession – see Plato's *Protagoras* 339C–347A.

32 Aristotle has three words for 'human,' *anthrōpikon* (the one used here), *anthrōpinon* and *anthrōpeion*. The last of these occurs only twice in *EN* (1175a4, 1181b15), and is a colourless word meaning 'pertaining to human beings.' *Anthrōpinon* is neutral in tone, and means whatever is appropriate to the human condition; *anthrōpikon* tends to be belittling or compassionate, 'all-too-human.'

   The word *kechōrismenē* is used by Aristotle almost as a technical term, to mean the 'separate' existence of a mind or a Platonic form from the physical world: mental operations, as we have seen, have no physical counterparts and do not follow physical laws (proving a conclusion is not causing it to happen).

33 Aristotle uses the ordinal word 'secondarily' here, without adding the partitive word 'fractionally' (*pollostōs*) which he applies to the occasional pleasures of second-rate people at 1176a29.

34 Note the verbal contrast between Aristotle's verbs *athanatizein*, performing the activities appropriate to an immortal being, and *anthrōpeuesthai*, which I should like to construe as 'getting on with the business of being the humans we are' – compare *aristeuein* in Homer (note 7 above), 'behave as the hero you really are,' and Aristotle's own use

of *alētheuein* for 'being a truthful person' (1127a19) and 'succeeding in knowing the truth' (1139b13). Verbs in -*izein* are about doing what you make a practice of doing, verbs in -*euein* are about being what you are.

35 To speak of mind as having bulk, however small, is a category mistake, recognized as such by Aristotle though he had not read Ryle. But one might compare Plato's *Republic* VI 427E, where the analogous point is made about the city's wisdom: the policy makers are numerically the smallest group, but the most important, because the city's wisdom depends on them. One might also compare Gorgias's *Praise of Helen* 8: '*Logos* is a great power, who with the smallest and most unapparent body achieves the most divine works.'

36 The quartet of virtues named here is implicit at the beginning of Book IV, 1119b23–6.

37 Cf. Lesher 1992, 78–119. Aristotle's former pupil Alexander of Macedon, by the way, was beginning to be worshipped as a god; Aristotle's comment that real gods would not be warriors or administrators is in point. He never mentions Alexander, for obvious reasons; but he often seems to have him in mind.

38 This is not the first time that *theōria* has been used in an extended sense: compare 1141a25, where it is implied (in striking contrast with the present passage) that animals have *theōria* and *phronēsis* because they exercise a sort of practical forethought in their own affairs.

39 Arendt 1959.

40 The description of the *megalopsuchos* at IV iii seems to imply possession of intellectual excellence as well; if it does, the life of such a person is clearly the best of all. But the conclusion of this account among the moral virtues suggests that scientific prowess is no part of the relevant supremacy, and it can have no functional relationship to the rest. In any case, what is said in the text holds of the *megalopsuchos* who is not also an intellectual.

41 This is implied by II ix, 1109b18–21. It might be argued that this is a misunderstanding: Aristotle could be taken to mean rather that the concept of precision is inapplicable in practical concerns, in accordance with his general position that precision is not to be looked for in moral philosophy (1094b12–28). But the latter point is immaterial, for it has to do with generalizations about what things are good or bad, not with the merits of individual actions. The definition of moral virtue as an extreme, and of the mean as an intermediate point rather than a range, shows that either Aristotle thought a precision of virtue attainable but an approximation tolerable or he was inconsistent on

this issue. The wording of II ix suggests the former: since it is all right to make a few mistakes, it is at least thinkable that no mistakes should be made.

42 Some would add that, in Aristotle's view, it is better to be a man than a woman, since a woman's virtue is necessarily incomplete in that she is not allowed, and hence not able, to take charge of her own affairs. But this is a fact about economic and political arrangements, not about the necessities of human life – see § 1.11341.

43 Ramsauer, followed by Susemihl and others, rejects this passage as an interpolation, the language being in some respects uncharacteristic of Aristotle. But textual surgery on this scale calls for a strong scenario to explain who was kidding whom. See Gauthier and Jolif 1958, II 910–13.

44 We have seen throughout how deeply Aristotle is imbued in Plato's conceptual world, how much he relies on the basic problematics of the *Meno* and the *Gorgias,* and how closely he follows the inner argumentation of the *Republic.* But there is also a curiously close parallel between certain features of the argumentative layout of the *Ethics* and the *Republic,* which I have explored elsewhere (Sparshott 1982a).

7 *Postscript*

1 Few commentators notice this lack of reforming zeal, partly because (despite its considerable length, about the same as X vii–viii) they take little interest in X ix. I suppose they consider it an extraneous appendage. Rather similarly, few commentators on the *Republic* seem to realize that in the imaginary city everyone except the army and the government carries on pretty much as before.

2 The *banausos* appears in the *Ethics* only at 1123a19, where the connotation is vulgarity. Generally, it appears that *banausia* is the quality of people engaged in forging and such, occupations so centred on continuous muscular exertion that those engaged in them are preoccupied with their bodies.

Appendix

1 I have explored some of these features further, from a different point of view, in Sparshott 1987.

2 The place of species in the cosmos partly explains Aristotle's invocation of an *ergon* for humanity. It also goes far to explain his reliance on the *phainomena,* the observed and agreed facts about human life –

though the existence and nature of cities means that that reliance cannot be complete (see nos. 15 and 16 below).

3 The importance of species in the economy of the universe explains Aristotle's repeated insistence on and neglect of 'what life means to' the individual; it also explains why he says so little of the virtues peculiar to specific stations in life, which figure prominently in the *Politics*.

4 Since these 'minds' are reached by different arguments, one wonders whether the 'mind that makes all things' in *On the Soul* III 5 is the same entity as the self-thinking mind of *Metaphysics* XII. There is no way of answering this question. The argumentative contexts are exotic enough that 'common sense' is no guide. The question is not worth discussing without a reasoned answer to the general question how minds are to be individuated; but this seems not to deter people from discussing it.

5 Richard Sorabji (1980, 175–6) says that 'another idea that would have struck Aristotle as anti-teleological is the great wastage involved in the discarding of unfavourable mutations. This would have seemed to go against the principle that "nature does nothing in vain." ' Maybe, but Aristotle was able to reconcile that principle with the great wastage of young animals that never reach maturity; to see what such a 'principle' means one has to see what it is applied to, not simply treat it as a slogan.

6 The uniqueness and importance of Greek philosophy and science go far to explain Aristotle's shameless cultural chauvinism, on which Nussbaum comments (1986, 245–6): there must be some explanation of why the Greeks made this great breakthrough while others did not, and Aristotle fastens on a supposedly happy coincidence of racial characteristics and climate (cf. *Politics* VII vii 1–3). For a more recent explanation of the phenomenon, see Lloyd 1990.

7 Catastrophe theory and the consequent rarity of philosophy explains the part played by the life 'according to mind' in the *Ethics*: the work of discovery develops historically, but its aim of discovering the whole truth about the cosmic order is one that is capable of fulfilment and the actual unfolding of that order is what is delightful – working out the details of an ingenious but mistaken hypothesis would not be the same thing at all.

Glossary

Several Greek words appear in my text without an accompanying translation. This is done when no English equivalent exists or is suitable in the context, either because the Greek concept is one we do not have or because Aristotle gives it a special sense or exploits its ambiguities. Aristotle's argument depends throughout on the conceptual repertory and relationships established in his native language, and it is easy to be seduced by the language of a translation. The following is a list of the terms used without accompanying translation, with their common English 'equivalents' and (sometimes) an explanation of the problems about the word's meaning.

Adikēma, 'wrongdoing,' a willing offence against a law one accepts as just.

Adikon, 'unjust,' an offence against fairness or rightness; the word is used in contexts where we would say 'wrong,' but combines the notions of wrongness and illegality.

Aitios, 'responsible.' A person who is *aitios* for something has caused it or is rightly accused of doing it; an *aitia* is an accusation as well as a cause.

Akrasia, 'moral weakness' or 'lack of self control,' the condition of people who act against their moral convictions. I have used 'weakling' to translate *akratēs*, the word for a person in this condition.

Aporia, 'difficulty.' Literally an impassable obstacle on a track, used in philosophical writings to designate the sort of apparent contradiction with which Socrates paralysed his opponents. An *aporia* in Socratic philosophy has the same sort of place that antinomies do in Kant.

Archē, 'beginning' or 'principle': any source of authority or power.

Aretē, 'virtue' or 'excellence.' Philosophers use it, like our word *goodness*, to cover whatever makes something good of its kind; ordinary people used it to cover the public value of warriors and statesmen, the richness of soils and fleeces, the power and handsomeness of steeds, and so on. Your virtues are the qualities of character that you are rightly praised for having. What Aristotle means by it appears best from his discussions. No adjective is formed from this noun; a person who has *aretē* may be called *agathos*, or *spoudaios*, or *epieikēs*.

Banausos, banausia, 'vulgar,' 'vulgarity.' Literally, manual labour, especially work at the forge.

Deon, 'needful,' applied to whatever is called for in a given situation, not necessarily with any moral connotations.

Dianoētikē, 'intellectual' in 'intellectual virtue.' *Dianoia*, from which the word derives, refers specifically to the discursive use of the mind, so that the virtues thus designated would not necessarily be expected to involve intuition.

Dokei, 'it seems.' Aristotle uses this word to introduce beliefs generally accepted in the circles to which he and his readers belong. In Greek generally, the word may mean 'it seems true' or 'it seems good'; it is not always clear which Aristotle means, nor can we always tell whether he endorses the beliefs thus introduced.

Energeia, 'activity' or 'realization,' contrasted with an unrealized potentiality. Aristotle makes much use of this word in his metaphysics; etymologically, it means engaging in one's work or performing one's function.

Entelecheia, 'realization.' A word apparently coined by Aristotle to mean the full or complete realization of a potentiality (cf. *Metaphysics* 1050a23).

Ephiesthai, 'desire,' both etymologically and actually to go after or go for something.

Epieikeia, 'equity,' in a legal context means looking to the intent of the lawgiver rather than to the letter of the law. In other contexts it means more generally 'reasonableness' or simply 'worthiness' – see next entry.

Epieikēs, 'worthy' or 'respectable,' the word most often used by Aristotle for the conventionally virtuous person. *Spoudaios* (q.v.) may be an exact synonym, but has that extra meaning of being serious and taken seriously, while the suggestion in *epieikeia* (q.v.) is rather that of being reasonable.

Ergon, 'function.' It is the common Greek word for 'work,' suggesting sometimes laboriousness and sometimes simply one's job. Aristotle follows Plato in using it as a semi-technical term; cf. §1.211.

Ēthikē is the word translated 'moral' in 'moral virtue,' and 'ethics' in the title of *EN*. The word seems to be Aristotle's coinage; it is derived from *ēthos*, which is used for the lairs of beasts, for the customs of societies, and for the characters of individuals as described in *EN* II. Not to be confused with *ethos* with a short e, and its derivatives, which refer to habituation.

Euboulia, 'good counsel,' the ability to give good advice to oneself and others; Aristotle identifies it with the ability to deliberate well.

Eudaimonia, 'happiness.' To call people happy is to felicitate them on the quality of their lives, not on how they are feeling at the moment; for the rest, it has many of the same connotations as the English word. Etymologically it suggests 'having a good guardian spirit'; *eudaimōn* is what you would be if an all-powerful spirit were watching out for your interests.

Haplōs, 'simply,' 'absolutely,' 'without qualification'; a tricky word, meaning that the word used is to be taken in its least qualified sense – but it is not always clear what would count as a qualification.

Hexis, 'condition' or 'habit.' A *hexis* is neither a temporary state nor a permanent quality, but a stable condition that is likely to endure.

Horos, 'definition' or 'criterion,' literally a boundary marker; a *horismos* is a formula defining the meaning of a term.

Hupolēpsis, 'supposition' or 'assumption,' something taken for granted within the context of the present argument.

Kairos, 'the right moment.' A typical use is in medical practice, where it means the exact moment to administer a cure, neither too soon nor too late. Great importance was attached to this, and its detection was a skill that could be acquired only through experience.

Kakia, 'vice,' badness and deficiency in the most general sense, suggesting absence of excellence rather than evil.

Kakodaimōn, 'ill-starred,' the converse of *eudaimōn* ('happy').

Kalokagathia, 'distinction,' the quality of a fine gentleman; a favourite word for epitaphs.

Kalon, 'fine' or 'fair' or 'beautiful,' much more widely used than any comparable English word. To act 'for the sake of the *kalon*' is to act idealistically; but the word is also applied to personal beauty, poetic excellence, honour, the fineness of a fine day.

Kerdos, 'gain' or 'pay-off' or 'profit.'

Kinēsis, 'movement' or 'change.' In Aristotle's usage, the word covers locomotion, alteration, growth, dwindling, coming into being – any sort of process whereby a state of a physical system gives place to a *different* state of the *same* system.

Kurios, 'lord' or 'in charge.' The word can be applied to whoever or whatever is in legitimate control in an organization or situation.

Logos, 'reason.' This is essentially the power of conceptualization and articulate speech; it is also used in mathematics to mean 'ratio.' It covers everything that depends on the use of language and similar symbol systems. See §1.212. The activities of reason are not typically ascribed to *logos* as an agency but to *to logon echon*, 'that which has reason,' presumably because the psychology and epistemology involved are so desperately obscure that it is unwise to be specific.

Makarios, 'blessed.' Sometimes this is used as a synonym for *eudaimōn*, but usually implies an exceptional degree of happiness, such as a god might enjoy.

Meson, Mesotēs, 'mean.' A *meson* is an intermediate point between extremes; a *mesotēs* is an intermediate condition.

Mochthēros, 'wicked,' morally depraved; Aristotle's world of specifically moral condemnation (as distinct from *phaulos* and *ponēros*, qq.v.).

Nomikos, 'lawful,' complying with actual law (as opposed to justice).

Nous, 'mind.' The word is used generally for a perceptive intelligence that notices and understands what is going on around it. Aristotle uses it specifically for the intellectual ability to formulate and grasp first principles in an intellectual domain, as distinguished from the ability to reason correctly or fruitfully from those principles.

Oikeion, 'one's own'; literally, domestic, at home as opposed to abroad, hence what belongs peculiarly to oneself.

Pathos, 'passion' or 'suffering.' A *pathos* is something that just happens to a person or thing, and specifically a feeling that just comes over one.

Phainomena, 'appearances.' As Aristotle uses this word, these are not what a dispassionate observer would observe but the facts that are agreed on: the emphasis is not on perception but on actual judgment. But there is an ambiguity between appearance (as contrasted with reality) and perceptibility (as opposed to obscurity).

Phaulos, 'cheap, easy, slight, paltry,' and of people 'low in rank, mean, common' (LSJ); but not necessarily *mochthēros* or even *ponēros* (qq.v.).

Philos, 'friend' or 'beloved' or 'one's own.' See §4.23.

Phronēsis, 'good sense,' traditionally 'prudence.' The quality of people who conduct themselves intelligently in private or public life. In everyday language the word was used quite broadly and vaguely; Aristotle's use (§§ 2.3123, 2.32ff.) tidies things up.

Pleonexia, 'greed,' etymologically as well as lexically the desire and tendency always to get more than other people have, or more than one already has oneself, of goods and services.

Polis, 'city' or sometimes 'city-state' – the word is often left untranslated in political theory. It stands for the effective political unit in Aristotle's Greece, a self-governing community of free citizens centred on a town with its sustaining hinterland.

Ponēros, 'worthless,' 'good-for-nothing.' About halfway between *phaulos* and *mochthēros* (qq.v.).

Praxis, 'action' or 'practice.' The word can be applied to anything anyone does – whatever 'does' means; but especially to the things that practical people do.

Scholē, 'leisure,' rest, ease; specifically, freedom from business.

Skopos, 'aim,' a target to aim at or a mark to steer for, something to keep one's eye on.

Sophia, 'wisdom'; Aristotle has a chapter on this concept (cf. §2.3125). Etymologically, 'philosophy' means the attempt to achieve *sophia*, so Aristotle uses *sophia* to stand for the ideal of intellectual endeavour as he understood it; but, as he admits, the word was ordinarily used for any sort of expert or sophisticated use of the mind.

Sōphrosunē, 'moderation' or 'temperance.' Notoriously untranslatable, this word stands for the quality of quiet and discreet people who do not make disturbances, obedient children, 'modest' women. Aristotle rather oddly takes its literal meaning to be moderation in eating, drinking, and sex.

Spoudaios, 'serious.' This sometimes and principally means approaching the relevant activity seriously and in earnest rather than playfully, but may also mean being the kind of person who is to be taken seriously, a respectable or conventionally virtuous one. Aristotle seems to exploit the ambiguities.

Spoudē, 'zeal' or seriousness, the quality one shows in taking something seriously.

Taxis, 'order.' The sort of order shown by a military unit on parade; also, one's place in such an order or hierarchy. The central idea is that of assigning units a determinate place in a series or system.

Teleion, 'perfect,' having the character of a *telos*. Systematically ambiguous as between 'complete' and 'ideal.'

Telos, 'end.' A word of very various use (see LSJ): performance or consummation of a task or mission; degree of completion or attainment; termination (especially natural death). Aristotle chiefly uses it to mean the end or purpose for which something exists, with the implication that the end is actually achieved.

Theion, 'divine.' Since the Greeks acknowledged many gods, the adjective might connote any sort of superhuman excellence, but especially exemption from change and mortality.

Theōria, 'thinking.' Customarily translated 'contemplation,' but it is the usual word for sightseeing and spectatorship, and is regularly applied by Aristotle to scientific and philosophic concern with 'theoretical' truth.

References

Adkins, J.W.H. 1960. *Merit and Responsibility*. Oxford: Clarendon Press

Aquinas, St Thomas. 1949. *S. Thomae Aquinatis in Decem Libros Ethicorum Aristotelis ad Nicomachum Expositio*. Turin: Marietti

Arendt, Hannah. 1959. *The Human Condition*. New York: Doubleday

– 1963. *On Revolution*. New York: Viking Press

Arrighetti, Graziano, ed. 1973. *Epicuro: Opere*, 2d ed. Turin: Einaudi

Aubenque, Pierre. 1963. *La Prudence chez Aristote*. Paris: Presses universitaires de France

Auden, W.H. 1962. *The Dyer's Hand*. New York: Random House

Baier, Kurt. 1958. *The Moral Point of View*. Ithaca, NY: Cornell University Press

Bonitz, H. 1870. *Index Aristotelicus*. Berlin, 1870; repr. Graz: Akademische Druck– u. Verlagsanstalt 1955

Broadie, Sarah. 1991. *Ethics with Aristotle*. New York: Oxford University Press

Burnet, John. 1900. *The Ethics of Aristotle*. London: Methuen

Burnyeat, M.F. 1980. 'Aristotle on Learning to Be Good,' in Rorty 1980, 69–92

Charlton, W., ed. and trans. 1970. *Aristotle's Physics I and II*. Oxford: Clarendon Press

Chesterton, G.K. 1987. *Collected Nonsense and Light Verse*. London: Xanadu Publications

Chroust, Anton-Hermann. 1973. *Aristotle, New Light on His Life and Some of His Lost Works*, 2 vols. Notre Dame, IN: University of Notre Dame Press

Clark, Stephen R.L. 1975. *Aristotle's Man*. Oxford: Clarendon Press

Cooper, J.M. 1973. 'The Magna Moralia and Aristotle's Moral Philosophy,' *American Journal of Philosophy* 94, 327–9

– 1975. *Reason and Human Good in Aristotle*. Cambridge, MA: Harvard University Press

– 1980, 'Aristotle on Friendship,' in Rorty 1980, 301–40

Cornford, F.M. 1912. *From Religion to Philosophy: A Study in the Origins of Western Speculations.* London: Edward Arnold

Diels-Kranz, Hermann. 1951. *Die Fragmente der Vorsokratiker*, 6th ed., ed. by Walther Kranz. Berlin: Weidmann

Dirlmeier, Franz. 1962. *Aristoteles*, Nikomachische Ethik. Berlin: Akademie-Verlag

Dodds, E.R. 1951. *The Greeks and the Irrational.* Berkeley: University of California Press

Dover, K.J. 1974. *Greek Popular Morality in the Time of Plato and Aristotle.* Oxford: Blackwell

Düring, Ingemar. 1957. *Aristotle in the Ancient Biographical Tradition.* Stockholm: Almquist and Wiksell

Edel, Abraham. 1982. *Aristotle and His Philosophy.* Chapel Hill: University of North Carolina Press

Engberg-Pedersen, Troels. 1983. *Aristotle's Theory of Moral Insight.* Oxford: Clarendon Press

Fortenbaugh, W.W. 1968. 'Aristotle and the Questionable Mean-Dispositions,' *Transactions of the American Philological Association* 99, 203–31

– 1969. 'Aristotle on Emotion and Moral Virtue,' *Arethusa* 2, 163–85

– 1975. *Aristotle on Emotion.* New York: Barnes and Noble

Furley, David. 1967. *Two Studies on the Greek Atomists.* Princeton, NJ: Princeton University Press

– 1978. 'Self-Movers,' in Rorty 1980, 55–67

Gauthier, R.-A., and J.-Y. Jolif. 1958. *L'Éthique à Nicomaque*, 2 vols. Louvain: Publications universitaires de Louvain

Glotz, Gustave. 1904, *La Solidarité de la famille dans le droit criminel en Grèce.* Paris: Fontemoing

Gottschalk, Hans B. 1990. 'The Earliest Aristotelian Commentators,' in Richard Sorabji, ed., *Aristotle Transformed: The Ancient Commentators and Their Influence.* Ithaca, NY: Cornell University Press

Grant, Alexander. 1874. *The Ethics of Aristotle*, 2 vols. London: Longmans, Green and Co.

Hardie, W.F.R. 1968a. 'Aristotle on the Freewill Problem,' *Philosophy* 43, 274–8

– 1968b. *Aristotle's Ethical Theory.* Oxford: Clarendon Press

Hare, R.M. 1952. *The Language of Morals.* Oxford: Clarendon Press

Heath, T.L. 1931. *A Manual of Greek Mathematics.* Oxford: Oxford University Press

Hutchinson, D.S. 1986. *The Virtues of Aristotle.* London: Routledge and Kegan Paul

Huxley, Aldous. 1928. *Point Counter Point.* New York: Harper and Bros

Irwin, Terence. 1977. *Plato's Moral Theory: The Early and Middle* Dialogues. New York: Oxford University Press

– 1980a. 'The Metaphysical and Psychological Basis of Aristotle's Ethics,' in Rorty 1980, 35–53

– 1980b. 'Reason and Responsibility in Aristotle,' in Rorty 1980, 117–55

– 1980c. Review of Kenny 1978, *Journal of Philosophy* 77, 338–54

Joachim, H.H. 1951. *Aristotle, The* Nicomachean Ethics. Oxford: Clarendon Press

Just, Roger. 1989. *Women in Athenian Law and Life*. London: Routledge.

Kahn, Charles H. 1988. 'Discovering the Will: From Aristotle to Augustine,' in *The Question of Eclecticism*, ed. by J.M. Dillon and A.A. Long, 234–59. Berkeley: University of California Press

Kenny, Anthony. 1963. *Action, Emotion and Will*. London: Routledge and Kegan Paul

– 1978. *The Aristotelian* Ethics: *A Study of the Relationship Between the* Eudemian *and* Nicomachean Ethics *of Aristotle*. Oxford: Clarendon Press

Kenyon, Frederic G. 1951. *Books and Readers in Ancient Greece and Rome*, 2d ed. Oxford: Clarendon Press

Kraut, Richard. 1989. *Aristotle on the Human Good*. Princeton, NJ: Princeton University Press

Lear, Jonathan. 1980. *Aristotle and Logical Theory*. Cambridge, UK: Cambridge University Press

– 1988. *Aristotle: The Desire to Understand*. Cambridge, UK: Cambridge University Press

Lee, H.D.P. 1937. 'The Legal Background of Two Passages in the Nicomachean Ethics,' *Classical Quarterly* 31, 129–40

Léonard, Jean. 1948. *Le Bonheur chez Aristote*. Brussels: Académie Royale de Belgique, Classe des lettres et des sciences morales et politiques, t. 44, fasc. 1

Lesher, J.H. 1992. *Xenophanes of Colophon*, Fragments: *A Text and Translation with a Commentary by J.H. Lesher*. Toronto: University of Toronto Press

Liddell, Henry George, and Robert Scott. 1940. *A Greek–English Lexicon*, new ed. by Henry Stuart Jones. Oxford: Clarendon Press

Lloyd, G.E.R. 1990. *Demystifying Mentalities*. Cambridge, UK: Cambridge University Press

Lloyd-Jones, Hugh. 1971. *The Justice of Zeus*. Berkeley: University of California Press

LSJ. See Liddell, Henry George, and Robert Scott (1940)

MacIntyre, Alasdair. 1982. *After Virtue*. Notre Dame: Notre Dame University Press

Maritain, Jacques. 1930. *Art and Scholasticism*. London: Sheed and Ward

Marx, Karl. 1959. *Economic and Philosophic Manuscripts of 1844.* Moscow: Progress Publishers

Mill, John Stuart. 1861. *Utilitarianism,* in his *Complete Works,* vol. 10. Toronto: University of Toronto Press 1969

Modrak, Deborah K.W. 1987. *Aristotle: The Power of Perception.* Chicago: University of Chicago Press

Monan, J. Donald. 1968. *Moral Knowledge and Its Methodology in Aristotle.* Oxford: Clarendon Press

Moraux, Paul. 1951. *Les Listes anciennes des ouvrages d'Aristote.* Louvain: Études universitaires de Louvain

– 1957. *À la recherche de l'Aristote perdu: Le Dialogue 'Sur la Justice.'* Louvain: Publications universitaires de Louvain

Mulgan, R.G. 1977. *Aristotle's Political Theory: An Introduction to the Study of Political Theory.* Oxford: Clarendon Press

Nowell-Smith, P.H. 1954. *Ethics.* Harmondsworth: Penguin Books

Nussbaum, Martha Craven. 1978. *Aristotle's De Motu Animalium.* Princeton, NJ: Princeton University Press

– 1980. 'Shame, Separateness, and Political Unity: Aristotle's Criticism of Plato,' in Rorty 1980, 395–435

– 1986. *The Fragility of Goodness.* Cambridge, UK: Cambridge University Press

Olmsted, E. Harris. 1948. 'The "Moral Sense" Aspect of Aristotle's Ethical Theory,' *American Journal of Philology* 69, 42–61

Pears, David. 1980. 'Courage as a Mean,' in Rorty 1980, 171–87

Perry, R.B. 1923. *A General Theory of Value.* New York: Scribners

Ramsauer, Gottfried, ed. 1876. *Aristotelis Ethica Nicomachea.* Leipzig: B.G. Teubner

Rawls, John. 1971. *Theory of Justice.* Cambridge, MA: Harvard University Press

Rist, John M. 1985. 'The End of Aristotle's *On Prayer,'* *American Journal of Philology* 106, 110–13

– 1989. *The Mind of Aristotle.* Toronto: University of Toronto Press

Robinson, Richard 1945. 'L'Acrasie, selon Aristote,' *Revue philosophique de la France et de l'étranger* 145, 261–80

Rorty, Amélie Oksenberg, ed. 1980. *Essays on Aristotle's Ethics.* Berkeley: University of California Press

Rowe, C.J. 1971. *The Eudemian and Nicomachean Ethics: A Study in the Development of Aristotle's Thought.* Cambridge, UK: The Cambridge Philological Society [Proceedings, Supplement no. 3])

– 1975. 'A reply to John Cooper on the Magna Moralia,' *American Journal of Philosophy* 96, 160–72

Sacks, Oliver. 1973. *Awakenings*. London: Duckworth

Sartre, Jean-Paul. 1960. *Critique de la raison dialectique*. Paris: Gallimard; English translation, London: NLR Books 1983

Schwyzer, Eduard. 1959. *Griechische Grammatik*. Mürich: C.H. Beck

Sibley, Frank N. 1959. 'Aesthetic Concepts,' *Philosophical Review* 68, 421–50

Sorabji, Richard. 1980. *Necessity, Cause and Blame: Perspectives on Aristotle's Theory*. London: Duckworth

Sparshott, F.E. 1966. 'Socrates and Thrasymachus,' *Monist* 50, 421–59

– 1970.'Five Virtues in Plato and Aristotle,' *Monist* 54, 40–65

– 1978. 'Zeno on Art: Anatomy of a Definition,' in J.M. Rist, ed., *The Stoics*, 273–90. Berkeley: University of California Press

– 1982a. 'Aristotle's *Ethics* and Plato's *Republic*: A Structural Comparison,' *Dialogue* 21, 483–99

– 1982b. *The Theory of the Arts*. Princeton, NJ: Princeton University Press

– 1985. 'Aristotle on Women,' *Philosophical Inquiry* 7, 177–200

– 1987. 'Aristotle's World and Mine,' in Mohan Matthen, ed., *Aristotle Today: Essays on Aristotle's Ideal of Science*. Edmonton, AL: Academic Printing and Publishing

Spicq, C., O.P. 1953. 'Le Verbe *agapaō* et ses dérivés dans le grec classique,' *Revue biblique* 60, 372–97

Stephanus, Henri Estienne. *Thesaurus Graecae Linguae*, 8 vols., ed. by C.B. Hase et al. Paris: A. Firmin Didot 1831–65

Stewart, J.A. 1892. *Notes on the* Nicomachean Ethics *of Aristotle*, 2 vols. Oxford: Oxford University Press

Suits, Bernard. 1978. *The Grasshopper*. Toronto: University of Toronto Press

Taylor, Charles. 1989. *Sources of the Self: The Making of the Modern Identity*. Cambridge, MA: Harvard University Press

Thorpe, W.H. 1963. *Learning and Instinct in Animals*, 2d ed. London: Methuen

Torr, Cecil. 1979. *Small Talk at Wreyford*, 2d series. London: Oxford University Press; (first published 1921)

Tracy, Theodore James, S.J., 1969. *Physiological Theory and the Doctrine of the Mean in Plato and Aristotle*. The Hague: Mouton

Urmson, J.O. 1973. 'Aristotle's Doctrine of the Mean,' in Rorty 1980, 157–70 (rprtd from *American Philosophical Quarterly*)

– 1988. *Aristotle's* Ethics. Oxford: Blackwell

Vinogradoff, Paul. 1908. 'Aristotle on Legal Redress' (*Columbia Law Review*, November 1908), in his *Collected Papers*, vol. 2, 1–14. Oxford: Clarendon Press 1928

– 1922. *Outlines of Historical Jurisprudence*, 2 vols. London: Oxford University Press

Vlastos, Gregory. 1975. *Plato's Universe*. Seattle: University of Washington Press
– 1991. *Socrates, Ironist and Moral Philosopher*. Ithaca, NY: Cornell University Press
Wedin, Michael V. 1988. *Mind and Imagination in Aristotle*. New Haven, CT: Yale University Press.
Wilkes, Kathleen V. 1980. 'The Good Man and the Good for Man,' in Rorty 1980, 341–57
Wollheim, Richard. 1984. *The Thread of Life*. Cambridge, MA: Harvard University Press

Index

458 Index

soul 193, 214, 401; – on pleasure
412; – politics of 76; – on sage
and politician 78; – on soul 337;
Republic I, Cephalus in 233, 422;
– on function 41, 44, 381; –
Polemarchus in 157, 397, 399,
400; – Thrasymachus in 165,
186–7, 188, 271, 385, 396; *Republic*
II 321, 373; *Republic* III 429;
Republic IV 30, 93, 246, 375, 381,
407, 416; *Republic* V 219, 355–6;
Republic VI–VII 27, 345, 366, 373,
409, 434; *Republic* VIII 417;
Republic IX 133, 257, 263, 291,
316, 339; *Republic* X 322, 337, 354,
413, 422; *Statesman* 293, 393, 417;
Symposium 62, 93, 274, 378, 422,
432; *Theaetetus* 23, 343, 344, 433
play 318, 326, 327. *See also* pastimes
pleasure 12, 89–91, 111–12, 241–2,
252–62, 301, 307–23, 351; and
activity 253–4, 308; concept 59,
254–6; and enjoyment 428; evaluation of 315–16; and life 312; as
prescriptive 409; as supervenient
312–15
pleasures 256, 259–60, 301–2,
318–19; as activities 427; and
lifetimes 316–17
pleonexia 157, 159–60, 161, 166, 188,
385, 395–6; concept 441
Plotinus 370, 405, 414
Plutarch 370, 388, 427
poiein 404
poiēsis 209
polis: as community of communities 105; concept 441; as educational system 137, 283; equality
in 76, 269–70; and human nature
82, 147, 226, 321; inclusiveness of
282, 372; as recurrent phenom-

enon 367; shared values in 279;
size of 373. *See also* city, political
community
political: animal 261; community
161, 197, 267–8; justice 176–96;
life 351–2; philosopher 308, 406,
410; virtue 178
politics 195, 355–6; as architectonic
18–20, 235, 252, 388; domain of
178; and ethics 18–20, 225–6, 373,
402; as way of thinking 18–20,
209; and welfare 211
ponēros 51, 261, 441
Porphyry 4, 370; tree of 95
posthumous fate 67, 69
potentiality 105, 359
power 328
practical syllogism 121, 246–7, 249,
409, 410
pragmateia 370
praise 335; and blame 76–7,
116–17, 130, 134, 251, 388, 421
prattein 404
praxis 106, 209, 261, 265, 324, 327,
337; concept 49, 78, 83, 441
pre-emptive values 376
Priam 65–6, 67, 120
price 174–5
pride 151–3, 353
Prince Regent (George IV) 416
principle. *See archē*
process 258, 260, 310–11; and activity 411. *See also kinēsis*
Prodicus 29, 58–9, 310, 312
prohairesis 371, 388. *See also*
choice
proportions, theory of 401
pros hen concepts 274
Protagoras 23, 85, 378, 379
psychological egoism 188
publication 3, 370
Pythagoreans 172, 181, 218, 299,